THE OFFICIAL® GU

COIN GRADING
AND COUNTERFEIT DETECTION

PROFESSIONAL COIN GRADING SERVICE

Scott A. Travers, Editor

John W. Dannreuther, Text Author

David Hall, Foreword

Jay W. Johnson, Introduction

Bruce Amspacher, Counterfeit Dectection Co-Author

Richard Montgomery, Counterfeit Detection Co-Author

Ed Reiter, Numismatic Editor

Thomas K. DeLorey, Technical Editor

Michael W. Sherman, Project Coordinator

John Bahner, Photography Editor

Second Edition

House of Collectibles

New York

The Official Guide to Coin Grading and Counterfeit Detection, 2nd Edition
Scott A. Travers, Editor
John W. Dannreuther, Text Author

Copyright © 1997, 2004 by Professional Coin Grading Service

This is a revised and updated edition of THE OFFICIAL GUIDE TO COIN GRADING AND COUNTERFEIT DETECTION, published in 1997 by House of Collectibles, a member of The Random House Information Group, a division of Random House, Inc.

This book is available for special discounts for bulk purchases for sales promotions or premiums. Special editions, including personalized covers, excerpts of existing books, and corporate imprints, can be created in large quantities for special needs. For more information, write to Special Markets/Premium Sales, 1745 Broadway, MD 6-2, New York, NY, 10019 or e-mail specialmarkets@randomhouse.com.

Please address inquiries about electronic licensing of reference products for use on a network, in software or on CD-ROM to the Subsidiary Rights Department, Random House Reference, fax 212-572-6003.

Visit the Random House Web site: www.randomhouse.com.

Library of Congress Cataloging-in-Publication Data is available.

0 9 8 7 6 5 4 3 2

March 2004

ISBN: 0-375-72050-2

Cover design by Geraldine Sarmiento

On the cover: 1804 Class I Draped Bust Heraldic Eagle silver dollar graded Proof-68 by PCGS and sold for $4.14-million by Bowers & Merena in August 1999; portrait side of Statehood quarter graded Proof-70 Deep Cameo by PCGS. (Photos by the Professional Coin Grading Service)

CONTENTS

4 Professional Coin Grading Service Grading Standards

5 Elements Of A Coin's Grade

6 Grading U.S. Copper Coins

7 Grading U.S. Nickel Coins

8 Grading U.S. Silver Coins

9 Grading U.S. Gold Coins

10 Grading U.S. Commemorative Coins

11 Doctored Coins

14 Frequently Seen Counterfeit Coins

ACKNOWLEDGMENTS

A book of this magnitude cannot be carried from concept to completion without the collective efforts of many talented and dedicated people. The Professional Coin Grading Service was fortunate to have some of the most knowledgeable and talented experts in the numismatic field involved in this project, and the success of the finished product testifies eloquently to the many long hours and Herculean efforts they devoted to the task. It became, quite literally, a labor of love.

Scott A. Travers made the book possible by recognizing the urgent need for a definitive coin-grading guide and bringing together the principals—PCGS and Random House—in a perfect marriage of talent and technology. Scott assembled the team that produced and polished the text and prepared the illustrations. In a very real sense, he was not only the editor of this book but the driving force behind it.

John W. Dannreuther wrote most of the book, drawing upon his comprehensive knowledge of U.S. coinage—knowledge, which encompasses not only grading and marketing aspects but also production procedures. "J.D." combined prodigious productivity with painstaking attention to detail. Without this world-class numismatic genius, this book never could have been produced.

Bruce Amspacher, John Dannreuther, and Rick Montgomery drew upon their years of experience to author the chapters on counterfeit detection. Rick's knowledge of this subject and Bruce's and John's writing skills give this part of the book the greatest possible accuracy, authoritativeness, and readability.

Ed Reiter, former Numismatics columnist for the *New York Times,* helped write several of the non-technical portions of the book and edited the technical parts with an eye to making the text readily comprehensible to even the average layman.

Thomas K. DeLorey, a professional numismatist with long experience as both a journalist and a coin grader, checked the manuscript patiently and carefully for technical accuracy, serving as an invaluable safety net.

PCGS also wishes to extend special thanks to the following, all of whom played vital roles in helping to bring this project to fruition:

Anibal Almeida; Jon Bahner; Q. David Bowers; Nick Buzolich; Bill Caldwell; Myra Dannreuther; Victor John "Dan" Dannreuther (deceased); Beth Deisher; Silvano DiGenova; Michael R. Fuljenz; David Hall; James L. Halperin; David Harper; Dorothy Harris; Michael Haynes; Ron Howard; Jay W. Johnson; Timothy J. Kochuba; Randy Ladenheim-Gil; Alex Klapwald; Denis Loring; Steve Mayer; James L. Miller; Tom Mulvaney; Donn Pearlman; Maurice Rosen; Mike Sargent; B.J. Searles; Michael W. Sherman; Keith Simpson; Michael Standish; Scott Thompson; Simon Vukelj; John Whitman; and Gordon Wrubel.

FOREWORD
by David Hall

"What's it worth?" is perhaps the most frequently asked question in all collectible fields. Whether a person has seven figures in a collectibles investment portfolio or merely a few trinkets picked up at a flea market, the overriding question is value. There are three components to value for a collectible: rarity, importance, and condition. This book is about condition.

In all collectibles fields, it is the seller who is usually the expert. It is the professional dealers who have the most knowledge about the item, the best handle on current market prices, and the necessary experience to determine the quality of each item. It is the sellers who are the grading experts. This puts the buyer at a tremendous disadvantage, and the fact is that in all collectible fields, misrepresentation of the quality of the product is a huge problem.

In February 1986, the Professional Coin Grading Service (PCGS) presented the rare coin industry with a solution to this problem. Under the PCGS system, the world's top professional coin graders would use a consensus-of-opinion method to grade coins by an industry-accepted grading standard. Coins would then be sonically sealed in tamper-evident holders, thereby attaching the grade to the coin. The idea was so good that PCGS immediately began receiving between 30,000 and 50,000 coins per month for grading according to these standards. It was an idea whose time had come.

Now, after over seventeen years as the preeminent coin grading service, the PCGS consensus-grading method has spread to other collectible fields, most notably sports cards and stamps. PCGS remains the largest coin grading service, although others have entered the field since the first edition of this grading book was published in 1997.

Before PCGS, every coin dealer was literally a separate grading standard. Everybody graded coins slightly differently. What PCGS did, in one way, was to gather the top dealers in the market together and have them agree on a single grading standard, a standard that would be set and administrated by one third-party arbiter of quality. To set the standards, PCGS sought the input of many major dealers. The standards were set and represented by actual coins. PCGS formed a grading set of coins that were used as examples of the PCGS grading standards. Today, PCGS is still the only grading service with an extensive set of grading standards examples.

But while the grading set is a wonderful way for the PCGS graders to implement the PCGS grading standard, the grading set is merely the physical example of the standards. What was needed was a detailed description of the grading standards that were used by the coin market. What was needed was a published set of grading standards. And because grading is so important, what was also needed was a detailed description of what those grading standards meant, how rare coins were graded, and explanations of the numerous issues involved in the grading and authenticating of rare coins. What was needed was a grading book written by the top rare coin-grading experts in the world. The award winning 1997 first edition of *The Official Guide to Coin Grading and Counterfeit Detection* was that book. Now, you hold in your hands the second edition of that guide – in a more compact format with several additional areas added. I have been told on countless occasions by both dealers and collectors that the first edition of the grading guide sits on their desks within arm's length reach, as it has become one of the most consulted references in all of numismatics. The detailed grading descriptions and photos are invaluable, as are the photos and detailed discussions of the counterfeit sections.

This book, as well as the first edition, is the work of some of the top rare coin experts of all time. The PCGS grading book is a true team effort. PCGS founder and Numismatic Research Director John Dannreuther, who is considered to be one of the top numismatic technicians in the world, did the bulk of the technical writing for this book. Several top experts, including PCGS founders Gordon Wrubel and Bruce Amspacher, reviewed the grading standards and made salient suggestions. PCGS graders, including current head grader Ron Howard, as well as Miles Standish and Mike Sargent, also reviewed the standards and made important contributions. Bruce Amspacher wrote the counterfeit detection section based on the notes of John Dannreuther and Rick Montgomery. In addition, many of the ideas, definitions, and concepts were formulated by the PCGS Numismatic Advisory Board, which consists of world-class rare coin experts David Akers, Bruce Amspacher, Jack Beymer, Del Bland, Q. David Bowers, Mike Brownlee (deceased), Jack Collins (deceased), John Dannreuther, Bill Fivaz, Jeff Garrett, Ron Guth, Jack Hancock (deceased), Larry Hanks, Ron Howard, Don Kagin, Denis Loring, Andy

Lustig, Wayne Miller, Lee Minshull, Paul Nugget, Tony Terranova, Rick Tomaska, and Gordon Wrubel.

Just as PCGS brought the top grading experts in the world together to form an industry-wide grading standard and a new way of grading and trading coins in 1986, the PCGS grading book, once again, brings together the top grading experts in the world, this time to put it all down on paper for you to learn from and enjoy. The demand for a smaller format that would be more transportable resulted in the second edition of this book. The second edition also includes two important enhancements: descriptions of grading standards for Statehood quarters and information about the impact of the now very influential PCGS Set Registry™ program.

This book is a testimony to how advanced the rare coin market is in comparison to all other collectibles fields. The rare coin market provides more information, liquidity, and safety than any other collectibles field. *The Official Guide to Coin Grading and Counterfeit Detection, 2nd Edition* makes a significant contribution to the information available to all coin enthusiasts, just as the first edition did, but the second edition is in the easy-to-transport smaller format. If you love rare coins, this is a book that I am sure you will benefit from greatly and enjoy thoroughly. The new second-edition format will make this an often-seen reference on the bourse floor, at auctions, and anywhere there is a gathering of serious numismatists. This edition of the PCGS grading guide will give you page after page of important numismatic information and hopefully many hours of numismatic enjoyment.

Have fun with your coins!

INTRODUCTION
by Jay W. Johnson
Former Director, United States Mint

My tenure as Director of the United States Mint was educational and illuminating.

Prior to that, like most Americans, I looked upon coins as utilitarian objects—useful little disks that came in handy for making calls from a pay phone, or feeding a parking meter, or buying a snack from a vending machine to feed myself. I soon learned that coins are much more than pieces of metal stamped with a monetary value. They possess history, artistry, beauty, romance, and sometimes great rarity and value—value that is determined not by what the government stamped on these coins when it made them, but by what they are deemed to be worth by a dedicated and knowledgeable group of people called collectors.

I also became aware that a process know as "grading" plays a fundamental part in determining how much these coins are worth by establishing their degree of quality and, indirectly, their rarity. And I learned that a company called PCGS—the Professional Coin Grading Service—is by far the best in the business at rendering grading verdicts, judgments that collectors accept and respect as authoritative and accurate year after year.

Quality was a matter of constant concern to me at the Mint. It's a daunting challenge to maintain the highest standards when you're dealing with products made by the billons each year, but quality control was a very high priority for me and the people who worked for me. That's why I took it as a personal setback whenever some dramatic mint-error coin turned up in circulation. That's also a major reason why I am so impressed by the track record PCGS has achieved for consistency and reliability—for being right on the money—in short, for *its* quality control.

PCGS deals with quality on two different levels. Judging quality—grading coins—is its stock in trade. But in carrying out this mission, the people at PCGS bring to bear a level of expertise unequaled by any other company. And this, too, is a form of quality.

This book is an extension of the high-quality service the company renders to its clients—and more than that, to the coin collecting hobby as a whole. By furnishing a simple, yet detailed guide to the art—and yes, the science—of grading coins, PCGS has demystified this process and made it easy for ordinary collectors to understand the elements that go into determining the number that appears on a grading holder. The lavish illustrations simplify the experience even more. On a personal note, I found myself marveling at the sharpness and detail of the exceptional coin photographs and at how clearly they showed, at a glance, the points being made in the text. Truly, each of these pictures is worth a thousand words. In this book, however, the words are lucid and well worth pondering, too.

My time at the Mint taught me volumes about the technical process of manufacturing coins. I left with a deep appreciation for the myriad details that the artists, craftsmen, technicians, and workmen must master in the course of their daily work. Fashioning designs, preparing hubs and dies, operating presses—these and other exacting details are essential to the production of high-quality coins worthy of a mighty nation such as ours.

In reading this book, however, I found myself discovering important new details about the minting process and fascinating insights into how that process has impacted collectible U.S. coins through the years. In a way, I felt like Dr. Watson looking on with admiration and a little bit of awe as he watched Sherlock Holmes unravel complex mysteries with skillful deductions. *The Official Guide to Coin Grading and Counterfeit Detection, 2nd Edition* is not a detective novel; it deals with fact, not fiction, and with coins, rather than crimes. But this is required reading for anyone interested in reconstructing the profiles of scarce and valuable coins, analyzing the "fingerprints" that identify them or, for that matter, following the trail of evidence that can help expose the real-life villains who prey upon the unwary in this field.

Reading this book will make you an expert—a Sherlock Holmes, so to speak—at grading genuine coins and detecting those that are counterfeit, altered, or otherwise questionable. It will give you the necessary tools to make informed judgments on these matters, and it will help you to understand the elements that determine the grade of a coin.

I have read other books on how coins are made and how they are graded. Some of these have been helpful to me during and since my service at the Mint. Evaluating older coins was not part of my job description as Mint Director, but maintaining excellence in new collector coinage was an important duty. Of all the books I examined and studied, however, none came close to providing so much pertinent information—and showcasing it so well—as *The Official Guide to Coin Grading and Counterfeit Detection 2nd Edition*. Knowing what I do today about the high standards and consistent excellence of PCGS in serving its constituency over the years, I am not at all surprised. This company is first-class all the way, and that's one of the reasons why it is first and best in its field. It is a grading service that stresses both the *grading* and the *service*.

I hope you enjoy this book as much as I have. I am sure you will. And I have a word of advice: keep it on a shelf where you can reach it easily. You'll be using it often.

1 WHAT ARE COINS? WHAT IS GRADING? HOW DO YOU DO IT?

What are coins, and how and why do people grade them?

Those are simple, straightforward questions, but answering them properly is much more complicated. At the very least, an explanation of how the production of coins evolved, both historically and technically, is required.

We think of coins today as small, round disks of metallic money that are stamped with a statement of value and are used to pay for merchandise or services. Our early ancestors had no such "pocket change," however—if, indeed, they had any pockets at all. The world's first "money" was anything of value that one person could trade to another for something else of value. Cattle, grain, pottery, tools—all served as money in the barter systems that flourished in ancient times. Only when gold, silver, and other precious metals were recognized as precious did coins come into being, and that did not occur until the sixth century B.C. in the Asia Minor kingdom of Lydia.

The Evolution of Coins

At first, metallic money consisted of ingots, rather than coins. These hunks of metal, made primarily of gold, silver, and copper, were more compact and convenient than the cumbersome commodities used in most transactions before that time, and thus represented a great leap forward. They were primitive, however, at the start—often just amorphous lumps of metal—and evolved only gradually into sizes and shapes that resembled the coins we know today.

As time passed, these ingots were hammered into coins through the use of crude dies. In modern terms, dies are pieces of hard, engraved metal—typically tempered steel—used for stamping coins or medals (coin-like metallic objects lacking a statement of value). Ancient minters used the hardest metals available, but often those would be no harder than bronze and tin—and there were even occasions when dies were fashioned from wood.

Then, as now, there was one die for the obverse (or "heads" side) of a coin and one for the reverse. The design would be engraved into each of these dies in mirror-image fashion—the opposite of the way it would appear on the coin itself. Thus, when the coin was struck, the design would look normal. With rare exceptions throughout history, dies have also been cut with the elements of the design "incuse," or recessed below the surface. That way, the design is raised on the coin itself—appearing in what is known as "relief" above the surface. Early minters would set up one die in a fixed position, place an ingot on top of it, align another die above the ingot, and then strike the upper die with a hammer or other heavy instrument to drive the ingot into the lower die.

The very first coins had no real design, generally being stamped only with a statement of their weight and fineness or perhaps a simple seal denoting their official status. Portraits came later, along with inscriptions and dates, as more and more governments, church officials, monarchs, and minor princes started issuing coinage. For more than 2,000 years, "hammered" coins continued to be the rule.

The Evolution of Coins
Obverse and reverse of a hammered-die coin-an ancient Roman Egyptian coin of Antoninus Pius.

The minting process underwent major refinements, of course, but the basic process remained much the same: coins were produced by using human force to *hammer* the designs into a "planchet" (or blank piece of metal in the shape of a coin).

The Screw Press

Sometime in the late fifteenth century, a major breakthrough took place in coinage technology. The resourceful Italian architect and inventor Donato Bramante devised a new kind of minting machine that imparted the design to a planchet not with a blow from a hammer, but rather by the turn of a screw. Bramante's ingenious machine consisted of a massive screw-like mechanism with a die attached to a sleeve along its head. This die was aligned above a second die, a planchet was placed between them, and workmen then turned large metal arms protruding from the screw to drive the upper die into the planchet, imparting the design from both above and below.

Bramante was seal-master to the pope, and initially his "screw press" was used not for coining but instead for producing heavy lead papal bulls (official seals) and elaborate papal medals. It soon was adapted for use in coinage as well, because it had important advantages over hammering: it permitted the production of larger-size coins, and the coins were more uniform and generally had a higher quality.

When they first appeared on the scene, screw presses actually slowed production; the coins they turned out were better, but they took longer to make than through the hammering process. Then, too, many minters were slow to accept the new technology, fearing it might jeopardize their livelihood. As a consequence, the old and new methods coexisted for more than two centuries—far longer than logic would have dictated, for well before then, enhancements had made screw presses more efficient. By the early eighteenth century, the screw press had emerged as the dominant means of minting and few new hammered coins were being produced, although older ones lingered in circulation for several generations thereafter.

The Early United States Mint

By the time the United States had gained its independence and had established a federal mint of its own, in the early 1790s, the screw press was firmly entrenched and became the obvious choice for use at the fledgling Philadelphia Mint—which served for nearly a half century thereafter as the source of all U.S. coinage and remains to this day the nation's mother mint.

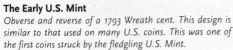

The Early U.S. Mint
Obverse and reverse of a 1793 Wreath cent. This design is similar to that used on many U.S. coins. This was one of the first coins struck by the fledgling U.S. Mint.

Men and horses provided the power to run the machines used in the production of the earliest U.S. coins. During that period, individual tools were used to punch the lettering and date into each die. As a result, no two dies were exactly the same, and this resulted in the creation of hundreds of so-called "die varieties" when the coins were struck. These are avidly collected by hobbyists who specialize in early U.S. coinage.

Technology grew apace in the early nineteenth century, and the U.S. Mint strove to keep up with it. Steam engines were replacing men and horses as the source of power at European mints, and Uncle Sam followed suit—first on a limited basis in 1816, then for all production in 1836. Another innovation at the Philadelphia Mint, in 1828, was the introduction of the close collar—a device that functioned essentially as a third die to strike the edge of each coin. This collar was slightly larger than the planchet being struck; thus, when the upper die was driven into the planchet, the metal expanded not only into the recesses of the upper and lower dies but also into the collar, which finished the edge. The coins that resulted were more uniform, their rims higher and more regular. This process can be used only for coins whose edges are plain or reeded—that is, struck with sharp, vertical lines; thus, it signaled the

end of lettered-edge coins—coins with inscriptions on their edges—as a major component of U.S. coinage. (Several of the earlier U.S. coins had been of that type.)

The combination of the close collar and the powerful new steam-driven presses enhanced both the Mint's productivity and the quality of U.S. coins from 1836 on, although at the sacrifice of the teeming die varieties that make the earlier coins so distinctive and appealing. Later, oil and coal were used to generate steam for the presses, and still later, electrical engines became the standard. Each was an improvement, and with every step the resultant coinage became even more consistent. Electric-powered presses, in particular, increased the potential striking power behind the dies. Furthermore, improved reducing machines made production of the dies more standardized.

Minting and Grading

What do the minting process and the type of equipment used in making coins have to do with grading? For that matter, why are coins graded at all?

With coins, as with any other collectible, quality is a major consideration; the purchaser wants the best example available, or at

Classification of Coins—Uncirculated
Uncirculated 1880-S Morgan dollar with original luster and no trace of wear.

Classification of Coins—Proof
Proof 1894 Morgan dollar. Because Proofs are struck with higher pressure and given two or more blows from the dies, the detail is extremely crisp. Also note the mirrored fields resulting from highly polished dies and planchets.

least the best that he or she can afford. Whether the object in question is a painting, an antique dresser, a music box, or a coin, the best examples are in the greatest demand and bring the highest prices. Knowing how a coin was made provides important insights into the various attributes that a perfect—or near-perfect—specimen of that coin should possess. These, in turn, serve as reference points in determining the *grade*, or level of preservation, of specimens that are less than perfect.

Over the years, coin collectors developed a set of terms to denote the conditions—or grades—of the coins they encountered. This made it easier for them to communicate with other collectors when discussing their mutual interests or when arranging to buy, sell, or trade. At first, the terms they used were quite broad: Coins were described as poor, fair, good, fine, excellent—or sometimes just "new" or "used." The value of an *excellent* coin was not dramatically higher, as a rule, than that of a similar coin that was merely good. For that reason, there was no pressing need to develop more specific degrees of gradation.

By the mid-twentieth century, price differentials had started to expand. As more and more people began collecting coins, the demand for better specimens intensified, putting greater pressure on their supply, which

in most instances was relatively small compared with that of lower-grade examples. Intermediate grade levels came into general use; coins might be described as *very fine* or *extremely fine*, or perhaps *about uncirculated*. These sufficed for a while, but by the 1970s, tremendous emphasis was being placed on quality, to the point where one high-quality coin might bring a far higher price than another one that was only slightly less perfect. That led to the establishment of formal grading standards, recognized and used throughout the rare coin market, and set the stage for the founding of the Professional Coin Grading Service (PCGS).

Classifications of Coins

Generally, there are three categories of coins that will be discussed in this book:

- *Uncirculated*, or *Mint State*, coins. These are coins produced in what is known as *business-strike* quality—the kind of coins used in everyday commerce but which show no sign of ever having been used in circulation. The planchets on which they were struck, and the dies used to strike them, were of the same type regularly used in ordinary production.

- *Proof* coins. These are presentation-quality coins, struck on flawless planchets with highly polished dies at a slower rate than production-level coins and usually with mul-

Classification of Coins—Circulated
Circulated Morgan dollar with wear evident on the hair, cap, and other head devices such as the cotton bolls.

Factors that Determine Value—Quality
Uncirculated 1916 Lincoln cent obverse. Note the detail of the beard, hair, and face.

tiple impressions. The term Proof refers not to the condition of these coins, but rather to the method by which they are made. In earlier times, Proofs were often made as gifts for important dignitaries—even heads of state. Today, they are produced primarily for sale at premium prices—individually or in sets—to collectors.

- *Circulated* coins. These are coins that have undergone wear, however slight, as a result of use in circulation or mishandling. They can range in condition from Poor, a grade that denotes a coin that can barely be identified, all the way to *About Uncirculated* (AU, for short), right on the threshold of being a Mint State coin. Business-strike coins and Proofs both come under the heading of *circulated* coins if they exhibit wear. Circulated Proofs are said to be *impaired* and retain the term "Proof" as part of their grade.

These three classes of coins will be examined separately, for the most part, in this book. However, there are numerous parallels and areas in which some of these coins' characteristics overlap.

Factors That Determine Value
Three factors determine the value of a coin:

- *Rarity*—the number of pieces produced and, more important, the number that survive. In some instances, coins with relatively high mintage figures—showing that many were produced—may be scarce or even rare because large numbers were melted or otherwise lost through the years. This is especially true of certain gold and silver coins, which have been melted in vast numbers at various times because of either government intervention or bullion-market conditions that made them worth more as metal than as money.

- *Quality* or *grade*—the level of preservation. People will pay more—often much more—to get a coin that is well-preserved and pleasing to the eye, just as they will pay more for a new car or a low-mileage used car than they will for a similar model with 100,000 miles on the odometer. The premium differential will not be as great if large numbers exist in high grades. However, the value of a lustrous Mint State coin may go through the roof if the number of pieces available in "factory-fresh" condition is very small.

- *Popularity*—the level of demand for a given coin. Some coins appeal to great numbers of hobbyists. Lincoln cents, for instance, have an enormous following; so do Morgan silver dollars, which were issued by Uncle Sam between 1878 and 1921. Other coins are not collected as widely. For example, the pool of collectors is considerably smaller for half dimes—silver five-cent pieces issued until 1873—than it is for Indian Head (or "Buffalo") nickels, which are also obsolete but hold powerful appeal to many hobbyists. Because there are more collectors pursuing them, Lincoln cents and Buffalo nickels are considered scarce at mintage levels that in other series would be looked upon as being relatively normal. The 1914-D Lincoln cent, produced at the Denver Mint and bearing a "D" mint mark below the date, has a mintage of nearly 1.2 million, yet may sell for hundreds of dollars even in circulated grade levels. By contrast, the 1843 half dime, with an almost identical mintage, brings well under $100, even in grades approaching Mint State. That is because the Lincoln cent has many more collectors seeking to acquire it. In short, the prices reflect supply and demand, and while the supplies are similar, the demand is decidedly not.

By now, the rarity (or lack of rarity) of most older U.S. coins has been fairly well established. Reliable mintage figures are available for virtually all of the coins produced by the U.S. Mint since its inception, and these figures are easily obtained in widely disseminated books and periodicals. Popularity is cyclical to some extent; various series of coins experience peaks and valleys in the marketplace. In broad terms, however, the "haves" and "have-nots"—the popular and not-so-popular coins—tend to remain much the same as time goes by.

The one remaining factor in determining market value—the quality or grade of a coin—has come to the fore in recent years and has triggered considerable discussion, controversy, and concern. For more than a decade, PCGS has striven to remove the confusion and doubt from this sometimes contentious area and bring a sense of confidence to the marketplace. This book is intended to demystify grading even more by explaining in detail the process by which PCGS determines the grades it assigns to various coins, and to quantify in print the standards that it uses to distinguish one grade from another.

The 1-70 Grading Scale

In the mid-1970s, the American Numismatic Association (ANA), the nation's largest coin club, recognized the need for uniform grading standards to bring order out of the chaos that existed in this regard in the coin market at the time. Vague terms such as "gem," "choice," and "brilliant uncirculated" were being used to describe Mint State coins, and purchasers were essentially being asked to buy a pig in a poke.

The panel appointed to draft the grading standards considered various options, including a system with grades from 1 to 100. In retrospect, that might have made more sense. However, the panel decided to turn instead to a system already being used in a much more limited way to denote the condition of large cents—the pure copper one-cent coins issued by the U.S. Mint from 1793 to 1857. Dr. William H. Sheldon, a prominent collector of these coins, had promulgated this system in his 1949 book *Early American Cents*, which was subsequently revised and reissued as *Penny Whimsy*.

Sheldon described his system as a "quantitative grading of condition." It was based upon the value of the 1794 large cent, a bellwether coin in the series, in various levels of preservation during the second quarter of the twentieth century. Sheldon observed that cents of that date in the lowest collectible condition—"identifiable and unmutilated"—were selling for about one dollar apiece, so he established $1 as the *basal value* and assigned a grade of 1 to coins in that level of preservation. Noting that examples in Good condition were selling for about four dollars each, he assigned these a numerical grade of 4. Continuing in this manner, Sheldon came up with numerical grades of 7 to 10 for Very Good, 12 to 15 for Fine, 20 to 30 for Very Fine, 40 for Extremely Fine, 50 for About Uncirculated, and 60 to 70 for Mint State.

The relative values reflected in Sheldon's scale may have been accurate for one given coin—the 1794 large cent—at the time he first proposed them as grade levels. However, they have never been reliable barometers for U.S. coin values as a whole. In choosing to base its own grading system on Sheldon's version, the ANA apparently was influenced by the fact that the 1–70 scale was a known commodity, already being used in at least one portion of the coin market.

This scale has shortcomings. Its most obvious deficiency is that of the 70 numbers available, only 11—those from 60 to 70—are set aside for Mint State coins and unimpaired Proofs. These coins have assumed far greater importance than circulated coins during the last quarter-century, and it would be desirable to have more space for them on the grading spectrum to reflect their degrees of difference more precisely. Nonetheless, PCGS has used the 1–70 scale since opening for business in 1986, because by that time the system enjoyed wide acceptance among both collectors and dealers.

Grade	Description
PO-1	Identifiable date and type
FR-2	Mostly worn, though some detail is visible
AG-3	Worn rims but most lettering is readable though worn
G-4	Slightly worn rims, flat detail, peripheral lettering nearly full
G-6	Rims complete with flat detail, peripheral lettering full
VG-8	Design worn with slight detail
VG-10	Design worn with slight detail, slightly clearer
F-12	Some deeply recessed areas with detail, all lettering sharp
F-15	Slightly more detail in the recessed areas, all lettering sharp
VF-20	Some definition of detail, all lettering full and sharp
VF-25	Slightly more definition in the detail and lettering
VF-30	Almost complete detail with flat areas
VF-35	Detail is complete but worn with high points flat
EF-40	Detail is complete with most high points slightly flat
EF-45	Detail is complete with some high points flat
AU-50	Full detail with friction over most of the surface, slight flatness on high points
AU-53	Full detail with friction over 1/2 or more of surface, very slight flatness on high points
AU-55	Full detail with friction on less than 1/2 surface, mainly on high points
AU-58	Full detail with only slight friction on the high points
MS/PR-60	No wear. May have many heavy marks/hairlines, strike may not be full
MS/PR-61	No wear. Multiple heavy marks/hairlines, strike may not be full
MS/PR-62	No wear. Slightly less marks/hairlines, strike may not be full
MS/PR-63	Moderate number/size marks/hairlines, strike may not be full
MS/PR-64	Few marks/hairlines or a couple of severe ones, strike should be average or above
MS/PR-65	Minor marks/hairlines though none in focal areas, above average strike

MS/PR-66 Few minor marks/hairlines not in focal areas, good strike

MS/PR-67 Virtually as struck with minor imperfections, very well struck

MS/PR-68 Virtually as struck with slight imperfections, slightest weakness of strike allowed

MS/PR-69 Virtually as struck with minuscule imperfections, near full strike necessary

MS/PR-70 As struck, with full strike

The Advent of Certified Grading

The introduction of official coin-grading standards by the ANA in the late 1970s represented a major step forward. Prior to that time, there was no uniform yardstick for measuring the grade of a given coin. On the contrary, the coin market was almost as chaotic as a Middle Eastern bazaar and as unrefined as a frontier town in America's Wild West. In the absence of a recognized set of values, coin buyers had relatively little guidance regarding what an "uncirculated" coin really was, or how a "gem" uncirculated coin differed from one that was "choice." The only choice involved, it seemed, was how each dealer chose to describe his merchandise, since there was no law of the land—and, for that matter, no sheriff to enforce even rudimentary frontier justice.

The process of bringing order from chaos began in earnest in March 1979, when the ANA Certification Service (ANACS), established seven years earlier to authenticate the genuineness of coins, started grading coins submitted for its review, using standards based on the Sheldon scale. The timing could not have been better; the coin market was booming, and the new grading service gained immediate acceptance from buyers and sellers alike as a welcome source of stability—a means to instill greater confidence, thereby reinforcing the bull market.

Unfortunately, neither the bull market nor confidence in the ANACS grading lasted very long. As prices began to fall in the early 1980s, dealers who had earlier complained that ANACS was undergrading now complained that the same coin with the same certificate was overgraded. ANACS came under intense new scrutiny, much of it hostile. Coin dealers, plagued by plummeting profits, complained that the ANACS grading was partially to blame, terming it inconsistent and all too often inaccurate. They further complained that the ANACS graders lacked the levels of competence and experience needed for such demanding work and that they were out of touch with commercial considerations in the marketplace.

The controversy threatened to wipe out the gains made during ANACS's formative years—the progress that had taken place in bringing uniformity to grading. Commercial grading, it appeared, had indeed become inconsistent; a coin that was Mint State-65 in a hot market would shrink to Mint State-63 when the marketplace was depressed and the dealer who had sold the coin was buying it back. And confidence in the process was shrinking, too.

In 1985, a group of prominent coin dealers headed by David Hall came up with a solution that not only restored the market's confidence in the grading process but literally revolutionized the way rare coins are bought and sold. Hall and his associates—John Dannreuther, Bruce Amspacher, and Gordon Wrubel—established the Professional Coin Grading Service. In doing so, they created more than a new company: PCGS represented a new and more sophisticated approach to grading coins. Instead of the photo certificates used by ANACS, PCGS encapsulated coins in sonically sealed, hard plastic holders, thus providing physical protection for the coins and safeguarding against possible tampering with the grading documentation. The company also pioneered the use of consensus grading: each coin would be examined by three different experts who then would assign a grade—and after that,

The Advent of Certified Grading
PCGS-graded 1883 Proof double eagle. Shown in sonically sealed holder with insert listing date, denomination, and grade. Also included are a bar code, the PCGS coin number, and the unique seven-digit identification number.

Co-founders of PCGS, David Hall and John Dannreuther.

another grader would view it, weigh the individual grades, and determine the actual grade by means of consensus.

From the outset, PCGS dedicated itself to standardizing grading, so any fluctuations in the value of a coin would be limited to price swings, rather than to market-related changes in the grade. A Mint State-65 coin would still be the same in any market—hot, cold, or neutral. The price might change but the grading would not—and *could* not—because the coin was encapsulated along with a unique serial number and a fixed grade.

The company carefully assembled a master grading set to guide its expert graders, choosing the contents from coins that had been examined and graded by preeminent dealers and collectors. This was the very first set of consensus-graded coins. It was—and is—the standard by which all coins are graded at PCGS. Many of the coins in this set are illustrated in this book.

The Attributes of Grading

Whether they are Mint State, Proof, or circulated, all coins are graded on the basis of certain elements. These elements, or *attributes*, may be positive, negative, or neutral—and the positive and negative attributes are broken down further into very positive, positive,

or slightly positive, or, on the downside, into slightly negative, negative, and very negative. Each element of a coin's grade is analyzed and given a rating from very positive to very negative.

The primary attributes that make up the grade of a Mint State or Proof coin are marks, luster, strike, toning, and eye appeal. Some of these elements have less importance with circulated coins, or are factored into the grade in a different way. With circulated coins, for example, wear tends to outweigh marks as a grading determinant, especially in lower grade levels. Similarly, surface preservation takes the place of luster as a focal point. Strike is considered an adjunct of wear. And toning is not a factor for most coins graded below Very Fine.

The elements of grading will be explored in detail in chapter 5. Basic familiarity with these attributes is essential, however, before we proceed. Here, then, is a summary of what they are and how they can be identified.

Marks

Marks are associated primarily with Mint State coins and can take many different forms. Among other things, graders look for bag marks (resulting from contact with other coins in bags or kegs), roll marks (from contact with other coins in rolls), scratches (from

The Attributes of Grading—Marks
*1880-S Morgan dollar with marks, which are most notice-
able on the cheek and chin.*

The Attributes of Grading—Luster
*1881-S Morgan dollar with vibrant luster. Note the frosty
devices against the flashy fields.*

contact with a foreign object), reeding or milling marks (from contact with the reeded edge of another coin), gouges (from deep contact with another coin or foreign object), hairlines (finer lines than scratches, usually caused by some type of cleaning), album slide marks (caused by sliding an album's plastic insert across the high points of a coin, leaving parallel lines similar to hairlines or scratches), cabinet friction (slight contact from being stored in an old-style coin cabinet), and flip rub (from contact with the plastic flip in which some coins are stored).

With circulated coins, marks result mainly from contact with foreign objects, although bag marks from other coins are common in the higher circulated grades. Other types of marks on circulated coins parallel those on Mint State coins; however, some of them—cabinet friction, roll marks, and flip rub, for example—are part of the coins' overall wear. In the lower grades, marks are much less important; the amount of wear visible on such coins takes the place of marks as an attribute used to determine grade. With Proof coins, the most commonly found marks are hairlines. These are usually caused by cleaning, although they may result from even light contact from a finger or from paper or some other object, because of the delicate nature of Proof coins' surfaces.

Luster

Luster, too, is associated most commonly with Mint State coins, since Proof coins generally have brilliant, mirror-like surfaces and circulated coins usually have no luster in grades below Very Fine. With Proof coins, reflectivity replaces luster as a grading attribute; with circulated coins, surface preservation is weighed instead. With Mint State coins, luster is the result of light reflecting from the surface. As a coin is struck, the metal flows into the recesses of the die because of the pressure applied by the coining press. The metal flow is usually in a radial pattern, i.e., outward toward the rim. On some coins, the flow lines—or metal stress lines—are visible to the unaided eye. On other coins, these lines are all but invisible but are still present microscopically. The degree of luster is determined by how, and how intensely, light reflects from these flow lines. Sometimes this luster "cartwheels" around the fields (or background areas) of a coin as it is tilted back and forth under a good light source. Mint State luster is categorized in several ways: flat (flow lines are invisible to the unaided eye, as often happens when coins are struck from worn dies), satin (flow lines may be slightly visible but there is little cartwheel effect), frosty (flow lines are usually visible with a cartwheel effect, ranging from slight to heavy), semi-prooflike (light flow

The Attributes of Grading—Strike
Well-struck 1938-D Indian Head (Buffalo) nickel. Details of hair, braid, and face are sharp and crisp.

Weakly struck 1926-D Buffalo nickel obverse. Note weakness in hair, LIBERTY, and date.

Weakly struck 1926-D Buffalo nickel reverse. Note weakness at head and tail of bison.

lines may be visible but most are not, being replaced by slightly mirrored fields that have a slight cartwheel effect), and prooflike (no flow lines are visible, with the fields now mirror-like, but with virtually no cartwheel effect). With brilliant Proof coins, the surfaces of the planchets and the dies are highly polished. These coins are often struck multiple times, resulting in coin surfaces that are highly reflective. Flow lines are present even on these brilliant Proofs, but only in microscopic form. When flow lines become visible on a Proof die, the die will normally be repolished. With circulated coins, smooth, original surfaces are rated more positively than rough, impaired surfaces.

Strike

Strike is most important as an element of grading on Mint State coins and the highest-grade circulated coins. Proof coins are almost always fully struck, or at least well struck, with only an occasional example being found with a weak strike. With circulated coins graded Very Fine and lower, strike is incorporated with wear as a grading element. There are several ways in which a coin may lack the intended detail—that is, be weakly struck. When the striking pressure is inadequate to cause the metal to flow into the deepest recesses of the dies, the resultant coin lacks detail on the highest points. (The deepest part of a particular die, which is incuse, corresponds to the highest point of the struck coin, which is raised, or in relief.) When the dies are spaced too far apart, the metal does not flow into the deepest parts of the dies, resulting in coins that are incompletely struck. This type of weakness of strike is difficult to distinguish from weakness on coins struck

The Attributes of Grading—Toning

Toned 1897 Barber half dollar. Even toning is seen throughout the entire obverse.

Brilliant 1878-S Morgan dollar. This white coin shows no evidence of toning.

with insufficient pressure. Sometimes the dies are not level in the coining press—a problem that most often involves just one die, although on occasion both dies may be out of plane. When this occurs, weakness of strike will be localized in a particular quadrant of the coins that are produced. Coins struck from worn or eroded dies also are said to be weakly struck—although technically this is not totally accurate, since a coin from worn dies may be "fully struck" and still be missing significant detail. When this detail is worn or eroded from the dies, no amount of striking pressure can impart it to the coins struck from those dies, since it is detail that does not exist. During the 1920s, some dies used at the Denver and San Francisco mints were not hardened properly before use, causing them to mush down and lose detail almost immediately. However, they normally would be left in the coinage press for a full press run. Most coins struck from such dies have mushy or fuzzy detail in the area where the die wear has occurred. Weakness of strike on Proof and circulated coins is caused in the same ways but, as noted, is usually very minor on Proof coinage and is factored along with wear on circulated coins.

Toning

Toning is the result of elements combining with the metals in a coin. Technically speaking, when a coin leaves the coining die it begins to tone at once, as the reactive metals begin to combine immediately with reactive elements in the atmosphere. There are, however, coins that appear to have no toning; these coins are said to be brilliant. (They are sometimes referred to as "white specimens," although silver coins are the only ones that are truly whitish in color.) Coins that have a clear, milky, or slightly opaque creamy color are also sometimes called brilliant, especially when the luster is unimpeded. When colors begin to appear on the surfaces, a coin is considered to have toning. These colors result primarily from metallic oxides and sulfides and are nearly infinite in their varieties and hues. Toning is evaluated in similar fashion for Mint State and Proof coins and, where applicable, for circulated coins. The various types of toning are examined in detail in chapter 5.

Eye Appeal

Eye appeal is the most difficult grading attribute to define and determine. This term refers to the overall appearance of a coin and is really a combination of the other attributes. Mint State coins that have very positive eye appeal are usually well struck, very lustrous, brilliant or attractively toned, and minimally marked. Mint State coins that have very negative eye appeal are poorly struck and have flat or dull luster, unattractive or splotchy toning, and noticeable or multiple marks. Of course, most coins fall between these two extremes, since the other grading attributes tend to vary. Brilliant Proof coins that have very positive eye appeal are well struck and highly reflective, have frosted devices and lettering, are brilliant or attractively toned, and have virtually no hairlines or other impairments. Brilliant Proof coins that have very negative eye appeal may be well struck but have impaired reflectivity, dull surfaces or unattractive toning, and multiple hairlines or other impairments. As with Mint State coins, most Proof coins have eye appeal that falls between these two extremes, with their individual attributes varying from very negative to very positive. With circulated coins, eye appeal often is determined primarily by surface preservation. Luster is a non-factor for most circulated coins and strike is a minor consideration, except in cases of extreme weakness. Marks are important in measuring this attribute, since they contribute to surface preservation. Toning, as noted previously, is not much of a factor with circulated coins, except in grades of Very Fine and higher.

Other Grading Factors

Other considerations also come into play in determining the overall grade of a coin, and many times these have nothing to do with the dies or the coining process. The planchets used for early U.S. coins often were defective, for example. Other factors affecting the overall grade are sometimes type-specific—that is, peculiar to one given kind of coin. These include the presence or absence of a "Full Head" on Standing Liberty quarters (not necessarily the result of striking weakness), color on Mint State and Proof copper coins (reflected in a grade as Red, Red and Brown, and Brown), and Full Bell Lines on Franklin half dollars (whose absence may be the result of worn dies, weak strike, or both).

All of the various attributes, or elements, are quantified and combined in determining the overall grade of any particular coin. This book will take you on a step-by-step journey into the mind of a grader and, with the help of photographs, will show you how the overall grade of every type of coin is determined.

In the final analysis, the correct market grade of a coin is a single grade at which you would *love* to sell the coin if you owned it. That "happy-to-sell-at" grade must also be the same grade at which you would like to buy the same coin. The grade of any coin is a combination of all of the attributes and variations, both positive and negative, that a grader takes into account. This book will explain how these attributes and variations are combined to arrive at the overall grade.

2 HANDLING AND STORAGE

All coins are not created equal. Some come into the world with sharper strikes than others . . . brighter luster . . . greater eye appeal. From a grading standpoint, however, all coins are as perfect as they are ever going to be at the moment of their creation—the very split second they are ejected from the coining dies.

It is all downhill from there; a coin's condition can only decline after that time—or, at best, remain the same. In most cases, in fact, a business-strike coin—the kind produced for use in circulation—loses its state of perfection (if it was truly perfect to begin with) on its very first bounce into the waiting hopper at the mint. Proof coins receive better treatment as a rule, but they, too, are in jeopardy of losing their pristine quality from the moment they leave the coining press.

The world is a cold, cruel place and too many coins end up in the school of hard knocks, shorn of their virginity and suffering wear and tear as they are buffeted about from mint bag to cash drawer to pocket, purse, and cookie jar. It is little wonder then that not many examples survive in top condition, especially in the case of early U.S. coins, whose production occurred at a time when dedicated collectors—people devoted to keeping the coins safe from harm—were few and far between.

Handling and *storage* play fundamental roles in determining the grade of a coin. That grade depends not so much on how well the coin was made, but rather on how well it was preserved.

The Odds Against Perfection

If someone were waiting to catch a coin in a glove the moment it left the coining dies, there is a chance—although a very slim one—that it might end up in a holder with a grade of Mint State-70 or Proof-70, denoting sheer perfection. The chance is slim because in practice, coins almost always incur imperfections, however slight, at some point in their life and thus fall short of the ultimate grade. More often than not, they begin incurring these flaws at the moment of their birth, precisely because there is not someone waiting to catch them in a glove and lovingly deposit them on a piece of velvet in a climate-controlled environment—or place them, as PCGS does, in a hard, inert, protective plastic holder. On the contrary, even Proofs are sometimes mishandled at the mint. (Today, the mint personnel are better trained and wear gloves, so Proof-70 modern coins are more abundant.)

In the real world, business-strike coins begin descending the grading scale almost at once: each tiny contact mark, however imperceptible it may be to the naked eye, pushes a coin down the scale from Mint State-70 to 69 to 68 and so on. And if a blemish is larger and visible without magnification, the push is that much harder and shoves the grade that much farther down the numerical ladder.

Even if a coin is fortunate enough to leave the mint unscathed, it still must run a gauntlet of formidable assaults upon its unblemished nature. If it is a business-strike coin, it will be tossed haphazardly into a canvas sack with hundreds of other coins for a bumpy ride to a bank. Then, after being unloaded amid further jostling, that bag will be flung to the floor in a vault where its contents may shift many times a day. Eventually, the bank may run the coins through a counting machine in order to wrap them in rolls, meanwhile exposing them to further risk of scratches, nicks, and gouges. It is no wonder that the number of flawless coins emerging from this obstacle course is downright infinitesimal.

Preserving Coins

The grade of a coin is a shorthand way of stating its level of preservation. A Mint State designation signifies that a business-strike coin has never entered circulation—never been subjected to the gradual erosion that comes from being passed from hand to hand. The Mint State range is a broad one, however, extending all the way from coins that are stunningly perfect to coins that are flat-out ugly, yet technically bear no evidence of ever having been in circulation. Naturally, those that are perfect—or very nearly perfect—are much more desirable than those that barely qualify as being in mint condition. This, in turn, translates into a higher market value; people will pay a premium—often a very large one—for coins in superior levels of preservation, and this gives collectors a very strong incentive to handle and store their coins with the greatest possible care to protect them from damage and resultant loss of value.

How to Handle a Coin

The first rule of thumb on how to handle a coin is not to place your thumb—or anything else, for that matter—directly on its surfaces. Coins should be gripped only by their edges. The likelihood is great that if you touch the obverse or reverse (the front or back) of a coin, your finger or thumb will leave a permanent mark. The chemicals in your body will react with the metals in the coin, creating potentially disastrous results. That fingerprint or thumbprint may not be obvious at first; it may not show up for months or even years. But when it does appear, it may be im-

possible to remove, short of causing damage to the surface of the coin in another way.

If at all possible, always keep something soft—perhaps a piece of velvet—underneath a coin while you are holding it. That way, if you drop the coin, it will have a safety net. A hard landing could have dire consequences; a single nick or gouge could send the grade and value of the coin plunging dramatically, even though the original fall may have been just a few feet or inches!

Proof coins have particularly delicate surfaces, and the slightest rub from a finger or other external contact may leave them with "hairlines"—very fine lines that may not be apparent to the unaided eye but that show up all too glaringly under magnification. These lines stand out on Proof coins, precisely because the surfaces of these coins are so flawless to begin with. In many instances, business-strike coins are expected to have such lines, but Proofs by their very nature aspire to perfection. They are made from special planchets, using polished dies, and are usually struck multiple times to give them their exceptional sharpness and detail. Therefore, every flaw, however minute it may be, is that much more readily detectable and detracting.

Slight mishandling of a coin may cause only slight damage—perhaps an almost imperceptible smudge. In that case, the effect on the coin's grade and value may be minor, even negligible. However, if the surface is disturbed more significantly—with hairlines or even slight wear beginning to appear—then the problem is more serious and the coin's grade will undoubtedly be reduced. The impairment may be so serious, in fact, that the coin will no longer qualify for a Mint State grade.

To prove to yourself how readily a Mint State coin can be impaired, take a full-red Lincoln cent from a brand-new late-date roll and rub it just slightly between your fingers. Then look at the coin under a five-power glass. Repeat this process several times. You will be surprised at the damage that can result from

How to Handle a Coin—Incorrect
Improper handling of coin. Oils and contaminants from hand will cause damage over time.

How to Handle a Coin—Correct
Correct handling of coin. All coins should be handled only by their edges.

How to Handle a Coin—Effects of Mishandling
Hairlines are seen in the field above the eagle on the reverse of a quarter eagle.

such seemingly minor contact. Even the slightest rub can leave hairlines on the surfaces, and these will cause graders—as well as potential purchasers—to view the coin less favorably.

Particular care must be exercised when placing a coin in a holder or removing it for viewing. The sliding plastic inserts used in certain albums can damage a coin's surfaces if the plastic and the metal come into contact; the friction can actually erode the metal's highest points, reducing the coin's grade from Mint State to circulated and, in the process, very likely slashing its market value. Similar friction is possible, with similar loss of value, when taking a coin out of—or placing it back inside—a plastic "flip." A single careless moment can leave a valuable coin with permanent and irreversible damage.

PCGS requests that each coin submitted for grading be placed first in a poly bag—a protective plastic covering—and that the bag then be placed in a soft vinyl flip. This enables the graders to remove the coin from its packaging without touching the surfaces. They then place the coin on a velvet pad, where it can be picked up easily by its edge. This affords maximum protection for the surfaces, with little risk of mishandling.

How to Store a Coin

Ideally, coins should be handled as seldom and as little as possible. Frequent handling greatly increases the chance that an accident may occur—a coin may be dropped, touched with a sweat-soaked finger, or rubbed with a plastic liner while being placed in an album or being removed. Proper *storage*, however, is every bit as important as proper *handling*.

How to Store a Coin

Proof Franklin half dollar in a poly bag. This soft bag is used to protect coins during shipment and for short-term storage. It is not recommended for long-term storage.

Soft plastic flip used to submit coins for grading. This is not recommended for long-term storage.

Coins can be impaired through unsafe storage just as surely as they can be through careless handling. The damage may take place more gradually, and you will not be aware of it right away. However it can be just as lasting and just as costly.

First of all, it is essential that you house your coins in holders that are chemically inert. The hard plastic holders used by PCGS contain no reactive chemicals, thus are entirely safe. Because they are sonically sealed, they also protect their contents from airborne contaminants and other external hazards. All of these qualities make them ideal for use in long-term storage.

Be particularly wary of soft plastic flips made with the substance polyvinyl chloride (PVC, for short). This compound is unstable and tends to break down over time, releasing harmful chemicals that actually may attack the surfaces of your coins, eating away at the metal and leaving unsightly scars. Many unfortunate hobbyists have learned this chemistry lesson the hard way—by opening their safe deposit boxes after months or years to discover that some of their coins were basically ruined.

At times, the safe deposit box itself may contribute to coins' deterioration. Ironically, this risk is likely to be greater in high-rent districts—banks where the box rental fee is higher than usual because special efforts are made to enhance the environment in the vault. Typically, this "enhancement" takes the form of increasing the humidity of the air. Banks do this because mortgages, wills, and other paper documents—the kinds of items generally found in safe deposit boxes—tend to grow brittle when the air is dry. But moisture is a coin's enemy: water serves as a catalyst for chemical reactions on coins' surfaces. Therefore, it is advisable to store your coins in a bank where the vault is not moisturized—and normally, that will be a bank with cheaper box rates.

Frequently, copper coins are kept in cloth pouches. These are basically inert and will cause little toning, but they also offer minimal protection. Two-by-two cardboard holders are unsatisfactory, too; flecks of the cardboard often come to rest on the surfaces of the coins being housed in these crude holders, setting the stage for chemical reactions that can leave the coins permanently spotted. Also, as a rule, these holders are sealed with staples, which can easily scratch a coin during its removal.

Simple folders with cutout holes may be satisfactory for circulated coins of no great value. But they certainly should not be used for Mint State coins or any coins worth more

How to Store a Coin
Whitman folder for Lincoln cents, which was very popular, especially from the 1940s through the early 1970s.

than a few dollars. The paper behind the slots contains reactive chemicals that will darken an untoned coin on the side placed against it. And the visible side of a coin housed in such a holder has little or no protection from the elements. Album-type holders are better than basic folders; at least the coins are covered on both sides. However, as we have seen, the sliding plastic liners typically found above and below the coins in many popular albums pose a threat of damaging the coins through inadvertent friction during the coins' insertion and removal. The hard plastic may touch the coins' high points as it is slid into place and may leave "slide marks" or hairlines. Furthermore, inserting coins into these albums can be just as hazardous as with the rudimentary push-in folders, since the fingers are just as likely to touch their surfaces.

3 GRADING TECHNIQUES AND TECHNICAL GRADING

There is no precise road map for grading coins. Even among professionals, different people may well approach the objective from somewhat different directions and still arrive at the same destination—that is to say, the same grade. However, the principal methods employed in grading coins are universal. There may be subtle differences in how they are applied, but the basic techniques are standard.

The attributes of grading described in chapter 1 come into play with every coin, no matter where—or by whom—it is evaluated. Some of these attributes are relatively easy to agree upon; others can be more subjective. For instance, experienced graders are likely to reach the same conclusions regarding the marks, luster, and strike of a given coin. On the other hand, their assessments may differ on the eye appeal of that coin, or on problems involving the planchet. These can be difficult matters to verbalize, much less quantify.

Tremendous insight can be gained about the grading process by examining graded coins—those already certified by professionals—at coin shows and auctions. Seeing such coins will help you understand why each coin received the grade it did and give you the knowledge you need to make correct grading judgments yourself. The more coins you study, the better equipped you will be. At PCGS, the graders routinely see an incredible variety of coins, and the breadth and depth of this exposure play fundamental roles in fine-tuning their skills.

At the outset, here are a few basic points to keep in mind:

- To grade a coin properly, you will need a good light source and a 5X to 10X (5- to 10-power) magnifying glass. The reasons are discussed later in this chapter in the section on Light Sources and Magnification.

- Coins can be graded on an "ivory-tower" basis—strictly by the book, with no regard for their value—or with what is known as a "market-related" approach, which takes into account the commercial implications of their grade. These will be examined in the section on Technical Versus Market Grading.

- "Technical" grading and "market" grading both are used at various times by professionals, including the graders at PCGS, as circumstances warrant. Certain kinds of coins tend to be technically graded, while other types are graded on a market-related basis.

- Often, a coin will merit a higher grade on one side than on the other. We will consider the implications of a "split grade" for the overall grade of a coin.

Learning from Observation

Coin shows and auctions are excellent classrooms for learning how to grade coins. By attending such events, you can examine hundreds of graded coins in just a few hours and gain valuable grading knowledge simply by observation. Although this will not make you an expert grader, it is an inexpensive way to view various types of coins of many grades. Examining a specific coin of a particular grade might not reveal too much about grading, but seeing multiple examples of a particular coin in a single grade is enlightening.

Grading Techniques and Technical Grading
A PCGS grader properly examining a coin with a magnifying glass.

Light Sources
Powerful halogen lamp used to detect imperfections on coins. This type of light is not used for ordinary grading, since the intensity prevents proper evaluation.

Firsthand examination of multiple coins of the same type and grade provides an excellent overview of why a coin achieves that grade.

Although all coins are different, many are similar and therefore receive the same grade. By studying coins that are graded the same, then comparing them with coins graded one point lower and one point higher, you will gain a clearer understanding of the "line" between the grades. Knowing why a coin receives a higher or lower grade involves an appreciation of distinctions that can be very subtle, and these will become increasingly apparent after you have viewed many different examples of graded coins. Coin shows and auctions give you the opportunity to do this. Auctions may not always contain quantities of similarly graded coins, but most of them do provide considerable variety, making them fertile areas for study. By looking at different coin series, types, and denominations in a variety of grades, you will gain an excellent grounding in how to assess the variances you will encounter in grading coins of different metals and types.

Light Sources

A good light source is essential to accurate grading. Whether you use a normal incandescent grading lamp, tensor lamp, halogen lamp, or some other direct lighting source is often just a matter of convenience or personal preference. Your eyes can adjust to various lighting conditions—although in poor light, coins cannot be evaluated properly regarding their grade.

Coins do look different when viewed under varying light sources. Halogen lamps are so bright and powerful that even tiny hairlines may look like "trenches," while a 60-watt incandescent bulb may "wash out" the surface defects on a coin. Although each lighting source has its particular uses and each may be employed for specific purposes, the incandescent lamp and tensor lamp are the most common light sources used by the PCGS graders.

The eye is a very sensitive instrument and will adjust quickly. PCGS grades coins in a room with no extraneous outside light (i.e., no windows)—a condition not always possible to duplicate at coin shows or auctions, or even in one's own home. Often you will see someone at a coin show "disappear" momentarily under a table with a coin and a light source. Chances are, that person is examining a coin for hairlines or marks that might not be clearly visible without being scrutinized closely in a darkened area.

The use of incandescent, rather than fluorescent, light is related to the physics of light. The sun's light is incandescent, and this di-

Technical Versus Market Grading
Weakly struck 1884-O Morgan dollar. Note that the hair over the ear is extremely flat.

rect type of light reflects from a coin's surface and gives a true "picture" of its luster and other grading aspects. Fluorescent light is indirect and does not "bounce" off the coin's surface in the same way. The scattered nature of fluorescent lighting does not allow the grader to "read" the surface of a coin. Interestingly, however, fluorescent light does have a place in numismatics. A ring lamp sometimes is used in coin photography to negate the "light line" caused by incandescent lighting. This light line is caused by the reflection of direct light from the flow or stress lines—which, in turn, result from the flowing of the metal into the recesses of the die.

Magnification

Although some coins can be graded without using a magnifying glass, there are times when the unaided eye is not sufficient. A good-quality 5X to 10X magnifying glass is essential for some coins. Higher-powered aids, such as a stronger loupe (often 20X to 30X) or a microscope (50X to 200X or more), are useful in other instances. These more powerful devices are used primarily to detect fraudulently added mint marks, examine die characteristics, identify counterfeits, and conduct other microscopic examinations. Grading coins under a microscope is very difficult and not recommended in most cases.

In evaluating larger coins, most graders examine them first without the aid of magnification and then, if necessary, use a loupe. With smaller coins, a glass is almost always necessary, especially if toning is present. It can be quite difficult to distinguish slight friction from incomplete striking, and a magnifying glass can be a valuable tool in making this determination. Frequently, small die lines or planchet lines may be confused with hairlines if viewed with the unaided eye, and the truth will only become apparent under magnification. Likewise, a glass—or even a loupe or microscope—may be needed to discern grade-related peculiarities of a certain coin series or certain metals, such as distinctive characteristics of their strike. Although small coins may require closer examination under magnification than larger coins, a good loupe is useful on all.

Technical Versus Market Grading

As the name suggests, "technical" grading is a process of evaluation that considers only the degree to which a coin does or does not meet objective, hard-and-fast guidelines for a given grade level. This has also been described as an "academic" approach. "Market" grading, by contrast, broadens the equation to include commercial factors, as well, giving important weight to the way in which a coin is viewed by buyers and sellers in the marketplace.

There is no course or book that can teach you exactly which coins trade on their technical grade only, which trade on a combination, and which trade with little regard to their technical grade—that is, coins that trade at the market grade. A general analysis of why and how this process takes place is only part of the story. The implications vary for each metal, coin type, and denomination. Likewise, the process works in varying ways for coins with split grades—coins where the reverse is **MS-67** or better, for example, but the obverse barely grades **MS-63**. With those, the market's viewpoint is a key consideration.

When you hear a numismatist say that technically a coin is **AU-58** but it will *grade* **MS-61** or **MS-62**, what is he or she telling you? How can a coin "grade" two different ways? How can a coin be *almost* uncirculated and also be uncirculated? Can an **MS-66** coin have *friction*? Does my **MS-65** Saint-Gaudens double eagle have *roll friction*? Yes. Though a coin may have slight "friction" on its highest points, it may never have been in circulation, so technically speaking it is uncirculated. Technically, it also has slight friction—though the market dictates an uncirculated price, not an **AU** price. The **MS-66** coin may have slight "contact" on its highest points, though it may be friction from other coins. Most **MS-65** Saints have "roll" or "coin" friction on the breast and leg of Miss Liberty. In truth, the only Saints that do not have broken luster on their high points are the counterfeits! Luster breaks, cabinet friction, album slide marks, and other slight friction affect nearly all coins.

The amount of friction allowed for each type and denomination of coin varies, but the general rules are:

- The *larger-size* coins are allowed more friction than are the smaller coins. Coins with large, smooth devices show friction more obviously than those with intricate designs, although the amount allowed is not always greater than for those coins.

- The *softer the metal*, the more friction is allowed. Given this guideline, the greatest amount would be allowed on gold coins, followed in order by copper, silver, and nickel.

- Coins of *older* types are allowed more friction than are modern types.

- More friction is allowed on coins *struck with an open collar* than on those that are struck with a close collar, because it is more difficult to strike a coin fully in an open collar and, as a consequence, some of the "friction" on these coins is actually incomplete striking.

Finally, what does that split-grade coin really grade? In nearly all cases, the obverse determines the majority—or, in many cases, *all*—of the total grade. No matter how nice a coin's reverse may be, if the obverse is just **MS-63**, then the overall grade will be **MS-63**. Thus, while technically the "average" grade for a coin's two sides may be **MS-65** (**MS-63** obverse, **MS-67** reverse), market-wise the coin trades as **MS-63**. Split-grade coins are common in some series. Morgan dollars, Barber coinage, Liberty Seated coinage, and Capped Bust coinage are very common with superb reverses (**MS-66** or better) and lower-grade obverses (**MS-64** and lower).

4 PCGS GRADING STANDARDS

During the course of a typical day, the graders at the Professional Coin Grading Service (PCGS) examine hundreds of coins—coins that can include specimens from every denomination, series, size, and coinage metal. In each and every case, they bring to bear not only their personal knowledge but also the collective wisdom gained by PCGS in the course of evaluating millions of rare coins since 1986. That wisdom has been codified in the PCGS Grading Standards—a body of guidelines constantly reviewed, studied, and implemented by members of the grading staff.

Now, for the first time, those standards are being publicly promulgated in this book so members of the coin-collecting public can incorporate these carefully formulated guidelines into their own grading calculations.

Before we consider the grading standards, let us go behind the scenes at PCGS and look over the shoulder of one of the veteran graders as he goes about his work.

After coins are received and processed at PCGS, they are brought into the grading room and distributed in boxes by the grading room manager. Each box contains only the coins from a particular invoice, and each box is assigned a unique number. The boxes are generic, and the graders do not know what types or dates of coins they contain until they examine them. Of course, there is no reference to the owner of the coins on the box or available to the graders through their computers.

The grader begins by entering the box number into his computer; information regarding the first coin in that group then appears on the screen. He takes that coin from the box and carefully removes it from its plastic flip, examines the coin, makes a grading determination, then enters his grade into the computer.

Upon confirmation of this grade in the computer, the next coin listing appears on the screen and the grader returns the previously graded coin to its flip. He then removes the next coin from its flip and examines and grades it. The process is repeated until all of the coins in the box have been graded. The grader then enters another box number into the computer and begins the entire process anew.

Determining the Grade

What thought processes go into combining the elements of a coin and determining its overall grade? Obviously, the brain makes many subconscious evaluations before the conscious act of entering the final grade into the computer. First and foremost, it "measures" the coin's physical characteristics against those of previously seen coins.

Determining the amount of *wear*—or lack thereof—is usually the first element considered by the grader. At the outset, he or she decides whether it merits a grade of 60 or above or, on the other hand, a sub-60 grade. Once the grader has made this determination, he or she evaluates the *marks, strike,* and *luster.* The coin's *striking status*—whether it is a business strike or a **Proof**—will already have been determined. Sometimes coins are submitted as **Proofs** but are really business strikes, and vice versa. This determination has to be made before the other elements are considered, because Proofs and business strikes are evaluated differently. (There is an option in the computer to "switch" the coin's status, and the grader can do this when he or she considers its status different from the one listed.)

After reaching a preliminary conclusion, the grader will evaluate more technical elements, such as the planchet's condition and any striking irregularities, and factor these into the final grade. Before assigning the final grade, he or she also will consider any added designations, if these are applicable. These include a designation of color (**RD**, **RB**, or **BN**) for copper coins, prooflike or deep-mirror prooflike (**PL** or **DMPL**) status for Morgan silver dollars, full split bands (**FB**) for Winged Liberty Head (Mercury) dimes, full bands on the torch (**FB**) for Roosevelt dimes, full head (**FH**) for Standing Liberty quarters, full bell lines (**FBL**) for Franklin half dollars, and cameo and deep cameo (**CAM** and **DCAM**) for **Proof** coins. Finally, the grader will consider the *color* or *toning*, if any, and the *eye appeal*.

Judgments regarding color or toning are sometimes subjective. When a coin has beautiful original color or toning, this is almost universally viewed in a positive way. However, many coins have color or toning that may be considered differently by individual graders. *Eye appeal* is a combination of all of the other elements of a coin's grade, so there is often some disagreement on this factor as well. When a coin has blazing luster and is fully struck with almost no marks, the eye appeal is great and there is little or no controversy. As with color or toning, however, most coins do not fall into that category. A grader, then, makes a partly conscious, partly subconscious decision on a coin's eye appeal. These factors are then combined into a final grade.

This is a simplified walk-through of the grading process. Magnification is often used to examine the subtle nuances of the elements of grading. Many times, coins have been lightly cleaned, and this affects their luster

and eye appeal. Many coins have been exposed for years to reactive chemicals and their surfaces may have been affected, depending on the chemicals, storage procedures, length of exposure, and the coin's reactive metals. Graders make thousands of subconscious decisions during the grading process, and their experience and knowledge give them the insight to accurately make those evaluations.

When all of the graders have finished their evaluations, a coin is given a final grade. The coin is then encapsulated and verified. If the verifier disagrees with the final grade, the coin is tagged and given to the other graders for discussion and possible comparison to examples from the PCGS Grading Set. The Grading Set contains coins that visually illustrate the PCGS standards, and each grader routinely examines the entire set. Many of the coins in this set have been there since 1986, with new specimens being added when especially good examples of a particular grade are found. Once the other graders have determined the final grade, the coin is boxed and sent to the shipping room to be returned to the submitter.

Although grading is a combination of art and science, relatively few changes are made in the PCGS graders' evaluations. More than 95 percent of the grades they assign are not changed by the verifiers and other graders. The graders' broad knowledge and the indepth expertise many of them possess in specific areas of numismatics make PCGS consensus grading a very accurate process.

Note: At times, the following descriptions will include the term "if applicable." (1) This refers to Proof coins that may not be reflective due to the method of manufacture. For instance, a Roman-finish Proof or Matte Proof coin will not show reflectivity, but still can grade Proof-68. It also refers to Proof coins with unusual characteristics, such as 1889 Liberty Head nickels, 1886 three-cent nickels, and certain other issues that were minted without highly reflective surfaces. (2) "If applicable" also can refer to detail left on a coin after wear has taken place. For instance, detail that is worn away on the

PENNY WHIMSY

A Revision of

EARLY AMERICAN CENTS

1793-1814

An Exercise in Descriptive Classification with

TABLES OF RARITY AND VALUE

by

WILLIAM H. SHELDON, M.D.

With the collaboration of

DOROTHY I. PASCHAL

and

WALTER BREEN

Determining the Grade
Cover page of Penny Whimsy, the William Sheldon book about early large cents that introduced the 70-point scale to numismatists.

MS-70 *Morgan dollar obverse. A coin with no marks visible to the aided eye, appearing exactly as when the coin left the dies, except for toning, if that is present.*

MS-70 *Morgan dollar reverse. No marks are visible under magnification. This coin is in the same condition as when it left the dies.*

---

eagle's wing is applicable to the grade of a Morgan dollar, but obviously not to a gold dollar, since there is no eagle on that coin.

Also, the standards for EF/PR-45 and lower grades are essentially the same. Therefore, they are listed only under Mint State Standards.

Mint State Standards
MS-70: Perfect Uncirculated
MARKS: An **MS-70** coin has no defects of any kind visible with a 5X (5-power) glass. **Note: Minor die polish, light die breaks, and so on are not considered defects on business-strike coins.**

STRIKE: The strike is razor-sharp and will show 99+ percent of the detail intended.

LUSTER: The luster is vibrant and undisturbed in any way. Any toning will be attrac-

tive. Only the slightest mellowing of color is acceptable for red copper.

EYE APPEAL: The eye appeal is spectacular—the ultimate grade!

MS-69: Superb Gem Uncirculated
MARKS: A virtually perfect coin. It usually takes an intense study of the surfaces to ascertain why the coin will not grade **MS-70**. Only the slightest contact marks, nearly invisible hairlines, the tiniest planchet flaws, and so on are allowable for this grade.

Note: Slight die polish, medium die breaks, or slight incomplete striking are not defects.

STRIKE: The strike is extremely sharp and will show 99+ percent of the detail intended.

LUSTER: The luster will be full and unbroken. Any toning must be attractive. Only the

MS-69 *Morgan dollar obverse. No marks on the surfaces are visible to the unaided eye.*

MS-69 *Morgan dollar reverse. No marks on the surfaces are visible to the unaided eye.*

MS-68 *Morgan dollar obverse. Only the slightest imperfections are noted, mainly on the jaw.*

MS-68 *Morgan dollar reverse. No surface marks are noted with the unaided eye.*

slightest mellowing of color is acceptable for red copper, and only the slightest unevenness of color for red-brown and brown copper.

EYE APPEAL: Superb!

MS-68: Superb Gem Uncirculated

MARKS: A nearly perfect coin, with only slight imperfections visible to the unaided eye. The imperfections (tiny contact marks, minuscule hairlines, a small lint mark, etc.) will almost always be out of the range of the coin's focal points.

STRIKE: The strike will be exceptionally sharp.

LUSTER: The luster will be full (or virtually so) and "glowing." Any luster breaks will be extremely minor and usually restricted to the high points. Slight unevenness in toning is

acceptable, as long as it is still attractive. Red copper may show some mellowing, and there may be some unevenness of color for red-brown and brown copper.

EYE APPEAL: Exceptional, with no major detractions.

MS-67: Superb Gem Uncirculated

MARKS: Any abrasions on the coin are extremely light and/or well hidden in the design and do not detract from the coin's beauty in any way. As with **MS-68** coins, the fields on smaller coins are usually nearly flawless, especially on the obverse. On large silver coins with smooth devices (Morgan dollars, for instance), the flaws will usually be found in the fields; on large gold coins (such as Liberty Head $20s), the fields will usually be superb in this grade, with only minor flaws in the devices.

MS-67 *Morgan dollar obverse. Slight contact is noted on the face, with the field virtually perfect.*

MS-67 *Morgan dollar reverse. As with higher grades, the reverse is often mark-free to the unaided eye.*

MS-66 *Morgan dollar obverse. More marks are noted with the field, as well as the cheek, now showing some disturbances.*

MS-66 *Morgan dollar reverse. Reverses are often less marked than the obverses, with only slight disturbance noted for the field.*

STRIKE: The strike will be very sharp and almost always full.

LUSTER: The luster will be outstanding. Any toning (even if slightly uneven) must be attractive and not impede the luster in any way. Red copper can have mellowing of color, and there can be unevenness of color for red-brown and brown copper. Minute spotting, if present, should be virtually unnoticeable.

EYE APPEAL: In almost all cases, the eye appeal will be superb. Any negativity will be compensated for by another area that is spectacular.

MS-66: Gem Uncirculated
MARKS: There may be several noticeable, but very minor, defects. If marks or hairlines

are in an important focal area, they must be minimal and compensated for by the rest of the coin's superbness.

STRIKE: The coin will be well struck.

LUSTER: The luster will be above average (usually far above average), and any toning should be attractive and should only minimally impede the luster. Red copper can have mellowing of color, and there can be unevenness of color for red-brown and brown copper. Very minor spotting may be present, although it should be noticed only upon close examination. A dipped coin must be "fresh" in appearance and never give the impression of having been cleaned.

EYE APPEAL: The eye appeal will almost always be above average for a gem-quality coin, and many **MS-66** coins will be superb in

MS-65 *Morgan dollar obverse. Light marks are noted on the face, jaw, neck, and field.*

MS-65 *Morgan dollar reverse. Slight marks are now noted on the breast, with other slight disturbances in the field.*

this category. Any negative factors must be compensated for in another area.

MS-65: Gem Uncirculated

MARKS: There may be some scattered marks, hairlines, or other minor defects. If the flaws are in a main focal area, they must be minor and few. Hidden marks and hairlines can be larger. On dime-type and smaller, they almost always must be in the devices or must be very minor if they are in the fields. On larger coins, there can be marks/hairlines in the fields and in the devices, but no major ones.

STRIKE: The coin will be well struck.

LUSTER: The luster will be at least average (almost always above average), and any toning can only slightly impede the luster. Copper coins can have mellowing of color for red and unevenness of color for red-brown or brown coins. **Note: There can be a little minor spotting for copper coins.**

EYE APPEAL: The eye appeal will be average or above. This is a very nice coin. However, there are many ways a coin can grade **MS-65**. This grade (or **MS/PR-64**) may have the largest range of eye appeal. A coin may grade **MS-65** with scattered light marks, but with great luster and strike—or a coin with virtually no marks but a slightly impeded

luster also could be **MS-65**. The overall eye appeal still must be positive or the coin does not merit **MS-65**.

MS-64: Choice Uncirculated

MARKS: There may be numerous minor marks/hairlines, several significant marks/hairlines, or other defects. There may be a few minor or one or two significant marks/hairlines in the main focal areas. On minor coinage (dime coinage and lesser), there may be several marks/hairlines in the fields or main focal areas, but none should be too severe. On larger coins, these marks/hairlines may be more severe in the fields or main focal areas. However, a severe mark/hairline would have to be of a size that would preclude grading the coin **MS-65**, though not so severe as to reduce the coin to **MS-63**. If there are several fairly heavy marks/hairlines in obvious areas, the coin would grade **MS-63**.

STRIKE: The strike will range from average to full.

LUSTER: The luster can be slightly below average to full, and toning can impede the luster. On brilliant coins, there may be breaks in the luster caused by marks or hairlines. Red copper can be considerably mellowed. There may be noticeable spotting for this grade, although heavy or large spotting would reduce the grade to **MS-63** or below.

MS-64 *Morgan dollar obverse. The face, neck, and field all have noticeable marks, though none too severe.*

MS-64 *Morgan dollar reverse. More marks are noted, including a medium-sized one below the bow.*

MS-63 *Morgan dollar obverse. Marks on the face, neck, hair, and field are moderate in size, but plentiful in number.*

MS-63 *Morgan dollar reverse. The reverses of most coins, especially large ones, usually have fewer marks than the obverses. Note that the marks are now found on the wing feathers as well as on the breast and in the field.*

EYE APPEAL: The eye appeal can range from slightly negative to very positive. This is a nice coin, so anything too negative would preclude the **MS-64** grade. Balance is a key. A coin with marks/hairlines in obvious focal areas would have to have great luster or some other positive factor to attain **MS-64**. A coin with less severe marks/hairlines hidden in devices could have impaired luster or some other problem and still be graded **MS-64**. Coins with deficiencies and no redeeming characteristics are graded **MS-63** or lower.

MS-63: Choice Uncirculated

MARKS: There may be numerous marks/hairlines, including several major marks/hairlines in main focal areas. If there are distracting marks/hairlines on the major devices, the fields should be relatively clean. If there are distracting marks/hairlines in the fields, the devices should have fewer disturbances.

STRIKE: The strike will range from slightly below average to full.

LUSTER: The luster can be below average to full. The toning can seriously impede the luster. On brilliant coins, there can be significant breaks in the luster. Red copper can be considerably mellowed. There can be noticeable spotting, including several large spots or a group of small ones.

Note: If the luster is poor, the coin would not be graded **MS-63**, even with a full strike and acceptable marks/hairlines for the grade.

EYE APPEAL: The eye appeal can be slightly negative to very positive. The "average" **MS-63** will have neutral eye appeal (noticeable marks/hairlines, average to above-average strike, and average luster). However, quite a few coins are graded **MS-63** because of their negative appearance. If either the luster, strike, or marks/hairlines are below the standards set forth here, then one of the other criteria must be exceptional for the coin to attain **MS-63**.

MS-62: Uncirculated

MARKS: The marks/hairlines may cover most of the coin. If the marks/hairlines are light, they may be scattered across the entire coin. If there are several severe marks/hairlines, the rest of the coin should be relatively clean.

STRIKE: The strike can range from very weak (some New Orleans Mint Morgan dollars, for example) to full.

LUSTER: The luster can range from poor to vibrant.

EYE APPEAL: The eye appeal will be negative to slightly positive. The negativity in this grade usually involves excessive marks/hairlines and/or the strike and/or lack of luster and/or unattractive toning. There can be one to three of the major criteria that contribute to negative eye appeal. Even coins with overall positive eye appeal usually have one or two areas that are negative. Thus, a coin with numerous marks/hairlines but with average strike and luster may grade **MS-62**, while a coin with just a few marks (probably in the wrong places) and weak strike and luster also may grade **MS-62**.

MS-61: Uncirculated

MARKS: There may be marks/hairlines across the entire coin. There may be several severe contact marks/ hairlines. If there are numerous large marks/hairlines in the main focal areas, the fields should be cleaner, although they still could have some contact marks/hairlines. On larger coins (half dollars and larger), there may be areas with almost no marks/hairlines.

STRIKE: The strike can range from very weak to full.

LUSTER: The luster may be poor, average, or full.

EYE APPEAL: The eye appeal will be very negative to very slightly positive.

MS-60: Uncirculated

MARKS: Numerous. The marks/hairlines will probably cover the coin's entire surface. On larger coins (half dollars and higher), there may be some areas that have few or no marks/hairlines. The marks/hairlines can be large and in prime focal areas.

Note: Sometimes the mark is not from "normal" contact with other coins or from circulation, thus would be considered damage and the coin might not be graded.

STRIKE: The strike can range from very weak to full.

LUSTER: The luster may be poor, average, or full.

EYE APPEAL: The eye appeal can be very negative to neutral.

Circulated Standards
AU-58: Choice About Uncirculated

WEAR: There will be slight wear on the highest points of the coin. In some cases, 5X magnification is needed to notice this wear, and sometimes it can be noticed by slowly tilting the coin in the light source. This method often may show the slight friction as discoloration. Very often, the obverse will have slight friction and the reverse will be full Mint State (often **MS-63** or higher).

MARKS: There are usually very few marks for this grade. Instead of marks, the principal detractions on the typical **AU-58** coin are rub or hairlines. The few marks should not be major or in prime focal areas. A coin that would grade **AU-58** from a wear standpoint, but has numerous marks, would be graded **AU-55** or lower.

STRIKE: The strike can range from below average to full.

MS-62 *Morgan dollar obverse. Marks on the face, neck, hair, cap, and field are now more severe, with several (below the eye and the middle of the cheek) very noticeable.*

MS-62 *Morgan dollar reverse. Marks for this grade range from minute to fairly severe.*

MS-61 *Morgan dollar obverse. Marks are numerous, with almost the entire surface covered with light-to-heavy scuffs and marks.*

MS-61 *Morgan dollar reverse. Marks are quite noticeable, with the breast and field showing several fairly large ones.*

MS-60 *Morgan dollar obverse. Many heavy and lighter marks cover the entire surface, especially noticeable on the face.*

MS-60 *Morgan dollar reverse. Although this reverse is relatively mark-free, some marks are seen in the field. Seldom are the reverse marks heavier than those of the obverse.*

AU-58 *Morgan dollar obverse. Slight friction is noted on the hair above the ear, as well as on the cheek.*

AU-58 *Morgan dollar reverse. Only light friction is noted for the high points of the eagle's breast.*

Note: A very weak strike would be downgraded to AU-55 or lower.

LUSTER: The luster can range from poor to full. There will be noticeable breaks in the luster on the high points. These areas will be visible to the unaided eye, but should be less than 10 percent of the surface area.

EYE APPEAL: The eye appeal is usually very good. Since marks are usually very minor, mainly strike, luster, and originality will determine the eye appeal. Many **AU-58** coins are lightly cleaned or dipped uncirculated coins that are no longer considered uncirculated because of the light cleaning or rubbing that is now present. These coins can be just as attractive as coins that are graded **AU-58** because of slight circulation—and sometimes even more so. Often these coins will have fewer marks than low-grade uncirculated coins.

AU-55: Choice About Uncirculated

WEAR: There will be slight wear on the high points and some friction in the fields. The reverse will now usually show wear similar to that on the obverse. In a few instances (coins stored face up that have acquired friction), the reverse will still be uncirculated.

MARKS: There usually will be several minor marks/hairlines and a couple of major ones.

These should be scattered between the devices and fields, with nothing too severe on the prime focal areas.

STRIKE: The strike will range from slightly weak to full.

LUSTER: The luster can range from poor to full, although the areas of wear will not show full luster. There will be breaks in the luster covering 10 to 25 percent of the surface.

EYE APPEAL: The eye appeal is usually good. The main criteria will be surface preservation, lack of and placement of marks/hairlines, the luster remaining, and originality.

AU-53: About Uncirculated

WEAR: There will be obvious wear on the high points. Friction will cover 50 to 75 percent of the fields.

MARKS: There usually will be several minor and major marks/hairlines. These will be scattered, or there can be small concentrated areas of them, including prime focal areas.

STRIKE: The strike will range from weak to full.

LUSTER: The luster can range from poor to full; however, rubbed areas will not exhibit as much luster as the protected areas. There

AU-55 Morgan dollar obverse. Friction is noted on the hair, cap, and face, and light wear is evident in the field around the head.

AU-55 Morgan dollar reverse. The eagle, mainly the breast area, shows noticeable wear, with the field lightly rubbed.

AU-53 Morgan dollar obverse. Wear is seen over most of the surface, with only the protected areas around the devices and lettering seen without friction.

AU-53 Morgan dollar reverse. Flatness is seen on the breast and leg feathers, with friction covering most of the surface.

will be noticeable breaks in the luster over one-half to three-fourths of the coin.

EYE APPEAL: The eye appeal now is a function of surface preservation, lack of and placement of marks/hairlines, the luster remaining, and originality.

AU-50: About Uncirculated

WEAR: Wear is evident. There can be friction in the fields, ranging from half to all of the unprotected areas. The high points will have wear that is very obvious to the unaided eye.

MARKS: There may be many marks/hairlines. However, many minor marks/hairlines will be worn away, as much of the original surface shows wear.

STRIKE: Ranges from weak to full.

LUSTER: The luster can range from poor to full. Fifty to 100 percent of the surface may have luster disturbance. In some cases, the only luster remaining will be around protected devices.

EYE APPEAL: The eye appeal is now a function of surface preservation, lack of and placement of marks/ hairlines, the luster remaining, and originality.

Note: Coins that grade EF/PR-45 and below are graded essentially the same for regular and proof strikes. As such, from here on, the criteria is the same for both, with exceptions noted.

EF-45: Choice Extremely Fine

WEAR: The amount of wear will be noticeable, with all details still sharp and clear and definition between individual parts of the de-

AU-50 *Morgan dollar obverse. Wear is very apparent on the face, neck, hair, and cap, with friction across the entire coin.*

AU-50 *Morgan dollar reverse. Breast feathers are mostly flat from wear, with the tips of the wing feathers showing noticeable wear. Friction is seen across the entire coin.*

EF-45 *Morgan dollar obverse. The entire coin shows wear except in the protected areas. The hair has slight flatness from the top to the area above the ear.*

EF-45 *Morgan dollar reverse. The breast feathers are flat in the center, with only the edges showing any remaining detail. The wing feathers are separate but worn.*

vices. Approximately 95 percent of the original major detail is still evident.

MARKS: There may be a couple of very minor marks.

LUSTER: There can be some luster in the devices. Sometimes there can be considerable luster in the fields. However, if there is no luster present, a coin still can grade **EF-45** if the detail is exceptional.

STRIKE: The strike will range from below average to full. For weakly struck coins that show wear consistent with **EF-45**, the grade would probably be **EF-40** or lower.

EYE APPEAL: The eye appeal will be determined by the cleanness of surface, lack of or placement of marks, and originality.

EF-40: Extremely Fine

WEAR: The amount of wear is now quite evident. Some of the highest points of the coin's detail are worn away. Some definition of individual parts of the devices will be worn down. Approximately 90 percent of the original major detail is still evident.

MARKS: There may be a few minor marks or perhaps one medium-size mark.

LUSTER: There will be minimal luster remaining. For many coins, there may be no luster except for slight amounts around devices such as stars, arrows, and so on.

STRIKE: Ranges from below average to full.

EYE APPEAL: Eye appeal will be determined by clean surfaces, lack of and placement of marks, and originality.

EF-40 *Morgan dollar obverse. Slightly more flatness is noted in the hair from the top to above the ear. The hair below the ear is slightly flat.*

EF-40 *Morgan dollar reverse. The breast feathers show only slight detail on the edges. Some of the wing feathers have begun to blend into each other, though they are mostly separate.*

VF-35 *Morgan dollar obverse. Areas of the hair from the top to above the ear are totally worn together. The hair below the ear has areas that are worn together.*

VF-35 *Morgan dollar reverse. The breast and leg feathers are worn smooth, with only slight detail remaining. The wing feathers, especially those at the tips, are worn together in places.*

Note: (1) Since luster is seldom evident for grades VF-35 and below, luster is not listed as a criterion for these grades. Some VF grades will exhibit minor amounts of luster, but these are the exceptions. (2) Since circulated coins are graded mostly by the amount of wear or lack thereof for grades VF-35 and lower, strike will be incorporated into the criteria for wear.

VF-35: Very Fine
WEAR: The devices are sharp and clear, but there is noticeable wear in the individual components of the devices; however, little blending of detail is evident. Approximately 60 to 80 percent of the detail survives.

MARKS: At most, expect several minor marks or one or two medium-size ones, although on large coins such as silver dollars and twenty-dollar gold pieces, there may be multiple medium marks and a few heavy marks.

EYE APPEAL: Any eye appeal will be due to clean surfaces, lack of and placement of marks, and originality.

VF-30: Very Fine
WEAR: The devices will be sharp and somewhat clear, with very little blending among the details. Approximately 50 to 75 percent of the original detail survives in this grade.

MARKS: At the most, expect several minor marks or one or two larger ones—but, as noted under **VF-35,** large coins may have more and heavier marks.

EYE APPEAL: Any eye appeal will be due to clean surfaces, lack of and placement of marks, and originality.

VF-30 Morgan dollar obverse. More flatness is noted in the hair above and below the ear. The hair directly above the ear is worn smooth.

VF-30 Morgan dollar reverse. The breast and leg feathers are worn smooth. Several of the wing feathers will have blended together. The wreath's leaves are beginning to lose detail.

VF-25 Morgan dollar obverse. Only the deepest strands of hair still have detail, with other areas—the cap, cotton bolls, and so on—now showing obvious wear.

VF-25 Morgan dollar reverse. The breast and leg feathers are flat from wear, with about half of the wing feathers still separate. The top leaves of the wreath are worn smooth.

VF-25: Very Fine

WEAR: The devices are clear, but some sharpness is lacking, and minor detail is starting to blend. Approximately 50 to 60 percent of the original detail is evident.

MARKS: There may be minor and/or medium marks or, as noted previously, multiple medium and large marks on larger coins.

EYE APPEAL: Any eye appeal will be due to clean surfaces, lack of and placement of marks, and originality.

VF-20: Very Fine

WEAR: There will be detail in major devices, although some blending may be evident. For types with LIBERTY, all of the letters will be visible, but some may be indistinct. For re-

verses with eagles, breast feathers will be mostly worn away and wing feathers will show most of their detail.

MARKS: There may be minor, medium, or large marks, but not enough to detract from the overall grade.

EYE APPEAL: The cleanness of surface and lack of marks constitute most of the eye appeal. The originality of the coin also is a factor in the eye appeal and ultimately the grade. Lightly cleaned coins are almost always penalized one or more grading points. Light cleaning on lower-grade coins (i.e., **F-15** and below) is not quite as important to the overall grade.

Note: Heavy cleaning is *not* acceptable (or even gradable) except for the very low grades (P-1 through AG-3).

VF-20 *Morgan dollar obverse. The deep recessed areas of the hair still show slight detail. The other devices—the cap, cotton bolls, and so on—are worn but still separate.*

VF-20 *Morgan dollar reverse. No breast or leg feathers are present, even on the edges. Half or fewer of the wing feathers show separation.*

F-15: Fine

WEAR: The major devices have moderate detail, and some distinctness of design is evident. For series with LIBERTY, most of the letters are at least partly visible. For types with eagles, the breast feathers may be worn completely and wing feathers will show from 25 to 50 percent of their detail.

MARKS: There may be minor, medium, or large marks, but nothing too severe.

EYE APPEAL: Any eye appeal is due to surface preservation and lack of marks.

F-12: Fine

WEAR: There will be some detail visible in the major devices. For series with LIBERTY, there will be four or five letters partly or wholly visible.

MARKS: There may be minor, medium, or large marks, but nothing too severe.

EYE APPEAL: Any eye appeal will be due to clean surfaces and lack of marks.

VG-10: Very Good

WEAR: There will be some detail visible in the major devices, although most are worn smooth. All devices/lettering will be quite clear. For series with LIBERTY, there will be from one to three letters visible or parts of up to five letters evident.

MARKS: A few minor, medium, and large marks may be evident, but they cannot be too severe. There should be no major marks. If the marks are too severe, the coin will not be graded.

EYE APPEAL: Any eye appeal is due to clean surfaces and lack of marks.

VG-8: Very Good

WEAR: There will be a few details visible in the devices. The peripheral devices/lettering will be sharp and clear. The rims will be complete for all series. For coins with LIBERTY, there will be one or two letters visible or parts of several letters evident.

MARKS: There should be no major marks, since most will be worn away.

EYE APPEAL: Any eye appeal is due to clean surfaces and lack of marks.

G-6: Good

WEAR: All devices will be worn smooth, but the outlines will be sharp. The minor devices/lettering around the periphery will be clear.

Note: For some series (Barber coinage, in particular), there will be slight wear into the reverse rim that touches some letters.

F-15 *Morgan dollar obverse. The hair is very flat, with only the deeply recessed areas below the ear showing detail. Some of the devices—the cotton bolls, wheat stalks, and so on—have begun to blend.*

F-15 *Morgan dollar reverse. Slight feather detail is seen on the neck, with the breast and leg worn smooth. The wing feathers will show some detail, though most feathers will be blended.*

F-12 *Morgan dollar obverse. Only slight hair detail re-mains. The cap and other head devices are worn mostly smooth, with areas that are blended.*

F-12 *Morgan dollar reverse. Most of the wing feathers are blended, as are most of the leaves of the wreath.*

VG-10 *Morgan dollar obverse. Most of the hair is worn to-tally flat. Slight detail is seen in some of the head devices, though most are worn smooth.*

VG-10 *Morgan dollar reverse. Some wing feather detail is present, but only the lower feathers have much definition. The wreath is quite worn, with only the recessed leaves showing detail.*

VG-8 *Morgan dollar obverse. All of the hair from the top to the ear is worn smooth. Slight detail is seen in the lower hair. Only the deep recessed areas of the other head devices have any detail.*

VG-8 *Morgan dollar reverse. Nearly all of the wing feathers are worn, though the lower feathers still show some detail. The leaves are worn smooth, but there are some that still show separation.*

G-6 *Morgan dollar obverse. Only the deeply recessed areas of the head show detail. The hair, face, neck, and cap are worn smooth and are blended.*

G-6 *Morgan dollar reverse. The neck, breast, and leg feathers are worn flat and blended. Slight wing feather detail is seen, as well as slight leaf detail in the wreath. The rims are nearly worn through all of the dentils.*

MARKS: There can be some minor marks, but major ones will be worn away.

EYE APPEAL: Any eye appeal will be due to clean surfaces and lack of marks.

G-4: Good
WEAR: Only the outlines of the major devices are still visible. The minor devices/lettering around the periphery will be worn but still clear.

Note: For some series (Barber coinage, in particular), there will be some wear into the top parts of the reverse lettering.

MARKS: There may be marks, but they should not be severe.

EYE APPEAL: Virtually no eye appeal, but nice, even wear can be pleasing to the eye.

AG-3: About Good
WEAR: The wear will be considerable, with the rims mostly gone, sometimes blending with devices.

MARKS: There may be numerous marks, but usually the surfaces are smooth from wear.

EYE APPEAL: None.

FR-2: Fair
WEAR: There will only be partial device detail visible. The date can be weak or almost missing. The rims may be completely worn.

MARKS: There may be numerous marks, but usually the surfaces are smooth from wear.

EYE APPEAL: None.

G-4 *Morgan dollar obverse. The head is worn mostly smooth, with only slight detail in the recessed areas. The rim is worn through the dentils and is slightly blended into the field.*

G-4 *Morgan dollar reverse. The eagle is worn smooth with only slight detail seen in the lower wing feathers. The wreath will show slight detail. The rim is worn through most of the dentils and into the field.*

AG-3 *Morgan dollar obverse. The head is worn very smooth, with only LIBERTY and a few recessed areas, such as the ear, still showing detail. The rims are worn through all of the dentils and into the stars and lettering.*

AG-3 *Morgan dollar reverse. The eagle is very flat, with slight wing feather detail present. The wreath is outlined, but shows no detail. The rims are worn into the tops of the lettering.*

PO-1: Poor

WEAR: The amount of wear is so massive that sometimes only the date and a few details are visible. If the date is not visible, the coin can be graded only if it is a one-year type (Chain cents, 1796 quarters, and so on).

MARKS: There can be numerous marks, although when a coin is this worn, the marks are usually worn down also.

EYE APPEAL: None.

Proof Standards
Proof-70: Perfect Proof

MARKS: There can be no defects visible with a 5X glass. A **Proof-70** coin is 100 percent free of hairlines, planchet flaws, lint marks, and any other mint-caused or post-striking defects.

STRIKE: The strike is full, showing all of the intended detail.

LUSTER: The surfaces are fully reflective (if applicable) and undisturbed in any way. Any toning must be attractive. Red copper must have no breaks in the color, and only the slightest mellowing is acceptable.

EYE APPEAL: Nothing short of spectacular.

Proof-69: Superb Gem Proof

MARKS: This coin will appear perfect to the unaided eye. Upon magnification, one or two minute imperfections (extremely minor hairlines, a previously hidden lint mark, a flake from the planchet, etc.) will be evident.

FR-2 *Morgan dollar obverse. There is almost no detail seen on the head, but* LIBERTY *is still clear, as it is deeply recessed. The rims are worn deeply into the lettering and touch the date and stars.*

FR-2 *Morgan dollar reverse. Slight lower wing detail is seen, though the eagle is worn very flat. The rims are worn deeply into all of the peripheral lettering.*

PO-1 *Morgan dollar obverse. Heavy wear is seen, with the rims deeply worn into the field. The date is discernible.*

PO-1 *Morgan dollar reverse. Only the central area still has detail. The reverse may be worn nearly smooth on some specimens.*

Note: Slight die polish, very minor die breaks, or very minor incomplete striking will not preclude a coin from attaining this grade.

STRIKE: The strike will be full, showing all of the detail intended.

LUSTER: The surfaces must be fully reflective (if applicable) and not negatively affected by toning or patina. Any toning must be attractive. Slight mellowing of color is allowed for red copper and only the slightest unevenness of color for red-brown and brown copper.

EYE APPEAL: Superb!

Note: Darkly toned proof coins will not grade Proof-69.

Proof-68: Superb Gem Proof
MARKS: A **Proof-68** coin will have minor defects barely visible to the unaided eye—defects that usually go unnoticed at first look. These will usually include one of the following: virtually undetectable hairlines, a small planchet flaw, or an unobtrusive lint mark. Such defects, no matter how minor, should not be in a conspicuous place such as Liberty's cheek or the obverse field.

STRIKE: The strike will be full, showing virtually all of the detail intended.

LUSTER: The coin must be fully reflective (if applicable) or virtually so. Any toning must be attractive, but slight unevenness is allowable. Some mellowing of color is allowed for red copper and some unevenness of color for red-brown and brown copper.

EYE APPEAL: The eye appeal will be exceptional. Any hint of negativity will be compensated for in another area.

Proof-67: Superb Gem Proof

MARKS: Any defects visible to the unaided eye will be minor. These could include unobtrusive hairlines, one or more very minor contact marks, a stray lint mark or two, a well-hidden planchet flaw, and so on. If the eye is immediately drawn to a defect, that will almost always preclude the coin from grading **Proof-67**.

STRIKE: The strike will be full or exceptionally sharp.

LUSTER: The reflectivity must be nearly full (if applicable). Toning may be dark or uneven, but not both. Red copper can have mellowing of color, and there can be unevenness of color for red-brown and brown copper. Minute spotting, if present, should be virtually unnoticeable.

EYE APPEAL: Superb, or nearly so. Any negativity must be compensated for in another area. Darkly toned coins are almost always penalized at least one grade point at this level—for example, a **Proof-67** coin that is dark would grade at least **Proof-68** if the toning were attractive or nonexistent.

Proof-66: Gem Proof

MARKS: A **Proof-66** coin can have a few light contact lines/hairlines, but nothing detracting or concentrated in one area. It may have small lint marks or planchet flaws, but any defects must be minor. If the eye is drawn to a flaw, the rest of the coin must be superb to compensate for it.

STRIKE: The strike must be sharp and will almost always be exceptionally sharp.

LUSTER: The reflectivity will usually be excellent (if applicable). Any toning must be positive, and reflectivity must be good (if applicable). A **Proof-66** coin may have some extremely positive attributes that offset slightly too much negativity in another area. For instance, Coin X has two or three too many hairlines to qualify as **Proof-66**, but the ton-

ing is fantastic, the devices are heavily frosted, and the eye appeal is outstanding, so the coin is graded **Proof-66** anyway. Red copper can have mellowing of color, and there can be unevenness of color for red-brown and brown copper. Very minor spotting may be present.

EYE APPEAL: Overall eye appeal for this grade is great, since this coin just misses **Proof-67**. Any deficiency in toning (too dark for **Proof-67** because of impeded reflectivity, "splotchy" almost to the point of being negative, etc.) will be slight. If the coin is brilliant, the deficiency usually will be minuscule—contact/hairline/slide marks that preclude a higher grade.

Proof-65: Gem Proof

MARKS: There may be several minor problems. These may include light contact, hairlines, lint marks, planchet flaws, or other minor defects. Since there may be several minor problems, there are many ways to attain the grade of **Proof-65**. For example, a coin with virtually no hairlines may have slight contact/slide marks on the high points and still grade **Proof-65**. In another case, a coin with no contact/slide marks might still grade no higher than **Proof-65** because of minor but noticeable hairlines. Any other minor defects, such as lint marks or planchet flaws, should be unobtrusive.

STRIKE: The coin will be well struck and, in most cases, very sharp.

LUSTER: The reflectivity will be average or above. Any toning present can impede the reflectivity only slightly. On untoned coins, the reflectivity can be moderately subdued, but coins with "washed-out" surfaces cannot be graded **Proof-65**. Red copper can have mellowing of color; copper coins can have minor spotting.

EYE APPEAL: The eye appeal will be average or above. This is a coin almost everyone finds attractive. The comments for eye appeal under **MS-65** are just as relevant for **Proof-65**. There is a wide range in the appearance of **Proof-65** coins. Any slightly negative factors must be compensated for in another area.

Proof-64: Choice Proof

MARKS: There may be numerous minor problems. These may include contact marks, many small hairlines, or several large hairlines. Other defects—such as lint marks or planchet flaws in focal areas—may be allowed.

STRIKE: There can be some weakness in strike.

Note: This is the highest Proof grade where some distracting weakness of strike in the major devices is allowable. Weakness in stars and other minor devices is not usually enough to reduce the grade.

LUSTER: The reflectivity can be impeded. If the coin is toned, the reflectivity can be noticeably subdued. On untoned coins, there can be dullness or a "washed-out" appearance, but these coins should have fewer contact lines/hairlines than a coin with more of the mirror surface intact. Red copper can be considerably mellowed. There may be noticeable spotting for this grade, although large or numerous spots would reduce the grade to **Proof-63** or lower.

EYE APPEAL: The eye appeal can range from slightly negative to very positive. This is an attractive coin. However, there can be some negativity in toning (too dark, hazy, splotchy, etc.)—or, with untoned coins, there can be dullness in the mirrored surface. The amount of hairlines acceptable for this grade is directly proportional to the eye appeal. If a coin has great contrast (frosted devices), the hairlines or other defects can be quite noticeable. On a coin that has less contrast and is either darkly toned or dull brilliant, the hairlines must be minor.

Proof-63: Choice Proof

MARKS: There may be immediately noticeable defects. There may be quite a few contact marks/hairlines or a group of concentrated hairlines, lint marks in prime focal areas, medium-to-large planchet flaws, or a combination of these or other defects.

Obvious "slide marks," which usually result from an album's plastic sliding across the devices, will almost always result in a grade of no higher than **Proof-63**.

STRIKE: The strike can range from average to full. This is the highest **Proof** grade where considerable weakness of strike is allowed. If the coin is poorly struck, a grade of **Proof-62** or below would be appropriate.

LUSTER: The reflectivity can be below average to full. On untoned coins, the surfaces are often dull—and on toned coins, there can be dark or uneven toning that will seriously impede the amount of reflectivity. Red copper can be considerably mellowed. There can be noticeable spotting, with several large spots or numerous small ones.

Note: If the mirrored surface is almost totally obscured, the grade of Proof-63 will not be attained and a grade of Proof-62 or lower is warranted.

EYE APPEAL: The eye appeal can be slightly negative to very positive. The "average" **Proof-63** coin will have neutral eye appeal (noticeable hairlines, well struck, slightly dulled surfaces). Some coins can still grade **Proof-63**, even if one or more of the major criteria are negative, but that must be compensated for by strength in another area.

Proof-62: Proof

MARKS: There may be some light contact marks, numerous light hairlines, medium-to-heavy hairlines, or a combination of the above covering most of the coin's surface. There also may be concentrated patches of hairlines, with some areas remaining relatively free of contact marks/hairlines.

STRIKE: The strike can range from very weak to full. (Of course, there are very few **Proof** coins that are very weakly struck, since most **Proof** issues were struck at least twice. This comment applies to all **Proof** grades from hereon.)

LUSTER: The reflectivity can range from below average to nearly full. On toned coins, there may be very little of the mirrored surface left, and with brilliant coins the reflectivity may be almost completely impaired by hairlines.

EYE APPEAL: The eye appeal will be negative to slightly positive.

Proof-61: Proof
MARKS: The surfaces may have some contact marks and numerous light-to-heavy hairlines. There may be several small marks hidden in the devices. The entire surface may be covered with contact marks/hairlines, or there may be several areas with concentrated hairlines and some others relatively free of them.

STRIKE: The strike can range from very weak to full.

LUSTER: The reflectivity will range from poor to slightly impaired.

EYE APPEAL: The eye appeal will be very negative to very slightly positive.

Proof-60: Proof
MARKS: The surface may have quite a few contact lines or myriad medium-to-heavy hairlines and may have several marks. There should be no large marks for this grade. If there are large marks, the grade would be Proof-58 or lower.

STRIKE: The strike can range from extremely weak to full.

LUSTER: The reflectivity may range from poor to slightly impaired.

EYE APPEAL: The eye appeal can be very negative to neutral.

Proof-58: Circulated Proof
WEAR: There usually is very little wear on the high points. With Proof coins, wear usually takes the form of slight friction in the fields. Since the mirrored surfaces of Proof coins are so delicate, any minor circulation or mishandling will cause marks and hairlines to become immediately apparent. In some cases, the reverse may have no impairment and will grade Proof-60 or higher.

Note: It is much easier to discern wear on a Proof than on a business strike. Proofs and prooflike business strikes reveal marks/hairlines much more easily because of the mirrored surface.

MARKS: There could be a few major marks. There can be scattered contact marks, with a few allowed on the devices and in the fields. If there are more than a few marks, a Proof coin would be graded Proof-55 or lower.

STRIKE: Ranges from average to full.

Note: A very weak strike would be downgraded to Proof-55 or lower.

LUSTER: The reflectivity will be somewhat impaired. This is not always true with Proof-58 coins, since many coins in this grade will have full reflectivity, which is disturbed only by hairlines, marks, or minor wear.

EYE APPEAL: The eye appeal is usually very good. There usually is nothing other than slight contact marks/friction on Proof-58 coins. Appearance is usually not the problem with this coin.

Proof-55: Circulated Proof
WEAR: There will be slight wear on the high points and up to half of the fields will have friction. The reverse will now be impaired in most cases.

MARKS: There may be several marks and quite a few contact marks/hairlines. These should be scattered about and should not be concentrated on prime focal areas.

STRIKE: Ranges from slightly weak to full.

LUSTER: The reflectivity may be severely impaired. Up to 50 percent of the mirrored surface is now slightly to fairly severely impaired. There can be a few areas that have lost complete reflectivity.

EYE APPEAL: The eye appeal is usually good. The main criteria will be surface preservation, lack of and placement of marks/hairlines, reflectivity remaining, and originality.

Proof-53: Circulated Proof

WEAR: There will be obvious wear to the high points. Friction will cover 50 to 75 percent of the fields.

MARKS: There may be several minor and major marks/hairlines. There can be scattered marks/hairlines in all areas of the coin, including prime focal areas, but a severe disturbance in those prime areas will result in a lower grade. Some small areas may have heavy concentrations of hairlines.

STRIKE: Ranges from below average to full.

LUSTER: The reflectivity may be severely impaired. The amount of "mirror" still visible will depend on the original depth of the mirrored surface.

EYE APPEAL: The eye appeal now is a function of surface preservation, lack of and placement of marks/hairlines, reflectivity remaining, and originality.

Proof-50: Circulated Proof

WEAR: Wear is evident. There can be friction in the fields ranging from half to all of the unprotected areas. High points will have wear that is very obvious to the unaided eye.

MARKS: There may be many marks/hairlines. Many times, hairlines and small marks will now start to "blend" into the surfaces. These will appear as discolored areas.

STRIKE: The strike will range from below average to full.

LUSTER: The reflectivity may be completely impaired. There may be parts of the surface with no mirror at all. The **Proof** surface may be visible only around protected devices.

EYE APPEAL: The eye appeal is now a function of surface preservation, lack of and placement of marks/hairlines, reflectivity remaining, and originality.

Note: Coins that grade PR-45 and below are graded essentially the same as regular strikes. Since the criteria for determining the overall grade will mostly be the same for both mint state and Proof coins, these grades are listed only under the mint state standards mentioned earlier, with any exceptions noted.

5 ELEMENTS OF A COIN'S GRADE

The overall grade of a coin is determined by evaluating all of the various elements that enter into that grade, then arriving at a composite figure.

The interrelationship of these factors can be complicated. Does a strong strike compensate for poor luster? Does the hidden mark in the hair keep that Morgan dollar from grading MS-68? The various elements of a coin's grade must be defined before these and other more complex questions can be answered.

This chapter will dissect each component and examine the effect it has on grading. Then, in the final section, the grading process itself will be reviewed.

Learning the Language

Although there is no way every aspect of grading can be verbalized, many technical terms can be explained in an effort to provide a better understanding of how a coin is graded. Only experience will make clear how all of the aspects interrelate and how they are combined to arrive at the overall grade. However, by learning the language of grading, you will be one important step closer to becoming a good grader.

Some elements of grading are well-defined; these include *strike, luster,* and *the number of contact marks.* Others are more abstract—*eye appeal* and *incomplete striking*, for example. Still others are gray areas somewhere between the tangible and the abstract—among them determinations of whether a coin is *prooflike, deep-mirror prooflike, red,* or *red-brown*. When there is any doubt about such a determination—Full Head designation for a

Standing Liberty quarter, for instance, or the degree of color for a copper coin—PCGS follows a simple philosophy: if the area in question is not clear-cut, then the element is regarded as the lesser of the two alternatives. In other words, a coin will not be called Full Head, Red, Prooflike, and so on, unless it indisputably fits the definition.

Some coins that are called Red-Brown will have 10 percent red remaining, while others will have 90 percent red. Some Standing Liberty quarters that are *not* designated Full Head will have "dished" heads, while others will show 95 percent or more of the intended head detail.

These controversial "break" points can be learned by experience, just as experience will teach you how to "blend" the various grading elements to determine the overall grade. Learn the basic elements and grading will become a subconscious application of these elements.

Wear vs. Incomplete Striking

Perhaps the most difficult task when grading a coin is distinguishing wear from slightly incomplete striking. To cite just one example, experts constantly disagree over whether Capped Bust half dollars have wear (usually slight friction on the cheek) or are incomplete strikes (also usually on the cheek). Indeed, there may be more arguments about this than about any other aspect of coin grading.

The simple explanation is that wear "discolors" the surface of a coin, while an area with incomplete striking has the same color as the surrounding portion of the coin. In reality,

Wear

1941 Walking Liberty half dollar obverse showing slight friction. Note the discolored areas, which actually are spots of
light wear.

1941 Walking Liberty half dollar reverse with slight friction.
Discoloration on the head, neck, breast, and leg of the
eagle is actually slight wear.

however, the distinction is much more complicated than that. Even though the luster
may break slightly on incompletely struck
coins and cause some "discoloration," this
does not keep a coin from being uncirculated.
Likewise, there are other ways coins can have
slight "friction" and still be uncirculated.
When coins are in bags or rolls, for example,
they pick up bag or roll friction.

The only Saint-Gaudens double eagles that
do not have luster breaks on the breast and
knee, usually caused by contact with other
coins, are the Proofs and counterfeits! Even
the single 1910-S Saint graded MS-68 by
PCGS has minute breaks on the high points
(the breast and the leg). There is even evidence of slight "contact" on the eagle's feathers.

There also is the problem of "slide marks"
and "cabinet friction." Sometimes uncirculated coins are slightly mishandled and develop friction. The vinyl plastic flips also
sometimes cause "flip rub." When these
problems become more than slight, a coin
might no longer be graded Uncirculated—
no wonder there is confusion!

Thus, what appears to be wear is sometimes
incomplete striking, bag/roll friction, album
slide lines, cabinet friction, flip rub, slight
mishandling, or actual wear from slight cir-

culation. The grades involved are **AU-58** and
higher. This element of grading is not just
about the difference in **AU-58** and **MS-60**,
since there is slight wear or friction in grades
up to **MS-67**. This is not really wear, but incomplete striking or one of the other "problems."

Often the best way to understand something
is to understand what it is not. When coins
are truly worn (those coins grading **AU-55**
and lower), it is not difficult to "see" the wear,
so following the discussion of wear there will
be an analysis of incomplete striking, bag/roll
friction, "slide" marks, "cabinet" friction,
"flip rub," and slight mishandling.

Determining Types of Wear
True wear mainly comes from circulation
and usually there is some discoloration.
When the wear is from one of the other
"problems," there may not be discoloration.
Plastic in album slides and flips will not cause
the same discoloration as will contact with
cloth or human hands, or other ways in
which coins become circulated. Since wear
from circulation usually causes discoloration,
comparing the affected area with pristine
areas by tilting the coin under a good light
source will determine whether the luster is
really broken by actual wear. When a coin is
worn enough to grade **AU-55** or lower, dullness is observed by a casual glance at the coin.

Incomplete Striking

1946-S Walking Liberty half dollar obverse with striking weakness. Note the missing hand and leg detail often noted for some-date Walking Liberty half dollars.

New Orleans Morgan dollar reverse with slight striking weakness. Note the incomplete breast feathers.

If you need magnification to see the "wear," it is either not wear or it is wear that is so slight as to not prevent the coin from grading Uncirculated. Unless you put the coin in your own pocket, how can you determine whether the "contact" on a coin came from circulation or slight mishandling?

Incomplete Striking

Incomplete striking is usually caused by insufficient striking pressure. The amount of pressure that was used to strike different series varied with the size of the coin and the metal in which it was struck. When the pressure was not sufficient to cause the metal to flow into the recesses of the die, the coin is said to be incompletely struck, or weakly struck if this deficiency is severe. Actually, severe incomplete striking is much easier to determine than slight incomplete striking. If there are large areas of a coin that are weak and the luster still "rolls" across the coin, it is quite obvious the coin is still Uncirculated, such as some New Orleans Mint silver dollars that have extreme weakness of strike over the ear and on the breast feathers.

There are incomplete strikes in virtually every series of U.S. coins, although modern coins other than mint errors are rare with this characteristic. Poorly struck coins usually grade no higher than **MS-62** or **MS-63**.

Sometimes insufficient-pressure strikes have areas that look somewhat granular or pebbly. On some coins, the roughness of the planchet is visible where the incompleteness shows as crisscross lines or planchet abrasions. Most Peace dollars have the granular or pebbly look in the hair on the obverse and the entire length of the eagle's feathers on the reverse. On coins with smooth devices that are the high point (Morgan dollars, Liberty gold coins, three-cent nickels, etc.), the incompleteness will usually be the crisscross lines or planchet abrasions. Morgan dollars can show both types: the ear may be flat and the lower part of the smooth cheek may have visible planchet abrasions, or as with some 1902-S Morgan dollars, long, large roller marks may appear across almost the entire coin, probably due to incorrectly spaced dies instead of improper pressure.

When the incompleteness on the highest points of a coin is minor, the grade usually is not affected. Only in the very highest grades of **MS-68** and above will slight incomplete striking affect the grade.

Two other "incomplete" strikings must be mentioned. Dies are made of tempered or quenched steel to maximize the number of strikings. However, die steel was expensive, so dies were used until they became worn out

Bag/Roll Coin Friction
Close-up of Saint-Gaudens double eagle with arrows pointing to areas of bag or roll friction. These slightly darker areas are seen on many Uncirculated gold and silver coins.

Slide Marks
Close-up of Eisenhower dollar with album slide marks. The mostly parallel lines are noted mainly on the cheek and jaw.

Bag Marks
1946 Walking Liberty half dollar obverse with bag marks. Light marks are noted on the leg, sun, and fields.

or shattered. Worn or broken dies result in different looks. On a worn die, the details of the devices will appear fuzzy or mushy. An example of this would be an Indian Head or a Buffalo nickel with a full horn but an eroded look with full luster, though the luster usually will not be as vibrant as with sharp dies. (These coins often suffer from insufficient striking pressure, as well as the worn dies.) Broken dies also can result in "missing" detail. On many early coins, the Mint kept striking coins even when the die broke in half, resulting in missing detail. Luster will sometimes be impaired when the die is broken, but usually not as severely as with worn dies.

Bag/Roll Coin Friction

When coins rub together in a bag or roll, the highest points of the coins come in contact

with each other and may "break" the luster slightly. This bag or roll friction is usually noticed on larger coins (dollars, eagles, double eagles, etc.), but other series also may suffer from this (Standing Liberty quarters are especially vulnerable). On Saint-Gaudens double eagles, the frost on the breast and leg of Miss Liberty often is broken, the field remaining undisturbed. These coins are heavy, and slight rubbing among the coins results in this type of wear. Upon observing real wear on a Saint, one notices the brown or grayish look as opposed to the bright look of coin-against-coin friction. The missing frost is "skinned" off the coin by other coins, but the luster should still "roll" when tilted in a good light source. Standing Liberty quarters also have this skinned look on the knee of Miss Liberty. Friction from circulation discolors the knee, where coin-on-coin contact is still silvery-looking. When a coin is not frosty on the high points, coin-on-coin friction is more difficult to detect.

Slide Marks

Slide marks are tiny, concentrated lines across the high points of a coin, usually running horizontally across the surface, caused by the plastic insert of a coin album. When a coin is placed in a "slide" album, the plastic insert is closed by pushing it toward the side of the album page. If the coin is not fully recessed into the opening in the album, the plastic sleeve may rub across the exposed part of the coin. This may result in slide lines on the delicate surfaces of the coins. These lines are almost always seen on the obverse, as most people tend to use only the top slide and never move the back slide in the page. Barber coins, Bust coins, Liberty Head coins, and other coins with large, smooth devices often show these slide lines, especially where the coin is thick and does not drop into the hole below the level of the slide. On Liberty Seated coinage, Miss Liberty's knee usually develops these lines. The amount of contact can range from a minute line or two to many heavy slide lines; the coin's grade is reduced accordingly. In extreme cases, the coin may no longer grade Uncirculated, although the lines would have to be very severe to cause a grade lower than **AU-58**.

Cabinet Friction

Cabinet friction is mostly a problem of the past. Before there were albums or plastic holders, coins were often kept in trays in wooden cabinets especially made for storing coins. Collectors would often dust or rub the coins with a cloth, creating fine lines or "cabinet friction." This type of friction, like album slide marks, usually is confined to the obverse, although in random directions. On Draped and Capped Bust coinage, this friction is commonplace. These fine lines usually do not interfere with the luster, but when the friction discolors the luster, the coin probably will grade no higher than **AU-58**. Another type of cabinet friction may occur on the reverses of early U.S. coins, where the cabinets'

wooden trays were slid in and out and the coins moved back and forth across the felt pads lining the holes in the trays.

Flip Rub

This is a modern phenomenon, since plastic flips were not developed until the middle of the twentieth century. There are two basic types of plastic flips. The soft, pliable flip has fewer problems with "rubbing" coins, but usually contains PVC (polyvinyl chloride), a chemical that softens the plastic, which can cause the surface of the coin to become oily. This gooey substance later dries to become what is known as PVC damage; this is the green, chalky-looking residue seen on coins stored too long in this type of flip. In the presence of moisture, the chloride component of PVC can form hydrochloric acid. The hard, brittle flip does not contain the dreaded PVC but is stiff, and improper insertion or removal of coins may result in hairlines or flip rub, similar to album slide marks, although these lines or rubs are often not as severe as those seen from album slides.

Mishandling

When coins are handled improperly, the surfaces can develop slight blemishes. There are instances where inexperienced collectors or non-collectors have mishandled Uncirculated coins. When this mishandling results in noticeable wear, the coin will not grade Uncirculated. In general, this type of friction will be difficult to discern from ordinary circulation. If there is no discoloration and the luster is still intact with only very slight breaks, the coin still will be considered Uncirculated. Marks from a coin or heavy object dropping on another coin are considered in the same way as bag marks or contact marks.

Contact Marks

Contact marks can occur on coins in many ways. When business-strike coins are ejected from the coining dies, they drop into a container. In 1792, this was a small receptacle; today, large hoppers are used for this purpose. Most business-strike coins have contact marks before they leave the mint! After the

Contact Marks
Close-up of high-grade 1896 Proof "V" nickel obverse and reverse.

receptacle became full, it was emptied, and the coins were placed into kegs or, later, cloth bags. (Today, most coins are shipped from the mints in the large hoppers or the new "super" bags that can hold up to several hundred thousand coins!) Transportation to banks in kegs and later in cloth bags also accounts for some of the contact marks. Banks then opened the kegs or bags and placed the coinage into cash drawers, again allowing for more coin-on-coin contact. When looking through bags of coins, one may find a coin or two with almost no marks. This is a minor miracle, when one thinks of the weight (50+ pounds for a bag of 1,000 silver dollars) and the miles traveled in stagecoaches, trains, and later, trucks. Obviously, the heavy coins (half dollars, silver dollars, ten dollars, etc.) are more prone to these types of marks than are smaller coins. Also, the softer-metal coins (gold, silver, and copper) are more likely to receive these marks than are nickel coins. If a coin survived from the mint to the bank drawer relatively unscathed, and a collector obtained it immediately thereafter and preserved it, a high-grade coin existed. Most coins were not so lucky.

There are other ways coins can survive with few contact marks. It was common practice to sell coins to visitors of the early Mint or present them to visiting dignitaries. The Lord St. Oswald coins discovered in England

in the 1960s are examples of these. The Lord St. Oswald 1794 silver dollars are relatively free of marks and may have been caught in a glove from the coining presses. The coins saved from the melting pots by members of the annual Assay Commission are another way relatively mark-free coins may have survived. All of the mints had to send coins for assay to this commission, although usually only a random sample was destroyed in the assay process. Obviously, there were some Assay Commission members who saved certain of the survivors; many of the 1873 rarities are believed to have been rescued by the Assay Commission members. An 1893-S Morgan dollar graded MS-67 by PCGS is rumored to have survived in this way. Indeed, the coin is free of the contact marks seen when coins are placed in bags, and it and other coins may have survived relatively mark-free in this manner. J. M. Clapp started obtaining coins directly from the various mints in the late 1800s and his son sold his collection to Louis Eliasberg Sr. through Stack's, in 1942, for a reported $100,000. Mr. Clapp was a visionary, and some of the most mark-free coins, especially gold coins, come from this source.

There are two basic types of coin contact that are encountered. The edge of one coin hitting the surface of another is one of these, causing what sometimes are referred to as reeding marks, although for plain-edge coins this would not be technically correct. These are also called bag marks, but not all of these marks occur in bags, so again this is not technically correct. These marks also may result from an object other than another coin hitting the surface of a coin. The second type of coin contact is sometimes called bag or roll friction. This is characterized by friction or contact, often just slight luster breaks, on the high points of coins, often confused with wear. (See the previous discussion of Wear for a more in-depth view of this.) There are other variations of coin "contact." These also are discussed under Wear and include hairlines, album slide marks/lines, cabinet friction, and flip rub.

Strike

Strike is one of the most important elements of higher-grade coins. In grades of **MS-65** and **PR-65** and higher, the coin must be well struck. If a coin has nearly perfect surfaces but is not well struck, PCGS will assign a grade no higher than **MS-64**. (Proof coins must be well struck in **Proof-64** and higher.) In the highest grades, **MS/PR-67** through **MS/PR-70**, a coin must be fully struck, or nearly so. Strike is so important on some issues (Morgan dollars, Peace dollars, etc.) that collectors will pay huge premiums for fully struck coins. In grades of **MS-63** and below, there may be considerable weakness of strike and, in some cases, that is the main reason for the grade. In **PR-63** and below, some weakness is allowed, although a "flat" struck Proof coin would probably be graded no higher than **PR-60** or **PR-61**.

Why aren't all coins fully struck? There are several answers. Insufficient striking pressure is the most common reason a coin does not strike up fully. If a coin is struck with sufficient pressure, then all areas of the dies are filled with metal upon impression, including the collar, which is a third die. (**Note: On coins struck in open collars, full strikes are the exception.**) The highest points of a coin are, obviously, struck from the deepest recesses of the coin dies. Upon striking, the metal heats up and "flows" into the recessed areas of the dies. The planchet, before striking, is slightly smaller than the collar. The outward expansion into the collar causes radial "erosion" lines to appear in the surfaces of the dies. "Flow" or "stress" lines are visible on some coins and produce the "cartwheel" luster effect. Even when they are not noticeable, there usually is still some "cartwheel" effect seen when the coin is tilted back and forth under a light source. (On Proof and prooflike coins, the radial flow lines are present, but almost never are visible.) When the metal "flows" to all parts of the coin dies, the coin is said to be fully struck. On almost all issues, the weakness of strike will be found in the central section of the coin. The exceptions are the issues where the high points are not located in the central part of the coin or where there is a die problem that causes weakness in one particular area (i.e., the "flatness" of the head area in Standing Liberty quarters, flat peripheral lettering on Mercury dimes, etc.) This type of weakness may be confined to the periphery (dentils and stars), and can be caused by die breaks, die wear, filled dies, misaligned hubbing, and so on. Some early U.S. dies "sank" in selected areas, causing those parts of the design to be weak or missing. Sometimes the entire coin can be weak (obverse and/or reverse dies out of alignment, vastly insufficient striking pressure, etc.). Whatever the reason for weakness or incompleteness, the strike is very important to the overall grade.

The amount of necessary striking pressure varies from metal to metal and also is directly related to the relief of the issue and the size of the coin. A large gold coin such as the regular-relief 1907 Saint-Gaudens double eagle requires less striking pressure than does a High-Relief double eagle, but a gold dollar, in approximately the same degree of relief as the regular-relief Saint-Gaudens twenty, will require less pressure to strike fully. Since gold is the softest of the four major coin metals (gold, silver, nickel, and copper), the least amount of striking pressure will be required for fully struck coins of similar sizes. Nickel is the hardest of the four metals to strike. Even Proof nickel coins, which are usually

Strike

1830 Lettered Edge Capped Bust half dollar obverse, an example of an open-collar strike. Note the weak stars on the left side, as well as the slight incompleteness of the drapery. Dentils are weak and irregular.

1839 Reeded-Edge Capped Bust half dollar obverse, an example of a close-collar strike. Slight weakness is still seen on some stars and the drapery, but the dentils are very strong and even-sized.

Close-up of Indian Head cent obverse, with four diamonds fully struck.

given more than one blow from the dies, may not strike up fully. This weakness, or incompleteness of strike to be more accurate, is often seen as a "rough" or "pebbly" area on the high points of a coin, where the surface of the original planchet survives. This may look like wear or rub but will not usually have the discoloration associated with circulation.

Because die steel was expensive, dies were repolished from time to time to remove clash marks or other die injuries. When excessively polished, a die may "lose" detail. If the detail has been partially polished away, the best a coin can be is well struck, since fully struck implies full detail. If some of the detail is "missing" from the die, no amount of striking pressure will result in a "fully struck" coin. Thus, some coins such as three-cent nickels with "weakness" in the Roman nu-

merals on the reverse may only grade **MS-64** or **PR-64**. If this weakness is minor (i.e., the lines in the numerals are slightly weak but still have some separation), higher grades may be warranted. The regular-strike 1856 half dime is often seen with weak or missing dentils. Unless most of the dentils are present and separated, these coins will be graded no higher than **MS-64**.

Coins struck in open collars are the ones where it is most difficult to determine whether the incompleteness is the result of die wear or striking pressure. Since the edges of the planchet were imparted by a Castaing machine before they were put in the dies for striking, the size of the planchet had a lot to do with whether a coin struck up fully. The planchet is work-hardened on the edge after passing through the Castaing machine, whether lettering or reeding is added. Because of this edge hardening, after the planchet was struck by the dies, it would remain roughly the same size as when it left the Castaing machine. Thus, a smaller planchet might strike up "better" than a larger one. (The smaller planchet has the same amount of metal in a smaller area, thus more metal would flow into the recesses of the dies. A larger planchet struck with the same pressure would not flow as deeply into the recessed areas.) A coin struck from worn or excessively polished dies also will show less detail than intended. Since these are usually unique die states, one must examine each series, date by date, to determine whether the incomplete areas result from insufficient striking pressure, die deterioration, excessive polishing, and so on.

Improperly aligned dies also can cause weakness of strike. This usually will be confined to a specific quadrant of the coin. This type of weakness is difficult to distinguish from worn dies, excessive polishing, filled dies, and the like. If a coin is otherwise well struck and weak only in one quadrant, then improperly aligned dies are probably the culprit. Also, there should be a corresponding weak area on the opposite side of the coin when the dies are improperly aligned, while the opposite quadrant of the coin may be well struck if the fitting of the dies caused them to be closer together at that point.

Luster

Luster is the reflectivity of a given coin. It is caused by light reflecting off the flow, or stress, lines of a coin. When a coin is struck, the metal flows into the recesses of the die. Small cents were struck with approximately 40 tons of pressure and silver dollars with approximately 160 tons of pressure. For larger coins, more pressure is needed to obtain a full strike, and this is also the case with harder metals such as nickel. Five-cent coins (75 percent copper, 25 percent nickel) require approximately the same amount of pressure, 60 tons, as do the larger quarter dollars (90 percent silver, 10 percent copper). When the

planchet is stamped by the presses, the metal flows out from the center of the die and is pushed down into the lower or anvil die, and flows upward and out into the upper, or hammer, die. Most of the time, the obverse is the upper die and the reverse is the lower die, but at times this was reversed. This is mentioned because the radial stress lines, caused by the metal flow into the upper die, are usually more predominant than those caused by the lower die (there are exceptions to this also). These flow, or stress, lines are actually visible on some coins and are the cause of the "cartwheel" effect that is a main aspect of luster. A Morgan dollar obverse usually has more cartwheel luster than the reverse. The amount of cartwheel luster, or lack thereof, is determined by other factors as well. Heavily polished dies have prooflike luster, or in the case of Proofs, they have Proof luster.

Below is a breakdown of luster for the four basic metal groups (copper, nickel, silver, and gold) and the types of luster within each group. The copper-nickel alloy (88 percent copper, 12 percent nickel) for Flying Eagle cents and Copper-Nickel Indian Head cents is listed under copper, though it could just as easily be listed under nickel. The nickel alloy coins, which as stated above are 75 percent copper and 25 percent nickel, also could be listed under copper, since that is their predominant metal. For silver coins 1834 and later, the alloy is 90 percent silver and 10 percent copper, except for the star three-cent silver Type I, which was 75 percent silver and 25 percent copper. There are also the cupronickel coins dated 1965 and later (except for half dollars, which were 40 percent silver and 60 percent copper through 1970) and some anomalies: the zinc-coated steel cents of 1943, the silver/manganese/copper alloy for the silver five cents of 1942–45, and so on.

Copper
Flat Luster
Copper coins that are struck with insufficient pressure, worn dies, or dies that have cracked usually will have this type of luster. Sometimes these coins are referred to as "dead." This means that when you tilt the coin into a

Luster
1946 Walking Liberty half dollar obverse and reverse. After repeated dips in a commercial solution, the luster "washes" out and becomes lackluster.

1939-D Walking Liberty half dollar obverse and reverse with blazing original luster.

light source, there is very little cartwheel effect. When this is a result of insufficient pressure, lightweight planchets or worn dies, the flow, or stress, lines will often be visible to the unaided eye. Even full mint-red coins will be dull with mushy surfaces. Flat-luster coins will negatively affect the grade, with more "discount" in higher grades than for lower-grade coins.

Satin Luster

Many copper coins, including most copper-nickel alloy coins, have this type of luster. These are usually coins struck with sufficient pressure from the middle life of the dies. This is why many coins, whether copper or other metal, have either this type of luster or frosty luster. This type of luster is characterized by a slight-to-moderate cartwheel effect and little reflectivity. When the dies become

worn, flow lines become noticeable and the luster becomes duller.

Frosty Luster

Some copper coins have swirling, cartwheel luster, although they do not usually have the contrast between the devices and fields of silver or gold coins. Half and large cents of the 1840s and 1850s are the large copper coins mostly seen with this type of luster. Some early copper coins have this type of luster but are rare in full original mint red, so it is not as evident as the later dates, which may still retain the mint-red color. The small cents exhibit this frosty luster for most years. The copper-nickel coins occasionally have frosty luster. Frosty luster is imparted to coins struck with sufficient pressure from lightly used dies on full-weight planchets.

Semi-Prooflike Luster
Many times dies are basined, or polished, re-sulting in fine polish lines in the fields of the dies. Since these lines are in the dies, the re-sulting struck coin will have fine *raised* lines—not to be confused with hairlines. These usually are parallel and sometimes cover the entire field area. Most people asso-ciate semi-prooflike and fully prooflike coins with Morgan dollars, but most U.S. coin se-ries have these luster types. Copper coins do not seem to have these fine die polish lines as often as the other metals.

Prooflike Luster
When dies are polished as described above or are more heavily polished to a mirrored fin-ish, the coins struck have prooflike luster. There is still a cartwheel effect, though it is not as evident as with semi-prooflike luster. There are usually no flow lines visible, but they are still present in microscopic form.

Proof Luster
Proof dies are polished even more rigorously than are regular-strike dies and, when fin-ished, often glisten as if they were nickel-plated. (Today, Proof dies are chrome plated to prolong use and impart deeply mirrored fields.) Usually the planchets are burnished as well, the resulting coins having deeper, more "watery" mirrored surfaces than prooflike coins. These still have the cartwheel effect, but even a microscope may not reveal any flow or stress lines. These coins sometimes have a "watery" look to the surfaces, resulting from the burnished planchets, higher striking pressure, and heavily polished dies—this term refers to the almost wavy nature of the surfaces. There is another kind of Proof luster for copper coins in addition to the brilliant Proof luster described above. From 1909 to 1916, Matte Proof Lincoln Head cents were struck. These are really closer to the Roman Matte Proof gold coins of 1909–10. Although the exact method of preparing these dies and the striking procedures are not known, it ap-pears that the dies were sandblasted or pick-led in acid after the basining process. These copper coins were not sandblasted after strik-ing, since there are usually fine die lines or

striations visible on most dates, and the edges are shiny. The luster of these coins is similar to the satin luster described previously. There also are some anomalies: some 1829–31 large-cent planchets were bronzed before striking, and these Proofs have flat luster; the 1936 Lincoln Head cent Type I and some 1950–54 cents are satinlike in luster, having prooflike surfaces with a satiny effect.

Nickel
Flat Luster
Since nickel is the hardest of the four major metal groups, many nickel coins exhibit flat luster. The fact that the alloy in most such coins contained only 25 percent nickel is fur-ther testament to the metal's hardness. These coins were so difficult to strike that many dies cracked after only a few thousand strik-ings. Insufficient striking pressure, worn dies, cracked dies, and underweight plan-chets are some of the causes of flat luster on nickel coinage. Many Liberty Head and In-dian Head nickels have this flat luster. When tilted under a light source, these coins will have little cartwheel effect.

Satin Luster
The majority of nickel coins have satin luster. With the difficulty in striking these coins, this is to be expected. These coins are character-ized by a slight-to-medium cartwheel effect.

Frosty Luster
A few nickel coins exhibit this type of luster, but cameo devices usually are seen only on Proof nickel coinage. Frosty-luster nickel coins do not usually have the "blast" associ-ated with silver or gold frosty-luster coins.

Semi-Prooflike Luster
When the dies are polished as described pre-viously, the resulting coins have semi-prooflike luster. If the die striations are light and not distracting, the resulting look can be quite attractive. Many three-cent nickels and Shield nickels exhibit this type of luster. It is rarer on the Liberty Head type and very rare on the Indian Head or Jefferson nickels. The parallel die striations are almost never visible on nickels after the Liberty Head type.

Prooflike Luster

There are few business-strike nickel coins with deep prooflike luster. Some dates of three-cent, Shield, and occasionally Liberty Head nickels have prooflike luster. There are only a few Indian Head nickels (1915-S, 1916-S, etc.) and almost no Jefferson nickels with prooflike luster, and those that do have it are not very deeply mirrored.

Proof Luster

Proof luster has a greater cartwheel effect on nickel coinage than on any other metal. The hardness of the metal makes deeply mirrored fields difficult to obtain. There are some Proof nickel coins (1886 three-cent nickels, 1889 Liberty Head nickels, etc.) that actually fall between satin luster and semi-prooflike luster. The Matte Proof 1913–16 Indian Head nickels have satin luster. (See comments under Proof Luster for copper, with the comments on 1936 Type I and 1950–54 Proof cents also applicable for nickels.)

Silver

Flat Luster

Silver coins struck with insufficient pressure from worn or broken dies, or on underweight planchets, have flat luster. These coins with diminished luster occur with less frequency than with copper coinage and with much less frequency than with nickel coinage. Cleaned coins often exhibit this type of luster, although they undoubtedly were more lustrous before the cleaning.

Satin Luster

When silver coins are struck with correct striking pressure from dies that are not excessively worn or broken, the luster is described as satin luster. These exhibit some cartwheel effect and usually have a pleasing look, with a slight "glow" to the surfaces.

Frosty Luster

There are many frosty-luster silver coins. The swirling, cartwheel luster on these coins makes them among the most attractive of all U.S. coinage. When observing a Liberty Seated dime, Reeded-Edge half dollar, Morgan dollar, and so on with this type of luster, one wonders why all coins do not look like this. Often the luster on these coins is described as "blast" or another descriptive moniker. The terms *moose, wonder coin,* and *killer,* for example, are heard on bourse floors and in auction viewing rooms, and when you look at the coin, invariably it is a frosty-luster coin. Often, the devices are frosted on these coins, which contrasts with the frosty-luster fields.

Semi-Prooflike Luster

Silver coins are common with semi-prooflike luster. The polishing of the dies that cause this look and luster type are often associated only with Morgan dollars; however, many silver series have this type of luster to varying degrees. The coins also may have frosted devices.

Prooflike Luster

Like semi-prooflike luster, prooflike luster has mainly been associated with Morgan dollars, but there are some other series that exhibit prooflike luster. Capped Bust coinage is much rarer with full prooflike luster than are Liberty Seated and Barber issues (to impart this type of luster, extra care was needed in the polishing of the dies, and Mint practices varied). Morgan dollars sometimes have frosted devices, contrasting with and providing an even more mirrorlike appearance to the fields. These are called *cameo prooflike* and *deep cameo prooflike.* (See the section on Surface Designations later in this chapter and the section on Morgan dollar grading as well.)

Proof Luster

After improved die and planchet polishing techniques were developed in the 1830s, presumably by Christian Gobrecht, deep Proof luster was possible. The silver coins struck after 1836 usually have deep, "watery" fields, with stress lines usually invisible even under magnification. Before the dies were polished, the devices were also treated, either sandblasted or pickled, to produce a frosty effect. This contrast between the devices and fields makes the mirrored fields seem even deeper. Many Proof coins of all denominations

Semi-Prooflike Luster
Morgan dollar reverse with semi-prooflike surfaces. Note the slight "cartwheel" luster that keeps this coin from the PL designation.

Prooflike Luster
San Francisco Morgan dollar with deep mirror prooflike (DMPL) reverse, with near Proof-quality depth mirrored surface with no "cartwheel" effect.

Proof Luster
Proof Morgan dollar reverse. Note the heavy frost on the devices and lettering contrasting with the deeply mirrored surfaces. This is often called a black-and-white cameo.

struck in 1900–08 are fully brilliant with no contrast. The non-mirrored Proofs are the Matte Proof Peace dollars of 1921–22, the Satin Proof 1921 Peace dollar, the variants of the 1922 regular-relief Peace dollar, the Type I 1936 issues, and the 1950–54 satinlike Proof coins, plus various Proof commemoratives.

Gold
Flat Luster

Not many gold coins have flat luster. Since gold is the softest metal used for coinage, it is easy to impart luster to these coins. Only severely worn dies, vastly insufficient striking pressure, massive die breaks, or underweight planchets result in flat luster. Some early Draped Bust and Capped Bust gold coins have this luster, although they are still exceptions.

Satin Luster

Most gold coins exhibit satin luster. Satin luster on gold coins has been compared to the look of velvet. Probably half or more of the gold coinage, especially after 1836, will exhibit satin luster.

Frosty Luster

Quite a few gold coins have frosty luster. Although the percentage of frosty-luster gold coins is probably less than that for silver coins, it is higher than for nickel and copper coinage. Although the flow lines are evident, especially under magnification, on many of the frosty-luster gold coins they do not really detract from the look.

Semi-Prooflike Luster

The die polish seen on gold coins occasionally can be as predominant as on silver coins, and since gold is softer, they usually remain in the die longer. There are some scarcer-date gold dollars, for example, that have parallel die striations on almost all strikes from those dies. The polish lines give the coins semi-prooflike luster that ranges from swirling frosty to almost fully prooflike.

Prooflike Luster

The percentage of prooflike gold coins is less than for silver coins. Additionally, they usually do not have as much contrast between the devices and the fields as do silver issues. Some of the first-year gold coins (1795 for example) have prooflike luster.

Proof Luster

The "watery" mirrored fields of copper and silver coins are replaced by "orange-peel" mirrored fields for brilliant Proof gold coins. The depth of the mirrored fields is as deep as that of silver coins, with the lack of "cartwheel" about the same. The softness of gold no doubt is one of the main causes of the orange-peel effect. Upon striking gold coins, the hard steel of the dies crystallizes the gold surface, resulting in this peculiar mirrored surface. There also are more types of Proof luster for gold coins than for other metals. The Matte Proofs of 1908 and 1911–15 have no cartwheel effect (these were sandblasted after striking). The Roman Proofs of 1909–10 (there are a couple of 1908s with this finish also) have some cartwheel effect. The dies were sandblasted or pickled, though the coins do not appear to have been treated after striking. The Satin Proofs of 1910 (possibly other dates) have satin luster, but with a more velvet look than business strikes. There also are other controversial Proof gold coins, among these the High-Relief double eagles, Rolled-Edge eagles, and Wire-Edge eagles. These have satin surfaces, and if they are Proofs, they are similar to the 1910 Satin Proofs.

Eye Appeal

Eye appeal is the most subjective part of coin grading. When numismatists say a coin has a great appearance or great eye appeal, they mean different things for different coins. When the terms *premium quality* or *high end* are used, these are often euphemisms for good eye appeal. A low-grade coin such as a G-4 large cent can have good eye appeal, as can a MS-67 half eagle, which, of course, always has great eye appeal. How can such diverse coins both have good eye appeal? The answer is perhaps simpler than it would appear. Eye appeal is a combination of marks, luster, strike, toning (if applicable), planchet condition, and surface preservation. It also is a very complex mixture of these attributes, and only years of experience will make you an expert in determining eye appeal. As stated previously, eye appeal is the most subjective part of coin grading and unless a coin is one extreme or the other (great-looking or ugly), there is sometimes disagreement. By breaking down the basic metals, types, and grades, one can better understand this difficult area of grading.

Supposedly, Albert Einstein was once asked to provide a layman's interpretation of his Theory of Relativity. His reply was that a finger on a hot stove for a few seconds seems like an eternity and an hour with a pretty girl seems like a few seconds. I wish eye appeal could be explained as easily. Since it cannot, we must break it down to comprehend its various parts. For lower-grade coins (EF-45 and below), eye appeal often comes down to placement of marks, or lack thereof, and surface preservation. Strike is also important (although in the lower grades it becomes part of the wear factor) and planchet condition can be a consideration if there are problems with the planchet. In these lower grades, the planchet "problems" (cracks, small flaws, etc.) are often worn away, so they become less important. Since there can be attractive or unattractive toning on these lower grades, that also must be considered. Luster, of course, has no bearing on grades below VF, since it is gone by the time a coin has wear over the entire surface. On higher-grade coins (MS-67 or PR-67 and above), there is very little negative eye appeal or the coin would not be given such a lofty grade. Thus, the "tough-to-determine" eye-appeal coins are the middle grades of **AU-50** to **MS-66**, and the corresponding Proof grades. Since there are many coins in these grades and there are probably as many ways to examine eye appeal as there are opinions about it, we will look at the four basic coin metals (copper, nickel, silver, and gold) and use these three basic grading groups for our analysis.

Copper
Lower Grades
For **G-4, F-12, VF-30,** and other lower-grade copper coins to have good eye appeal, marks, if there are any, must be minor or not in the prime focal areas, and the surfaces should be smooth and even. Since there is usually no luster in these lower grades (some coins have luster in grades down to **VF**), the relatively mark-free and smooth-surface coins are said to have good eye appeal. When there is porosity, flaking of the surface, a rough planchet, and so on, a copper coin is not considered to have good eye appeal, unless these problems are minor.

Middle Grades
Coins in grades of **AU-50** to **MS/PR-66** may have poor to great eye appeal. How can this be possible? Well, there is more controversy in "grading" eye appeal than in any other aspect of coin evaluation. A copper coin with a great planchet, good strike, and nice luster will have very positive eye appeal. When one or more of these aspects is deficient, eye appeal is diminished. The toning on copper coins, if present, must not be too dark, streaky, or splotchy, or it will not possess good eye appeal.

Higher Grades
The grades of **MS/PR-67** and higher must have good or great eye appeal. An **MS/PR-67** coin with poor eye appeal is an oxymoron, since it will not receive a lofty grade unless it contains minimal marks, has booming luster or reflectivity, and has a great strike, thus, positive eye appeal.

Nickel
Lower Grades
Eye appeal in low-grade nickel coins is a combination of good strike, decent planchet,

and lack of major marks. The lack of marks on the surface is probably the major factor in the appearance of these lower-grade coins.

Middle Grades
The eye appeal of **AU-50** to **MS/PR-66** coins is related to the luster, toning, strike, planchet, and lack of major marks. The luster and strike are related, since a poorly struck coin will rarely have good luster. The toning is usually light on nickel coins, but, like other higher-grade coins, some have spectacular toning and color. Planchets varied in quality, and some years even late-date coins, such as 1955 Jefferson nickels, almost exclusively had poor planchets. It is difficult to find good eye appeal with these coins. Marks or hairlines on nickel coins are fewer and generally smaller than on the other metal coinage, since nickel is a harder metal. Because the hardness of nickel makes good luster, full strike, and decent planchets more difficult to find, there are fewer nickel coins with good eye appeal than with other metals.

Higher Grades
The appearance of higher-grade nickel coins is often spectacular. Although many nickel coins suffer from poor planchets, weak strikes, die wear, marks, discoloration, or other maladies, there are good eye-appeal coins. Early strikes with sufficient striking pressure on good planchets produce great-looking coins. Often Proof nickel coins, especially in the 1880s and later, have blue "tissue" toning that adds to the attractiveness; occasionally, the business strikes seem to have been stored in this manner as well, or have acquired their vibrant colors from storage in holders with reactive chemical content.

Silver
Lower Grades
The grades of **EF-45** and below have good eye appeal when the combination of few marks/hairlines and decent strike is present. Most silver planchets are of good quality, and this is usually not a problem. However, some coins have impurities that cause dark areas on coins, sometimes called "drift marks," which are like planchet flaws, their negativ-

ity being mainly a factor of size and placement.

Middle Grades

The eye appeal of the grades from **AU-50** to **MS/PR-66** is mostly dependent upon the marks/hairlines, luster, toning, and strike. Planchets are usually of good quality. Some coins with few marks, good luster, and decent strike may have unattractive toning that will reduce the eye appeal. Obviously, any weak aspect will reduce the eye appeal, but unattractive toning is perhaps the single aspect for reduction of appearance.

Higher Grades

The same aspects as for middle-grade silver coins determine the eye appeal for grades of **MS/PR-67** and higher. Again, spectacular colors or vibrant toning will enhance the eye appeal of silver coins, more so than coins of other metals. No **MS/PR-67** or higher coin would be graded that high without good or great eye appeal. Since many of these high-grade coins are toned, color and toning are one of the main components of eye appeal in the higher grades. A coin cannot grade **MS/PR-67** with poor luster/reflectivity, and/or weak strike, and/or heavy marks/hairlines; therefore, if any of these aspects are lacking, the coin will not achieve these high grades.

Gold
Lower Grades

Gold is the softest metal, so eye appeal is related to marks/hairlines, or even more properly, the lack thereof. When luster disappears in the lower **VF** grades, the lack of marks/hairlines is the basic determinant of eye appeal. Only on poorly struck coins or coins with rough planchets does anything other than the marks/hairlines issue affect appearance. Many branch-mint gold coins do have poor planchets and weak strikes, often combined with worn dies.

Middle Grades

The lack of marks/hairlines and the intensity of the luster are the main factors in eye appeal for the grades of **AU-50** to **MS/PR-66**. Although many early issues and branch-mint

coins are plagued by weak strikes and poor planchets, most gold coins nonetheless have good eye appeal, because this is more dependent on the lack of marks/hairlines and the intensity of the luster.

Higher Grades

The highest-grade gold coins, **MS/PR-67** and above, have super-clean surfaces, great strike, superior luster, and problem-free planchets. These coins often have a deep-green or rich gold color that adds to the appearance. The Eliasberg gold sale in 1982 contained many of the **MS-67** and higher certified gold coins; John M. Clapp obtained most of these coins from various mints in their years of issue.

Planchet and Striking Errors

Planchets, or coin blanks, are sometimes made by the Mint and sometimes come from outside contractors. In the early days of the Mint, both sources had varying problems with planchets. Whether the planchets had defects from an alloy that did not mix properly, had foreign matter adhering to the surface, or had defects resulting from the rolling machines, they were almost always still used for coinage. Only the truly defective planchets were not used, these being melted for reuse. The coins that were struck on these less-than-perfect planchets sometimes exhibit these defects. Sometimes the striking process would obliterate the defects, but impurities and foreign matter on blanks usually do not disappear upon striking.

Sometimes planchets are stamped from the ends of the strips or from the areas of the strips that are too thin. The first may result in ragged edges that do not strike completely, as the affected edge does not have enough metal to fill the die. When the planchet is too thin, the entire coin might not have enough metal to sufficiently fill the die, resulting in missing detail over most or all of the coin. Sometimes the ragged edge causes no more than a crack to develop in the planchet, and coins with such defects are still graded unless they are severe.

Planchets of gold and silver that were over-weight were filed to remove the excess metal. At first, this was done across the planchet. These "adjustment marks" sometimes were struck away, but often were still visible after striking, especially on the high points. Later, the Mint changed the process, filing only the edges, any trace of which was usually struck away by the coining process. After the close collar was introduced, a very distinct rim resulted and the striking process almost always obliterated any adjustment of the planchet.

On early Proof coins, another planchet defect is noted. Before Proof coins were first mass-produced in 1858, the burnishing lines on the planchet were not always struck away. These lines are most often seen on coins struck before 1836, when Christian Gobrecht and other Mint employees began updating many Mint procedures. They are similar to die polish or die striations seen on some coins, which are *raised* lines on the struck coin. However, the burnishing lines are fine *recessed* lines on the struck coin, the result of the planchet being polished or burnished to impart a deeper mirrored surface for Proofs. These fine lines often are confused with die polish lines or hairlines. The differences among die polish lines, or striations, burnishing lines, and hairlines can sometimes be distinguished only under strong magnification. Die polish lines are *raised* and go *under and through* lettering and devices, burnishing lines are *recessed* and go *under and through* lettering and devices, and hairlines are *recessed* and go *over* lettering and devices.

Striking errors can occur in many ways. The really unusual striking errors are graded as error coins by PCGS and are noted by an E that proceeds the PCGS coin number. These include off-center strikes (more than 5 percent off), clipped planchet strikes (extremely minor clipping is acceptable), broadstruck specimens, brockage strikes, wrong planchet size strikes (a Draped Bust dollar struck on a large cent planchet), or any other major striking or planchet error. Off-metal strikings also are graded as error coins.

A list of the various planchet and striking errors on coins that *may be* graded by PCGS follows. The severity of the defect determines by how much the overall grade is affected. Although many minor planchet and striking defects do not seriously affect the grade, they will be included here. When the "defect(s)" is/are major, the coin will probably be graded as an error coin.

Improper Alloy

Improperly mixed metals can result in a variety of planchet problems. This may cause only streaky toning on some copper coins or even large gas bubbles under the surfaces, which sometimes explode, leaving a planchet flake or flaw. If poor mixing of the alloy leads only to streaky toning, the effect on the grade is minimal. This type of streaking is actually quite common on 1908-S and 1909-S cents, including the 1909-S VDB. Large planchet flakes or flaws are sometimes so severe, especially on major devices, that the coin will be graded as an error coin. Improper mixing may leave streaks in the planchet before the coins tone (see the following section on Foreign Matter for other types of planchet streaking).

Foreign Matter

This type of planchet defect may be a piece of tiny foreign matter or a large chunk of "charcoal" which, if too large, may result in the coin being graded as an error coin. These charcoal-looking areas are sometimes called planchet "drift" marks. Another type of foreign matter, probably strings of cloth from rags used to wipe the dies after polishing, results in lint marks. When this type of foreign matter is on the planchet when it is struck and then falls off the surface, the results are lint marks, ranging from short, basically straight to long, squiggled marks. When the foreign object is large, the defective area may be large, and if it is centered on a device, the coin will be graded as a strike-through error. At some point in the 1800s the planchets were dried in wood chips or sawdust, and the wood clung to the planchets and became embedded in the surface upon

Roller Marks
1888-S Morgan dollar obverse with roller marks. Note the parallel lines especially visible on the face. Proper die spacing usually "strikes" away these lines unless they are severe, as these are.

Rough Planchets
Half cent reverse with rough planchet. No amount of striking pressure will eliminate the deep imperfections seen on this planchet.

striking. This is most common on New Orleans dollars.

Roller Marks

This term is often a misnomer, as most of the long, straight, parallel, and indented lines called roller marks are actually from a different device called a drawing bench. At some point in the nineteenth century, gold and silver ingots were first rolled to just more than the desired thickness of a finished planchet, at which point the tapered leading edge of the rolled strip was fed through a rectangular gate in a block of steel mounted on the drawing bench. The bench gripped the leading edge and pulled the strip through the gate, reducing the strip to the *exact* desired thickness. Planchets punched from this strip would thus be the exact weight, eliminating the need for adjustment. Unfortunately, any irregularity or burr on the edge of the gate would leave a long scratch in the strip; multiple irregularities left parallel scratches. The planchets cut from these strips often retained these roller marks, which look like adjustment marks but are more uniform in size and depth and are usually straight and parallel. Usually these marks disappear in the striking process as the metal heats and flows into the recesses of the dies, although with insufficient die pressure or improper die spacing they are not struck away. Certain coins,

such as 1902-S Morgan dollars, commonly have roller marks, with the number, length, and depth of the marks determining how much the overall grade is affected.

Rough Planchets

Sometimes planchets were inferior because of an improper alloy mix or some other problem, and these have rough surfaces. Many Charlotte and Dahlonega coins were struck on these rough planchets, leading to coins that were not very attractive right off the presses. Occasionally, these planchets may have been cut from thin parts of the strips, thus they may have been lightweight, leading to a weakly struck coin.

Ragged-Edge Planchets

Planchets, when cut from the ends or edges of strips, often had ragged edges. Since the ragged edges were usually too thin, the detail might not strike fully in these areas. However, they are usually graded as a regular coin unless there is a considerable amount of detail missing or unless the ragged area covers more than 5 to 10 percent of the coin – those coins will then be graded as error coins. The coins struck from these defective planchets often develop cracks, but such coins are graded as non-error coins, unless the cracks are too large or too deep. Large or deep cracks mean the coin will be graded as an error coin.

Clipped Planchets
Connecticut colonial with clipped planchet. This type of clip is the result of a planchet cutter's error. He was too close to a previously cut-out planchet hole, this planchet overlapping the edge of the cut-out. This is a minor clip covering less than 5 percent of the surface, so this coin would be graded.

Clipped Planchets

When the planchet is cut from the strips of mill-rolled ingots, and it is cut over an edge, a straight-edged clipped planchet results. When the planchet is cut from an area from which a planchet has already been cut and overlaps the cut-out area, a curved-edged, clipped planchet is produced, and this is more common than straight-edge clipped planchets. PCGS will grade some coins with slight (less than 5 percent) clips, among these being Colonials, Territorials, and certain other issues. Federal issues and other coins with clips larger than 5 percent are graded as error coins.

Thin Planchets

When the milled strips are finished, they usually are of uniform thickness. They are then placed in another device that draws the strips to the proper thickness; planchets are then cut from these drawn strips. Occasionally the strips had areas, usually on the ends, that were not of the proper thickness. The planchets cut from these areas will be thin and probably underweight. If they were still within weight tolerances for silver or gold, however, these planchets were used for coinage. The thin copper and nickel planchets often were used even when they were below the acceptable weight. The resulting coins often do not show full, intended detail and can be differentiated

from improperly spaced die strikes by weighing them.

Adjustment Marks

In the early days of the Mint, it was common practice to take heavy planchets and file them to bring them within weight tolerances. At first this was done across the surface of the planchet. If these crisscross lines were deep, they remained there after striking. The lighter, shallow adjustment marks were sometimes struck away. At some point in the 1800s, the Mint started adjusting the planchet weights by filing the edges instead of the surfaces. After the close collar was introduced in 1828, the rim became more pronounced and usually obliterated the edge adjustment filing.

Burnishing Lines

These fine, polishing lines are sometimes seen on pre-1836 Proof coins. The close collar introduced in 1828 for dimes, and over the next few years for other coinage, allowed better metal flow, thus obliterating most of these burnishing lines. These lines are very fine and sometimes are visible only upon magnification. As mentioned earlier, these are usually parallel and very fine lines that go under and through lettering and devices.

Off-Center Strikes

When the blank did **not center** directly over the anvil die **and the coin** was struck, the coin is said to be off center. PCGS will grade coins that are slightly (less than 5 percent) off center for certain series (as with slightly clipped planchets as noted above). When the coin is more than slightly off center, it is considered a major error and is graded as an error coin.

Wrong-Metal Strikes

A coin struck on a correct-size planchet that is of the wrong composition is considered a wrong-metal strike. Such coins are considered major mint errors and are graded as such by PCGS. When coins are intentionally struck in a different metal, they are called die trials or set-up pieces. Examples of die trials are the copper, nickel, and aluminum strikings of regular-die gold issues. These also are graded by PCGS and can be found among the pattern issues.

Color and Toning

When the subject of color (or toning) arises, eyebrows are raised. Only eye appeal generates this kind of emotion from serious numismatists. There seem to be two basic camps: nature's beautiful work or nature's wrath. In fact, both are correct. Any color on any metal is some form of corrosion or oxidation. Yet, sometimes a coin's grade is "enhanced" by lovely, original color or toning. Although toning is technically a form of corrosion, there is no reason to always view it negatively. With proper preservation, which is only one of an encapsulated coin's great features, there is no reason why the beauty of originally toned coins cannot be maintained. When you see an 1800 Bust half dime in **MS-68** with nearly perfect surfaces and beautiful, original toning, you are transported through time to the early United States, when some collector plucked this beauty from a bank, merchant, or perhaps a visit to the first U.S. Mint. It was carefully put away, perhaps being wrapped in cloth or paper. It then was passed from generation to generation until it ended up in a famous collection auctioned a few years ago. Like all artifacts, such coins allow us a glimpse into the past.

A technical discussion of color and toning and an aesthetic view of negative, neutral, and positive color and toning follow. Although it would be nice to have pictures and discuss every aspect of all types of color and toning, that is impossible here. There are, however, basic types of color and toning that can be explained.

Technically, toning really relates only to copper, nickel, and silver, since gold does not oxidize except at extreme temperatures. However, gold and silver coins are alloyed with copper, which does oxidize and imparts color and toning to these coins. Silver also reacts with sulfur to form silver sulfides, which constitute a large percentage of the toning on toned silver coins. The term "when applicable" may be employed on certain types of toning. Also, toned copper is not usually as desirable as toned silver, nickel, or gold. When toning is called "positive," that may only be true for coins of these three metals and not copper coins.

Peripheral

Although almost all peripheral color or toning is considered positive, there are some exceptions. On copper, nickel, and silver coins that were improperly stored, dark, often black, unattractive color resulting from sulfur or other chemical reactions can appear. Since all four major coin alloys contain copper, all could be affected like this. However, it is virtually unheard of for a gold coin to have peripheral toning so thick that the coin is ungradable. Another way peripheral toning is acquired is from Wayte Raymond type cardboard holders, very popular in the 1930s, 1940s, and 1950s, which contained sulfur and other chemicals that reacted with the coins from the edge inward, leading to the golds, blues, reds, yellows, and other colors many coins acquire. Storage in these holders led a to a few cases where the edges of the coins became too deeply toned to be attractive. This color and toning is among the most desirable, along with target toning (see the later section on Target toning). In fact, most target toning originates from these types of holders and began with peripheral toning.

When copper receives this light bright color or toning on the periphery, the coin may still be designated Red. When the color covers most of the coin and begins developing darker shades, the coin is designated Red-Brown.

Light Even

This is a very common color or toning occurrence. When a coin is stored without touching a reactive chemical in its holder, the resultant toning is mainly from the oxidation process caused by exposure to the atmosphere. Of course, the "air" is different in Miami, New York, Phoenix, and other divergent climates, resulting in different air toning. What colors appear depends on the mix of chemicals in the air, the humidity, other atmospheric conditions, the type of holder, and the storage location. This type of toning is only a few microns deep, and sometimes it is difficult to see unless it is viewed under good lighting conditions. Sometimes this toning is so light that, as noted earlier, it is ignored. If a coin has good luster that blooms through a light color, this has virtually no effect on the grade.

Medium Even

This type of toning also is very common. The colors are deeper and range from light-to-medium blues, reds, yellows, and other light colors. If the colors approach gray and black, they are considered deep toning, discussed later. In general, medium, even toning is positive. When coins lack luster intensity, this type of toning may be viewed as neutral, especially on silver coins. It is hard for medium, even color or toning to be anything but positive on nickel and gold coins.

Dark Even

When the colors and toning become deep blue, charcoal, or black, they generally are viewed neutrally at best. Sometimes intense-luster coins will be viewed as positive with deep or "electric" blue color. When the luster is impaired by the color and toning, or the colors approach charcoal or black, the coin is said to have negative toning. Some coins have such deep toning that PCGS will not grade them, and they are returned, unsealed, as environmentally damaged. (See later section.)

Mottled

When toning is splotchy or uneven, it is said to be mottled. When this is light or the colors are vibrant, the coins are considered to have neutral to positive toning. Some mottled toning is beautiful, and when it is the result of storage in original holders, such as those issued with some commemorative coinage, it can enhance the premium by multiples. Toning from these holders turns out uneven for several reasons. The reverse is usually flat against the holder, but the obverse may have a tab or flap that causes this uneven toning. When the colors are not vibrant or fall into the grays, browns, and charcoals, and the mottling is very uneven, mottled toning may be negative or only neutral. When the shades of color become darker and move toward the gray and brown scale, the vibrancy of the luster often becomes subdued. If the coin has booming luster, the toning may still be positive, but many coins with average or below-average luster often look "dead" and unattractive with this type of color or toning. When a coin has resided for many years in a holder, or the holder has a high concentration of sulfur or other reactive chemicals, the resulting coin may have very deep, heavily mottled color or toning. Often the vibrancy of the coin is almost completely obscured. The colors may range from pretty greens, blues, reds, and yellows to unsightly browns, grays, charcoals, and black. If the colors are from the first group and the mottling is heavy, but not totally obscured, the toning may be neutral or even slightly positive. Most darkly toned, heavily mottled coins are negative, sometimes excessively so.

Streaky

Although streaky toning could be considered a variation of mottled color or toning, there are some coins other than mottled ones that are worth mentioning. The wood-grained toning found on some copper coins is considered attractive by many. The alloy probably was not mixed properly, resulting in this type of toning seen on business strikes and Proofs, ranging from light streaks to heavy "walnut" streaking. Streaky toning also is seen on nickel coinage. Although original nickel coinage may tone in a streaky way, the most-often-seen streaky toning on nickel is the result of improper rinsing after dipping. The chemicals in commercial dips often leave a residue, which, if not rinsed off, will cause a streaky brown toning to appear after a time. Curiously, streaky toning also can result from too much rinsing after dipping, especially if a copper-nickel coin is left in a dish of water. The oxygen in the water can cause copper-rich areas of the surface to oxidize quickly. The same results are noted from improper rinsing of silver and gold coins, except the streaking is usually minor. The streaky toning is seen on silver coins from other sources, however, and may be the result of unusual storage methods and/or holders.

Hazy

Although, technically, hazy toning is not clearly defined as toning, it does not fit into any other category. Sometimes appearing as no more than a clear film on the surface of a coin, the haze is often the result of a PVC flip. Although nickel, silver, and gold coins exhibit such haze most frequently, copper is occasionally seen with it. The luster is not often obscured by this haze, so only the overall look of the coin is used to determine how negatively the haze affects the grade. The term "dusky" is often used for coins with hazy toning and little luster showing through the toning; commemoratives often have this look. Gold coins repatriated from Europe often have a milky haze—if this is not thick and too mottled-looking, it will usually be treated neutrally.

Target

This also is called "bullet" toning, and is often seen on silver coins, although it can be found on copper, nickel, or gold. This is the result of toning from the outside inward. When a coin is left for years in a slide-type holder that grips the coin by the edge in a cardboard liner that is chemically reactive, this type of toning may result. Often the colors will start with blue on the edge and fade to red, green, yellow, or other lighter colors, making this one of the most attractive kinds of toning found on coins. It is sometimes called "Wayte Raymond" toning, because the holders he developed often cause this type of toning. If the coin was original when it was placed in the holder, then the colors are rich and vibrant. A dipped coin may not have the depth of color and vibrancy, although these are often very attractive and positive on such a coin. This and peripheral toning overlap, whereas target or bullet toning begins as peripheral toning and progressively moves to this variation.

Holder

Although this type of toning has been discussed somewhat in the earlier descriptions under Mottled and Target, there are many types of "holder" toning. Commemoratives were issued in many types of holders, and the commercial holders of the past and present are varied. Since the reactive chemicals in the holders differed and climate and storage affect the colors and toning, holder toning covers a broad spectrum. Most holder toning is attractive, unless it ranges to the dark, mottled, streaky, or other unattractive areas. Many multicolored toned gems are the result of toning in holders.

Tab

Tab toning is a type of holder toning. It is mainly associated with commemoratives, since the issue holders often had a tab to hold the coin in place. This type of toning is similar to target toning, because there is a central focus, although tab toning usually will have a line across the coin and a central circle. The length of time spent under the tab and the climate and storage environment will affect the depth and range of colors.

Envelope

The coins toned in envelopes (small 2 X 2 white or manila "Kraft" type are the most often seen) often are difficult to distinguish from other types of toning. The resulting colors and toning are quite varied and can range from light, smooth colors to darker, mottled colors. Since these envelopes are so varied and their chemical content so different, this is predictable. The climate and storage also have a great effect. Heating a coin in an envelope or placing the enclosed coin on a window-sill can simulate this type of toning. However, the resultant toning "floats" on the surface of the coin. True envelope toning is deeper into the surface, thus appears "bonded" to the coin. This is a difficult concept to verbalize, but after seeing examples of both it usually is obvious. If a coin has been dipped, however, the toning may not adhere as it would with an original coin, and the toning may not be as deep.

Tissue

Before 1955, Proof coins often were stored in mint tissue that contained sulfur, among other reactive chemicals (business strikes also were stored in this type of tissue, but they are much less often seen with such toning than Proof coins). The resulting colors from storage in this manner are sometimes spectacular. This usually produces fairly even toning, although the folds of the tissue touching the surface of the coin sometimes leave areas of unevenness. When the tissue is used for copper coins, the resultant colors range from reds to purples, with many shades in between. Some nickel coinage has a blazing blue color that highlights the surfaces, and many of these coins have even toning with no streaks, smudges, or splotches. Silver coins stored in this tissue have the most colors, with reds, yellows, and greens being mixed with the usually dominant blues. Gold coins were probably also stored in this manner; however, most Proof gold does not have much toning, as only the copper tones and imparts color to gold coins, usually in very subtle pastel colors.

Bag

The first coins struck in the United States were shipped in wooden kegs. Sometime in the nineteenth century, coins began to be shipped in cloth bags. With the Bland-Allison Act of 1878, which authorized the purchase of huge quantities of silver to be coined into silver dollars, large quantities were struck that were not needed and did not circulate. Throughout the country, large groups of silver dollars lay in bank vaults, usually held as reserves, acquiring spectacular toning in cloth bags. This toning usually is crescent-shaped or "patterned." The crescent shapes came from coins being placed on top of other coins, pressed against the inside of the cloth bag, which often left the patterned or checkered cloth design. Since these bags had reactive chemicals in them, the colors produced were often bright blues, reds, and yellows. Some collectors pay large premiums for rainbow-colored silver dollars with explosive colors.

Unusual

This is a catchall category, but the term "unusual" often is apt with coins stored in peculiar ways, acquiring peculiar colors and toning. Sometimes copper coins acquire vivid, multicolor toning. Nickel coins sometimes have a pink color that dominates, instead of blue. Silver has so many color and toning variances that to single them out as unusual is futile. If the toning does not fit the other categories, it often is referred to as unusual toning, which may be a "square" patch of color or some other geometric shape acquired in an unusual way. The same may be true of gold coins; however, it is often subtle. Unusual colors may sometimes appear in the recesses of the incuse Indian Head design as well.

Second

Technically, second toning is not a type of color or toning, but it is important to understand what causes it and the consequences thereof, since the grade may be affected. Once a coin is dipped or cleaned, a second toning will "lie" differently on the surface of the coin. The toning may "float," similar to artificial toning, and lack the "depth" and "bonded" look of first toning. Although dipping and cleaning may sometimes be the best solution for some coins, originality is appreciated by true numismatists. Once a coin has been dipped or cleaned, nothing can bring back the originality. The surfaces have been changed and the colors and toning of the entire life of the coin are gone. The second toning is never going to look the same as the first because of the "leaching" effect. The secondary metals in a coin, which are responsible for some of the color and toning, leach to the surface, and when the coin is dipped or cleaned are removed in higher concentrations than the primary metal. For instance, on an original gold coin, the colors come from the cupric sulfides and oxides, and after dipping or cleaning, those are removed from the coin. An X-ray diffraction of the surface of the coin may show less copper than before the dipping or cleaning, leaving less metal that may tone. The second toning will almost always be less intense and colorful, which is not to imply that second toning is always negative, because it may be positive.

Environmental Damage

When toning is no longer pretty and becomes dark, thick, and unsightly, the coin is considered environmentally damaged. At what point does a coin change from being toned to being environmentally damaged? When stored for long periods of time with reactive chemicals, the surface of a coin will change from light, pastel-type colors to deep, rich colors to dark, luster-inhibiting colors. There also may be a black buildup that resembles charcoal. When these factors are in place, the coin is labeled environmentally damaged and will not be graded by PCGS. Although this is usually seen on copper, nickel, and silver coins, a few gold coins also are found in this category. (See Doctored Coins, chapter 11 for further explanations about environmental damage and how it occurs.)

Artificial

Artificial toning is the most controversial area of color and toning and one of the most controversial subjects in all of numismatics. This is the "ugly" aspect of color and toning. Although some "artificial" toning is ugly, some of it is attractive. Some will say there is no such thing as artificial toning, since chemicals and atmospheric conditions cause both natural and artificial toning. At PCGS, intent is often all one can use, since second toning and artificial toning are sometimes virtually indistinguishable. If the suspected toning occurs over marks or hairlines, there is a good chance Mother Nature had help in her chemical reactions, achieved in a variety

of ways, as discussed in Doctored Coins, chapter 11. The main points of emphasis are the "floating" toning, bright "crayon" colors, and marks or hairlines hidden directly under suspected toning. PCGS realizes this is a tough area and when there is doubt, the correct solution is to not grade the coin. Although there can be legitimate disagreements over some color and toning, when a coin is absolutely original there is no question about the color or toning. By not putting questionably toned coins in holders, PCGS ensures that the "coin doctors" are less likely to attempt their trade. If a coin has been dipped or cleaned, it is much more desirable in whatever its current state may be than it would be after applying chemicals that, over time, will only reduce the remaining surface luster or reflectivity. A coin that has been "burned" by repeated tonings can never improve. Just as over dipping a coin will eventually remove its luster or reflectivity, multiple artificial tonings will "wreck" the surfaces. (See Doctored Coins, chapter 11, for more information.)

PCGS Designations

Designations refer to the suffixes added to some grades in certain series, which expand and elaborate on the numerical grade. There are three basic areas:

Color Designations: Red, Red-Brown, and Brown for copper coins—**RD, RB, BN.**

Strike Designations: Full Steps for Jefferson nickels, Full Bands for Mercury dimes, Full Bands on the torch for Roosevelt dimes, Full Head for Standing Liberty quarters, and Full Bell Lines for Franklin half dollars—**FS, FB, FB, FH, FBL.**

Surface Designations: Deep Mirror Prooflike and Prooflike for Morgan dollars and Deep Cameo and Cameo for Proofs—**DMPL, PL, DCAM, CAM.**

Color Designations
Red (RD)

Red (RD) is the designation that follows the numerical grade of **MS/PR** copper coins that are still in full mint bloom, with original color as struck and only slight diminishing of the luster or reflectivity is allowed. There must be at least 95 percent of the red color on both sides of the coins. In the highest grades (MS/PR-69/70), only the slightest mellowing of color is allowed. In the high grades (MS/PR-67/68), slight mellowing to some mellowing of color is allowed, but if a coin has exceptional luster/reflectivity, the mellowing that is allowed is proportional to these elements. In the middle grades (MS/PR-64/66), some mellowing is expected. The amount of mellowing is now proportional to the luster/reflectivity and the spotting allowed for each of these grades. In the lower grades (MS/PR-60/63), considerable mellowing of the color is allowed, and since spotting is often the reason for these grades, it is the factor that often determines the amount of mellowing allowed.

Red-Brown (RB)

Red-Brown (RB) is the designation following the numerical grade of **MS/PR** copper coins that have lost some (5 to 95 percent) of their original mint color. This is a very wide spectrum of colors. The coin's colors can range from nearly full mint red to mostly brown or tan. Mint State coins tend to have more brown mixed with the red color and Proof coins seem to have more tan mixed with the red color, but there are exceptions (some Proof Indian cents have a purple color, etc.). Severely faded red coins, (which may have little or no brown) are called RB instead of RD. Also, coins with very little red (i.e., 5 percent) that are almost completely brown are designated RB. Spotting is allowed, although in higher grades (MS/PR-65/66) this will be extremely minor, usually noticeable only under magnification. In grades **MS/PR-67** and above, spotting is almost never allowed; however, a minor spot or two may be allowed if compensated for by superior luster/reflectivity or intensity of color. In lower grades (**MS/PR-64** and below), excessive spotting can result in the coin's not being graded (obviously, no coin would attain **MS/PR-65** or higher with noticeable spotting).

Note: A coin with one side full original red and the other side fully brown, or with only traces of red, will be designated RB.

Brown (BN)

Brown (BN) is the designation following the numerical grade of **MS/PR** copper coins that usually have 5 percent or less of their original color. Most coins with this designation will have either a smooth, light-to-dark brown color or a light-to-streaky tan color with only tinges of red, if any at all. Some coins will have up to 10 percent red on one side of the coin and no red, or only trace amounts of red, on the other side, and will be designated BN. Although unevenness of color is nonexistent for smooth brown or tan coins, for streaky brown or tan coins the amount of unevenness allowed in **MS/PR-67/69** is very minor. For grades **MS/PR-64/66**, a moderate amount of unevenness of color is allowed. For **MS/PR-63** and below grades, streaky or uneven color is common (usually one of the reasons for the grade). Minor spotting is allowed in the higher grades (**MS/PR-65** and above), although for grades above **MS/PR-66** this must be microscopic. For grades **MS/PR-64** and below, there may be considerable spotting, but excessive or massive spotting will always reduce the grade and in some cases may result in the coin's not being graded.

Note: Many BN coins will have diminished luster or reflectivity, with a few having lost almost all bloom (this, of course, will negatively affect the numerical grade). Some BN coins will still retain exceptional luster or reflectivity.

Strike Designations
Full Steps (FS)

Full Steps (FS) is the designation following the numerical grade of some regular-strike **MS-60** or higher Jefferson nickels that have at least five separated steps (lines) at the base of Monticello. Any major disturbance or interruption of these steps or lines, whether caused by contact, planchet problems, or another source, will result in the coin not being designated FS. Only the slightest weakness on any step (line) is allowed for this designa-

Full Steps (FS)
Close-up of Jefferson nickel reverse with full steps (FS). All six steps are complete and separate, with no disturbances.

Partial Steps
Close-up of Jefferson nickel reverse with non-full steps. A very poorly struck coin with fewer than two steps present, one partial and another basically complete.

tion. Some issues are almost never seen with Full Steps and may command a significant premium.

Full Bands (FB)

Full Bands (FB) is the designation following the numerical grade of some regular-strike Winged Liberty Head (Mercury) dimes that have fully separated horizontal bands on the central part of the fasces (the bundle-of-rods design on the reverse). There can be no interruption in the trough of the bands due to strike, contact, planchet problems, or any other damage, whether mint-caused or not.

Note: Although the central bands must be fully separated with no interruption, it is not necessary to have full roundness to the bands—the so-called "McDonald's Arches" that are sometimes referred to as Full Split or Full Rounded Bands. For some dates (i.e., 1945-P, etc.) this ultimate state almost never occurs, thus may command a significant premium.

Full Bands (FB)

Full Bands (FB) is the designation following the numerical grade of some regular-strike Roosevelt dimes that have fully separated horizontal bands on the top and bottom of the torch on the reverse. There can be no major interruption in the trough of the bands due to strike, contact, planchet problems, or any other damage, whether mint-caused or not. This is different from the criteria noted for full bands on Winged Liberty Head (Mercury) dimes, which can have no interruption in the central bands. The Roosevelt dime standard is closer to the Franklin half dollar full bell line criteria, where slight disruptions are allowed so long as the continuity of the lines is maintained.

Full Head (FH)

Full Head (FH) is the designation that follows the numerical grade of some Standing Liberty quarters that have full detail in the head and cap of Miss Liberty. For coins that grade **AU-50** and higher, this designation is assigned when full head and cap detail is present for the four varieties of the two major design types (Type I—1916, 1917; Type II—1917–1924, 1925–1930). The Type I exhibits only slight differences between the 1916 and 1917 head detail. The Type II has even slighter differences between the raised (1917–1924) and recessed (1925–1930) date varieties. This occurs only on certain date and mint-mark combinations. The most noticeable Type II modification of the head area is a small slit for the ear hole instead of a small, round hole. Since different criteria for the four basic varieties will determine whether FH status is assigned, the descriptions and minimum detail necessary for Full Head status are listed separately.

Full Bands (FB)
Close-up of Mercury dime reverse with full bands (FB). Note the uninterrupted line between the horizontal bands.

Partial Bands
Close-up of Mercury dime reverse with not quite full bands. This just-miss specimen has the bands touching slightly near the center, along with a disruption on the right side.

Flat Bands
Close-up of Mercury dime reverse with flat bands. The horizontal bands have only slight separation and are basically blended together.

Full Bands (FB)
Close-up of Roosevelt dime reverse with full horizontal bands (FB) at the top and bottom of the torch.

Note: The exception to the AU-50 and higher rule for FH designation is that PCGS will designate 1918/7-S quarters as Full Head, when they attain FH, in grades of EF-40 and above.

1916 Type I

The minimum head and cap detail required for the 1916 Standing Liberty quarter is the most difficult to verbalize. Since there is *not* a great deal of detail in the original head design, consisting mainly of very fine lines or strands of hair, one must look for overall sharpness in this area to determine FH status. Some coins of this date will have full, intended detail but have some slight overall mushiness and still qualify for FH status. Others may have bolder lines without the general mushiness, but with slight weakness in several strands and still attain the FH designation. As long as the hair is distinct and the

strands do not blend into Miss Liberty's head or cap, the coin will be designated Full Head.

Note: 1916 Standing Liberty quarters with both exceptionally bold strands of hair and no mushiness or blending of the hair detail are the exceptions and may command a significant premium.

1917 Type I

The head detail is slightly modified and strengthened considerably for the 1917 Type I issues. Instead of hair strands, cords are now present and the mushiness associated with the majority of the 1916 issues is absent. If these hair cords are well-defined and distinct, the FH designation is warranted. There should be a distinct separation between these hair cords and the cap of Miss Liberty, with any blending being extremely

Full Head (FH), Type I
Close-up of Type I Standing Liberty quarter obverse with a full head (FH). All intended detail is sharp and crisp. The hair and helmet are very sharp, with the curls rounded and distinct.

Flat Head, Type I
Close-up of Type I Standing Liberty quarter obverse with a flat head. The top part of the head and the hair curls are flat, not from wear but from strike.

Full Head, Type II
Close-up of Type II Standing Liberty quarter obverse with a full head (FH). The modified design shows the hair and helmet fully detailed, with three sprigs, the hairline, and the ear hole complete.

Nearly Full Head, Type II
Close-up of Type II Standing Liberty quarter obverse with a just-miss full head. This coin nearly qualifies for FH status, with three sprigs and nearly complete hair detail. However, the hairline is not complete down the face and the ear hole is missing.

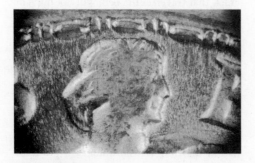

Flat Head, Type II
Close-up of Type II Standing Liberty quarter obverse with a flat head. Less than half of the head detail is present, with part of the sprigs, no hairline, and no ear hole.

minor. This date is the best-struck Standing Liberty quarter, including not only the head area, but also the entire coin, which often is 100 percent fully struck.

Note: Almost all Philadelphia Mint 1917 Type I quarters have Full Heads, and many Denver Mint coins are Full Head; only the San Francisco Mint 1917 Type I quarters are not often seen with Full Heads.

1917–1924 Type II

In mid-year 1917, a major modification occurred in the entire design, with the head detail totally changed. Now there is a distinctive helmet-like cap with a three-leaved, or sprigged, wreath; an outline that runs down the face and curves back below the ear; hair detail that is cordlike; and a small, round hole for an ear. For the FH designation, 95 to 100 percent of the detail intended must be present. In most cases, this means there must be three complete and distinct leaves present (they must be separate from each other and the other details of the hair, with only the slightest blending); the outline must be distinct all the way around the face; the hair detail will be distinct, although some slight weakness or blending is allowed; and the ear hole must be present. If any of the above is not present to the degree specified, the Full Head designation will not be assigned.

Note: On certain Denver and San Francisco issues, the outline that runs down the face may have some slight weakness in the curve at the point where it turns to the back of the head. If all the other details are exceptionally strong (i.e., the three leaves are very distinct, the hair is bold, and there is a strong ear hole), this slight blending of the outline into the face will not keep the coin from receiving Full Head status. Also, a coin with a very distinct outline, bold hair, and a distinct ear hole may have slightly less distinctness and separation in the three leaves or sprigs and still attain the FH designation.

1925–1930 Type II

The criteria for this modified variety are basically the same as for the previous style (1917–1924). The major difference is that for certain date and mint-mark combinations, the ear hole will be a narrow slit instead of a round hole. Many of the problems (filled dies, striking pressure, etc.) of the early Type II coins (1917–1924) are less prevalent for the recessed-date variety, thus a greater percentage of many dates and mint marks attain Full Head status.

Note: A few issues (1926-D, 1926-S, 1929-D, etc.) were still plagued by problems with head detail and are exceptions. These issues are seldom seen with all the criteria to attain Full Head status and may command multiples of non-Full Head prices.

Full Bell Lines (FBL)

When the bottom set of lines across the Liberty Bell is complete and uninterrupted, a regular-strike Mint State 60 or above Franklin half dollar receives the designation Full Bell Lines (FBL). If these lines are obscured by marks, strike, planchet defects, or other sources, the coin will not receive the FBL designation. A few marks across the lines will not prevent a coin from receiving this designation, as long as the continuity of the lines is not disturbed. Multiple marks, scratches, scrapes, or other detractions that interfere with the continuity of the lines will prevent a specimen from receiving the FBL designation. Slight incompleteness of the bell lines, immediately to the left or right of the crack that traverses the bell, will not prevent a coin from receiving the FBL designation. Premiums for some dates, such as some of the San Francisco issues, may be multiples of the non-FBL coins.

Surface Designations
Deep Mirror Prooflike (DMPL)

Deep Mirror Prooflike (DMPL) is the designation that follows the numerical grade of some regular-strike Morgan dollars that have fields with very deep reflectivity. The depth of surface, in some cases, will be near-Proof quality, and in a few cases (1889, 1896, etc.) the coins are so close to Proof quality that they are often labeled as such by experi-

Full Bell Lines (FBL)
Close-up of Franklin half dollar reverse with full bell lines (FBL). The bottom three bell lines are complete and uninterrupted.

Partial Bell Lines
Close-up of Franklin half dollar reverse with non-full bell lines. The bottom three lines not only are incomplete but are interrupted by a disturbance near the crack.

enced numismatists. The surfaces must have clear reflectivity at a distance of six inches, with no distortion caused by striations or frost. Minute striations usually will *not* impede the reflectivity, but if they do cause slight distortion, the coin would be designated PL instead of DMPL. For a few dates (especially some Carson City issues), there may be small patches of frost around the major devices. As long as this does not detract from the overall look of the coin, it may still qualify for DMPL status. The devices may be frosted, in some instances with a strong cameo effect as seen on some Proofs. On some later dates (1899–1904), the devices will have little or no frost.

Note: Coins that usually come with deep frost on the devices (such as many Carson City issues) usually will not command a premium, while other dates that are seldom seen with strong cameos will bring extraordinary premiums.

Prooflike (PL)
Prooflike (PL) is the designation that follows the numerical grade of some regular-strike Morgan dollars that have considerable reflectivity, with clear reflection in the fields at a distance of two to four inches. A slight amount of cartwheel luster may be evident, but this must not impede the clarity of reflec-

tion. If the cartwheel effect or the striations cause an area to lose clarity, the designation of PL will *not* apply. Contrast, or frost, may be present for some dates and mint marks. (See comments under DMPL.)

Note: The easiest way to examine a coin for PL or DMPL status is to hold the coin perpendicular to a flat, white surface with either writing or a design across the item. The clarity of reflection, or lack thereof, will be obvious at this viewing angle. If there is fading or obscurity at the designated distances, the coin will not attain PL or DMPL status.

Deep Cameo (DCAM)
Deep Cameo (DCAM) is the designation following the numerical grade of some Proof coins that have deep, unbroken frosted devices on both the obverse and reverse. There will be strong contrast between the mirrored fields and frosty devices. If the major devices have any frost fade or recessed areas where there is diminished frost or even tiny areas of "brilliance," the coin will not attain DCAM status.

Note: Certain dates and denominations of modern Proof coins (1951, 1958 Franklin halves, etc.) are seldom seen with DCAM and will command significant premiums over CAM coins of the same date and denomination.

Deep Mirror Prooflike (DMPL)
1881-S Morgan dollar obverse with deep mirror prooflike surfaces (DMPL). The heavy frost on the head contrasts with the near-Proof quality reflective fields.

San Francisco Morgan dollar reverse with deep mirror prooflike surfaces (DMPL). Highly polished dies give the surfaces their mirrorlike reflectivity. Only the first strikes from the dies have the depth seen on coins such as this.

Prooflike (PL)
1885-O Morgan dollar obverse with prooflike surfaces (PL). These mirrorlike surfaces have only a slight "cartwheel" effect. An object should be clear at two to four inches in these surfaces.

1885-O Morgan dollar reverse with prooflike surfaces (PL). Although not as reflective as deep mirror prooflike or Proof surfaces, this field has clarity at two to four inches.

Cameo (CAM)

Cameo (CAM) is the designation following the numerical grade of some Proof coins that have light-to-moderate frosting of the devices. Both sides must have frosting to attain CAM status; however, if there are some small areas (preferably the reverse devices) where the frost fades slightly or that have small patches of "brilliance," the coin may still qualify for the CAM designation. Some CAM-designation coins exhibit even, light frost. Others may have some unevenness of frost, ranging from light to heavy cameo.

Note: If a Proof coin conforms to DCAM criteria on one side and CAM criteria on the opposite side, the CAM designation is used. Most dates and denominations of modern Proof coins are available in CAM status, though some are quite scarce.

The Grading Process

Combining all of the different elements of coin grading into an overall grade is the PCGS grader's task. After the coins are received and processed, they are brought into the grading room and distributed by the grading room manager. The boxes contain only coins from a particular invoice, and each box has a unique box number. The boxes are generic and the graders do not know what types of coins or dates are contained until they examine them. The grader enters the box number into his or her computer and the first coin listing appears on the screen. The first coin is then taken from the box and care-

Deep Cameo (DCAM)

1962 Franklin half dollar obverse with deep cameo devices (DCAM). The recessed areas of the die are specially treated at the Mint to produce the highly frosted surfaces seen here. This creates a cameo effect with the deeply reflective Proof surfaces.

Franklin half dollar reverse with deep cameo devices (DCAM). Note that the deep frost is uninterrupted, with no shiny areas.

Cameo (CAM)

1957 Franklin half dollar obverse with cameo devices (CAM). Although there is frost over the entire head it is not heavy and there are some areas that fade slightly.

Franklin half dollar reverse with cameo devices (CAM). Completely frosted, but the central part of the bell is not as heavily frosted, leading to the CAM designation instead of DCAM.

fully removed from the plastic flip. The grader examines the coin, makes the grading determination, and enters his or her grade into the computer. Upon confirmation of this grade in the computer, the next coin listing appears on the screen and the grader replaces the previously graded coin in its flip. The next coin is then removed from the flip and examined and graded. The process is repeated until all of the coins in the box are graded. Another box number is then entered into the computer and the entire process begins anew.

What are the thought processes involved in combining the elements of a coin's grade and determining the overall grade? Obviously, the brain makes many subconscious evaluations before the conscious act of entering the

final grade into the computer. The physical characteristics are "measured" against previously seen coins. Determining the amount of wear, or lack thereof, is usually the first element considered by graders. Once this determination has been made (the grader decides whether a grade above or below 60 will be assigned), the marks, strike, and luster are evaluated. Sometimes coins are submitted as Proofs and are business strikes, and vice versa. The grader has to make this determination before the other elements are considered, as Proofs and business strikes are evaluated differently. (There is an option in the computer to "switch" the status, which is done when the grader considers a coin different from the listed status.) After the **MS/PR** status has been decided, other elements are considered. Planchet condition and striking irregularities are evaluated and factored into the final grade. Before the final grade is assigned, the designations, if applicable, are evaluated. Finally, the color or toning, if present, is considered and eye appeal is evaluated to determine the overall grade.

When a coin has beautiful original color or toning, it is almost universally agreed upon as such. However, many other coins have color or toning that may be considered differently by various graders. Eye appeal is a combination of all the other elements of a coin's grade. When a coin has blazing luster and is fully struck with almost no marks, eye appeal is great and there is little or no controversy. Again, as with determining positive or negative color/toning, most coins' eye appeal does not fall into that category. A grader's decision about eye appeal is a partly conscious, partly subconscious combination of the elements of grading. These factors are then combined into a final grade.

This simplified walk-through of the grading process does not include all the criteria a grader will use. Other tools, such as magnification, are often used. Since many coins have been lightly cleaned, this affects the luster and eye appeal elements. Also, many coins have been exposed to reactive chemicals; the surfaces are changed forever and the grade may be raised or lowered depending on the grader's decision about the color or toning caused by the reactive chemicals. Since graders make thousands of subconscious decisions during the grading process, their experience and knowledge allow them the insight to make those evaluations.

When graders finish their evaluations, the coin is encapsulated with that final grade, and verified. If the verifier disagrees with the grade assigned, the coin is tagged and given to the senior graders for reevaluation and possibly comparison to examples from the Grading Set. The Grading Set contains coins that illustrate the PCGS standards, and the entire set is examined by each grader on a regular basis. Most of these coins have been in the Grading Set since 1986, with new specimens added when good examples of a particular grade are found. Once the final grades are determined, the coins are boxed and sent to the shipping room, then returned to the submitter.

Few changes are made from the PCGS graders' evaluations. More than 95 percent of the grades assigned are left unchanged by the verifiers and senior graders. The combination of highly skilled graders calling upon in-depth knowledge and expertise makes the PCGS consensus grading process extremely accurate.

The PCGS Set Registry™

The **PCGS Set Registry**, located on the PCGS website (www.pcgs.com), is an interactive community where collectors can list and build their collections with coins that have been certified by PCGS. The **PCGS Set Registry** consists of the world's finest coin collections. If you love coins and are proud of your collection, you are a potential registrant.

Because sets are ranked in order of grade point average, completion and rating, collectors participating in the **PCGS Set Registry** program enjoy "friendly competition." The Registry provides a safe place on the Internet to show off your collection and compete with others who share the same interests as you.

Interestingly, the Set Registry concept started not with coins, but with baseball cards. In 1996, PCGS co-founder David Hall collected, among other things, sportscards. He had become friendly with two other very prominent card collectors and in an effort to compare his 1952 Topps baseball set to theirs, he made a record of each card in each collector's set. He called this recording the "Set Registry."

Because PCGS was very well established, and since rare coin collecting has been popular for a long time, the logical place to first begin an "official" registry program was with coins. So in 1998, the first **PCGS Set Registry** booklet was printed. It listed many of the important sets from years past, as well as current collections. For several years this format continued, then in 2001, the **PCGS Set Reg-**

istry was launched on the Internet. Using interactive and very user-friendly software, the Registry was an immediate success. Within months, hundreds of collectors were competing to see who had the best sets. In just two years, 1,600 collectors were displaying over 7,000 sets in the Registry!

The **PCGS Set Registry,** which offers categories for nearly every U.S. coin, is organized by "All-Time Finest" and "Current." Every set listed as "Current" is an active set. Sets listed in the "All-Time Finest" area may include retired sets that were complete at one time, but have since been dismantled. Sets from the famous Eliasberg, Childs, Price, and other collections are listed in the Registry, many of these sets containing auction records and other historical information. The **PCGS Set Registry** has not only become a place where today's collectors can experience the joy of watching their own personal collections grow, but it also offers an opportunity to compare their sets with the great collections of past generations.

There is no fee to register a collection in the **PCGS Set Registry**. Users log into an administration area with a private username and password, then enter their coins using the PCGS certification numbers that appear on each coin's insert. The collector is able to update his or her set as frequently as needed. In addition, he or she can add images of the coins to further enhance the set listing. Collectors can choose to use their own name in the Registry or they can remain completely anonymous.

Coins within each set composition are "weighted" on a 1-10 scale according to the overall rarity of the coin, i.e., the rarity in all grades, the rarity in the highest 2 or 3 grades, and the price (because this is an indication of demand and importance to collectors). The grades of the coins are then multiplied by the weight to calculate the grade point average and the set rating.

Each year, PCGS awards the top five best sets in the following categories:

- Best Classic Set (1792-1964)

- Best Modern Set (1965 to Present)

- Best New Set

In addition, the registrant with the finest collection (at least 50% complete) within each set listing receives a "Best of the Registry" certificate of recognition.

Annually, some of the greatest "All-Time Finest" collections ever assembled are inducted into the **PCGS Set Registry Hall of Fame.** Hall of Fame collections and the contest winners are selected based on a vote of PCGS coin experts.

The **PCGS Set Registry** is dedicated to those who have collected the best and provides a unique and exciting way to recognize these great sets. Some of the sets listed in the Registry are, without a doubt, the finest in the world and are significant accomplishments to be admired by all coin enthusiasts.

6 GRADING U.S. COPPER COINS

Mint State and Proof copper coins are graded in part according to the color of the metal. Coins with original red color are deemed most desirable, while those with brown toning are considered somewhat less desirable. PCGS follows this market practice by assigning such coins one of three designations: Red (or RD, for short), Red-Brown (RB), and Brown (BN). In some cases, full-red specimens command far higher premiums than those that are red-brown or brown, reflecting the fact that they are much scarcer—sometimes all but nonexistent—in such pristine condition.

Half Cents
Flowing Hair Half Cent or Liberty Cap Left Half Cent (1793)
Circulated Examples
In **AU-55/58**, there is slight wear on the cheek directly in front of the ear and the hair behind the ear. There may be incompleteness due to strike in the hair and the central lettering of the reverse. The wreath will have slight wear in this grade, mainly on the leaves. In **AU-50/53**, the wear on the cheek will be very noticeable and there will also be friction in the neck and shoulder areas. The hair will have wear on all the major curls. The reverse will have wear on the leaves of the wreath, with some flattening.

The hair and entire face will show obvious wear in grades of **EF-40/45**, with 80 percent or more of the hair detail still present. There may be some luster, the protected areas of the reverse showing more than the obverse. The wreath's leaves will have obvious wear—some of them flat, with only outline detail.

For **VF-20/35**, there is considerable wear on the hair and face. There will be 50 to 75 percent hair detail still present, with weakly struck coins showing slightly less detail (25 to 50 percent). Weak central reverse lettering is noted on incompletely struck specimens. The leaves will almost all show full outlines, though inner detail is gone.

In **F-12/15**, 10 to 40 percent of the hair detail is present, depending on the strength of the strike. The face will still have complete definition, but it will be quite worn. The leaves of the wreath will be quite flat, with other details of the wreath worn. The central lettering may be missing on weak strikes, although this affects the grade only minimally.

Only the deepest hair curls are present in **VG-8/10**, with only the outline of the face. LIBERTY may be worn but still complete. The reverse wreath will have only the outline, and some of the legend may be worn away. The central lettering may be partially missing due to strike.

In **G-4/6**, the outline of the face and hair may partially blend into the field. LIBERTY may be partially worn, with the rim also incomplete in places. The reverse will usually have an outlined wreath with worn lettering; however, the central lettering may be completely missing due to strike.

The head, LIBERTY, and the date will be visible, but not distinct, in **AG-3**. The reverse will still show most of the wreath, with some lettering missing. Central lettering is partially visible on strong strikes, totally gone on weak strikes. The **FR-2** coin will be even more worn with the head, LIBERTY, and the date barely visible. The reverse will have little more than slight wreath detail.

In **PO-1**, the coin is identifiable as to type, with LIBERTY and the date possibly completely worn away. The reverse may have only part of the wreath visible and little or no readable lettering.

Mint State Examples

MARKS: These coins were small; thus, the marks are usually minor. Some coins will have fairly deep marks, since copper is a soft metal.

LUSTER: Most coins have satin to slightly frosty luster. Some deeply frosted coins are known, but they are exceptions. Full-red and prooflike coins are unknown, though they are possible. Glossy brown specimens are seen; these are often the result of judicious brushing from a camelhair brush.

STRIKE: This one-year type coin is generally well-struck, but die failure on one variety results in weakness in HALF CENT. Dies were made individually in this Mint era, with some varieties having more chiseled hair and leaves—and determining what is strike weakness can be a daunting task. When luster is still present on the high points, strike weakness usually is the cause of any flatness of the detail.

EYE APPEAL: Since full-red and prooflike specimens are essentially unknown, the glossy brown or red and brown specimens have the best eye appeal. Coins with good strike, few marks, and superior luster are difficult to find, but are available on occasion.

Liberty Cap Right Half Cent—High Relief/Regular Relief (1794–1797)

Circulated Examples

This is a difficult series to grade in both circulated and uncirculated grades. With much more pronounced detail on the high-relief coins than on the regular-relief pieces, the wear in **AU-55/58** is much easier to notice, with slight wear on the hair strands around the ear and on the face directly in front of the

ear. On regular-relief coins, the detail is much less pronounced, with wear in approximately the same area. The reverse will show nearly full leaf detail except on weakly struck specimens, which may have localized weakness. In **AU-50/53**, all the hair strands have definite wear on both types. The cheek may appear to be more worn on high-relief specimens, since there is higher detail. The reverse leaves are slightly flattened, with little interior detail. Localized strike weakness should not affect the overall grade.

For **EF-40/45** coins, there is considerable hair flatness on both types, with 70 to 90 percent of the detail visible, depending on the strike. The face will have wear but will still have roundness on the high-relief coins. The flat face on regular-relief coins makes it difficult to discern between **AU** and **EF**, with hair detail the main focus for grade. The reverse leaves will be mostly flat, though quite separate with some inner detail. The lettering should be complete except for localized strike weakness.

In **VF-20/35**, high-relief coins have approximately 30 to 70 percent of the hair visible. Regular-relief coins usually will have less than half the hair distinct. LIBERTY will be distinct except for occasional local weakness. On weakly struck coins of both types, surfaces are also used to determine the overall grade. The reverse will have flattened leaves with no inner leaf detail on most specimens. The lettering will be complete, except for the central lettering of weakly struck specimens.

The **F-12/15** grade has 15 to 30 percent of the hair visible on high-relief coins, slightly less on regular-relief examples. LIBERTY is complete, except for occasional strike weakness. Wreath leaves show only outlines and may be slightly worn into each other or other wreath components. The lettering usually will be readable and weak only in areas of strike weakness.

In **VG-8/10**, the hair will show only in the deepest recesses on high-relief coins and will be mostly flat on regular-relief specimens. LIBERTY is weak but complete. Strike is not as important when coins become worn to this point. The leaves may blend into each other or other wreath components. Some reverse lettering may be illegible due to wear or strike.

The **G-4/6** high-relief coin may have slight hair detail visible; there will be no hair detail with outline blending for regular-relief coins, with LIBERTY mostly complete. Rims may be worn into the peripheral lettering on the reverse. Wreath leaves are worn into each other, the wreath, and the field. The central lettering on some varieties is very weak, though localized weakness due to die cracks and so on also is noted.

In **AG-3**, the head is flat even on the high-relief variety, and the rim is worn into LIBERTY. Reverse lettering may only be 50 percent complete, with the wreath showing only major detail, and weakness of strike is commonplace. In **FR-2**, there is less detail, but the date and LIBERTY are still readable; the reverse lettering is mostly worn away. The wreath and central lettering may be very weak in some places.

PO-1 will have major details visible, with enough of the date present to positively identify the year.

Mint State Examples

MARKS: High-relief coins, because of the raised obverse design, are more prone to marks than are regular-relief pieces. The cheek is one of the most marked areas, though marks in the field are noted for both types. The marks in the hair are sometimes hidden by the design of the high-relief type, though they are easily seen on the regular-relief coins. The reverse has a less open field than the obverse, and marks tend to be more hidden on the reverse. Marks are more difficult to note for the "bunched" leaf wreath than for the cent-type wreath.

LUSTER: Luster variations range from flat to nearly full prooflike, with the average coins satin to slightly frosty. There are quite a few satin-to-slightly frosty glossy brown coins, just as in other copper series.

STRIKE: The chiseled hair of the high-relief type does not always strike up fully, and this area should be examined carefully to determine whether there is friction or weakness of strike. Several of the reverses for the high-relief coins are completely hubbed. The Mint immediately abandoned this approach for half cents, but periodically this die-making method was tried on other denominations until it became standard procedure for all dies in the 1840s. The Mint's equipment at the time was not powerful enough to sink the hubs sufficiently into the die steel, and this led to weakness in the devices and lettering. These weak areas sometimes were strengthened by hand, but the overall striking quality of these hubbed dies was inferior to that of hand-punched dies until the Mint acquired more powerful presses. Cut-down cent blanks or inferior planchets resulted in many poorly struck coins from 1795 to 1797. Die breaks, wear, and die failure led to many coins with localized weakness, with fully struck coins not often seen.

EYE APPEAL: Well-struck, lustrous, mark-free coins are seen for this series—and those with original red color are of course the most attractive, with glossy brown specimens next on the list. As with most early U.S. coin series, some of these issues have inferior planchets, dies, and striking qualities. Coins with these deficiencies will not be graded as high as coins of equal luster and marks but with superior strikes.

Draped Bust Half Cent (1800–1808)
Circulated Examples

Draped Bust half cents have such slight wear in **AU-55/58** that it is difficult to discern unless the coin is severely discolored on the wear points. The cheek and bust of Miss Liberty are the flat areas that first show wear. Minor wear on the high points of the hair is noticed mainly by the dullness and discoloration associated with friction. The reverse is similar to the Liberty Cap reverse, with the wreath showing slight wear and nearly complete leaf detail. The **AU-50/53** coin has more noticeable wear on the cheek, bust, and hair, with areas of dullness covering 50 percent or more of the surfaces. The reverse has some slight flatness on the wreath leaves, and the lettering now exhibits wear.

In **EF-40/45**, there is more apparent wear on the cheek, bust, and hair, with approximately 70 to 80 percent of the hair still present. There may be slight luster on the obverse, though the protected reverse areas may have luster into **VF** grades. The reverse leaves will have flatness, with most detail still visible, but the central lettering, the bow, and other parts of the wreath may have localized strike weakness.

The grades of **VF-20/35** have hair detail ranging from several to most strands visible, with 30 to 70 percent of the detail intact. Of course, strike affects the amount of hair visible, and surface preservation should always be considered. The cheek, bust, and drapery will be well worn. The reverse will have most leaves separate, but with little inner leaf detail. Strike weakness will affect some coins, with some varieties always weak.

F-12/15 coins have 15 to 20 percent of the hair detail remaining, although on very weakly struck coins little detail is evident, with the percentage of remaining hair detail overlapping with the **VF** grade because of strike variances. The cheek and bust are usually very flat, with outlines only. Most of the wreath's leaves will be worn into each other or other components of the wreath, with none showing detail. The lettering and rims will usually be complete, but localized rim weakness is occasionally noted.

In **VG-8/10**, there may be little or no hair detail remaining, depending on the strength of the strike. The bust will be complete, but with very little detail remaining. LIBERTY may have slight weakness in the tops of the letters, with rims worn into some areas. The wreath will be outlined. The rims may be indistinct in some areas, with slightly worn lettering.

For **G-4/6** coins, the bust is completely outlined, with little or no definition showing. LIBERTY and the date may exhibit weakness.

Rims may be slightly worn in places on the obverse, with slightly more incompleteness on the reverse. The tops of the reverse lettering may be slightly worn, with the wreath worn flat and blended in areas.

In **AG-3**, the bust will be mostly outlined, with LIBERTY partially worn and the date readable. The rims may be incomplete; sometimes the reverse rims are completely missing, with less than half of the peripheral lettering intact. The wreath may be worn away in places, and the central lettering may be obscured by strike and/or wear. The **FR-2** coin will have most of the bust indistinct, with LIBERTY and the date mostly gone. The peripheral lettering may be completely worn away and only sections of the wreath may be visible. The central lettering usually is completely missing.

PO-1 coins must have a discernible date, though not much more. The reverse may be worn completely away; however, slick-reverse coins seldom trade for much money unless they are rare dates or varieties.

Mint State Examples

MARKS: Marks are fairly common on these coins, with the hair, face, and neck of Miss Liberty and the field in front and back of the head the most affected. Only heavy digs or scratches are noted, as a rule, in the intricate hair. Reverse marks are less noticeable, because there is much less open and flat area.

LUSTER: These early copper coins usually have satin-to-slightly frosty luster. Fully prooflike coins are not seen for this series. Glossy brown specimens are fairly common for most dates except 1802, which is extremely rare in high grade. Frosty, mint-red specimens are known from several hoards, though there is little surface difference between the devices and fields.

STRIKE: Poor planchet quality plus the cutdown blanks employed for many of these coins led to numerous poorly struck coins. Die deterioration and die breaks were also common. Many of these coins will have incomplete detail, especially in the hair around the ear. The upper part of the wreath and HALF CENT are also seen weak—especially for certain dates and varieties, as die steel was expensive and dies were used until they failed completely. Fully struck coins are very scarce and bring premiums among knowledgeable numismatists.

EYE APPEAL: Although glossy brown specimens are attractive when well-struck and mark-free, the most attractive of the Draped Bust half cents are the full-red coins that are encountered infrequently. These coins, especially the 1806, often have slight weakness of strike that detracts from the overall eye appeal—but the mint-red color and frosty luster are strong positive attributes.

Classic Head Half Cent (1809–1836)

Circulated Examples

AU-55/58 coins will have slight wear on the cheek, the bust, the hair curls above and below the ribbon, and the central area. Weakness of strike is specifically noted on the hair curl above the eye and the surrounding areas. Strike weakness, improperly aligned dies, filled dies, and so on may cause weakness in the stars and LIBERTY. The reverse leaves are broader and slightly longer than previously, with wear and strike weakness difficult to distinguish. The grades AU-50/53 have more flatness on the hair curls, cheek, and bust. The stars will have slight wear, and dullness will be present on up to 50 percent or more of the surface. The reverse leaves will have definite wear, with the uppermost leaf of each group flat.

In EF-40/45, wear is immediately noticeable, but 70 to 80 percent of the detail is still present. High points of hair curls will be flat, with recessed curls still full. The cheek and bust will have wear over their entire surfaces. Most of the stars will have flat tops blending the crosshatched lines. Wreath leaves will be flat, though separate, with some detail.

Grades VF-20/35 have 40 to 70 percent of the hair detail present, depending on the strike and the amount of wear. The cheek and bust will have considerable wear, the jaw line beginning to disappear. Stars are mostly flat, but some lines are usually visible. Some wreath leaves are totally flat, with some slightly blended.

In F-12/15, hair detail is 20 to 40 percent intact, although strongly struck coins have more hair detail. The cheek and bust are worn flat, with the adjacent hair curls blended into the face. Reverse leaves are blended into each other in some instances, with little detail. Rims and lettering will be complete.

VG-8/10 coins have little hair detail, and LIBERTY may have several weak letters. John Reich's Classic Head design had relief not seen since the high-relief Liberty Cap coinage, therefore has detail on coins down to the lowest grades. The bust is almost always boldly outlined, the obverse rim usually bold. Wreath leaves will be worn into each other, but the wreath is usually well outlined. Reverse rims may be slightly incomplete, with weakness in the upper parts of the lettering.

For G-4/6 specimens, the bust will be outlined and LIBERTY will be readable, though weak. The date and rims should show slight weakness. The leaves will show little or no separation, and the wreath's outline may not be distinct. Reverse rims will be slightly worn into the tops of some lettering.

AG-3 coins have the obverse rim worn into the field, sometimes obscuring the stars. The bust is partially outlined, and LIBERTY will have some letters visible. The reverse will have much of the peripheral lettering obscured, the wreath flat and blended. The central lettering is still readable, except on very weak strikes. The FR-2 coin will have a readable date and some details of the bust still present. The reverse may be nearly completely worn away, with sporadic device and lettering seen.

In PO-1, the date must be discernible, but not much else is necessary. Various parts of the bust are still partially visible. The reverse may be totally slick or have only parts of the wreath and central lettering.

Mint State Examples

MARKS: The face and field in front of the face are the areas where marks are most noticeable. The field behind the head is small and the hair very curly, making marks unobtrusive unless they are severe. The reverse has slightly more open field area than previous types—although, as with wreath designs, unless the marks or scratches are severe, they are not very apparent.

LUSTER: Classic Head half cents are the first half cent series to have all the variations in luster types. Flat-luster to fully prooflike specimens are known for most dates. Prooflike coins are more prevalent for the coins after 1825, as the presses improved striking quality and dies were more likely to be basined before striking. Typical coins of the early years, 1809 through 1811, are satin to slightly frosty. Examples dated 1825 and later are slightly frosty to very frosty, with more semi-prooflike and prooflike specimens encountered.

STRIKE: Striking quality improved for the Classic Head half cent, although localized star weakness, flat hair curls, and indistinct wreath leaves are encountered. General central-die weakness is less often seen with these coins, but die breaks and deterioration are still noted. Some star weakness is the result of improperly aligned dies. If the stars on one side of a coin are very flat and those on the other side are very strong, improperly aligned dies are usually the cause. In 1828, the Mint introduced the close collar (1831 for half cents), and overall striking quality for all coins was much better from then on. The collar allowed the metal to be squeezed into the deepest recesses of the dies, leading to more fully struck specimens. Some post-1831 half cents still have slight weakness, as striking pressure, die alignment, and light planchets continued to affect overall striking quality.

EYE APPEAL: Hoards of various dates have surfaced over the years, and most of the attractive high-grade specimens can be traced to these sources. These coins range from glossy brown to spotted red to full red, and luster runs the gamut of variations—though slightly frosty to frosty is the luster most often seen.

Proofs

HAIRLINES: Light cleaning was commonplace among early collectors, and many of the Classic Head Proof half cents were affected. Hairlines, mainly attributable to this wiping, tend to be light, with the obverse usually having more lines, as would be expected on coins that reposed face up in coin cabinets.

REFLECTIVITY: The coins struck after the introduction of the close collar, including the restrikes, have deeply reflective fields. Those struck earlier, 1829 and prior, are very rare and do not have as deeply reflective surfaces. The latter strikings may have cameo on the devices that the earlier coins lack.

STRIKE: Careful striking methods for Proofs were employed beginning in the 1820s. The quality of the original Proofs is high, but the open-collar Proofs (1829 and prior) are not as well struck as the close-collar ones (1831 and later). The rims of the open-collar coins are more rounded, and the detail does not appear as chiseled. The original close-collar coins have chiseled detail, but the rims are still slightly rounded, as the old-fashioned screw press used to hand strike proofs until c. 1900 was not powerful enough to force the metal completely into the collar. The restrikes of the 1831 and 1836 coins have squarer rims than the originals, suggesting that a larger screw press intended to strike metals was employed to strike these coins and metal flowed into the collars, creating flatter, broader rims.

EYE APPEAL: The close-collar Proofs and the restrikes have deeply reflective fields and often have frosted devices. They are seen mostly in brown and red-brown—but when these coins have red color and are mostly free of hairlines, they are the most attractive of the Classic Head half cents. Spotting, discoloration, hairlines, and light marks are the detractions most often seen.

Braided Hair (Coronet Head) Half Cent (1840–1857)

Circulated Examples

On **AU-55/58** coins, friction is first noticed on the cheek of Liberty and on the hair directly above and below the headband. Discoloration is evident on many coins and is a sign of slight friction. On brown coins, a good light will often be the only way to see the dullness caused by wear. The reverse will have slight wear on the leaves and bow of the wreath. When worn slightly more, to **AU-50/53**, the cheek will have more obvious wear and the hair will be flatter above and below the headband. The stars will still show complete hatch lines except for localized weakness, where several stars may be totally flat. Reverse leaves will have nearly full detail, with the top parts slightly flat.

EF-40/45 half cents will have obvious wear on the cheek and neck, with the hair flat above and directly below the headband. The stars will all show wear, though well-struck coins may still show some star detail. The reverse will show the top leaves flat, but adjoining leaves should show nearly full detail. The field will be worn, and luster, if present, will exist only in the protected areas.

For **VF-20/35**, the cheek and neck area will be worn and the hair will be flat on the high points, with detail in the recessed areas. The beaded hair cords should still be strong, except on very weakly struck specimens. The stars will be worn mostly flat. The top wreath leaves will be worn flat and will blend into the adjacent leaves. Some porosity of the surface is allowed in this grade, though it must be minor.

The detail should be sharp, but quite worn, for **F-12/15**. The face and hair will be flat, and the beaded hair cords may have slight wear. Detail in the recessed areas, especially the hair curls, will still show. The reverse will have the top and adjacent leaves worn into each other. The bow will be mostly flat, with slight detail. The surfaces may show more porosity, but heavily porous coins are not graded.

With wear to **VG-8/10**, the head will be completely outlined, with only the deepest recessed areas showing detail. LIBERTY will usually be complete, with slight weakness on the tops of the letters, except on poorly struck coins, which may have the first few letters only partially showing. The stars will be very flat, and the rim should still be bold. The reverse wreath will be outlined, with only slight detail still visible. The lettering around the periphery should be complete, with a strong rim still present.

G-4/6 coins will have an outlined head with almost no detail visible, except for a partial LIBERTY and the deep recesses. The date and stars will be very flat, with the obverse rim beginning to show areas of incompleteness. The reverse will have an outlined wreath, with almost no fine definition. The rim may be worn into some of the lettering—partly from uneven striking and partly from wear.

The **AG-3** and **FR-2** coins will show progressively less detail. The head may be complete and the date may be only partial, but readable. The stars will be incomplete to completely missing, especially on **FR-2** coins. The reverse will have a complete wreath, though half of the lettering may be missing in **AG-3** and up to 90 percent may be missing in **FR-2**.

The date and type will be identifiable for **PO-1**, but very little other detail will be present, other than Miss Liberty's head.

Mint State Examples

MARKS: Although these have about the same amount of obverse head and field area as Classic Head half cents, they seem to be slightly more prone to marks in the face and field. The hair is not as intricate as with Classic Head coins, and marks tend to be more noticeable. The reverse is similar to the Classic Head type, but the wreath is more delicate and there is no center dot or line below cent. As before, there is little open field area on the reverse, with the wreath hiding all but very heavy marks.

LUSTER: As with the Classic Head coins, Braided Hair half cents are known in all luster variations. Most coins are satin to frosty in luster, with flat-luster and prooflike coins occasionally seen. A few dates are not often seen in original mint red, with 1849, 1850, and 1853 all very scarce with red color.

STRIKE: No half cents were struck in 1837–39, and only Proofs were struck from 1840–48. When produced for commerce again starting in 1849, these are well struck, with slight weakness sometimes seen on the hair above the ear and the braids below LIB-ERTY. The tip of the coronet and the back bun also may show slight weakness, as will the tops of some of the wreath leaves. Star weakness is sometimes seen—and when it is on one side or the other only, it probably is the result of improperly aligned dies. This die alignment problem persisted through the nineteenth century, affecting some Barber and Liberty Head coins, among others.

EYE APPEAL: A few dates are seen with full red color and frosty luster—and these, when mark-free and well-struck, are the most attractive of the Braided Hair half cents. Glossy brown or red-brown specimens of some dates are all that are seen, and these will be the most attractive coins for certain years.

Proofs

HAIRLINES: For the first years, 1840 through 1848, only Proofs were struck; these were made for collectors and sometimes were part of complete Proof sets. Light hairlines from wiping or cleaning are commonplace, especially for the obverse, and hairline-free coins are the exceptions. The years 1856 and 1857 saw increased Proof coin production, though light hairlines are still often noted for these years.

REFLECTIVITY: Although restruck on numerous occasions, the originals have the same deeply reflective fields. There are coins with full red color and frosted devices that make the fields seem more deeply mirrored than non-frosted coins. Although the fields are slightly muted when the red fades and eventually becomes brown, the fields still have good reflectivity in nearly all cases.

STRIKE: Striking quality of the originals and restrikes is very good, with broad, flat rims seen on these close-collar coins. Weakness is sometimes seen for stars and the hair above the ear. The upper part of the wreath, as well as the bow at the bottom, may be slightly flat.

EYE APPEAL: There are some originals and restrikes with full red color and glistening surfaces, and these are the most attractive of the Braided Hair half cent Proofs. Coins whose surfaces are unimpaired, whether by a haze or hairlines, have the most eye appeal. Red-brown and brown coins can also be quite attractive if the surfaces are mostly free from impairments.

Large Cents
Flowing Hair Chain Cent (1793)
Circulated Examples

In **AU-55/58**, Chain cents have slight friction on the cheek of Miss Liberty and on the tips of her hair, above and below the ear. There is slight wear on the tops of the interlocking chains and the lettering inside them. Many Chain cents have chiseled hair, and the friction, when present, is obvious. There are some softly struck coins that have indistinct hair—so discoloration, or the lack thereof, should be used in determining what is wear and what is incomplete striking. When the wear is enough to lower the grade to **AU-50/53**, the cheek will have flatness and the hair will no longer have a chiseled look. There are coins that never had sharp, chiseled hair, and overall surface condition should be used to arrive at their final grade. There will be friction in the fields and the chain will show wear, but all the detail will still be sharp. On well-struck coins, the links will be rounded and separated where they join. There will be wear on the lettering.

As Chain cents wear to **EF-40/45**, the hair becomes flattened, especially along the neck and above the ear. The cheek will be flat, and luster will be almost gone from the obverse, remaining only in the recesses. The reverse will have a complete, strong chain, though some of the interlocking areas will begin to lose sharpness. The lettering and field will have obvious wear, with luster in only protected areas.

VF-20/35 coins will have from one-third to two-thirds of the hair detail still present, depending on the strike. On well-struck coins, the hair may still have a chiseled look, though on weakly struck coins the hair may resemble the Wreath cent, with a more rounded appearance. The head should be complete, but on some weakly struck specimens there may be areas that are not sharp. The reverse will have a full, though obviously worn chain, with central lettering clear. The peripheral lettering on weakly struck coins may have letters that are partially complete.

The **F-12/15** Chain cent is graded primarily by the reverse. The head of Miss Liberty will be complete, but it may blend into the field in places and there will be little hair detail remaining. LIBERTY and the date may show incompleteness. The chain will still be complete, though the linked areas will be flat and lacking detail. On well-struck coins, the central and peripheral lettering will be complete. Surface condition should be used in combination with the amount of detail present to assess the final grade.

The Chain cent in **VG-8/10** will have a complete but quite worn head that will blend into the field. The date and LIBERTY will be complete on well-struck coins, though partially missing on weakly struck ones. The surfaces may be smooth and worn or slightly porous. The reverse will have a complete chain, but it will be worn flat. Lettering may be very incomplete, depending on the original strike.

G-4/6 coins will have several areas of the head worn into the field. The date and LIBERTY may be very weak and partially missing. Porous surfaces are common in this grade and smooth, even wear is the exception. The reverse will have a full, but very worn, chain, with much of the lettering weak. The central lettering may be missing on weakly struck coins.

The lower-grade Chain cents, **AG-3** and **FR-2**, all have various problems. There may be porosity, missing lettering or a missing date, and marks or nicks. The head will be present, though quite worn into the surfaces. Remarkably, the chain is still usually complete, even down to these grades. The lettering of the periphery may be missing, especially in **FR-2**, and the central lettering may be completely gone.

PO-1 coins will have a partial head, but not much else, on the obverse. LIBERTY and the date are usually completely gone. Rough surfaces are very common and are expected. The chain will still be partially visible. Lettering is usually nonexistent, although partial letters inside the chain may be visible.

Mint State Examples

MARKS: Large cents, in general, have more marks than half cents. The larger size caused more severe marks when transported and Chain cents often have marks, hairlines, nicks, scratches, gouges, and other impairments to their surfaces. The obverse has the intricately detailed hair, the cheek, and field areas, where marks are easily noticed. The reverse has a large open area around the chain, and this, along with the chain, central lettering, and fraction, is susceptible to marks, nicks, gouges and so on.

LUSTER: Most Chain cents have flat to slightly frosty, glossy brown luster. There are few coins with any original mint red, and no coins are known with heavily frosted devices. A few semi-prooflike and prooflike coins are known, but they are the exceptions.

STRIKE: Fully struck Chain cents are seen, but many coins are seen with weakly struck hair, mostly around the ear. Some varieties are almost always seen with this flatness. Most of the reverses are well struck, with slight weakness sometimes noted for ONE CENT—though the chain is not often affected. In addition, the date, LIBERTY, and the reverse peripheral lettering are sometimes incomplete, which may be the result of incomplete or uneven striking. Since each letter or numeral typically was punched individually during this period, many weak letters or numerals are the result of uneven punching into the dies.

EYE APPEAL: Centered, well-struck, minimally marked Chain cents with good luster are encountered now and then, and these coins have great eye appeal. Glossy brown or red-brown surfaces on coins that have smooth planchets are the pinnacle of our first large cents. Rough or discolored copper planchets were a problem for the early half cent and cent coinage, resulting in less-than-perfect surfaces on newly minted coins.

Specimens

HAIRLINES: These coins are the ultimate rarity, and the few known specimens have been carefully preserved by collectors. Only the lightest lines are visible on these coins.

REFLECTIVITY: The screw press, the Mint's equipment in 1793, produced specimen strikes with only lightly mirrored fields. These specimen coins were struck in open collars by hand, and there is no way the reflectivity will match that of the close-collar coins struck by steam or hydraulic presses.

STRIKE: The very few known specimen strikes have chiseled hair detail, with the chain bold and all of the lettering quite strong. As would be expected, these few coins were given careful attention when struck and are the finest examples of the Mint's early copper strikings.

EYE APPEAL: The known specimens have glossy brown surfaces with chiseled strikes. Obviously, the Mint's first coinage was struck with care; thus, these are the cream of the early copper coinage.

Flowing Hair Wreath Cent (1793)
Circulated Examples

In **AU-55/58**, there is slight wear on the cheek directly in front of the ear and on the highest points of the hair. There may be in-

completeness due to strike in the hair and the central lettering of the reverse, but the surfaces should still be nearly completely lustrous. The wreath will have slight wear in this grade, mainly on the leaves. In **AU-50/53**, wear on the cheek will be very noticeable and there will also be friction on the lower part of the face. The hair will have wear on all the major strands, with some slightly flattened. The reverse will have wear on the leaves of the wreath, and some of them will have begun to flatten.

The hair and entire face will show obvious wear in grades **EF-40/45**, with 80 percent or more of the hair strands still present, except on weakly struck specimens. There usually is some luster, though the reverse will often show more in the protected areas than the obverse. The leaves of the wreath have obvious wear and many of them may be flat, but all should be distinct.

For **VF-20/35**, there is considerable wear on the hair strands and face. There will be 50 to 75 percent hair detail still present, though weakly struck coins may show as little as 25 to 50 percent. The front part of the hair will be mostly worn smooth, with the back part showing separation. There may be weak lettering on the reverse in cases where the strike is incomplete. The leaves will show full outlines, but nearly all will be flat. The lettering will still be distinct, except on very weak strikes.

In **F-12/15**, 20 to 40 percent of the hair detail is present. About half of the hair will be totally flat, with only the back strands still having visible detail. Though quite worn, the date and face will still have complete definition. The wreath leaves will be quite flat, with wear into the other details of the wreath. The central lettering may be obscured on weakly struck coins, but this should not affect the grade.

The hair detail in **VG-8/10** is mostly gone, with only the backmost strands still visible. The face will show only slight definition, with LIBERTY worn, though still complete. The reverse will have only the outline to the leaves, berries, and branches of the wreath, with the legend slightly worn. The central lettering may be partially missing due to strike and should not be used as a grading criterion.

In **G-4/6**, the outline of the face and hair will be mostly complete, with areas that may blend into the field. LIBERTY may be worn and several letters indistinct, with the rim also incomplete. The reverse will usually have an outline to the entire wreath, with the rim worn into the lettering in places. On particularly weakly struck coins, the central lettering may be completely missing.

The head, LIBERTY, and the date will be visible, though only partially, in **AG-3**. The reverse will still show most of the wreath, but the lettering will be partially to mostly missing. The central lettering is usually only partially visible on strong strikes and may be totally gone on weak strikes. The **FR-2** coin will be even more worn, with the head, LIBERTY, and the date barely visible. The reverse will have little more than slight wreath detail. The central lettering may be totally missing.

In **PO-1**, the coin is identifiable as to type, with LIBERTY and the date possibly completely worn away. The reverse may have only part of the wreath visible and little or no readable lettering.

Mint State Examples

MARKS: The only difference for the obverse between marks on Chain cents and Wreath cents is that the hair on the Wreath cent is slightly coarser, resulting in marks that are slightly less noticeable. The cheek and field are open areas where marks and other impairments will be readily noticeable. Reverse detail is more intricate than on the Chain cent and marks are more easily hidden among the wreath detail.

LUSTER: For uncirculated Wreath cents, the luster is generally satin to slightly frosty. There are more coins with original mint red

than for Chain cents and certainly more coins with glossy brown surfaces. Flat-luster coins are sometimes seen, and the occasional semi-prooflike coin is also noted.

STRIKE: Although many of these coins are well struck, few are fully struck. Slight weakness is noted for the hair, especially around the ear. The top and bottom—affecting LIBERTY and the date, respectively—are also sometimes weak, which may be due to out-of-parallel dies. The reverse may show slight weakness in the center and in some letters of ONE CENT, as well as in the top peripheral lettering and the fraction at the bottom. Some of the leaves and the bow may be slightly incomplete.

EYE APPEAL: Well-struck, lustrous, mark-free coins are seen, and these are among the most attractive and desirable of the Mint's early coinage. Glossy brown or red-brown coins often have a "glow," combined with good planchets, good strikes, and minimal marks, resulting in very attractive specimens.

Specimens

HAIRLINES: Although there is one nearly perfect specimen strike known for Wreath cents, slight hairlines would be expected on other coins. These would be the result of light cleaning or wiping and should be very minor. These should not be confused with burnishing lines, which result when the planchet is polished before striking.

REFLECTIVITY: As with early Mint specimen strikes, the mirrored fields are not as deep as with later strikings. There are no cameo devices, and the overall depth would not be called deep mirror prooflike, compared with a Morgan silver dollar. However, it is obvious that special care was taken in striking these coins.

STRIKE: The strike is extraordinary for the specimen strike, as the hair is chiseled and the wreath is boldly impressed. Only the slightest bit of incompleteness can be discerned on the high points of a few strands of the hair and a couple of the leaves of the wreath, and that only with the aid of magnification.

EYE APPEAL: It is hard to imagine a full original red specimen strike Wreath cent. Yet the coin does exist and it has a razor-sharp strike, no marks, no noticeable hairlines, and incredible eye appeal. Examining this coin, one can comprehend the true meaning of "eye appeal."

Liberty Cap Cent—Beaded Border/ Denticled Border (1793–1796)

Circulated Examples

In **AU-55/58**, the wear is much easier to notice on the high-relief coins, with slight wear on the hair strands around the ear and on the face directly in front of the ear. On regular-relief coins, the detail is much less pronounced and therefore more difficult to discern, although it is in approximately the same areas. The reverse will show nearly full leaf detail, except on weakly struck specimens. In **AU-50/53**, the hair has definite wear on the strands across the entire head on both the high- and regular-relief coins. The reverse leaves are slightly flattened and have little interior detail.

For **EF-40/45** coins, there is flatness on high-relief coins and even more on regular-relief coins, with 70 to 90 percent of the hair detail visible. The hair detail should be the main focus for regular-relief coins. Most of the leaves are now flat, though quite separate, with some inner detail. The lettering should be complete, with only localized strike weakness.

In **VF-20/35**, approximately 30 to 70 percent of the hair is visible on high-relief coins, with less than half of the hair distinct on the regular-relief specimens. LIBERTY will be distinct, except for occasional local weakness. The reverse will have flat leaves, along with flatness in the other components of the wreath. The lettering will be complete, except on weakly struck specimens.

The **F-12/15** grade has 15 to 30 percent of the hair visible on high-relief coins and slightly less on regular-relief examples. LIBERTY is complete, except for localized weakness. Leaves will show only lines and may be slightly blended. The lettering will usually be readable, and weak only in areas of strike weakness.

In **VG-8/10**, the hair will show only in the deepest recesses of high-relief coins and will be mostly flat on regular-relief specimens. LIBERTY is weak, but complete. Strike is not as important when coins become worn to this point. The leaves will blend, and the reverse lettering may have illegible letters.

The **G-4/6** coin may have slight hair detail visible for high-relief coins and no hair detail, with outline blending in some places, for regular-relief coins. Most letters of LIBERTY are complete and legible. The rim may be worn into the peripheral lettering of the reverse. The leaves will be mostly blended. Central lettering on some varieties is very weak, with localized weakness due to die cracks and so on also noted.

In **AG-3**, the head is flat even on high-relief coins, and the rim is worn into LIBERTY, which may have most letters incomplete. The lettering on the reverse may be incomplete, with only the wreath showing major detail. In **FR-2**, there is still less detail, though the date remains readable and some of LIBERTY may be visible. The reverse peripheral lettering will be mostly worn away. The wreath and the central lettering are visible, but they may be incomplete in some areas.

PO-1 coins will have major details visible, with enough of the date present to identify. LIBERTY may be completely worn away. Reverse peripheral lettering, central lettering, and the wreath will be mostly gone.

Mint State Examples

MARKS: Marks and other surface impairments are easily noted for the obverse of the high-relief and regular-relief cents, especially on the cheek and the coarser hair (compared to Chain/Wreath cents). The reverse is similar to the Wreath cent, with marks sometimes hidden in the leaves of the wreath.

LUSTER: Although the luster variations are similar, there are probably more glossy brown, frosty-luster specimens seen than for the Chain and Wreath cents, because of a few hoards. Although flat-luster coins are seen, there are no prooflike coins reported and virtually no semi-prooflike specimens. Full original red surfaces are almost nonexistent, though coins with some red color are known.

STRIKE: Striking weakness is caused by several factors. For some coins, such as some 1793 beaded-border coins, the die broke fairly early and caused weakness, especially for ONE CENT. The obverse of some coins is similarly affected, with die cracks causing odd striking patterns with local or general weakness. Other coins suffer from central weakness, leading to flatness of the hair curls from the top of the head down past the ear to the flowing curls at the back of the head. The reverse will show weakness in ONE CENT on these coins. As with most early coins, some top and bottom weakness is noticed from out-of-parallel dies. Occasionally other localized weakness is noted, such as on the front of the bust, the lower back curls, and the left and right bottom wreath leaves.

EYE APPEAL: Well-struck, minimally marked, glossy brown or red-brown coins with good planchets are the most attractive Liberty Cap large cents. These are found with some regularity, as noted previously, from old hoards dispersed over the years.

Draped Bust Cent (1796–1807)

Circulated Examples

In **AU-55/58**, the cheek and bust of Miss Liberty are the flat areas that first show wear. High points on the hair curls may have strike weakness or wear that are differentiated by dullness and discoloration. The reverse is similar to the Liberty Cap reverse, with nearly complete detail in the leaves. The **AU-50/53** coin has more noticeable wear on the cheek, bust, and hair. There are areas of dullness that may cover half or more of the coin.

There is more flatness on the leaves, and the lettering now exhibits wear.

In **EF-40/45**, there is wear on the cheek and bust, with 70 to 80 percent of the hair intact but worn flat in one or more places. The leaves will have most detail still visible. The reverse central area is sometimes weakly struck, affecting not only the lettering but also other sections of the wreath.

Grades of **VF-20/35** have hair detail ranging from 30 to 70 percent. Of course, strike affects the amount of hair visible and surface preservation should be considered. The cheek, bust, and drapery will be worn. The leaves are separate, with little detail remaining. Certain varieties are very weak in late states.

F-12/15 coins have 15 to 50 percent of hair detail, though on weakly struck coins, little detail is evident. The cheek and bust are usually flat, with outlines only. Most of the leaves will be worn into each other, with none showing detail. The lettering and rims will be complete, except for localized strike weakness.

In **VG-8/10**, there may be little or no hair detail. The head will be complete, the rims will be worn down to field level, and there will be weakness in the top of LIBERTY. The wreath will be outlined, though few leaves have separation. The rims may become indistinct in some areas, with the lettering becoming slightly worn.

For **G-4/6** coins, the head is completely outlined, with little definition showing. LIBERTY and the date may exhibit weakness. Rims may be slightly worn on the obverse, with the reverse slightly more so. Lettering is often worn on the tops, with the leaves blending into other parts of the wreath or field.

In **AG-3**, the bust will be mostly outlined, with LIBERTY and the date readable. Rims may be incomplete on the obverse and reverse, with less than half of the peripheral lettering intact. The wreath may be worn away in places and the central lettering may be obscured. **FR-2** coins will have most of the bust indistinct, with LIBERTY and the date mostly gone. Peripheral lettering may be completely worn away and only sections of the wreath may be visible. Central lettering is usually missing.

PO-1 coins must have a discernible date, though not much more is necessary. The reverse may be worn completely away or show slight detail.

Mint State Examples

MARKS: As with the Liberty Cap large cents, the Draped Bust large cents have coarse hair, and the open areas of the face, neck, bust, and field are all subject to marking. Keg marks (or bag marks) are very common on these coins and finding coins that are mark-free is unusual, as these are mainly hoard coins.

LUSTER: Nearly every luster variation is seen for this series, though semi-prooflike and prooflike coins are rare. The average coin is glossy brown with slightly frosty to frosty luster, the typical Nichols hoard specimen. Some years had inferior planchets, notably 1799, 1800, and 1803, and the Mint records refer to these as "black copper"—with the resulting coins having poor luster. Full original red coins are seen, and these usually have slightly frosty-to-very frosty luster.

STRIKE: There are perhaps more blundered dies, failed dies, die cracks, eroded dies, and odd situations in this series than with any other U.S. type coin. Weakness of all kinds is encountered, with strike weakness noted in numerous spots. Some coins from this series are well struck, but the dies that struck these superior specimens sometimes were used to the point that later states have coins with missing lettering and partial devices. When there is insufficient pressure, the hair above the forehead, around the ear, and behind the neck may be incomplete, with strands blended. The reverse may have part of ONE CENT, parts of the wreath, and peripheral lettering weak or missing. When the dies were out of parallel, there may be specific weak quadrants, with corresponding areas of the reverse also weak. Common areas seen with such die alignment weakness are the bust, the

lowest hair curls, and sections of the wreath and peripheral lettering.

EYE APPEAL: Strike and planchet problems are the most common distractions on these coins. Fully struck, mark-free, clean-planchet, and lustrous coins are the pinnacle of Draped Bust large cents.

Classic Head Cent (1808–1814)

Circulated Examples

AU-55/58 coins will have slight wear on the cheek, the bust, and the hair curls above and below the ribbon and in the central area. Weakness of strike is specifically noted on the hair curl above the eye and the surrounding areas. Strike weakness, improperly aligned dies, filled dies, and so on may cause star weakness. LIBERTY is usually complete, though weakness is noted on some coins. The leaves are broader and slightly longer than on the previous types, with wear and strike weakness difficult to distinguish. **AU-50/53** coins have more flatness on the hair curls and noticeable wear on the cheek and bust. Stars will have slight wear, and dullness will be present on up to 50 percent or more of the surface. The leaves will have definite wear, with the uppermost leaf of each group flattened.

In **EF-40/45**, 70 to 80 percent of the detail is still present. The high points of the hair curls will be flattened, with recessed curls still full. The cheek and bust will have wear over their entire surfaces. Most of the stars, except on extremely sharp strikes, will have flat tops blending the crosshatched lines. Most of the leaves will be flattened, though nearly all will still show some detail and separation.

Grades **VF-20/35** have from 40 to 70 percent of the hair detail present. The cheek and bust will have considerable wear, with the jaw line beginning to disappear. Stars are all flat, but most still have some lines visible. The leaves are totally flat, mostly separate, with slight detail.

In **F-12/15**, the hair detail is 20 to 40 percent intact. The cheek and bust are worn mostly flat, with the adjacent hair curls blended into the face. The leaves are blended into each other with little detail. The rims will be complete and not worn into the lettering.

VG-8/10 coins have little hair detail, and LIBERTY may have several weak letters. John Reich's Classic Head design had relief not seen since the high-relief varieties of the Liberty Cap cents, with detail down to the lowest grades. The bust is almost always boldly outlined, and the obverse rim is usually bold. The leaves will be worn into each other and have little detail, though the wreath is usually well outlined. Reverse rims may be incomplete, causing slight weakness to the upper parts of the lettering.

For **G-4/6** specimens, the bust will be outlined and LIBERTY will be readable. The date and rims should show only the slightest weakness. The leaves will show little or no separation and the wreath's outline may not be distinct. Reverse rims will be worn into the tops of some or all of the lettering.

AG-3 coins have the obverse rim worn into the field, sometimes obscuring stars. The bust is partially outlined and LIBERTY will have some letters visible. The reverse will have up to 50 percent or slightly more of the peripheral lettering obscured, with the wreath flat and blended. Central lettering is still readable, except on very weak strikes. The **FR-2** coin will have a readable date and some details of the bust still present. The reverse may be nearly completely worn away, with sporadic devices and lettering.

In **PO-1**, the date must be discernible, though not much else is necessary, with various parts of the bust still visible. The reverse may be totally slick or with minimal detail.

Mint State Examples

MARKS: The more intricate hair detail hides some marks on the obverse, but the face and field are just as open as previously, subject to the usual marks and other surface impairments. Reverse open area is slightly larger, so marks are slightly more apparent than for the previous reverse types.

LUSTER: Some of the planchets for this series were similar to some of the early 1800-era Draped Bust blanks and were very dark and sometimes porous. Luster is poor for these coins and tends to be very flat to slightly satin in appearance. On some of the better planchets, luster is sometimes glossy with slight frost. Prooflike coins are nonexistent, with semi-prooflike surfaces very rare. Coins with any red color are extremely scarce, with full original red coins unknown.

STRIKE: It has been speculated that the die steel received by the Mint was of a higher quality, as more coins were produced per die with Classic Head cents than for previous issues. There were still poorly struck coins, because extended die use led to worn dies and there were coins struck with insufficient striking pressure. Worn-die coins have a fuzzy overall look, while central weakness is characteristic of insufficient striking pressure. The hair above LIBERTY and the eye may be weak, as will be some of the curls in the central area. Star weakness is often the result of die wear or dies that are slightly out of parallel. The reverse may show slight weakness in ONE CENT, but most of the reverse weakness is noted in the tops of the leaves. Occasional coins with weak peripheral lettering are usually the result of dies not in parallel.

EYE APPEAL: Clean planchets and full strikes are tough to find for this series. Finding minimally marked and lustrous coins is difficult, but these are occasionally seen and, when found, they are very attractive. Original coins with mint red or red-brown are quite scarce, but they are among the most desirable and attractive large cents to type and date collectors.

Coronet Head/Braided Hair Cent (1816–1857)

Circulated Examples

The friction seen on **AU-55/58** coins is first noticed on the cheek and on the hair, directly above and below the headband. Discoloration is evident on red and red-brown coins and is almost always a sign of slight friction. On brown coins, this is much more difficult to discern, and tilting the coin in a good light source often will be the only way to see the dullness caused by wear. The reverse will have slight wear on the leaves and bow. Since striking problems are seen for many years, care should be taken to determine whether the "wear" is from slight circulation or striking weakness. When worn to **AU-50/53**, the cheek will have more obvious wear, and the hair will start to flatten above and below the headband. Stars will still show complete hatch lines, except for localized weakness, where several stars may be totally flattened. The reverse will have leaves with nearly full detail, with the top parts slightly flattened.

EF-40/45 Coronet Head and Braided Hair cents will have obvious wear. The cheek and neck will exhibit wear, and the hair will be flat above and directly below the headband. All stars will show wear, but will show some detail. The top leaves will be flattened, though the adjoining leaves should show nearly full detail. The field will be worn, and luster, if present, will exist only in the protected areas.

For **VF-20/35**, the cheek and neck area will be worn and the hair will be flat on the high points, with detail in the recessed areas. The hair cords should still be evident, except on very weakly struck specimens. Stars will be worn mostly flat. The top leaves will be worn flat and blended. Some porosity is allowed in this grade, though it must be minor.

The detail remaining should be sharp, but quite worn, for **F-12/15**. The face and hair will be flat from wear, and the hair cords may show slightly. Detail in the recessed areas, especially the hair curls, will still show definition. The top and adjacent leaves will be worn into each other, with some detail remaining. The bow will be mostly flat, with slight detail. The surfaces may show more porosity, but heavily porous coins are not graded this high.

With wear to **VG-8/10**, the head will be outlined, with only the recessed areas showing detail. LIBERTY will be complete, except on poorly struck coins, which may have only parts of the first few letters. Stars will be complete, though very flat, and the rim should still be bold. The wreath will be outlined, with only slight detail. Lettering around the periphery should be complete, with a strong rim still present.

G-4/6 coins will have an outlined head, with almost no detail visible except for a partial LIBERTY and the recessed areas. Date and stars will be very flat, with the obverse rim incomplete in areas. The reverse will have an outlined wreath with almost no definition. The rim may be worn into some of the lettering.

The **AG-3** and **FR-2** coins will show progressively less detail. The date may only be partial, with the stars incomplete to completely missing, especially on **FR-2** coins. The reverse will have a complete wreath, though half of the lettering may be missing in **AG-3** and up to 90 percent missing in **FR-2**.

The date and type will be identifiable for **PO-1**, though very little other detail, other than Miss Liberty's head, will be present.

Mint State Examples

MARKS: For both types, marks are very easily seen in the hair. The open areas of the obverse, such as the face, neck, and field, are often seen with marks and other surface impairments. The reverse is similar to the Classic Head reverse, with slightly more open area than the early large cents. Marks on the leaves are noticed more easily than for the Draped Bust type, which had more intricate leaf detail.

LUSTER: Luster variations run the gamut from flat to fully prooflike. During the production of these coins, many improvements were made to the Mint's equipment, leading to higher striking quality. Most Coronet Head and Braided Hair large cents have slightly frosty-to-very frosty luster, though satin-luster coins are also common. Semiprooflike and prooflike coins are more often seen for the later-dated coins, since those struck after 1836 were produced from more carefully polished dies prepared for use with the new steam-powered presses.

STRIKE: These long-lived series have many striking peculiarities. Striking weakness is noted on the hair above LIBERTY; the peak of the coronet, with the L of LIBERTY sometimes weak; the hair around the ear, the hair braid at the back of the head, and the lower hair curls. These areas are not usually all weak on the same coin, although a few coins may have such overall weakness. Stars are sometimes flat in sectors, and this is usually attributable to out-of-parallel dies. The reverse is sometimes seen with central striking weakness, when the central area of the obverse is weak. The tops of the wreath's leaves and the bow are sometimes incomplete, with striking weakness, die wear, and improperly spaced dies being possible contributors. Because of the introduction of the close collar and the steam-powered presses, the Braided Hair type has more well-struck coins than the Coronet type.

EYE APPEAL: Many coins with superb eye appeal are known for both types. Full, original red specimens are known for many dates, and these have the best eye appeal when they are well-struck and mark-free. Glossy brown or red-brown coins are common too, and are attractive as well.

Proofs

HAIRLINES: As with many Proof coins, large cent Proofs were cleaned or wiped on occasion. Light hairlines are noted, especially for the obverse, on many of these coins. These lines may be difficult to notice unless the coin is tilted under a good light source.

REFLECTIVITY: The early Proof strikings in open collars have good reflectivity, compared with the early large cents, though they are not nearly as deeply mirrored as the coins struck in 1836 and later. These later strikings have superb reflectivity on nearly every coin.

STRIKE: Some of the Coronet Proofs have slight weakness in some stars and occasion-ally in some of the other high points. These would be the tip of the coronet, the hair above LIBERTY, and the hair around the ear. Reverse weakness is occasionally seen on the high points of the leaves or in the bow. Braided Hair cents are usually seen with full strikes—though they, too, sometimes have localized weakness. Coins struck after the close collar was introduced usually have broad, flat rims.

EYE APPEAL: As with most Proof copper coins, those with original mint red or red-brown and few or no hairlines are the most attractive specimens. Blazing, full original red coins are encountered, and these have superb eye appeal. Glossy brown coins that still have "blast" also are highly desirable.

Small Cents
Flying Eagle Cent (1856–1858)
Circulated Examples

The wear on the obverse of **AU-55/58** Flying Eagle cents is noted on the eagle's breast and tip of the left wing and along the leading feathers of the right wing. As would be expected, the coins with weakness in strike are also weak in those areas. Also, as the dies wore, the lettering around the periphery deteriorated, and this "washing away" of the lettering is sometimes seen with—and confused with—weakness of strike. The reverse has slight wear on the leaves of the cereal wreath. Coins with striking weakness may show some areas of the wreath flat. Determining what is wear and what is weakness of strike is paramount in arriving at the overall grade. If a coin has full luster, a weak strike is usually the cause of the apparent wear. On circulated coins, especially for **AU-50/53**, the fields are rubbed and often discolored. The breast and the tips of the wing feathers will have more noticeable wear, and the wreath will have top leaves that show very little central detail.

EF-40/45 coins show wear that flattens the breast feathers, with the trailing edge of the left wing and the leading edge of the right wing becoming flat from wear. Striking weakness also affected the eagle's tail feathers and the reverse central lettering. These letters, ONE CENT, were sometimes hubbed unevenly into dies, aggravating the situation when combined with weakness of strike. The reverse has wear that causes flatness on the top leaves and the bow, with some leaves losing almost all detail.

Half or more of the feathers on **VF-20/35** coins are now worn. The tail feathers will show wear and, except for weak strikes, still have separation. The top leaves and the bow now are very flat, with only a few still having central detail, and with some blending into adjacent leaves and stalks.

Except for weakly struck coins, **F-12/15** examples may have 20 to 50 percent of the feather detail still evident. The fields may be marked, but no major marks are allowed in this grade. The rim is strong for both sides and the lettering should be clear, except in instances of strike weakness or die deterioration. The reverse will have some separation of the leaves and stalks, though only the recessed ones show detail.

VG-8/10 coins will have some feather detail, though in some cases just in the very deep recessed areas. The rim will be complete and the lettering and date strong, except in cases of strike weakness or die wear. Leaves and the bow are very flat and worn, with only slight detail in the recesses.

For the **G-4/6** grade, the eagle will exhibit virtually no detail, but will have a complete outline. The lettering of the obverse may have the rim worn into the tops of the letters. The reverse will have an outlined wreath with slight detail, flat leaves, and flat bow. The rim may be incomplete in a few places.

In **AG-3** and **FR-2**, the obverse will lose the lettering completely, the date will be readable but worn, and a slick eagle will blend into the field. The reverse will have a nearly completely flat wreath and areas blending into the field. The rim may be worn into the field and into the wreath in **FR-2**, with only

slightly more detail for **AG-3**. In either grade, some or most of the lettering may be weak or missing.

PO-1 coins will be identifiable as to date and type. Part of the eagle and the date may be all that is visible on the obverse, and parts of the wreath and some lettering may be all that is left on the reverse.

Mint State Examples

MARKS: Although these coins are harder than the pure copper large cents, marks are still evident on many coins. Since these coins were harder and smaller than the large cents, the marks are usually smaller than previously. In relation to their size, however, the marks are sometimes severe. Fairly large nicks and other surface impairments are found on the eagle and in the field on the obverse. Reverse marks are seen on the wreath and the denomination in the center, and in the field.

LUSTER: Striking these coins was difficult because of the hardness of the copper-nickel alloy, and most coins have satin-to-slightly frosty luster. There are some flat-luster coins, with semi-prooflike and prooflike coins fairly common.

STRIKE: Even using the reverse as the hammer die did not prevent many of these new-alloy coins from having striking weakness. The hardness of the copper-nickel alloy caused the dies to wear quickly, with die erosion a big problem. Crumbling letters and devices are commonplace for this series, and die breaks are seen fairly often. Weakness is seen in the eagle's feathers at the tip of the right and left wings, the breast, and the tail. The entire body of the eagle, including the head, is also sometimes seen with incompleteness, some undoubtedly due to die wear and improperly spaced dies. The Mint, in an attempt to prolong die life, spaced the dies as far apart as possible, sometimes leading to these very weakly impressed specimens. One other problem with these coins should be mentioned, as the Mint realized this problem, which led directly to the Indian Head cent design. Some of the deepest parts of the obverse die were directly opposite some of the deepest parts of the reverse die. This caused the metal to not flow completely into either cavity, resulting in much of these coins' incompleteness. Coins also are seen that came from dies not in parallel, and these will have localized weakness on the obverse and reverse.

EYE APPEAL: Since striking these coins was difficult, fully struck, lustrous coins with frosty or prooflike surfaces are the most attractive Flying Eagle cents. Many of these coins have discoloration, smudging, or haze, and these are negative eye appeal attributes.

Proofs

HAIRLINES: Although the copper-nickel alloy is hard, these coins easily hairline. Many of the Proof Flying Eagle cents encountered have light or moderate hairlines, noticeable mainly in the obverse field.

REFLECTIVITY: Although most 1857 and 1858 Proof Flying Eagle cents have deeply reflective fields and some frosting on the devices and lettering, most 1856 coins do not. The typical 1856 Proof cent has very lightly mirrored fields, with little frosting on the devices and lettering.

STRIKE: Although the 1857 and 1858 Proof Flying Eagle cents are usually very well struck, many 1856 Proofs are not. Deeply mirrored fields and some contrast usually are noted for the 1857 and 1858 coins, while the Proofs of 1856 often do not have either. Debates have raged for years as to whether the Mint was striking Proofs or business strikes in 1856. Since the quality of these strikings is not up to the Proof standards of the day, one must wonder whether all of them were just well-struck Mint State examples with some prooflike surface. Do not expect the full chiseled strikes for 1856 issues, as most have rounded lettering, slight weakness in the eagle, and less than razor-sharp wreaths.

EYE APPEAL: As mentioned previously, the 1857 and 1858 Proofs have deeply mirrored

fields, usually with some frost on the devices, thus they have good eye appeal. Since most of the 1856 coins do not have the deeply mirrored fields and cameo devices, they usually are not as attractive. Spotting, discoloration, hairlines, nicks, scratches, and other surface impairments are obviously negative attributes.

Indian Head Cent (Copper-Nickel)— No Shield/Shield (1859–1864)
Circulated Examples

The change in 1859 to the new Indian Head design was not accompanied by a metallic change. The new "nickel" cents were popular with the public, and it was only because of striking problems—incorrectly attributed to the Flying Eagle design—that Mint officials directed Chief Engraver James Longacre to prepare a new design. The copper-nickel composition was changed to bronze five years later, after the striking problem was correctly linked to the alloy, and not the design.

AU-55/58 examples of both the no-shield and shield types have slight friction on the tips of the headdress feathers, the cheek, the hair above and behind the eye, the lowest hair curl, and the ribbon. The reverse of the no-shield type has slight wear on the laurel wreath, while the reverse of the shield type has slight wear on the high points of the oak wreath. More wear on the previously noted areas of the obverse is seen in **AU-50/53**. The ribbon area is one of the strike-weakness points, and the lack of four diamonds on the ribbon should not be used as a grading element. The reverse has slightly more wear on the laurel or oak leaf wreaths, with flatness on the top leaves.

EF-40/45 coins will have more wear evident on the cheek and headdress feathers, with flatness in the hair above and behind the eye and the lowest curl. Although nearly all Extremely Fine Indian Head cents have a full and strong LIBERTY, the four diamonds on the ribbon cannot be reliably used to grade Indian Head cents. The laurel wreath reverse will have minor wear, with slight flatness. The oak wreath will have some detail missing from the top leaves of the wreath and slight flatness on the bow.

With **VF-20/35**, the job of grading copper-nickel Indian Head cents becomes tougher. On weakly struck coins, a full, sharp LIBERTY is not always present, and the feather detail and surface preservation are more reliable grading elements. Half the headdress feathers may be worn away or show only partial detail. The reverse will have flatness in the laurel leaves, with the recesses having separation. The oak leaves will start to blend together, as will the details of the bow in the shield type.

As with the other grades, **F-12/15** coins should not be graded solely based on the presence of LIBERTY, which is present on many coins that grade Fine but is not complete on others that are weakly struck. There will be little headdress or hair detail visible in this grade. The reverse will have some deep detail visible on the laurel wreath. The oak wreath will have many leaves blending together. The bow will be worn to the point where the ribbon around the arrows may no longer be visible.

VG-8/10 coins may have parts of three letters of LIBERTY present, but this is not a reliable guide for the grade. The presence of any detail in the headdress feathers is a better indicator than the letters of LIBERTY. There is a complete rim on the obverse and reverse. The reverse will have an almost completely flat laurel wreath, though the oak leaf wreath will show recessed detail, with the bow and ribbon worn mostly flat.

There is an outlined head in **G-4/6**, but very little fine detail is present. The rim, especially on **G-4** pieces, may be worn into the tops of some of the lettering. The reverse will have a completely flat laurel wreath and very little detail for the oak leaf wreath. The rim should be incomplete in just a few spots.

AG-3 and **FR-2** coins will have incomplete lettering, although on About Good coins most of the lettering should be readable. The reverse will have the rim worn into the field for **AG-3** and into the wreath for **FR-2**. The central lettering may be weak or partially missing for both grades.

Part of the date and Indian may be all that is visible for **PO-1** coins. The reverse will have parts of the wreath and central lettering visible.

Mint State Examples

MARKS: As with Flying Eagle cents, these coins were struck in copper-nickel alloy. Resultant marks and other surface impairments are noticeable to about the same degree for the obverse. The reverse of the first type, with no shield and a thin laurel wreath reverse, shows marks and other detractions more easily than the second type, with a shield and the more complex oak wreath.

LUSTER: As with Flying Eagle cents, all types of luster variations are seen, with the typical coin having satin to slightly frosty luster. Flat-luster, semi-prooflike, and prooflike specimens are fairly common. There is seldom frost on the devices and lettering, and the surface texture is usually very uniform.

STRIKE: The problems encountered with striking the copper-nickel alloy continued with the cents of 1859–64, though the new design allowed for better striking. Slight weakness for the obverse is often seen in the tips of the headdress feathers, the hair below LIBERTY, the diamonds on the ribbon, the lowest hair curls, and the tip of the bust. The reverse may show weakness in the leaves and bow of the 1859 type, with the shield, leaves, bow, ribbon, and arrows sometimes weak on the 1860–64 type. Some coins are seen with a mushy look, and this is attributable to worn and/or improperly spaced dies. These coins will have incomplete feathers and diamonds.

EYE APPEAL: Strike and luster are the two areas that are usually deficient. Spotting, discoloration, and other surface impairments also may be noted, although there are coins with blazing luster and minimal marks. Finding all positive attributes for these coins may take some time, but exceptional coins are available.

Proofs

HAIRLINES: Although, like Flying Eagle cents, these are hard-alloy coins, light-to-moderate hairlines plague many of them. Lines are generally confined to the fields, but some may also be noted on the face and high points of the wreath—especially on the thin wreath of the no-shield type.

REFLECTIVITY: Almost all of these coins have deeply reflective fields and many, if not most, have frosted devices and lettering. Some have discoloration, spotting, or haze, thus they appear less deeply reflective.

STRIKE: Proofs are of much higher quality, and most are very well struck. Many of the 1860 Proofs and some from a few other years have beveled rims. Slight beveling on the very edge of the rim is sometimes seen on coins that at first glance appear to have broad, flat rims. The feathers and diamonds are usually very sharp on all dates. Strike is seldom a problem with these coins.

EYE APPEAL: Since strike is usually not a problem for these Proof coins, the detractions are usually hairlines, discoloration, spotting, tiny nicks, or other surface impairments. Blazing, deeply reflective coins with little or no surface disturbance are found, however, and these have superb eye appeal.

Indian Head Cent (Bronze) (1864–1909)

Circulated Examples

Although the striking problems with the copper-nickel alloy were alleviated somewhat with the change to bronze, they were not totally eliminated. The **AU-55/58** Bronze Indian Head cent has slight friction on the tips of the headdress feathers, the cheek, the hair above and behind the eye, the lowest hair curl, and the ribbon. The reverse will have slight wear on the high points of the oak wreath and bow. More wear on the obverse is seen in **AU-50/53**. The ribbon area is one of the strike weakness points, and the lack of four diamonds on the ribbon should not be used as a grading element. The diamonds are visible only on well-struck coins in grades below Uncirculated.

EF-40/45 coins will have more wear evident on the cheek and headdress feathers, with flatness in the hair above and behind the eye and the lowest curl. Although nearly all EF Indian Head cents have a full LIBERTY, the four diamonds on the ribbon cannot be reliably used to grade them. The reverse will have slight wear on the leaves, with some detail missing from the top leaves and slight flatness on the bow.

With **VF-20/35**, the job of grading Indian Head cents becomes tougher. On weakly struck coins, a full LIBERTY is not always present, and the feather detail and surface preservation are more reliable grading elements. The lack of diamonds on the ribbon should not keep a weakly struck coin from grading Very Fine, although the overall grade is affected by strike weakness. Half the headdress feathers may be worn away, and there may be little hair detail remaining. The reverse will have flatness in the leaves, with some of them starting to blend, as will the bow.

F-12/15 coins should not be graded solely based on the presence of LIBERTY, which is present on many coins that grade Fine but is not complete on others that are weakly struck. The feather detail, which should show some intricate design, is a more reliable grading element. There will be little hair detail visible. Many leaves will be blended, though much fine detail will still be visible. The bow will be worn to the point that the ribbon around the arrows may no longer be visible.

VG-8/10 is similar to the previous grades in the common misconception that three letters of LIBERTY must be visible to attain the **VG** grade. Although this is true for many coins, the presence of any detail in the headdress feathers is a better indicator than the letters of LIBERTY. There is a complete rim in this grade. The wreath will show recessed detail, with the top leaves, bow, and ribbon worn mostly flat.

The outlined head is visible in **G-4/6**, though very little fine detail is present. The rim, especially on **G-4**, may be worn into the tops of

AU-58 *1902 Indian cent obverse. Slight friction is seen on the cheek and band with diamonds.*

AU-58 *1902 Indian cent reverse. Slight friction is seen on the wreath and shield.*

AU-55 *1898 Indian cent obverse. Slightly more friction is seen on the cheek and band with diamonds.*

AU-55 *1898 Indian cent reverse. Slightly more friction is seen on the wreath and shield.*

AU-53 *1907 Indian cent obverse. Friction is now noted in the field as well as on the cheek.*

AU-53 *1907 Indian cent reverse. Friction is seen in the field as well as on the wreath and shield.*

AU-50 *1907 Indian cent obverse. Friction is seen over most of the head and field, with slight flattening.*

AU-50 *1907 Indian cent reverse. Friction is seen in the field and slight flattening is noticed on the wreath.*

EF-45 *1905 Indian cent obverse. Wear on the feathers and band with diamonds is more noticeable.*

EF-45 *1905 Indian cent reverse. The wreath and shield show noticeable wear.*

EF-40 *1908 Indian cent obverse. Some of the tips of the feathers, as well as the band with diamonds, are flat.*

EF-40 *1908 Indian cent reverse. The upper leaves are now flat in spots.*

VF-35 *1907 Indian cent obverse. Flat hair, feather tips, and band with diamond as well as cheek and neck are seen.*

VF-35 *1907 Indian cent reverse. Most of the upper leaves are flat, with the ribbon around the arrows slightly blended.*

VF-30 *1908 Indian cent obverse. Slightly more wear is seen in the noted areas.*

VF-30 *1908 Indian cent reverse. This shows about the same amount of wear as for VF-35.*

the lettering. The wreath is completely flat, with very little fine detail visible. The wreath should be complete, however, and the rim should be incomplete in just a few spots.

AG-3 and **FR-2** coins will have incomplete lettering, but on **AG** coins most of the lettering should be readable. In Fair, very little lettering is readable. The reverse will have the rim worn into the field for **AG-3** and into the wreath for **FR-2**. Central lettering may be partially missing for both grades.

Part of the date and Indian may be all that is visible for **PO-1** coins. The reverse will have parts of the wreath and central lettering visible.

Mint State Examples

MARKS: The change in 1864 to bronze cents, from the previous copper-nickel alloy or

pure copper, made a significant difference in surface preservation. The softer bronze is more easily marked than the copper-nickel, but it is slightly harder than pure copper, thus, the marks are more muted and not as sharp. Also, the small cents did not bang against each other as severely in shipping, leading to smaller and less severe marks. The reverse is fairly intricate, hiding all but the most severe marks.

LUSTER: The new bronze-alloy cents have all luster variations, though the typical coin is satin to slightly frosty for the early years, 1864 through the 1880s. Coins from the later 1880s through the end of the series in 1909 are usually slightly frosty to very frosty. The red color varies from year to year, ranging from tan to a golden color to bright red, with many variations in between.

VF-25 *1908 Indian cent obverse. Most of the feathers have blended, as have the hair and band with diamonds.*

VF-25 *1908 Indian cent reverse. All of the upper and some of the lower leaves are flat, with the shield lines mostly blended.*

VF-20 *1908 Indian cent obverse. Upper feather tips are flat, as are the hair and band with diamonds.*

VF-20 *1908 Indian cent reverse. All leaves show flatness and the ribbon around the arrows is completely blended.*

F-15 *1908 Indian cent obverse. Some letters of LIBERTY are weak or partially missing. The hair shows only deepest detail.*

F-15 *1908 Indian cent reverse. All of the leaves are flat, and some have begun to blend.*

F-12 *1908 Indian cent obverse. LIBERTY is weak in several places.*

F-12 *1908 Indian cent reverse. More leaves are blended.*

VG-10 *1908 Indian cent obverse. Parts of LIBERTY will be present.*

VG-10 *1908 Indian cent reverse. Most of the leaves will show blending.*

VG-8 *1908 Indian cent obverse. Some LIBERTY is present, though most other detail is flat.*

VG-8 *1908 Indian cent reverse. Some leaf detail is present, though most is flat.*

G-6 *1887 Indian cent obverse. The Indian is flat, with deeply recessed detail only.*

G-6 *1887 Indian cent reverse. Only slight detail is visible in the wreath.*

G-4 *1883 Indian cent obverse. Slight Indian detail is seen, with rims slightly worn into field in spots.*

G-4 *1883 Indian cent reverse. An outlined wreath with rims complete (slightly worn into the field on some examples).*

STRIKE: The new bronze alloy alleviated many of the striking problems seen with the copper-nickel alloy Indian Head cents. Die life improved, as the new alloy was much softer and easier to strike. Weakly struck coins are still seen, however, as the dies were sometimes used too long and deteriorated. The tips of the headdress feathers, the hair below LIBERTY, the hair around the ear, the diamonds, the lowest hair curls, and the tip of the bust are seen weakly impressed on some coins. The earlier dates are more often seen with these weaknesses. Also, the reverses still show occasional weakness, with the shield, leaves, bow, ribbon, and arrows sometimes affected. The bottom part of the N of ONE is also seen weak on some business strikes from the hub used from 1864 to 1870 and again in 1877, which had this letter weakly impressed. Crumbled dies are still

seen, mainly in the earlier issues, which often are characterized by partial lettering, dates, hair, diamonds, and feathers. The San Francisco Mint started striking cents in 1908, and many of the 1908 and 1909 San Francisco coins have weakness in the tips of the feathers and an overall mushy look.

EYE APPEAL: There are many different looks that have good eye appeal for bronze Indian Head cents, though obviously those with full strikes, original mint red, no spots, minimal marks, and blazing luster are the most attractive. Once the red color starts to fade and becomes red-brown or brown, then the other factors become paramount in determining eye appeal. Strike, spotting, marks, and luster are the important factors on coins that are less than full original red. Issues from the early years, the 1860s and 1870s, do

AG-3 *1881 Indian cent obverse. Rims are worn into the field in most areas, into the tops of the lettering.*

AG-3 *1881 Indian cent reverse. An outlined wreath with rims slightly worn into the field.*

FR-2 *1882 Indian cent obverse. Rims are worn into lettering or, as with this example, into the rough field.*

FR-2 *1882 Indian cent reverse. Rims are worn into the field or, as with this example, the rough field.*

PO-1 *1882 Indian cent obverse. Rims are worn deeply into the lettering and date.*

PO-1 *1882 Indian cent reverse. Rims are worn into the field with a partial wreath.*

not have the blazing red color of some of the later years, and one should not expect an 1872 Indian cent to have the same color as an 1899.

Proofs

HAIRLINES: Hairlines are most easily noticed on the obverse of Indian Head cents, with the field and the cheek the most affected areas. Reverse lines are noticed in the open area inside the wreath and among the letters of the denomination. Coins from several years after 1900 have extremely fine die polishing that is often confused with cleaning. These parallel lines may be the result of an overly zealous Mint employee or some type of experimental die polishing, since this was an era of unusual surfaces for Proof coinage. Many Proof Indian Head cents obviously were not handled carefully at the Mint, as quite a few coins also have tiny nicks that are the result of contact with other coins. Reports from this era confirm that minor Proof coinage was often kept loosely in drawers in the cashier's office at the Mint.

REFLECTIVITY: When seen with full original mint red, the surfaces of bronze Indian Head cents are deeply mirrored. Cameo or frosted devices are not often seen, and the typical Indian Head is either lightly frosted or mirrored across the entire coin. Reflectivity diminishes as the red color fades to red-brown or brown and also is diminished by spotting, haze, and hairlines. Some of the issues in the 1880s, mainly those with beveled rims, also do not have the depth of reflectivity of those issued before and after.

STRIKE: Proofs are generally very well-struck, with the Indian and the wreath sharply impressed. Broad, flat rims are the norm except for the 1885–89 issues, which are mainly seen with beveled rims. Some other dates, mainly in the 1870s, are sometimes seen with slightly beveled rims—though not usually as pronounced as with the 1886–89 coins.

EYE APPEAL: Since there are many different shades of red color for Proofs, just as there are for business strikes, eye appeal for

some dates will not be as positive as for others. Some dates from the 1860s, 1870s, 1880s, and 1890s do not have fiery red color, even when properly preserved, and may not be as attractive as dates that have bright red color. Hairlines, discoloration, spotting, nicks, and other surface impairments are the main factors affecting eye appeal after the red color begins to fade.

Lincoln Head Cent—Wheat/Memorial Reverse (1909 to date)

Circulated Examples

In the **AU-55/58** grades, there will be slight wear on the cheek, forehead, and jaw of Abraham Lincoln. There also may be slight friction in the hair above and around the ear and coat. The wheat stalks will have only slight rubbing and, except for weakly struck specimens, will be completely separated. The Memorial-type reverse will have slight friction on the building. There will be more rub for **AU-50/53** coins, and the fields may now show rubbing. Red color may be present down to these grades and even below, though red color is not necessary for these grades. The reverse will still show only slight wear, with wheat stalks still separate, except on poorly struck or worn-die specimens. Memorial-reverse coins will have definite wear on the high points, especially across the base of the building, including the steps.

The wear across Lincoln's face, head, hair, and coat is obvious in **EF-40/45**, and these areas are usually a different color, often lighter brown, than the field. The detail of the hair is still very good, flat from wear only on the highest curls. The wheat stalks will have definite wear but, except on weakly struck coins, will have clear and separate stalks. The Memorial building now has wear across the top and on the columns, as well as on the base and steps.

VF-20/35 are difficult grades, because determining strike versus wear in Very Fine is tough, and in the lower grades it is usually factored in with wear. A full ear and bow tie are not present on some weakly struck coins in **AU** or higher grades. Thus, the wear on

AU-58 *1937 Lincoln cent obverse. Slight friction is seen on the forehead, cheek, jaw, and coat.*

AU-58 *1937 Lincoln cent reverse. Slight friction is seen on the wheat lines.*

the craggy face of Lincoln is on the forehead, cheek, and jaw, with the depressed areas between them still defined. The weakly struck **VF** coins will have stalks that blend together, and only on the higher-grade and well-struck **VF** coins will the stalks be full and totally separate. The Memorial reverse is not usually found in this grade and below, though the amount of wear on the building would be enough to blur the detail of the top and base.

The central head area will be quite worn on **F-12/15** coins, with some of the ear visible but the hair flat around it. The hair at the top and back of the head will show some detail. Detail of the coat will still be evident, though the bow tie may not be distinct on poorly struck coins. Although on well-struck coins the majority of the lines of the wheat stalk will be evident, poorly struck coins may have few if any stalk lines visible and should be graded mainly by surface preservation. Memorial reverse coins are seldom seen in this grade and almost never in the Very Good and below grades.

VG-8/10 coins will have little detail visible on the head, with a few hair curls and possibly part of the ear noted. The coat will show the deepest folds of the lower part, with the upper area worn flat. The rim should be strong on both sides. The wheat stalks will

have some lines, though little separation is seen.

For the obverse of **G-4/6** coins, the head will be worn smooth, with only slight folds in the lower part of the coat visible. The rim, especially for **G-4** coins, may be worn into the tops of the lettering. The reverse rim also may have indistinct areas. An outline will be the only part of the wheat stalks that is present, though some of the detail of the lower part may still be visible.

AG-3 and **FR-2** coins will have almost no detail on the head and coat of Lincoln. For **AG-3** coins, the rim may be worn up to halfway into the lettering, and on some **FR-2** coins parts of some letters may be totally gone. The reverse will have the rim into the letters and wheat stalks on **AG-3** coins, and some of the lettering may be missing for **FR-2** coins.

The date will be readable for **PO-1** coins and some letters also may be, with the head and coat blended into the field in several places. The reverse will have some of the central lettering readable, with little of the peripheral letters seen and the wheat stalks blended with the rim and field.

Mint State Examples

MARKS: For the obverse, the face, head, and coat of Lincoln are prime areas for marks

AU-55 *1909 VDB Lincoln cent obverse. Slightly more friction is seen on the head, face, and coat.*

AU-55 *1909 VDB Lincoln cent reverse. The wheat lines show slight friction.*

AU-53 *1938-D Lincoln cent obverse. The field now shows friction, as do the face and coat.*

AU-53 *1938-D Lincoln cent reverse. All wheat lines are separate, but show slight wear.*

AU-50 *1938-D Lincoln cent obverse. Most of the field shows friction, with flatness now noted on the hair.*

AU-50 *1938-D Lincoln cent reverse. Slight flatness is seen on the grain of the lower wheat stalk.*

EF-45 *1909 VDB Lincoln cent obverse. Flatness is seen on the hair, cheek, beard, and coat.*

EF-45 *1909 VDB Lincoln cent reverse. The grain on the lower wheat stalk is obviously worn.*

EF-40 *1917-D Lincoln cent obverse. The ear is slightly blended, along with flatter hair, cheek, beard, and coat.*

EF-40 *1917-D Lincoln cent reverse. All wheat lines are separate, though worn (weakly struck coins will not exhibit this). The grain on the lower wheat stalk is mostly flat.*

VF-35 *1938-D Lincoln cent obverse. Some hair detail is very flat, the ear about half blended.*

VF-35 *1938-D Lincoln cent reverse. Some of the wheat lines are beginning to blend.*

VF-30 *1909 VDB Lincoln cent obverse. The hair is slightly detailed, the ear mostly blended, with missing coat detail that blends at the neck line.*

VF-30 *1909 VDB Lincoln cent reverse. Some wheat lines are blended, but most are still separate.*

VF-25 *1913-D Lincoln cent obverse. The beard is flat, with the upper coat line now blended with the neck.*

VF-25 *1913-D Lincoln cent reverse. Some separate wheat lines are seen with some blending.*

VF-20 *1935 Lincoln cent obverse. Slight detail is seen in the upper hair and behind the ear.*

VF-20 *1935 Lincoln cent reverse. Most wheat lines are blended, with a few separate.*

F-15 1915-D Lincoln cent obverse. Slight hair and coat detail is seen.

F-15 1915-D Lincoln cent reverse. Parts of a few wheat lines are visible.

F-12 1913-D Lincoln cent obverse. The cheek and beard are worn nearly level with the face.

F-12 1913-D Lincoln cent reverse. Parts of a few wheat lines are visible.

and other surface impairments. The open field areas in front and back of the head are also locations where marks are noted, though the high-relief design and the high rims protect the field. Reverse marks are generally found in the denomination and lettering of the central area, with some marking also noted on the wheat stalks.

LUSTER: Most Lincoln Head cents are satin to frosty in luster, though nearly every luster variation is found. Deeply prooflike coins are virtually unknown, however, and semi-prooflike coins are not often seen except for the modern Memorial-reverse issues. Flat to satin luster is seen on many of the early Denver and San Francisco issues, as the dies were used until they were excessively worn. Some of these were polished to remove clash marks, and semi-prooflike luster resulted on

the strikings immediately after the dies were polished. However, detail was weakened sometimes by this polishing, and after successive strikings the luster diminished with the detail.

STRIKE: Strike is not a problem for most Lincoln cents produced in Philadelphia. Many Denver and San Francisco coins do have striking and die wear problems. The most famous weakly impressed issue is the 1922 "Plain" coin, struck in Denver. Some dies were polished that year to remove clash marks, and this effaced much of the detail, including the mint mark. Some Uncirculated coins from these dies have no separation in the wheat stalks and only slight hair detail. The lettering is indistinct, with some parts of Lincoln's coat also missing. Although this is the worse example of strike and die weak-

VG-10 *1917-S Lincoln cent obverse. The face is worn smooth, and the field shows several marks. (These may be present in all circulated grades, though severe ones may result in the coin's not being graded).*

VG-10 *1917-S Lincoln cent reverse. A few wheat lines are partially visible.*

VG-8 *1913-D Lincoln cent obverse. Slight detail is seen in the hair and coat.*

VG-8 *1913-D Lincoln cent reverse. There may be slight or no wheat lines present.*

G-6 *1915-D Lincoln cent obverse. Slight detail is seen in the hair and coat.*

G-6 *1915-D Lincoln cent reverse. No wheat lines are visible, usually, though parts of several may show.*

G-4 *1910G-4 Lincoln cent obverse. A flat head is seen with slight coat detail.*

G-4 *1910G-4 Lincoln cent reverse. Only slight detail is seen in the lower wheat stalk.*

AG-3 *1913-D Lincoln cent obverse. The figure is nearly totally flat; rims are worn in the L of LIBERTY and the tops of a few other letters.*

AG-3 *1913-D Lincoln cent reverse. Flat detail is seen, with rims worn into the lettering and wheat stalks.*

FR-2 *1913-D Lincoln cent obverse. Flat head is seen, with rims worn into the field and lettering.*

FR-2 *1913-D Lincoln cent reverse. Rims are worn into all of the peripheral detail.*

PO-1 *1913-D Lincoln cent obverse. There is a readable date, with some lettering missing.*

PO-1 *1913-D Lincoln cent reverse. Slight central detail is visible.*

ness, there are many Denver and San Francisco coins from the teens and twenties that are poorly impressed. Most of the coins struck after the mid-1930s, including the branch-mint issues, are much better struck. The modern Lincoln cents with the Memorial reverse are of a much higher quality, with the obverse detail strengthened, giving Lincoln's hair and coat more chiseled detail. The modern Mint equipment leads to very uniform, well struck coins.

EYE APPEAL: Although the red color varies from year to year and mint to mint, there are full red, well-struck, minimally marked coins known for nearly every issue. Some rare issues, such as the 1914-S and 1922 "Plain" coins, are nearly impossible to find with blazing red color—and obviously, a full-strike 1922 "Plain" coin is an oxymoron. For some years, Lincoln cents have a golden red color, and these coins do not have the "blast" of the full red issues of other years.

Proofs

HAIRLINES: For the Matte Proof coins of 1909–16, hairlines are difficult to detect. The matte-like surface, which is really closer to Satin or Roman Proof than the Matte Proof look of gold coins, "hides" hairlines. These coins often have die polish, and making the distinction frequently requires careful examination. The brilliant Proofs from 1936 and

later often have light-to-moderate hairlines from mishandling or cleaning. The field of the obverse is the most noticeable area affected by hairlines, with the central area among the denomination and lettering of the reverse also affected.

REFLECTIVITY: The Matte Proofs do not have reflectivity; their surface is best described as satin. When original, these coins have a soft "glow" that is very attractive, though not reflective. The brilliant Proofs of the later years, except the 1936 Type I, have deeply mirrored fields and often have frosted devices. After 1968, almost all Lincoln cents have deeply frosted or cameo devices that contrast superbly with the deeply reflective fields.

STRIKE: Almost all Lincoln cent Proofs are well struck. The Matte Proofs of 1909–16, brilliant Proofs of 1936–42, and the 1950–64 and 1968-to-date Proofs are excellent examples of the Mint's ability to produce high-quality coinage. The bow tie is sharp and distinct, as are Lincoln's hair and coat. The inner borders of the rims are nearly square with the fields, and broad, thick rims are found on nearly every coin. Nearly 100 percent of the modern Lincoln Memorial proofs are razor-sharp strikes.

EYE APPEAL: The most attractive coins of both Proof types have original mint red. The color for the Matte Proof coins is usually not as fiery as for the brilliant Proofs, with other factors determining eye appeal for the Matte coins. Spotting, discoloration, hairlines, and other surface impairments affect both types—and the presence, or lack, of these deficiencies determines the eye appeal.

Two-Cent Pieces
Shield Two-Cent Piece (1864–1873)
Circulated Examples

AU-55/58 two-cent pieces are difficult to distinguish from slightly weak-struck uncirculated coins, since the tips of the leaves are generally the areas that are weakly struck and also one of the first places slight wear is noted. In these grades, the WE of the motto IN GOD WE TRUST may have slight rub on the scroll, and there may also be weakness on the arrow tips and the bottom of the shield. The reverse will have slight wear on the high points of the wreath and the bow. The leaves are more flattened on **AU-50/53** coins, with some of the center leaves of each group lacking sharp detail. Other areas—including the lines of the shield, which may be slightly blended—will now have wear, though on weakly struck coins it is hard to distinguish which incompleteness is due to strike and which is due to wear. The reverse will usually have separation on all the details of the wreath, though some intricate parts of the design may now be indistinct.

On **EF-40/45** coins, some of the leaves around the shield will lack central detail. The vertical and horizontal shield lines will blend in some spots, and the WE of the motto will have noticeable wear. Some components of the wreath and bow will have obvious wear and may be blended. Poorly struck coins may have considerable flatness, especially in the horizontal lines of the shield and the leaves of the obverse. The numeral 2, CENTS, and the leaves/grains of the wreath also may have strike weakness.

If the **VF-20/35** coin is well-struck, then the leaves and the lines of the shield will be mostly separate. On weakly struck coins and lower-graded **VF** coins, this distinctness may

disappear. The WE of the motto will be readable, though it may have some weakness. The leaves and grain of the reverse wreath should all be present, but some of the leaves may be only outlined. The bow and the leaves will be blended.

Although the WE of the motto is readable on many **F-12/15** coins, this should not be used as a grading key for weakly struck coins. Details of the leaves will be weak, and many of them will not show separation. The horizontal lines of the shield will be nearly all flattened, as will the vertical ones. Most of the leaves on the reverse will have no detail and will be blended, though most of the wheat grains will still have separation.

VG-8/10 specimens will have separation in some leaves, but almost none with any detail. The WE of the motto may show slightly, and the other letters will be worn but readable. The vertical and horizontal shield lines will be mostly worn away. The rims should still be complete and raised. The wreath will have worn leaves with little separation, and some of the grains will be plain though quite worn.

With the wear down to **G-4/6**, the obverse has little intricate detail remaining, with only the outline of the shield visible. Some of the motto may show, though usually only parts of some letters. The rim is usually complete in this grade, but parts of it are no longer raised.

An **AG-3** or **FR-2** coin will have rims worn into the date and fields, with **FR-2** rims blending into the wreath, which will show only the deeply recessed detail. The reverse will have wear into the lettering and the wreath blending into the field.

For **PO-1** graded coins, only a readable date, the central part of the shield, part of the reverse wreath, and some of the central and peripheral reverse lettering may be present.

Mint State Examples
MARKS: With the intricate design of the obverse, there are many places for marks to

"hide" between the wreath and shield. There is very little open field area for the obverse, with marks and other impairments mainly confined to the ribbon, wreath, and shield. Those on the horizontal lines of the shield and in the open area between the vertical lines are the most obvious and detracting. The reverse surface detractions are usually seen in the central area on the denomination or in the open area around it. The wreath and the peripheral lettering also may be marked, though the intricacy of the wreath makes it difficult to detect marks there.

LUSTER: Most Shield two-cent pieces have satin to frosty luster. Original color ranges from tan to fiery red, with coins from the early years mostly red and those from later years mostly tan or golden. All luster variations are seen, though prooflike coins are unusual for most dates except the lower-mintage dates such as 1871 and 1872.

STRIKE: Although these coins were struck with the relatively soft bronze alloy, weak strikes are seen fairly often. Very poor strikes are uncommon, however, and the typical weak coin will have slight weakness in the motto, the center leaves of the wreath, and the upper part of the shield, including the horizontal lines. Occasionally, the lower part of the shield will have slight weakness, with the ball and arrow feathers having slight incompleteness. The reverse, when weak, will have incompleteness on the wreath and bow. The 2 CENTS is sometimes seen with slight weakness, though this is rare. A few coins are seen from improperly spaced dies, resulting in large areas of the obverse and reverse being very incomplete. These are seen much less frequently, however, than are similar Flying Eagle cents.

EYE APPEAL: Since the red color varies with the date, some issues will not have the "blast" seen for certain years. Fully struck, minimally marked, original mint red coins are available for every year, and these are very attractive, even when the red color is not fiery. As the color fades, other factors such as spotting, discoloration, marks, and other surface impairments become the primary determinants of eye appeal.

Proofs

HAIRLINES: As with many pre-1900 Proof issues, two-cent pieces were wiped or cleaned by their owners. The resulting hairlines are noticed by tilting the coin under a good light source, revealing the lines within the shield, around the outside of the wreath, and sometimes across the wreath and shield. The reverse hairlines are mainly noted in the open areas, though sometimes they are seen across the lettering and the wreath. Small nicks and scratches are noted on some coins, and some of these may be the result of improper handling by careless Mint employees.

REFLECTIVITY: Most of these coins have fairly deep-mirrored fields. Slight frost may be noted on the devices and lettering, though heavily frosted coins are unusual. Spotting, discoloration, hairlines, haze, and the fading of the original red color to red-brown or brown also affect the depth of the reflectivity.

STRIKE: Most Shield two-cent Proofs are well-struck, and many are fully struck. Slight incompleteness on the tops of the center leaves of the obverse wreath is occasionally seen. Most of these coins have broad, flat rims, though coins from a few years are seen with slight beveling.

EYE APPEAL: As with Mint State coins, Proof two-cent pieces with full original red color, minimal hairlines, and full strikes are the most attractive coins. As the color fades, the other criteria, such as hairlines, spotting, and discoloration, become the most important elements of eye appeal. Still, there are attractive coins that have faded to brown but retain unimpaired mirrored surfaces.

7 GRADING U.S. NICKEL COINS

Nickel is the hardest metal regularly used in U.S. coinage. For that reason, the dies employed in striking coins with high nickel content tend to wear out more quickly than those that strike coins made primarily of a softer metal, such as gold or silver. The coins that emerge from these dies look worn themselves, even at the second they are struck, and that can create serious problems for graders.

Some countries, such as Canada, have issued pure-nickel coins. Because of the metal's hardness, however, the U.S. Mint has chosen not to do so. In fact, it has never issued a coin whose primary component has been nickel. Even the five-cent pieces commonly known as "nickels" actually contain three times more copper than nickel; the alloy used in these coins is 75 percent copper and only 25 percent nickel.

When struck from new dies under adequate pressure, nickel five-cent pieces and other coins with a high nickel content are excellent specimens of U.S. coinage and are relatively easy to grade. All too often, though, nickel coins have been struck through the years with worn dies and under inadequate pressure. The wear and pressure problems go hand in hand: in an effort to extend the life of the dies, Mint production workers have sometimes aligned them slightly farther apart than the optimum distance—and though this has reduced die wear, it also has reduced the fullness and sharpness of the strike. To make matters worse, the planchets used for nickel coins have not always been of even quality.

Three-Cent Nickels
Liberty Head Three-Cent Nickel (1865–1889)
Circulated Examples

For **AU-55/58**, only the cheek on the obverse and the top of the wreath and the Roman numerals on the reverse will have slight wear. This is usually manifested on the obverse by a slight discoloration on the cheek. If there is no discoloration on the cheek, the coin has either been dipped and the wear is difficult to notice, or the "disturbance" may be the rough planchet, still visible because of an incomplete strike. The lines on the Roman numerals are completely separated except on coins with poor strikes, which may show incompleteness. The grades of **AU-50/53** will show more wear, thus more discoloration. Up to half, or slightly more, of the surface will show rubbing.

In **EF-40/45**, there is wear across the entire coin. Up to 20 percent of the detail will be worn away.

VF-20/35 examples will have 25 to 50 percent of their detail missing. On strong strikes, there will be half or more of the hair detail visible and some line separation on the Roman numerals.

In **F-12/15**, there will be 10 to 20 percent of the hair detail visible on strong strikes, and most of the leaves of the wreath should be separated. Well-struck coins will have some lines of the Roman numerals visible, though on poor strikes there may be none.

In **VG-8/10**, the hair detail will be worn mostly smooth, with detail in only the recesses. Rims will be worn nearly to field level, but still intact. Leaves may be worn smooth, with only slight or no separation.

In the **G-4** grade, the rim will be completely worn into the fields, but it should not touch the letters of the obverse or the wreath of the reverse. The hair detail will be worn away, though LIBERTY is recessed and visible. Leaves will be worn nearly flat. The **G-6** should have nearly complete rims, with approximately the same amount of other detail.

If the rims have worn into the letters and the wreath, the coin will have lost 90 to 95 percent of its detail to wear and will grade **AG-3**. **FR-2** coins will have less than 5 percent of the original detail, with no rims and very little, if any, lettering still evident.

The grade **PO-1** will show less than 5 percent of the original detail. There will be no rims visible, and the lettering may be completely gone. The rim will be totally blended into the field.

Mint State Examples

MARKS: These were small coins, so bag marks are not as prevalent as with larger coins. They were stored and transported in bags, so tiny nicks and scratches sometimes are noticeable, mainly on the cheek and on and about the Roman numerals and the wreath. Slide marks from plastic album pages are sometimes seen, though nickel is a hard metal and this is not as much of a problem as with other metals. As noted previously, many of these coins are incomplete on the cheek and Roman numerals. (See below under Strike and chapter 5 under Strike for a more thorough discussion.)

LUSTER: Luster ranges from flat to frosty for the 1865–69 group, with a few semi-prooflike and full prooflike specimens. The 1870–76 group has more frosty, semi-prooflike, and full prooflike specimens than the earlier group. The 1879–81 coins usually have frosty, semi-prooflike, or full prooflike luster. The 1882–87 dates are usually prooflike or semi-prooflike, though a few frosty examples are known, and these bring added premiums. The 1888–89 coins are almost always seen with frosty and semi-prooflike luster.

STRIKE: The strike of the 1865–69 coins ranges from "flat as a pancake" to fully struck. The weakly struck coins, especially 1865–67, sometimes have totally flat hair and no vertical lines on the numerals. Clashed dies were very common—and if the coins were polished to remove the clashing, detail is sometimes lost. The 1868–69 coins are usually better struck than the earlier dates, and the 1870–89 coins have fewer strike problems than either. The occasional clashed-die specimen is seen, though coins from the 1880s seem to have fewer than those from the 1870s, with one exception: There are many 1881 clashed-die specimens.

EYE APPEAL: The coins dated 1865–69 usually have average eye appeal, with poor strikes and inferior luster. The group from 1870–76 usually has a better appearance than the early years. The alloy seems brighter and the poor strikes are fewer. The coins of 1879 and later usually have the best eye appeal. The low-mintage coins have superior luster and strike, with fewer clashed-die specimens than in previous years.

Proofs

HAIRLINES: The 1865–69 coins are difficult to find without hairlines. Coins from these years often show small nicks on the cheek or the numerals of the reverse. The 1870–76 Proofs often have striations that are confused with hairlines, though these coins are easier to find with fewer hairlines than those from the previous years. Coins dated 1877–89 are seen with the fewest hairlines or marks. Many hairline-free coins of this period are downgraded from the loftiest grades because of slight spotting or slide marks (lines) on the cheek.

REFLECTIVITY: The 1865–69 coins usually have deep mirror surfaces. The 1870–76 Proofs often have die striations, thus lack deep reflectivity. Proofs from 1877–89 usually have good reflectivity. Some Proofs have enough "Mint State luster" or frost that they are sold as the rarer Mint State examples. When there is doubt regarding the **MS/PR** status, examining the edge for reflectivity is useful in making this determination.

STRIKE: Proofs of the first two groups, 1865–69 and 1870–76, are not as well struck as those from the later years. They will sometimes have weakness in the high points of Miss Liberty's curls and incomplete lines on the Roman numerals. This problem is seen somewhat more often in the first group. The 1877–89 Proofs are generally well-struck, though clashing was occasionally a problem. When the clashing is polished away, some detail is lost, as on 1879 and 1880 Proofs, where detail is missing in some areas of the wreath.

EYE APPEAL: The 1865–69 Proofs usually have good eye appeal, but they may be downgraded when the strike is deficient. The 1870–76 Proofs have decent eye appeal, though striated coins are usually not as attractive. The Proofs after 1877 are often fully struck, with good reflectivity. Even the less-than-fully mirrored Proofs often are attractive. The 1880s issues also come with "mint-tissue" blue color, making these coins the most attractive three-cent nickel Proofs and also the highest-graded.

Nickels
Shield Nickel Five Cent—Rays/No Rays (1866–1883)
Circulated Examples

In **AU-55/58**, there is little noticeable wear. The leaves and the shield show slight friction. The reverse will show slight wear on the stars (and the rays, when present). There should be nearly full luster in the fields. When worn to **AU-50/53**, the leaves and shield have begun to flatten with wear. The stars (and rays) of the reverse will show wear.

In grades of **EF-40/45**, the wear is immediately noticeable on the leaves and the shield. The field will be dull, with only vestiges of luster. The reverse will have wear across the entire coin, with luster remaining around the stars (and rays), which should show most of their detail.

In **VF-20/35**, the coins will have lost from 25 to 50 percent of their detail. The leaves will be separated but worn, and the shield will show most of the lines with separation. The reverse will show flatness on the stars with blended lines. Most of the rays should be separate, but indistinct.

In **F-12/15**, the leaves will mostly be worn flat, with very little detail, though some separation. The lines of the shield will mainly be gone, but a few may still show. The stars (and the rays) are flat.

In **VG-8/10**, there is a full rim; however, only the detail of the shield and the leaves will be outlined. The reverse will have a full rim, with flat stars (and the rays, when present, will have no separation).

In **G-4/6**, the rim will be mostly full, but not distinct, and may be worn into the tops of the lettering, though in **G-6** the rim should be almost complete. There will be a complete outline, but with no fine detail in the shield and leaves. The reverse will have outlined stars (and rays) and indistinct rims.

If the rims have worn into the top part of the lettering, the coin will grade **AG-3**. The shield may be indistinct in places, and there is little detail. In **FR-2**, the rims will be worn into the date and lettering, and the stars (and rays) of the reverse will be totally flat and indistinct.

In **PO-1**, the rims will be worn into the lettering, date, and shield, with the leaves showing no detail. Some of the lettering may be obscured, and some of the stars (and rays) of the reverse will be worn away.

Mint State Examples

MARKS: These are small coins struck in a hard metal, so marks are generally not a great problem. They usually are small and first noticed on the shield lines and in the fields. The reverse will have marks on the 5 in the center and scattered about the field and stars (and rays). Hairlines are found on Mint State coins, but both 1866 and 1867 Shield nickels With Rays sometimes have striated dies, as do several other dates.

LUSTER: The luster on all Shield nickels is usually satiny to frosty. The luster on the With-Rays and early No-Rays coins (1866–73) is usually satiny to slightly frosty, with few semi-prooflike or prooflike coins. The 1874–76 coins and the 1879–81 business strikes are found satiny, frosty, striated semi-prooflike, and prooflike. The 1882 and 1883 are usually found satiny to fully frosty, though striated reverses are seen, as well as full prooflike. The alloy varied through the years, and more difference in luster is found in nickel coins than in copper or gold coins, although less than in silver.

STRIKE: Striking problems caused the Mint to suspend coinage of nickels with rays in January 1867 and resume with the No-Rays reverse in February. Many With-Rays nickels are characterized as weakly struck, some so poorly made that the leaf detail is worse than on a fully struck coin in **VF**! Sometimes the lines of the shield are missing and the corresponding 5 of the reverse is weak. The stars (and rays) also often show weakness. No-Rays coins were better-struck, though there were still problems, especially with the early dates. When the hub was changed in 1870, some of the defects in the die were fixed, and the striking qualities of coins from 1869 and again in 1872 onward were slightly better. Coins from nearly every date show some striking weakness, although it is usually minor—mainly on the leaves and shield lines, but also in the 5 and in the stars of the reverse.

EYE APPEAL: When Shield nickels With Rays are fully struck with satiny or frosty luster, they are great-looking coins, but only a small minority of the coins meets these criteria. It is nearly impossible to find one of these coins in MS-67 or better. The early No-Rays coins (1867–73) do not have the "flash" of some of the later issues, thus have slightly less

eye appeal. The striated No-Rays coins often have better luster and a better appearance than those from the early years. The 1874–76 and 1879–83 coins usually have good eye appeal. When free of marks, these are the most attractive business-strike Shield nickels.

Proofs

HAIRLINES: Minor Proof coins were treated with little respect by Mint employees, sometimes being kept loosely in cash register-type drawers and mishandled, often resulting in small nicks and hairlines. Also, collectors sometimes cleaned them with abrasives, leaving tiny hairlines. Even though nickel is very hard, the delicate Proof surfaces are easily hairlined. The combination of light hairlines and small marks is noted on many of the pre-1877 With-Rays and No-Rays Proofs. The 1877 and later coins do not usually have these tiny marks, but hairlines are still noted. The highest-grade Proof coins, those with the fewest hairlines, are those dated 1877 and later. In fact, through April 2003, PCGS had certified just *sixteen* coins PR-67 prior to 1877—and none higher! Careful storage by collectors accounts for some of this discrepancy, though sloppy Mint personnel probably were responsible for many of the marks/hairlines of the pre-1877 coins.

REFLECTIVITY: Because of the striking difficulties, some Proof With-Rays Shield nickels lack deep reflectivity. The 1866 issue is more deeply mirrored than the 1867. The coins from 1867–73 and 1877–83 are usually deeply mirrored specimens. Just as with three-cent nickels, where there probably was an alloy problem, the mid-1870s No-Rays Proofs are often seen with die polish and the resultant diminished reflectivity. The 1877–78 coins also are seen with less-than-deeply mirrored fields. The Mint obviously was not as careful burnishing the blanks and sometimes struck them only once.

STRIKE: The strike on Proofs is usually full; however, some slight weakness is sometimes noted on the tips of the leaves and some of the stars (and rays). Certain 1867 With-Rays nickels and some No-Rays issues, the 1873 in particular, had overly polished dies and a resultant loss of detail. These coins are usually deeply mirrored, though the leaf and other details are missing because of over polishing.

EYE APPEAL: Fully struck With-Rays Proofs with full-mirrored surfaces are quite attractive and have nearly the superb eye appeal of the late-date No-Rays Proof coins. The appearance of the No-Rays Proofs is usually good. The years with striations lack deep reflectivity and do not have the "blast" of the early or late years. The 1879 and later coins often have a gorgeous blue color, usually from storage in the mint tissue.

Liberty Head Nickel Five Cent—No Cents/With Cents (1883–1912)

Circulated Examples

In **AU-55/58**, there is slight wear on the cheek and hair curls. Stars will show only slight wear and, unless weakly struck, will have clear lines. The reverse will show only slight friction on the high points of the wreath and the V. The corn may not be fully struck. In **AU-50/53**, the cheek has noticeable wear and the hair of the forehead and above the ear is beginning to flatten. Stars will start to show wear, though the lines should still be mostly complete. The wreath will be slightly flat on the high points.

An **EF-40/45** coin has obvious wear on the cheek, and the hair will be worn together in places, especially below LIBERTY, which should be full. Some of the star lines will be worn away. The reverse will have flatness on the wreath, with some of the "flowers" obviously worn. The V has noticeable wear.

VF-20/35 coins have up to half of their detail worn away. LIBERTY will still be complete. The hair detail is fairly separated behind the ear, but there is little separation below LIBERTY, with wear on the face and neck. The stars will be worn, with little or no line separation. The wreath is worn, though there is some detail. The V is fully outlined.

F-12/15 coins will have 75 percent or more of their detail worn away, but LIBERTY will still

be complete, but weak. The hair will show little detail below LIBERTY, and only a few strands may show separation behind the ear. The stars will be worn mostly flat. The entire wreath will show separate small devices, though they will almost all be worn flat. The V may blend slightly into the field.

VG-8/10 coins will show a few letters of LIBERTY, but sometimes only one letter may be complete. The hair will show almost no detail and the stars will be totally flat. There should be complete rims, and all lettering will be clear. The wreath will show all small devices, though they will show little or no detail. The lower part of the V may blend into the field.

G-4/6 coins will show no LIBERTY and no hair detail. There may be an ear and some detail visible above LIBERTY, and the stars will be outlined. The obverse usually has a full rim, even in **G-4**, though the reverse may be worn slightly into the lettering in **G-6** and almost always worn into the lettering in **G-4**. The V will blend into the fields, especially on the lower part.

An **AG-3** coin will have the date visible, though the obverse rim will be worn into some of the stars. The reverse rim will be worn deeply into all of the lettering, obscuring some. The V will be visible, with little of the wreath seen. A **FR-2** coin will have some detail of the obverse visible, but the date may be very weak and few stars may show. The reverse will show the V and little else.

A **PO-1** coin will be worn nearly slick, with the date barely visible, a poorly defined head, and no stars visible. The reverse may be worn completely, with no detail seen except for part of the V.

Mint State Examples

MARKS: These light (5 grams) coins in hard alloy received few marks from each other. When they did strike each other with sufficient force to cause nicking, the results were small, sharp marks. These marks usually appear on Miss Liberty's face, the V of the reverse and surrounding area, or occasionally in the wreath and fields. More common are the lines seen on the face and other areas as a result of cleaning, album slides, and the like. The 1883 no-Cents type has slightly more small marks, possibly because quantities existed for years stored in bags instead of rolls, as with other years.

LUSTER: The luster of business-strike examples varied from year to year. Coins from 1883–99 generally have frosty luster, though 1886–89 coins are usually seen with satin luster. The 1900–12 coins are more satiny, though there are many frosty and semi-prooflike coins as well.

STRIKE: The strike of most years is similar. The main weaknesses are in the upper hair and headband of Miss Liberty and the reverse wreath, especially the corn on the lower left. This area of the reverse is directly opposite the high point of the obverse and would be expected to show weakness when the obverse does. The years 1886 through 1889 seem to have adequate detail, though the rims are often beveled, perhaps from die spacing as opposed to insufficient striking pressure. Coins from 1908 through 1912 often have a mushy look, perhaps due to die wear or even possibly a worn master hub. The Denver and San Francisco issues of 1912 are often seen with mushiness, and San Francisco coins are rare with strong hair detail.

EYE APPEAL: Good eye appeal is the result of a good strike, planchet, and luster, and the absence of marks and hairlines. Most dates have some coins that meet these criteria. Although the issues before 1900 seem to have a frostier luster than those after 1900, coins with good eye appeal can be found for every date.

Proofs

HAIRLINES: As with Shield nickels, some Liberty Head Proofs have tiny nicks—some perhaps from mishandling in the Mint. The early dates seem to have more hairlines than those after 1900, but that is usually true for all coins, since preservation improved over time.

Coins were still cleaned, but probably not as harshly as previously. Coins from several years after 1900 have extremely fine die polish that often is confused with cleaning. These parallel lines may be traceable to an overly zealous Mint employee or some type of experimental die polishing, since that was an era of unusual Proof techniques.

REFLECTIVITY: The first several years of Liberty Head nickel Proofs had good reflectivity and contrast, continuing the quality seen for the last few years of Shield nickel Proofs. At some point in 1885, this changed—and from 1886 through 1889, nearly all Proof Liberty nickels lack deep reflectivity. This problem came to a head in 1889, and most of the Proofs from that year are *semi-prooflike to satiny* and are often sold as "rare" Mint State coins. The rims of most of these coins are beveled, and the surfaces look like those of business strikes. From 1890 to 1900, most Proofs have decent reflectivity and contrast, with 1895 through 1897 nickels often being seen with cameo devices and deep reflectivity. After 1900, the cameo devices are often missing. Post-1900 coins often are brilliant across their entire surface, as with other series of U.S. Proofs. The "look" of the post-1900 Proofs may have resulted from intentional Mint experimentation. After 1909, many Liberty Head nickel Proofs have frosty devices. The 1913 coins appear to have been struck on unprepared planchets and may have been struck only once. They probably were made in haste, and there is doubt as to whether they are Proofs or business strikes. In fact, St. Louis coin collector Eric P. Newman, who owned all five known examples, called two of them Proofs and three of them business strikes!

STRIKE: The strike of most Proofs is good-to-excellent. A few coins are sometimes seen with mushiness, and even fewer are seen with overall weakness, perhaps due to the use of excessively light planchets. Beveled-rim Proofs seen in the mid- to late 1880s are usually well struck, with neither more nor less weakness than those before or after. Weakness on the high points of Miss Liberty's hair

PR-65 *1883 No Cents Liberty nickel obverse. A low-end specimen with streaky surfaces.*

PR-65 *1883 No Cents Liberty nickel reverse. A few streaks and light disturbance are seen on this low-end specimen.*

PR-65 *1909 Liberty nickel obverse. A high-end coin with a pristine field.*

PR-65 *1909 Liberty nickel reverse. A small toning streak is the only thing that mars the clean surface of this high-end coin.*

curls and the corresponding corn ear of the reverse is seen much less often than on business strikes. Although most Proof coins are struck twice, it appears that nickel coinage did not receive the careful attention afforded gold and silver Proofs. Some of the 1908–12 Proof Liberty Head nickels suffer from the mushiness seen on some of the business strikes. The 1913 coins are similar to these late-date coins, as the strike is slightly mushy.

EYE APPEAL: The tissue-toned Proofs with deep blues and vibrant yellows are usually the most attractive Liberty Head Proofs. The cameo coins of the mid-1890s are great-looking coins, whether toned or not. The lack of hairlines or tiny nicks is, of course, a primary factor in eye appeal. Coins after 1900 with little or no contrast are not as appealing as those prior to 1900. The fine die polish seen on

some of these post-1900 coins is considered quite negative, and these coins seldom receive high grades unless they have other outstanding attributes.

Indian Head (Buffalo) Nickel Five Cent—On Mound (Type I) / On Base (Type II) (1913–1938)

Circulated Examples

AU-55/58 coins have very little noticeable wear on the obverse. There may be slight friction on the Indian's cheek and the hair immediately above the braid. Wear is noted on the reverse, with the bison's head and shoulder and the upper hindquarters showing slight friction. These areas on the obverse and reverse also show the effects of weakness of strike and die wear. If the areas in question have complete luster and no discoloration,

AU-58 *1937-D Buffalo nickel obverse. Wear is seen on the high points of the hair and cheek. The braid is weak from strike, not wear.*

AU-58 *1937-D Buffalo nickel reverse. Slight friction is seen on the head and hind portion of the bison.*

AU-55 *1938-D Buffalo nickel obverse. Friction is seen on the hair, forehead, and cheek.*

AU-55 *1938-D Buffalo nickel reverse. Friction is seen on the head, shoulder, and hind part of the bison.*

the coin is probably Uncirculated. In **AU-50/53,** wear will be noticeable on the obverse, with the cheek and hair above the braids showing discoloration. The shoulder and hindquarters now have blatant friction. The luster will be missing in these areas on both Type I and Type II coins.

In **EF-40/45,** there is wear across most of the Indian and bison, with diminished luster. The reverse will have wear on the head and across the entire body of the bison, especially on the front shoulder and hindquarters. On most coins, a full, sharp horn will be visible. Some 1926-D coins, and other dates, never had a full horn. Knowledgeable numismatists realize that some date and mint-mark combinations are almost never seen fully struck, so circulated examples of these coins do not have the detail expected for the grade.

The grades of **VF-20/35** have up to half of their detail worn away. There will be wear across the entire obverse, including the protected areas. There is hair detail, though much of the sharpness is gone. On some coins, the rim may touch the top of LIBERTY, especially in the lower **VF** grades. The reverse will have wear across the entire bison and in the protected areas. Normally, the horn will be full, but the tip may be slightly worn. In lower **VF** grades and on coins that were weakly struck, the tip of the horn will not be present. On some coins, the rims may touch the head and tail of the bison.

F-12/15 coins will have lost up to 75 percent or more of their detail, but LIBERTY will be sharp and usually is separated from the rim. The hair will show little detail, and the hair braid will probably be visible only in outline.

AU-53 *1937-D Buffalo nickel obverse. Friction is seen on the hair, forehead, and cheek, with slight flattening evident.*

AU-53 *1937-D Buffalo nickel reverse. The hair on the head and shoulder is slightly flat, with friction over most of the bison.*

AU-50 *1937-D Buffalo nickel obverse. The face, hair, and field show friction, with some hair detail incomplete.*

AU-50 *1937-D Buffalo nickel reverse. The hair above the head is mostly flat, with friction over most of the bison and surfaces.*

EF-45 *1937 Buffalo nickel obverse. Wear is seen over the entire surface, with the hair mostly present.*

EF-45 *1937 Buffalo nickel reverse. Hair is flat on the head and shoulder, with the hump very flat.*

EF-40 *1937-S Buffalo nickel obverse. Hair is detailed, though obviously worn.*

EF-40 *1937-S Buffalo nickel reverse. Most of the hair above the head and on the shoulder is flat. The hump is blended with the hind portion.*

VF-35 *1937-S Buffalo nickel obverse. The hair and feathers show recessed detail.*

VF-35 *1937-S Buffalo nickel reverse. The tip of the horn is complete (on weakly struck coins this is not always true). Some hair detail is seen on the head and shoulder.*

VF-30 *1936-S Buffalo nickel obverse. The hair and feathers show recessed detail.*

VF-30 *1936-S Buffalo nickel reverse. The tip of the horn is complete (not on weakly struck specimens). Most other bison detail is flat, with recessed areas clear.*

VF-25 *1936 Buffalo nickel obverse. The hair and feathers show slight detail.*

VF-25 *1936 Buffalo nickel reverse. The tip of the horn is complete, but blurry. Recessed detail is clear.*

VF-20 *1929-S Buffalo nickel obverse. Much of the hair and feather detail is worn.*

VF-20 *1929-S Buffalo nickel reverse. The tip of the horn is blended slightly, with recessed bison detail.*

The date should be full, though it may not be sharp. The reverse has some detail on the bison, and approximately half to two-thirds of the horn will be present. As noted previously, weakly struck coins will exhibit less of this feature. The rim will be complete, but it may be flat in some areas.

VG-8/10 coins will have a full LIBERTY, though the rim may be worn into some of the letters. The hair will have detail in only the recessed areas. The date will be complete, but some numerals may be weak. The bison will show detail only in the recessed areas, and the horn will show up to half. The rim will be worn to the level of the field, but it should not touch any lettering.

G-4/6 coins will show LIBERTY, but the rim may be worn into all of the letters. The In-

dian will be very worn, and only the deepest recesses will show detail. The date should be complete, though the numerals will be indistinct. The bison will show an outline and slight detail. The rim will be worn down into the lettering, even on **G-6** coins. There will be no horn detail, even on well-struck coins.

AG-3 coins will have a partial date, and the obverse rim will be worn well into LIBERTY. The Indian will still be well outlined, with some detail present. The reverse will have an outlined bison and wear into all of the lettering. **FR-2** coins will have an outlined Indian head, but little else. LIBERTY may be completely missing, and the date may be barely readable. The reverse will have a mostly outlined bison, though much of the lettering may be obscured because the rim has worn into it.

F-15 *1930-S Buffalo nickel obverse. Only the top hair has much detail remaining.*

F-15 *1930-S Buffalo nickel reverse. Two-thirds of the horn is present on strong strikes, with the bison mostly flat. The rim may touch the head and tail.*

F-12 *1929-S Buffalo nickel obverse. Slight upper hair detail is present.*

F-12 *1929-S Buffalo nickel reverse. From one-half to two-thirds of the horn is present. Most detail of the bison is flat. The rim touches the head and tail.*

A **PO-1** coin will be worn nearly slick, with the date barely visible and little or no LIBERTY present. The reverse may be worn completely, with the only visible detail being the bison, which will be worn flat.

Mint State Examples

MARKS: The marks and hairlines on Mint State examples are usually confined to the Indian, though they are often hidden by the hair detail. Only sharp nicks on the cheek are really obvious—and since nickels are light, these are usually not numerous. The reverse has more field area, and small marks are sometimes seen below the bison, as well as on it. Hairlines are usually confined to the body of the bison.

LUSTER: The luster on most Philadelphia business strikes is good, ranging from satiny to very frosty. On some dates, such as 1921, 1923, and 1924, it is superior, with dripping mint frost. Little frost is seen on the devices, though the luster can still be called frosty on many of the Philadelphia issues and on some of the Denver and San Francisco issues. Satiny luster is predominant on most dates, especially the Denver and San Francisco issues. Very few extremely frosty coins are seen for the Denver and San Francisco coins, but several dates—such as the 1915-S and 1916-S—are seen with semi-prooflike surfaces.

STRIKE: Some date and mint-mark combinations command huge premiums when they are fully struck. The areas most affected on the obverse are the back part of the face, the braid, and the hair directly above the braid; on the reverse, the areas to check are the head, shoulder, and hindquarters—espe-

VG-10 *1927 Buffalo nickel obverse. Only deeply recessed hair and feather detail are present.*

VG-10 *1927 Buffalo nickel reverse. This specimen has one-half of the horn, though this is not necessary. The bison shows recessed detail only. The rim touches the head, tail, and tops (and bottoms) of some letters.*

VG-8 *1926 Buffalo nickel obverse. The rim may touch part of LIBERTY.*

VG-8 *1926 Buffalo nickel reverse. Less than one-half of the horn is present on this specimen. The rim may touch the head and lettering, and may be worn slightly into the tail.*

G-6 *1923-S Buffalo nickel obverse. The rim is worn into LIBERTY and the field. The date is incomplete.*

G-6 *1923-S Buffalo nickel reverse. Only the bottom part of the horn shows. The rim is worn into the head, tail, lettering, and field.*

G-4 *1930 Buffalo nickel obverse. The rim is worn into LIB-ERTY and the field, with a partial date visible.*

G-4 *1930 Buffalo nickel reverse. A very flat bison is seen, with no horn detail. The rim is worn into the head, tail, lettering, and field.*

AG-3 *1930 Buffalo nickel obverse. Slight recessed detail is seen, with the rim worn into one-half or more of LIBERTY, now touching the hair and feathers. A partial date is present.*

AG-3 *1930 Buffalo nickel reverse. The rim is worn into all of the lettering and deeply into the head and tail.*

FR-2 *1930 Buffalo nickel obverse. A heavily worn rim is seen, with a partial date. Little detail is visible.*

FR-2 *1930 Buffalo nickel reverse. A heavily worn rim is seen, with basic design present.*

PO-1 *1930 Buffalo nickel obverse. A partial date is seen, with little other detail.*

PO-1 *1930 Buffalo nickel reverse. Little detail is present, with part of the bison and lettering visible.*

cially the tail—of the bison. LIBERTY, the date, and other areas of the obverse may also have striking weakness. On the reverse, the horn can be affected in several ways, since worn or filled dies can contribute to weakness, just as well as striking pressure can. The presence of a "split" tail is almost unknown on several issues. Apparently, the branch mints were not hardening their dies properly in the mid-1920s—for all denominations— and on the nickel coins, the dies sometimes became so eroded that the mint mark is difficult to distinguish.

EYE APPEAL: When Indian Head nickels are well-struck, as with the 1937 and 1938-D, the eye appeal can be great. These are also seen with "target" toning from storage in cardboard holders and sometimes with an even, blue color. These toned coins can be spectacular and very high-grade when a good strike, superior luster, and lack of marks are combined. No amount of amazing color can compensate, however, for a poor strike, eroded die luster, and numerous marks, and coins with these deficiencies will not have good eye appeal.

Proofs

HAIRLINES: The marks sometimes seen on earlier nickels are not often encountered on Proof Indian Head nickels. Hairlines are

seen, though the early proofs (1913–16) are Matte Proofs and do not "show" hairlines as easily as brilliant Proofs. (There is controversy over reports of 1917 Matte Proofs, and PCGS has never seen one, but they may exist.) The 1936–37 brilliant Proofs do exhibit hairlines, but spotting is more of a problem than hairlines with nearly all nickel Proofs. The 1936 Type I Proofs are hybrids and are called Satin Proofs. These show hairlines more than mattes, though less than brilliant Proofs.

REFLECTIVITY: There is, of course, almost no reflectivity on the Matte Proofs of 1913–16. This finish has a satiny surface with no mirrorlike appearance. The Satin Proof 1936 coins do have some reflectivity, though it is best described as semi-prooflike. The 1936–37 brilliant Proofs have deeply mirrored fields, but only some of them have the cameo devices to contrast with the reflective fields.

STRIKE: Almost all Indian Head nickel Proofs—matte, satin, and brilliant—are fully struck. Occasional minor weakness is noted.

EYE APPEAL: Some Matte Proof coins are seen with almost no toning, others with spectacular colors splashed across the surface or around the periphery. The appearance is usually great, though spotting is a problem, as it is

MS-67 *1938-D Buffalo obverse. This coin has blazing lus-ter, with unmarked Indian and field.*

MS-67 *1938-D Buffalo reverse. Full, crisp detail, with un-blemished bison and field, is seen here.*

MS-66 *1936-S Buffalo nickel obverse. This coin has a small mark on the cheek, with minor scuffs elsewhere.*

MS-66 *1936-S Buffalo nickel reverse. A pristine field with full detail is seen on this coin.*

MS-65 *1938-D Buffalo nickel obverse. A few scattered marks and scuffs are seen on this coin.*

MS-65 *1938-D Buffalo nickel reverse. This coin has a minor tick here or there.*

MS-64 *1930 Buffalo nickel obverse. Slight scuffing and a few minor marks are seen on this coin.*

MS-64 *1930 Buffalo nickel reverse. Slight contact marks appear on the bison.*

MS-63 *1916 Buffalo nickel obverse. A few marks appear on this coin, mainly on the face.*

MS-63 *1916 Buffalo nickel reverse. Slight marks and contact on the bison's body and legs are seen here.*

MS-62 *1926-S Buffalo nickel obverse. Although the surfaces are not heavily marked, the strike is slightly incomplete.*

MS-62 *1926-S Buffalo nickel reverse. Besides the marks, there is incompleteness on the head and tail.*

with all nickel coinage. The Satin Proofs of 1936 and the brilliant Proofs of 1936–37 were issued with mint tissue and often have the pretty blues and yellows associated with this storage method. When they are free of hairlines and spots, these colorful coins receive the high grades that they deserve.

Jefferson Nickel Five Cent—Copper-Nickel/Copper-Silver-Manganese (1938 to date)

Circulated Examples

The slight friction in **AU-55/58** is seen mainly on Thomas Jefferson's cheekbone and sometimes in the hair. The reverse will show some wear on the columns of Monticello and the areas directly above and below—the area below being the steps. The steps are often weakly struck, so weakness there and nowhere else is almost always strike-related and not a function of wear. Wear is more apparent for **AU-50/53**, and discoloration is noticed across the face and hair. The reverse will have nearly full detail, with only traces of wear in the central area of Monticello.

The wear on **EF-40/45** coins is noticeable across the face and hair of Jefferson, but detail is still almost full. The reverse has wear on all of Monticello, and the center has lost some detail.

The hair will lack up to half of its detail in **VF-20/35**, and the cheek will have lost some definition. The reverse will have columns visible, with the rest of Monticello showing only the most general detail.

In **F-12/15**, the hair and cheek detail will be worn away, with only recessed detail visible. Jefferson's coat will have wear, but major detail will be visible. The reverse will have some detail visible in Monticello, though the columns will be indistinct.

VG-8/10 coins will have no detail in the hair, with the cheek and coat very flat. The columns will be visible, though most of the detail in Monticello will be worn away. The rims may touch some of the lettering.

In **G-4/6**, the hair detail will be completely flat and the rims will be worn into the lettering. Monticello may have only the outline clear and no central detail. The rim may be complete on the reverse.

AG-3 coins will have a clear outline of Jefferson, but the rim will be worn into much of the lettering. The reverse will have Monticello outlined, and the rim will be worn into the lettering. **FR-2** coins will have Jefferson outlined and the lettering mostly gone. The reverse will have Monticello worn flat, possibly worn into the field, and the rims obscuring much of the lettering.

PO-1 coins may have almost no lettering and the date nearly worn away. The reverse will have Monticello worn into the field, and the lettering will be mostly obscured.

Mint State Examples

MARKS: The face and hair are sometimes seen with light marks or hairlines. The fields of the obverse and the reverse are also sometimes seen with light marks. Monticello is seen with light marks as well.

LUSTER: Most have satin luster, but there are some with frosty luster and some semi-prooflike and prooflike coins. The luster is usually frosty on the silver war nickels, though all variations are seen.

STRIKE: The strike is usually nearly full to full, but coins from the early 1950s are exceptions. The only weakness usually seen, other than that on the mushy coins from the early 1950s, is on the steps of Monticello and the other features of the building. On some dates, the area that comprises the steps, plus the detail around the steps, is flat—as is the corresponding part of the obverse, where it usually is noted as weakness in the lower part of the hair.

EYE APPEAL: Except for the poor-planchet coins of the early 1950s, the appearance of most coins is good, though not spectacular. Occasional spotting and excessive marks are noted, but they are the exceptions. The silver war nickels sometimes toned nicely and have good eye appeal when this occurs on a well-struck, lightly marked specimen. Now and then, other nickel-alloy dates also have toning that is attractive, often with shades of blue, yellow, or pink.

Proofs

HAIRLINES: Jefferson nickels in Proof were handled better by the Mint than earlier Proof nickel coinage. The 1938–42 coins were sometimes distributed in mint tissue and often exhibit tissue toning. Some complete sets were issued in boxes with cellophane sleeves. The hairlines seen on these early issues, including the 1942 Type II Proof, are usually from cleaning, not mishandling, as with some of the earlier Proofs. Some of the Proofs issued and stored in the cellophane sleeves acquired hairlines because these plastic sleeves disintegrated. The 1950–55 coins also were issued in mint tissue and cellophane sleeves, usually in boxes. In 1955, this was changed and Proof sets were issued in Pliofilm "flat packs" in paper envelopes. If the coins were superb specimens when sealed, they often remained so until they were cut out of the Pliofilm. However, some light hairlines probably were acquired in these holders also, as the coins could move around slightly. In 1968, the Mint started issuing Proof sets in hard plastic holders—and if they were hairline free upon encapsulation, they usually remained so. The hairlines acquired on post-1964 Proof nickels are usually from mishandling after removal from their holders.

REFLECTIVITY: Most Jefferson nickel Proofs are deeply mirrored coins. The coins from 1938–42, including the 1942 Type II, sometimes have cameo devices. Some of the 1950–53 coins are not deeply mirrored. After 1953, cameo devices are quite common and the surfaces are deeply mirrored. The coins struck in 1968 and later in San Francisco are almost all deeply mirrored, with cameo devices.

STRIKE: Nearly all Jefferson nickel Proofs are fully struck, including the steps of Monticello, which are often weak on business strikes. Slight weakness is seen in the steps and other detail on some strikings.

EYE APPEAL: The eye appeal of the 1938–42 Proofs is often great. Many toned and brilliant examples are virtually free of hairlines. The cameo-device coins of 1938–42, 1950–64 and 1968 to date are very attractive when they are nearly hairline-free. Sometimes coins from these years are nicely toned as well. The post-1964 Proof Jefferson nickels are almost always superb in appearance. Deeply mirrored fields contrasting with deep cameo devices are the norm, and the only detractions usually seen are shiny spots on the high points when the frosted dies have lost some of their frost.

8 GRADING U.S. SILVER COINS

Silver coins present special challenges to a grader, primarily because the metal can tone in a myriad of ways, attractive and otherwise. The colors that comprise the toning on silver coins make them interesting—and sometimes very difficult—to grade. Often, subtle differences in alloy composition gave various batches of silver their own unique coloring and identity, providing a kind of fingerprint for coins from a certain year and mint. Coins produced in some years toned quite spectacularly, while coins from other years seemed almost resistant to toning.

The machinery utilized to strike silver coins also had an impact on the "look" of these coins, thus the grade assigned to them today. The introduction of the close collar in 1828 and the steam-powered presses in 1836 greatly changed the look of all business-strike U.S. coins, but silver coins reflected this more than most. Conversely, the use of worn dies resulted in poor detail and subdued luster on many silver issues over the years. Very early Proof U.S. coins—those struck prior to 1836 and especially those struck in open collars—lack the deeply mirrored fields often found on later Proof issues, largely because the method used to polish their dies was so much cruder. Curiously, historians tell us that as late as 1900, Proof U.S. coins were made with screw presses whose giant arms were moved, in each case, by two workmen.

Silver is a fairly hard, durable metal, easier to strike than nickel, but more difficult than gold. A full strike requires correctly spaced dies and sufficient pressure to force the metal into all areas of the dies. Then, too, the planchet must be the correct weight; a lightweight planchet might not emerge fully struck, and a heavy planchet would have to be filed beforehand to remove the excess weight, leaving adjustment marks.

Marks and hairlines pose a particular problem on silver coins. On copper and nickel coinage, these defects tend to be more subdued, especially on coins that are worn or toned. But silver is a bright metal, and problems of this nature are more likely to "shine"—especially in the case of a fresh mark, scratch, nick, or hairline. Toning can hide these problems on silver coins as well, thus reducing the apparent severity of the defect.

Three-Cent Silvers
Star Three-Cent Silver—Type I/Type II/Type III (1851–1873)
Circulated Examples

Although Type I three-cent silvers are not of the normal alloy (75 percent silver, 25 percent copper), they do not look very different from Type II and Type III coins and thus are included in the grading analysis for those types. In 1854, the alloy was changed to the normal 90 percent silver and 10 percent copper mixture and the design was modified for the star three-cent silver Type II and III coins. Lines outline the star and a bundle of arrows was placed below the Roman numerals, a sprig of leaves above. **AU-55/58** coins will have slight wear on the shield and star, and the silvery look of the standard alloy makes the difference between slight friction and incomplete striking easier to determine than for the debased alloy of the Type I coins. Strike is a problem for all three types and the shield is still not complete on some specimens. The reverse will have slight wear on the "C" design and the Roman numerals. The arrows below and the leaves above also are commonly seen with strike weakness, which manifests itself as waviness in these features. In **AU-50/53**, the wear is across the shield and star, with rubbing in the field now apparent. The reverse will have definite wear on the "C" design and the Roman numerals.

The shield and star may not be complete on weakly struck **EF-40/45** coins and may blend into the field. There is wear across the entire star, though the detail should still be strong. The reverse will have wear on the "C" design, the Roman numerals, the arrows, and the leaves. All details, including the lines of most stars (when present), should still be evident, except for localized areas of weakness.

Many **VF-20/35** coins have a completely outlined shield and star, though blended areas may be from strike weakness and not wear. The reverse will have an outlined "C" design and Roman numerals, but the detail in the "C" is not sharp. The arrows, leaves, and stars will be outlined, but with little detail.

F-12/15 Type II and III coins will have the lines around the star blended into the field (on Type I coins the star itself blends into the fields), as will the shield, which will have incomplete detail. The reverse will have some detail visible in the "C" design, arrows, and leaves. The Roman numerals and stars may be weak but are outlined.

If the **VG-8/10** coin is well-struck, there is still some detail in the shield, with some of the lines around the star still visible (the outline of the Type I star will still have slight definition). Rims should be complete, with the lettering, date, and stars complete as well. The "C" design, Roman numerals, arrows, and leaves should be outlined, though with little detail.

The rims may begin to blend into the lettering and the date for **G-4/6** coins. The lines around the star (the outline of the star itself

on Type I examples) may still be partially visible, and the shield should have slight detail. The reverse may have the rim worn into some stars in places and will be worn smooth, with little detail.

AG-3 specimens may have the rims of the obverse worn into half or slightly more of the lettering and the date. On well-struck coins, some star and shield detail may be present. The reverse may show only parts of the design. The **FR-2** coins will have some lettering, a partial date, and a partially outlined star visible (on Type I coins the star will have some definition around its periphery). The reverse may have slight parts of stars, the "C" design, Roman numerals, arrow, and leaves present.

PO-1 coins will have a readable date and may have part of the shield and star. The reverse may be worn completely flat, though some detail may still be evident.

Mint State Examples

MARKS: These small coins are more likely to have hairlines, slide marks, and other minor disturbances than marks. The shield and star are the areas where disturbances are usually found, though the entire obverse surface may have hairlines. Reverse impairments are noted on the Roman numerals, the "C" design, the leaves, and the arrows.

LUSTER: With the return to the normal silver alloy for Type II/III issues, these coins are usually more lustrous than the Type I coins, with most specimens satin-to-frosty in luster. Type I coins also will come in all luster variations, although most are more subdued due to the lower silver content. Some of the low-mintage Type III issues are usually found very frosty, semi-prooflike, or prooflike, often with heavy die polish in the fields. Some of the frosty-luster specimens are seen with about equal amounts of frost on the devices and the fields, while others have the devices frostier than the fields.

STRIKE: The Type II/III coins are usually better struck than the Type I three-cent silver

MS-65 *1852 Type I three-cent silver obverse. This coin is well-struck, original, lustrous, and nearly mark-free.*

MS-65 *1852 Type I three-cent silver reverse. Slight weakness is seen in the stars, otherwise this coin is extremely well-struck, lustrous, and nearly mark-free.*

MS-64 *1851 Type I three-cent silver obverse. This coin is lustrous, with very light scuffing and slight weakness noted on the rim from 2 o'clock to 4 o'clock.*

MS-64 *1851 Type I three-cent silver reverse. As with the obverse, slight weakness is seen on the rim, with most of the stars also flat. Minor marks are noted on the devices and in the field.*

MS-63 *1852 Type I three-cent silver obverse. Localized weakness is noted in the shield, star, and lettering, especially the E of AMERICA. The lines around the rim from 6 o'clock to 10 o'clock are planchet lines that were not obliterated by striking.*

MS-63 *1852 Type I three-cent silver reverse. Weak stars and light planchet lines are noted, with light surface abrasions.*

issues. However, all three types are still found with weakness in the lettering, shield, star, star outlines (when present), Roman numerals, "C" or crescent-shaped device, reverse stars, leaves, and arrows. The leaves and arrows added to the reverse design for the Type II/III issues are often incomplete, with the central part of the arrows being very susceptible to this weakness.

EYE APPEAL: All three types have many spectacular-appearing coins, with brilliant, lightly toned, or brightly toned examples common with the Type III issues and, of course, rarer for the Type I and II coinage. Many of the most spectacular Type III coins, therefore, are brilliant or beautifully toned 1863–1872 issues that have minuscule mintages and were not widely distributed for commerce.

Proofs

HAIRLINES: Since the known Type I Proofs have die striations, these coins must be examined carefully to determine whether the "lines" present are hairlines or polishing lines. If they are only in the fields, they are likely die-polishing lines. The Type I Proofs are excessively rare with only a couple of examples known, so most of the comments to follow relate to Type II/III examples. These Type II/III coins are often found with light-to-moderate hairlines. Both types are found with hairlines and album slide marks. Often, these coins were cleaned, with the resultant hairlines covering the entire coin. Many of these coins, especially the Type II issues, have fine die-polish lines in the fields and should be examined carefully to determine whether the lines are hairlines or die polish.

REFLECTIVITY: Most of the Type II and Type III Proofs have deeply mirrored fields. (The only known Type I examples are not deeply reflective because of excessive die polish.) The Type II/III coins that lack deep reflectivity also are those that have die striations that slightly inhibit reflectivity. As noted before, some of these coins have been cleaned, which dulls the fields, reducing reflectivity. Repeated cleaning sometimes results in fields that are gray and lifeless, the resultant coins resembling business strikes. With the rare, low-mintage Type III issues, many times these cleaned Proofs are sold to less knowledgeable numismatists as the rarer business strikes. Examining the edge for the brilliance and squared-off look of Proof coinage is sometimes the easiest way to determine the status of these coins, since cleaning rarely affects the edge.

STRIKE: All three types are usually well struck. Slight incompleteness is still seen in the central shield, star, and outlines (when present). Reverse striking deficiencies are noted in the stars, leaves (when present), and arrows (when present), with the Roman numerals and the "C" design usually well-struck.

EYE APPEAL: Many of these coins are found with light, medium, or dark toning, and these are attractive Type II and Type III Proofs. Since most of the Type II/III coins have deep reflectivity and are well-struck, the most important attributes are usually the number and size of the hairlines, or lack thereof, and the toning. Some dipped specimens are also very attractive when free of impairments.

Half Dimes
Bust Half Disme (1792)
Circulated Examples

These coins are seen in all circulated grades, as many of them obviously spent many years as pocket pieces, probably some as mementos given directly to the owners by George Washington. In **AU-55/58** there is slight friction on the cheek, tip of the bust, and high points of the hair, mainly around the ear. This hair area is also an area of strike weakness, as are the breast and leg of the flying eagle on the reverse. The breast and leg of the eagle are also the first point of wear, with slight friction also sometimes noted on the eagle's head, neck, and wing feathers. Wear associated with **AU-50/53** is seen in the same areas, though now it is obvious friction easily differentiated from strike weakness. There will also be rubbing in the fields, with the eagle now having obvious wear on the breast, leg, neck, and wing feathers.

Note: As with many early coins, pre-striking adjustment marks are fairly common and are part of eye appeal when determining overall grade. This applies to circulated and Uncirculated examples. The size and placement of the adjustment marks are the main criteria used to determine how much they affect the grade. In VF and below, they are basically ignored, unless they are severe.

EF-40/45 coins will have wear over most of the cheek and most of the hair, save the curls around the outline. The bust will have noticeable flatness and the field will have friction. The eagle will now have wear across the entire body, with some loss of detail. Strong strikes will have some breast and leg feathers visible and nearly all the wing feathers complete.

VF-20/35 coins have from one-half to two-thirds of the hair complete, flattened above the forehead and around the ear, with only the deeper curls present. The cheek and bust will be worn and the eye will have lost some detail. There will be flattened feathers on the breast and leg, with from one-third to two-thirds of the eagle's wing feathers intact. All of the lettering should be clear and readable, but there may be some slight incompleteness.

In F-12/15, there is little detail left on Miss Liberty, with only deep hair curls visible. The eagle will show only slight feather detail. Uneven strikes may result in areas of the rim and lettering that are incomplete.

VG-8/10 coins have an outlined Miss Liberty, blending into the field in some places. There should be a complete legend, though sometimes with some of the lettering weak. The reverse will have an outlined eagle, with some blending and little fine detail. The lettering may be weak in areas of localized weakness.

With coins that grade G-4/6, much leniency is given to localized strike weakness. Miss Liberty will be worn flat, with blending in

spots, as will the reverse eagle. Rims may be worn into the tops of the letters.

Many AG-3 coins will have parts of the rim intact, though the majority of it will be worn into the letters. The head will be mostly complete, and there may be some rough areas. The reverse will have a partial eagle and some of the lettering may be missing. There will be little lettering visible for FR-2 coins, and only part of Miss Liberty will be present. The reverse will have little detail and a partial eagle, lettering is not required, and some coins may be worn nearly completely smooth.

PO-1 specimens will have only sporadic detail, and a readable date is not necessary.

Mint State Examples

MARKS: These examples of our first coinage sometimes are well-preserved, since some were saved as souvenirs. Marks are usually found on the face, hair, and bust, with minor impairments sometimes noted in the fields. Slide marks are sometimes seen on the high points, but these should not be confused with pre-striking planchet adjustment marks. The reverse may have minor marks on the eagle, as well as on the field and lettering.

LUSTER: Most luster variations are seen on this issue, with slightly frosty, frosty, and semi-prooflike luster seen more often than the others. There is not much contrast noted between the devices and fields.

STRIKE: Since the Mint did not have a building or its own presses until March 1793, these coins were struck on inferior blanks under less than ideal conditions. Many of these coins have unevenness of strike, with the hair and the eagle's feathers weak. The hair curls around and below the ear are often flat, with the head, bust, and lettering sometimes also weak. The eagle's breast feathers are often flat, with the wing feathers usually better struck. Sometimes the peripheral lettering and the denomination also are weak. Dentils are sometimes missing on Uncirculated specimens. When the dies were out of parallel, quadrants of the coin may be extremely weak or partially missing.

EYE APPEAL: When found decently struck, minimally marked, and lustrous, this issue is extremely attractive. Finding coins with a decent strike and no planchet adjustment marks is usually more of a problem than finding coins without marks, hairlines, or other surface impairments.

Specimens

HAIRLINES: These ultra-rarities are the souvenirs presented to dignitaries and, as such, have been well-preserved. There may be slight hairlines on some of these from minor mishandling, but most should have nearly pristine surfaces.

REFLECTIVITY: Since these issues were struck before the Mint occupied its first building, the preparatory and striking equipment was not of superior quality. The resultant coins were struck on planchets that were not burnished as heavily as later ones and on a press that was less than ideal. Therefore, reflectivity is not as deep as on silver issues struck at the new Mint.

STRIKE: Intricate hair detail for Miss Liberty and the feather detail on the eagle are noted on the few specimen strikes reported. These coins were obviously given special care when they were struck, though there may be slight incompleteness on the highest points of the hair and the eagle's breast.

EYE APPEAL: These are often spectacular in appearance, notwithstanding the often-inferior planchets and coining press, exhibiting the extra care with which they were struck. These ultra-rarities are the best examples possible under the circumstances, and the reflective surfaces highlight the head and eagle, creating a spectacular-looking coin.

Flowing Hair Half Dime (1794–1795)
Circulated Examples

These tiny coins have slight wear on the cheek, the forehead, and the hair strands around the ear for **AU-55/58**, though these

are also the general areas of strike weakness. The reverse will have slight friction on the eagle's neck, breast, legs, and upper parts of the wing feathers. The wreath will have slight friction on the highest points, mainly the leaves. Worn to **AU-50/53**, the friction is fairly easy to distinguish from strike weakness. There will be friction across the face and neck, and most of the hair will display some wear, as will the field. The eagle and the wreath will now have definite wear.

With grades **EF-40/45**, the hair strands will still be distinct, though worn. The entire face and neck area will have wear, as will the field. Some of the stars will still have detail, though this is not necessary for the grades, as some coins may have flatness even in Uncirculated grades. The reverse will have feather detail only on strong strikes, with the highest leaves now worn flat with slight blending.

There will be from one-third to two-thirds of the hair strands still visible for **VF-20/35** coins, strongest mostly in the lower part of the hair. The wear will now blend most of the hair details into the face, and most of the stars will be flat. Rims should be complete, though unevenly struck coins may have weakness. The eagle may have no fine detail on poorly struck coins and up to half the feathers present on good strikes. Leaves of the wreath will be worn smooth, and some will blend into the adjacent devices.

F-12/15 coins may have from slight to nearly half of the lower hair details still present, though poorly struck coins may only have the back strands. The head, LIBERTY, and the stars should be complete. Rims should be complete, except for localized weakness. There may or may not be wing feathers present, depending on the original strike, but the eagle and wreath should be outlined, though indistinctly.

Although marks are usually seen on all circulated (and most Uncirculated) examples, these coins should have only small marks. Even in **VG-8/10**, large marks are not acceptable. The head should be outlined, with only the back strands of hair visible. Rims, stars, and lettering should be complete, save for unevenly struck coins. The eagle and wreath will be worn nearly smooth, with only slight detail.

G-4/6 specimens will have Miss Liberty worn smooth, with parts blending into the field. The rims probably will have several indistinct areas, possibly blending almost to some of the stars. LIBERTY and the date should be clear, save for uneven strikes. The eagle is worn smooth, and the wreath will blend into the adjacent devices and field. Rims will touch some of the lettering.

With the **AG-3** grade, there may be some stars totally missing and part of the date may be gone. Miss Liberty will blend into the field in several areas, with little detail remaining. The reverse will have areas where the lettering is completely gone. The eagle and wreath will be incomplete in places and will have no fine detail. **FR-2** coins will have a readable date and some parts of the head, LIBERTY, and the stars will be present. The reverse may be worn smooth.

A **PO-1** coin must have a readable date, with the head partly visible. The reverse may be worn smooth.

Mint State Examples

MARKS: These coins are usually found with no more than light marks, with hairlines and other minor impairments seen with about the same regularity. Obverse marking is easily noticed on the face and neck, with the field also occasionally noted with marks. The hair will "hide" light marks or ones that go with the flow of the hair. Marks on the reverse are usually noted on the eagle, though the wreath and the small open field occasionally have some disturbances.

LUSTER: All luster variations are seen for the two years of issue, with more prooflike 1794 coins seen and more frosty-luster coins for 1795, plus numerous satin-to-slightly frosty-luster coins seen for both years. The satin-luster coins have a sheen unlike the larger-denomination issues, a more delicate-looking surface perhaps imparted because of the small size.

STRIKE: Most coins from this era have central or peripheral weakness, the hair around the ear for the obverse and the neck, breast, and leg for the reverse. This ranges from slight weakness to extreme flatness for the hair, face, stars, LIBERTY, and date for the obverse. The reverse may have flat wing feathers, peripheral lettering, and areas of the wreath, as well as the eagle's head, breast, and leg.

EYE APPEAL: There are incredible specimens of both 1794 and 1795 issues, with brilliant, lightly toned, and deeply toned surfaces. These coins are attractive, with satin, frosty, semi-prooflike, or prooflike luster when the surfaces are mark-free and well-struck. Eye appeal often hinges on attributes that are so superior that slight weakness of strike would be offset by blazing luster and vivid original toning.

Specimens

HAIRLINES: These first half dimes were struck in the Mint's own building on its own equipment and would have been highly prized when acquired in the year of issue. The mirrored fields are very delicate, and any contact with almost any object will leave hairlines or other impairments. Light wiping no doubt caused many of the hairlines seen.

REFLECTIVITY: The surfaces of these coins are more reflective than those of the 1792 Bust half disme, but not as reflective as those of the Capped Bust half dimes. Some of the 1794 coins have near-Proof quality surfaces, with a slight watery look as seen on close-collar Proofs.

STRIKE: Specimen-strike Flowing Hair half dimes have chiseled hair and feather detail. There should be only the slightest incompleteness on the highest points of the hair and the eagle's head, breast, and legs. The stars, date, wreath, and lettering should be extra-sharp, with only the slightest incompleteness noted.

EYE APPEAL: These coins are the pinnacle of the Mint's first half dime production. Miss Liberty's flowing hair and the eagle's feathers are super-sharp on these special coins, and when combined with nearly hairline-free original surfaces, make these miniature works of art.

Draped Bust Half Dime—Small Eagle/ Heraldic (Large) Eagle (1796–1805)

These diminutive cousins to the Draped Bust Dime are so similar to them and are graded in essentially the same way. Therefore, one can find the grading analysis under the dime section in the Draped Bust coinage section (1796–1807).

Capped Bust Half Dime (1829–1837)

In 1829, the reintroduction of the half dime, not struck since 1805, came one year after the first use of the close collar, which resulted in a raised rim, allowing better protection of the devices and fields. Therefore, they are graded like the Capped Bust dimes struck in close collars and their analysis is found under the dimes in the Capped Bust Large Dentils/Small Dentils coinage section (1809–1837).

Liberty Seated Half Dime—No Stars/ Stars/Stars with Arrows (1837–1859)

No Stars, Stars, and Stars with Arrows coinage spans decades, and though the design was modified several times creating these new types, the basic grading of these coins remains very similar. Also, the grading for these half dimes is nearly identical to their dime counterparts. See Liberty Seated dimes No Stars/Stars/Stars with Arrows for the grading of the same type half dimes.

Liberty Seated Half Dimes—Legend (1860–1873)

Although similar to the earlier Liberty Seated coins, the Legend-type half dime is graded slightly differently, since the plain Gobrecht wreath is replaced by the intricate cereal wreath and the legend is moved to the obverse, replacing the peripheral stars. However, the half dimes are graded like the corresponding Legend dimes, and their analysis is found under the dime section with the Liberty Seated Dimes Legend/Arrows varieties.

Dimes
Draped Bust Dime—Small Eagle/ Heraldic (Large) Eagle (1796–1807)
Circulated Examples

AU-55/58 Draped Bust dimes have slight wear on the cheek, the hair around the ear, the bust, and the shoulder. (As previously mentioned under half dimes, the criteria for dimes also applies to their smaller brethren – the Draped Bust half dime. One can simply substitute the word half in front of dime at any time for these two types.) Almost all dates have coins with weakly struck centers. The central hair detail and the head, breast, and leg area of the eagle on Small Eagle coins are sometimes weak (the shield on the Heraldic coins is also an area of weakness, as are the adjacent wing feathers around the shield). The reverse will have slight friction on the wreath, head, breast, and leg of the Small Eagle coins, with the breast, shield, clouds, tail feathers, and tip of the wing feathers having slight wear for the Heraldic type. In **AU-50/53**, wear is now apparent on the same areas, with rubbing now in the obverse field in front of Miss Liberty. The reverse field is well-protected; thus only the devices mentioned usually show friction.

With wear to **EF-40/45**, there is friction now obvious on the face, hair, and bust, with the hair around the ear flat. Small Eagle reverse coins will have most wing feather detail, though the breast feathers are usually flat. Wreath detail is still very clear, with only the highest leaves flattened. Wear on Heraldic reverse coins is seen on the head, breast, clouds, shield and tips of the wing feathers, with most of the latter still present. Unevenly struck coins are sometimes seen, with areas of the legend weak or partially missing, slightly affecting the grade.

VF-20/35 specimens will have from one-third to two-thirds of the hair detail, depending upon the grade level of **VF** and the original striking quality. The bust area is often worn smooth in this grade. Small Eagle

MS-65 *1861 Legend half dime obverse. A well-struck, lustrous coin with surface contact marks and abrasions.*

MS-65 *1861 Legend half dime reverse. Good strike with a few light marks and abrasions. A mark is noted on the corn husk, but the apparent "marks" in and around the* ME *of* DIME *are clash marks from the obverse die.*

MS-64 *1866 Legend half dime obverse. A well-struck coin with a few surface marks, though none is major.*

MS-64 *1866 Legend half dime reverse. Slight scuffing is noted on the wreath and in the central field.*

MS-63 *1868 Legend half dime obverse. Light marks are scattered around the body and in the field.*

MS-63 *1868 Legend half dime reverse. No severe marks are seen but light, scattered ones appear on the wreath and in the field.*

coins will have a flat head, breast, and leg, with up to one-half of the wing feathers present. The wreath will have flat leaves that are mostly separate from each other. On Heraldic specimens, the shield will have blending of the vertical and horizontal stripes, with up to one-half of the wing feathers visible. The clouds, arrows, olive branch, and tail feathers will be worn, with blending apparent.

The hair detail on **F-12/15** coins ranges from a few strands visible to about one-third present, depending upon the original strike. The rims should be complete in this grade, except for uneven strikes. Small Eagle coins will have a flat wreath, with blending and little fine detail, and a worn eagle with a few feathers still showing. On well-struck Heraldic reverse coins, up to one-third or slightly more of the wing feathers may still be present. The clouds and shield will show only slight separation and are mostly worn smooth.

VG-8/10 coins have little detail on Miss Liberty, sometimes with the very back hair curls still intact. Rims may show slight areas of incompleteness. On Small Eagle–type reverses, the wreath and eagle will be worn smooth with almost no fine detail. Wing feathers of the Heraldic coins may show sporadic detail. The clouds, shield, arrows, and olive branch will have much blending and are worn almost flat.

Many **G-4/6** coins will have incomplete rims, partly due to uneven striking and partly due to wear. Miss Liberty will have little detail and may blend into the field. Stars should be visible, except in areas of rim weakness. Although the wreath and the eagle of the Small Eagle reverse are worn very flat, there still may be slight detail in the eagle and some separation in the wreath. The reverse rims of the Heraldic type will be worn into the tops of the lettering, with some letters missing in the areas of rim weakness. The clouds, eagle, shield, arrows, and olive branch will be quite worn, with slight fine detail.

AG-3 coins have a partial date, LIBERTY, and stars, with a head that blends into the field.

The reverse will have wear into the lettering for both types, with the central devices worn smooth. For **FR-2** coins, that wear will obliterate part or all of the stars and LIBERTY, though a partial date must show. The reverse may have only part of the eagle present for both types, with most of the lettering worn away.

A **PO-1** coin will have a discernible date and detail to determine type. The reverse is often worn completely away.

Mint State Examples

MARKS: Sometimes the incompleteness of strike seen on many of these coins is mistaken for tiny marks when the granular effect of weak strike is present. Larger marks are not likely to be mistaken for incomplete striking and are mainly seen on the face, neck, bust, and open field. The hair may camouflage tiny marks and nicks, especially those in line with the hair flow. On the reverse of the Small Eagle type, marks are mainly noted on the eagle, wreath, small open areas, and lettering. With little open field area on the Heraldic type, marks are usually found on the eagle, shield, and clouds, though the lettering, other devices, and open areas are also seen with disturbances.

LUSTER: One would expect the luster to be diminished, since many of these coins are weakly struck, but all luster variations are seen. Even deeply prooflike specimens are seen, though they still may have slight incompleteness. Although most specimens of both types have satin-to-frosty luster, semi-prooflike and prooflike coins are much more common for the Small Eagle type.

STRIKE: As with the half dimes, Draped Bust dimes often are softly struck in the central areas. Most dimes are not as flat as the half dimes, however, usually with only slight weakness seen on the obverse hair covering the ear, bust, and drapery. For Small Eagle coins, the eagle's head, breast, and leg may have less-than-full feather detail, though not usually as "pancake" flat as the half dimes. Heraldic reverses may show weakness in the clouds, stars, head, ribbon, neck, shield, inner wing, tip of the wings, tail, and claws. Other localized weakness is sometimes noted for the stars, date, LIBERTY, and other parts of Miss Liberty, such as the eyes, nose, upper hair, and lower hair. On the reverse, localized weakness is noted in the wreath on Small Eagle coins and the arrows and leaves of Heraldic coins. Quadrants of the obverse and corresponding reverse areas may be weak due to improperly aligned dies. Some parts of the coins, such as dentils, stars, and lettering, may be missing, even for Uncirculated coins.

EYE APPEAL: These first examples of U.S. half dime and dime coinage are occasionally found with all attributes positive. Well-struck, lustrous, minimally marked examples are available, especially for the 1796 Small Eagle type and 1805 and 1807 Heraldic type. Strike is often the one area where these coins are lacking, as their small size makes marks less of a problem, and lustrous coins are fairly available.

Specimens

HAIRLINES: There probably will be light-to-moderate hairlines on these ultra-rarities, the first half dimes and dimes struck by the fledgling Mint. Cleaning was commonplace, and though these coins would have been highly prized, they may not exist in pristine, original condition. The fields are very delicate and are easily marred by the slightest contact.

REFLECTIVITY: These coins are as deeply mirrored as the Mint's equipment and technology could make them. These open-collar strikes are not as reflective as close-collar strikes, but will have deeper surfaces than prooflike Mint State examples. There should be frost on the devices and lettering that will contrast with the mirrored fields.

STRIKE: There are no Heraldic specimen strikes known for either the half dimes or dimes. For the Small Eagle type, the hair, bust, and drapery detail for Miss Liberty is exceptional, with only the slightest incompleteness. The reverse may have slight weakness on the head, neck, breast, and leg, but

feather detail should be extremely sharp. All other devices, the date, and the lettering should be bold, with only the slightest incompleteness noted.

EYE APPEAL: These coins are the first examples of the Mint's dime production, and special care was obviously given to striking them. The strike, surface, and look of these coins are spectacular, with preservation being the one area where some problems are found. The delicate nature of the surfaces, plus the propensity to clean coins, makes field disturbances the main area of concern. When these areas are positive, the coins are incredible examples of our nation's first dime coinage.

Capped Bust Dime—Large Dentils (Large Size-Open Collar) / Small Dentils (Small Size-Close Collar) (1809–1837)

Circulated Examples

Open-collar, Large Dentils dimes do not have the high protective rims of the close-collar, Small Dentils coins, though by tradition they have been graded basically the same since they are almost identical. (The Capped Bust half dimes, as noted under the half dime section, are graded like the Small Dentil dimes.) In lower grades there are slight differences in the dimes because of the rims, but in **AU-55/58** they are graded the same, with slight friction on the cap, the cheek, the hair below the ribbon, the hair around the ear, and the bust. Strike weakness in the center of the coin mainly affects the curls of hair below the ear, along with the clasp and drapery. The reverse will have slight friction on the tops of the wing, neck, shield, leg, and claws, with strike weakness noted for the neck, shield, leg, and claws. In **AU-50/55**, the amount of wear is enough to distinguish it from strike weakness with the field also rubbed, mostly in front of Miss Liberty. The reverse will have obvious wear on the neck, leg, and claws, with slight wear on the motto, shield, and top of the wings.

Though striking weakness is noted on quite a few Capped Bust dimes, especially the pre-1828 open-collar strikes, in **EF-40/45** the amount of wear is the main focus for the grade. Unless the strike is horrendous, weakness will affect the grade only slightly. The cap, cheek, and bust will have noticeable wear and nearly all of the hair curls will be flat. Stars will have most of the crosshatch lines visible, but many open-collar coins have localized weakness, mainly from out-of-parallel dies, which cause flat stars. The reverse will have flatness in the top of the wings, neck, leg, and claws, with wear on the high points of the wing feathers. The fields of both sides will have obvious wear.

On well-struck **VF-20/35** coins, there still is considerable hair detail present, but all of the curls will have flatness on the high points. The cap and drapery will have blending. Stars may have some lines still present, and the open-collar coins may still exhibit the hole in the center. The reverse will have strong wing detail still present on well-struck coins, with the neck and leg feathers mostly flat. The shield may have some separation in the lines, with the claws worn flat but separate.

F-12/15 graded coins will have some recessed cap and hair detail showing, with the cheek and bust worn quite smooth. LIBERTY should be full, though some of the letters may show weakness and the stars will be worn flat. The reverse will have from one-third to one-half of the wing feathers showing some detail, though mostly worn flat. Shield lines and claws will blend into the adjacent devices and fields. On open-collar strikes, the dentils may be weak or missing. The rims on close-collar coins should still be bold.

With wear to **VG-8/10**, the head will be worn mostly smooth, with a few letters of LIBERTY still visible. Rims of open-collar coins may be worn into the dentils in spots. The stars should be outlined but very flat. The reverse will have an eagle that has only slight detail and may be slightly blended. The lettering should be full, though some of the motto may be missing.

On close-collar half dimes and dimes, the **G-4/6** coins may still have full rims, but open-collar dimes will often have the rim worn to

the tips of some stars. The head should be outlined though slightly worn into the field. Reverse rims of open-collar coins will touch the tops of some of the lettering and, as with the obverses, close-collar coins may still exhibit fairly strong rims. The eagle will be worn totally flat, with only some slight shield detail. The motto, claws, olive branch, and arrows will have only outlines, with slight detail.

AG-3 coins of both types will have rims that are worn into the stars and date of the obverse. The head will be worn into the field. The reverse will have the eagle blended into the field and the rims worn into the lettering. **FR-2** coins will have a very worn head, possibly with no stars present, and a partial date. The reverse will have minimal detail, with possibly all of the peripheral lettering missing.

PO-1 specimens must have a readable date and slight obverse detail, though the reverse may be gone.

Mint State Examples

MARKS: Both types are usually seen with only minor marks, but severe marks and disturbances are seen. Light album slide marks, nicks, hairlines, scuffs, and minor scratches are as common on these coins as are marks, especially on the obverse, with the cap, face, neck, and bust often exhibiting one or more of these impairments. The obverse field, especially in front of the face, will also often have disturbances, as will the hair, though the curls camouflage some light marks. The eagle and shield usually have most of the reverse detractions, with the field, other devices, and lettering occasionally affected.

LUSTER: Most of the Large Dentils coins have satin-to-slightly frosty luster, and the Small Dentils coins are usually found with slightly frosty-to-very frosty luster. However, every luster variation is seen for both types, with more semi-prooflike and prooflike coins seen for the Small Dentils. Some coins have frosted devices, along with frosty, semi-prooflike, or prooflike fields. In some in-

MS-65 *1825 Large Dentils Capped Bust dime obverse. A well-struck lustrous coin with original even toning, with no noticeable marks or abrasions. The hair curls above the clasp are slightly weak, common with open-collar strikes.*

MS-65 *1825 Large Dentils Capped Bust dime reverse. This beautiful example has lovely toning, with near mark-free surfaces. As with the obverse, slight weakness is noted on the top right part of the shield and on the feathers above it.*

MS-64 *1835 Small Dentils Capped Bust dime obverse. A well-struck close-collar striking with light, even toning over surfaces, with light marks and scuffing.*

MS-64 *1835 Small Dentils Capped Bust dime reverse. This coin is nearly fully struck, with only slight surface contact, for example, above and to the left of the eagle's right wing (left wing to the observer).*

MS-63 *1821 Large Dentils Capped Bust dime obverse. A few light scuffs and marks are noted on this fairly well-struck coin. Localized weakness is noted for a few stars and most of the dentils on the right side.*

MS-63 *1821 Large Dentils Capped Bust dime reverse. On this coin, slightly more weakness is noted on the reverse. Along with most of the dentils on the right side, the arrow feathers and eagle's claws are very flat.*

stances, the deeply prooflike specimens with frosted devices are so spectacular that they have been mistakenly sold as Proofs.

STRIKE: Although they are nearly identical in design, the striking quality of Large Dentils and Small Dentils Capped Bust dimes is quite different. The Large Dentils coins, struck in open-collar dies, have obverse weakness almost always seen on the stars, the cap, the hair above the eye, the hair around the ear, the hair down the back of the neck, the clasp, the drapery, and the bust. Reverse weakness is noted on the motto, especially the first few letters opposite the bust of the obverse, the denomination, and the peripheral lettering. The eagle often has weakness in the head, neck, shield, feathers around the shield, upper wing feathers, leg, claws, leaves, and arrow feathers. Flat, stretched dentils are commonplace, as the striking process often elongated these devices. The Small Dentils coins, produced in close collars, are much better struck. The same areas of striking weakness are noted, though to a lesser degree, and the dentils are almost always uniform, not elongated. (There were leftover obverse and reverse Large Dentils dies used in 1828 and 1829 with the new close collar; the coins struck from these dies have sharper detail than do open-collar strikes. The dentils are not quite as uniform as on the Small Dentils coins, but they are not stretched or elongated as with open-collar strikes.)

EYE APPEAL: As with the half dimes, Capped Bust dimes are found with lustrous surfaces, minimal marks, and attractive brilliant, or toned, fields. Although the Large Dentils strike is not usually as sharp as for the Small Dentils coins, both types are found well struck. There are satin, frosty, semi-prooflike, and prooflike coins seen for both types, and when any of these luster types are combined with minimally marked surfaces and attractive toning, the resulting coins are great examples of Capped Bust dimes.

Proofs

HAIRLINES: These coins are typical of most early Proofs and are usually found with light-to-moderate hairlines, slide marks, and other disturbances. The low rims of the Large Dentils, open-collar coins offer little protection for the fields and devices, resulting in impairments on most of these coins. The Small Dentils, close-collar strikes have high protective rims (the half dimes also have this feature), but most of these coins often have some impairments, though more of these are seen with light disturbances. Both types have exposed flat areas of the head, resulting in hairlines, album slide marks, and other detractions on the cheek and bust.

REFLECTIVITY: The Small Dentils, close-collar strikings are usually extremely reflective, often with the watery look of later Proofs. The Large Dentils, open-collar coins may have die polish and/or burnishing lines still evident, as well as small field areas with frost; thus the reflectivity is not as deep for these coins. Both types usually have frosted devices and lettering contrasting with the mirrored fields. On a few of both types of these coins, there may be a tiny field area that lacks the mirrored look. Also, this is very common with the half dimes, as the smaller the die, the more difficult it becomes to fully polish all the field areas.

STRIKE: Proofs from the Large Dentils, open-collar dies are not as well struck as those from the Small Dentils, close-collar dies. Slight incompleteness is usually noted for the Large Dentils coins on the highest hair curls, drapery, and bust on the obverse. Reverse weakness may be noted in the neck, shield, inner wing feathers, leg, and claws. The close-collar, Small Dentils Proofs also have higher, flatter rims and when viewed from the edge, are squared off, with little beveling. Only slight incompleteness is noted for the close-collar strikings (both half dimes and dimes), though these areas will be the same as on the open-collar strikings.

EYE APPEAL: Although the Large Dentils coins do not have as deeply mirrored surfaces as the Small Dentils coins, and occasionally have slight weaknesses, the Proofs are usually still spectacular. There are examples of both types with minimal hairlines, combined with the usually frosted devices and lettering, which make these Proofs the most attractive Capped Bust coinage. The spirited bidding for these examples at auctions is evidence of the dealer's, investor's, and collector's high esteem for these little jewels.

Liberty Seated Dime—No Stars/Stars/Stars with Arrows (1837–1860)

Circulated Examples

Although these coins were modified to create the Liberty Seated Stars and Stars with Arrows coin types, the basic grading remains very similar to that of the No Stars type. As noted under the half dimes, the grading standards for the identical types of half dimes are basically the same as for the dimes. Therefore, one only needs substitute the word half in front of dime to learn the criteria for the three types of half dimes. For **AU-55/58** coins, the wear is first noted on the head, breast, and upper legs of Miss Liberty. Sometimes the head, shoulder area, and central area, including the shield, are weakly struck, so these areas must be examined carefully to determine whether there is really wear or just weakness of strike. The reverse will have slight wear on the high points of the leaves and the bow. The upper leaves, bow, and central lettering are areas that sometimes exhibit striking weakness so, as with the obverse, flatness in these spots should be examined closely. Obviously, if the central and lower leaves are very sharp and the upper leaves are flat, strike weakness is the reason, not wear. **AU-50/53** specimens will have more noticeable wear on the head, breast, and upper legs, with wear now apparent in the field and on the stars. The reverse will have more wear on the leaves and bow, though there should be separation and nearly full detail except for localized areas of weakness.

EF-40/45 grades will have wear that now includes the arms, shield, and lower part of the legs, plus the stars, when present. The stars, when present and except for weakly struck ones, will have only slight wear and should

have complete crosshatch lines. The field now has obvious wear and only the protected areas may still exhibit luster. Reverse wear will now be more apparent and the top leaves may have lost some detail, though they should still be separate from the adjacent leaves.

With wear to **VF-20/35**, the head, breast, and gown folds are now worn into adjacent areas. LIBERTY should still be strong, except on coins that are weakly struck in the shield area. The lines of the shield will be quite worn, though most will still be separate, with the stars, when present, still showing some of the lines. Leaves on the reverse will have flat areas, but most will still be distinct and sharp. The bow will be worn; however, the knot will be clear save for coins that are poorly struck in that area.

F-12/15 graded coins will have most stars flat, when present, and detail still present in the deeply recessed areas of the gown. LIBERTY should still be present, though it may have some weak letters. Wear into these grades will have the top leaves flat and only the adjacent ones will show any detail.

A few letters or partial letters of LIBERTY will still be present in grades **VG-8/10**. Miss Liberty will have only slight detail, mainly in the deep folds of the gown and some lines of the shield. The rims should be complete, though many of the dentils may be worn together. The reverse will have the leaves and bow outlined, but little fine detail will be evident and many of the leaves will be blended together.

G-4/6 coins will have an outlined Miss Liberty with almost no fine detail, and the rims may be worn slightly into the field, with most of the dentils now gone. The reverse will have nearly all of the leaves blended together with almost no fine detail. Rims may touch the tops of some of the lettering.

Although **AG-3** coins will have a visible Miss Liberty, the edges may be worn into the field in places and some of the stars, when present, may be missing. The reverse will have wear into the peripheral lettering, with up to half or slightly more of the letters missing. **FR-2** specimens will have only a partial Miss Liberty and all the stars, when present, may be worn away. The reverse may have some of the peripheral lettering present, though this is not necessary. The wreath will be quite worn and some of the central lettering may be incomplete.

The **PO-1** coin will have a readable date, but Miss Liberty may be mostly incomplete. Some reverse detail may be present, though this is not necessary.

Mint State Examples

MARKS: For all three types, marks and other distractions are seen on Miss Liberty, as well as in the surrounding field, with disturbances in the field especially noticeable on the No Stars type. As with most small coins, tiny hairlines, slide marks, minor scuffing, and other detractions are equally as prevalent on these coins as are marks. The reverses have the most noticeable marks in the open field, with the wreath, lettering, and mint mark also found with impairments. As with the obverse, but not to as great a degree, there are often hairlines or other minor disturbance as well.

LUSTER: Although all luster variations are seen on these coins, the Philadelphia and San Francisco issues usually have frosty surfaces and the New Orleans coins have satin-to-frosty surfaces. **(Note: Half dimes of these types were struck only at Philadelphia and New Orleans.)**

Some of the low-mintage Philadelphia coins are usually found with semi-prooflike or prooflike surfaces, though common Philadelphia and New Orleans issues are also found with these luster variations. Many of the poorly struck New Orleans issues have a flat-to-satin luster, but some of these weakly struck coins are sometimes seen with semi-prooflike luster.

STRIKE: Liberty Seated dimes struck at Philadelphia and San Francisco usually show nearly full detail, with the New Orleans issues usually showing some weakness. Obverse weakness is noted for the dentils, stars,

when present, head, breast, upper leg, shield, and foot. Some coins may have only the head weak, others only the foot, and others may have all of these areas weak. New Orleans coins, as noted, often have many, or all, of these areas showing incompleteness. Reverses often have weakness in the dentils, peripheral lettering, wreath, including the bow, denomination, and mint mark, when present. New Orleans issues often have the top leaves and the bow of the wreath incomplete.

EYE APPEAL: Superb examples are found for all three types—the No Stars, Stars, and Stars with Arrows. There are some dates and mint marks that are not found in superb condition, but that is true with any long-lived series. Blazing luster, minimal marks, good strikes, and attractive brilliant or toned surfaces are found on many coins. Collectors from the nineteenth century should be commended for preserving these high-grade specimens, for many of these coins have obviously been carefully handled as they were passed from generation to generation.

Proofs

HAIRLINES: These small coins, as with most early Proof issues, are often found with light-to-moderate hairlines and occasionally with fairly heavy ones. Most hairlines and other minor impairments are usually noted in the obverse field, though the figure of Miss Liberty also is sometimes found with hairlines, slide marks, or other detractions, mainly on the breasts and right knee. Reverse hairlines and other disturbances are found across the lettering and in the open field, but rarely are they more severe than the obverse impairments.

REFLECTIVITY: Most of the coins struck in 1854 and later have the deep reflectivity associated with modern Proof coinage, especially the watery look associated with later issues. Frosted devices are commonplace among these later issues, which contrast with the mirrored fields, making the surfaces appear even deeper. The Proofs struck prior to 1854 are often found with light-to-moderate die polish, creating fields that are mirrored but sometimes not as deeply reflective as those of the later coins.

STRIKE: Striking quality for Proof Liberty Seated dimes varies according to the era. Those struck in 1854 and later are of an even more exceptional quality than those struck before 1854. More incompleteness is noted on the highest points of the earlier coins such as the dentils, head, stars, when present, drapery folds, shield, and wreath. The 1854 and later strikings are usually fully struck, or nearly so, with only very slight incompleteness.

EYE APPEAL: Although the quality of the early issues is not quite as high as that seen on the 1856 through 1859 Proofs, there are still many great-looking examples from the inception of the Liberty Seated design. Even though they are quite rare, some No Stars and Stars with Arrows coins have superb surfaces and attractive toning. These, along with the Stars specimens, are the pinnacle of the Mint's production of Liberty Seated dimes from 1837 through 1860.

Liberty Seated Dimes—Legend/ Legend With Arrows (1860–1891)

Circulated Examples

The Legend type is graded slightly differently from the Stars type, since the legend from the reverse replaces the stars around the obverse. The plain Gobrecht wreath is replaced by the intricate cereal wreath on the reverse. Of course, half dimes of the Legend type are graded the same as the dimes and their criteria are found in this analysis. For **AU-55/58** coins, wear is first noted on the head, breast, and upper legs. The lower part of the shield, the head, and sometimes the central area show strike weakness, as well as slight friction. The reverse will have full detail on the wreath, with slight wear on the highest points. The reverse may show slight strike weakness in the wreath's top and the bow. If the lower part of the shield is weak, the corresponding area of the reverse, the wreath's upper left part, will have a dished effect, obscuring much of the detail. In **AU-50/53** grades, the wear is now apparent and the fields will also have noticeable friction.

The reverse will have more wear on the wreath, with some flattening of the topmost detail.

EF-40/45 coins now have wear on the head, breast, arms, legs, shield, and gown, but the fine detail is still very sharp. The wreath will still be sharp, though the topmost detail will be worn and slightly flattened. On some coins, strike weakness may obliterate localized areas of the wreath.

VF-20/35 graded coins will have a full LIBERTY except for weakly struck specimens, and the recessed detail of the gown will still be present. The wreath will still show most detail, though the top parts will be quite flat, especially in the lower **VF** grades.

Coins graded **F-12/15** usually have a full LIBERTY, but some letters may be weak or missing on lightly struck ones. The deeply recessed areas of Miss Liberty, under the arms and below the legs, still exhibit detail. The head and breast area are very worn and blended. The reverse will have the high points of the wreath worn flat, with the recessed parts showing some detail.

Worn to **VG-8/10**, the figure will have only the deep recessed areas showing detail, with the legs still having separation. LIBERTY will have some letters or parts of letters visible. The reverse wreath will be worn flat, with the deeper recessed areas having slight, though fuzzy, detail.

G-4/6 specimens will have only slight detail in Miss Liberty and the shield. The obverse rim will be worn into the dentils, though not into the field. The reverse will have a completely flat, boldly outlined wreath, with the rim worn deeply into all dentils and slightly into the field in areas.

With **AG-3** coins, the rim will be worn into the letters and possibly the date, with Miss Liberty having only the deep areas with detail and some areas blending. Rims of the reverse will be worn into the field, the wreath worn flat, blending into the field, with some central lettering weak or missing. **FR-2** coins will have some or all of the obverse legend and date missing, with part of Miss Liberty present. The reverse may only show part of the wreath and the central lettering may be partially or totally missing.

A **PO-1** grade requires a readable date and some obverse detail. Reverses may show slight or no detail.

Mint State Examples

MARKS: These small coins are found with scuffing or other minor impairments as often as they are found with marks. The obverse figure and field are the main areas where detractions are found, but the peripheral lettering is sometimes affected. Album slide marks are sometimes found on Miss Liberty's breast and right knee. The reverse has much less open field area than the previous Stars types, so marks are commonly found on the wreath or the denomination. Slight scuffing or small marks are still seen in the field—above and below the denomination, as well as on the tiny open areas between the wreath and rims.

LUSTER: All luster variations are seen on these coins, though the common Philadelphia and San Francisco issues usually have satin-to-frosty luster. New Orleans coins were struck in the first and last years of the Legend type, 1860 and 1891, both dates showing a satin-to-semi-prooflike luster. The early Carson City issues, 1871 to 1874, are very rare and seldom encountered in Uncirculated condition, though they are likely to be semi-prooflike or prooflike when found. The later Carson City coins, 1875 to 1878, are usually found satin-to-very frosty, but these too are sometimes found semi-prooflike and prooflike. The rarer Philadelphia coins usually are found with frosty-to-prooflike luster, sometimes with blazing luster accompanied by frosted devices. The San Francisco coins that are elusive in Uncirculated condition often are found with the usual satin-to-frosty luster of the common issues.

STRIKE: With more powerful presses in use at the various minting facilities, one would expect nothing but fully struck Liberty Seated Legend dimes. Although there are many well-struck coins, weakness is still noted. Obverse incompleteness is noted on the peripheral lettering, head, breast, drapery folds, foot, rock, and lower part of the shield. Reverse weakness is seen in the upper left part of the wreath, opposite the rock and lower part of the shield of the obverse. Some coins, however, may have weakness in the entire wreath, including the bow and the denomination. Dentil weakness is not as prevalent as with the previous types. New Orleans issues, 1860–1891, San Francisco, 1863–1891, and Carson City coins, 1870–1878, are usually weaker in these areas than Philadelphia coinage. There are also some striking abnormalities for some issues, such as those resulting from the heavily rusted obverse die used for some 1876 Carson City issues.

EYE APPEAL: Blazing luster, minimal marks, and full strikes abound for Legend dimes of most dates, though a few dates are not found pristine. Many Philadelphia and San Francisco issues are found in superb condition, often with spectacular toning, but only the common Carson City coins are usually seen in the highest grades. The Arrows type is not quite as rare as for the other denominations, as there was a hoard of spectacular 1874 dimes with blazing luster and very attractive toning.

Proofs

HAIRLINES: As with the Legend half dimes, the dimes are sometimes found with nearly pristine surfaces. When hairlines are present on the obverse, they are usually light-to-moderate and are mainly found in the field. Miss Liberty is found impaired on coins with heavier hairlines and other detractions, but album slide marks are usually confined to the breasts and right knee. Although there is little open field area on the reverse, the area above and below the denomination is found with impairments. The wreath and denomination may have hairlines and other disturbances.

REFLECTIVITY: Most of these coins have deeply mirrored fields and usually have heavily frosted devices and lettering. Almost all of these coins have the watery look associated with the post-1854 Proof coinage. Several years are found with die polish, impairing reflectivity, though these are not as prevalent as in the Legend half dime series.

STRIKE: Proof Legend dimes are almost always well struck. There are coins seen with slight weakness in the rock and lower shield on the obverse and the corresponding upper left part of the wreath on the reverse. Some issues also exhibit flatness in the head and the corresponding area of the reverse, the bow.

EYE APPEAL: Nearly every date, 1860–1891, is found in pristine condition. The Mint had excellent technical capability in this era and produced many outstanding coins. Deeply mirrored, watery-looking coins are found minimally hairlined, with brilliant, lightly toned, medium toned, or vividly toned surfaces.

Liberty Head (Barber) Dime (1892–1916)

The obverses of Barber dimes, quarters, and half dollars are all graded essentially the same, but of course the reverse of the dime is nearly identical to that of the Legend dime. The reverses of the quarter and half dollar are newly designed, with the eagle's wings raised instead of folded. Therefore one can find the criteria for Barber dime obverses under the Barber half dollar section and the criteria for their reverses under the Liberty Seated-Legend/Legend with Arrows section. Of course, the dimes have the legend around the periphery of the obverse, while the quarters and half dollars have 13 stars circling the head. This is a very minor difference and the grading of the three denominations obverses is not affected by this difference.

Winged Liberty Head (Mercury) Dime (1916–1945)

Circulated Examples

AU-55/58 Winged Liberty Head, or Mercury, dimes have slight friction on the cheek, along the top of the hair down the back of the face, the top of the wing, and the hair above where the ear would be. Reverse wear is found on the top, center, and bottom horizontal bands and diagonal bands. In **AU-50/53**, wear is now noticed on the neck and the above-mentioned areas. The reverse will have blending of the horizontal bands with each other, and the diagonal bands will start to blend with the vertical lines of the fasces. The fields will now exhibit slight friction, though they are more recessed than on many coins.

Hair and wing feathers are still sharp in **EF-40/45**, the high points now flattened. The face, neck, and fields will have obvious wear. The bands, both horizontal and diagonal, will be mostly flat, with little separation and some blending, and the vertical lines of the fasces will still be separated, except on weakly struck coins.

VF-20/35 coins have the hair along the back of the face very worn and blended. Wing feathers are worn flat along the edges, with the central part still showing some detail. The lower jaw line will still be very distinct at the juncture with the neck. The top, center, and lower horizontal bands will be worn flat with the diagonal bands evident, though slightly blended. Most vertical lines of the fasces will be separated, but slight blending is acceptable, especially in the lower VF grades and on weakly struck specimens.

The hair along the back of the face will show slight detail, and the wing will have only a few feathers present in the **F-12/15** grades. The jaw line will start to blend into the neck, though there is clear separation. The diagonal lines will be blurry in the centers, and the horizontal bands will be totally flat. About one-half or slightly more of the vertical lines of the fasces are still clear.

The rims are very high, so in **VG-8/10** some areas may be worn slightly into the fields; however, the date should still be clear. Only slight detail is still present in the hair and feathers, the jaw line worn into the neck in some places. Some vertical lines of the fasces will be seen, but all will show blending. Horizontal bands will appear solid and are worn into adjacent areas. The rim should not touch any of the reverse lettering, but parts of it may be worn into the field.

G-4/6 coins have rims worn to the tops of the peripheral letters and slightly into part of the date. There will be slight detail in the head, with the jaw line blended into the neck. The reverse will have the rim worn into the tops of some letters. The fasces will be outlined, but worn almost completely smooth.

In **AG-3**, the rims will be worn into the letters of the obverse and reverse, and the date will be only partially visible. The head will show only slight detail and be worn mostly flat. The leaves of the reverse will show detail, the fasces worn smooth. **FR-2** specimens will have only part of the head and IN GOD WE TRUST present, with the date mostly worn away. The reverse will have only part of the fasces and some of the leaves still evident.

With **PO-1** coins, only a readable date and part of Miss Liberty will be present. The reverse may show only slight leaf detail and part of the fasces, with some specimens worn smooth.

Mint State Examples

MARKS: The face and neck are the main areas where marks and other impairments are noted. The hair, "winged" cap, and fields are found with disturbances, though they are often free of impairment. Album slide marks, common for this highly collected series, are noted across the face, neck, hair, and "winged" feathers. Reverse disturbances are found on the fasces and in the field, with occasional markings on the lettering. The vegetation around the fasces is intricate, and only large marks are noted in the leaves and branches.

LUSTER: Although most luster variations are seen, the majority of these coins have a satin-to-frosty luster, with few noted at the luster scale extremes. Some early issues have scaly, grainy surfaces like Matte Proofs. Some Denver and San Francisco coins were struck from worn dies, subduing the luster and resulting in some examples with excessive stress, or flow, lines and/or rough areas near the rims.

STRIKE: Most striking weakness for Mercury dimes is minimal. Slight incompleteness, especially for early Denver and San Francisco issues, is seen on the hair and the front and top of the wing feathers. Reverse weakness, besides the center bands, is usually in the stalks of the fasces, the diagonal bands, and the horizontal bands at the top and bottom. Weakness in the date and the corresponding area of the reverse, part of STATES, is also noted and is severe in a few cases. The top part of the fasces may also be slightly incomplete on some of these coins that show this extreme weakness.

EYE APPEAL: Finding spectacular coins for this series is fairly easy, as rolls of every date were saved. Although some of the rarer date and mint-mark combinations are not often seen, this series can be assembled in superb condition, the first dime series for which this can be fairly easily accomplished. Also, there are many lightly toned, medium toned, and some vividly toned specimens that have good strike and blazing luster and are minimally marked. The only problem usually seen for this series is with the strike of some of the Denver, San Francisco, and a few Philadelphia coins. Those weakly struck coins seldom grade higher than MS-64, many of them being lackluster.

Proofs

HAIRLINES: The reported, but unverified, Matte Proof coins would "hide" any hairlines, much like the Matte Proof gold issues. Brilliant Proof issues were struck from 1936 until 1942, and these coins are sometimes found pristine or with only slight hairlines in the fields. Album slide marks are sometimes encountered and are usually found on the face, neck, hair, and "winged" feathers. There are coins with hairlines across their entire surfaces.

REFLECTIVITY: Some of the 1936 issues have been reported with the satin, or Type I, finish like the cent and nickel, although these are excessively rare. Most of these coins have deeply mirrored, watery-looking surfaces, often accompanied by frosted devices, sometimes with deep frost. Some coins have no contrast with the surfaces and are brilliant across the entire coin.

STRIKE: Only the slightest weakness is noted for Proof Mercury dimes, though some dates, especially 1941–1942, have flat center bands and slight incompleteness on the obverse hair. In rare instances, this weakness may be more than slight, and some of the vertical stalks may be incomplete.

EYE APPEAL: There are incredible specimens known for this series, the early years being much more difficult to find virtually free of hairlines. There are numerous brilliant, lightly toned, cream-colored, and vividly toned specimens encountered. Most have good strikes and deeply mirrored fields, so the toning, or lack thereof, the absence of hairlines and other impairments, and the presence of frosted devices will mainly determine the eye appeal, positive or negative.

Roosevelt Dime—Silver/Copper-Nickel (1946 to date)
Circulated Examples
For **AU-55/58** Roosevelt dimes, slight friction is seen on the hair above the ear, the cheek, and the neck. The torch will show slight rub, and the high points of the leaves will be slightly flattened. Worn to **AU-50/53**, these coins will now have more obvious rub on the hair, cheek, and neck, with a slight dulling of the fields. The leaves and torch will be slightly flatter, and dulling on the fields is evident, though the busy design protects most of the fields, even into the lower grades.

EF-40/45 specimens have some hair slightly flat but most detail is still sharp. The cheek, jaw, and neck now have obvious wear, but the major features are bold. On well-struck coins, the flame, torch, and leaves will all be flattened slightly, but all the lines in the torch

will still be separate. Poorly struck coins will not have distinct lines, even in Uncirculated grades, and these can be missing in the higher circulated grades.

About one-half of the hair detail is still clear in **VF-20/35**, with wear seen across the cheek, face, and neck. Flame and torch lines are indistinct, and the leaves are flat on the high points, though still separate. Roosevelt dimes are not often seen, or collected, in grades below Uncirculated, but someday they probably will be.

F-12/15 coins have slight hair detail, with the deepest lines present. The cheek, jaw line, and ear are flat. Some lines in the torch will show, especially at the top, and the leaves are all flat, though almost all still separate.

With wear to **VG-8/10**, hair detail is slight and the jaw line is worn into the neck area. A few torch lines are visible, with the leaves flat and slightly blended.

G-4/6 coins will have very slight hair detail, with the ear flat and the jaw line worn into the neck. The rim may be only very slightly worn into the field on the obverse, though the reverse may touch a few letters. The torch will be flat, as will the leaves, which are blended in multiple spots.

Roosevelt dimes are almost never seen below the Good grade, though they would be graded per the PCGS standards set forth in chapter 4.

Mint State Examples
MARKS: Obverse marks and other disturbances are mainly found on the face, neck, and hair, with the field and lettering being the secondary areas of marking. The reverse is more intricately designed, with the torch being the main area where marks and other impairments are noted. As with many coins, the reverse is often found pristine, or nearly so. Markings and other disturbances are noted for other reverse devices and the field, but seldom are they more severe than obverse detractions.

LUSTER: These coins are usually found with a satin-to-frosty luster, but flat and semi-prooflike luster coins are sometimes seen. On rare occasions, a prooflike luster example is noted, though there is only slight reflectivity. Most coins have little contrast between the devices and fields, with uniform luster being the norm.

STRIKE: More striking weakness is noted for San Francisco issues than for Philadelphia and Denver issues. The ear, hair above the ear, and hair at the top of the head are sometimes softly struck. Peripheral weakness is noted for some coins, but not necessarily the coins with central striking weakness. The reverse weakness is mainly in the torch, with the flame and base often mushy. Other areas that might be weak are the central part of the torch, the two groups of leaves on either side of the torch, and the motto.

EYE APPEAL: These coins are found in superb condition for every date and mint mark. The only negatives to eye appeal are the occasional weakness of strike, the lackluster appearance, or the unattractive toning. There are many brilliant, well-struck, and lustrous examples of every date, as well as many toning variations on other superb coins. In fact, those coins in the series that are the rarest in higher grades are the 1959 and later ones that never came in the cardboard Mint Sets, these coins often having vivid colors. The Mint Sets were issued in flexible plastic sleeves from 1959 onward, with little attractive toning resulting, plus many coins in these sets have marks and other imperfections.

Proofs

HAIRLINES: Many of these coins are found with nearly hairline-free surfaces, with the obverse field the main area where lines, when present, are noted. The reverse is often pristine, even when there are slight lines or impairments on the obverse. Album slide marks are sometimes noted on the face, hair, and neck, as coins broken out of their original Proof sets were sometimes placed in albums that had spaces for the Proofs among the Mint State examples. There are also albums made exclusively for Proofs.

REFLECTIVITY: Although some of the 1950 issues have swirling die polish and satin-like surfaces, most of these coins have deeply mirrored surfaces. Many coins are found with deeply frosted devices and lettering. Starting in 1968, these coins were struck in San Francisco, and nearly every coin has deeply frosted devices and lettering surrounded by extremely reflective fields.

STRIKE: Most Proofs are very well struck with strong, chiseled detail. Many coins have frosted devices, which make the detail even more distinct. Slight weakness is noted only occasionally.

EYE APPEAL: The coins from the 1950s, the earlier ones being even rarer, are much more difficult to find, with deep frosting on the devices and lettering than those from the 1960s. Issues from 1955 and later also are more common with pristine, or nearly pristine, surfaces. The coins until mid-1955 were still issued in boxes with Mint tissue, these coins often acquiring attractive toning. The most attractive coins are brilliant and have light or vibrant toning, deep frosting, and virtually no hairlines.

Twenty Cents
Liberty Seated Twenty-Cent Piece (1875–1878)
Circulated Examples

This odd denomination is graded similarly to the Liberty Seated series but has LIBERTY raised on the shield instead of incuse, causing this to wear away much faster.

For **AU 55/58** coins, slight friction is seen on the head, breast, and upper legs, and all detail, including LIBERTY, should be sharp. The reverse should have light wear on the neck, breast, legs, and upper wing feathers, though some coins have striking weakness in the upper wing feathers. This area of weakness, mainly the eagle's upper right wing, corresponds to the shield area of the obverse, which also will be weak. **AU-50/53** specimens will have slightly more wear in these spots and friction in the field. The reverse will have slight flattening of the neck, breast, leg, and wing feathers, but most of these areas will still have strong definition.

In **EF-40/45**, loss of hair detail with more obvious friction on the breast and the upper legs will be seen. LIBERTY and shield lines may still be sharp, except for poorly struck coins that may have the central letters weak (usually "BER"). The arms, lower legs, and stars will now have noticeable friction, but detail should still be strong. The neck, breast, leg, and upper wing feathers will now be slightly flat. Since most of the middle and lower wing feathers are recessed, these should still be almost fully detailed.

In **VF-20/35**, there may be weakness in LIBERTY, especially "BER." There will be slight hair detail, the breast and legs now blending, and there is some loss of definition in the gown. Stars will still have some lines present, except for localized weakness. The neck, breast, leg, upper wing feathers, and area along the edges of the wings will now be flattened, but some detail is present. Central parts of the wing feathers are now slightly worn, though most detail is still fairly sharp.

F-12/15 specimens will have a partial LIBERTY, with "BER" worn away. The head, breast, legs, and arms will all be quite worn, with slight detail. Stars will be flat and only the deeper parts of the gown will still have detail. Although the central part of the wing feathers will still be fairly sharp, the neck, breast, leg and upper/outer wing feathers are now flat, with slight detail.

For **VG-8/10**, some part of LIBERTY is present, but only parts of a letter or two may be discernible. Only the deepest gown lines will be present, with the head, breast, and legs now worn into the adjacent areas. Reverse feathers will be present in the wing's central areas, with other parts worn nearly smooth.

The detail remaining for **G-4/6** will be slight, with only a few deeply recessed areas evident. Rims should be full, though worn through most of the dentils and slightly indistinct in a few areas. The eagle will have slight central feather detail, with some peripheral lettering weak, though probably readable.

AG-3 coins have the rim worn into the stars and date. Miss Liberty will be worn smooth, with blending. The reverse rim will be worn into the lettering, and the eagle will have only slight detail. For **FR-2** coins, a few stars may still be present, as well as a partial date and a partial, very worn Miss Liberty. The reverse may have some of the peripheral lettering still apparent and a flat, worn, and blended eagle.

The **PO-1** specimen will have slight detail and a readable date. Reverse detail may be slight or none.

Mint State Examples

MARKS: This short-lived series, issued in just 1875 and 1876 for the business strikes, is mainly found with light-to-moderate marks. More often these coins have hairlines, album slide marks, or other disturbances, with the head, breast, shield, and legs, along with the surrounding field, being the main areas where these impairments are noted. Other parts of Miss Liberty also may have impairments, though marks, sometimes fairly significant ones, are mostly noted on the above-mentioned areas. The eagle, especially the breast and wings, is the main area of the reverse where marks are noted. Hairlines and other disturbances are sometimes noted, but slide marks are seldom encountered on the reverse. The field, other devices, and lettering also are areas of the reverse showing marks or other detractions.

LUSTER: All luster variations are found for this series, but the Philadelphia issues are usually found satin, frosty, semi-prooflike, or prooflike, while the single San Francisco product, 1875, is mainly found satin to very frosty. There are a few semi-prooflike and prooflike examples of the 1875-S. The Carson City Mint struck coins in 1875 and 1876. The 1875-CC is usually found with a satin-

MS-65 *1876 Liberty Seated twenty-cent obverse. Glittering surfaces are seen with a few light contact marks, on the right arm above the wrist and in the field immediately to the left.*

MS-65 *1876 Liberty Seated twenty-cent reverse. As with most coins, the reverse often has fewer marks, and this reverse is virtually mark-free.*

MS-64 *1875-S Liberty Seated twenty-cent obverse. Light marks and scuffs are noted on the body and field of this coin, though no large disturbances are seen.*

MS-64 *1875-S Liberty Seated twenty-cent reverse. A few light marks are seen, mainly to the left of the eagle's head, with full luster. The irregular line through the bottom of the lettering is a die break that does not affect the grade.*

MS-63 *1875-S Liberty Seated twenty-cent obverse. A few obverse marks are seen, none severe, with several in the field in front of the knee.*

MS-63 *1875-S Liberty Seated twenty-cent reverse. A few light contact marks are seen above and around the well-struck eagle, with slight weakness on the top edge of the wings.*

to-frosty luster, though semi-prooflike luster coins are occasionally seen. The excessively rare 1876-CC is usually seen frosty.

STRIKE: Areas of strike weakness are in basically the same areas as the other Liberty Seated coinage, even though William Barber's design is slightly different from the Gobrecht one. The stars, head, breast, knee, foot, rock, and shield all are areas of possible strike weakness. Some San Francisco coins, struck only in 1875, have weakness in all of these areas. Reverses may be weak on the head, neck, breast, upper right wing, legs, and claws, and sometimes parts of the peripheral lettering also are weak. Some coins, especially the 1875-S, may have the upper right wing feathers totally flat, with the top left wing incomplete as well. Business strikes from Philadelphia only, issued in 1875 and 1876, are usually well-struck.

EYE APPEAL: There are brilliant, blazing-luster specimens that have very positive eye appeal, as well as many attractively toned specimens. Strike is a problem with the common date, 1875-S, so weakness must be minor to obtain the highest grades. Coins must have other superior attributes to compensate for their slight weakness of strike.

Proofs

HAIRLINES: Struck from 1875 to 1878, most Proofs have light-to-moderate hairlines. There are cleaned examples that have fairly severe hairlines, as well as coins with slide marks and other impairments. Obverse hairlines are noted mainly in the field, with slide marks seen on the head, breasts, and right leg. Reverse lines are usually found in the field, with coins also found with lines across the entire surfaces.

REFLECTIVITY: Most of these coins have deeply mirrored surfaces, with light-to-moderate frosting on the devices and lettering. Light die polish is noted on some 1875 examples and, occasionally, on 1876 examples. These light polishing lines do not usually interfere much with the reflectivity. Most of the 1877–1878 coins have deeply reflective, watery-looking fields, often contrasting with frosted devices and lettering.

STRIKE: Most Proofs are very well struck, with any incompleteness seen on the highest points, especially the head, when the rest of the coin is well struck. The reverse may show slight weakness in the breast and claws, with the upper right wing sometimes failing to strike up completely. The corresponding part of the obverse—the rock and lower part of the shield—is also affected.

EYE APPEAL: These coins are usually found lightly to darkly toned, with brilliant coins dipped or cleaned, often revealing hairlines obscured by toning. There are coins with extremely light, original yellow, or cream toning. Perhaps the most attractive coins are the vividly toned ones, sometimes the result of their being stored in Mint tissue, protecting them from impairment while giving them their spectacular colors.

Quarter Dollars
Draped Bust Quarter—Small Eagle/Heraldic (Large) Eagle (1796–1807)
Circulated Examples

In **AU-55/58**, Draped Bust quarters have slight wear on the cheek, the hair around the ear, the bust, and the shoulder. Central hair detail and the eagle's head, breast, and leg for the one-year-only Small Eagle issue, the 1796, are sometimes partially missing, even on high-grade Uncirculated specimens. On Heraldic coins, struck from 1804 to 1807, the shield replaces the breast, thus will be the area of weakness. The reverse will have slight friction on the wreath, head, breast, and leg of the Small Eagle coins, with the breast, shield, clouds, tail feathers, and tip of the wing feathers showing slight wear for the Heraldic type. In **AU-50/53**, wear is now apparent on the aforementioned areas, with rubbing in the obverse field in front of Miss Liberty. The reverse field is well-protected; thus only the devices usually show friction.

With **EF-40/45** coins, friction is obvious on the face, hair, and bust, with the hair around the ear now flat. Small Eagle-reverse coins will have most wing feather detail, though the head and breast feathers are usually flat except on well-struck coins. Details of the wreath are still very clear, with only the highest leaves flattened. Wear on Heraldic-reverse coins shows on the head, breast, clouds, shield, and tips of the wing feathers, with most wing feathers visible except on poorly struck coins. Unevenly struck coins are sometimes seen with areas of the legend weak or partially missing. Adjustment marks also are common, and unless they are severe, they will only minutely "discount" the grade.

VF-20/35 specimens will have from one-third to two-thirds of hair detail, depending on the level of **VF** grade and the original striking quality. The bust area is often worn smooth, especially on weakly struck coins. Small Eagle coins will have a flat head, breast, and leg, with up to one-half of the wing feathers present. The wreath will have flat leaves, mostly separate. On Heraldic specimens, the shield will have blending of the vertical and horizontal stripes, with up to one-half of the wing feathers visible. The clouds, arrows, olive branch, and tail feathers will be worn, with blending.

The hair detail on **F-12/15** coins ranges from a few strands visible to about one-third present. Rims should be complete, except for uneven strikes. Small Eagle-reverse coins will have a flat wreath, with blending and little fine detail and a worn eagle with a few feathers still showing. On well-struck Heraldic-reverse coins, up to one-third or slightly more of the wing feathers may be present. The clouds and shield will show only slight separation and are mostly worn smooth.

VG-8/10 coins have little head detail, sometimes with the very back hair curls still intact. Rims may show areas of incompleteness, though this should be slight. On Small Eagle-reverse types, the wreath and eagle will be worn smooth with almost no detail. Wing feathers of the Heraldic coins may show sporadic detail. The clouds, shield, arrows, and olive branch will have much blending and are worn almost flat.

Many **G-4/6** coins will have incomplete rims, partly due to uneven striking and partly due to wear. Miss Liberty will have little detail and may blend in places. Stars should be visible except in areas of rim weakness. Although the wreath and eagle of the Small Eagle reverse are worn very flat, there still may be slight detail. Reverse rims of the Heraldic type will be worn into the tops of the lettering, and areas of rim weakness may have some letters missing. The clouds, eagle, shield, arrows, and olive branch will be quite worn, with slight fine detail.

AG-3 coins have a partial date, LIBERTY, and stars with a head that blends into the field. The reverse will have wear into the lettering for both types, with the central devices worn smooth. For **FR-2**, the wear will obliterate part or all of the stars and LIBERTY. The reverse may have only part of the eagle present for both types, with most of the lettering worn away.

A **PO-1** 1796 issue may be graded with no discernible date, if reverse detail is identifiable as the Small Eagle type. Heraldic types must have a readable date, though the reverse is often worn completely away.

Mint State Examples

MARKS: Larger coins are more prone to disturbances than are smaller coins, though quarters are usually not as banged up as half dollars or dollars. The face, neck, bust, hair, and field of the obverse are prone to impairments, ranging from light hairlines to more severe marks. Reverses of the Small Eagle type ordinarily have fewer disturbances than do the obverses, with the eagle, wreath, and open field being the areas most affected. Heraldic reverses have a slightly less open field area, with impairments usually found on the eagle and shield, with the clouds, stars, open field, and lettering sometimes also showing marks.

LUSTER: Although all luster variations are found for both types, most of the Small Eagle coins are seen with frosty-to-prooflike surfaces, while the Heraldic Eagle coins are usually found with satin-to-frosty surfaces. Many of the Small Eagle coins saved were early strikes, obviously souvenirs of the first quarter coinage, accounting for the inordinate number of prooflike examples.

STRIKE: Almost all Draped Bust Small Eagle quarters have striking weakness, along with many, if not most, of the Heraldic coins. These coins have weakness in the central areas, with the hair and eagle's head, neck, breast, and leg feathers affected. Small Eagle coins almost always have the head weak. The reverse of the Heraldic coins usually has weakness in the clouds, stars, head, ribbon, neck, shield, wing tips, tail, and claws. The peripheral lettering and denomination, when present, also are sometimes weak from uneven striking. Dentils and other details are sometimes missing on Uncirculated specimens. When the dies were out of parallel, there might be quadrants of the coin that are extremely weak.

EYE APPEAL: For the Small Eagle type of 1796, strike is of paramount concern. These coins are fairly often seen with minimal marks and good luster, so the weakness of strike prevents them from attaining the higher grades. There are quite a few attractively toned or brilliant specimens known for the Heraldic type, though there are very few Mint State 1804 quarters.

Specimens

HAIRLINES: These first examples of the Mint's output of quarter dollars were carefully struck. However, some cleaning or mishandling is usually noted. The delicate fields are easily marred by any contact, and light disturbance is expected. The reverse will probably have less contact than the obverse.

REFLECTIVITY: The burnishing of the planchet, along with the extra care in striking these first examples, resulted in deeply mirrored fields. Although these open-collar strikes do not usually have the watery look, there usually is some device and lettering frosting to contrast with the reflective fields.

STRIKE: There are no Heraldic coins known in specimen-strike quality. The few Small Eagle coins found have exceptional detail, with only the slightest incompleteness in the hair and on the eagle. The head, which is almost always weak, should be nearly full on these coins.

EYE APPEAL: The deep prooflike fields on these coins contrast with the design, creating the ultimate early quarter dollars. These coins are difficult to preserve, so the lack of hairlines and other impairments are paramount to eye appeal as well as to the originality of the surfaces. When original surfaces are nearly hairline-free on specimen strikes, these are the pinnacle of the Mint's early quarter production.

Capped Bust Quarter—Large Size/Small Size (1815–1838)
Circulated Examples

As with the open- and close-collar Capped Bust dimes, the two quarter types are graded similarly. The Small Size coins do not have a motto, and the eagle is moved upward, leaving the bottom of the reverse less crowded. **AU-55/58** coins have slight friction on the cap, face, bust, hair below the ribbon, and most high points of the rest of the hair. On the reverse, the neck, leg, claws, and tops of the wings have slight wear. Quite a few Large Size and some Small Size coins have striking weakness in the central area, the hair below the ear, the upper part of the drapery, and the clasp. The corresponding area of the reverse will also exhibit weakness, with the shield and leg being the spots affected. Also, the Small Size coins have a more rounded and raised cheek; thus friction is more easily noticed than on the flatter Large Size type. Worn to **AU-50/53**, there is obvious friction on the noted areas with some hair curls and feathers now slightly flat. The cap and cheek, especially on the Small Size, will also have noticeable friction, with the field showing rub.

The **EF-40/45** specimens have more friction in the same places mentioned above, with the cap and hair curls now flat on the high points. The bust area will have parts worn into the surrounding area, and stars will be flat, though all lines should still show. Some unevenly struck coins will have some flat stars, even in Uncirculated grades. Reverse wear will now flatten the tops of most of the neck, leg, and wing feathers. The motto on Large Size coins will show wear, the claws will be flat and start to blend together, and the olive branch and arrows will have flat, high points, though separate.

Wear on **VF-20/35** coins is marked by flat stars with little detail, flat hair with recessed areas sharp, slight detail in the cap and the hair directly below the ribbon, and drapery worn into the bust. Reverse detail will range from one-third to two-thirds of the feathers still present. The motto, when present, will still be sharp on well-struck coins, and the leaves, arrows, and claws will be flat and worn into adjacent areas.

F-12/15 specimens will have a full, strong LIBERTY, as this is recessed. Up to one-half or slightly more of the recessed hair detail may be present, though the high points will be quite flat, the cap and bust worn nearly flat. Stars will all be outlined with strong rims on the Small Size, close-collar products. The reverse will have some feather detail and some lines of the shield separate. The claws, leaves, and arrows will be very flat with blending. The motto on Large Size coins may still be complete.

Rims of **VG-8/10** coins may now be slightly worn into the dentils, though less so for the Small Size type. LIBERTY may be partial to full, and there still may be considerable recessed detail. Only a few feathers may still be apparent for the Large Size coin, and the motto may show only partially. Small Size coins may have more feathers because of the protective rims and deeper, chiseled feathers.

With **G-4/6** grades, Large Size coins separate from their smaller brethren. The rims probably will be worn to the tips of some of the stars, and Miss Liberty will be nearly worn

smooth, with only a few letters of LIBERTY present. Small Size coins will probably still have the rims only worn into part of the dentils, and the head of Miss Liberty may still show some detail, with more of LIBERTY usually still evident. The reverses are similar, with the rims worn into the tops of the lettering for the Large Size and the eagle quite flat with only the shield showing detail. The scroll will be flat with no E PLURIBUS UNUM present. The Small Size rims may be worn through most of the dentils, but only the very tips of a few letters will be touched. Some feather and shield detail should be present.

AG-3 coins will have missing stars and Miss Liberty worn into the field, but a few partial letters of LIBERTY may still show. The rim will be worn into the lettering of the reverse, with a flat, smooth eagle and only a partial shield. Claws, leaves, and arrows will be very flat and worn into the surrounding areas. For **FR-2**, few or no stars will be visible, the date now partial. Miss Liberty and the eagle will have no detail and will be worn into the fields. The reverse rims will be worn deeply into all of the lettering.

A **PO-1** coin must have a readable date, but other detail may be minimal.

Mint State Examples

MARKS: As with half dime and dimes, the Capped Bust quarters usually have obverse marks or other disturbances on the face, neck, bust, and open field, with the cap, hair, stars, and date sometimes showing impairments. Hairlines and other line-related marks are also fairly common on these coins, as the larger-size coins are heavier and broader than lower-denominations coinage. Reverse marks are noted on the eagle, the other devices, and the open field of both types. The higher rims protect the fields on the Small Size coins, but the head and eagle are in higher relief, leaving them just as vulnerable to disturbances.

LUSTER: Both types are found with all luster variations, with satin-to-frosty luster being the norm for the Large Size coins. Most of the Small Size coins are found with slightly frosty-to-very frosty luster. Semi-prooflike and prooflike examples of both types are encountered, though not as often as Capped Bust half dimes and dimes. On both types, frosted devices and lettering are sometimes seen.

STRIKE: The striking quality of Large Size and Small Size quarters is quite different, but the designs are very similar. The Large Size coins were struck in open-collar dies, with weakness almost always seen on the stars, cap, hair above the eye, hair around the ear, hair down the back of the neck, clasp, drapery, and bust. Reverse weakness is noted on the motto, especially the first few letters that are opposite the bust of the obverse, as well as on the denomination and peripheral lettering. The eagle often has weakness in the head, neck, shield, feathers around the shield, upper wing feathers, leg, claws, leaves, and arrow feathers. Flat, stretched dentils are commonplace, as the striking process often elongated these devices. The Small Size coins are struck in close collars and are much better struck overall. The same areas of striking weakness are noted to a lesser degree, with the dentils almost always uniform, not elongated.

EYE APPEAL: Both types of Capped Bust quarters are found with good eye appeal. However, the close-collar dies produced coins with frostier luster, thus slightly more high-quality specimens. Also, the higher rims of the Small Size coins give slightly more protection to the fields. Both types are rare in the very highest grades, with the most attractive coins seen with near mark-free surfaces, great luster, and either brilliant, lightly toned, or vibrantly toned fields.

Proofs

HAIRLINES: These large coins have very delicate surfaces, with the Large Size coins having very low rims affording little protection for the devices and fields. The Small Size coins have much higher rims but, as noted previously, the head and eagle are in higher relief, negating most of the protection provided by the taller rim. Hairlines are found in the fields of both types, with slide marks and other impairments also noted on the face, cap, and bust.

REFLECTIVITY: The open-collar strikings of the Large Size quarters are not as deeply mirrored, as are the close-collar strikings of the Small Size coins. Often, light burnishing marks are still evident on the planchets of the Large Size coins, these not being struck away during the minting process. These are different from hairlines or die polishing lines; burnishing lines are incuse in the coin like hairlines but do not "move" when the coin is tilted under a good light source. These burnishing lines prevent the surfaces from having the glass-smooth fields seen on the Small Size strikings. Both types usually have medium-to-heavy frosting on the devices and lettering, which contrasts with the reflective fields. At least one Proof 1838 coin is known with heavy, though very fine, die polish across the entire fields. This condition is also noted on a Proof 1838 half eagle and may represent some type of experimentation by Mint personnel.

STRIKE: Proofs from the open-collar dies are not as well struck as those from the Small Size, close-collar dies. Slight incompleteness is usually noted for the Large Size coins on the highest hair curls, drapery, and bust. Reverse weakness is seen in the neck, shield, inner wing feathers, leg, and claws. The close-collar Small Size Proofs also have higher, flatter rims and, when viewed from the edge, are squared with little beveling. Even less incompleteness is noted for the close-collar strikes, though the same areas are affected.

EYE APPEAL: These coins usually have cameo devices and lettering. Some of the Small Size coins have deep frost, creating the effect seen on many of the later Proof strikings, that of deeply frosted devices and lettering that appears to float on watery-looking mirrored fields. When either type is found with minimal abrasions, brilliant or attractively toned, these coins are among the most attractive of all Proof quarters.

Liberty Seated Quarter—All Types (1838–1891)

There are six types of Seated Liberty quarters, but the grading criteria are essentially the same for all of them. In fact, the quarters are graded like the Liberty Seated half dollars, which have the same six types. Go to the half dollar section for Liberty Seated half dollars to find the grading analysis for Liberty Seated quarters.

Liberty Head (Barber) Quarter (1892–1916)

As noted under the Dimes section, the grading of the obverses of Barber dimes, quarters, and half dollars is very similar, but the quarter and half dollar have a different reverse than the dime. The only difference (besides size), however, in the quarter and half dollar is the denomination at the bottom of the reverse. The grading analysis for the quarters is so similar to the half dollars that one can simply substitute the word quarter for half dollar in that section and have no problem grading Liberty Head or Barber quarters.

Standing Liberty Quarter-Type I/Type II (1916–1930)

Circulated Examples

There are slight variances in grading Type I and Type II Standing Liberty quarters, but there are more similarities than differences. The head and shield detail and the lack of the three stars under the eagle are the most obvious differences between the two types, but in circulated grades this is insignificant. (See Chapter 5, Color, Strike and Surface Designations on designations to learn the differences in the two types.) In **AU-55/58** grades, the first points of wear are the head, breast, shield, and right leg. Slight friction is noted in these areas, with strike weakness also seen in these spots, plus in the central part of Miss Liberty. Flatness on the head, shield, and knee is often seen on Uncirculated coins. When these areas are still silvery-looking, they are weakly struck, and a brown or dull

look for these spots indicates wear. The reverse will have slight friction along the front edge of the eagle's right wing and along the body. Weakness of strike is also noted in these areas, with the front of the right wing often quite flat. With wear to **AU-50/53**, the friction is now obvious, especially on the right leg, which will now be flattened somewhat. The field of the obverse is well-protected, and only slight friction is noticed, with the reverse having slight friction in the field. With weakly struck coins, the wing and body feathers may not be sharp.

The head, shield, breast, and knee will exhibit obvious wear in **EF-40/45**, with flatness in the shield and knee. The reverse will have flatness along the front part of the eagle's right wing and along the body. The left wing will have slight friction at the front part, though most wing feathers will still be sharp.

VF-20/35 coins will show wear down the entire leg, with the shield, head, and central area now missing at least one-third of their detail. Friction is now quite evident on the wall around Miss Liberty, but most of the detail is still sharp. The date on the Type II coins from 1917 through 1924 will be worn but still complete. The date for Type I and 1925–1930 Type II coins will be very sharp. About one-half of the wing feather detail is present, but the front edge of the right wing and the body will be mostly worn flat.

Though Type I and 1925–1930 Type II coins have strong dates in **F-12/15**, the 1917–1924 Type II coins may have weakness. The head, breast, and shield are slightly blended, with the leg worn flat. Only the deeply recessed feathers of the right wing will have detail, as the left wing feathers and body will be worn smooth.

VG-8/10 coins will have the shield and central areas blended, the recessed areas of Miss Liberty and the wall evident though worn. The date on the Type I and Type II coins of 1917–1924 may be slightly incomplete, though still very readable, with the 1925–1930 coins still exhibiting a complete date. The reverse will only have slight

MS-65 *1912 Barber quarter obverse. This coin is well-struck and lustrous, with only slight contact, such as the tiny lines on the cheek. Very slight incompleteness is noted on the hair below* LIBERTY *and stars 7 and 11.*

MS-65 *1912 Barber quarter reverse. The slight weakness in the claw and arrow feathers is noted on many Barber quarter and half dollars, as this area is directly opposite the deepest part of the obverse die, the hair below* LIBERTY.

MS-64 *1916-D Barber quarter obverse. A nearly fully struck coin with a few contact marks on the face and neck, and in front of the face.*

MS-64 *1916-D Barber quarter reverse. The claw and arrow feathers are nearly full on this nearly perfect reverse, for which many Barber coins are noted.*

MS-63 *1908-D Barber quarter obverse. A few more marks are noted here, such as the one between the I and N of IN and on the face and neck.*

MS-63 *1908-D Barber quarter reverse. Slight surface contact is noted, though it is very minor.*

feather detail in the right wing, with the rest of the eagle worn smooth.

Many **G-4/6** specimens of the Type I and 1917–1924 Type II coins will have only a partial date, but the 1925–1930 Type II issues still have most digits strong. The deeper recessed areas will still have detail, though Miss Liberty is very worn. For both Type I and Type II coins, the rim of the obverse may be worn through most of the design that replaced the dentils of previous designs. The reverse rim has a plain inner border and may be worn down to the tops of the lettering for the Type II coins, though most Type I coins still have a strong reverse rim. The eagle will show only slight feather detail in the right wing.

AG-3 coins will have a partial date for Type I and 1917–1924 Type II coins, with the later Type II coins having a nearly complete date with the rim slightly worn into the lower parts of the digits. The rims of the obverse will be worn through the design, slightly into the lettering, with Miss Liberty quite flat, showing only deeply recessed detail. The reverse will have a very worn eagle, with only the recessed areas of the right wing feathers showing slight detail. **FR-2** specimens will have only a readable date for the Type I and 1917–1924 Type II coins, with a partial date for the later Type II coins. The rims of the obverse and reverse will be worn into the lettering, stars, and fields. Miss Liberty may show only slight inner detail and will be quite flat. No feathers will be visible, with some lettering and stars totally obliterated.

PO-1 coins are usually seen only for the 1925–1930 Type II coins, as a readable date is necessary. Though little else is necessary, some detail is usually present on these coins. Many pre-1925 coins have much better detail than the Poor grade but do not have a readable date. The 1916 coins have a slightly different design from the 1917 Type I coins and can be identified by these features. This is one of the few instances (Chain and Wreath Cents, Arrows and Rays coins, etc.) when a readable date is not necessary for a gradable coin.

Mint State Examples

MARKS: Although marks are fairly common on these coins, the most prevalent "problem" is rubbing on Miss Liberty's right leg. Marks, when present, are fairly evenly distributed across the obverse, with the shield, body, and "wall" perhaps more marked than other areas. Album slide marks are very common for this highly collected series, with the head, breast, shield, and right knee being the most affected areas. The reverse has a much more open field area, with marks seen on the eagle and in the field with equal regularity. Another type of "mark" is noted for this series and successive series—namely, the burn or wheel mark resulting from the coin's passing through a counting machine. The rubber wheel that draws the coin through the counter is sometimes set too low, causing a "mark" that looks like a concentrated patch of hairlines. When this wheel mark is more than very minor in nature, the coin will *not* be graded by PCGS.

LUSTER: These coins are found only with flat-to-frosty luster. A few coins have some slight claim to semi-prooflike luster, but there is really no reflectivity. Most Philadelphia coins have satin-to-very frosty luster, no matter what the striking characteristics. Denver and San Francisco issues are mainly found satin-to-slightly frosty, with some of the early issues seen with a flat luster and some later issues seen with a very frosty luster.

STRIKE: Strike again became a problem with the introduction of the Standing Liberty quarter. Many of these coins show weakness in the head, breast, shield, and leg of the obverse and in the wing and body of the reverse. The 1917 Type I coins are the best-struck Standing Liberty quarters, with only the head and shield, the eagle's body, and the leading part of the wing showing incompleteness. The redesign in 1917, resulting in the Type II coins, was not an improvement as far as striking was concerned. Many coins, Denver and San Francisco issues especially, have weakness in the head, breast, shield, and right leg and these are usually found incomplete. On the reverse, the leading edge of the eagle's right wing and the body almost always has some incompleteness. The date, especially on the 1917–1924 variety, is also an area of weakness. Some dates, 1924-D for example, are often seen with one-half or less of the date, even on Uncirculated specimens.

EYE APPEAL: These coins were saved by the roll for most dates, with many brilliant, lightly toned, or attractively toned specimens. Strike is the major problem with many of the Type II issues, as luster is often good and finding coins with minimal marks is usually not too difficult. Sharp strike, bright luster, mark-free surfaces, and either brilliant color or attractive toning are ingredients for the highest grades. Those coins with Full Heads are not graded differently from coins that do not have Full Heads, but these are more desirable and bring premiums that vary with their rarity in this condition.

Washington Quarter—Silver/ Copper-Nickel (1932–1998)

Circulated Examples

Washington quarters are usually collected in Uncirculated condition, and only a few rare dates are valuable in the grades below **VF**. The wear on **AU-55/58** specimens is seen on the hair at the top of the head, the cheek, the hair around the ear, and the neck. Reverse wear is easily seen on the breast first, with slight friction noted for the legs and edges of the wings. **AU-50/53** coins have more noticeable friction in these areas and slight friction in the obverse field. The reverse has a protected field, so more wear is noted for the breast, legs, and outer edges of the wings.

Flatness will show on nearly all of the hair curls in **EF-40/45**, with the curls around the ear being noticeably flat. The face and neck will exhibit wear, as will the field. The hair has been strengthened several times, and modern cupro-nickel alloy Washington quarters have much more detail than do their silver alloy brethren. The breast and leg feathers are now flat, with slight flatness on the outer edges of the wing feathers and slight wear on the inner feathers. As with the

obverse, the eagle of the modern Washington quarter has more detail than do the silver alloy coins.

VF-20/35 Washington quarters have slight hair detail, but some areas will be very flat. The face and neck show wear across their entire surfaces. The reverse will have flat breast and leg feathers, with some of the inner wing feathers now slightly incomplete, and the outer feathers showing little detail.

With wear to **F-12/15**, the hair detail will show only in deeply recessed areas. The top part of the head will be worn nearly smooth, as will the face and neck. Only the inner wing feathers will still show detail, as the breast, leg, and outer wing feathers are worn smooth.

VG-8/10 coins will have only slight hair detail, with the face and neck very worn. The rims may touch the tops of the lettering. Only one-half or so of the wing feathers will still have detail, and this is incomplete.

Rims may wear slightly into the lettering and date for **G-4/6**, and Washington's head will be worn nearly smooth, with only the jaw line and other slight detail seen. There will be slight feather detail, though it will be indistinct. The reverse rim may be slightly worn into the lettering.

With **AG-3** coins, the rims may be worn nearly halfway into the lettering and date. The head will have slight detail and a few eagle feathers will be seen. The wing's edge may be worn into the field. For **FR-2** coins, a partial date and lettering will be seen, with the head of George Washington and eagle incomplete.

PO-1 specimens will have a readable date, with some parts of the head and eagle present.

Mint State Examples

MARKS: These coins have Washington's bust in high relief, with the hair, face, and neck often found with marks and other impairments. The open fields are somewhat protected by the rims but sometimes have marks or other disturbances, especially on coins that have been transported in bags. As with other coins, these were often rolled before shipment, so "roll friction" is noted on the high points of some coins, often seen as tiny scrapes on the highest points. On the reverse, the eagle receives most of the marks and other disturbances, with the neck, breast, wings, and legs usually bearing the brunt of these impairments. There is very little open field area on the reverse, though the other devices and lettering are found with marks. As with most coins, the reverse is usually less marked than the obverse.

LUSTER: Most Washington quarters have a satin-to-frosty luster, with other variations scarce to very rare. Flat-luster and semi-prooflike coins are seen, but not often, while full prooflike specimens are essentially unknown. The reflection on semi-prooflike specimens is slight, as the design, especially on the reverse, is not conducive to prooflike fields. Most of the Philadelphia issues have a frosty luster, with most Denver and San Francisco issues having a satin-to-frosty luster.

STRIKE: Though in general Washington quarters are decently struck, there are some San Francisco coins that are weak. Occasionally, Philadelphia and Denver coins will also exhibit slight weakness. The earliest examples show IN GOD WE TRUST weak, which was due to a die problem. The areas of weakness are the hair, especially around the ear, and the eagle's head, breast, and legs. Sometimes the upper wing feathers will also show slight incompleteness, as will the claws. The modern Washington quarters (1965 and later) have had several makeovers, and nearly all of these coins are fully struck. Also, the hair and feather detail on the modern coins is much sharper, because of the modifications.

EYE APPEAL: Every date and mint mark combination is available in higher grades, though obviously some are much rarer than others. Finding brilliant, lightly toned, or attractively toned examples of most dates is the result of the existence of rolls or bags. Well-struck coins with light contact and lustrous fields are also found in the government-issued cardboard Mint Sets, but nearly all of these specimens have toning, often quite spectacular. The modern cupro-nickel coins, especially those from the reworked master dies, are all found in superlative condition, but very few have more than slight toning.

Proofs

HAIRLINES: These coins, as with most modern Proofs, are sometimes found with pristine surfaces. Album slide marks and hairlines are found on some coins, with the hair, cheek, and neck of Washington, along with the field, being the affected areas. Reverse hairlines are less common and more difficult to notice because of the intricate design. As with nearly every Proof series, album slide marks are seldom found on the reverse. Those coins in government plastic holders are usually found in near-perfect condition.

REFLECTIVITY: The modern Mint equipment has imparted deep reflective fields to nearly every Washington quarter. Often these deeply mirrored fields are accompanied by frosty devices and lettering. This is the norm for the San Francisco Proofs, struck since 1968, with most having deep, rich frost on the devices and lettering. As with nearly all of the 1950 Proofs, the quarters are sometimes found with swirling die polish, giving the surfaces a satin-like quality with diminished reflectivity.

STRIKE: Nearly all Proof Washington quarters are well struck. Only slight weakness is seen on the 1936–1942 and 1950–1964 coins. Those coins struck after the resumption of Proof coinage in 1968 are almost always fully struck and almost universally have frosted devices.

EYE APPEAL: The early issues, 1936–1942, as well as 1950–1955, which were wrapped in Mint tissue, often have lovely toning. These plus the blazing white cameo coins are the most attractive of the silver-issue Washington quarters. The 1968 and later cupronickel coins almost always have deep cameo devices and lettering to contrast with the deeply mirrored surfaces. Since these coins were issued in hard plastic holders, they are often superb, though few have more than light toning, often only a peripheral wisp of color.

Washington Quarter—Statehood Copper-Nickel/Silver (Proofs only) (1999 to Date)

Washington quarters were substantially changed starting in 1999. To honor the states of the Union, each year five different Statehood quarters are being issued. The first thirteen Statehood quarters were issued in the order the states ratified the Constitution. After those thirteen quarters were issued, the order for the remaining thirty-seven states was determined by their admittance to the Union. In order to allow enough room on the reverse for each state's design, the obverse of the Washington quarter was modified. The date was moved to the reverse, LIBERTY was moved to the left of the head, UNITED STATES OF AMERICA was placed around the top periphery, and IN GOD WE TRUST was moved to the right of the head. The only thing on the obverse that remained in the same position was the head and it was flattened and given a new hair treatment. The mint mark, however, is in essentially the same place, right behind the lowest part of the head on the right, but moved further away from the head, centered under IN GOD WE TRUST. These coins have created more interest in coins than almost anything the Mint has done in its more than 200-year history. Casual collectors have been created by the millions, no doubt some of them becoming collectors of other United States series as well. The grading of the obverse of Statehood quarters is essentially the same as the previous Washington quarter. The flattened Washington head is less likely to receive coin or bag friction, but is subject to marks in about the same frequency. The reverse is changed five times each year, so this is not the place for a detailed analysis of each reverse design. Suffice it to say, that some designs are quite plain, while others have very intricate layouts. Since most collectors are able to obtain Mint State or Proof examples, no circulated criteria will be discussed.

Mint State Examples

MARKS: These coins have Washington's bust in low relief, with the hair, face, and neck often found with marks and other impairments, although coin and bag friction is less likely than for the previous head design, as previously noted. The fields are not as open as the previous obverse design, so there is less area to receive marks. As with most coins, the reverse is usually less marked than the obverse and with some of the intricate designs, some have numerous protected areas. Those examples with plain, relatively open designs (i.e. the Pennsylvania quarter) are more prone to scuffing and marking in the open areas.

LUSTER: Nearly every Statehood quarter, from both the Philadelphia and Denver Mints have satin-to-frosty luster. Occasionally, prooflike examples are seen, mainly with the most reflective surfaces on the obverse.

STRIKE: Almost every Statehood quarter encountered will have a full or almost full strike. The modern mints have equipment and technology on their side. Strike is really no longer a problem with modern coins.

EYE APPEAL: Every reverse design is different, but all Statehood quarters have great eye appeal. With great strikes and luster, one only has to find a minimally marked example to have a coin with eye appeal. Of course, some may find fault with some of the designs, but that is a personal preference and eye appeal is not affected by someone's bias toward or against a particular Statehood quarter.

Proofs

HAIRLINES: These coins, as with most post-1968 Proofs, are usually found with pristine surfaces. In fact, PCGS will remove Proofs from their Mint packaging and grade them,

MS-69 *Indiana Statehood quarter dollar obverse. Near perfect example with no obvious marks.*

MS-69 *Indiana Statehood quarter dollar reverse. Fully struck with no marks visible to the unaided eye.*

MS-68 *Indiana Statehood quarter dollar obverse. Only a few minor marks are visible, though a glass is necessary to view them.*

MS-68 *Indiana Statehood quarter dollar reverse. The design may have a few very minor ticks, although the fields should be without any disturbances.*

MS-67 *Indiana Statehood quarter dollar obverse. There may be a few minor marks, though none can be in the focal areas.*

MS-67 *Indiana Statehood quarter dollar reverse. The only marks noted will be on the devices and they must be very minor.*

MS-66 *Indiana Statehood quarter dollar obverse. There may be a couple of minor marks, though the focal areas and fields should be nearly mark-free.*

MS-66 *Indiana Statehood quarter dollar reverse. The only marks will usually be confined to the devices with the fields nearly mark-free.*

eliminating the collector's worry about damaging them in the removal process. Therefore, Proof Statehood quarters routinely receive grades of **PR-68** and **PR-69**, as well as the occasional **PR-70** designation. Almost all these coins receive the moniker **DCAM** after their grade, as nearly 100 percent of these modern marvels have intensely frosted devices.

REFLECTIVITY: The modern Mint equipment imparts deeply reflective fields to every Statehood quarter.

STRIKE: As noted under the regular Washington quarters, those coins struck after the resumption of Proof coinage in 1968 are almost always fully struck and almost universally have frosted devices.

EYE APPEAL: The Proofs are similar to the Mint State Statehood quarters with superb eye appeal for nearly every example.

Half Dollars
Flowing Hair Half Dollar (1794–1795)
Circulated Examples

Flowing Hair half dollars suffer from the same striking weaknesses as the Flowing Hair half dimes, but fewer coins are affected and the area of weakness is smaller in proportion to their sizes. These larger coins have slight wear on the cheek, forehead, and hair

strands around the ear for **AU-55/58**, though this is also the area of strike weakness. The reverse will have slight friction on the eagle's neck, breast, legs, and upper parts of the wing feathers. When weakly struck, the entire central part of the eagle is affected, with the wing feathers possibly weak also. The wreath will have slight friction on the highest leaves. In **AU-50/53**, the friction is fairly easy to distinguish from strike weakness. Friction will be seen across the forehead, face, and bust, and most of the hair and field will display some wear. The eagle and wreath will now have definite wear, though the field is well-protected, showing slight rubbing.

For grades **EF-40/45**, the hair strands will still be distinct, though worn, and missing only the detail around the ear on poor strikes. The forehead, cheek, and bust areas will show wear, as will the open field. Some of the stars will still have detail, though they do not have crosshatch lines and are of the pointed variety, with sloping sides to each ray. The reverse will have central feather detail only on strong strikes, but there is some wing feather detail, with the tops of the wings worn smooth. The highest leaves and berries will now be worn flat, with slight blending.

One-third to two-thirds of the hair is still visible for **VF-20/35** coins, and mostly worn away from the ear up. Most of the hairline blends into the face, and most stars will be flat. Rims should be complete, though unevenly struck coins may have slight weakness. The eagle may have no fine detail, but up to one-half of the feathers are present on good strikes. The leaves and berries of the wreath will be worn smooth, with some blending.

F-12/15 coins may have slight to nearly one-half of the lower hair strands still present, poorly struck coins only the back strands. The head, LIBERTY, and the stars are complete. Rims should be complete, except for localized weakness. If any eagle feathers are present, they will be seen on the lower wing and tail areas, though the eagle and wreath should be outlined. Only the fine parts of the wreath will be distinct.

Although some marks are present in all circulated (and most Uncirculated) grades, these coins should have only small- or medium-sized marks. Even for **VG-8/10** grades, large marks or huge rim nicks are not acceptable. The head should be outlined with only the back strands of hair visible. Rims should be complete, save for unevenly struck coins, with stars and lettering also complete. The eagle and wreath will be worn almost smooth, with only slight detail present.

G-4/6 specimens will have Miss Liberty worn smooth, with parts blending. Rims probably will have several indistinct areas, possibly blending to some stars. LIBERTY and the date should be clear, save for uneven strikes. The reverse will have a flat, smooth eagle and blending of the wreath. Reverse rims will touch some of the lettering.

For the **AG-3** grade, some stars may be totally missing and part of the date may be gone. Miss Liberty will blend into the field, with little detail. The reverse will have areas where the lettering is completely gone. The eagle and wreath will be incomplete in places and have no fine detail. **FR-2** coins will have a readable date and some parts of the head, LIBERTY, and stars present. The reverse may be almost totally worn smooth, with sporadic detail.

The **PO-1** coin must have a readable date with some detail visible, and the reverse may be worn smooth.

Mint State Examples

MARKS: As a rule, the larger and heavier the coin, marks become more frequent and heavier. Flowing Hair half dollars are no exceptions, with the face, neck, and hair often found with marks and other impairments. The open field around the head, the stars, LIBERTY, and the date is also seen with disturbances, in some cases severe. The reverse is more intricately designed, with the eagle, wreath, and lettering covering most of the surface. Often, marks are hidden among these devices and lettering. These coins, especially the ones dated 1795, are sometimes seen with album slide marks on the face, neck, and hair.

LUSTER: Although these coins were the first half dollars struck, there are no prooflike and very few semi-prooflike coins seen. Most coins have satin-to-slightly frosty luster. Why no prooflike coins were struck is a mystery, since there are examples known for most other denominations and the Draped Bust half dollar that follows is fairly common in that state.

STRIKE: As with nearly all coins, Flowing Hair half dollars have strike weakness—the central hair of the obverse, sometimes with the stars, upper hair, high points on the very back of the hair, and bust. LIBERTY, the date, eyes, lips, and other areas may have localized weakness or punching weakness, as each letter or device was punched individually to different depths. Reverse weakness is seen on the head, neck, breast, upper wing, legs, perch, and wreath. The lettering may also be weak for the same reasons as on the obverse. Rim irregularities are sometimes the result of the edge-letter machine, making the edge look like a piecrust.

EYE APPEAL: Well-struck, lustrous Flowing Hair half dollars with minimal marks and brilliant or toned surfaces are occasionally found, though seldom pristine. The few great-looking coins available were undoubtedly saved as the first examples of half dollar coinage. Finding coins with all of the positive attributes is difficult, as many of these coins had adjustment marks, weakness of strike, subdued luster, and other negative characteristics.

Draped Bust Half Dollar—Small Eagle/Heraldic (Large) Eagle (1796–1807)

Circulated Examples

AU-55/58 Draped Bust half dollars have slight wear on the cheek, the hair around the ear, the bust, and the shoulder. Almost all dates have some coins with weakly struck centers. On Small Eagle coins, the central hair detail and the head, breast, and leg areas of the eagle are sometimes partially missing, even on Uncirculated specimens, with the head notoriously flat on some coins. Heraldic Eagle coins have the shield instead of breast feathers, and sometimes the stripes are obliterated. The reverse will have slight friction on the wreath, head, breast, and leg of the Small Eagle coins, with the breast, shield, clouds, tail feathers, and tip of the wing feathers showing slight wear for the Heraldic type. In **AU-50/53**, wear is now apparent on the aforementioned areas, with rubbing in the obverse field in front of Miss Liberty. The reverse field is well-protected; thus only the devices usually show friction.

Worn to **EF-40/45**, there is obvious friction on the face, hair, and bust, with the hair around the ear now flat. Small Eagle coins will have most wing feather detail, though the breast feathers are usually flat. Wreath detail is still clear, with only the highest leaves flattened from wear. Wear on the Heraldic reverse coins is seen on the head, breast, clouds, shield and tips of the wing feathers, with most of the wing feathers visible. Unevenly struck coins are sometimes seen with areas of the legend weak or partially missing.

VF-20/35 specimens will have from one-third to two-thirds of the hair detail. The bust area is often worn smooth, especially on poorly struck coins. The Small Eagle coins will have a flat head, breast, and leg, with up to one-half of the wing feathers present. The wreath will have flat leaves that are mostly separate. On Heraldic specimens, the shield will have blending, with up to one-half of the wing feathers visible. The clouds, arrows, olive branch, and tail feathers will be worn, with blending apparent.

Hair detail on **F-12/15** coins ranges from a few strands to about one-third visible. Rims should be complete, except for uneven strikes. Small Eagle coins will have a flat wreath, blending, little fine detail, and the eagle worn, with few feathers showing. On well-struck Heraldic-reverse coins, up to one-third or slightly more of the wing feathers may be seen. The clouds and shield will show only slight separation, being mostly worn smooth.

VG-8/10 coins have little detail on Miss Liberty, with sometimes the very back hair curls still intact. Rims may show slight areas of incompleteness. On Small Eagle types, the wreath and eagle will be worn smooth, with no fine detail. The wing feathers of the Heraldic coins may show sporadic detail. The clouds, shield, arrows, and olive branch will have much blending and are worn almost flat.

Many **G-4/6** coins will have incomplete rims. Miss Liberty will have little detail and may blend into the field. Stars should be visible, except in areas of rim weakness. Although the wreath and eagle of the Small Eagle reverse are worn very flat, there still may be slight eagle detail and some separation in the wreath. Reverse rims of the Heraldic type will be worn into the tops of the lettering. The clouds, eagle, shield, arrows, and olive branch will be quite worn, with slight fine detail.

AG-3 coins have a partial date, LIBERTY, and stars, with a head that blends into the field. The reverse will show wear into the lettering, with the central devices worn smooth. For **FR-2** coins, the wear will obliterate part or all of the stars and LIBERTY. The reverse may have only part of the eagle present, with most of the lettering worn away.

A **PO-1** coin will have a discernible date and detail to determine type, the reverse often worn away.

Mint State Examples

MARKS: As with all larger coins, these coins are usually found with some markings. The head is seen with disturbances on the face, neck, bust, and hair, the open field also seen with impairments. The date, stars, and LIB-ERTY are also sometimes seen with impairments. The reverse of the Small Eagle type has more field area than does the Heraldic type, though both have much less than the Capped Bust type that follows. The reverse of the Small Eagle type is similar to the Flow-ing Hair, a perched eagle with spread wings surrounded by a wreath and lettering. These Small Eagle coins also have the fraction 1/2 below the wreath's bow. Heraldic-reverse coins have very little field area, with the eagle and shield being the areas for disturbance. The clouds, stars, other devices, lettering, and open field are secondary areas for im-pairment.

LUSTER: Small Eagle coins have slightly frosty-to-prooflike luster, with many speci-mens seen with semi-prooflike and prooflike surfaces. The Heraldic coins are usually seen with satin-to-very frosty surfaces, with semi-prooflike coins scarce and fully prooflike coins quite rare.

STRIKE: Although there are well-struck Small Eagle coins, many are poorly struck. When the upper die was the reverse for the Heraldic coins, from 1801 through part of 1806, the coins are slightly better struck on the obverse than those coins struck after mid-1806, when the obverse was the upper die. Conversely, reverse detail is usually slightly better for the second die arrangement than for the first. Obverse weakness is first noticed on the hair above the ear, around and below the ear, and the bust, with other weakness noted in the top of the stars, the lettering, the date, the hair, the ribbon, and the drapery. Reverse weakness for the Small Eagle type is first noticed on the head, neck, upper wings, breast, and legs. With the Heraldic type,

weakness is noted in the clouds, stars, head, ribbon, neck, breast, shield, inner wings, wing tips, and claws. The right part of the clouds and the right stars are opposite the tip of the bust of the obverse on the Heraldic type, and on some coins these areas may be very weak. Other weak areas noted are the wreath on the Small Eagle type and the ar-rows, branch, and inner wing feathers on the Heraldic coins.

EYE APPEAL: As with the quarters, for the Small Eagle coins of 1796 and 1797 strike is a major concern. The Heraldic coins are some-times found with near-full strikes. Since these large coins are fairly often seen with some marks, finding examples with good luster and only slight weakness of strike is often difficult, especially for the Small Eagle type. More Heraldic-type coinage is brilliant or attractively toned than the Small Eagle type, due to the overall rarity of the Small Eagle type. A few of the spectacular 1796 coins are seen that were obviously saved as souvenirs of the first year of the type.

Specimen Strikes

HAIRLINES: These coins are among the most prized examples of the Mint's early coinage. The delicate nature of the surfaces plus the large size of half dollars made preservation a difficult task. Known speci-mens often have light-to-moderate hairlines, mainly in the obverse field. The reverse may have hairlines or other impairments in the small open field areas, as well as on the eagle, wreath, and lettering.

REFLECTIVITY: These coins were struck with special care, the dies heavily polished. The specimen-strike planchets were bur-nished before striking, allowing the dies to impart deeply mirrored fields. Some frosting on the devices and lettering of these examples is noted.

STRIKE: True specimen strikes have ex-traordinary strikes. Both varieties of 1796 may exist in specimen strikings, though no other date Draped Bust half dollars are known to exist in Specimen Strike. There may be slight incompleteness on the hair in the central areas and on the head, neck, breast, and leg of the reverse eagle.

EYE APPEAL: These are the pinnacle of early half dollars, with deep prooflike fields contrasting with the devices. These large coins have very delicate fields, so the lack of impairments is paramount to the eye appeal, along with the originality. When original surfaces are combined with nearly hairline-free surfaces, specimen-strike coins are the finest examples of the Mint's early half dollar production.

Capped Bust Half Dollar—Lettered Edge/Reeded Edge (1807–1839)

Circulated Examples

This is probably the toughest series to grade in American numismatics. Although similar to the other Capped Bust series, the half dollars are almost never seen without either friction or weak strike. In **AU-55/58**, coins range from being well-struck, with slight friction on the cap, the cheek, the hair below the ribbon, the hair at the back of the neck, and the bust, to weakly struck, with wear in the same spots. The weakness is usually seen in the bust, clasp, drapery, hair curl on the neck, and hair curls behind the neck. Obverse stars should have full detail except for localized weakness. The reverse will have slight friction on the neck, leg, claws, and upper parts of the wings, with striking weakness affecting the neck, shield, leg, and claws. The legend E PLURIBUS UNUM is often incomplete. The part of the motto that often shows weakness is opposite the bust area of the obverse die. **AU-50/53** specimens will have more obvious wear in the same regions, with friction now in the field. There will be more flatness on the cap, hair, and bust, with friction now quite evident on the cheek. Stars have slightly flat tops. The reverse will have more flatness in the neck, leg, and claws, with the central wing feathers now showing wear. The leaves and arrowheads will be strong, with only slight rub.

EF-40/45 coins that are well struck will have full detail but blatant wear on the cap, cheek,

bust, and all the high points of the hair curls. The field will now have friction. Reverse detail is very sharp on well-struck coins, with the neck, leg, and wing feathers complete, showing only slight flatness on the high points. The shield will now have a slight blending of the stripes, though completely outlined. Weakly struck coins will have the central hair incomplete, with the shield weak and blended.

Although many **VF-20/35** specimens have very sharp detail, many do not. The absence of a particular detail required for **VF** should not be used as the primary reason for denying a particular grade. Average or well-struck coins will have one-third to two-thirds of hair detail, with the high points flat. The cap and bust will still show major detail, but the high points will be flat and blended. The stars, if well struck, will have some detail remaining. Eagle detail will usually have the neck and leg feathers quite flat, with from one-third to nearly all of the wing feathers visible, though flat. Shield horizontal lines are mostly intact with only slight blending, with the vertical lines mostly blended. The claws, leaves, and arrowheads will be worn smooth but separate. The motto should still be bold, with missing letters related to striking deficiencies.

In **F-12/15**, parts of the cap, hair, and bust are worn into the surrounding areas, but up to one-half of the detail may be present. The stars are now flat, with rims worn down slightly into the dentils for the Lettered Edge type, though not for the higher-rim Reeded Edge type. Eagle feathers range from one-fourth to one-half, though all of them will be well worn, with the neck, leg, and tops of the wings worn smooth. The shield lines are worn together. The claw, leaves, and arrowheads will be very worn, with slight blending.

VG-8/10 coins have from one-fourth to one-third of hair detail, slightly more for Lettered Edge coins. LIBERTY should be strong as it is recessed, with the stars mostly flat. Feathers will be scarce, and the shield will have only a few horizontal lines visible, with most of the outline blended. The claws will all be flat and blended, with the leaves and arrowheads worn flat though still separate.

G-4/6 specimens will have an outlined Miss Liberty, slight detail present such as a partial LIBERTY, and traces of hair curls and drapery. Rims should be mostly complete, but, worn through most dentils. Stars will be outlined though quite flat. The reverse will have only a few feathers visible, but the shield may have some lines. The lettering will be complete, with the rims worn into most dentils.

With the **AG-3** grade, rim wear will show into the stars and date, with Miss Liberty blended. The reverse rims are worn into the lettering, and the eagle may be worn into the field. **FR-2** coins will have some stars and part of the date present, with more areas of Miss Liberty worn into the field. The reverse may have some lettering completely worn away. The eagle will be worn into the field in several spots.

PO-1 coins will have a readable date and some part of Miss Liberty, with little or no reverse detail.

Mint State Examples

MARKS: These coins are usually found with disturbances, slight on some specimens to quite heavy on others. The obverse cap, face, neck, bust, and hair of Miss Liberty as well as the field around the head are found with marks and other impairments. Combined with incomplete striking, very common for this series, very few coins are found disturbance-free. The eagle and shield, as well as the open area above the eagle, are commonly seen with impairments, though less than with obverses. The other devices, lettering, and open field areas are sometimes seen with disturbances.

LUSTER: All luster variations are seen for this long series, with most examples seen with satin-to-very frosty luster. Those coins struck in the early part of the series, 1807–1820, are usually satin-to-slightly frosty. Coins from the middle to later part of the series usually are seen slightly frosty-to-very frosty, with the other luster variations also common. With the introduction of the steam-powered presses and close collar, most Reeded Edge–type coinage has a slightly frosty-to-very frosty luster. There are minor variances in dies, planchets, and minting equipment, which give the different eras their distinct looks.

STRIKE: There are many areas of weakness of strike, at least until the close collar and steam-powered presses were introduced in 1836. A greater percentage of these coins will show strike weakness than any other U.S. coin series. Areas of weakness include the stars, cap, tip of the band, hair above the eye, hair above the ear, all the hair from the ear down, clasp, drapery, and bust. The date, eye, nose, mouth, and other areas may also show localized weakness. Reverse weakness usually includes the motto, head, neck, shield, inner wings, upper wings, leg, and claws. Sometimes the lettering, denomination, leaves, arrows, and central wing feathers may show incompleteness. Reeded Edge coins are sometimes weak in the above-mentioned areas but overall are much better struck. The exception for Reeded Edge coinage is the very rare 1839, Type of 1840 reverse, which is always weakly impressed.

EYE APPEAL: Although these coins are difficult to find pristine, they are much more available than are the previous half dollar types. The longevity of the series, 1807–1839, is one reason why more of these coins are available in the higher grades. Luster and surfaces, brilliant or toned, are often found positive on these coins, with the strike and marks being the areas where problems usually occur. Nearly every coin has at least slight weakness of strike, with impairments common on these large coins. Finding all attributes positive produces the high-grade specimens, mainly the common dates. Many varieties and rare dates are not known in the highest grades, so a complete date set of even MS-65 coins is probably not possible.

Proofs

HAIRLINES: Nearly every Proof has light-to-moderate hairlines, with some coins showing heavy lines from old cleanings. Although these coins were highly prized even then, the surfaces are extremely delicate and easily impaired. Hairlines are mainly noted in the fields, with album slide marks, when present, usually seen across the cheek and bust. The higher rims of the Reeded Edge coins provided slightly more protection for the fields, with fewer and lighter hairlines noted for this type. Miss Liberty is in higher relief for this type, so the extra protection of the higher rims is offset by the higher relief, with the result that album slide marks and hairlines on the face and bust are as common as for the Reeded Edge type.

REFLECTIVITY: Those coins struck prior to 1836 in open collars do not have the depth of reflectivity seen on the Reeded Edge coins, which were struck in close collars. Also, the so-called "crushed-edge" coins of 1834–1836, which had lettered edges but were struck in close collars, have more deeply mirrored fields than do the open-collar strikes. The open-collar strikings also are sometimes seen with planchet burnishing lines still visible, these impairing the reflectivity slightly and occasionally resulting in areas of "frost" in the fields, especially near devices. Frosted devices are seen on most Proofs, whether open- or close-collar strikings, though the heaviest frost is almost always seen on close-collar strikings.

STRIKE: The open-collar Lettered Edge Proofs are not as well struck as the close-collar Reeded Edge Proofs. There is almost always some slight weakness on the Lettered Edge–type Proofs. It may be slight weakness in the hair, plus the shield, leg, and claw on the reverse. The crushed-edge strikes of the 1834–36 Lettered Edge coins are restrikes struck in close collars with much better strikes.

EYE APPEAL: When found with original surfaces and minimal hairlines, these are attractive early Proof coins. There are some very spectacular open-collar Proofs with heavy frost, contrasting with the mirrored fields. These cameo Proofs are the most attractive of the Lettered Edge coins, along with the "crushed-edge" restrikes. The close-collar, Reeded Edge coins are very high-quality Proofs. Finding coins with minimal contact and original surfaces is still difficult, with only a few superb specimens still in existence.

Liberty Seated Half Dollar—All Types (1839–1891)
Circulated Examples

There are six types of Seated half dollars, as there are quarters, but the grading criteria are essentially the same for all of them. As noted under the Liberty Seated quarters, their grading criteria are found here with the half dollar analysis. The arrows, rays, and motto are all added features and do not strongly affect the overall grading. For **AU-55/58** coins, the first areas to show wear are the head, breast, and upper legs. Areas commonly found with strike weakness are the head, clasp, upper legs, and shield, and the neck, shield, leg, claws, and arrow feathers of the reverse, which may be very flat on some coins. The wear on the reverse is noted on the neck, top wing feathers, feathers around the shield, legs, and claws. With **AU-50/53**, the wear is obvious from strike weakness, the fields now showing noticeable rubbing, in addition to increased friction on the head, breast, and upper leg. The reverse will have light friction on the high points of the feathers, as well as in the noted areas, and the No Motto coins will have rubbing above the eagle in the open field. Motto types will have slight friction on the ribbon with IN GOD WE TRUST.

EF-40/45 grades have obvious friction on the head, breast, shield, upper and lower legs, and on the lower gown folds. The recessed gown folds are still sharp, with most of the shield lines still distinct, though weakly struck coins may have incompleteness. Stars, except for localized weakness, will still show most of the radial lines. Reverse wear will now be evident across all of the feathers, with noticeable flatness on the neck and leg. The claws, leaves, and arrowheads will be worn but separate. Motto coins will have full lettering, except on the occasional weakly struck specimen.

Most **VF-20/35** specimens will have a full strong LIBERTY, with exceptions noted for localized shield weakness. The head, breast, and many of the gown folds will be worn with only slight detail. Some of the stars will still have some crosshatch lines. The eagle will have one-half or more of the feathers visible, but the neck and leg will be very flat. The claws, leaves, and arrow feathers will be mostly flat, with some blending. On Motto coins, the legend may show some weakness but should still be readable.

A full LIBERTY is usually found on **F-12/15** coins, though localized weakness may obscure some letters. Only the deeply recessed details of Miss Liberty will still be visible, with the shield having only slight separation in the horizontal lines. Stars may have slight detail remaining. Wing feathers will be well-worn, with only the deeper details evident and much blending of the neck, leg, and upper/lower wing feathers. The outline of the shield will blend into the surrounding feathers, and the claws, leaves, and arrow feathers will be worn smooth. Several letters of the motto may be weak.

VG-8/10 graded coins will have some of the LIBERTY visible, with the deepest recessed areas showing slight detail. Stars will be worn flat, and the rim may be worn into nearly all of the dentils. The reverse will have sporadic feather detail, and most of the vertical shield lines will be visible but blended. The claws, leaves, and arrow feathers will be worn smooth. Some dentils may still be present, though the rims will be worn into most of them. Motto coins may have some of the lettering present.

There may be slight rim wear into the field, but all of the stars should still be outlined in **G-4/6**. Miss Liberty will be worn smooth, fully outlined except for localized areas of weakness. The reverse may have the rims worn into the tops of some of the lettering, and for Motto coins the lettering may be worn away. The eagle will be worn smooth, with only the vertical lines of the shield still apparent.

AG-3 specimens will have the rim worn into the stars and date. Miss Liberty will be totally flat and may be blended in spots. The reverse will have the rims worn into the peripheral lettering, with one-half or more of the letters obscured. The eagle will show only the deeply recessed vertical shield lines and may blend into the field. The motto ribbon will be worn smooth, with some parts worn into the field. **FR-2** coins will have a partial Miss Liberty and date, with no stars present. The reverse may show no peripheral lettering and a well-worn eagle.

The **PO-1** coin will have a partial Miss Liberty and a readable date, with little or no reverse detail.

Mint State Examples

MARKS: Obverses of most coins usually have light, medium, or heavy marks, depending on the storage, distance transported, and other factors. The body is seen with marks and other disturbances, as is the open field. Marks may range from light contact on the head, breast, and legs, to heavy digs, gouges, and other disturbances. Reverse markings, common with nearly every series, are mostly light contact marks on the eagle or shield, or in the open field. The Arrows and Rays coinage as well as the Motto coinage may have marks or other disturbances on these devices. Album slide marks, when present, are mainly noted on the obverse on the head, breast, and upper legs of Miss Liberty.

LUSTER: Every luster variation is seen on these coins, from flat to deeply prooflike. Philadelphia issues, at least for the common dates, usually have a satin-to-very frosty luster, with the lower-mintage issues usually found very frosty, semi-prooflike, or prooflike. New Orleans coins are usually found with more subdued luster, though some issues are seen with very frosty, semi-prooflike, and occasionally deeply prooflike surfaces. In fact, some 1860-O coins are so deeply reflective that they may have been struck as branch-mint Proofs. When the San Francisco Mint opened, half dollar coinage commenced in 1855 and continued until 1878. Most of the rarer dates are found frosty to prooflike, with the large-mintage issues usually found with satin to very frosty surfaces. Carson City struck half dollars in the first year of its existence, in 1870, with the issues 1870–1874 mainly found frosty to deeply prooflike, while the more common Carson City coins, 1875–1878, usually are found frosty.

STRIKE: Philadelphia issues are usually decently struck, as are the San Francisco and Carson City coins, with the New Orleans issues often weak. Weakness is noted on the stars, head, breast, knee, foot, rock, and shield of the obverse. Reverse incompleteness is noted on the head, neck, shield, inner wing feathers, upper wing feathers, right leg, claws, leaves, and arrow feathers. The motto, when present, also may show weakness. New Orleans coins nearly always have the eagle's right leg flat, often with no feathers visible. Dentil weakness is not often seen, though New Orleans issues sometimes exhibit this weakness.

EYE APPEAL: As with the quarters, there are many superb half dollars, since the series was issued, uninterrupted, from 1839–1891. This workhorse series had many years with multiple millions struck, though some date and mint mark combinations had minuscule mintages. These coins are found with many variations, some with brilliant, frosty surfaces, and others with toned, prooflike fields. The 1839 No Drapery issue is by far the most difficult type to find superb, with the Arrows and Rays being the next most difficult type. The Arrows, Motto type is the next most difficult type to find pristine and the Arrows, No Motto type is the next most difficult type to find in the higher grades, though many more of these are available than for the Arrows, Motto type. The Motto type is more common than the No Motto type, but there are quite a few nice No Motto coins. The

very highest-grade coins are usually only seen for the Motto series, these coins usually being seen with blazing luster and brilliant, lightly toned, or vibrantly toned surfaces.

Proofs

HAIRLINES: These large and delicate-surface coins are seldom found with pristine surfaces, though the Motto type is more often found than the others. Obverse hairlines and other impairments are usually noted in the open field in front of the figure, with others behind. Album slide marks, when present, usually are found on the head, breast, and upper legs of the figure, with the arms and lower legs also sometimes seen with lines. The reverse of the No Motto coins often has hairlines above the eagle. Motto coins generally have lines in the same area, though the motto affords some field protection.

REFLECTIVITY: Those coins struck prior to 1854 do not usually have the deep, watery-looking fields of the coins struck in 1854 and later. Sometimes the devices and lettering are not as deeply frosted, and the lettering may not be as flat and squared. It should be noted that the Mint was also not as careful striking some of the Proofs of the 1880s, as these coins are sometimes found with rounded lettering instead of the square, heavily frosted letters usually seen. Some of the early issues may also still have slight die striations present in the fields, which impair the reflectivity. The Arrows and Rays Proofs, of which only five were struck, also have heavy die polish that results in diminished reflectivity.

STRIKE: Coins struck in 1854 and later are of very high quality. Weakness is only seen occasionally, and this usually will show as a slight flatness in the stars, head, and foot of the obverse. Reverse weakness is usually confined to the upper right wing, right leg, and claws. A few later coins with more than slight weakness are sometimes seen, as are some pre-1854 issues.

EYE APPEAL: As with other Liberty Seated series, these coins are split into two groups.

Those coins struck in 1853 and before are not of as high striking quality as the later issues, with far fewer high-grade specimens seen. In fact, all of the 1855 and prior half dollars are rare-to-ultra-rare in Proof, with very few specimens known. For these coins, finding original coins with minimal hairlines and abrasions is a near-impossible task. The later Proofs, especially the Motto type and particularly the coins of 1880–1891, are found pristine, or nearly so. Many of these coins were stored in Mint tissue and have acquired attractive, vibrant toning. There are brilliant, lightly toned, or spectacularly toned examples of most of the Motto and later No Motto issues.

Liberty Head (Barber) Half Dollar (1892–1915)

Circulated Examples

As noted under the Dimes and Quarters sections, the grading of the obverses of Barber dimes, quarters, and half dollars is very similar but the quarter and half dollar have different reverses from the dime, and the dime's obverse legend is now replaced with stars for the quarter and half dollar. As mentioned, the dime and quarter obverse criteria are found here, while the quarter reverse analysis is here, but the dime is found under the Liberty Seated Legend dime series. Obverse wear is first noticed on the cheek for **AU-55** and **58** coins, with slight wear also noted for the hair below LIBERTY and the tops of the leaves in the laurel wreath. The hair below LIBERTY and the leaves right above the ear are areas that sometimes show strike weakness. Reverse weakness is noted in the neck feathers, the wing feathers around the shield, the shield, the tail feathers, and the eagle's right claw. Weakness is not always seen in all of these areas, as some coins may only have the claw weak. (The claw is opposite the hair below LIBERTY of the obverse, thus often leading to weakness in these areas and no others.) The reverse wear is noted on the neck, upper wing, wing tips, and tail. When worn to **AU-50/53**, more of the face and neck will have slight wear and the fields will ex-

hibit rubbing. More wear is now evident on the neck, wing, and tail feathers, with the raised shield now having some lines blurred.

EF-40/45 coins have the hair flat below LIBERTY and some of the ends of the leaves will be indistinct, though still outlined. The LIBERTY will be strong, except for weakly struck issues such as the New Orleans coins, which often have marks from clashed dies also. The cheek and neck will have obvious wear and the stars will be flat, though with most radial lines. The eagle feathers and the shield will have obvious friction, with the tips of the wing feathers now starting to flatten.

Many **VF-20/35** specimens have a fairly strong LIBERTY, but lower **VF** grades and weakly struck coins may not. The hair below LIBERTY will be worn smooth, and quite a few leaves of the wreath will be blended. Stars will have some lines still evident, though little in the lower **VF** grades. Tips of the wings will be worn flat, and only the deeper feathers will still be visible. The neck, tail, and shield will have much blending, with one-half or less of the detail present.

Having the top leaves of the wreath fairly well outlined is a better indicator for **F-12/15** grades than the traditional full LIBERTY, since weakly struck coins may have letters partially missing. The bottom leaves of the wreath are mostly worn into the adjacent areas. There is a slight separation for the bottom of the face and neck, and the stars will be mostly flat, with only occasional lines visible. Wing feather detail is evident only in the deeply recessed parts, with the neck, tail, and shield showing slight detail.

VG-8/10 specimens usually have a few letters, or partial letters, of LIBERTY. Parts of the top leaves of the wreath are visible, with little or no separation between the face and neck. Only part of the ear is still visible. There is an outlined eagle with slight detail, with the neck, tail, and shield worn quite flat.

Worn to **G-4/6**, most Barber coins have only part of the eye socket and ear remaining, but

Miss Liberty is still outlined. Rims may be worn through the dentils and slightly into the field, with wear into the tops of the reverse letters. The eagle is well-outlined, but there is only slight detail remaining around the shield.

AG-3 coins will have rims worn into the stars and possibly into the date. The head will be worn smooth, with some blending into the field in places. Lettering will be partially missing for the reverse, and the eagle will be worn into the field in places. In the **FR-2** grade, no stars may be evident and there may be only a partial date, with Miss Liberty indistinct. Reverse detail may consist only of a partial eagle, with a few stars, leaves, and arrows present.

A **PO-1** coin will have a discernible date and partial head of Miss Liberty, with the reverse usually worn smooth.

Mint State Examples

MARKS: The large, smooth open area of the face and neck is a magnet for marks and other disturbances. Nearly every coin has minor, moderate, or major impairments in this area. The cap, wreath, and fields are secondary areas showing marks. Reverses are found with much lighter marks, with some coins having near-pristine surfaces often several grades higher than the obverse. Marks, when present, are usually found on the neck, shield, wings, and tail, with areas surrounding the eagle less often seen with disturbance.

LUSTER: Every luster variation is seen on coins from all of the mints. Most Philadelphia coins are seen with slightly frosty-to-very frosty surfaces. New Orleans issues, as noted previously, do not usually have as vibrant a luster as the other issues, being mostly seen with a flat-to-frosty luster. Very frosty, semi-prooflike, and prooflike specimens are encountered from this mint, though many of these coins still exhibit slight weakness of strike. San Francisco issues generally have satin-to-very frosty surfaces, with many semi-prooflike and some prooflike coins also seen. Denver Mint issues are mostly seen

with a frosty luster, but often with more of a satin look than Philadelphia and San Francisco coinage.

STRIKE: The Barber half dollar reverse is the same as that of the quarter, thus striking weakness is noted in the same areas. The hair below LIBERTY is seen with incompleteness, as are the stars, wreath, and ribbon. The reverse may have weakness in the head, neck, wing tips, shield, inner wing feathers, tail, and claws, with the right claw weak on many coins. As with the dimes and quarters, New Orleans issues often show weakness in all of these locations. Philadelphia, Denver, and San Francisco mint coins are usually decently struck, though on occasion they also show some weakness. On some coins, such as the 1907-O and 1908-O, there is a bulge on the cheek and neck caused by die clashing and improperly hardened dies.

EYE APPEAL: Although Barber half dollars are rarer than the quarters and much rarer than the dimes, there are still many great examples of most date and mint mark combinations. There are more weakly struck coins than for quarters or dimes, so for some issues this is a concern. Although there are probably not as many blazing-luster half dollars, many coins do have good luster. There are numerous lustrous, well-struck coins, and when combined with minimal marks, obviously more common on these larger coins, half dollars are great examples of the Barber series. There are many brilliant white, lightly toned, or spectacularly toned examples of most date and mint-mark combinations.

Proofs

HAIRLINES: Although some of these coins are found nearly hairline-free, light or moderate hairlines are seen on the majority of Barber half dollars. Album slide marks are also prevalent, with the face and neck being most affected. Hairlines are sometimes found across the entire obverse, but most examples show impairment in the open field, mainly in front of the face. The reverses have little open field area, but on cleaned specimens hairlines will be seen in the field among the devices and lettering.

REFLECTIVITY: Nearly every coin seen has deeply mirrored fields, most with frosted devices and lettering. The hub was changed in 1901, resulting in coins that for several years had less frosting on the devices and lettering, but heavily frosted coins are seen for the later years, from 1907 through 1915. All years have the deeply reflective, watery look, and nearly every specimen encountered will have these surfaces.

STRIKE: As mentioned earlier, the Mint had little problem striking Proofs in the latter part of the nineteenth century. Nearly all examples of Barber Proofs are well struck or fully struck. Slight weakness is occasionally seen in the dentils, stars, hair, feathers, shield, and claws.

EYE APPEAL: As with the dimes and quarters, many coins were stored in Mint tissue, acquiring vibrant toning. Strike is usually excellent, so finding coins with minimal hairlines and abrasions with original surfaces is not difficult. There are also many examples with deeply frosted devices and lettering, which, when combined with pristine surfaces, make incredible examples of these large coins. This is a highly collectible series, so target-toned coins from albums are also seen.

Walking Liberty Half Dollar (1916–1947)
Circulated Examples

Although the Morgan modifications in 1918 strengthened the skirt lines, some other areas seemed not to strike up as well as the 1916–1917 issues. Most noticeably, Miss Liberty's left hand is often weakly struck. For **AU-55/58** coins, the left hand is also one of the first areas of wear, along with the head and left leg. Wear along the breast of the eagle is the first area of the reverse where friction is noted, along with the left leg and upper part of the left wing. Strike weakness is seen for the breast feathers and leg of the eagle. Worn to **AU-50/53**, obvious friction is seen from the head down to the bottom of the

left leg, with friction now evident in the field. The reverse will have some of the breast and left leg feathers slightly flat in these grades, and slight friction will now extend to most of the wing feathers.

EF-40/45 coins have flatness in the head, breast, left hand, and skirt lines of the left leg, with blending of the breast, hand, and skirt lines. The breast, upper wing, and leg feathers will be worn mostly flat, and some wear is evident on the central wing feathers.

Although on the modified Morgan dies the skirt lines are usually evident, some branch-mint issues will still have skirt-line weakness, which should be a secondary grading factor. **VF-20/35** specimens will have flatness along the body from the head to the bottom of the leg. With the breast and leg feathers worn flat and the upper wing having only slight detail, the central wing feathers will be the only feathers still showing detail.

The modified Morgan design will have some skirt lines present in **F-12/15**, but the Weinman dies may not. The head, breast, and hand will be worn smooth, with flatness in the flag and foliage around the upper part of the body. The reverse will have some wing feathers present, though little fine detail.

VG-8/10 graded coins will have a mostly flat Miss Liberty, with the flag, foliage, and skirt lines showing slight detail, though weakly struck, and Weinman-die coins may not have skirt lines present. The rims should still be strong and the inner border still distinct. There will be slight wing feather detail.

Miss Liberty will be very flat in **G-4/6**, with the deeply recessed areas showing some detail. The rim may be worn into the tops of a few letters, though some inner border should be present. The date may have some slight wear on the bottom part of the numerals, and there may be a few wing feathers slightly visible.

With **AG-3** coins, the rims will be worn into the lettering and the date may be partially incomplete. Miss Liberty will show slight recessed detail, blending into the field and adjacent devices. The reverse will have an eagle that is worn nearly flat. **FR-2** specimens will have a partial date and lettering, with Miss Liberty quite worn and blended. The reverse may have some peripheral lettering obliterated, with a flat eagle.

PO-1 coins will have a discernible date and some of Miss Liberty, with the reverse worn smooth, though a mint mark must be present for branch-mint coins.

Mint State Examples

MARKS: These coins were stored in bags and rolls, so some examples have only the "roll friction" on the high points, while others may have slight-to-heavy bag marks. When contact comes from other coins in a roll, the marks are seen down the center of the coin, including the head, breast, hand, and leg. Other obverse marks and impairments are found on and about the figure, as well as in the open field, other devices, and lettering. Reverse contact from other coins in a roll is usually seen on the neck, breast, and left leg of the eagle, as well as along the tops of the wings. Bag marks and other disturbances on the reverse are mainly found on the eagle, with the slight open field, other devices, and lettering being secondary marking areas.

LUSTER: Most coins are seen with satin-to-very frosty luster. There are a few flat-luster and semi-prooflike coins found and, very rarely, prooflike specimens, though with little reflectivity. Some early coins, especially the 1916 and 1917 issues, have a scaly surface similar to Type I Standing Liberty quarters that really defies luster categorization. These coins sometimes have a satin look and other times have a booming luster that would otherwise be labeled "very frosty," save for the "orange-peel" look of the surface. Most Philadelphia issues have good luster, ranging from slightly frosty to very frosty. Denver and San Francisco issues, especially those from the teens and twenties, usually have satin-to-slightly frosty surfaces. Most of the coins in the 1930s and 1940s from all three

mints have frosty luster, but satin, semi-prooflike, and occasionally prooflike specimens are seen.

STRIKE: Although there is not quite as great a percentage of weakly struck Walking Liberty half dollars as Standing Liberty quarters, there are certainly as many poorly struck Walking Liberties. Some Denver and San Francisco coins have "dished" centers, with parts of the breast, belly, arm, hand, and left leg totally missing. On the reverse, the entire breast may be missing, with part of the left leg and wing missing as well. Other coins that show slight weakness of strike may have incompleteness on the head, breast, arm, hand, and left leg. Other areas that may show weakness are the flag, foliage, sun, feet, and date. Most reverse weakness will be in the upper wing, the upper edge of the lower wing, the breast, and the left leg, with other weakness seen in the head, right leg, lower feathers, perch, foliage, and lettering.

EYE APPEAL: The design of this coin is considered by some to be the most attractive of all regular-issue half dollars. The highest grades, in which most of the later dates and some of the earlier dates are available, are extremely attractive coins. They are found with almost no marks, are very well struck and lustrous, and have brilliant, lightly toned, or spectacularly toned surfaces. These coins are found in many variations in the higher grades since rolls, and in some cases bags, of many dates exist. Brilliant or light cream-colored toning comprises the greatest number of superb specimens, these obviously having been cherry-picked from rolls or bags by astute collectors in the past.

Proofs

HAIRLINES: If Proofs are verified for 1916 or 1917, the matte or satin surfaces would mask all but fairly heavy hairlines and other impairments. For the brilliant Proofs struck from 1936 through 1942, the obverse hairlines are usually noted in the open field, in front of and behind the figure. On heavily cleaned specimens, lines may be present across the entire surface. Album slide marks,

MS-67 *1942 Walking half dollar obverse. Well-struck, with only minor contact.*

MS-67 *1942 Walking half dollar reverse. Nearly mark-free surfaces, with full detail.*

MS-66 *1942 Walking half dollar obverse. Slight contact, with a few light "hits" above the left hand.*

MS-66 *1942 Walking half dollar reverse. A few very light marks are seen on the eagle's breast and leg, as well as a toned area in the upper right quadrant.*

MS-65 *1946 Walking half dollar obverse. Light marks are seen on the rays and body, and in the field.*

MS-65 *1946 Walking half dollar reverse. As with many coins, the reverse is nearly mark-free.*

MS-64 *1946-S Walking half dollar obverse. Marks and weakness of strike are noted for this specimen, with an especially weak motto.*

MS-64 *1946-S Walking half dollar reverse. Weak strike, light marks, and "drift" marks are found on this coin. Note the very weak breast and leg feathers.*

MS-63 *1946-S Walking half dollar obverse. Marks on the sun, rays, and body and scuffs in the right field are noted, with strike weakness on the left hand and right leg. The missing skirt lines are from striking weakness.*

MS-63 *1946-S Walking half dollar reverse. Several obvious marks are seen on the leg and lower wing feathers, with strike weakness in the breast, leg, and upper wing feathers.*

MS-62 *1946-S Walking half dollar obverse. Marks are noted around the obverse, with several seen on the sun, left leg, and the field above the motto.*

MS-62 *1946-S Walking half dollar reverse. Marks are scattered around the eagle, and several are seen in the field.*

when present, are noted on the head, breast, arm, and left leg of the figure. Reverse lines are usually minor, though some coins have been cleaned, leaving behind lines that are most noticeable on the wing and breast.

REFLECTIVITY: Of course, the Matte or Satin Proofs, if verified, would have no reflectivity and would look similar to the Matte and Satin Proof gold, nickel, and copper coins of the era. The brilliant Proofs have the deeply mirrored, watery-looking surfaces of most modern Proof issues. There are quite a few coins that have frosted devices and lettering. The deeply frosted coins contrast with the mirrored surfaces, making the fields appear even more reflective. There are rumors of 1936 Satin Proofs like the cent and nickel, but they are unverified.

STRIKE: A Matte or Satin Proof of 1916 or 1917 would have extraordinary detail with sharp inner borders, and all of Miss Liberty's fine detail would be fully struck, as would the eagle's. The brilliant Proofs struck from 1936 through 1942 are almost all well struck or fully struck. An occasional coin showing slight central weakness is seen. Coins without the designer's initials are the result of polishing, possibly when the dies were being made mirrorlike.

EYE APPEAL: There are brilliant, lightly toned, medium toned, and Mint tissue toned specimens seen in the highest grades. These coins are found with near hairline-free surfaces, and quite a few have frosted devices and lettering, though not many with deep frost. This popular design is extremely attractive when found in the highest Proof grades, with strong demand from collectors for the spectacularly toned, frosted, or other impressive specimens.

Franklin Half Dollar (1948–1963)
Circulated Examples
Most Franklin half dollars are collected in Mint State, but a few dates are worth premiums over their silver content in the higher circulated grades. Hair detail is not sharp,

even in **AU-55/58** grades, as the design does not have much intricate detail. The top of the head, the cheek, the hair around the ear, and the shoulder will show slight wear. The reverse will have slight wear on the bar holding the bell, the top of the bell, and the lower part of the bell with the lines. Weakness of strike is noted for the obverse in the hair, mainly around the ear. For the reverse, the inscription and bell lines show areas of weakness. Worn to **AU-50/53**, the surfaces now exhibit slight friction, as do the aforementioned areas of the obverse and reverse.

EF-40/45 coins have wear in the same places, though now the hair behind and below the ear will be flat on the high points. The reverse may show part of the inscription and bell lines on well-struck coins, with little evident on poorly struck specimens.

Though not often collected, **VF-20/35** Franklin half dollars will have some detail in the hair at the back of the head, with the top hair flat. On the reverse, detail of the bar holding the bell and the bell itself will be slight. The deeper bell parts will still have slight detail, such as the crack and the bell lines at the edges.

F-12/15 specimens have a well-worn head, with only the deepest hairlines showing any detail. The reverse will have the bar holding the bell and the bell itself worn smooth, with a few slight details such as the straps holding the bell and the bell crack still evident.

Franklin half dollars are not usually seen below Fine, though PCGS general standards explained in chapter 4 would apply.

Mint State Examples
MARKS: Many of these coins are found with roll contact as well as bag marks. Most of these coins have light contact marks from other coins across the bust, with the hair, cheekbone, and shoulder being the main areas of contact. Other impairments are common on the hair, face, neck, and shoulder, as well as in the open field. Reverse roll contact marks are seen mainly on the bell, usually its

middle and lower parts. Marks and other disturbances are also found on the upper part, along with the bell holder and open field.

LUSTER: Most Franklin half dollars have slightly frosty-to-very frosty surfaces. There are coins that have a satin luster and a few coins are semi-prooflike, but full prooflike specimens are virtually unknown. Philadelphia and Denver coins usually have slightly more frosty surfaces than do the San Francisco coins. Some San Francisco issues are softly struck, with satin-to-slightly frosty surfaces, but some of these weakly struck coins have quite frosty surfaces.

STRIKE: Although the bell lines are the point of interest for Franklin half dollar collectors, this is only one area of strike weakness. The obverse has striking weakness noted in the top hair, the hair that flows around the ear, the two waves of hair at the bottom, the cheek behind the mouth, and the lower bust line. Reverse weakness, besides the bell lines, includes the ropes and lettering, with other areas showing slight weakness. When the lower set of bell lines is full, these coins are designated Full Bell Lines (FBL).

EYE APPEAL: Most early dates are either found brilliant, high-grade examples usually from rolls, or toned, usually from government-issued Mint Sets. The last of the cardboard Mint Sets was issued in 1958, so the 1959–1963 coins are almost always found brilliant or with light creamy toning, these having been cherry-picked from rolls. Finding coins with minimal marks, whether brilliant or toned, is the most difficult problem with most years. Strike is a problem with many San Francisco issues, though luster is generally good. Superb coins are found for nearly every date, but FBL examples are rare for some issues.

Proofs

HAIRLINES: These coins were in plastic sleeves in boxes until mid-1955, when they were then packaged in the familiar "flat packs" that contained all of the coins in one large flexible plastic "envelope." These coins,

however, often are hairlined from sliding in these holders, with the field in front of and behind the head usually being the affected area. There are many pristine coins, as not all have acquired hairlines. On cleaned specimens, hairlines may be seen across the entire surfaces, with light-to-moderate lines usually seen.

REFLECTIVITY: Nearly every year, except some 1950 issues that have satiny prooflike surfaces, has a deeply reflective, watery, mirrored field. Many coins have medium-to-very heavy frosted devices and lettering, though some years are scarce. Some coins are seen with mirrored surfaces across the entire coin, with no hint of frosting on the devices or lettering.

STRIKE: Proofs are much better struck but may still have slight incompleteness on some coins. The fuzzy reverse lettering and bell lines may be more from worn dies than from striking weakness. There is not a lot of detail in the hair, so weakness is difficult to detect on the obverse.

EYE APPEAL: These coins usually are brilliant or lightly toned, with varying degrees of frosted devices and lettering. There are coins with no frost on the devices and lettering, but most have light-to-moderate frosting. Some of the early dates are very rare with deep frost on the devices and lettering, but the early dates are much rarer.

Kennedy Half Dollar (1964 to Date)
Circulated Examples

There is no premium for Kennedy half dollars in circulated grades, even for the silver alloy 1964 coins. In **AU-55/58** grades, slight friction is seen on the hair around the part, the cheek, and the neck. The reverse will exhibit slight wear on the neck, shield, upper wing, and tail of the eagle. For **AU-50/53** coins, slightly more friction will be seen in the noted areas, with slight friction now evident in the obverse field.

For grades of EF and below, Kennedy half dollars would be graded by the general standards set forth by PCGS, described in chapter 4. Technical grading would apply to all grades.

Mint State Examples

MARKS: Roll contact marks are common on the 90 percent silver, 40 percent silver, and cupro-nickel specimens of the Kennedy half dollar, with the hair, face, and neck of the obverse seen with these marks. Roll friction for the reverse is usually very minor, much less than for the obverse, with only slight contact on the neck, shield, and tail.

LUSTER: For the 90 percent silver issues, most coins are slightly frosty-to-very frosty in luster, with the 40 percent silver issues mainly satin to frosty. The clad issues struck in 1971 and later are like most cupro-nickel issues, with a satin-to-slightly frosty luster. Other luster variations are sometimes seen for all three alloys, with flat and semi-prooflike specimens occasionally seen and prooflike specimens rare.

STRIKE: The hair of the Kennedy half dollar is only slightly more detailed than that on the Franklin half dollar. Obverse weakness is noted on the upper part of the hair, the cheek, and the lower bust line. For the reverse, the stars, ribbon, head, wing tips, shield, and tail may show weakness of strike. This detail is not crisp on new dies, so when the dies wear, there may be even more incompleteness.

EYE APPEAL: When found superb, these coins are usually brilliant or have a hint of toning. Specimens are occasionally seen that have been in envelopes or other sulfur-containing enclosures that show vibrant red, blue, green, yellow, and other colors. These coins, when nearly mark-free and lustrous, often bring premiums higher than brilliant specimens in the same grade.

Proofs

HAIRLINES: Most of these coins have very few hairlines. All three alloys are seldom found with more than very minor hairlines. The coins struck in 1968 and later were issued in hard plastic holders and unless re-

moved carelessly from their holders, they are usually found pristine.

REFLECTIVITY: All three alloys have deeply mirrored fields, with many coins and nearly all of the 1968 and later examples showing frosted devices and lettering.

STRIKE: Proofs are nearly all fully struck, with those struck in 1968 and later showing frosted devices and lettering. Only those coins struck from slightly worn dies will show anything but full intended detail.

EYE APPEAL: Coins with heavily frosted devices and lettering are the most attractive of the Kennedy half dollar Proofs. All three alloys are found with heavy frost and near-perfect fields. The cupro-nickel alloy examples from 1971 and later are mostly found with this deep frost, while some of the 90 percent and 40 percent silver alloy specimens are found with heavy frost.

Silver Dollars
Flowing Hair Dollar (1794–1795)
Circulated Examples

Since Flowing Hair dollars are large coins, marks are more prevalent than for all lower denominations. Slight wear on the cheek, bust, and hair strands around the ear are found on **AU-55/58** coins, with strike weakness sometimes noted in the hair around the ear. The 1794 coins were struck on the Mint's first presses and are almost universally weak on the first few stars and the corresponding area of the reverse. This weakness is more the result of the dies not being parallel than of striking weakness. The eagle's head, neck, breast, legs, and upper parts of the wing feathers will show friction. When weakly struck, the entire central part of the eagle and possibly the wing feathers are affected. The wreath will have slight friction on the highest points, mainly the leaves. When worn to **AU-50/53**, the friction is fairly easy to distinguish from strike weakness. There will be friction in the field and across the face and neck, with some of the hair displaying slight wear. The eagle and wreath will now have definite wear, though the field is well-protected and should show only slight rubbing.

For grades **EF-40/45**, the hairlines will still be distinct on strong strikes with only slight wear, flat around the ear on poor strikes. The entire face and neck area will show wear, as will the field. Some of the stars will still have detail. Breast feathers will be worn mostly flat, with only a few visible when the strike is strong. The reverse will show most of the wing feather detail on strong strikes only. The highest leaves will now be worn flat, with slight blending into the surrounding devices.

On well-struck coins, from one-third to two-thirds of the hairlines will be visible for **VF-20/35** coins, strongest mostly in the lower part of the hair. The wear will now blend most of the hairline into the face, and most of the stars will be flat, though they are sometimes quite sharp. Rims should be complete, though unevenly struck coins may show slight weakness. As noted earlier, almost all 1794 dollars are weak in the lower left quadrant of the obverse and corresponding part of the reverse, obliterating the rim in these areas. The eagle may have no fine detail on poorly struck coins, with up to one-half the feathers present on good strikes. Leaves of the wreath will be worn smooth, with notable blending.

F-12/15 coins may have from slight to nearly one-half of the lower hairlines still present, but poorly struck coins will have only the back strands. The head should be complete, as should LIBERTY and the stars. Rims should be complete, except for localized weakness. There may or may not be wing feathers present, depending on the original strike, though the eagle and wreath should be outlined. Only the recessed parts of the wreath will be distinct.

Some marks are usually present in circulated (and most Uncirculated) grades. However, even in **VG-8/10**, large marks or huge rim nicks are not acceptable. The head should be outlined, with only the back strands of hair visible. Rims should be complete, save for

unevenly struck coins, with the peripheral stars and lettering also complete. The eagle and wreath will be worn almost smooth, with only slight detail.

G-4/6 specimens will have Miss Liberty worn smooth, with parts blending into the field. Rims may have several indistinct areas, possibly blending almost to some of the stars. LIBERTY and the date should be clear except for uneven strikes. The reverse will have a flat, smooth eagle and blending of the wreath, with the rims touching some of the lettering.

The **AG-3** grade may have some stars and part of the date missing, as the rim will be worn in most areas. Miss Liberty will blend into the field in several areas, with little detail. The reverse will have areas where the lettering is completely gone. The eagle and wreath will be incomplete in places and will have no fine detail. **FR-2** coins will have a readable date and some parts of the head, LIBERTY, and stars present. The reverse may be almost totally worn smooth, with sporadic detail evident.

The **PO-1** coin must have a readable date, with part of the head visible, and often the reverse is worn smooth.

Mint State Examples

MARKS: These large coins are usually found with marks and other disturbances, with the face, neck, bust, hair, and open field often noted with impairments. The date, stars, and LIBERTY are secondary areas where markings are found. The eagle is the first place marks and other impairments are found with the wreath, open field, and peripheral lettering being the secondary areas of marking. Album slide marks are sometimes found on the obverse, with the face, neck, and bust being the usual areas seen with these lines.

LUSTER: All luster variations are found for both 1794 and 1795 issues, but most of the 1794 coins have a satin-to-slightly frosty luster, while the 1795 coins were struck on stronger presses, resulting in most of this issue having a frosty luster. Semi-prooflike coins are found for both dates, but full prooflike examples are rare.

STRIKE: As noted, nearly all 1794 Flowing Hair dollars have strike weakness, especially on the lower left part of the obverse, with the first few stars almost always weak. The corresponding part of the reverse, the upper left quadrant, also will usually be weak, as the dies were not in parallel. The 1795 coins were better struck, with the more powerful press introduced in 1795. The central hair of the obverse is sometimes weak, along with the stars, the upper hair, the high points on very back of the hair, and the bust. The LIBERTY, date, eyes, lips, and other areas may have localized weakness or weakness from punching, as each letter or device was punched individually to different depths. Reverse weakness is seen on the head, neck, breast, upper wing, legs, perch, and wreath. The lettering may also be weak for the same reasons as on the obverse. The edge-lettering machine sometimes causes rim irregularities, the resultant edges resembling a piecrust.

EYE APPEAL: These coins, the largest silver coins struck, are beautiful when found with positive attributes. Well-struck, lustrous coins with minimal marks and either brilliant or toned surfaces are occasionally found. There are a few great-looking coins that were saved by visitors to the early Mint, such as the Lord St. Oswald specimens, with the other superb specimens undoubtedly saved as the first examples of silver dollar coinage. As noted, finding coins with all of the attributes positive is difficult because many of these coins had adjustment marks, weakness of strike, subdued luster, and other negatives.

Specimens

HAIRLINES: The first coins struck of this largest-denomination silver coin were obviously very highly prized by their owners. However, their sheer size and the delicate nature of the surfaces make them very difficult to preserve, thus light, moderate, or even heavy hairlines are expected, with the obverse field being the main area where these would be found. On the reverse, there is very little field area, though that around the eagle may have some hairlines.

REFLECTIVITY: Although a new, more powerful coining press was introduced in 1795, the 1794 specimen strikes have deeply prooflike surfaces. These coins have surfaces as deeply mirrored as most of the open-collar strikings of other denominations. The devices and lettering have moderate frosting that contrasts with the mirrored fields.

STRIKE: Striking quality of the known 1794 specimen-strike dollar is extraordinary for the era. Although not fully struck, all the stars are present, though several of the first ones are slightly flat. Overall detail for this 1794 coin is extremely sharp, and any 1795 specimen-strike dollars would also have this sharpness. Only the slightest weakness would be acceptable for a coin to qualify for specimen-strike status.

EYE APPEAL: The first of the largest silver coin struck at the new Mint are, without question, the most incredible examples of its production. Mirrored surfaces highlighting the Flowing Hair design make these early specimens among the most treasured U.S. coins.

Draped Bust Dollar—Small Eagle/ Heraldic (Large) Eagle (1795–1804)
Circulated Examples

AU-55/58 Draped Bust dollars have slight wear on the cheek, the hair around the ear, the bust, and the shoulder. Almost all dates have some coins with weakly struck centers. The central hair detail and the head, breast, and leg area of the Small Eagle coins (the shield and adjacent wing feathers on the Heraldic coins are areas of weakness) are sometimes partially missing, even on Uncirculated specimens. The reverse will have slight friction on the wreath, head, breast, and leg of the Small Eagle coins, with the breast, shield, clouds, tail feathers, and tip of the wing feathers showing slight wear for the Heraldic type. In **AU-50/53**, wear is now apparent on the aforementioned areas, with rubbing now in the obverse field. The reverse field is well-protected; thus only the devices usually show friction.

With wear to **EF-40/45**, friction is now obvious on the face, hair, and bust, with the hair around the ear flat from wear. Small Eagle coins will have most wing feather detail, though the breast feathers are usually flat. Details of the wreath are still very clear, with only the highest leaves flattened from wear. The wear on Heraldic-reverse coins appears on the head, breast, clouds, shield, and tips of the wing feathers, with most of the wing feathers visible. Unevenly struck coins are sometimes seen, with areas of the legend weak or partially missing.

VF-20/35 specimens will have from one-third to two-thirds of the hair detail, depending on the level of **VF** grade and the original striking quality. The bust area is often worn smooth in this grade. The Small Eagle coins will have a flat head, breast, and leg, with up to one-half of the wing feathers present. The wreath will have flat leaves that are mostly separate. On Heraldic specimens, the shield will show a blending of the stripes, with up to one-half the wing feathers visible. The clouds, arrows, olive branch, and tail feathers will be worn, with blending apparent.

The hair detail on **F-12/15** coins ranges from a few strands to about one-third present, depending on the original strike. Rims should be complete in this grade, except for uneven strikes. Small Eagle coins will have a flat wreath, with blending and little fine detail, and a worn eagle with few feathers showing. On well-struck Heraldic-reverse coins, up to one-third or slightly more of the wing feathers may be present. The clouds and shield will show only slight separation and are mostly worn smooth.

VG-8/10 coins have little detail on Miss Liberty, with sometimes the very back hair curls sometimes still intact. Rims may show incompleteness, though this should be slight. On Small Eagle-reverse types, the wreath and eagle will be worn almost smooth. Wing feathers of the Heraldic coins may show sporadic detail. The clouds, shield, arrows, and olive branch will have much blending and are worn almost flat.

Many **G-4/6** coins will have incomplete rims. Miss Liberty will have little detail and may blend into the field. Stars should be visible, except in areas of rim weakness. Although the wreath and eagle of the Small Eagle reverse are worn very flat, there may be slight detail and some separation in the wreath. The reverse rims of the Heraldic type will be worn into the tops of the lettering. The clouds, eagle, shield, arrows, and olive branch will be quite worn, with slight fine detail.

AG-3 coins have a partial date, LIBERTY, and stars with a head that blends into the field. The reverse will have wear into the lettering, with the central devices worn smooth. For **FR-2** coins, the wear will obliterate part or all of the stars and LIBERTY, with a partial date. The reverse may have only part of the eagle present, with most of the lettering worn away.

PO-1 coins have a discernible date and enough detail to determine type, with little or no reverse detail.

Mint State Examples

MARKS: Large coins equal large marks, and many of these coins have marks and other disruptions. Obverse marks are found on the face, neck, and bust, along with the field, though the hair may disguise small marks. The Small Eagle reverse is similar to the Flowing Hair, and marks are similar. Heraldic-reverse coins have an intricately designed reverse with less open field area. The eagle and shield are the main areas with marks, with the other devices, open areas, and lettering also seen with impairments.

LUSTER: All of the luster variations are found, with most of the Small Eagle coins seen with satin-to-frosty luster, and the Heraldic coins mostly frosty. There are probably a higher percentage of semi-prooflike and prooflike examples known for the Small Eagle type. There are quite a few examples of both types with very frosty luster, as the Mint was quite adept at striking these large silver coins.

STRIKE: Although well-struck Small Eagle coins can be found, many are poorly struck. Obverse weakness is first noticed on the hair above the ear, around and below the ear, and the bust, with other weakness noted in the top of the stars, lettering, date, hair, ribbon, and drapery. Reverse weakness for the Small Eagle type is first noticed on the head, neck, upper wings, breast, and legs. With the Heraldic type, weakness is noted in the clouds, stars, head, ribbon, neck, breast, shield, inner wings, wing tips, and claws. The right part of the clouds and the right stars are opposite the tip of the bust on the obverse of the Heraldic Eagle type, and on some coins these areas may be very weak. Other weak areas noted are the wreath on the Small Eagle type and the arrows, branch, and inner wing feathers for the Heraldic coins. The lettering around the periphery may be weak, and unevenness of strike is sometimes seen, but severe cases are rare. Most coins struck from out-of-parallel dies for Draped Bust dollars have slight weakness.

EYE APPEAL: When found lustrous, minimally marked, well struck, and with light or attractive toning, these are some of the most spectacular coins of any denomination or metal. The silver dollar, in its various incarnations, has always been popular. Fully struck coins are rare—so well-struck specimens with lustrous, near mark-free surfaces are usually the best examples available. Though there are not many coins known in the very highest grades, there are some very spectacular coins seen for most dates of both types.

Proofs

HAIRLINES: These so-called originals, dated 1801–1804 but struck in 1834–1836, were made for dignitaries and issued in special boxes, while the restrikes, circa 1858–1860 or later, were made primarily for collectors. Therefore, extra care would have been given to these ultra-rarities, and many of them are still relatively free of hairlines. The obverse field is the main area where hairlines and other impairments are found, though some coins show hairlines on the head and other areas. The reverse hairlines are usually very minor, with little open field area available for impairment.

REFLECTIVITY: The original strikings were made with stronger presses than were the coins of the early 1800s, and the resultant surfaces were more deeply reflective, similar to the coins of the era in which they were struck, 1834–1836. The restrikes were struck much later, with even more powerful presses and with close collars, resulting in coins that had deeply mirrored, watery looking surfaces. Frosted devices and lettering are seen, though the close-collar coins have a slightly deeper frost.

STRIKE: Coins dated 1801–1804 actually were struck in 1834–1836 and later, with striking quality far superior to the earlier issues. Slight weakness may be noted in the obverse hair, stars, drapery, and bust. Reverse detail is very sharp, with only slight weakness noted in the head, breast, wing, and tail.

EYE APPEAL: The Draped Bust dollar and eagle are the only examples of Draped Bust coinage found in Proof condition. These spectacular examples illustrate the superb design in its ultimate state. They are the *crème de la crème* of Draped Bust coinage and are sometimes so spectacular that even experienced numismatists often do double takes when examining them. They have a medal-like quality that accents the superb design by highlighting the devices and lettering, with deeply reflective fields. Many of these coins have nice original toning, as the owners obviously stored them with care.

Liberty Seated (Gobrecht) Dollar— Flying Eagle–No Stars Obverse/Stars Obverse (1836–1839)

Circulated Examples

Though issued only in Proof, these coins were delivered for commercial use to the

Bank of the United States and are often seen circulated. Although they are similarly graded to the Liberty Seated Perched Eagle coins, discussed next, some slight differences are noted. **PR-55/58** coins have slight friction on the head, breast, and upper leg. The reverse has slight wear on the breast feathers and along the tips of the wing feathers. Specimens in the **PR-50/53** grades will show friction in the fields, as well as wear on the shield and lower leg. Some flatness on the breast and upper wing feathers is now evident, with the central wing and tail feathers showing slight friction as well. The starry reverse coins will show less friction in the fields than will the No Stars reverse.

In **PR-40/45** grades, the head and breast areas will be worn and slightly blended. There will be a slight loss of detail in the gown, though most folds will be present. LIBERTY should still be very bold. The eagle will have flatness on the breast and upper wing feathers. The central wing, body, and tail feathers will have wear but will still show major detail.

In **PR-20/35** grades, the body will have all recessed detail still evident, but the head, breast, right arm, and legs are flat. LIBERTY will begin to show letters partially worn away, especially in the lower **VF** grades. Feather detail will be partial, with the body, upper wing, and tail of the eagle worn flat.

PR-12/15 specimens will have only the deepest folds of the gown still present. LIBERTY may have several letters partially or totally missing. Most of the feathers will be worn smooth, with slight detail remaining. The lower part of the left wing may have most feathers visible.

The grades of **PR-8/10** may have only slight detail of Miss Liberty remaining, and LIBERTY may now be mostly worn away. The reverse will have a few worn feathers, mainly those in the lower part of the left wing.

In grades **PR-4/6**, only slight detail is present for Miss Liberty and LIBERTY is now worn completely away. The reverse may have the eagle worn completely smooth, though some slight detail is still possible.

For coins that grade **PR-3**, Miss Liberty will only show an outline, and the rims will be worn into the field of the No Stars type and into some of the stars of the Stars type. The reverse will have an outlined eagle, the rims worn into some of the reverse lettering. **PR-2** coins may have a partial date, and Miss Liberty may blend into the field. The reverse may have some lettering still evident around the periphery, with the eagle worn into the field.

PR-1 coins do not have to have a date, as the two types are identifiable from the reverse stars, or lack thereof. Some other identifying characteristics, such as a partial date or obverse stars, must be present if the reverse is worn smooth.

Proofs

HAIRLINES: Since this is the only Proof issue that was released into ordinary commercial channels, many of these coins have marks, nicks, scratches, and other contact marks, as well as hairlines. The obverse field, especially on the No Stars type, has the most open area of any silver coin, with the body of Miss Liberty being the secondary area of marking. Album slide marks are seen on these popular coins, with the head, breast, and right leg the main areas showing these. The reverse has many stars of varying size, with a much less open field area than the obverse. However, many hairlines and other impairments are found on and among these stars.

REFLECTIVITY: These have deeply mirrored and watery-looking fields. Moderate to heavy frosting on the devices and lettering is commonplace, contrasting with the mirrored fields to make the surfaces appear to have even deeper reflectivity.

STRIKE: Since all of these coins were Proofs, strike is usually superb. Slight weakness for the obverse is sometimes noted in the head, breast, leg, drapery folds, foot, shield, and stars, when present. Reverse weakness is occasionally noted in the upper tips of the wings, breast, leg, tail, and stars.

EYE APPEAL: When found with light hairlines and little impairment, these coins are the pinnacle of what Christian Gobrecht intended when he designed the Liberty Seated coinage. These coins are occasionally found with attractive, original toning, and when this is not too thick, these are among the most attractive of all Liberty Seated coinage. Since these Proofs were deposited into commercial channels, that is, the Bank of the United States, many coins have small marks, nicks, and other abrasions. Finding pristine examples of the original 1836 and 1839 issues is nearly impossible, with most superb specimens being restrikes from 1858 and later.

Liberty Seated Dollar—Perched Eagle No Motto/Motto (1840–1873)

Circulated Examples

Many Liberty Seated dollars show weakness of strike that, for the obverse, is noted on the head, breast, or central part of Miss Liberty. The reverse may show this weakness in the neck, upper right wing, and right leg of the eagle. **AU-55/58** coins will have slight wear on the head, breast, and upper legs, though these are areas noted earlier as strike weakness spots as well. The reverse will show slight friction on the feathers of the neck, both upper wings, and the legs. These are large coins, so slight friction and scattered marks in the fields are to be expected, even in these higher circulated grades. With wear to **AU-50/53**, the head, breast, entire legs, shield, rock, and lower gown folds now exhibit friction. The field now has rubbing, and scattered marks, small and large, are present. The reverse will have flatness on the neck, upper wing, and leg feathers, with wear now evident on the high points of all of the wing feathers.

The shield with LIBERTY wears much faster than for other Seated Liberty series, though not as quickly as with the raised LIBERTY of the twenty-cent coins. Therefore, **EF-40/45** coins that are decently struck should still

have fairly sharp letters for LIBERTY, but some wear will be evident on "BER." On poorly struck coins, the "BER" may be totally missing. The head, breast, and upper leg of Miss Liberty will be flat from wear, with the rock, shield, and lower leg also exhibiting friction. All gown folds will be present, though worn on the high points. Stars should still show most lines. The reverse will have all feathers present, except for areas of strike weakness, though the neck and leg feathers will be flatter than the wing feathers. Claws, leaves, and arrowheads will be separate, but the high points will be flat.

VF-20/35 specimens may have a partially missing LIBERTY, especially in the lower **VF** grades. As noted, "BER" may be missing entirely on some coins. The head and breast will be worn mostly flat, with blending evident. Gown detail will still be sharp in the recessed areas, though some lack of detail is noticed around the legs. Star lines will show only on the edges, with the central parts worn flat. Reverse feather detail should still be evident in the wings, but the neck, upper wing, and leg feathers will have only slight detail remaining. Claws, leaves, and arrowheads will be mostly flat, with blending evident.

F-12/15 coins may have an incomplete LIBERTY, with "BER" and other letters missing entirely, but some letters must be partially visible. Major gown detail is still present, though blending of the gown lines, breast, and shield lines is very evident. Some feather detail is still visible, but all of the feathers are well-worn. Those central wing feathers will have some sharpness, with the neck and leg feathers mostly flat. Some detail remains in the claws, leaves and arrowheads, but these are worn together in places.

A few letters or partial letters of LIBERTY may be present for **VG-8/10**, but this is not necessary. Some recessed gown detail is still evident, though this is slight, such as the drapery at Miss Liberty's left elbow and next to her right arm. The shield will be present, but it will have blended lines, and a few wing feathers may still show. The claws, leaves, and arrowheads will be mostly worn flat and blended.

G-4/6 coins will have a smooth figure of Miss Liberty, with only slight recessed detail. The rim may be slightly worn into the fields and the lettering of the reverse may be weak, with the rim touching the tops of a few letters. Only the shield will usually have any detail, with the eagle worn smooth though fully outlined. Claws and leaves will be flat and very indistinct, with the arrowheads flat but separate.

AG-3 coins will have the rims worn into the stars and date and the lettering around the reverse. Miss Liberty will be totally flat and worn into the field in spots. Some lettering will be readable, while some will be nearly illegible. A few lines of the shield may be present, with the eagle worn smooth and into the field. For **FR-2**, there will be a partial Miss Liberty, date, and stars, though the stars may be obliterated. The reverse will have a partial eagle with some or no lettering present.

In **PO-1**, all that is necessary are a date and mint mark, if present, and some slight detail. The reverse may have slight eagle detail or be worn smooth.

Mint State Examples

MARKS: As with all large coins, these are more often than not seen with marks and other impairments. Small, medium, and heavy marks are found, along with hairlines and other disturbances. The body is the main area affected, though the field is a close second. Reverse marks are found across the surfaces, with the area above the eagle on the No Motto coins often having multiple markings. Although most obverses have more markings, there are some coins with as many or more reverse marks.

LUSTER: All luster variations are found for both types, with most Philadelphia coins showing satin-to-very frosty surfaces, except for the low-mintage dates, which are usually frosty, semi-prooflike, or prooflike. New Orleans coins are usually found with frosty sur-

faces, though satin, semi-prooflike, and prooflike examples are seen, especially for the common 1859–1860 issues. San Francisco coins are very scarce, with the 1870 issue excessively rare in Uncirculated, the 1859 extremely rare, the 1872 rare, and the 1873 unknown in any grade. The few Mint State specimens found have satin or slightly frosty surfaces, with an occasional frosty or semi-prooflike coin seen. Carson City issues are all low-mintage, with most specimens seen either semi-prooflike or prooflike, and only a few frosty or satin specimens encountered.

STRIKE: Although similar to other Liberty Seated coinage, dollars have more striking problems than do smaller issues. Part of this is due to the difficulty in striking large coins. Weakness on the obverse is often noted for the stars, head, breast, legs, gown, foot, rock, and shield. Reverse weakness is seen on the head, neck, shield, upper wings, especially the right wing, legs, claws, and arrow feathers. On the Motto type, occasional weakness is noted, usually in the first few letters that are opposite the rock and shield of the obverse. Other slight weakness is sometimes noted in the date, lettering, and other devices.

EYE APPEAL: These large coins are usually found with medium-to-heavy marks and other impairments. Finding pristine examples of some date and mint mark combinations is nearly impossible, with some dates extremely rare in any Uncirculated grade. Well-struck, lustrous, lightly marked, and brilliant or attractively toned examples are available for some issues, however, and when these coins are offered they are always highlights of the collection or auction in which they appear. Obviously, finding mark-free or lightly marked coins is difficult with both the No Motto and Motto types.

Proofs

HAIRLINES: These large silver coins are seldom found pristine. In fact, they are probably the most commonly seen silver type coin with hairlines, often quite heavy and concentrated. The obverse field is commonly seen with hairlines and other impairments, with the figure regularly seen with impairments as well. Album slide marks, when present, are usually seen on the head, breast, and right leg, and often these are fairly severe. Both types usually have hairlines and other impairments above the eagle on the reverse, with the No Motto type especially affected. Other areas of the field on the reverse also reveal hairlines, but, as with most coins, they are often lighter and less concentrated than those on the obverse.

REFLECTIVITY: Deeply reflective fields are found on the coins struck in 1854 and later, as well as on the restrikes of the early dates, which were probably struck in 1858 and later. Some of the original 1840–1850 issues may have die polish still evident in various areas, which may slightly impede the mirrored surfaces. Frosted devices and lettering are seen on most coins, and are light to heavy in nature.

STRIKE: Almost all Liberty Seated dollars, including Proofs, show slight weakness. Although this may be seen only in a few flat stars, weakness in the head, upper right wing flatness, a flat right leg, or weak claws, there is usually some area that has some weakness. Fully struck coins are the exception, and for some dates, 1857 for instance, no *fully* struck Proofs are known.

EYE APPEAL: These coins are extremely attractive when found with minimal impairments, whether with brilliant, lightly toned, or attractive medium or dark toning. The heavily frosted specimens that contrast with deeply mirrored fields are perhaps the best looking of all Liberty Seated dollars, with more Motto coins usually seen in superb condition than No Motto examples. When either type is offered in superb condition, the price is also likely to be spectacular.

Trade Dollar (1873–1885)
Circulated Examples
Slight wear is evident for **AU-55/58** Trade dollars on the head, breast, and left leg. Slight friction might also be seen on Miss Liberty's arm and LIBERTY on the banner across the

cotton bale. The eagle will have slight friction on the neck, breast, upper and outer parts of the wing, and the legs, especially the left one. Areas of striking weakness for the obverse are Miss Liberty's head, her central part, and the left foot, plus the surrounding area. For the reverse, the eagle's head, upper right wing feather, motto, breast, left leg, left claw, plus the surrounding areas, are places where weakness is sometimes noted. **AU-50/53** coins will have more friction in these areas, plus the obverse and reverse fields will now show rub. Both legs and the other obverse devices will now also show wear, as will the central wing feathers.

For **EF-40/45** coins, more friction will be found on Miss Liberty's body, though most folds of her gown are still evident. The frond of grain behind the cotton bale will show slight flatness, as will the stars, but these should still have most of the radial lines. The LIBERTY and IN GOD WE TRUST will be strong, with no weakness unless it results from the strike. Wear will have flattened most of the neck, the outer and upper wing, and some of the breast and left leg feathers. Most of the central wing feathers are still clear, though slightly worn on high spots, with the claws flat and indistinct.

VF-20/35 coins usually have a very readable LIBERTY and IN GOD WE TRUST, but some letters may be slightly weak. Some areas of the gown are worn and blended, though recessed areas are still sharp. Miss Liberty's head and the breast area will still have some detail, though some areas are blended. The cotton bale is still sharply detailed, as are the fronds next to it. On the reverse, save for localized areas of weakness, E PLURIBUS UNUM will be strong, since it is incuse in design. Flatness of most neck, breast, and leg feathers is evident, with slight detail remaining. The outer wing feathers will be worn smooth, with the central wing feathers still fairly sharp, though obviously worn.

With **F-12/15** Trade dollars, Miss Liberty will show only the deepest recessed gown lines and other detail. The cotton bale and fronds are worn, with loss of detail very evident, and now LIBERTY is slightly weak, with some letters indistinct, as is IN GOD WE TRUST. The legend E PLURIBUS UNUM on the reverse will have indistinct letters and about one-half of the feathers will still show detail. The neck, outer wing, and both leg feathers are worn mostly smooth, as are the claws.

VG-8/10 coins show Miss Liberty very worn, with only slight deep details still evident. The LIBERTY is worn away, as is most of IN GOD WE TRUST, and the cotton bale has only some of the bands still present. The reverse may have part of E PLURIBUS UNUM still evident and a few central wing feathers.

For grades G-4/6, only deeply recessed parts of Miss Liberty, the cotton bale, and the fronds are still evident, with other areas worn smooth. There will be no evidence of LIBERTY or IN GOD WE TRUST. The rims are worn completely through most of the dentils and even slightly into the field, though they should not touch the stars or lettering. The eagle will be worn nearly smooth, with the E PLURIBUS UNUM worn away and with only the ribbon remaining.

In AG-3, the rims are worn into some of the stars and part of the date, with the reverse rims worn into some parts of the lettering. The obverse will still have some deep details of Miss Liberty and other devices, but some areas will be worn into the field. The reverse eagle will be totally flat and worn into the field in places. FR-2 coins may have some stars and part of the date present, with a partial Miss Liberty. The reverse may have the weight and fineness as the only lettering still present, with the eagle flat and worn into the field.

PO-1 coins should have a readable date and mint mark, if present, and little else save a partial Miss Liberty and eagle. There may be some lettering on the reverse, or possibly the entire surface may be worn smooth.

Mint State Examples

MARKS: These coins were struck to facilitate trade with the Orient, hence their common name. Since they were usually sent long distances, many of the coins have bag marks, hairlines, and other disruptions. Also, this series is commonly found with an unusual "impairment" seldom found on any other series of any denomination. The chop marks of various Oriental merchants are found on these coins, sometimes multiple marks, as the coins were passed in commerce. These chop-marked coins are now graded by PCGS, and they are avidly collected. Obverse marks and other impairments are found on the figure of Miss Liberty and the associated devices, as well as in the open field. Album slide marks, when present, are seen on the head, breast, arm, and left leg of Miss Liberty. The reverses often have as many marks as the obverse, or even more, with the eagle and surrounding field the main areas affected and the lettering and other devices being the secondary areas of disruption.

LUSTER: All luster variations are found on coins struck at each of the three issuing mints. Most Philadelphia coins are found with satin-to-very frosty luster, though semi-prooflike and prooflike examples are fairly common for several dates. San Francisco issues are usually found frosty, with quite a few satin, semi-prooflike, and prooflike specimens encountered, some with both sides showing the same luster variations and others showing varying luster combinations. Most Carson City issues have a frosty luster, with satin and semi-prooflike coins encountered fairly often. Deeply prooflike coins are less common for this mint, though they are occasionally encountered.

STRIKE: Mint Chief Engraver William Barber turned Miss Liberty around on this coin, now facing left. Striking weakness is noted for the stars, head, breast, central body, legs, foot, cotton bale, grain shafts, and base. Occasional weakness also is noted for other areas, such as the right hand holding the olive branch. Reverse weakness is noted on the motto, head, neck, breast, upper wings, especially the right wing, legs, and claws. Weakness is sometimes noted for other reverse areas, such as the lettering, leaves, and arrows.

EYE APPEAL: There are quite a few very attractive Mint State Trade dollars, but, as with all silver dollars, marks are found on nearly every specimen. When these impairments are light and the example has good luster, strike, and either brilliant, lightly toned, or attractively toned surfaces, these are the highest-grade Trade dollars. Finding some date and mint mark combinations in the highest grades is very difficult, as most of these coins were used in Far East trade. There are some spectacularly toned examples that look as though they were preserved from their year of issue, probably by collectors.

Proofs
HAIRLINES: These coins were mainly sold to American collectors, in contrast with the business strikes, which were mainly exported. They are more often found with hairlines and other impairments than Morgan dollars, but usually with less severe ones than seen on the Liberty Seated series. There are quite a few more pristine specimens of the Trade dollar seen than for the Liberty Seated series. The obverse field is especially vulnerable to hairlines, with the figure and associated devices also sometimes seen with impairments. Album slide marks are fairly often seen, with the head, breast, arms, and left leg being the most affected areas. The reverse field around the eagle is the most often seen hairlined area, though often the lines are lighter and less concentrated than those on the obverse.

REFLECTIVITY: Deeply mirrored fields are the norm for this series, with watery-looking fields on nearly every specimen, especially on the coins struck in 1877 and later. Heavy frost on the devices and lettering is commonplace, again, more so on the 1877 and later issues. Some of the later coins appear to have even deeper reflective fields than most Liberty Seated dollars, mainly due to the heavy frost present.

STRIKE: Most Trade dollar Proofs are well struck, more so than Liberty Seated dollars. Slight weakness is sometimes noted for the obverse stars, head, breast, central area, and foot. Reverse weakness is usually seen in the neck, upper wing, breast, leg, and claws.

EYE APPEAL: These coins are found with pristine surfaces, deeply frosted devices and lettering, and spectacular toning. Many of these coins were obviously stored in the Mint tissue of the era, preserving the surfaces and imparting beautiful blue, red, yellow, and other vibrant colors, which created some of the most spectacular Proof dollar coins. These coins are much more available in the highest grades than are the Proof Liberty Seated dollars.

Liberty Head (Morgan) Dollar (1878–1921)
Circulated Examples
There are three main styles of reverses for Morgan dollars that affect grading. The first is the flat-breast variety, seen on some 1878–1880 coins; the second is the round-breast variety, seen on most 1878–1904 issues; and the third is the groove-breast, seen only in 1921. Wear looks different for these reverses, and in the higher circulated grades this should be considered when determining remaining feather detail. The obverses are of two varieties, the one used from 1878–1904 and the one used only in 1921. These are graded similarly, though there is more relief on the 1878–1904 variety. Wear on the hair, especially above the ear, looks much different for the 1921 variety. That said, **AU-55/58** Morgan dollars have slight friction on the hair below LIBERTY, the hair above the ear, and the cheek. Reverse wear is noted on the eagle's head, breast, wing tips, legs, and claws. The wreath will have only slight friction on the highest points of the center leaves, with full detail except for localized weakness. Since some of these areas are often seen with strike weakness, careful examination is necessary. When wear is present, the surfaces are usually dull and discolored—strike weakness examples still having a bright, silvery look. When increased wear is present, as with **AU-50/53**, the friction is more obvious in the hair and is now seen on the entire high

part of the face plus the front of the neck. The field is now rubbed, obvious wear often being accompanied by marks. Reverse wing feathers will now have slight friction, though all should still be very sharp. The breast feathers, especially on the round-breast variety, will be slightly flattened for these grades, as will the leg feathers and claws. The wreath will have slight friction on the high points of the leaves, with some slight loss of detail.

EF-40/45 specimens have wear across all of the high points of the obverse. The back of the cap, the hair below LIBERTY, the hair above the ear, the hair at the back of the neck, the cheek, and the neck will all have noticeable wear. Some of the hair will be worn sufficiently to be blended, particularly the hair above the ear. Reverse wing feathers will have noticeable wear on the tips, with some feathers now blended, and light wear will be seen on the central wing feathers. The breast feathers of the round-breast variety will be flattened slightly on well-struck coins but will show sharply around the edges. For poorly struck coins and the flat-breast variety, the central part of the breast may have feathers that are completely flat. The leg feathers will be mostly flat in these grades with detail on their edges, the claws flat though not blended with the branch and arrow shafts. The leaves will have the high points worn, with some loss of detail, though separate.

Wear to **VF-20/35** will result in the blending of much of the hair detail, with one-half or more of the detail missing. The hair behind the neck will be flattened slightly and will have blending. Breast feathers on well-struck coins will be very flat in the center, with slight edge detail. Poorly struck and flat-breast coins will usually have no breast feather detail. Wing feathers will have worn slightly together in the outer and upper feathers, with most lower feathers separate. For lower **VF** grades, up to one-third or slightly more of the wing feathers may show some blending. Head and neck feathers will now show slight wear, though they should still be complete in the higher **VF** grades.

Leg feathers will be very flat with slight edge detail, and the claws will be flat and blended. Higher **VF** coins will have some flattened wreath leaves with slight blending, while the lower grades of **VF** will have most of the leaves flat and blended.

F-12/15 coins will have some deeply recessed hair detail present, but the high points will be well-worn and blended. Much of the cap will be worn flat. Reverse wing feathers will show most feathers, though nearly all will show some blending; however, the upper wing is very flat. Breast and leg feathers will be totally worn smooth and the claws will be blended into the branch and arrow shafts. The neck and head feathers will now show only slightly. All of the leaves of the wreath will be flat and blended.

Wear to **VG-8/10** will result in most of the upper hair being worn smooth, with only slight deep detail, the hair below the ear having only the recessed areas present. For the cap area, some slight detail is still present, with the cotton bolls worn smooth but mostly outlined. There may be a few wing feathers still showing, mainly those nearest the breast, while the breast and leg feathers will be worn flat. The head and neck feathers will now be worn smooth, as will the claws. Only the deeper leaf detail will still be present, as the upper leaves are all flat and worn together.

G-4/6 specimens will have all of the upper hair worn flat, with only slight deep detail remaining in the hair below the ear. Little detail remains in the cap ornaments with all of the elements, including the cotton bolls, worn smooth and blended. The rims will be worn through most of the dentils and may touch the tops of some of the reverse lettering. Only a few wing feathers around the breast will still have any detail, with the breast, head, neck, and most of the wing feathers worn smooth. The wreath will be outlined, but there will be no leaf detail.

For **AG-3** coins, a full LIBERTY, a partial ear, and a few deeply recessed spots in the lower hair are still present, and Miss Liberty still should be outlined. The rims will be worn into part of the lettering, stars, and date of the obverse. On the reverse, there may only be one-third or less of the peripheral lettering, as the rims of the reverse wear more quickly than the obverse. The eagle should be outlined except for the upper tips of the wing feathers. Amazingly, there still might be slight wing feather detail in the recessed areas at the lower part of the wing next to the breast. The wreath will be totally flat, with slight recessed detail and some blending. In **FR-2**, the obverse may have a totally flat Miss Liberty, but LIBERTY may still be partially present. The lettering, stars, and date may be mostly worn away. The reverse will have a partial eagle with no peripheral lettering and only IN GOD WE TRUST partially present. For branch-mint coins, a mint mark must be present, though it may be very indistinct.

PO-1 coins will only be graded when a date and mint mark, when applicable, are readable. There may be only a partial head of Miss Liberty, and the reverse may be worn nearly smooth.

Mint State Examples

MARKS: Morgan dollars were usually transported in bags; thus most have marks and other surface impairments. Finding any date, other than the most common ones, in grades of MS-67 and higher is nearly impossible. Light contact on the highest points is evident even in the highest grades, as those coins that were stored in rolls also received some contact. For the lower grades of MS-60 through MS-62, marks are plentiful, with the face usually bearing the brunt of the impairments. The large, smooth cheek of Miss Liberty is a magnet for marks, with the field also being a very common area of impairment. Album slide marks are also common, as this is one of the most popular and highly collected series of any denomination. The reverse has less field area and sometimes marks are hidden in the eagle's feathers. The breast area is a high point, and severe marks are often seen on this device.

LUSTER: All of the luster variations are found for Morgan dollars, and the immense

quantities in which they were issued make all of these variations common. Flat-luster coins are seen for some New Orleans and Philadelphia issues. Satin luster is seen from all mints, with perhaps a majority of Morgan dollars being of this type and frosty luster. Very frosty luster coins are also common, with many Philadelphia, San Francisco, and Carson City coins having this type of surface. Semi-prooflike, prooflike, and deep prooflike specimens are found for most dates, though some dates are obviously much rarer than others. The early San Francisco issues are often found with this type of surface, as are many of the Carson City coins. The surfaces of many of the coins from 1900 to 1904 are gray and not the silvery white luster of the pre-1900 issues. Prooflike coins from these years are usually duller than those of previous years, though some dates, 1903–1904-O, for example, have the deeply mirrored, silvery fields. Frosted devices are seen on coins that range from slightly frosty to deep prooflike. Some dates, when encountered in prooflike condition, do not exhibit frosted surfaces and have prooflike devices.

STRIKE: There are very few fully struck Morgan dollars. As with most large coins, striking them fully was difficult. The Philadelphia and San Francisco mints had the most success striking these coins, with New Orleans having the least success. Denver struck these coins only in 1921 and had limited success, with many coins having striking irregularities. Carson City issues are only slightly inferior in striking quality to Philadelphia and San Francisco issues. The central areas are the most affected sections of these coins. The highest point of the obverse is the hair directly above the ear, which is almost always incomplete except for the redesigned 1921 issues. Other exposed areas for the obverse are the stars, the hair all the way from the ear up to the forehead, the cap, the cotton boll, the ear, and the lower hair curls. The reverse high point is the central part of the breast, with the head, neck, tips of the wings, legs, and claws also often showing weakness. The arrow feathers, tail feathers, bow, and wreath are also sometimes weak.

Other striking abnormalities are noted for these coins, such as filled dies that might obscure the lettering, date, or other devices.

EYE APPEAL: In the highest grades, the common-date Morgan dollars are found with many varying and interesting looks. There are satin, frosty, semi-prooflike, prooflike, and deep prooflike luster coins that are well struck with almost no marks. These coins have brilliant white, lightly toned, rainbow toned, and other spectacular toning combinations. Although these heavy coins are more often found with marks and other impairments, they are sometimes found pristine. These coins, especially the common San Francisco issues, mainly are from bags and rolls that were not shipped back and forth. Rarer-date issues in the higher grades were probably cherry-picked from rolls or bags by astute collectors or, in some cases, may have originated as assay coins that were not melted. Finding well-struck coins is a major problem for most New Orleans issues, while well-struck Philadelphia, San Francisco, and Carson City coins are available for most dates. Finding coins with all attributes positive is therefore more difficult for most New Orleans issues, making fewer superb coins available from that mint than from the others. There are more superb San Francisco examples than for the other mints, though there are spectacular Philadelphia and Carson City coins. Denver struck coins only in 1921, with most of these being average strikes with marks.

Proofs

HAIRLINES: Although there are quite a few pristine or very lightly hairlined Morgan dollars, these coins are found with every degree of impairment. Coins are found with heavy hairlines that are quite concentrated, as well as the aforementioned pristine examples. The open field of the obverse and the smooth face and neck of Miss Liberty are the main areas where hairlines, album slide marks, and other impairments are usually found. The reverse has quite a bit of open field area, though it is broken up by the eagle, wreath,

lettering, and other minor devices. As with most coins, the reverses usually are less hairlined than the obverses, though some coins have equal or more impairment on the reverse.

REFLECTIVITY: Nearly every coin is deeply mirrored, usually with the watery look seen on the later-date Liberty Seated and Trade dollars. Frosted devices and lettering peaked in the mid-to-late 1890s, and most of the coins struck from 1900 through 1904 have brilliant surfaces across the entire coin or lightly frosted devices and lettering, due to the new obverse and reverse hubs that were employed for these coins. Occasionally, these dates are found with fairly heavy frost, but they are the exceptions. The Chapman Proofs of 1921 have deeply reflective fields with frosted devices and lettering. The 1921 Zerbe Proofs often have heavy die polish that makes these coins less mirrored than many of the deep mirror prooflike business strikes. The Zerbe Proofs do not have much frost on the devices and lettering, as they were not as carefully made as the Chapman Proofs.

STRIKE: Some Morgan dollars are almost always weakly struck in Proof, such as the 1893, with weakness on the hair above the ear, the breast feathers, the legs, and the claws. Some of these coins will have other areas, such as the arrow feathers, tail feathers, bow, and wreath, exhibiting weakness. Even on well-struck coins, such as those from 1897, there may be slight weakness in these areas. The flat-breast Proofs of 1878 and those from 1921 may also show slight weakness, though the nature of the design hides some of this weakness.

EYE APPEAL: Every date is found in pristine, or nearly pristine, condition, but some dates are much tougher to find than others. There are many coins found with Mint tissue toning, ranging from light colors to very deep blues and purples. Some of the most attractive Proofs are found with this tissue toning, and when the surfaces are free of impairment, these are some of the most spectacular Proof silver coins of any denomination. This series has been highly collected, so coins that were stored in albums are found, with some of these examples acquiring target toning or other attractive toning. Whether with brilliant or spectacular toning, Proof Morgan dollars are extremely attractive when found with minimal impairments.

Peace Dollar—High Relief/Regular Relief (1921–1935)

Circulated Examples

For the two types of Peace dollars, the High Relief and the regular relief, grading is very similar. Strike is a problem for both types, though most Philadelphia-issue regular-relief coins are decently struck. High Relief coins from 1921 and the branch-mint issues, especially those from San Francisco, are notoriously weakly struck. Striking problems with the High Relief coins led to the modification of the dies, resulting in the regular-relief type issued from 1922 through 1935. **AU-55/58** coins show wear in the same places for both types, however, and slight friction on the cheek and the top of the hair is noted for these grades. Weakness of strike is seen on the central hair, and for the High Relief type may result in a large area of hair with little or no detail. In the higher Uncirculated grades, this becomes a large negative influence on the grade, but on circulated coins this is treated as a minor deficiency. The reverse will show slight friction on the neck, shoulder, and wing feathers, with strike weakness seen along the wing feathers in the central part of the eagle. In **AU-50/53**, this wear is more evident, with the neck and field now showing rub on the obverse. The entire eagle and the field now show slight wear, with some slight flattening of the top wing feathers.

EF-40/45 Peace dollars will have flatness on the tops of the hair strands, with the recessed detail still sharp. The cheek and neck will have obvious wear in these grades. For 1921 High Relief coins, central hair detail that is totally flat may be seen, the result of incomplete striking and wear. Reverse wing feathers will be flat on the high points, though most of the feathers will still show separation. There will be noticeable rub on the rock upon which the eagle is perched.

With wear to **VF-20/35**, much of hair detail is lost. The lower-grade **VF** coins may have only the deepest hair strands with slight detail, while the higher-grade **VF** coins may show half or more of the hair. Strike, of course, will affect the amount of hair detail remaining. All of the major hair groups, except the ones exactly where the ear would be, should still be outlined, though quite flat. The reverse will have some feather detail still present on well-struck coins, but on poorly struck coins and lower-grade **VF** coins there may be only slight detail in the neck and tail feathers, with the wing feathers worn smooth. The PEACE inscription on the rock should still be sharp, though the rock will now have much wear on the top part. Individual letters of some inscriptions may be weak from localized strike weakness or filled dies and should not affect the grade.

F-12/15 coins will have most hair detail worn flat, the deeply recessed lines visible with the strands blended. Reverse feather detail will be slight, with only the lowest set of tail feathers still visible. Slight feather detail may still be present on the lower part of the neck and the upper edge of the wing down to the top set of tail feathers. The rock will be very worn and may blend slightly into the tops of PEACE.

Worn to **VG-8/10**, Peace dollars will have most of the hair strands very flat and blended. The obverse rim should still be strong, the inner border present. The reverse rim may be worn through the inner border but should not be worn into the field. Only slight detail will show in the lowest set of tail feathers, with the wing feathers very flat. The word PEACE may have wear into the top half of the letters, and the rock will be worn smooth on the top half.

G-4/6 coins will have hair worn and blended, with only the lowest strands showing slight deeply recessed detail. The rims of the obverse will be worn through the inner border and may touch the tops of a few letters or the bottom of the date. Reverse rims may touch the peripheral lettering and the end of the tail feathers, and are usually weaker than the obverse rims. Some of the lettering may be weak or missing due to wear or poor striking quality. The word PEACE may show parts of a few letters, but the rock will be worn smooth and deeply into most of the letters.

AG-3 Peace dollars will have rims worn into the lettering, rays, and date of the obverse. The head may still have slight deeply recessed hair detail, but most of the hair is worn smooth. Only a few feathers at the juncture of the neck and wing will still be present, with the eagle blended into the field. The reverse lettering may be worn to the point of being totally illegible, though some letters at the top should still be partially visible. The rock is worn very smooth, with no trace of PEACE. Many Peace dollars that would otherwise qualify for this and lower grades may not be gradable, as the mint mark area may be too worn to discern whether a mint mark is present. For **FR-2** coins, a partial head of Liberty will be seen, and a partial date, and possibly some of LIBERTY, will still be visible. Reverse detail will be very slight, though a mint mark, if present, must be discernible for the coin to be graded. As noted earlier, most Peace dollars will not meet this standard.

For **PO-1** graded coins, usually only the 1921 High Relief coins qualify, as the mint mark area on regular-relief coins, as previously noted, is usually too worn to be able to discern a mint mark. If the mint mark is visible, the coin probably is a higher grade.

Mint State Examples

MARKS: As with the Morgan series, Peace dollars are usually found with marks and other detractions. Finding coins that have pristine surfaces is difficult, with roll and bag contact common as well as other disturbances. The obverse is commonly found with markings on the hair, face, and neck, with the field also seen with impairments. Slide marks are also very common, as this series is

short and easily completed. These marks are usually found on the obverse on the hair, face, and neck. Reverse marks are very common also, with the eagle and field both commonplace with light-to-heavy detractions.

LUSTER: Most of the Philadelphia issues have a satin-to-frosty luster, with some issues having a frosty luster. Some of the 1922–1924 coins have a scaly or grainy surface that may have a satin, slightly frosty, frosty, or occasionally very frosty luster, though all of these luster variations have a different look with this type of surface. Some Philadelphia coins have surfaces that approach semi-prooflike, though these coins have very little reflectivity. Most Denver issues have a satin or slightly frosty luster, but very frosty and even semi-prooflike coins are seen for some dates. The reflectivity on Peace dollars is nowhere even near the depth seen on most semi-prooflike Morgan dollars. San Francisco coins have a satin-to-frosty luster, though there are many weakly struck coins, including some that have semi-prooflike surfaces, the dies having been worn and then polished to strike a few more coins before they were retired.

STRIKE: As noted, the High Relief coins are almost always weak in the central areas of the obverse and reverse. The hair may be extremely flat on some of these coins, with the central wing feathers missing. Even on well-struck coins, slight incompleteness on the highest curls of the hair and the tops of the wing feathers is noted. Wing feathers immediately above the right leg are incomplete, even on well-struck High Relief coins. For regular-relief coins from Philadelphia, strike is usually adequate. There may be slight weakness on the highest points of the central hair curls and along the feathers down the back of the eagle. Denver issues are not quite as well-struck as are those from Philadelphia and often have a pebbly look on the high points. San Francisco coins are almost always poorly struck, with incompleteness seen on the hair curls of the obverse and on the feathers along the entire back and tail of the eagle. The neck, leg, and rock are often weak, with

MS-66 *1922 Peace dollar obverse. Only light scuffs are noted on the face and in the left field.*

MS-66 *1922 Peace dollar reverse. A few light marks and scuffs are noted, mainly on the eagle.*

MS-65 *1922 Peace dollar obverse. A light mark on the neck and lightly scuffed fields are seen.*

MS-65 *1922 Peace dollar reverse. Scuffs and marks are often just as common on Peace dollar reverses, found on the rays and tail feathers.*

the pebbly look being very common for nearly all of the San Francisco coins.

EYE APPEAL: Strike is very important to this series, with the High Relief type and most of the San Francisco issues being very difficult to find even well-struck. Fully struck coins from Philadelphia and Denver are found, with well-struck coins readily available from both of these mints. Peace dollars are not usually found with the varying toning combinations that are seen on many Morgan dollars, and the luster variations are also more limited. Therefore, the highest-grade Peace dollars are often Philadelphia or Denver coins, with a satin-to-frosty luster and little or no toning. Since finding mark-free coins is the most difficult task for most of these issues, however, San Francisco coins are seldom found pristine.

Proofs

HAIRLINES: These are difficult to detect on the textured fields of Matte Proof coinage, with only fairly heavy lines readily seen. More often, these coins are found with scuffs or "shiny" spots similar to the areas seen on Matte Proof gold coins. The other Proof variations display hairlines in varying degrees, with the controversial Satin Proofs easily showing them and the sandblasted or acid-pickled surface coins being similar to the Matte Proofs, usually having scuffs or shiny spots.

REFLECTIVITY: There is no reflectivity on the Matte Proofs, as with all coins having this finish. In fact, there is less direct light reflected from these "rough" surface coins than with any of the luster variations seen on the regular strikes. The other experimental

MS-64 *1922 Peace dollar obverse. Marks and scuffs are noted on the hair, face, and field.*

MS-64 *1922 Peace dollar reverse. The wing and tail feathers have several marks, though none is very severe.*

MS-63 *1923 Peace dollar obverse. Marks, especially on the neck, are scattered, but none is severe. The lines through the neck and rays above the hair are die breaks and do not affect the grade.*

MS-63 *1923 Peace dollar reverse. Marks are seen on the eagle and in the field.*

MS-62 *1923 Peace dollar obverse. Discoloration and marks as well as weakness of strike are noted.*

MS-62 *1923 Peace dollar reverse. A severe mark on the eagle's head is seen, with discoloration and other scuffing prominent.*

PR-67

1901 quarter eagle obverse. A nearly flawless specimen with extremely light hairlines, too minute to be visible without magnification.

PR-67

1901 quarter eagle reverse. Extremely light hairlines are visible in the field only upon magnification.

PR-66

1901 quarter eagle obverse. Very light hairlines appear in the left obverse field.

PR-66

1901 quarter eagle reverse. A very light hairline appears above the eagle.

Close-up of PR-66

1901 quarter eagle obverse. An enlarged area is seen in front of the face, with hairlines.

PR-65

1883 double eagle obverse. Light hairlines are seen in the field around the head.

PR-65

1883 double eagle reverse. Light hairlines are noted in the open field area.

Close-up of PR-65

1883 double eagle obverse. Enlarged area is seen behind the head, with hairlines.

PR-64

1902 quarter eagle obverse. Light hairlines are noted in the field, mainly in front of and behind the head.

PR-64

1902 quarter eagle reverse. Light smudges and hairlines appear in the open field.

Close up of PR-64

1902 quarter eagle obverse. Enlarged field area is seen with noticeable hairlines.

Close-up of PR-64

1902 quarter eagle reverse. The enlarged area above the eagle is seen with light hairlines.

PR-63
1886 quarter eagle obverse. Diagonal hairlines appear across the field and head.

PR-63
1886 quarter eagle reverse. Hairlines are visible across most of the field.

Close-up of PR-63
1886 quarter eagle obverse. Enlarged area in front of the face is seen with noticeable hairlines.

Close up of PR-63
1886 quarter eagle reverse. Enlarged area above eagle is seen with obvious hairlines.

PR-62
1905 quarter eagle obverse. Many hairlines appear across the face and field.

PR-62
1905 quarter eagle reverse. Many hairlines appear in the field, with heavy lines above the eagle.

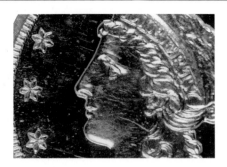

Close-up of PR-62
1905 quarter eagle obverse. An enlarged face and field area is seen with many hairlines.

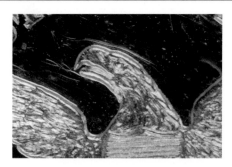

Close-up of PR-62
1905 quarter eagle reverse. An enlarged area shows heavy hairlines around the eagle's head and beak.

PR-61
1905 quarter eagle obverse. Numerous heavy hairlines appear across the entire obverse.

PR-61
1905 quarter eagle reverse. Heavy hairlines are seen in the field and across the devices and lettering.

PR-60
1896 quarter eagle obverse. Heavy hairlines appear across the face and field.

PR-60
1896 quarter eagle reverse. Dense hairlines are noticeable mainly in the field, though they also traverse the eagle and lettering.

Close-up of PR-60
1896 quarter eagle obverse. An enlarged area in front of the face is seen, with dense hairlines.

Close-up of PR-60
1896 quarter eagle obverse. An enlarged date area is seen with heavy, dense hairlines.

1936 Proof
Buffalo nickel obverse with great eye appeal. This coin has it all—blast, no hairlines, and great color, creating the ultimate look for a Buffalo nickel.

1936 Proof
Buffalo nickel reverse with great eye appeal. As with the obverse, this is the ultimate look for a Proof Buffalo—color, lack of hairlines, and blast.

Adjustment Marks
1805 Draped Bust half eagle obverse with adjustment marks. Criss-cross lines across the face and top of the cap are the result of a file. Overweight planchets were adjusted to the proper weight by Mint employees by filing off slight amounts of metal.

Peripheral Toning
Morgan dollar reverse. Light-reddish color around the edge of this coin may be the result of its storage in a cardboard album or some other holder.

Even Toning
1897 Barber half dollar obverse. Even toning covers the entire surface, slightly thicker around the edge.

Mottled Toning
1880 Morgan dollar obverse. This toning is characterized by multiple shades in splotchy toning patterns.

Target Toning
Proof Type III three-cent silver reverse. Like rings of a target, the colors change from blue to red to golden to white as they "move" toward the center of the coin.

Tab Toning
Robinson-Arkansas half dollar obverse. This commemorative was stored in an original tab holder, acquiring peripheral toning and the "tab" toning area in the center.

Bag Toning
1880-S Morgan dollar obverse. Another coin rested on part of this coin while the darker area was in contact with the cloth of a bag. The chemicals in the bag toned the darker area while the other coin prevented toning.

Environmental Damage
1925 Peace dollar obverse. This coin was not graded by PCGS because the surface was damaged by the environment in which it was stored, probably a holder with a highly reactive chemical. It is returned to the submitter in what is commonly called a "body bag."

Full Red (RD) Color *on a 1917 Lincoln cent obverse. This coin has full blazing original color that looks as though it was just struck.*

Red and Brown (RB) Color *on a 1909-S VDB Lincoln cent obverse. Original Lincoln cent with the red color faded in areas to a light-brown. This specimen has well over half of its original red color, with only slight fading.*

Brown (BN) Color *on a 1909-S VDB Lincoln cent obverse. This coin has a slight red color clinging to a few protected areas, but over 95 percent of its surface is an even-brown color.*

MS-63 RB
1834 Classic Head half-cent obverse. This well-struck specimen has light contact with a splendid red and brown color.

MS-63 RB
1834 Classic Head half-cent reverse. A few surface abrasions are seen on the original red and brown surfaces.

MS-64 RB

1855 Braided Hair large cent obverse. A cent's worth of copper when it was issued, this coin retains some of its original red color mixed with light brown across nearly mark-free surfaces.

MS-64 RB

1855 Braided Hair large cent reverse. The faded red color is blended with brown over surfaces, with slight contact.

Dipping and Retoning

1853 Braided Hair large cent obverse. Once the original color has faded, copper coins sometimes are dipped to "freshen" the surfaces, resulting in a bright pink color. Other chemicals are applied to the surfaces to "dull" the pink to resemble the original red color.

Dipping and Retoning

1853 Braided Hair large cent reverse. The original red color is simulated by first brightening the surfaces by dipping and then chemically treating them to try to create "original" red.

MS-67 RD

1900 Indian cent reverse with positive eye appeal. This coin has nearly perfect original surfaces with vibrant red color.

MS-67 RD

1900 Indian cent obverse with positive eye appeal. This coin has blazing original color and luster over nearly mark-free surfaces.

MS-64 RD
1904 RD Indian cent obverse. A full red example with a few marks.

MS-63 RD
1907 Indian cent obverse with negative eye appeal. Spots and discoloration mar these original surfaces, resulting in the MS-63 grade.

MS-63 RD
1907 Indian cent reverse with negative eye appeal. Spots lower the grade of all coins.

Copper Spots (Stains)
Liberty Head quarter eagle reverse. The copper alloy reacts and forms the brown spots and stains that are found on many gold coins.

Hairlines
1896 Proof Liberty Head quarter eagle obverse. Many hairlines are seen in the field and on the head.

Hairlines
1879 Proof Flowing Hair Stella or four-dollar obverse. Hairlines are found in the field in front of and behind the head, as well as above the date. The parallel lines horizontally across the face are roller marks and are not impairments.

MS-67

1923-D Saint-Gaudens double eagle obverse. This coin has lustrous surfaces and beautiful color, with almost no marks. Very minor contact is seen on the breasts and knees.

MS-67

1923-D Saint-Gaudens double eagle reverse. On this coin, only slight contact is seen on the high points over fully lustrous, colorful surfaces.

MS-66

1928 Saint-Gaudens double eagle obverse. This coin has a few contact marks here and there, none serious, with minor contact on the breasts and knee.

MS-66

1928 Saint-Gaudens double eagle reverse. A few marks appear in the wing feathers, though no major marks are present.

Liner MS-65/66

1928 Saint-Gaudens double eagle obverse. A few too many marks appear to qualify for the MS-66 grade—a very high-end MS-65 specimen.

Close-up of liner MS-65/66

1928 Saint-Gaudens double eagle. Marks and contact on the breasts, knee, and legs prevent the MS-66 designation.

MS-65
1928 Saint-Gaudens double eagle obverse. This coin has light marks, nothing major, noted mainly on the breasts, knees, and legs, with minor field contact.

MS-65
1928 Saint-Gaudens double eagle reverse. A few marks appear, mainly on the eagle and sun with the field, with only minor contact.

Liner MS-64/65
1927 Saint-Gaudens double eagle obverse. This coin has a few too many marks to qualify for the MS-65 grade.

Close-up of liner MS-64/65
1927 Saint-Gaudens double eagle. Enlarged area is shown with arrows illustrating marks too severe for a higher grade—a high-end MS-64 specimen.

MS-64
1924 Saint-Gaudens double eagle obverse. Marks are noted on the body and field, though nothing major.

MS-64
1924 Saint-Gaudens double eagle reverse. Scattered marks are seen on the eagle, sun, and rays, with light contact in the field.

Liner MS-63/64
1927 Saint-Gaudens double eagle obverse. Marks on the body and in the field make this a high-end MS-63 coin, just short of the MS-64 grade.

Close-up of liner MS-63/64
1927 Saint-Gaudens double eagle. Arrows mark the areas that have marks, too many to qualify for the MS-64 grade.

MS-63
1927 Saint-Gaudens double eagle obverse. Scattered marks appear on the body and in the field though nothing very severe.

MS-63
1927 Saint-Gaudens double eagle reverse. Scuffing and minor marks appear on and around the eagle.

MS-62
1908 No Motto Saint-Gaudens double eagle obverse. Marks and scuffs, several fairly large, are noted over most of the coin.

MS-62
1908 No Motto Saint-Gaudens double eagle reverse. Marks, most notable on the eagle, are numerous.

MS-61

1908 No Motto Saint-Gaudens double eagle obverse. Numerous marks, heavy and light, dot the surface.

MS-61

1908 No Motto Saint-Gaudens double eagle reverse. As with most coins, the reverse may have fewer and more minor marks—this reverse grades higher than the obverse.

MS-60

1924 Saint-Gaudens double eagle obverse. Heavy and numerous marks appear over the surface.

MS-60

1924 Saint-Gaudens double eagle reverse. Heavy marks and scuffing appear over the surface.

Originally Toned

1897 Barber half dollar obverse. The colors are even and "deep" into the surface.

Originally Toned

1897 Barber half dollar reverse. Color adheres tightly to the eagle and lettering.

Artificially Toned
1908 Barber half dollar obverse. The "crayon" colors "float" on the surfaces. Note that the color is missing around devices such as the stars.

Artificially Toned
1908 Barber half dollar reverse. The colors are not deep and are lacking around the lettering and devices.

Artificially Toned
1882 Liberty Seated quarter obverse. This coin has a light color, probably added by sulfur or related chemicals.

Artificially Toned
1882 Liberty Seated quarter reverse. There is nothing "heavy" in this toning, just light pastel.

Artificially Toned
1880 Morgan dollar obverse. This coin has a red and russet color added by chemicals. This is fairly even, with no "depth."

Dipped and Artificially Toned
1869 Indian cent obverse. The unevenness of the color and its pink hue give away this scarce-date Indian cent.

Dipped and Artificially Toned
1869 Indian cent reverse. The surface has been stripped and chemically treated to simulate the original red color.

Artificially Toned
Lafayette dollar obverse. This coin has light mottled toning, added by chemicals.

Artificially Toned
Lafayette dollar reverse. Some original color possibly was left on this specimen, with other color being chemically added.

Smoked/Hazed
1858 Type III Indian Princess gold dollar obverse. The field here is "hazed" by smoke or chemicals to hide hairlines and contact.

Smoked/Hazed
1858 Type III Indian Princess gold dollar reverse. The cloudy field here has been smoked or chemically "hazed" to cover imperfections.

Close-up of "Thumbed"
Morgan dollar obverse. The thumb has oils that, when rubbed across the surface, cover minor surface blemishes, which often turn the surface brown after a period of time.

"Thumbed"
San Francisco Morgan dollar reverse. The breast feathers, the spot usually "thumbed," may have a somewhat shiny area that is slightly dulled by the process.

Chromium-like Alteration
Proof 1858 Liberty Seated dollar obverse. The surfaces of this specimen have been treated to hide hairlines and other imperfections. This process gives a "chromelike" glisten to the surfaces that is very unnatural. Microscopic examination reveals the imperfections under the "new" surface.

Chromium-like Alteration
Proof 1858 Liberty Seated dollar reverse. At first glance, this type of alteration makes the coin appear spectacular—too good to be true! Of course, it is, since the surfaces are not original.

Artificially Frosted Proof
1942 Mercury dime obverse. This coin has been chemically altered to simulate the frosted cameo effect found on the devices and lettering of many Proof issues. Note the lines and marks "under" the frost.

"Added" Full Head *on an altered Standing Liberty quarter. This is a rather crude try, but other examples seen have been more deceptive, including attempts to "punch" a new ear hole.*

Proofs, which are very controversial, have varying degrees of reflectivity, while the Satin Proof coins have slight reflectivity and the sandblasted or acid-pickled coins have none.

STRIKE: The High Relief Matte Proofs show the detail intended for this coin and are the examples by which the business strikes should be measured. Detail is crisp and the hair curls of the obverse show fully. Wing and leg feathers are usually complete, with only the slightest weakness. The regular-relief Proofs have extraordinary detail, but the textured surfaces obscure this.

EYE APPEAL: Matte Proof coins seen in the highest grades have delicate textured surfaces that are disturbed by the slightest contact. Finding examples without scuffing or shiny spots is extremely difficult, though a few do exist. These examples are light to medium gray in color, and the most attractive examples have an even color over the entire coin. The other types of Proof Peace dollars, the Satin and regular-relief Matte coins, are usually seen with slight impairments, but some high-grade coins are seen.

Eisenhower Dollar—Eagle Reverse/ Liberty Bell–Moon Reverse (1971–1978)
Circulated Examples
Eisenhower dollars are usually seen in Mint State or Proof condition and are seldom encountered in any circulated grades below **AU**. The general PCGS grading standards described in chapter 4 apply to grading circulated Eisenhower dollars. These, as all modern issues, would be graded very technically.

Mint State Examples
MARKS: Most of the cupro-nickel specimens are found with roll contact or bag marks—the hair, face, and neck of Dwight Eisenhower commonly seen with markings, as well as the surrounding field. Reverse marks are noted on the eagle, surrounding field, and other devices on the Eagle Reverse type. The Liberty Bell–Moon Reverse type usually has marks on these devices, as well as in the surrounding field. As with most coins, the reverses of both types often have fewer marks than the obverses. The silver issues are usually more mark-free, as they were issued in sealed plastic sleeves. Quite a few of these coins have near-pristine surfaces when they are removed from their holders.

LUSTER: The cupro-nickel issues usually have a satin-to-slightly frosty luster, with other luster variations seldom, if ever, seen. The silver issues usually have frosty surfaces, though some have a satin luster and a few have surfaces that approach a semi-prooflike luster, but they are best described as very frosty.

STRIKE: Most silver issues are well-struck and quite a few are fully struck. The cupro-nickel strikings often have incompleteness for the obverse, most evident on the high points of the hair above the ear and about halfway between the ear and the top of the head. The eyebrow, down to and including the cheekbone and jawline, but not the sunken area between them, is also affected. Other areas that might have incompleteness are the ear, nose, and chin. The reverse of the regular eagle design has incompleteness on the eagle. Slight incompleteness is noted elsewhere, such as on the branch, lettering, and moon. Weakness of strike is noted on the Liberty Bell and Moon Bicentennial issues for the upper bell lines, the lettering between the upper lines, the lettering below the upper lines, the left part of the upper group of lower bell lines, and the moon.

EYE APPEAL: Obviously, the best examples are the silver-alloy coins that were issued in protective holders. These coins are found well-struck, with great luster and minimal marks. Cupro-nickel issues are much more difficult to find pristine, as most of these are from bags or rolls. Very few coins of either alloy have anything more than light toning and they are seldom colorful. Finding coins that are well-struck with light marks is not difficult, but there are not many cupro-nickel issues of the very highest grade.

Proofs
HAIRLINES: The silver Proofs were issued in hard plastic holders, with the cupro-nickel

coins issued with the Proof sets also in hard plastic. Thus nearly all of these coins are found pristine, with only light hairlines usually found on a few specimens.

REFLECTIVITY: Deeply mirrored fields are found on virtually every coin, but the frosted devices and lettering are sometimes not as heavy as with other modern Proof issues.

STRIKE: Nearly all Proof strikings, of both type and metal varieties, are well-struck or fully struck. Some of the copper-nickel strikings show slight incompleteness on the highest points. For the obverse, this may be seen just on the jawline. Reverse incompleteness may be evident on the neck, breast, leg, and leading edge of the wings for the Eagle Reverse type. The Bicentennial type may show only slight incompleteness on the lettering and lines of the bell.

EYE APPEAL: Eye appeal is usually superb, especially for most of the silver issues, with cameo devices being commonplace. Since strike is not a problem, finding coins with virtually no hairlines is the most difficult task for these Proofs, though there are quite a few coins of both alloys available. As with the Mint State issues, the silver Proofs are usually more often found pristine.

Susan B. Anthony Dollar (1979–1981, 1999)
Circulated Examples

Susan B. Anthony dollars are almost always found in Mint State or Proof, with a few **AU** specimens encountered. Strict, technical grading is employed for this series, as with nearly every other modern series. The general standards outlined in chapter 4 would apply to circulated Anthony dollars.

Mint State Examples

MARKS: These coins were very unpopular because of their confusion with quarters of approximately the same diameter. Therefore, they were not shipped from bank to bank and most coins have minimal marks. The hair, face, and neck of Miss Anthony are

sometimes found with light roll contact or small bag marks or other disruptions, with the reverses usually mark-free, or nearly so.

LUSTER: These coins are almost always found only with satin-to-slightly frosty surfaces. Very frosty coins are seldom encountered, and semi-prooflike and prooflike coins are extremely rare.

STRIKE: Most of these coins are well struck or fully struck, as with most modern issues. Slight weakness may be noted in the hair around the ear, as well as the central part of the eagle on the reverse.

EYE APPEAL: These coins were struck for only three years, and there are very few Mint State coins that could be called spectacular. The rather dull design does not help the eye appeal, and appearance is based mainly on the lack of contact, as the luster and strike are mostly uniform.

Proofs

HAIRLINES: Most of these coins are pristine, with hairlines caused by slight mishandling or improper storage.

REFLECTIVITY: Deeply mirrored surfaces with heavy frosted devices and lettering are the norm, with only a few coins encountered with less than these attributes.

STRIKE: Nearly every coin will have a full strike or at least be very well struck.

EYE APPEAL: Superb eye appeal is noted for nearly every specimen because of the heavy frost on the devices and lettering, combined with the deeply mirrored fields. Only those coins that have been mishandled or have cloudy fields caused by improper storage are less than spectacular.

Sacagawea Dollar—Copper/Zinc/ Manganese/Nickel (2000 to Date)
Circulated Examples

Sacagawea dollars, or golden dollars to which they are commonly referred, are almost always found in Mint State or Proof, with few circulated specimens encountered. Strict, technical grading is employed for this series, as with nearly every other modern series. The general standards outlined in chapter 4 would apply to circulated Sacagawea dollars.

Mint State Examples

MARKS: These coins are found with light roll contact or small bag marks or other disruptions, usually on the face and neck of Sacagawea and also in the fields. Both areas are smooth and readily show contact. The reverses can have marks but they are less frequently found than on the obverse.

LUSTER: These coins usually are found with satin-to-slightly frosty surfaces. Very frosty coins are seldom encountered, although semi-prooflike and prooflike coins are not uncommon.

STRIKE: Most of these coins are well-struck or fully struck, as with most modern issues. Slight weakness may be noted in Sacagawea's hair and in the center of the reverse.

EYE APPEAL: Some Mint State coins that have superior luster could be called spectacular. The ones that have the best eye appeal are, of course, the ones with lack of contact and either prooflike or satin luster.

Proofs

HAIRLINES: Nearly all of these coins are pristine, as they are handled with special care at the mint and are issued in hard plastic holders.

REFLECTIVITY: All examples have deeply mirrored surfaces with heavy frosted devices and lettering.

STRIKE: Nearly every coin will have a full strike or at least be very well-struck.

EYE APPEAL: Superb eye appeal is noted for nearly every specimen because of the heavy frost on the devices and lettering, combined with the deeply mirrored fields. Only those coins that have been mishandled or have cloudy fields caused by improper storage are less than spectacular.

9 GRADING U.S. GOLD COINS

Pure gold is very soft, so it has to be alloyed with harder, less malleable metals to be minted into coins that will circulate effectively—that is, retain their appearance without excessive wear and tear under normal use in commerce. All regular-issue U.S. gold coins were minted from an alloy of gold and copper, with gold coins minted up until 1873 containing from 1 percent to 5 percent silver as well. The chemically reactive copper in the alloy will tone—and this, along with other trace metals frequently found in gold ore, accounts for the soft pastel colors exhibited by some U.S. gold coins.

One of the anomalies encountered in grading gold coins is the lack of low-grade specimens in some series. This may seem puzzling, since the metal is so soft and susceptible to grade-reducing damage. There are logical explanations, however, for this phenomenon. For one thing, many gold coins were hoarded over the years or held by banks as part of their reserves. Then, too, higher-denomination gold coins represented tremendous sums of money during the periods of their issuance, so relatively few people had the occasion to use them when making purchases. This explains the limited wear seen on most eagles and double eagles ($10 and $20 gold pieces). Some issues—Saint-Gaudens double eagles, for example—are seldom seen in grades below Very Fine. Although low-grade coins are seldom encountered in such series, PCGS has seen nearly every U.S. gold coin type in grades as low as Good—and even lower.

Gold Dollars
Liberty Head Gold Dollar–Type I (1849–1854)
Circulated Examples

On **AU-55/58** Type I gold dollars, Miss Liberty's cheek may show only slight discoloration, since wear on gold is not easily seen. The existence of numerous weak strikes in some issues further clouds the confusion between what is wear and what is merely weakness of strike. Because of this, the flatness of the hair is not a certain sign of wear, and the special characteristics of each date and mint must be considered. Discoloration is usually noticed on the high points by the time a coin has enough wear to be graded **AU-50/53**, and the fields also begin to show dullness from slight friction.

EF-40/45 coins have wear across the entire surface and, depending on the strength of the strike, will show half to nearly all of the hairlines. Stars should have detail, though some weakly struck ones may be flat. The leaves of the wreath will have only slight wear and will show most of the detail on the inner leaf, except for weakly struck coins, which may be flat. There also may be weakness in the central lettering and date.

On **VF-20/35** coins, the hair will show some detail, especially in the recessed areas, but the areas above and around the ear will almost always be flat. Some of the stars may be flat, with no central detail. Weakly struck coins should be graded according to the surfaces and remaining luster. The reverse may have weakness in the lettering and date, especially on some of the branch-mint issues. The leaves will show some inner detail on well-struck coins, though weakly struck coins may not.

F-12/15 coins will have most of the hair worn flat, though LIBERTY will usually be complete except on poorly struck coins. The stars will have very little detail. The leaves will have little detail, and the central lettering and date will often be missing detail, especially on weakly struck coins.

Although gold coins are not often found in grades below Fine, some of the branch-mint coins are seen in the lower grades. **VG-8/10** coins will have little hair detail and part of LIBERTY may be missing. Stars will have outlines, though not complete. Rims will usually be complete, but some areas may be worn nearly flat. There will be a fully outlined wreath, but areas may be weak or missing due to problems with strike.

G-4/6 coins may have virtually no part of LIBERTY visible and some areas of the head worn slightly into the field. Some stars may be missing, especially weakly struck ones. Rims will begin to be worn into the fields and may be indistinct in several areas. The wreath will be outlined in most areas, with some central lettering and the date possibly worn or missing.

Very few examples of this coin are seen in **AG-3** and **FR-2**, with most being rarer branch-mint issues. The detail remaining in these grades is sporadic, with areas that have worn into the fields.

PO-1 coins will have enough detail to identify the date and type but little else. This grade is seldom seen for any gold coins.

Mint State Examples

MARKS: These tiny coins, with the smallest diameter of any regular-issue U.S. coin, are sometimes seen with marks, though most Uncirculated specimens have light hairlines instead of marks. Coins are occasionally seen with moderate-to-heavy marks, since they are 90 percent gold and mark easier than silver, nickel, or copper. Marks are usually seen on the cheek and field of the obverse, and on the reverse they are most noticeable on the "1" and the open area around it.

LUSTER: The Philadelphia-issued coins run the gamut of luster variations, with the typical coin having a satin-to-very frosty luster. The No "L" variety of 1849 is found deeply prooflike, with some other years also found prooflike, though usually not as deeply mirrored as the 1849 coins. Most other Philadelphia issues are usually found with a satin-to-frosty luster. Dahlonega and Charlotte coins are usually flat to slightly frosty in luster, but all luster variations are sometimes seen, even fully prooflike specimens. New Orleans coins are usually satin to frosty in luster, though all variances are seen. San Francisco coins have slightly frosty-to-semiprooflike surfaces; however, as with the other issues, most other luster variations are seen.

STRIKE: Philadelphia-issue coins are usually well struck, except for some 1849–1851 coins, which have the central hair behind the ear flat and blended. The reverse center of these coins will have part of DOLLAR and/or the date weak. New Orleans, Dahlonega, and Charlotte coins are a different story. Poor planchets, dies, and equipment caused striking problems for many of these coins. Poor hair detail, weak stars, incomplete lettering, and weak dates and mint marks are the norm for branch-mint issues. Some Uncirculated coins from these mints are so poorly struck that inexperienced numismatists sometimes grade them **VF** or less. Coins with full luster and no wear are Uncirculated, though they do not receive as high a grade as do well-struck coins with the same amount of luster and marks.

EYE APPEAL: There are several extremely high-grade examples that have almost no marks or hairlines and that have incredible planchets, luster, color, and strike. These are the most eye-appealing coins of this type, and their attributes are what one hopes for in a coin. Philadelphia coins usually have the best eye appeal, followed by New Orleans and San Francisco coins. There are superior eye-appeal coins from Dahlonega and Charlotte as well, but they are much more scarce than are coins from the other mints.

Proofs

HAIRLINES: On the few confirmed Type I Proofs, hairlines are mainly in the obverse field, with some also noted on the cheek of Miss Liberty. For the reverse, the most noticeable lines are in the open area around the "1." There may be small nicks or other surface impairments, also noted mainly on the obverse.

REFLECTIVITY: The few coins that are seen do not have the usual "orange-peel" surfaces, associated with brilliant Proof gold coins, that is, fields struck with such force that the mirrored surface is slightly crystallized, producing an "orange-peel" look to the surface. The surfaces are deeply reflective, but are similar to the silver coins of the era. Frosting on the devices and lettering is moderate, especially compared to the Type II and Type III issues.

STRIKE: These ultra-rarities have full strikes with the hair, star, wreath, and lettering all very bold. Any weakness would be in the stars or the very slightest weakness in the central portions of the obverse and reverse. There may be other very slight weakness due to strike or incompleteness in the dies.

EYE APPEAL: Although most of these coins do not have the deeply frosted devices of many of the Type II and Type III issues, these are spectacular Type I gold dollars. Miss Liberty is a miniature of the Liberty Head on the $20 gold piece designed the same year. The design was abandoned when the thinner and broader gold dollar was introduced in 1854. The lack of hairlines, the depth of mirror of the fields, the amount of frosting present on the devices and lettering, and the strike make up the eye appeal for these tiny gold coins.

Indian Princess Gold Dollar– Type II/III (1854–1889)

Circulated Examples

The Indian Princess gold dollar is thinner, therefore slightly broader, than the same-weight Liberty Head gold dollar. This resulted in poorer strikes and more difficulty in determining the slight wear of **AU-55/58** coins. The hair above and around the ear and the cheek are the two areas that first show slight friction. The top of the headdress will also show slight wear. The reverse will have full wreath detail, with only slight friction on the highest points. The reverse of the Type II is often weakly struck in the central area. For **AU-50/53** coins, there is more noticeable wear, especially on the cheek and in the field. The hair will have obvious wear and will be flattened above the ear. The top of the headdress will be obviously worn, as will the finer details of the reverse wreath.

For **EF-40/45** coins, the wear is apparent, though the weakly struck coins will sometimes have less detail than well-struck **VF** coins. The weakness is usually in the hair above and around the ear, but sometimes the area above the eye, including LIBERTY and the headdress, may exhibit weakness. The reverse will show corresponding weakness, and the wreath will have definite wear on the high points.

VF-20/35 coins will have flattened hair, especially with poor strikes, with detail in the recessed areas only. The wreath will be flat, with detail depending on the strength of the strike. Central lettering and the date will have considerable wear, and parts of them may be missing due to incomplete striking.

In **F-12/15**, the head will be fully outlined, with flat hair and some detail in the headdress. Peripheral lettering may show weakness, sometimes obliterating some letters. The "UN" of UNITED is weak on some issues (almost all 1861-D gold dollars have this characteristic). The wreath is outlined, with slight detail. The central lettering and date will be worn away in places, with strike weakness obliterating others.

The grades **VG-8/10** have an outlined head with little detail, the rim usually complete, except in cases of localized weakness. Lettering will sometimes be weak or missing, again depending on the original striking quality.

GOLD DOLLARS

215

The reverse will show little detail of the wreath, with areas worn into the field.

G-4/6 coins have indistinct rims, lettering, and the head worn into the field. The reverse is similar, with lettering, date, wreath, and rims very worn.

The lowest grades are seldom seen, though some coins were pocket pieces and are encountered in **AG-3** and **FR-2**. The detail of the **AG** coin is only slightly better than the Fair coin. Major devices and some of the lettering are usually visible for **AG-3** coins, with only a few letters seen on **FR-2** graded coins.

The **PO-1** will have some detail and a date that is readable.

Mint State Examples

MARKS: These coins are slightly larger in diameter, therefore slightly thinner, as they contain the same amount of gold as the Type I coins. These slightly broader coins often have more, and more severe, marks than Type I coins. Both Type II and Type III coins have rims that are not as high as Type I coins, which leaves the fields and high points vulnerable to marks, slide marks, and hairlines. These are noted on the face, neck, and open field around the head, with the headdress and hair also noted with surface distractions. Reverse marks are usually seen in the central area on and about the denomination and date, with impairments also noted on the wreath and the field between the wreath and rims.

LUSTER: These two types are seen in every luster variation, from flat to deeply prooflike for the coins of Philadelphia. The average Philadelphia coin is slightly frosty-to-very frosty, with many satin coins seen. Semi-prooflike and prooflike coins are known, mainly for the Type III issues. Deep frost on the devices is seen on many of the prooflike Type III coins, with the Type II issues rare in deep prooflike and seldom seen with semi-prooflike luster. The luster for the branch-mint issues is usually flat-to-slightly frosty

for the Dahlonega and Charlotte issues. New Orleans coins are usually satin-to-frosty in luster, with the San Francisco coins usually satin-to-frosty, but semi-prooflike and prooflike coins also are seen. Occasionally, Dahlonega, Charlotte, and New Orleans coins have semi-prooflike or prooflike luster.

STRIKE: Striking the new Indian Princess design should have alleviated the problems associated with the Liberty Head gold dollars. The new design was in lower relief and the diameter of the coin was slightly increased. However, most of the Type II coins, from both Philadelphia and the branch mints, have striking deficiencies. The hair above and around the ear, the lowest hair curls, the top of the headdress, the central lettering and date on the reverse, and the wreath are usually weak or sometimes nearly obliterated. This type of die problem would be encountered in the Mint a few years later with the Flying Eagle cent. Some of the deepest recesses of the obverse die were opposite some of the deepest recesses of the reverse die. This resulted in poor metal flow into the die cavity, leading to incomplete strikes. The date is a good example of this problem, since the high point of the hair on the obverse is directly opposite the date on the reverse. The head for the Type III coins was lowered in relief and made slightly larger to minimize this problem. Although it partially solved the striking problems, as the date is no longer as weak, Type III coins even from Philadelphia still sometimes have similar weakness in the same areas as the Type II coins. It was recently discovered by John Dannreuther that the Type III reverse is the exact reverse of the Type II gold dollar. Previous literature has incorrectly noted that the reverse was slightly changed. The coins from Dahlonega and Charlotte are slightly improved from the Type II issues, though deteriorated dies, poor planchets, and old minting equipment still caused most of these coins to exhibit weakness. New Orleans struck Type II coins in 1855, with most having some weakness in the strike or filled die problems. San Francisco struck Type II coins in 1856, and these are of a slightly better quality than the other branch-mint issues, about the same quality as the Philadelphia Type II coins. In 1860 and 1870, San Francisco struck Type III gold dollars, and they are better struck than the Type II coins.

EYE APPEAL: Philadelphia coins often have superior eye appeal, as they were well struck, had better planchets, and had better luster more often than the Dahlonega or Charlotte issues. Since many of the Dahlonega and Charlotte coins had defective planchets and were struck on inferior coining presses, the issues from those mints do not usually have the attractiveness of Philadelphia coins. San Francisco coins usually have better eye appeal than the Dahlonega and Charlotte coins, with quite a few coins similar to Philadelphia issues. The single New Orleans issue, 1855-O, falls between the San Francisco and Dahlonega/Charlotte issues, often with good luster and decent planchets but softly struck.

Proofs

HAIRLINES: These coins do not have high protective rims like the Type I coins, and hairlines are noted for most Type II and Type III gold dollars. Light-to-moderate hairlines are found on many coins, but some Type III issues, and occasionally a rare Type II issue, are seen nearly free of hairlines. Most of the lines are usually confined to the obverse cheek and field, with the reverse mainly having lines in the open area around the "1." There are coins that show lines across the entire coin, most likely the result of cleaning, while light lines in the fields are usually the result of slight mishandling.

REFLECTIVITY: Both types have deeply mirrored fields, with the majority of dates seen with cameo devices. These are the first gold dollars struck in significant numbers in Proof, which often have "orange-peel" surfaces, that is, fields struck with such force that the mirrored surface is slightly crystallized, producing an "orange-peel" look to the surface. Not all Type II and Type III Proofs have this type of surface, but if this type of surface is not present, the coin's Proof status is doubtful. Most issues have frosted devices

and lettering, with light-to-very heavy frost, which creates great contrast between the devices and fields.

STRIKE: The many striking problems encountered for the business strikes are not present for the Proofs. Striking quality is very high, with only slight weakness noted in the hair above the ear, the upper tip of the headdress, and the high points of the wreath. Most Proofs are well struck in these areas, some with chiseled detail. The rims are generally flat, with some having slight wire rims. A few of these also may have crumbling at the dentils, which is usually die-related and not a striking deficiency.

EYE APPEAL: Since strike is usually full or nearly full on Proofs, the number and degree of hairlines is of paramount concern for discerning eye appeal. Since many dates have frosted devices, which are an important attribute of eye appeal, these coins usually have the best eye appeal. When combined with superb surfaces, the frosted-device issues are considered some of the most attractive gold dollar Proofs.

Quarter Eagles
Capped Bust Right Quarter Eagle—No Stars/Stars (1796–1807)
Circulated Examples

In **AU-55/58**, the first wear on the obverse is seen on the folds of the cap, the hair around the ear, the cheek, and the folds of the drapery. The reverse is the Heraldic Eagle type only and the upper wing feathers, the breast feathers, and the lines of the shield are the first areas of wear. Strike is again a main factor, with the central areas often seen with weakness, though localized weakness of areas of the periphery is also seen. The grades of **AU-50/53** have more noticeable wear on these areas, and will also have rubbing in the field of the obverse. The reverse has little surface area that is not protected.

EF-40/45 coins will have about 75 percent of the hair detail sharp, though on weakly struck coins the central hair may be flat. The cap will show wear on the highest folds, with flatness evident. Localized weakness may cause some stars, when present, to show only outlines. The wing, breast, and shield are mostly complete on strong strikes, with up to one-third of the feathers and shield missing on poorly struck coins.

For **VF-20/35** grades, the hair and cap detail will range from approximately one-third remaining on lower **VF** grade and poorly struck coins to nearly full detail on higher **VF** grade and well-struck coins. The stars, when present, will be outlined, usually showing some detail. The wing and breast feathers may be only one-third complete on lower-grade or poorly struck **VF** specimens to mostly complete on higher-grade **VF** and well-struck coins. The shield and motto may be indistinct, especially on weakly struck specimens.

The deepest recesses of the hair and cap will be evident on **F-12/15** coins, with Miss Liberty usually having a complete outline. The With Stars type may have stars that are not completely outlined. There will be little feather or shield detail, though the eagle should be mostly outlined. The shield will probably have little or no separation in the lines, even on well-struck coins. The rims of the reverse, and also the obverse, may have localized weakness.

VG-8/10 coins have almost no hair or cap detail. The rims may have localized weakness. The eagle and shield will be outlined, with little detail and areas that blend into the field. The lettering may have slight weakness, though complete except in cases of localized weakness.

When worn down to **G-4/6**, the rim may be worn slightly in several places, the stars may blend into the field, and Miss Liberty will be flat. The reverse will have the rims worn into the tops of the lettering. The eagle and shield will show little detail, and weakly struck coins may have areas worn into the field.

AG-3 and **FR-2** coins will have some stars obliterated, with Miss Liberty having essentially no detail and blending into the field in several areas. The reverse will have half or less of the lettering obliterated in **AG-3** and half to all missing for **FR-2**.

The **PO-1** will have some detail of the obverse and reverse visible and a date that is discernible.

Mint State Examples

MARKS: For the obverse, the large open field of the No Stars type often has marks or other surface impairments. The face, cap, and hair of Miss Liberty are sometimes seen with small or moderate marks, with those in the hair possibly hidden. The stars slightly reduce the openness of the obverse field on the second type and provide some protection from contact. The reverse design is the same for both types, with little field area, so the marks are often hidden in the clouds, stars, eagle, or shield.

LUSTER: These are usually seen satin-to-frosty or semi-prooflike. All of these were low-mintage issues, with only the 1807 having more than a few thousand struck. There are prooflike specimens seen for the 1796 No Stars and most of the Stars dates. Even coins that were not fully struck still have prooflike luster sometimes, as the dies were obviously polished before striking commenced.

STRIKE: The central parts of many of these coins may be incomplete, with an almost dished appearance. The eagle's neck and breast feathers are sometimes totally flat, with part of E PLURIBUS UNUM sometimes weak or missing. Localized weakness is also noted for the stars, when present, cap, bust, LIBERTY, and date for the obverse. The reverse shield and tips of the wings are also sometimes weak, as are the peripheral lettering, head, claws, tail, arrows, olive branch, clouds, stars, and wing feathers. Almost any area may have localized weakness, as worn dies, broken dies, improperly spaced dies, and out-of-parallel dies are all contributing factors at various times.

EYE APPEAL: When these coins are well-struck, minimally marked, and have good luster, they are extremely attractive miniatures of Robert Scot's design. Die cracks and other die defects are noted for some issues, which may be slightly distracting. Overall eye appeal is probably affected more by strike and surface distractions than by luster, since this attribute is usually satisfactory.

Capped Bust Left Quarter Eagle— Large Size–Large Bust and Small Bust (1808–1827)
Circulated Examples

Both Large Bust and Small Bust types have slight wear on the cheek, the hair above the eye and behind the ear, and the cap above the ribbon in **AU-55/58**. Weakly struck coins have weakness in basically the same spots. The reverses of both types are nearly identical, with wear first seen on the upper wing feathers. The central area is almost always seen with slight-to-moderate weakness. The breast feathers and leg feathers, the eagle's upper right wing, and the shield exhibit softness on poorly struck coins, sometimes showing detail that appears to be several grades lower. Only with wear into **AU-50/53** does wear versus strike become obvious. Dullness across the broad, flat cheek is blatant evidence of wear.

The **EF-40/45** coin has wear across most of the face, hair, and cap. The detail ranges from approximately 70 percent on weakly struck coins to 90 percent or more for well-struck coins. The reverse will show wear on the upper wing feathers, the leg feathers, the eagle's inner right wing feathers, and the shield.

With the strike problems of the early Mint, **VF-20/35** coins may have less than 50 percent detail on lower-grade and poorly struck **VF** coins and nearly 90 percent detail on higher-grade and well-struck **VF** specimens. The poorly struck coins may have a mushy reverse central area and half of the wing feather detail. Well-struck coins may have much more detail.

The wear on **F-12/15** coins will leave only the deep recesses of the hair detail visible. LIB-

ERTY should be complete, though some letters may be weak, with the stars mostly flat. The reverse will have less than half of the feather detail, with some weakly struck coins showing only the deeply recessed areas.

The **VG-8/10** graded coins will have slight hair detail. LIBERTY may be missing parts of some letters. The stars will be mostly outlined. There will be slightly more detail in the recessed areas of the feathers than in the hair. Peripheral reverse lettering may have localized weakness.

The obverse should have most stars outlined, Miss Liberty complete, and some letters of LIBERTY visible for **G-4/6**. There may be localized rim weakness, with the peripheral lettering weak at the tops of some letters. The eagle will have little or no fine detail, though it should be well outlined.

AG-3 and **FR-2** coins will have worn rims, weak and missing stars, and Miss Liberty worn into the field. The reverse will have half or more of the peripheral lettering present on **AG-3** coins and less than half visible for **FR-2**. There will be a flat eagle worn into the field of the reverse.

PO-1 coins will be identifiable as to type, with the date readable.

Mint State Examples

MARKS: These coins are often seen with obverse marks that are noted on the cap and cheek or in the field in front of and behind the head. The hair is fairly intricate, making marks more difficult to detect than in the smooth open areas. The reverse has open areas above the eagle and below both wings, with surface detractions noted for these spots and on the eagle, though the wing's detail may hide small marks.

LUSTER: All luster variations are seen on these issues, with the typical coin having a satin-to-very frosty luster, with semi-prooflike and prooflike luster also fairly common. Most of these issues also had minuscule quantities issued, with only the 1821 having more than a few thousand coins struck. The dies, therefore, remained fresh and most coins have good luster, whether satin, frosty, or prooflike.

STRIKE: Both the Large Bust, struck only in 1808, and the Small Bust, struck from 1821 through 1827, were struck with open collars, which means the reeding was applied to the blanks and then the reeded blanks were fed into the coining presses and struck. More unevenness is noted in striking quality with central weakness commonplace. The hair around the ear is the general area where weakness is noted for the obverse, but the stars, the hair above the eye, the lower hair curls, and the front of the bust are sometimes seen with incompleteness. For the reverse, the neck, shield, right wing next to the shield, leg, and claws are often weakly impressed, sometimes with the detail obliterated. Localized weakness is also noted for the peripheral lettering, E PLURIBUS UNUM, the denomination, the laurel leaves, and the arrowheads. As with many early issues, die wear, improper die spacing, and out-of-parallel dies may be causes for some incompleteness. Insufficient striking pressure is another possible cause.

EYE APPEAL: Strike and marks are the main focus of eye appeal, as the luster is usually adequate or better. Well-struck and relatively mark-free coins are seen, and when these attributes are combined with a frosty or prooflike luster, these are very attractive coins.

Proofs

HAIRLINES: Hairlines are noted for most of the Proofs of this era. The obverse field is found with light-to-moderate hairlines, with the face sometimes showing slight lines, since the relief is low. The reverse lines are noted above the eagle and in the open areas below the wings. The storage method of the era was the coin cabinet, and most of the time coins were stored with the obverse facing up, thus receiving the brunt of any cleaning or wiping.

REFLECTIVITY: As with other open-collar strikings, the Proofs of these issues do not have quite as deeply mirrored fields as the close-collar strikings. However, frosted devices and lettering are usually found on these coins, which contrast with the mirrored fields, making them appear deeper.

STRIKE: No Large Bust Proofs are known. The Small Bust coins that are known in Proof are well-struck, with only slight incompleteness noted on a few hair curls, the shield, and a few central feathers. Though struck in open collars, these coins probably received extra blows from the dies.

EYE APPEAL: These coins often have superb eye appeal. The Mint was improving its ability to strike Proofs during the 1820s, and obviously the planchets were burnished along with the basining of the dies. When found with frosted devices and lettering, minimally hairlined, these are some of the most attractive of the early Proofs of any denomination or metal.

Capped Bust Left Quarter Eagle—Small Size (1829–1834)
Circulated Examples

The Small Size Capped Bust coins in **AU-55/58** have slight wear on the cheek, the hair above the eye and behind the ear, and the cap above the ribbon. These coins are in higher relief than are the Large Size Capped Bust coins and were struck in a close collar, leading to better overall striking quality. Though weakly struck coins are still seen, the close-collar strikes usually have only slight central weakness. The reverse wear is first noted on the upper wing feathers. Only with wear into **AU-50/53** does wear versus strike become obvious. Dullness across the cheek is evidence of wear, and the hair now has enough wear to discern between strike weakness and true wear.

The **EF-40/45** coin has wear across most of the face, hair, and cap. The detail ranges from approximately 80 percent to 90 percent or more for well-struck coins. The reverse will show wear on the upper wing, leg, inner right wing feathers, and shield.

VF-20/35 coins usually have 50 to 75 percent of the detail on most specimens. The coins with central weakness may have a very mushy reverse central area and half or slightly more of the wing feather detail. Well-struck coins may have much more detail.

The wear on **F-12/15** coins will leave only the deep recesses of the hair detail visible. LIB-ERTY should be complete, though some letters may be weak, with most stars flat. The reverse will have less than half of the feather detail, especially if the design was less than fully struck to begin with, and some weakly struck coins may show only the deeply re-cessed areas.

The **VG-8/10** graded coins will have some hair detail, but usually only slight. LIBERTY may be missing parts of some of the letters. The stars will be mostly outlined. The re-verse will have slightly more detail remain-ing in the recessed areas of the feathers than the obverse hair.

If the strike is decent, the obverse should have outlined stars, Miss Liberty complete, and some letters of LIBERTY visible for **G-4/6**. The eagle will have little or no fine detail, though it should be well outlined.

AG-3 and **FR-2** coins will have worn rims, weak and missing stars, and Miss Liberty worn into the field. The reverse will have half or more of the peripheral lettering pres-ent on **AG-3** coins and less than half visible for **FR-2**. There will be a flat eagle worn into the field of the reverse.

PO-1 coins will be identifiable as to type, with the date readable.

Mint State Examples
MARKS: These coins have the same basic de-sign as the previous type. Chief Engraver William Kneass modified Miss Liberty and the eagle with slightly higher relief. Now struck in close collars, these coins are very uniform. The higher rims of the close-collar strikings are offset by the higher relief of the head and eagle. The cheek is especially vul-nerable and is often seen with slide marks,

nicks, scratches, and other impairments. The amount of open fields is about the same as with the previous types, but the higher rims provide slightly more protection, therefore slightly fewer impairments are found in the fields. As noted, the eagle is in higher relief and therefore slightly more prone to mark-ing.

LUSTER: The coins of this type are all low-mintage issues, struck in close collars, allow-ing the metal to be limited in its outward flow, thus the luster is usually frosty to semi-prooflike in nature. Some satin and prooflike coins are also noted, with the dies remaining fresh from limited use.

STRIKE: The close-collar strikes of the Small Size Capped Bust coins are of very high qual-ity. A few specimens are noted with slight weakness in the central hair curls, the right wing feathers next to the shield, the shield, the right leg feathers, and the claws. As the reeding was imparted upon striking, the metal flowed more easily into the die cavities, as it was restrained by the close collar and could not spread.

EYE APPEAL: These first close-collar strik-ings are usually very uniform in strike, with the marks and luster varying. Frosty, well-struck coins with minimal marks are very at-tractive, as are the satin, semi-prooflike, and prooflike coins. Overall, these coins are usu-ally great examples of quarter eagles.

Proofs
HAIRLINES: With the higher rims imparted by the close collar, the fields are more pro-tected. However, the head of Miss Liberty is in higher relief, thus is more exposed to slide marks and hairlines. Light-to-moderate hairlines are noted on the cheek and the field in front of and behind the head. Reverse lines are mainly noted in the open areas above the eagle and below both wings. As with most coins, hairlines are usually less severe on the reverse than on the obverse.

REFLECTIVITY: These are the first Proof quarter eagles struck in close collars, and typically they are very deeply mirrored. Usually the surfaces are brilliant, similar to the silver Proofs of the era, without the "orange-peel" effect noted for the later Proof gold issues. Most have frosted devices and lettering, this contrast making the surfaces appear even more deeply mirrored.

STRIKE: Struck in close collars for the first time, Proofs are of very high striking quality. If any incompleteness is noted, it will be very minor, such as slight weakness on the central hair curls, the right wing feathers next to the shield, the leg, and the vertical lines of the shield. Broad, flat rims are also a result of the close collar, and when viewed from the edge there should be almost no beveling.

EYE APPEAL: There are several specimens known for this series that have deeply frosted devices and lettering, with nearly hairline-free, deeply mirrored fields. These coins have a great appearance, being the first quarter eagle Proofs struck in close collars, and are spectacular examples of the Mint's capabilities.

Classic Head Quarter Eagle (1834–1839)
Circulated Examples

The Classic Head design first shows obverse wear on the cheek, the hair curls above the ribbon, the hair above the eye, and the hair above and behind the ear for grades **AU-55/58**. The eagle will have friction on the upper edge of the wing, the neck, and the leg feathers. The feathers adjacent to the shield are sometimes weakly struck. For **AU-50/53** coins, more obvious wear is seen in the above-mentioned spots, with the entire cheek and neck showing friction. The reverse will have rub in the field above the eagle, and the feathers will develop flat spots that begin to blend together.

If the coin is well struck, **EF-40/45** coins will still show much detail in the hair, especially at the top of and behind the ear. The luster present will be seen in protected recessed areas and around the stars. The reverse will have feathers blended, with the neck and leg

areas showing considerable flatness, especially noticeable on weak strikes.

VF-20/35 coins will almost always have a complete LIBERTY, except on poorly struck specimens, though hair detail is now seen only in the very deepest recessed parts. Stars will be outlined, with only slight detail remaining. On higher-grade **VF** coins with good strikes, considerable feather detail remains, though many feathers will be flattened and blended.

The **F-12/15** grade may only have a partial LIBERTY visible, but well-struck coins usually have complete lettering. The hair is completely flat with slight detail, the stars flat with only an occasional line remaining. The reverse will have only the deepest feathers visible, less than half of them with any detail. The neck and leg feathers will be totally worn flat.

Many gold coins are not found in the lowest grades, but the Classic Head design is found in **VG-8/10** and below. There will be an outlined head with almost no detail, with the stars flat. The feathers will have slight detail.

With **G-4/6** coins, virtually no detail is seen on Miss Liberty, though a complete outline is present. The rims may blend slightly into the fields. The eagle will have little other than an occasional feather visible. The shield lines may blend into the field and some lettering may have the tops of the letters slightly worn.

The **G** and **VG** gold coins are scarce, but **AG-3** and **FR-2** gold coins are rare. The head will have no detail, but should still be outlined in these grades. The rims will be worn, especially with **FR-2** coins, and the lettering of the reverse will be partially missing. The eagle should be outlined, though the rims may wear into the tips of the feathers.

A **PO-1** coin will have a readable date and some detail.

Mint State Examples

MARKS: These coins have about the same field space for the obverse as the previous design, but the reverse does not have the motto above the eagle, leaving a large area that is a magnet for marks. The hair is more deeply chiseled than the previous designs, and marks, unless severe, are likely to be hidden in the hair. Light-to-moderate marks are normal for these issues. The reverse, as noted, has the open area above the eagle plus the spaces below the wings that often have marks and other surface impairments. Marks on the eagle, unless severe, are usually disguised by the intricate nature of the feathers.

LUSTER: These have every luster variation, with the typical Philadelphia coin having a satin-to-very frosty luster. Semi-prooflike and prooflike coins are seen, with some of the deep prooflike coins resembling Proofs. The Charlotte Mint struck coins in 1838 and 1839, Dahlonega only in 1839. These branch-mint coins usually are satin to slightly frosty, though other luster variations are sometimes seen. New Orleans struck coins in 1839, and these usually are satin to very frosty, with some semi-prooflike specimens seen.

STRIKE: These are often not as well struck as the preceding Small Size Capped Bust coins. The central hair curls are often mushy, with only the prooflike and semi-prooflike coins showing the razor-sharp hair detail intended by the designer. Reverse central detail, including the leg of the eagle, also suffers from this weakness. Christian Gobrecht's dies did not improve the striking qualities over the Kneass dies, and only the variety specialists note the differences, which are minor. There is less localized weakness noted for these coins, which is attributable to the introduction of the steam-powered presses in 1836. Dies not in parallel are much less common than before, and localized weakness is usually seen just in the stars.

EYE APPEAL: These are very attractive coins when seen well struck, lustrous, and relatively mark-free. Some of the semi-prooflike and prooflike as well as frosty specimens have frosted devices and lettering, and these are attractive and desirable.

Proofs

HAIRLINES: The obverse head is similar in relief to the previous type and may show slide marks, tiny nicks, or hairlines. The most prevalent areas for hairlines on the obverse, however, are the portions of the field in the front and back of the head. Light-to-moderate hairlines are noted in these areas, as well as in the reverse field above the eagle and below the wings. The area above the eagle is particularly vulnerable, as it is the largest open area on either side.

REFLECTIVITY: Proofs of the Classic Head design usually have deeply mirrored fields contrasting with frosted devices and lettering. Although not quite as deeply mirrored as the Liberty Head type to follow and mostly without the "orange-peel" look, these coins do show the watery look for the surfaces.

STRIKE: Proofs of the Classic Head quarter eagles are exceptionally sharp. The full, chiseled hair and wing feathers intended by the designers are evident on these coins. Only the slightest weakness in the very central hair and possibly some of the lines of the shield are noted for Proofs. Though broad, thick rims are not always present, when viewed from the edge there should be little or no beveling.

EYE APPEAL: These coins, when mostly hairline-free, are some of the most desirable and attractive of all gold Proof coins. These tiny Proofs have an incredible look when the frosted head, eagle, and lettering contrast with the deeply mirrored fields.

Liberty Head Quarter Eagle (1840–1907)
Circulated Examples

Liberty Head quarter eagles show wear first on the eyebrow, hair above the coronet, curls of hair above the eye and ear, hair curl below the ear, nose, and chin in grades AU-55/58. The reverse will show wear on the tops of the wing, neck, and leg feathers. The neck and leg feathers are also areas where strike weakness is noted, and for some of the branch-mint coins this area is almost never seen with much detail. Surface preservation should be the primary consideration when strike weakness is noted. **AU-50/53** coins will have more friction in the aforementioned regions, with some flatness noted for the hair above the ribbon and above the ear. The reverse will begin to show slight wear on all of the wing feathers, though there should be complete feather detail except on the neck and leg.

EF-40/45 specimens will have some of the hair detail missing or indistinct. The entire coin will show rubbing, and the stars and fields will show obvious wear. The eagle's feathers will show wear but still will be separate, save the neck and leg areas, which will often be completely flat except for well-struck coins. The leaves and arrows will be separate, with most detail still clear.

If **VF-20/35** coins are well struck, detail will still be plain on the obverse. The hair curls will have some separation, with the recessed areas distinct. The reverse will have the tips of the wing feathers worn together on well-struck coins in higher **VF** grades. Lower-grade **VF** and weakly struck coins may have very little feather detail. The leaves and arrows are still separate, but little detail is still visible.

Many **F-12/15** coins still have some intricate hair detail, with the curl on the neck sometimes still fairly sharp, though the stars are quite flat. LIBERTY should be complete, but some of the letters may have weakness. On well-struck coins, slight feather detail may be seen, with the leaves blended together. The arrows are flat, though still separate.

VG-8/10 and lower-grade Liberty Head gold coins are so seldom seen, except on rare dates and some branch-mint issues, that previous grading books have not bothered to define these grades. The head will have sporadic detail, with some of the letters of LIBERTY partially missing. The eagle will be outlined, with little or no intricate detail remaining. The lettering will be clear around the periphery.

G-4/6 coins will have a smooth head, with some of LIBERTY showing. The rim may be slightly incomplete and slightly worn into the reverse lettering. A flat eagle is present, with a full outline.

For **AG-3** and **FR-2** coins, a date, head, and some stars will be present. The **FR-2** may not have stars visible or just a few still seen. The reverse will have the rims worn into the tips of the wing feathers and lettering. The **FR-2** may have only parts of some lettering readable, with some parts obliterated.

PO-1 graded coins, almost never seen, will have a readable date and mint mark (if applicable), with slight detail.

Mint State Examples

MARKS: These are small coins, and they have about the same amount of open field space as the Classic Head design. Marks and other surface impairments are usually light-to-moderate; the face and the field around the head are the areas where distractions are noted. The hair is not as intricate as for previous designs, and marks are not easily hidden in the detail. Reverse markings are usually noted most in the open area above the eagle's head and below the wings. The shield is smaller than previously, leaving more of the eagle exposed, with surface distractions fairly well hidden in the feathers, unless they are severe in nature.

LUSTER: Luster for Philadelphia issues is noted in all variations, with the typical coin having a slightly frosty-to-very frosty luster. Flat, satin, semi-prooflike, and prooflike luster coins are seen with regularity; however, with some years, one luster variation or another predominates. Obviously, the low-mintage issues such as the 1875, with 400 struck, are nearly all prooflike, while higher-mintage issues such as 1853 or 1861 usually have a frosty luster. Branch-mint issues were struck at all of the mints except Carson City. Coins from the Charlotte and Dahlonega mints usually have a satin-to-frosty luster, though many of the planchets were of inferior quality and, when combined with antiquated minting equipment, did not produce highly lustrous coins. There are very few semi-prooflike and almost no prooflike coins known from these two mints. The New Orleans and San Francisco coins usually have a brighter luster, and many of these issues have a frosty luster. However, flat- and satin-luster coins are noted for both of these mints, as well as semi-prooflike and prooflike coins.

STRIKE: For the first years in Philadelphia, and for nearly all of the branch-mint coins, striking weakness is noted for Liberty Head quarter eagles. The main areas of weakness for the obverse are the stars, tip of the coronet, hair above the eye, hair curl above the ear, hair curl on the neck, hair curl going back from the ear, hair bun, and stars. All of these areas are not necessarily weak on all coins, though this is sometimes the case. The reverses have the tips of the wings, neck, shield, inner wing feathers around the shield, right leg, and claws showing weakness or sometimes totally flat. Many branch-mint coins were struck on inferior presses and central areas of the obverse-reverse sometimes have a dished appearance. Some branch-mint coins will also have wing feather weakness resulting in coins with obverses that appear to be a much higher grade than the reverses. Well-struck coins will receive a higher grade than poorly struck coins that have identical surface preservation.

EYE APPEAL: This design was used virtually unchanged from 1840 until 1907, and the eye appeal is dependent on many factors. Many of the branch-mint issues, especially from Charlotte and Dahlonega, were inferior strikes that do not often possess good eye appeal. There are attractive coins from these mints, as well as from New Orleans and San Francisco, but many of the high-grade coins are Philadelphia strikings.

Proofs

HAIRLINES: The quality and quantity of Proof gold coins increased after 1858. Those coins struck in 1859 and later are often found pristine, with minimal hairlines. Proof strikes prior to 1859 usually have light-to-moderate hairlines, as cleaning and storage in coin cabinets was still prevalent.

REFLECTIVITY: Deeply reflective "orange-peel" surfaces are the norm for these coins. A few early dates, especially those prior to 1859, sometimes have light die polish still evident, though one usually must tilt the coin in a good light source to note these parallel striations. Cameo devices are evident on coins from most years, which make the surfaces appear to have even deeper reflectivity. After 1900, the dies were modified and frosted devices are rarer, with many coins having brilliant reflectivity over the entire surface.

STRIKE: Proof Liberty Head quarter eagles are obviously much better struck than their business-strike counterparts. Some slight weakness is seen for pre-1859 and a few later issues, but this is usually confined to slight incompleteness in the hair on the obverse, especially the curl above the ear, with the reverse sometimes showing slight weakness in the eagle's right leg and both sets of claws.

EYE APPEAL: The Mint was experienced in striking Proof coins by the time the Liberty Head gold series was first issued in 1840. These coins usually had frosted devices and lettering contrasting with deeply mirrored, "orange-peel" surfaces. These tiny coins were easy to strike and when hairline-free, or nearly so, they are great examples of the Liberty Head coinage.

Indian Head Quarter Eagle (1908–1929)
Circulated Examples

With the incuse design of the Indian Head quarter eagle, **AU-55/58** are the most debated grades for circulated specimens. Slight friction on the cheek of the Indian is seen on Uncirculated coins, so other areas must be used to determine whether a coin is Mint State or not. Slight friction will be seen on the eyebrow, cheek, and feathers in these grades, and slight rubbing will be seen on the flat field. The reverse will show slight wear on the eagle's shoulder, though the 1908 coins are almost always soft in this area. The master hub was redone in 1909, and this spot now has distinct feather detail. The flat fields will have slight friction, though this will be difficult to discern in these grades. The grades of **AU-50/53** have more obvious wear on the previously noted areas, with the fields now obviously worn. The reverse will have definite wear on the shoulder feathers and the flat field above the eagle.

EF-40/45 coins that are well struck will have the dotted, zigzag design on the headband complete. The friction on the feathers and field will be evident in these grades. The reverse will have wear across the entire eagle and the flat field above. A few dates, such as the 1925-D, are sometimes seen with extreme strike weakness, and surface preservation must be used to evaluate these specimens.

Although these incuse coins were designed to combat counterfeiting and reduce wear, the opposite is probably true. Indian Head coinage is among the most copied of all coins and, when worn, actually appears to be more worn than normal designs. **VF-20/25** coins will have a flat cheek and very flat feathers with blending. The headband design will be partially to mostly worn away. The eagle's feathers will be totally flat on the shoulder and indistinct elsewhere. The leg feathers will be mostly flat.

F-12/15 specimens will show the deepest detail clear, with most of the feathers worn and blended. The cheek will be very flat, with other detail quite worn. The feathers of the eagle will be worn smooth, with only slight detail.

VG and lower-grade Indian Head gold are like most post-1900 gold series—almost never seen. **VG-8/10** coins will have only slight obverse detail in deeply recessed areas. The reverse has very flat feathers, and only the protected areas have any detail.

In **G-4/6**, the detail will be minimal, with only recessed areas showing any remaining design. The incuse lettering and design do remain, even in the lowest grades, but detail is almost nonexistent.

The **AG-3** and **FR-2** coins will have large areas of incomplete design. Since there is no rim to wear into the letters or devices, this is not a problem. Even if there was a rim, the incuse lettering and devices would not be affected. The stars and the area around them are sometimes worn into the adjacent field. The reverse is similar, with the lettering and devices remaining clear, though with little detail.

Pocket pieces sometimes grade **PO-1**, though only the stars may be missing or incomplete. The reverse should still have most of the lettering and devices evident, with some areas missing.

Mint State Examples

MARKS: These coins have no rims, so marks and other surface impairments are very common. The flat nature of the design along with the lack of rims makes most of the surfaces very vulnerable to marking. Obviously, the recessed areas of the incuse design are well-protected and marks are seldom found there. Hairlines and scrapes are seen as often, or perhaps more often, as marks. The eagle's neck and especially the wing feathers are also areas usually found with marks and scrapes. Hairlines are mainly noticed in the open areas and are difficult to notice on the intricate design of the headdress or wing feathers.

LUSTER: These coins are only found with a flat, satin, and frosty luster. The nature of the incuse design prevents the striking of coins with semi-prooflike and prooflike luster, though some of the very frosty coins sometimes have flat areas that are slightly prooflike. Most of the Philadelphia coins from 1908 to 1911 have satin-to-slightly frosty luster. Those struck in 1912 and later are generally frosty in luster, but flat- and satin-luster coins are seen. Some years, 1926 through 1929, for example, have a chalky look to the frost. The Denver issues are seen with flat, satin, and frosty luster. Many of the 1911 Denver coins have a matte-like surface that really does not fit any luster variation, though flat-to-satin is close. Denver also struck coins in 1914 and 1925, with those usually appearing frosty.

STRIKE: The 1908 issue came from a unique die, and full feather detail on the eagle's shoulder for this year is impossible. Only counterfeit 1908 quarter eagles have full shoulder feathers. The overall strike for most years is good, with any weakness noted in the headdress feathers and the band across the headdress. Reverse weakness is noted in the shoulder, middle wing feathers, and left leg, with other areas sometimes having slight weakness. One date in particular, 1925-D, should be mentioned, as it is sometimes seen with extreme weakness. For this date, sometimes the entire central parts of the obverse and reverse are flattened, with an almost "dished-out" appearance. Some coins also have a "rim" that starts around the innermost part of the lettering and bulges out, fairly level, to the edge. Coins struck with these "bulged rims" often show more weakness or incompleteness. Also, the mint marks for certain Denver issues, especially 1911 and 1914, are found weakly impressed, though these are more likely the result of filled dies. PCGS separately designates 1911-D coins as the Weak "D" variety when this occurs. The 1914-D coins with a nearly invisible "D" are sometimes sold as the rarer 1914 Philadelphia issue.

EYE APPEAL: This is a difficult series for which to quantify eye appeal. Obviously, well-struck coins, minimally marked with a satin or frosty luster, are the most attractive. However, as noted earlier, some coins from certain years and mints have unusual strikes and luster. Eye appeal for those issues is different from that of the frosty, well-struck coins. Some 1911-D coins may have great eye appeal for the year and mint, but would look totally different from a well-struck, frosty-luster Philadelphia coin from 1926.

Proofs

HAIRLINES: For the Matte Proofs, scuffs are usually more prevalent than are hairlines, and on the Roman Proofs, hairlines are more often seen, due to the coarser texture of the Matte Proofs, which makes hairlines more difficult to detect. The Roman Proofs have a finer, more brilliant texture, making it easier to notice hairlines. Obverses of Matte Proofs have shiny spots, or scuffs, usually first appearing on the cheek and then the headdress, the date area including the bust, and the field in front of and above the head. Matte Proof reverses often have shiny spots in the field in front of and behind the head of the eagle, with others on the wing feathers, leg, on and among the branch, the field around the lettering, and the peripheral lettering. If Satin Proof specimens are someday discovered for this series, they would show hairlines similar to the Roman Proofs.

REFLECTIVITY: Only the Roman Proofs can be said to have any semblance of reflectivity. The surfaces are the exact opposite of brilliant Proofs, and instead of reflecting light in straight lines, like a mirror, the textured surfaces diffuse the light and have no direct reflectivity. On Matte Proofs, this effect is magnified by the coarse texture of the surfaces, resulting in the most diffused reflectivity. Some dates, such as 1911, 1912, and 1913, have a glitter-like appearance, where the reflected light appears as diamonds or points of light against a darker green-gold background. The Roman and Satin Proof surfaces are finer in texture, with a more reflective surface and a somewhat scaly look. However, there is less direct reflectivity for any of these surfaces than for semi-prooflike business strikes.

STRIKE: These coins are struck with the experimental Matte and Roman Proof surfaces. The strike on these issues is difficult to discern, as the finishes obscure the detail. The Roman Proofs are the easiest on which to "see" fine detail, and these coins are obviously well struck. The Matte coins have a fuzzy look, but the strike is usually full, though indistinct, if one examines the coins with a magnifying aid.

EYE APPEAL: Eye appeal is based on the texture, color, originality, and lack of hairlines and shiny spots. Some of the surfaces, such as those on the Roman Proof issues, are more appealing than some of the darker, more textured Matte surfaces, such as those on the

1908, 1914, and 1915 issues. When hairline- and scuff-free, all of the dates are attractive if they do not have discoloring, haze, or fading of the surfaces.

Three Dollars
Indian Princess Three Dollar (1854–1889)
Circulated Examples

This design was also used for the Type III Indian Princess gold dollar. **AU-55/58** coins will have slight friction on the top of the headdress, the hair below the ribbon, and the cheek. The central area is often weakly struck, and the hair on the ear and the curls below are often indistinct. Apparent wear in these areas and the bow and central area of the reverse should be closely examined. If the luster is complete across these areas, strike weakness, not wear, is responsible for the incompleteness. The elements of the reverse wreath will have slight rubbing, though little detail is missing. For **AU-50/53** grades, the wear will be more evident and the cheek will now be obviously rubbed. The details of the leaves will be incomplete in the central parts, and the bow will now show definite wear.

When **EF-40/45** grades are seen, the hair will be flat above the eye, around the ear, and at the back of the neck. The top of the headdress will be worn, though detail will still be evident. The cheek will have obvious wear, as will the reverse wreath. The leaves and other wreath detail will be complete, but obviously worn. The bow area may be flatter than the rest of the wreath because of strike weakness.

In **VF-20/35**, the hair above the eye will be flat and blend into the face. The headdress will have detail only for the part above LIB-ERTY. The cheek will be very flat, as will most of the hair, with detail only in the recessed parts. There should be a complete LIBERTY, though a few letters may be slightly worn. The wreath detail will be distinct, but some parts may blend together, especially in the bow area.

F-12/15 coins have very little hair detail visible, a few strands intact, and the hair above the eye will be worn into the face. The head-dress will have the area above LIBERTY showing some detail, though the top feathers will be almost completely flat. LIBERTY may have several letters that have been partially worn away. The wreath will be outlined, but only the deeper recessed parts will still show any detail.

Worn to **VG-8/10**, the Indian is almost completely flat. Only slight detail is seen in the recessed areas, and LIBERTY may have wear on all of the letters. The wreath will still be outlined, with some detail.

Although many gold coins are almost never seen in **G-4/6**, three-dollar coins are fairly common in these grades and lower. Perhaps the unusual denomination accounts for the heavy circulation sometimes seen for this issue, as many were probably carried as pocket pieces. The rim should be complete for **G-6**, though certain parts may show some weakness. There will be little or no detail on the Indian in these grades, and the wreath of the reverse may start to blend into the field in some places.

AG-3 coins will have wear into the tops of the lettering, and the Indian may have some areas that blend into the field. The reverse rim may touch the wreath in spots. The lettering may be almost totally obscured for **FR-2** coins, with the head of the Indian blending into the field. The reverse will have the central lettering and date visible, though the wreath may be almost completely worn into the field.

A **PO-1** coin will have part of the Indian visible and a readable date on the reverse.

Mint State Examples

MARKS: These coins are similar to the Type II and Type III gold dollars in that they were designed to prevent confusion with quarter eagles and half eagles. Thus, they are quite broad and thin, leading to bending, marks showing through on the opposite side, and other surface problems. Also, the rim is not high in comparison to the relief detail, leading to slide marks and other impairments on the high points. The face, neck, and open field around the head are where most marks and other surface impairments are usually seen. The headdress and hair of the Indian are not very intricately designed, and may have noticeable impairments. The reverse marks and other distractions are usually noted in the central area on and around the denomination and date, with marks on the wreath and open area between the wreath and rims.

LUSTER: Philadelphia coins have all luster variations, with satin-to-very frosty coins mostly seen for the common dates and frosty-to-prooflike luster seen on most lower-mintage issues. Some very low-mintage coins are almost always seen semi-prooflike or prooflike, some so deeply mirrored that they are mistaken for Proofs. For New Orleans and Dahlonega issues, luster is usually flat-to-satin, with some slightly frosty-surface coins. Occasionally, the New Orleans coins are seen with semi-prooflike or prooflike surfaces. San Francisco issues are usually satin-to-frosty, with the other luster variations also occasionally seen.

STRIKE: Slight weakness of strike is commonplace for this unusual denomination. Overall, these coins are better struck than the Indian Princess Type II gold dollar and approximate the strike of the Type III gold dollar. Slight weakness is usually noted on the top of the headdress, the hair above the eye, the hair around the ear, and the lower hair curls for the obverse. Reverse weakness is usually confined to the date and bow area; however, some weakness is noted for some coins in the upper parts of the wreath and sometimes in the central area affecting the lettering and numeral. In 1854, Dahlonega and New Orleans struck this denomination, most softly struck, with the dentils of the Dahlonega issue almost always weak or missing. Actually, the design was slightly changed in 1855, with slightly higher relief noted for the head and wreath. The larger lettering is usually the only difference noted in the design, but the higher relief is immedi-

ately noted when comparing 1854 and 1855–1889 examples.

EYE APPEAL: These are extremely attractive coins when seen with minimal marks, good strike, and superior luster, whether satin, frosty, semi-prooflike, or prooflike. Some considers swirling mint luster seen on frosty-luster specimens the most attractive luster variation, but satin, semi-prooflike, and prooflike luster is also positive. Some of the frosted device and lettering coins have great eye appeal when the semi-prooflike or prooflike surfaces are nearly free of marks or other distractions. These coins sometimes have a glittering look and sparkle as if they were just struck. Other coins are noted with incredible color, usually pastels, making superb examples of this popular issue. Deep green-gold color is also sometimes noted, and these coins are usually considered to have superior eye appeal.

Proofs

HAIRLINES: Since the rims are not much protection for the surfaces or devices, hairlines and other impairments are seen on many of these coins. The face of the Indian and the surrounding field are often seen with light, moderate, or heavy hairlines, plus slide marks are sometimes noted on the cheek. Reverse hairlines and other distractions are mostly concentrated in the central area on and around the denomination and date. As with nearly every Proof coin, the reverse hairlines usually are lighter.

REFLECTIVITY: Nearly every date has deeply mirrored surfaces, most with the "orange-peel" look. Heavily frosted devices and lettering are the norm and contrast with the deeply reflective surfaces, making the fields seem even more deeply mirrored. On some coins, the head and wreath seem to "float" on the mirrored fields. There are some areas, mainly the area directly in front of the neck that sometimes do not have completely mirrored surfaces. This incompleteness is noted as slight porosity when viewed with magnification, and is caused by the depth of the reverse die opposite the incompleteness.

STRIKE: Slight weakness is still noted for Proof issues, though on most coins nearly all intended detail is present, with only slight weakness noted in the hair around the ear, the date, and the central reverse lettering. As noted under Reflectivity, an unusual effect seen on these coins is the slight incompleteness or porosity seen in the field directly in front of the neck. This is a "ghosting" effect from the reverse wreath, which results in the metal's not flattening completely in this spot, creating a granular area.

EYE APPEAL: These are some of the most attractive of all the Proof gold coins when found with minimal hairlines. Some coins have attractive, even toning, and when combined with frosted devices and superb fields, they have extremely positive eye appeal. Lint marks, planchet flaws, and other striking or planchet defects are noted for some years, and these detractions create negative eye appeal. On coins from several years, the frosted devices have interruptions in the frost from die problems, and these should not be confused with marks, though they slightly affect eye appeal.

Four Dollars
Flowing Hair/Coiled Hair Four Dollar (Stella) (1879–1880)
Circulated Examples

Although a Proof-only issue, the Flowing Hair type is commonly seen in circulated grades, mainly **VF** and above. The Coiled Hair type is usually seen only in **AU** and above grades. **PR-55/58** Stellas have slight wear on the cheek and hair. Both types usually come with central planchet striations, mostly noticeable on the obverse. If these coins had been given more blows from the presses or heavier striking pressure, the striations would have been "struck" away. Slight central weakness is noted on these coins, with striations present mainly on the cheek and the hair around the ear. The reverse will have slight wear on the star. The cheek and hair of both types will have noticeable wear in **PR-50/53**, with rubbing now also evident in the field. The star of the reverse will have notice-

able wear, and there will be slight disturbance in the field.

Stellas are still common in **PR-40/45**, with some flattening of the hair, especially on the Flowing Hair type, and obvious wear on the cheek. The fields are now rubbed, and luster is present only around the devices. The star will have obvious wear, though all of the numerals and lettering are still strong and readable. Some of the lines outlining the star are becoming indistinct.

PR-20/35 Stellas show one-third to one-half of hair detail and considerable wear on the cheek. The Coiled Hair type is not usually seen in this grade and below. The reverse will have some of the numerals and lettering worn and indistinct. The peripheral lettering is complete.

If a pocket piece is worn to **PR-12/15**, only the deep recesses of hair will be visible and the cheek will be worn smooth. The peripheral lettering and devices will be readable, though worn. The star will have missing and indistinct numerals and lettering, plus blending into the field.

Stellas are sometimes seen in **PR-8/10**, and these have an outlined Miss Liberty with little fine detail. The rims are still complete, with lettering and devices all readable but quite worn. There will be traces of numerals and lettering within the star.

Although these coins are rarely seen in **PR-4/6**, the grading would be similar to that of Indian Princess coinage. The head would be worn smooth, but outlined. The rims would be incomplete, especially for **PR-4**, but would not touch any of the lettering or devices. The reverse would have an outlined star, and the rims might touch some of the lettering.

The **PR-3** Stella would have rims that are worn into the lettering and devices. Miss Liberty might blend into the field in places. The reverse would have the rim worn halfway into the lettering. The star would be totally flat and blend into the field in places. **PR-2** coins might have all or part of the peripheral lettering and devices worn away.

For **PR-1** coins, there would have to be a discernible date, identifiable hair type, and little else.

Proofs

HAIRLINES: As noted, nearly all of the 1879 Flowing Hair Stellas and many of the other three issues have striations that were on the planchets before striking, caused by burnishing the blanks or roller marks. Blended with hairlines, these striations are sometimes very difficult to distinguish from hairlines, but the striations are almost always parallel and hairlines often run at angles to each other. Another test, though not infallible, is to tilt the coin under a good light source and note whether the lines "move" or appear to be stationary. If the lines "move," then they are probably hairlines and, if stationary, they probably are striations. Although hairlines are mainly present in the fields, they are also found on the face and star.

REFLECTIVITY: Although nearly all of these coins have deeply mirrored fields, the striations interfere slightly with the mirrored surfaces, and few of these coins have the "orange-peel" surfaces associated with most brilliant Proof gold issues.

STRIKE: As with all Proof coin series, these issues are well-struck overall. However, there is almost always slight incompleteness in the central areas. Slight softness is noted in the hair above the ear and the lettering inside the star, perhaps because the dies were not properly spaced or the proper striking pressure was never achieved, leading to the slight incompleteness seen on nearly all of these coins.

EYE APPEAL: When well struck, with minimum striations and hairlines, these are some of the most attractive of all U.S. gold coins. Highly prized by numismatists from the year of issue onward, these coins are attractively designed and very pleasing even to the untrained eye. Almost every coin has very frosted devices and lettering, which contrast with the mirrored fields, giving Miss Liberty and the star a floating or three-dimensional effect. Some of these coins have acquired beautiful toning, which adds to their attractiveness.

Half Eagles
Capped Bust Right Half Eagle— Small Eagle and Heraldic (Large) Eagle (1795–1807)
Circulated Examples

The slight wear of **AU-55/58** Capped Bust Right coinage is usually seen on the folds of the cap, the hair above and around the ear, the cheek, and the folds of the drapery on the bust. Weakness of strike, unfortunately, is sometimes located in these areas as well, and differentiating true wear from strike weakness is difficult. The upper areas of the wing feathers of the eagle will have slight friction, as will the breast feathers of the Small Eagle coins and breast feathers directly above the shield on Heraldic Eagle coins. These breast feathers and the shield lines of the Heraldic Eagle variety are the areas most often seen with strike weakness. As the coin is worn to **AU-50/53**, the obverse wear will become more apparent, with rub on the cheek, hair, cap, and bust causing discoloration. The reverse will have definite wear on the wing, breast feathers, and shield lines of the Heraldic Eagle coins. The central area may be missing considerable detail on poorly struck coins.

In **EF-40/45**, there is dullness across most of the coins' surfaces. The strength of the strike determines the amount of detail remaining, with strong strikes having nearly complete detail and weak strikes showing flatness in the hair and breast feathers. For the Heraldic Eagle reverse, the shield lines may be incomplete because of strike weakness. Localized weakness may affect some stars and lettering.

Worn to **VF-20/35**, Capped Bust coinage will have from 50 percent to nearly full detail in the hair, cap, and drapery of Miss Liberty. Stars will range from flat on **VF-20** and poorly struck coins to nearly full radial lines on higher-grade or well-struck **VF** coins. The reverse will have flat wing and breast feathers on weakly struck and lower **VF** coins, and sometimes better detail than weakly struck **EF** or some **AU** specimens.

Quite a few Capped Bust coins are worn to **F-12/15** condition, as some of these coins received considerable circulation. Five dollars was a lot of money in 1795, thus true "pocket" circulation is the cause of most of the wear seen on these coins. The hair detail will be less than half complete on well-struck coins and nearly gone on weakly struck ones. The wing and breast feathers will show almost no detail, and the shield of Heraldic Eagle coins will have only sporadic lines showing.

VG-8/10 coins will have an outlined bust of Miss Liberty, with only the deepest recesses of the hair showing detail. Stars will be flat and possibly worn into the field. The rims should be complete, except in areas of localized weakness. The reverse will have an outlined eagle with slight detail.

A **G-4/6** coin will have an outlined Miss Liberty with little detail. Rims will be worn into stars and the tops of some lettering on **G-4** coins. The eagle will be outlined, with very slight detail.

With **AG-3** and **FR-2** coins, the head of Miss Liberty may be worn into the field in several areas and the rims will obliterate some, if not all, of the stars. The lettering of the reverse may be one-half or more incomplete, with the eagle showing only slight detail.

PO-1 coins will have little detail, but the date must be readable, though seldom complete.

Mint State Examples

MARKS: The obverses of both types are the same, with marks and other surface impairments noted on the cap, face, bust, and hair of Miss Liberty, with the field in front of and in back of the head also areas of surface distractions. Marks in the hair are usually noticeable, except for minor marks or marks that blend with the flow of the hair. The reverse of the Small Eagle type has much more open field area than the Heraldic Eagle type, and marks are mainly noted in the open field, breast, and wing. The Heraldic Eagle type has little open field area, and marks are usually confined to the shield and wings of the eagle, with marks noticeable elsewhere only when they are severe.

LUSTER: All luster variations are seen for both types, with the Small Eagle type usually seen slightly frosty-to-prooflike in luster and the Heraldic Eagle type usually seen with slightly frosty-to-very frosty luster. This would be expected, as the Small Eagle dates had lower mintages than nearly all of the Heraldic Eagle dates. In fact, Heraldic Eagle coins are seldom seen with the deeply prooflike surfaces seen on some of the Small Eagle coins. There are many more frosty examples of the Heraldic Eagle type.

STRIKE: With the central parts of many of these coins showing incompleteness and the hair sometimes seen with an almost dished appearance, these coins should be graded mainly by surface preservation. Coins with extreme weakness would not be graded as high as well-struck coins if surface preservation is identical. The neck and breast feathers may be almost totally flat, with part of E PLURIBUS UNUM, for the Heraldic eagle type, sometimes missing. Also, the shield and tips of the wings are sometimes weak. Localized weakness is also noted for the stars, cap, bust, LIBERTY, and date for the obverse. Reverse weakness is sometimes seen in the peripheral lettering, head, claws, tail, arrows, olive branch, clouds, stars, and wing feathers. For the Small Eagle coins, the laurel wreath in the eagle's mouth may show weakness. Some localized weakness is noted in devices and lettering that is not deeply impressed into the individually made working dies.

EYE APPEAL: Both types are very attractive when found well struck, with minimal marks and superior luster, regardless of what luster variation is present. The heavily frosted Heraldic Eagle coins are often seen in the highest grades and have the most positive eye appeal for this type.

Specimens

HAIRLINES: Although only 1795 Small Eagle coins are reported in specimen strike, it is possible that other date Small Eagle coins may be discovered, as well as examples of the Heraldic Eagle type. Light-to-medium hairlines in the fields of the 1795 Small Eagle are expected, even though these coins would obviously have been very carefully struck and specially handled.

REFLECTIVITY: These coins have extremely deep reflective surfaces. Although they do not have the "orange-peel" surfaces of close-collar Proofs, the mirrored fields are more reflective than regular prooflike specimens. Frosted devices and lettering are present, though not the heavy cameo look of Liberty Head gold coins or other close-collar Proof strikings.

STRIKE: Nearly fully struck details are necessary for a specimen-strike Capped Bust half eagle. Razor-sharp hair and feather detail is present, and any weakness is slight.

EYE APPEAL: These coins are the pinnacle of Small Eagle coinage and represent the Mint's finest workmanship. The care used in striking these coins from specially prepared planchets resulted in spectacular examples of the first half eagles.

Capped Bust Left Half Eagle— Large Size–Large Bust and Small Bust (1807–1829)

Circulated Examples

Both Large Bust and Small Bust types have slight wear on the cheek, the hair above the eye and behind the ear, and the cap above the ribbon. **AU-55/58** coins will first show noticeable wear in these areas, though weakly struck coins have weakness in basically the same spots. The reverses of both types are nearly identical, with wear first seen on the upper wing feathers. The central area is almost always seen with slight to moderate

weakness. The breast, leg, upper right wing, and shield exhibit softness on poorly struck coins, sometimes having detail that appears to be several grades lower. Only with wear into **AU-50/53** grades does wear versus strike become obvious. Dullness across the broad, flat cheek indicates wear, which eliminates having to determine whether the hair has strike weakness or slight wear.

The **EF-40/45** coin has wear across most of the face, hair, and cap. The detail ranges from approximately 70 percent on weakly struck coins to 90 percent or more for well-struck coins. The reverse will show wear on the upper wing, leg, inner right wing feathers, and shield.

With the strike problems of the early Mint, **VF-20/35** coins may have less than 50 percent detail on lower-grade and poorly struck **VF** coins and nearly 90 percent detail on higher-grade and well-struck **VF** specimens. Poorly struck coins may have a very mushy reverse central area and half of the wing detail.

The wear on **F-12/15** coins will leave only the deep recesses of the hair detail visible. LIBERTY should be complete, though some letters may be weak. Stars will be mostly flat. The reverse will have less than half of the feather detail, and some weakly struck coins may show only the deeply recessed areas.

VG-8/10 graded coins will have some hair detail, though only slight. LIBERTY may be missing parts of some letters. Stars will be outlined and may blend into the field. The reverse will have slightly more detail remaining in the recessed areas of the feathers than the hair has for the obverse. The peripheral reverse lettering may have localized weakness, though all letters should be complete.

If the strike is decent, the obverse should have outlined stars, Miss Liberty complete, and some letters of LIBERTY visible for **G-4/6**. There may be localized rim weakness, with the peripheral lettering of the reverse weak at the tops of some letters. The eagle will have little fine detail, though it will be well outlined.

AG-3 and FR-2 will have worn rims, weak and missing stars, and Miss Liberty worn into the field. The reverse will have half or more of the peripheral lettering present on AG-3 coins and less than half visible for FR-2. There will be a flat eagle worn into the field of the reverse.

PO-1 coins will be identifiable as to type, with the date readable.

Mint State Examples

MARKS: These coins are similar to the Capped Bust quarter eagles, with marks and other surface impairments easily noticed on these low-relief, low-rim coins. The cap, face, bust, and open areas in front of and behind the head are flat, allowing any mark to be easily noticed. The reverse design has a large open area above the eagle and smaller ones below the wings, where marks are often noted. The eagle, especially the wings, may also have marks, though small ones may blend with the feathers.

LUSTER: Most of the first type Capped Bust coins are found with a satin-to-very frosty luster, with the other luster variations sometimes found. Small Bust issues usually have a frosty-to-prooflike luster, as most dates have much lower mintages than the Large Bust issues. Most of the prooflike coins have frosted devices and lettering, contrasting with the mirrored fields.

STRIKE: Both Large Bust coins, issued from 1807 until 1812, and Small Bust coins, issued from 1813 through 1829, were struck with open collars. More unevenness in striking quality is the result, and central weakness is noted on these coins. The hair around the ear is the area where weakness is mainly noted, though the stars, the hair above the eye, the lower hair curls, and the front of the bust are sometimes seen with incompleteness. For the reverse, the neck, shield, right wing next to the shield, leg, and claws are often weakly impressed, sometimes with detail obliterated. Localized weakness is also noted for the peripheral lettering, E PLURIBUS UNUM, the denomination, laurel leaves, and arrowheads.

As with many early issues, die wear, improper die spacing, and out-of-parallel dies may be causes for some incompleteness, as well as insufficient striking pressure.

EYE APPEAL: Both types have good eye appeal when found well struck, with minimal marks and superior luster, regardless of which luster variation is present. Frosty-luster coins, especially those with rich colors, have exceptional eye appeal when the other attributes are positive. Semi-prooflike and prooflike specimens are mainly seen for the Small Bust type, the prooflike coins sometimes mistaken for Proofs.

Proofs

HAIRLINES: Only coins of the second type, the Small Bust version, are known in Proof. As with most early Proofs, these coins sometimes were cleaned or wiped with a cloth by the early collectors. Light-to-heavy hairlines are noted on some of these coins, mainly in the fields, though the low rims do not protect the low relief of the devices. These coins do not have the upset rim of close-collar strikings, which leaves the fields and devices vulnerable to slide marks, hairlines, and other impairments.

REFLECTIVITY: Although not as deeply reflective as the close-collar Proofs, the surfaces are deeply mirrored and usually have frosty devices and lettering contrasting with the surfaces. The burnishing of the blanks and basining of the dies resulted in these superior fields' having the watery look associated with true Proofs, though they do not have the "orange-peel" surfaces found on most close-collar strikings.

STRIKE: Small Bust Proofs are well struck, with only slight incompleteness noted on a few hair curls, the shield, and a few central feathers. Though struck in open collars, these coins probably received extra blows from the dies, leading to their superior striking qualities. Blanks also would have been carefully weighed, so Proofs are almost always of correct weight or slightly higher.

EYE APPEAL: These coins are attractive open-collar Proofs, usually with great contrast between the frosted devices and lettering and the mirrored fields. When found with minimal hairlines and original color, these are some of the most attractive of all early Proof gold coins.

Capped Bust Left Half Eagle— Small Size (1829–1834)

Circulated Examples

AU-55/58 specimens have slight wear on the cheek, the hair above the eye and behind the ear, and the cap above the ribbon. These coins are in higher relief than the Large Size Capped Bust coins and are sometimes called the "Fat Head" type. They were struck in a close collar, leading to better overall striking quality. Though weakly struck coins are still seen, the close-collar strikes usually have only slight central weakness, resulting in a few hair curls, the shield, and the breast feathers exhibiting slight softness of detail. The reverse wear is first noted on the upper wing feathers. Only with wear into **AU-50/53** grades does wear versus strike become obvious. Dullness across the cheek indicates wear, and the hair now has enough wear to discern between strike weakness and real wear.

The **EF-40/45** coin has wear across most of the face, hair, and cap. The detail ranges from approximately 80 percent to 90 percent or more for well-struck coins. The reverse will show wear on the upper wing, leg, inner right wing feathers, and shield.

VF-20/35 coins usually have 50 percent to 75 percent of the detail. The coins with central weakness may have a very mushy reverse central area and half or slightly more of the wing detail.

The wear on **F-12/15** coins will leave only the deep recesses of the hair detail visible. LIBERTY should be complete, but some letters may be weak, with the stars flat. The reverse will have less than half of the feather detail, and some weakly struck coins may show only the deeply recessed areas.

The **VG-8/10** graded coins will have some hair detail, though usually only slight. LIBERTY may be missing parts of some letters. Stars will be outlined and may blend into the field. The reverse will have slightly more detail remaining in the recessed areas of the feathers than the hair will have on the obverse.

If the strike is decent, the obverse should have outlined stars, Miss Liberty complete, and some letters of LIBERTY visible for **G-4/6**. The eagle will have little or no fine detail, though it should be well outlined.

AG-3 and **FR-2** will have worn rims, weak and missing stars, and Miss Liberty worn into the field. The reverse will have half or more of the peripheral lettering present on **AG-3** coins and less than half visible for **FR-2**. There will be a flat eagle worn into the field of the reverse.

PO-1 coins will be identifiable as to type, with the date readable.

Mint State Examples

MARKS: These coins have the same basic design as the previous type, with Chief Engraver Kneass modifying Miss Liberty and the eagle, giving them higher relief. These close-collar strikings were issued in much larger quantities than the previous open-collar strikings, with these coins having a much more uniform look than previously. The higher rims of the close-collar strikings are offset by the higher relief of the head and eagle. The cheek of Miss Liberty is especially vulnerable and is often seen with slide marks and other impairments. The open field area is the about the same as with the previous type, but the higher rims provide slightly more protection, therefore slightly fewer impairments are noted for the fields.

LUSTER: Although the dates of this type are all fairly high-mintage issues, many of these coins were melted following the weight reduction of all gold coins in 1834. Since the close collar allowed the metal to be limited in its outward flow, the luster is usually satin-to-frosty in nature, with semi-prooflike and prooflike coins noted. Because the dies struck more coins than for the Capped Bust Small Size quarter eagles, there are more satin and frosty coins and fewer prooflike coins than for the quarter eagles.

STRIKE: Like the quarter eagles, the close-collar strikes of the Small Size Capped Bust half eagles are of very high quality. A few specimens are noted with slight weakness in the central hair curls of Miss Liberty, the right wing feathers next to the shield, the shield, the right leg feathers, and the claws. The metal flowed more easily into the die cavities, as it was restrained by the close collar and could not spread.

EYE APPEAL: Although the dies were used for more strikings than the quarter eagles of the same type, there are many half eagles with good eye appeal. These "Fat Head" coins when nearly mark-free, well struck, and lustrous are beautiful examples of the Mint's workmanship.

Proofs

HAIRLINES: Since the rims imparted by the close collar are slightly higher than for open-collar strikes, the fields are slightly more protected but the head is in higher relief, thus more likely to receive slide marks and hairlines. For the obverse, light-to-moderate hairlines usually are noted on the cheek and the field around the head. For the reverse, lines are mainly noted in the open areas above the eagle and below both wings. Hairlines are usually less severe on the reverse, as is true with most Proof coins.

REFLECTIVITY: These are the first half eagles struck in close collars and are very deeply mirrored. The surfaces are deeply brilliant but without the "orange-peel" effect noted for the later gold Proofs. Most of these coins have frosted devices and lettering, making the surfaces appear even more deeply mirrored.

STRIKE: These close-collar Proofs are of very high striking quality. Any incomplete-

ness noted will be very minor, such as slight weakness on the central hair curls, the right wing next to the shield, the leg, and the vertical lines of the shield. Broad, flat rims are also a result of the close collar, and when viewed from the edge should have only slight beveling. Some specimens may even have a slight wire rim, and when viewed from the edge these coins have the "squared-off" look of the later Liberty Head Proof coinage.

EYE APPEAL: These close-collar Proofs are of very high quality. Frosted devices and lettering contrast with deeply mirrored fields to create spectacular Proofs when relatively hairline-free. Obviously these coins are like other Proof issues and are sometimes found with cleaning and the resultant hairlines.

Classic Head Half Eagle (1834–1838)
Circulated Examples

Classic Head half eagles show obverse wear first on the hair curls above the ribbon, the hair above the eye, and the hair above and behind the ear. The cheek will also show friction in **AU-55/58** grades, and the stars will have slight wear. The eagle will have friction on the upper edge of the wing, neck, and leg feathers. The feathers adjacent to the shield sometimes are weakly struck. For **AU-50/53** coins, more obvious wear is seen in the above-mentioned spots, with friction across the entire cheek and neck. Rub will show in the field above the eagle, and the feathers will develop flat spots.

If well struck, **EF-40/45** coins will still show much detail in the hair, especially at the top and behind the ear. The reverse will have feathers blended together and the neck and leg area may have considerable flatness, especially noticeable on weak strikes.

VF-20/35 coins will almost always have a complete LIBERTY, though hair detail is now seen only in the deeply recessed parts. Stars will be outlined, with only slight detail. On higher-grade **VF** coins with good strikes, considerable feather detail remains, though many feathers will be flat and blended.

The **F-12/15** grade may only have a partial LIBERTY, with the hair completely flat and showing just slight detail. Stars are all flat, with only an occasional line remaining. The reverse will have only the deepest feathers visible, sometimes fewer than half of them showing any detail. The neck and leg feathers will be worn flat.

Many gold coins are not found in the lowest grades, but the Classic Head design is found in **VG-8/10** and below. An outlined head with almost no detail will be seen, with all of the stars flat. The feathers of the eagle will have a few areas with slight detail.

G-4/6 coins have virtually no detail on Miss Liberty, but a complete outline is present. The rims may blend slightly into the fields. The eagle will have little other than an occasional feather visible. The shield lines may blend into the field and some lettering may have the tops of the letters slightly worn.

The **G** and **VG** gold coins are scarce, but **AG-3** and **FR-2** gold coins are rare. The head will have no detail, but should still be outlined in these grades. The rim will be worn, especially with **FR-2** coins, and the lettering of the reverse will be partially missing. The eagle should be outlined, but the rims may wear into the tips of the feathers.

A **PO-1** coin will have a readable date, some stars partially visible, and Miss Liberty blended into the field in spots. The reverse may have little peripheral lettering.

Mint State Examples

MARKS: Although these coins have about the same field space as the previous design, the reverse does not have the motto above the eagle, thus marks are often seen in that area. Surface distractions are noted mainly on the face and the field in the front and back of the head. Marks in the hair, unless severe, are usually hidden by the deeply chiseled curls of the hair design. The reverse has an open area above the eagle plus spaces below the wings that often have marks and other surface impairments. Marks on the eagle, unless severe,

are usually disguised by the intricate nature of the feathers.

LUSTER: Though these coins are seen with every luster variation, the typical Philadelphia issue has a satin-to-very frosty luster. Semi-prooflike and prooflike coins are seen fairly often, with some of the deep prooflike coins resembling Proofs. The Charlotte and Dahlonega mints struck coins in 1838, which usually are satin-to-slightly frosty. A few semi-prooflike 1838 Dahlonega coins are seen.

STRIKE: As with the quarter eagles, Classic Head half eagles are often not as well struck as the coins that preceded them. The central hair curls are often mushy, with only the prooflike and semi-prooflike coins having the razor-sharp hair detail intended by the designer. Reverse central detail, including the leg of the eagle, also shows this weakness. Gobrecht's dies did not improve the striking qualities over the Kneass dies, and only the variety specialists note the minor differences. There is less localized weakness noted for these coins, attributable to the introduction of the steam-powered presses in 1836. Dies not in parallel are much less common than earlier, with weakness usually seen just in the stars.

EYE APPEAL: When seen well struck, lustrous, and relatively mark-free, these are very attractive half eagles. Some of the semi-prooflike and prooflike specimens have frosted devices and lettering, which are also very attractive and desirable. Some of the frosty coins also may have frosty devices and lettering, and these are some of the most eye-appealing coins of this design.

Proofs

HAIRLINES: Since the obverse head is similar in relief to the previous type, Miss Liberty may have slide marks, tiny nicks, or hairlines present. The field in the front and back of the head may reveal light-to-moderate hairlines. The field above the eagle and below the wings is found with light-to-moderate hairlines, with the area above the eagle particularly vulnerable, as it is the largest open area on either side.

REFLECTIVITY: Proof Classic Head half eagles usually have deeply mirrored fields contrasting with frosted devices and lettering. Although not quite as deeply mirrored as the Liberty Head Proofs to follow, and usually without the "orange-peel" surfaces, these coins do have the watery look for the surfaces. Some if not all of the Proofs of 1838 have fine die polish across the surfaces. These lines are also noted on Proof quarters of 1838 and may represent Mint experimentation with surface texture.

STRIKE: As with the quarter eagles, Proofs of the Classic Head half eagles are exceptionally sharp. Full chiseled hair and wing feathers are evident on these coins. Only the slightest weakness is seen in the very central hair and some of the lines of the shield. If there is more than very slight weakness in these areas, the coin is most likely an early business strike, with prooflike fields. Though broad, thick rims are not always present, when viewed from the edge there should be little or no beveling.

EYE APPEAL: When relatively hairline-free, these are some of the most spectacular of all Proof gold coins. The deeply reflective fields usually contrast with frosted devices and lettering, making these spectacular in appearance. The head of Miss Liberty and the eagle seem to float on the watery Proof surfaces, creating a three-dimensional effect.

Liberty Head Half Eagle—No Motto and Motto (1839–1908)

Circulated Examples

Half eagles of the Liberty Head design in **AU-55/58** first show wear on the eyebrow, the hair above the ribbon, the curls of hair above the eye and ear, the hair curl below the ear, the nose, and the chin. The reverse will have wear on the tops of the wing, neck, and leg feathers. The neck and leg feathers are also areas of strike weakness, and for some of the branch-mint coins this area is almost never seen with any detail. **AU-50/53** coins will have more friction in the aforementioned regions, with some flatness noted especially for the hair above the ribbon and ear. The reverse will have slight wear on all of the wing feathers, though there should be complete feather detail except on the neck and leg. Rubbing in the field above the eagle will usually be evident, though on the Motto type this area does not show rubbing as much.

EF-40/45 specimens will have some of the hair detail missing or indistinct. The entire coin will have some rubbing, and the stars and fields will have definite wear. The feathers of the eagle will have wear but will still be separate, save the neck and leg areas, which will usually be flat except for well-struck coins. The leaves and arrows will be separate, with most detail still clear.

If **VF-20/35** coins are well struck, a lot of detail will still be obvious on the obverse. The main hair curls will show some separation and the recessed areas will be distinct. The reverse will have the tips of the wing feathers worn together on well-struck coins in higher **VF** grades. Lower-grade **VF** and weakly struck coins may have very little feather detail. The leaves and arrows are still separated, though little detail is still visible.

Many **F-12/15** coins still have some intricate hair detail, with the curl on the neck sometimes still fairly sharp, but much of the hair and the stars are quite flat. LIBERTY should be complete, though some of the letters may have weakness. On well-struck coins, feather detail may be seen, though most of the eagle is now worn flat, the leaves now blended together. The arrows are worn flat, but still separate.

With **VG-8/10** and lower-grade Liberty Head coinage, specimens are so seldom seen, except for rare dates and some branch-mint issues, that previous grading books have not bothered to define these grades. The head will have sporadic detail and will be mostly flat, with some letters of LIBERTY partially missing. The eagle will be outlined, with little detail remaining. The lettering will be clear around the periphery.

G-4/6 coins will have a basically smooth head, with some of LIBERTY showing. The rim may be slightly incomplete and may be slightly worn into the lettering. A flat eagle is present with a full outline.

For **AG-3** and **FR-2** coins, a date, head, and some stars will be seen. The **FR-2** may not have stars visible. The reverse will have the rims worn into the tips of the wing and lettering. The **FR-2** may have only parts of some lettering readable.

PO-1 graded coins will have a readable date, partial head, partial eagle, and possibly no lettering.

Mint State Examples

MARKS: Marks and other surface disruptions are more prevalent for Liberty Head half eagles than for quarter eagles because of their heavier weight and larger size. Obverse surface impairments are mainly noted on the face and neck, as well as in the front and back of the head. The hair is not intricate, and marks are often noted unless they are very minor. For the No Motto type, the reverse has the same proportionate open field space as Liberty Head quarter eagles. Therefore, surface disruptions are mainly noted in the field above the head and below the wings for the No Motto type, with others noted on the neck, shield, legs, and wings. The motto is in the field above the eagle, with marks and other impairments noted in the same areas as for the No Motto type.

LUSTER: All luster variations are seen for the Philadelphia issues. For most of the common dates, satin-to-very frosty luster is usually seen, with flat, semi-prooflike, and prooflike coins occasionally noted. The rare Philadelphia coins, such as the 1875, are usually found semi-prooflike or prooflike, with scarce coins, such as the 1876, found frosty to prooflike. There are some common dates, such as 1899, that are mostly found with a satin-to-slightly frosty luster, often with a chalky-looking luster similar to many 1924 double eagles. The branch-mint coins are found in most luster variations, with the

Charlotte and Dahlonega coins usually seen with a flat, satin, or slightly frosty luster, with few very frosty or semi-prooflike specimens. Fully prooflike coins from these mints are seldom seen and, when found, usually have heavy die polish in the fields. San Francisco and Denver issues are usually satin to frosty in luster, though the other luster variations are sometimes found. There are more semi-prooflike and many more prooflike coins seen from these mints than from Charlotte and Dahlonega. The Carson City coins are mainly seen with a satin-to-slightly frosty luster, and since most of these are low-mintage issues, they are sometimes seen with semi-prooflike or proof-like surfaces.

STRIKE: As with the quarter eagles, the coins struck in the early years in Philadelphia, and nearly all of the branch-mint coins, have striking weakness. The main areas of weakness are the stars, tip of the coronet, hair above the eye, hair curl above the ear, hair curl on the neck, hair curl going back from the ear, and hair bun. All of these areas are not necessarily weak on all coins, but sometimes this is the case. The reverses, including many Philadelphia coins struck after 1900, have the tips of the wings, neck, shield, inner wing feathers around the shield, right leg, and claws showing weakness or sometimes totally flat. Many branch-mint coins were struck on inferior presses, and central areas sometimes have a dished appearance. Some branch-mint coins will also have wing feather weakness, which results in coins with obverses that appear to be a much higher grade than the reverses.

EYE APPEAL: There are many spectacular Liberty Head half eagles, more than for the heavier eagles and double eagles and slightly fewer than for the smaller and lighter Liberty Head quarter eagles. Some of the most incredible-looking half eagles are the deeply frosty, richly toned issues that were acquired in their year of issue by John Clapp and later sold to Louis Eliasberg. These are the pinnacle of Liberty Head half eagle coinage, coins that have almost no surface disruptions and are well struck, original, beautifully toned, and with a deep mint frost. Most high-grade half eagles are measured against these specimens, several of which have received the grade of **MS-69**, near perfection. Of course, most specimens do not equal these in attributes, but there are many coins that have good strikes, minimal marks, and original color.

Proofs

HAIRLINES: These are usually found with more hairlines than Liberty Head quarter eagles, often more concentrated and severe. The field in the front and back of the head is the most common area to view these lines, though the face is often found hairlined. Reverse hairlines are most often noted in the field above the eagle and below the wings for the No Motto type. The Motto type has hairlines in the same locations, but the motto protects the area above the eagle's head to some degree. Both types are sometimes noted with hairlines across the eagle, though these are more difficult to see because of the intricate design of the feathers. Other surface impairments are noted, some mint-caused and others post-striking impairments. These include lint marks, planchet flaws, die disruptions of the frosted devices, and other die or planchet impairments.

REFLECTIVITY: Most of these issues have deeply reflective "orange-peel" surfaces, especially the coins struck in the later years. Some of the early issues, especially those prior to 1859, sometimes have light parallel die polish still evident. Most years have frosted devices and lettering that contrast with the mirrored fields. After 1900, the dies were modified and frosted devices are rarer, with many coins having brilliant reflectivity over the entire surface or very lightly frosted devices and lettering.

STRIKE: Though usually much better-struck than their business-strike counterparts, Proof half eagles have more striking problems than do quarter eagles. Some slight weakness is seen for some pre-1859 and a few later issues, but this is usually confined to minor incompleteness in the hair, especially the curl above the ear, with the reverse hav-

ing slight weakness in the eagle's neck, both legs, and both sets of claws.

EYE APPEAL: Since these are larger and heavier than quarter eagles, more coins are seen with hairlines; therefore fewer specimens are found with great eye appeal. There are many spectacular Proofs, since many of these coins have frosted devices and lettering, original color, and minor hairlines.

Indian Head Half Eagle (1908–1929)
Circulated Examples

The incuse design of the Indian Head half eagle makes **AU-55/58** coins difficult to discern from Uncirculated specimens. Slight friction on the cheek is also seen on some Uncirculated coins, so other areas must be used to determine whether a coin is Mint State or not. There will be slight friction on the eyebrow, cheek, and feathers in these grades, and slight rubbing on the flat field. The reverse will have slight wear on the eagle's shoulder. The flat field will have slight friction, though this will be difficult to discern in these grades. The grades of **AU-50/53** have more obvious wear on the previously noted areas, with the fields now obviously worn. The reverse will have definite wear on the shoulder feathers and the flat field above the eagle.

EF-40/45 coins that are well struck will have the dotted, zigzag design on the headband complete. Friction on the feathers and field will be evident in these grades. The reverse will have wear across the entire eagle and the flat field. Some issues, especially those from San Francisco, are seen with softness of strike, with a mushy headdress and eagle feathers.

Although these incuse coins were designed to combat counterfeiting and reduce wear, the opposite is probably true. Indian Head coinage is among the most copied of all coins and, when worn, actually appears to be more worn than normal designs. **VF-20/35** coins will have a flat cheek and many blended feathers. The headband design will be partially to mostly worn away. The eagle's feathers will be totally flat on the shoulder and indistinct elsewhere. The leg feathers will be mostly flat.

F-12/15 specimens will have the deepest detail clear, with most of the feathers worn and blended. The cheek will be very flat, with other detail quite worn. The eagle's feathers will be worn smooth, with only slight detail remaining.

Very Good and lower grade Indian Head gold is like most post-1900 gold series—almost never seen. **VG-8/10** coins will have only slight obverse detail in the deeply recessed areas. The reverse is similar, with the feathers very flat and only the protected areas showing any detail.

If seen in **G-4/6**, the detail will be minimal, again with only recessed areas showing any remaining design. The incuse design does remain, even in the lowest grades, though detail is almost nonexistent.

AG-3 and **FR-2** coins will have large areas of incomplete design. The stars and the area around them are sometimes worn into the adjacent field. The reverse is similar, with the lettering and devices remaining clear, though with little detail.

Pocket pieces are sometimes found that grade **PO-1**, which will have a date and slight detail.

Mint State Examples

MARKS: As with the Indian Head quarter eagles, these coins have no rims, so marks and other surface impairments are common. The flat nature of the design makes most of the surface very vulnerable to marking. The recessed areas of the incuse design are well protected and are seldom marked. Hairlines and scrapes are seen as often as marks, or perhaps more often. On the obverse, the face, neck, and headdress are areas affected, along with the field in front of and above the Indian. The reverse has a large open field that usually has marks or other surface distractions. The eagle's neck and wing feathers are also areas usually found with marks and

scrapes. Hairlines are mainly noted in the open areas and are difficult to notice on the intricate design of the headdress or wing feathers.

LUSTER: Like their quarter eagle counterparts, these coins are found only in flat, satin, and frosty luster—semi-prooflike and prooflike luster are not seen. Philadelphia issues generally have a satin-to-slightly frosty luster, but very frosty coins are also seen. The Denver coins usually have slightly frosty-to-very frosty surfaces, though satin-luster coins are seen. Coins from San Francisco are often weakly impressed, but the luster is generally satin-to-slightly frosty.

STRIKE: Indian Head half eagles are similar in strike to the quarter eagles of the same type, but there are more weakly struck half eagles. The 1908 Indian Head half eagle may have slight weakness in the headdress feathers and braid, with the reverse shoulder feathers lightly impressed. Philadelphia and Denver coins are usually much better struck than those from San Francisco. Weakness in the central feathers of the headdress and eagle are very common for these San Francisco issues. Weak mint marks are common with 1908-S, 1909-O, 1913-S, 1916-S, and other dates.

EYE APPEAL: When well struck, lustrous, and minimally marked, these are great-appearing coins. Very popular with collectors and investors, Bela Lyon Pratt's unusual incuse design for this coin makes it highly prized when found with positive attributes. Rich colors, deep green or multi-hued, are sometimes found, and enhance the appearance of these coins, which have perhaps the most unusual design in numismatic history.

Proofs

HAIRLINES: Shiny spots, or scuffs, are usually more prevalent than are hairlines for Matte Proof Indian Head half eagles. With Roman Proofs, hairlines are more often seen and are easier to see than shiny spots, since they have brighter surfaces than the coarser-textured Matte Proofs. The cheek and headdress are the first areas where shiny spots usually appear on the obverse. Matte Proof reverses often have shiny spots, and sometimes hairlines, in the field in front of and behind the head of the eagle. Roman Proofs sometimes have light hairlines and occasionally shiny spots on the headdress, face, bust, and field in front of and above the Indian. Reverse hairlines and occasional shiny spots are usually first noticed in the open field in front and back of the eagle's head, with others seen across the wings, legs, branch, and lettering.

REFLECTIVITY: Roman Proofs have shiny surfaces, though the reflectivity is so diffused that it is nothing like a mirrorlike brilliant Proof surface. The surfaces, in fact, are the exact opposite of previous issues, and instead of reflecting light in straight lines, like a mirror, the textured surfaces diffuse the light and have no direct reflectivity. On Matte Proofs, this effect is magnified by the coarse texture of the surfaces, resulting in the most diffused reflectivity. Some dates, such as 1911, 1912, and 1913, have a glitter-like appearance where the reflected light appears as diamonds or points of light against a darker green-gold background. The Roman Proofs are finer in texture, with a more reflective surface and somewhat scaly look. However, there is less mirrorlike surface than for semiprooflike business strikes.

STRIKE: The experimental Matte and Roman Proof surfaces make the strike difficult to discern, as the finishes obscure the detail. The Roman Proof issues are the easiest on which to "see" the fine detail, and these are obviously well struck. Matte coins have a fuzzy look, though the strike is usually full if examined closely. The indistinct look on these coins is the result of sandblasting, which textures the surfaces.

EYE APPEAL: For Matte and Roman Proof incuse-design coins, eye appeal is based on the texture, color, originality, and lack of hairlines and shiny spots. Since the Roman Proof issues are more brilliant and flashy, they are usually considered to have better eye appeal than

some of the darker, more textured Matte surfaces. Some very attractive Matte Proof coins are found, however, and lack of scuffing, hairlines, haze, or discoloration are obviously the important factors in higher-grade coins. In any case, all of the dates are attractive when free of impairments such as discoloring, haze, or fading of surfaces.

Eagles
Capped Bust Eagle—Small Eagle and Heraldic (Large) Eagle (1795–1804)
Circulated Examples

The slight wear on **AU-55/58** Capped Bust coinage is usually seen on the folds of the cap, the hair above and around the ear, the cheek, and the folds of the drapery on the bust. Weakness of strike, unfortunately, is also sometimes located in these areas and differentiating wear from strike weakness is difficult. Slight wear on such coins is extremely difficult to detect. The upper areas of the wing feathers will have slight friction in these grades, along with the breast feathers of the Small Eagle coins and the breast feathers directly above the shield on Heraldic Eagle coins. These breast feathers, and the shield lines of the Heraldic Eagle variety, are the areas most often seen with strike weakness. As the coin is worn to **AU-50/53**, the wear will become more apparent, with rub on the cheek, hair, cap, and bust causing discoloration. The reverse will have definite wear on the wing and breast feathers and the shield lines of the Heraldic Eagle coins. The central area may be missing detail on poorly struck coins.

In **EF-40/45**, dullness is seen across most of the coins' surfaces. The strength of the strike determines the amount of detail remaining, with strong strikes having nearly complete detail and weak strikes showing flatness in the hair and breast feathers. For the Heraldic Eagle reverse, the shield lines may be incomplete because of strike weakness. Localized weakness may affect some stars and lettering.

Worn to **VF-20/35**, Capped Bust coinage will have from 50 percent to nearly full detail in the hair, cap, and drapery. Stars will range from flat on **VF-20** and poorly struck coins to nearly full radial lines on higher-grade or well-struck **VF** coins. The reverse will have flat wing and breast feathers on weakly struck and lower **VF** coins and sometimes better detail than weakly struck **EF** and **AU** specimens. The Heraldic Eagle reverse coins will have incomplete shield lines in **VF**, except for extremely well-struck coins.

Quite a few Capped Bust coins are worn to **F-12/15** condition, as some of these coins received considerable circulation. Some coins show evidence of "sweating," which is the result of banging coins in a bag to recover the slight amount of gold "knocked" off in this process. If the surfaces are heavily "sweated," the coin may not be graded. The hair detail will be less than half complete on well-struck coins and nearly gone on weakly struck ones. The wing and breast feathers will show almost no detail, and the shield of Heraldic Eagle coins will have only sporadic lines visible.

VG-8/10 coins will have an outlined bust, with only the deepest recesses of the hair showing any detail. The stars will be flat and slightly worn into the field. The rims should be complete, except in areas of localized weakness. The reverse will have an outlined eagle, with slight detail in the protected areas.

A **G-4/6** coin will have an outlined Miss Liberty, with almost no detail. The rims will begin to be worn into the stars and the lettering, with the tops of some lettering on **G-4** coins weak. The eagle will be outlined, with very slight detail.

With **AG-3** and **FR-2** coins, the head of Miss Liberty may be worn into the field in several areas and the rims will obliterate some, if not all, of the stars. The lettering of the reverse may be half, or more, incomplete, with the eagle showing only slight detail.

PO-1 coins will have little detail but the date must be readable, though seldom complete.

Mint State Examples

MARKS: Capped Bust eagles of both types have the same obverse design, with marks and other surface impairments noted on the cap, face, bust, and hair, as well as in the field. Most marks in the hair are easily noticed, though minor marks within the flow of the hair are sometimes hidden. Small Eagle type reverses have more open field area than the Heraldic type, with marks mainly noted in the open field as well as on the breast and wing. There is much less open field area on the reverse of the Heraldic type, and marks are easily noticed on the clouds, on and among the stars, and on the neck, shield, wings, and tail. Other marks are noted in the open areas, with marks also seen on devices or lettering.

LUSTER: Both types are found with nearly every luster variation, but the Small Eagle type is usually found satin-to-very frosty and with semi-prooflike and prooflike luster. The Heraldic Eagle type is usually seen with a satin-to-very frosty luster. There are not as many semi-prooflike and prooflike coins as with the Small Eagle type. The Small Eagle dates had lower mintages, plus fewer coins were struck per die, leading to more prooflike examples than for the Heraldic type.

STRIKE: Both Small and Heraldic types had many striking problems. Because these were larger coins, the Eckfeldt press, made at the Mint in 1795, was probably used to strike these issues. The central parts have incompleteness, with the hair sometimes seen with an almost dished appearance and the neck and breast feathers totally flat. Localized weakness is also noted for the stars, cap, bust, LIBERTY, and date. For the Heraldic type, part of E PLURIBUS UNUM, the shield, and the tips of the wings are sometimes missing. Reverse weakness is also seen for the peripheral lettering, head, claws, tail, arrows, olive branch, clouds, stars, and wing feathers for the Heraldic type. Small Eagle coins may also show weakness in the laurel wreath held in the eagle's mouth.

EYE APPEAL: Several spectacular Small Eagle coins are known with incredibly frosty surfaces, good strikes, and minimal marks. There are very attractive coins with other luster variations. The Heraldic Eagle coins are also seen with very frosty surfaces that are dripping with mint frost, and these usually have the most positive eye appeal for this type. As with the Small Eagle type, there are other luster variations that have good eye appeal.

Specimens/Proofs

HAIRLINES: Light-to-moderate hairlines are to be expected on both the Small Eagle specimen strikes and the 1804 Heraldic Eagle Proofs. The first 1804 Proof eagles were issued in 1834 and 1835 in presentation sets, housed in special cases that afforded some protection against mishandling. The Small Eagle coins, especially those of 1795, would have been carefully handled as examples of the Mint's first eagle coinage, though cleaning or wiping was commonplace at the time.

REFLECTIVITY: The specimen strikes have extraordinary surfaces, with deeply reflective fields for coins struck in open collars on human-powered presses. Frosted devices and lettering contrast with these fields, though they would not have the cameo look of the close-collar strikings. They also obviously do not match the Proof surfaces of the 1804 coins, which were struck on superior equipment in close collars. These coins have very frosty devices and lettering that contrast with the deeply mirrored fields.

STRIKE: Original specimen strikes for 1795 and 1796 were struck exceptionally. Only the highest hair curls, eagle's breast feathers, legs, and head might have any slight weakness. The 1804 Proof coins were struck for presentation Proof sets, such as the King of Siam and the Muscat of Oman sets. These are of exceptional quality, with very sharp detail and deeply mirrored fields.

EYE APPEAL: As with the half eagles, 1795 eagles were the first issues of this denomination, the highest-value denomination then

being struck. Specially prepared dies and planchets would result in incredibly attractive specimens of these coins. The 1804 coins are Proofs and, as such, have incredible eye appeal when found with minimal hairlines. The frosted devices and lettering create the contrasting look seen on other brilliant Proofs. These coins are fantastic-looking examples of an early design struck with advanced coining equipment.

Liberty Head Eagle—No Motto (Covered Ear and Uncovered Ear) and Motto (1838–1907)

Circulated Examples

In **AU-55/58,** wear is first seen on the eyebrow, the hair above the ribbon, the curls of hair above the eye and ear, the hair curl below the ear, the nose, and the chin. Large-letter coins of 1838 and 1839, with the swooping hair curl that covers the ear, quickly show friction in this area. The reverse will have wear on the tops of the wing, neck, and leg feathers. The neck and leg feathers are also areas where strike weakness is noted, and for some of the branch-mint coins this area is almost always weak. **AU-50/53** coins will have more friction in the aforementioned regions, with some flatness noted especially for the hair above the ribbon and above the ear. The large open area above the eagle on No Motto coins will have noticeable rubbing, though with the Motto type it is not as obvious. The reverse will begin to have slight wear on all of the wing feathers, but there should be complete feather detail except on the neck and leg.

EF-40/45 specimens will have some of the hair detail missing. The entire coin will have some rubbing and the stars and fields will have definite wear. The feathers will have wear but will still be mainly separate, save the neck and leg. The leaves and arrows will be separate, with most detail still clear.

If **VF-20/35** coins are well struck, a lot of detail will be seen on the obverse. The main hair curls will show some separation and the recessed areas will be distinct. The reverse will have the tips of the wing feathers worn to-gether in higher **VF** grades. Lower-grade **VF** and weakly struck coins may have very little feather detail. The leaves and arrows are still separated, though little detail is still visible.

Many **F-12/15** coins have some intricate hair detail, the curl on the neck sometimes still fairly sharp. LIBERTY should be complete, but some of the letters may have weakness. On well-struck coins, some feather detail may be present and the leaves are now blended. The arrows are flat, though still separate.

VG-8/10 specimens are seldom seen except for rare dates and some branch-mint issues. The head will have sporadic detail and will be mostly flat, with some letters of LIBERTY partially missing. The eagle will be outlined, with little detail remaining. The lettering around the periphery is complete.

G-4/6 coins will have a smooth head, with some of LIBERTY showing. The rim may be slightly incomplete and slightly worn into the reverse lettering. A fully outlined, com-pletely flat eagle is present.

For **AG-3** and **FR-2** coins, a date, head, and some stars will be seen. The **FR-2** may not have stars visible. The reverse rims are worn into the tips of the wing feathers and letter-ing. The **FR-2** may have only parts of some lettering readable.

PO-1 graded coins will have a readable date, partial head, partial eagle, and possibly no lettering.

Mint State Examples

MARKS: These coins are usually found with more marks and other surface impairments than the smaller Liberty Head quarter and half eagles. The face and neck are usually marked, as is the field in the front and back of the head. Unless small, marks are usually noticeable in the hair. Reverse marks for the No Motto type are found in the open areas above the eagle and below the wings. Both types sometimes have noticeable marks on the eagle. The Motto type may also show marks on the ribbon.

LUSTER: Philadelphia issues are found in all luster variations, though most issues have a satin-to-very frosty luster. Low-mintage dates are usually found semi-prooflike or prooflike, often with striations still present from the basining of the dies. Some common coins, such as the 1899, are found with satin surfaces, with a chalky look similar to 1924 double eagles. Among the branch mints, only Denver, San Francisco, New Orleans, and Carson City struck Liberty Head eagles. Most of the Denver and San Francisco coins have slightly frosty-to-very frosty surfaces, with quite a few semi-prooflike and prooflike coins. New Orleans coins are usu-ally satin-to-very frosty in luster, with the oc-casional semi-prooflike or prooflike specimen. Coins from Carson City are usu-ally low-mintage and are often seen frosty or semi-prooflike, with some fairly deep prooflike coins found.

STRIKE: As with the quarter eagles and half eagles, Liberty Head eagles from the branch mints are not as well-struck as those from Philadelphia. However, because Dahlonega and Charlotte did not produce eagles, there are fewer poor strikes known for the eagles than for the two smaller denominations. Larger coins are usually more poorly struck than smaller coins. More New Orleans and Carson City eagles have strike weakness than those from San Francisco. These coins show weakness for the obverse at the stars, the tip of the coronet, the hair above the eye, the hair covering the ear on the 1838–1839 type, the hair on and above the ear for the second type, the neck hair curls, the bun, the hair above LIBERTY, and occasionally the tip of the bust. Reverse weakness is noted for the motto, when present, and for the head, neck, shield, wing feathers around the shield, legs, claws, leaves, arrow feathers, and arrowheads.

EYE APPEAL: As with the half eagles, the most attractive Liberty Head eagles seen are the John Clapp–Louis Eliasberg specimens that were acquired in their year of issue and carefully preserved. Most of these high-grade specimens are San Francisco and New Or-leans coins which have swirling luster, spectacular color, near-full strikes, and almost no marks. The spectacular appearance of these coins is the pinnacle of Liberty Head eagle coinage. Some of the semi-prooflike and prooflike No Motto and Motto coins also have good eye appeal, though often the mirrored fields have marks, magnified by the delicate nature of the fields.

Proofs

HAIRLINES: These usually have more, and heavier, hairlines than quarter and half eagles. This is expected, since the larger and heavier coins are more difficult to preserve and the fields are just as delicate. Ten dollars was a lot of money in the 1800s and early 1900s, so their owners spent some of these coins in times of need. Obverse lines are mainly found in the open field in the front and back of the head, but many coins have hairlines across the entire obverse, easily noticed on the face and neck. Reverse lines are mainly noted in the field above the eagle and below the wings on both the No Motto and Motto types. As with the obverse, lines are sometimes found across the entire reverse, though the intricate nature of the eagle design makes them less visible than on the obverse.

REFLECTIVITY: Deeply mirrored fields with "orange-peel" surfaces are the norm for these coins, especially those struck in 1859 and later. Those struck before 1859 are extremely rare; they have slightly less deeply mirrored fields, and may have some minor die striations visible. Frosted devices and lettering are seen on nearly every coin prior to 1900. A change occurred in the dies after 1900, and some of the post-1900 Proofs have evenly mirrored surfaces across the entire coin. Those that have frosted devices and lettering usually are not as heavily frosted as previously.

STRIKE: Most Liberty Head Proofs are well struck. However, certain coins escaped Mint scrutiny and have weakness in the same places as business strikes, especially noticeable on the hair curl above the ear, the hair curl on the neck, the eagle's neck, the inner wing, the leg, and the claws.

EYE APPEAL: When seen with minimal hairlines with light toning or brilliant, these are spectacular examples of Liberty Head coinage. Heavily frosted devices and lettering seen on many specimens create great contrast with the deeply reflective surfaces. These cameo coins are probably the most attractive Liberty Head Proof eagles when found with light, or minimal, hairlines.

Indian Head Eagle—Wire Edge and Rolled Edge (1907)

Circulated Examples

The wire edge is seen with regularity in circulated grades, with only a few rolled-edge coins noted. In **AU-55/58**, the obverse has slight wear on the cheek and the hair above the eye and along the ribbon to the ear. There will be slight wear on the shoulder and head of the eagle. Wire-edge coins are often mushy-looking, the result of the heavy die polish and the failure to strike up completely. In **AU-50/53**, the wear is more apparent, with the headdress feathers now exhibiting wear. The cheek will be more noticeably worn, as will the hair. The feathers along the back as well as the leg feathers will have wear.

EF-40/45 coins will have some of the headdress feather detail worn away. Hair detail will be missing and blended in places, with the cheek now showing obvious wear. The reverse will have flatness on the eagle's shoulder and obvious wear down the back and the leg feathers.

With **VF-20/35**, almost all coins seen will be the Wire Edge type. The mushiness of strike and design on this coin, with the combination of striations, makes a **VF** coin difficult to grade. The hair will be quite flat in this grade, with considerable loss of feather detail in the headdress. The reverse will have one-fourth to one-half of the feathers worn away, with the shoulder completely flat.

These coins are seldom encountered in grades below **VF** and would be graded similarly to the regular Indian Head coins, discussed later.

Mint State Examples

MARKS: As these coins were not put into normal commercial channels, most of the marks and other surface detractions are from other wire-edge and rolled-edge coins. The fields of the Wire Edge type have an unusual finish, making any surface disruptions immediately noticeable. The face, neck, and headdress are areas where surface impairments are noticed. There is very little open field area on the obverse, but marks are sometimes found in these areas. Rolled Edge specimens have marks in the same places, but the surfaces are not as delicate; thus surface disruptions are not quite as obvious. The reverse has more open field area, but most marks are noted on the eagle for both types. Field marks are noted mainly in the open area above the eagle, with others seen in front and below.

LUSTER: Luster is difficult to describe for the Wire Edge type, but it is probably most like satin luster. The fine, often swirling die striations create a satin-like look that has a delicate sheen. Coins of the Rolled Edge type usually have a satin-to-slightly frosty luster similar to the surfaces on the regular-issue Indian Head eagles.

STRIKE: Both of these issues have strike weakness, but this manifests itself differently for each type. The Wire Edge type has so many die polish lines crisscrossing the fields that there is not much definition. These die striations even make the stars indistinct on these coins. Weakness beyond this die obscurity is noted in the hair covering the ear and in the central headdress area. The reverse will have flatness on the head, shoulder, and legs, with the entire wing sometimes weak. Coins of the Rolled Edge type have surfaces that are similar to the Indian Head coins, though the headdress and eagle still do not have the crisp, clear definition of those issues. Weakness is seen in the same areas as on the Wire Edge type.

EYE APPEAL: Although both of these coins can be very attractive, their appearances are dissimilar. Wire-edge coins do not have the crisp definition of the rolled-edge coins, but their satiny appearance, when free of marks, is attractive. Rolled-edge coins often have rich luster and color, combined with strong detail, which make them very appealing specimens when free of marks or detractions.

Indian Head Eagle—No Motto and Motto (1907–1933)

Circulated Examples

The modified designs that became the No Motto type in 1907 and the With Motto type in mid-1908 are basically the same designs as the Wire and Rolled Edge types. **AU-55/58** specimens will show slight wear on the hair and cheek. The feathers will be complete, save for slight friction or incompleteness of strike. Wear is most evident on the eagle's shoulder feathers, along with the head and neck areas. In **AU-50/53**, the hair and cheek show more wear, and now friction will be noticed in the field. Headdress feathers should be complete, though slight wear may blend some of the fine detail. The reverse will have friction in the field and the shoulder feathers will be flat. There will be wear along the eagle's back and legs.

EF-40/45 Indian Head eagles will have noticeable wear on the cheek and hair, with some parts of the hair blended. Headdress feathers will have some detail missing. Shoulder feathers may be worn up to one-fourth down the eagle's back. The leg feathers will have noticeable wear, but will still be detailed.

For **VF-20/35** grades, the hair will become more worn, with little detail remaining. The feathers will have from one-half to three-fourths detail present, though some areas will be flat. The reverse will have from one-fourth to one-half of the wing and leg feathers missing. There will be considerable wear in the field.

Some Indian Head eagles, such as the rare dates 1908-S, 1911-D, and 1913-S, are seen in low grade. **F-12/15** coins will have part of LIBERTY worn, with little hair detail present. Headdress feathers will show less than half of their detail. The eagle's feathers will be worn smooth across the entire wing and leg.

In **VG-8/10**, a full head will be visible, though much of the detail will be worn away. The eagle will be flat and show only slight detail. The rim may be weak, but still complete.

G-4/6 coins will have an outlined Indian head with almost no detail. The reverse will have an outlined eagle and minor detail visible. The rims are worn into the fields and may touch the reverse lettering.

AG-3 specimens have the rims worn into the fields, date, devices, and lettering. The head may blend into the field with almost no detail present. The reverse will have the eagle worn into the field and only minor detail visible. **FR-2** coins will have much of the head blended into the field and a partial date. The reverse will have much of the lettering missing with the eagle present, though quite worn and blended.

The **PO-1** grade will have a readable date and will have only part of the Indian Head visible.

Mint State Examples
MARKS: As with Wire and Rolled Edge eagles, marks and other disruptions are usually confined to the face, neck, and headdress. Field marks are usually minor, as there is little area to mark because the rims and devices protect it. Reverse marks are mostly noted on the upper part of the wing, though the neck, lower wing, tail, and legs are also found with marks. There is more reverse field area than for the obverse, but the rims and devices protect them somewhat and impairments are usually minor.

LUSTER: These coins are usually found only with flat, satin, and frosty luster, with most coins satin to frosty. Most of the Philadelphia issues have a frosty luster, though some coins, 1926 and 1932 issues, have surfaces that could be called slightly prooflike. Denver and San Francisco issues are usually satin to slightly frosty, though frosty-luster coins are found for some dates.

STRIKE: When IN GOD WE TRUST was added in 1908, the design was made slightly more chiseled in the headdress and eagle. The No Motto coins had more fine detail than the Rolled Edge type, and the 1908 modification strengthened the design even more. Weakness is still seen in the central areas (hair covering and around the ear, eagle's head, shoulder, and legs, etc.), with the upper headdress feathers, lower headdress feathers, and eagle's tail feathers also being areas of weakness.

EYE APPEAL: Fully struck, minimally marked, lustrous Indian Head eagles are great-looking coins that are splendid examples of the Saint-Gaudens design. High-grade coins are always prized, many of these being encountered with rich green-gold color or multicolored pastels. Some satin-luster coins are as attractive as the frosty coins, with some Denver/San Francisco issues having a delicate velvet-like surface that is very appealing.

Proofs
HAIRLINES: As with the other Proof issues after 1907, the Matte issues usually have shiny spots that are more evident than hairlines. Roman and Satin Proofs show hairlines more easily. For the obverse, most hairlines or scuffing will be noted on the face, neck, and headdress, with other slight disruptions in the protected field, but some coins have lines across the entire surface. Reverse hairlines or scuffing will be mainly noted on the neck, wing, and legs, though the field also may have impairments.

REFLECTIVITY: Roman and Satin Proofs have a shiny look, but the light is so diffused that there is little reflectivity. In fact, the surfaces are the exact opposite of previous brilliant Proofs and instead of reflecting light in straight lines, like a mirror, the textured surfaces diffuse the light. On Matte Proofs, this effect is magnified by the coarse texture of the surfaces, resulting in the most diffused reflectivity. Some dates, such as 1911, 1912, and 1913, have a glitter-like appearance where the reflected light appears as diamonds or points of light against a darker green-gold background. The Roman and Satin Proof surfaces have a somewhat scaly look, but there is less reflectivity than for semi-prooflike business strikes.

STRIKE: Indian Head eagles are struck with the experimental Matte, Roman, and Satin Proof surfaces, but the Satin Proof strikes are extremely rare. Strike on these issues is difficult to discern, as the finishes obscure the detail. The Roman and Satin Proof issues are the easiest on which to "see" the fine detail, and these coins are obviously well struck. The Matte coins have a fuzzy look, though the strike is usually full if one examines them with a magnifying aid.

EYE APPEAL: All three finishes are attractive when found nearly free of hairlines or shiny spots. High-grade pieces are excellent examples of the Saint-Gaudens design, and collectors have prized these low-mintage issues since they were issued.

Double Eagles
Liberty Head Double Eagle—
Type I/Type II/Type III (1849–1907)
Circulated Examples

Although the design of Liberty Head double eagles is similar to other Liberty Head coinage, their large size makes grading them slightly different. LIBERTY is also not as recessed as on the other Liberty Head coinage, thus wears more quickly. Weakness of strike also sometimes affects the "RTY," with the tops of these letters sometimes weak. In **AU-55/58**, slight friction is seen on the cheek and hair. The reverses usually have fewer marks and the friction is first noted on the eagle's neck, tail feathers, and wing tips and the high pints of the scroll. The fields for **AU-50/53** have more noticeable friction and often have more numerous, heavier marks. Obvious friction is now seen on the cheek and hair. Friction is evident on the entire eagle in these grades, including the shield and more parts of the scroll. If the marks become too severe or there is one very heavy mark, the coin may

not be graded or the grade may be lowered to **EF**.

With **EF-40/45** grades, the cheek will now have wear, except in the recessed areas, and the hair will be flat below the coronet, above the ear, and in the curls below the ear. The field will have obvious friction and the stars will be worn. The last three letters of LIBERTY may have slight striking weakness or may be worn slightly, but still complete. The reverse will have friction across the entire eagle, shield, and scroll, though all of the wing feathers will still show detail.

VF-20/35 coins will have wear across the entire face. The hair will be flat above the eye, above the ear, and on the top part of the curls below the ear. The stars usually will still have some lines visible. The "RTY" of LIBERTY will have slight incompleteness, especially in the lower **VF** grades and on weakly struck coins. Wing feathers will have some areas where detail is missing, though in the higher **VF** grades the feathers will be mostly complete. Some lines in the shield may be indistinct, as will be some feathers in the neck and the tail. The scroll will have some flat areas that blend into adjacent devices and the field.

Although most Liberty Head double eagles are found in the higher grades, **F-12/15** specimens sometimes are encountered. The face will be quite worn and the hair above the eye and around the ear will be flat. Only the deeper recesses of the hair will have detail, with the stars mostly flat. LIBERTY will be partially complete, with the last three letters worn on the tops. The reverse will have the neck, tail, and outer wing feathers worn flat, with the shield showing some separation of the vertical and horizontal lines. The scroll will have more flatness and blending, though the lettering should still be readable.

Rarer still are **VG-8/10** double eagles, which may have much of LIBERTY worn away, along with little hair and star detail. The reverse will have a complete eagle and outlined scroll, but very little detail will remain and some parts may blend into the field. The rims of both sides will be complete.

G-4/6 coins are almost never seen and will have an outlined head with little detail still visible. The stars will be flat and the rims may show areas of weakness. The eagle and scroll will be worn flat, and several areas may blend into the field. The rims may be incomplete and touch the top of the lettering.

Only rare dates have numismatic value in **AG-3** and **FR-2**; thus they are seldom encountered. The rims for **AG-3** will be worn and the lettering of the reverse may be partially missing. The obverse will have a mostly outlined head and some stars visible. The reverse will have the eagle visible, though worn smooth. **FR-2** coins will have even more wear, with some or all of the stars worn away and a partial Liberty head. The reverse may have most or all of the peripheral lettering missing and a partial eagle.

The **PO-1** coins will have a discernible date and enough detail to identify the type.

Mint State Examples

MARKS: These large coins are almost always found with marks or other surface disruptions. These impairments may be numerous and fairly minor, though many coins have both large and small disruptions. These are especially noted on the cheek and neck, but the hair is smooth and easily shows marks. The field in front of the face is the largest open area of the obverse and is often seen marked, but the entire field area is often seen with some disruptions. The reverse open field area has marks, most being confined to the eagle and the many devices on and around it. In general, markings are less severe for the reverses, with some high-grade and even some lower-grade specimens showing nearly mark-free reverses.

LUSTER: Although all luster variations are found, most Liberty Head double eagles have a satin-to-very frosty luster. Most of the Philadelphia issues have the usual satin-to-very frosty surfaces, with some of the lower-mintage issues, such as 1885, 1886, and 1891, mainly found semi-prooflike or prooflike. New Orleans coins are usually seen with a satin-to-frosty luster, but semi-prooflike and prooflike specimens are fairly common. San Francisco and Denver issues are found with deep prooflike surfaces, even for some of the higher-mintage issues, such as 1904-S and 1907-D, but most of these mints' output is frosty in luster. Carson City issues are mainly seen with frosty luster, though satin, semi-prooflike, and prooflike coins are also seen.

STRIKE: These large coins are better struck than the quarter and half eagles from the Dahlonega and Charlotte mints, but usually with slight striking weakness noted. This head is like that of the Liberty Head gold dollar and not like the quarter eagle, half eagle, and eagle. LIBERTY is on an unprotected band, leading to striking weakness usually confined to the "RTY" and the beads above it. The row of beads above LIBERTY is like the one on the Type One gold dollar, and it replaces the solid line of the other Liberty Head gold issues. The hair curls are much straighter and smaller, and a more modern-looking heraldic one replaces the perched eagle on the reverse. The hair covering and around the ear, the hair below LIBERTY, the upper hair, the bun, and the lower curls are areas where striking weakness is noted, along with the stars, the tip of the coronet, the eyebrow, the lips, and the tip of the bust. Reverse weakness is seen on the head, neck, shield, inner wing feathers, tips of the wing feathers, claws, leaves, arrow feathers, ribbon, and tail, with the motto weak, when present, along with the stars and rays above the eagle. The New Orleans coins usually do not have the chiseled hair seen on the Philadelphia coins. Also, the San Francisco coins are usually better struck than the Carson City coins.

EYE APPEAL: These large coins are difficult to find without marks, so great eye appeal mainly is dependent on minimal markings. Some of the best examples are the John Clapp–Louis Eliasberg coins, carefully preserved from their years of issue. These minimally marked coins are characterized by blazing luster, sometimes with deep, rich colors that make them the pinnacle of Liberty Head double eagles. Some spectacular Philadelphia issues are found, including an **MS-67** 1861 coin.

Proofs

HAIRLINES: These large issues are more often seen hairlined than any other series of brilliant Proof gold coinage. Obverse hairlines are found not only in the open field but also often across the entire face and hair. Small nicks and scratches are also sometimes noted, along with other surface distractions. Reverse hairlines are usually not as thick or concentrated as on the obverse, but often cover the entire surface.

REFLECTIVITY: Most of these coins have deeply mirrored fields with "orange-peel" surfaces, especially the coins struck in 1859 and later. Those struck before 1859 are rare and may have slightly less deeply mirrored fields, some with minor die striations. Frosted devices and lettering are seen on nearly every coin prior to 1900. A change occurred in the dies after 1900, and some of the post-1900 Proofs have mirrored surfaces across the entire coin. Some coins after 1900 have lightly frosted devices and lettering.

STRIKE: Proofs generally are very well struck, and the weakly struck coins are rarer than for half eagles and eagles. Slight weakness for the obverse is noted on the stars and the highest hair curls, mainly those over and around the ear. The reverse may have slight incompleteness on the head, neck, shield, claws, leaves, arrow feathers, ribbon, and tail.

EYE APPEAL: Though these large coins are not often found free of hairlines, when they are found without impairments they are spectacular. Some late issues, 1896 for example, have extremely deep frost on the devices and lettering, contrasting with the deeply mirrored fields and creating spectacular examples of James B. Longacre's design.

Saint Gaudens Double Eagle High Relief (1907)

Circulated Examples

The high-relief design of Augustus Saint-Gaudens proved to be difficult to strike, so slight weakness of strike and slight friction are difficult to distinguish. **AU-55/58** coins have slight friction on the breast and knee and on the breast and lower body and upper wing feathers of the eagle. The deep relief protects the fields in these grades, and they almost always have full luster. When worn to **AU-50/53**, the fields show friction. The breast and knee now are flattened from wear. The reverse will have flat breast and lower body and upper wing feathers, with friction seen on the rest of the eagle and the surrounding field. These are large, heavy coins and sometimes there are marks as well as friction. Very deep marks would obviously lower the grade.

The deep relief of these coins has the effect of making wear appear more severe than on lower-relief coins. **EF-40/45** specimens have very flat breasts and knees, and the fields have obvious rubbing. The eagle has a very flat breast and lower body and upper wing feathers, with other feathers also showing wear. The surfaces will have obvious friction. More and heavier marks may be noticed, though the dished effect of the design prevents some surface marks.

VF-20/35 coins will have a very flat breast and leg, with only recessed detail visible. Marks may be more severe and may now be present in the dished field. The reverse will have a flattened breast and lower body and upper wing feathers, but as with the obverse recessed detail is seen.

These coins were often kept as pocket pieces, so low-grade coins are fairly common. For **F-12/15** grades, Miss Liberty is quite flat, but recessed areas still have some detail. Marks may be quite severe and present on Miss Liberty, the eagle, or in the field. The reverse will have a very flat breast and lower body and upper wing feathers, with some feather detail still present.

With **VG-8/10** coins, some lack of distinctness may be seen between the flat rim and fields. Miss Liberty will be almost totally flat, though the deepest recesses will show slight detail. The reverse will be similar, with a flat eagle and deep detail still slightly visible. More prevalent marks may be noted, some quite severe.

G-4/6 coins will have indistinct rims and only very deep details present. There may be heavy marks, but some gouges are acceptable for this grade. The rim of the reverse will be worn into the lettering.

Although **AG-3** High Reliefs are scarce, they are found. The rims will be quite worn and little detail will be noted for Miss Liberty and the eagle. The **FR-2** coins will have no distinct rims evident and a very flat Miss Liberty and eagle.

A **PO-1** coin will have only enough detail evident to identify it as a High Relief type.

Mint State Examples

MARKS: These are large, heavy coins and are not often seen without some marks. Obverse marks or disruptions are often seen on the breast and knees of Miss Liberty, others on the body and deeply recessed field. These coins have broad rims that also often have marks or nicks—though, unless severe, these do not detract much from the overall grade. Reverse contact is first noted on the upper wing and body of the eagle, but often the impairments are minor, with more scuffing, scrapes, and hairlines than marks and nicks. The recessed areas of the body, the fields, and the sun are also sometimes seen with disruptions, though these are usually minor.

LUSTER: These coins are seen with flat, satin, and frosty luster, but most coins usually have satin-to-quite frosty surfaces. There are two minor varieties noted for this issue: the so-called Flat Edge and Wire Edge varieties. Most of the Flat Edge coins are seen with a velvet-like surface that is usually satin-to-slightly frosty, while the Wire Edge coins usually have frosty surfaces.

STRIKE: As with wire and rolled edge eagles vs. No Motto and Motto eagles, High Relief double eagles have a slightly different look from the No Motto and Motto types. Saint-Gaudens gave a softer, more medal-like look to Miss Liberty and the eagle, while the regular-relief dies prepared by Chief Engraver Charles Barber have more chiseled definition, but in much lower relief. High Relief coins often show slight obverse strike weakness on the head, nose, breast, belly, left knee and leg, torch, rock, and branch. Reverse weakness is noted along the upper wing feathers and along the entire body of the eagle, plus along the tail and claws. The top part of the sun is also sometimes slightly weak, as are some of the rays.

EYE APPEAL: This is perhaps the most popular regular-issue U.S. gold coin. It is not really rare, with almost all of the 11,250 coins produced still in existence. The sculptured relief and intricate design have made this issue immensely popular with collectors, hoarders, and investors. When found relatively free of surface impairments, these are spectacular coins. The medal-like design makes Miss Liberty appear as though she is about to walk off the coin, with the reverse eagle soaring in flight, floating above the sun's rays.

Standing Liberty (Saint-Gaudens) Double Eagle—Regular Relief– No Motto and Motto (1907–1933)

Circulated Examples

The redesigned double eagles were first struck in very low relief. These No Motto coins have flat knees, not from wear or strike, but from the design. The Motto type introduced in 1908 has a more rounded knee. For **AU-55/58** coins of both types, the friction is noted on the breast and leg of Miss Liberty. Although it is generally ignored, the eagle of the No Motto type is in lower relief than the Motto type. The wear is noted in the same places for both types—the breast and lower body and upper wing feathers of the eagle. When the coins are worn to **AU-50/53**, the fields now have obvious wear. The breast

AU-58 *1915-S Saint-Gaudens double eagle obverse. Slight friction is seen on the breasts and left knee.*

AU-58 *1915-S Saint-Gaudens double eagle reverse. Slight friction is seen on the upper wing, breast, and body of the eagle.*

and leg are flattened from wear, and the reverse eagle has noticeable wear on the breast and lower body and upper wing feathers. Although some coins are virtually mark-free, marks are also commonplace, but deep or exceptionally long marks may prevent the grade of **AU** or may prevent the coin from being graded at all.

Wear for **EF-40/45** coins is now evident on the entire body, with the breast and leg quite flat, though the recessed areas have fine detail. The fields will have wear across the entire surfaces. The eagle's breast and lower body and upper wing feathers will be worn flat, with other feathers also showing wear. Marks may be slightly more severe than for higher grades.

VF-20/35 specimens have wear that leaves only the deepest detail intact. The breast and legs are very flat, and some of the rays may blend into the field. The reverse will have the breast and lower body worn smooth and the line of the upper wing feathers will show almost no detail. The central feathers will still have detail, though they will be obviously worn.

F-12/15 specimens are seldom seen, with the breast and leg totally flat and only the deep recesses still showing detail. Many rays may blend into the field, and marks may be quite

severe. The reverse will show detail only on the central feathers.

VG-8/10 coins will have an outlined Miss Liberty with little fine detail. There may be heavy marks and the field may be quite rough. The eagle will be worn nearly smooth, with only slight detail. The rims should still be complete.

Mostly rare dates, 1908-S, 1913-S, and so on, are found in **G-4/6**. Stars may be slightly obscured by incomplete rims, with Miss Liberty outlined with almost no detail. The reverse rim may be worn into the tops of the lettering. Deep recessed areas of the eagle may show slight detail.

AG-3 coins will have incomplete rims with partial or missing stars, and parts of Miss Liberty may blend into the field. Rims on the reverse may be worn halfway into the lettering and the eagle may blend into the surfaces. Some slight feather detail may still be evident. For **FR-2** coins, the stars may be mostly worn, with only a partial Miss Liberty noted. The reverse lettering may be totally missing around the periphery and only slightly visible elsewhere, with virtually no feather detail seen on the eagle.

The date must be readable for **PO-1** specimens, but little else is necessary except for

AU-55 *1908-D Motto Saint-Gaudens double eagle obverse. Slightly more friction is seen on the breasts and knee. Slight friction is noted in the field.*

AU-55 *1908-D Motto Saint-Gaudens double eagle reverse. Upper wing friction is seen, with the breast and body slightly flat from wear. Slight friction is noted in the field.*

AU-53 *1908 Motto Saint-Gaudens double eagle obverse. Breasts and knee are slightly flat, with most of the field showing friction.*

AU-53 *1908 Motto Saint-Gaudens double eagle reverse. The upper wing, breast, and body are slightly flat. Most of the field has friction.*

AU-50 *1909-S Saint-Gaudens double eagle obverse. The breasts, knee, and other parts of the body are slightly flat. The field has friction, except in protected areas.*

AU-50 *1909-S Saint-Gaudens double eagle reverse. The upper wing, breast, body, and tail are slightly flat. Friction is noted in the field, except in protected areas.*

EF-45 *1910-S Saint-Gaudens double eagle obverse. The breasts and knee are very flat. Some of the other detail, such as the rock, is slightly flat.*

EF-45 *1910-S Saint-Gaudens double eagle reverse. Flatness is noted on the high points—the upper wing, breast, body, and tail.*

EF-40 *1911-S Saint-Gaudens double eagle obverse. Slightly more flatness is noted on the breasts and knee, with the head and other areas showing noticeable wear.*

EF-40 *1911-S Saint-Gaudens double eagle reverse. The wing feathers are starting to blend, with a flat upper wing, breast, body, and tail.*

VF-35 *1910-S Saint-Gaudens double eagle obverse. Detail is weaker in recessed areas, with a very flat face, breasts, and knee.*

VF-35 *1910-S Saint-Gaudens double eagle reverse. A very flat upper wing, breast, and body are seen, with the central wing and tail feathers slightly blended.*

1908 coinage. The motto, or lack thereof, must be evident.

Mint State Examples

MARKS: Like Liberty Head double eagles, these coins are almost always found with surface disruptions. There is less smooth surface on these coins, however, and marks are more easily concealed. Obverse detractions are seen on the breast and knees, with the other devices and field also noted with marks. There is almost always "frost" disruption on the breast and knee, with only the modern counterfeits showing complete frost in these areas. Reverse marks and other disruptions are noted across the entire eagle, but the upper wing and body often have the most severe markings. The fields are also seen with detractions, especially noticeable on the sun. These coins have been hoarded in quantity, especially by European banks. Another surface disruption should be mentioned—these are the only gold coins that are commonly found with "wheel marks," which are the result of the rubber wheel of a counting machine scraping the surface of the coin as it passes though the counter. Banks often sold coins to each other, and the coins would be emptied from bags into counting machines and counted before being replaced into the bags and sealed. These "marks" are like concentrated patches of hairlines, often covering a small area of the obverse or reverse.

LUSTER: These issues are found with all luster variations, but the prooflike-luster coins do not have the deeply reflective surfaces of Liberty Head gold coinage. The majority of coins have a satin-to-very frosty luster, with flat, semi-prooflike, and prooflike coins a distinct minority. Philadelphia issues are usually seen with smooth luster, whether satin, slightly frosty, or very frosty. Some issues, such as 1922, 1923, 1924, and 1927, are found with semi-prooflike and prooflike luster, often only seen on one side. Some of the 1924 coins are also seen with a "chalky" look to the surface that results in luster that is difficult to categorize, satin being the closest. Some 1924

and other Philadelphia issues also have a "scaly" surface like many of the early Denver and San Francisco issues, such as 1911-D, 1914-D, and 1914-S. This scaly surface is closest to a satin luster, though many of these coins have brilliance that is more intense than frosty-luster issues. The later Denver and San Francisco coins from the 1920s and 1930s are usually seen with slightly frosty-to-frosty surfaces, but some satin and semi-prooflike coins are found.

STRIKE: No Motto coins are usually very flat on the breast, left knee, and leg, with the head, nose, torch, and branch also showing weakness. Reverse weakness is noted along the upper part of the wings and the entire body of the eagle, including the tail and claws. This flatness is due to striking weakness and the very flat nature of the design. The top part of the sun and some of the rays sometimes show weakness. The Motto coins have slightly more roundness on the breast, left leg and knee, and eagle. However, weakness is noted in the same areas as the No Motto coins.

EYE APPEAL: Other than the High Relief, the Saint-Gaudens double eagles are probably the most popular regular-issue U.S. gold coins. Well-struck, lustrous, and minimally marked coins are great-looking examples of this desirable issue. The most eye-appealing coins are usually the satin-to-frosty luster examples, especially some of the deep green-gold or multi-colored Philadelphia coins of the 1920s.

Proofs

HAIRLINES: These coins are seen with Matte and Roman Proof surfaces. The Matte Proofs are more likely to have shiny spots, or scuffing, than hairlines because of the coarser texture of the surface. For the obverse, these are mainly seen on the high points of Miss Liberty, but they are seen in the open field also. Reverse scuffing is usually seen on the eagle, with the upper wing and body usually being the most affected areas. Roman Proofs show more hairlines than shiny spots because of the more brilliant nature of the finer-textured surfaces. The field is the most affected area of the obverse; however, hairlines are sometimes seen across the entire surface. Reverse lines are usually seen across the entire coin, though they may be slightly more concentrated in the field.

REFLECTIVITY: As with all Matte and Roman Proofs, reflectivity is minimal. Matte Proofs have no mirrored surface, with the light totally diffused by the coarse textured surfaces. Although slight reflectivity is seen on the scaly surfaces of the Roman Proofs, it is very minor and should not even be considered semi-prooflike.

STRIKE: Strike on these issues is difficult to discern, as the finishes obscure the detail. The Roman Proof issues are the easiest on which to "see" the fine detail, and these coins are obviously well struck. Matte coins have a fuzzy look, but the strike is usually full if examined with a magnifying aid.

EYE APPEAL: These rare issues are some of the most highly prized U.S. gold coins, with hairline-free and scuff-free examples considered extremely attractive. Eye appeal is mainly a factor of lack of hairlines and originality. Coins with original surfaces, not showing discoloration, are considered the most eye appealing.

10 GRADING U.S. COMMEMORATIVE COINS

For its first hundred years, the U.S. Mint devoted itself almost exclusively to regular-issue coinage—making coins for use in everyday commerce. The nation was young, and the Mint, like other elements of American society, was preoccupied with fulfilling its basic mission. Frills and extras would have to wait. The Mint did produce Proof and pattern coins in significant numbers from the 1850s onward, but those were related to existing or anticipated regular-issue coinage.

Not until 1892, its centennial year, did the U.S. Mint strike its very first commemorative coin. Strictly speaking, commemoratives are non-circulating legal-tender coins issued to mark a special occasion or to honor an important person, place, or event. Like regular-issue coins, they can be spent; however, they are meant to serve not as pieces of money but as mementos. Now and then, regular-issue coins are given a commemorative theme; this occurred, for instance, in 1976, when the Washington quarter, Kennedy half dollar, and Eisenhower dollar bore special designs tied to the Bicentennial of American Independence. Coins such as these are often described as "circulating commemoratives," but they are generally not included in listings of commemorative coins; rather, they are treated as part of the regular series to which they belong.

Typically, U.S. commemorative coins are offered for sale at a premium at the time of their issuance, and part of the extra money helps finance an undertaking linked to the subject of each coin. In 1986, for example, the Mint issued three commemorative coins to honor the Statue of Liberty on its 100th anniversary, and part of the proceeds helped defray the costs of restoring both the statue and the Ellis Island Immigration Center in New York Harbor.

Grading is now an important issue with modern U.S. commemoratives. Although these coins are almost always fully struck and in pristine condition, demand for **MS/PR-68** and higher graded examples has ballooned in recent years, in part due to the Set Registry. These coins are graded on a strictly technical basis, as with all modern issues, since the modern mint produces an extremely high-quality product.

Classic U.S. commemoratives, however, are a different story. Grading these coins can be tricky, since there are many nuances in the way in which they were struck and other characteristics affecting their grades. Some are normally well struck; others often exhibit weakness of strike. Some tend to be lustrous and appealing to the eye; others are encountered frequently with dull, unattractive surfaces.

What follows is an issue-by-issue breakdown of the grading peculiarities of U.S. commemoratives struck during the golden age of this fascinating series. The general criteria set forth in chapter 4 apply to all of these issues in Mint State, Proof, and Circulated grades.

Grading Commemoratives
Columbian Exposition Half Dollar (1892–1893)
Grading the very first U.S. commemorative requires an understanding of the way this

coin was struck. Although the Mint was issuing high-quality coins in 1892, the design of this coin caused problems in fully striking Charles Barber's portrait of Christopher Columbus on the obverse and George T. Morgan's likeness of Columbus' ship and rigging on the reverse. This weakness of strike is often mistaken for wear—and only after examining several coins with apparent "wear" in the same spots does this become apparent. The wear on lightly circulated coins is first noticed on the cheek and forehead on the obverse. Wear and weakness of strike affect the corresponding area on the reverse: the sails of the boat. A coin with weakness of strike will still have luster in the affected areas, while wear will usually lead to discoloration and dullness. Proofs are generally of very high quality, and the sharpness of detail on those coins shows us the intended detail of the design. The typical Columbian half dollar has a frosty luster, though all luster combinations can be found, including some prooflike coins that are so sharp that they have been sold as Proofs. The Proofs have sharper detail in the rigging and the watery look of a burnished planchet. There are many toned Columbian half dollars—some with beautiful colors and others with dull, unattractive, or splotchy toning. Many times, the toning has been rubbed from the high points, which usually lowers the grade slightly.

Columbian or Isabella Quarter (1892)

This is the only non-circulating legal-tender commemorative in the 25-cent denomination. The 1932 Washington quarter was a circulating commemorative, as was the 1776–1976 dated Bicentennial quarter with the drummer boy reverse. Most Isabella quarters are well struck. Their striking quality is much better than that of the Columbian half dollars. Weakness of strike, if present, will be evident in the hair detail and in Isabella's crown, with some specimens showing weakness in the detail of the clothing. On the reverse, any weakness can be seen mainly in the folds and other details of the costume. The figure's hand and hair also may exhibit

weakness on such strikings. The luster on these coins is usually satin to very frosty. As with Columbian half dollars, there are many spectacularly toned Isabella quarters, ranging from a light, mainly golden color to deeply colored coins with greens and blues. Prooflike coins are fairly common and are sometimes so deceptive that they are sold as Proofs. True Proofs have razor-sharp detail and show mirrored surfaces in every nook and cranny of the design. As with the 1892 Columbian half dollar Proofs, 103 Isabella quarters were struck in Proof and numbered.

Lafayette Dollar (1900)

The Lafayette dollar is the only non-circulating legal-tender silver dollar from the Classic Era of American numismatics. In fact, its denomination is shown as the "Lafayette Dollar," rather than as the "One Dollar" usually seen on regular-issue coins—a substitution unique in American numismatics. This coin, designed by Charles Barber, is seldom seen fully struck. Nearly every coin has slight weakness in George Washington's cheek and the corresponding central area of the reverse, especially the leg and boot of the rider, Lafayette. The luster is usually satin to frosty, with prooflike coins essentially nonexistent. A brilliant Proof is said to exist, though PCGS has never seen one. The very first example struck was given to the president of France, and presumably that coin would be as prooflike as they come. Lafayette dollars are seen with colors ranging from light golden to deep sea-green and blue. Numerous coins have the toning rubbed from the high points, which detracts slightly from the overall grade. The surfaces usually have marks, as with most large silver coins, and finding unmarked coins is unusual.

Louisiana Purchase/McKinley Gold Dollar (1903)

The first U.S. gold commemoratives were two gold dollars issued in 1903 for the Louisiana Purchase Exposition in St. Louis. One portrays the recently assassinated President William McKinley, during whose administration the exposition was approved;

the other honors Thomas Jefferson, the president who arranged the historic land purchase from France. Both coins were also struck in brilliant Proof, usually with frosted devices and lettering. Slight weakness of strike is noted on some of the McKinley coins, mainly in the hair and detail of McKinley's coat, with the central detail and lettering of the reverse sometimes slightly weak. A few coins were made with badly eroded dies; the effects are seen mainly in the peripheral lettering on both the obverse and reverse. Friction is noted on the cheek, hair, and coat on the obverse; the leaves of the branch and the lettering are the first places wear is noted on the reverse. These coins are found brilliant, lightly toned, or deeply toned—sometimes a deep green-gold, pastel colors, or reddish. Proofs often have a haze, resulting from their storage in the original holders.

Louisiana Purchase/Jefferson Gold Dollar (1903)

Like its McKinley counterpart, the Jefferson gold dollar was struck in both business-strike and brilliant Proof versions and is still occasionally found in original holders. These may be mostly brilliant, but unless removed from their enclosure and dipped, most of them have a film or haze. Friction is noted on Jefferson's cheek, hair, and coat and on the leaves of the branch and the lettering on the reverse. The hair and coat are areas where striking weakness is noted, while the branch and lettering of the reverse are sometimes found softly impressed. Crumbling of the dies also is seen with this issue, with the peripheral lettering on both sides being most affected.

Lewis and Clark Gold Dollar (1904–1905)

The gold dollar issued for the 1905 Lewis and Clark Centennial Exposition appeared in two consecutive years, and the coins are identical except for the date, with friction and weakness of strike seen in some of the same locations. Hairlines are also seen on some of these coins, which are found with semi-prooflike and prooflike luster as well as

with satin and frosty surfaces. The points of wear are the hair, cheek, and coat of each figure, with weakness of strike usually noted in the hair and coat areas. Crumbled peripheral lettering usually indicates deterioration of the dies, rather than weakness of strike. Proofs are reported for both issues, though extremely rare, and these will have exceptional detail, with frosted devices and lettering as well as deeply reflective fields. As with most commemorative gold coins, these are seen brilliant, lightly toned with pastel colors, multicolored reddish gold, and deep green-gold.

Pan-Pacific Half Dollar (1915)

Issued both singly and as part of complete sets, the five coins struck for the Panama-Pacific Exposition of 1915 are intricately designed examples of an early commemorative issue. They are usually found with a satin or slightly frosty luster, though some have deeply frosty surfaces. Gold, silver, and copper examples without the "S" mint mark were struck in Philadelphia before the dies were shipped to San Francisco. These are different in surface texture from most of the regular strikings, but it is uncertain whether they are Satin Proofs. Their surfaces are similar to those of regular-issue Matte or Satin Proof strikings of the era, such as the 1915 cent and nickel. Several experimental Proof strikings are known with the "S" mint mark; these may be Satin Proof or experimental-finish strikings as they are struck from the same dies as the gold, silver, and copper specimens without the "S." On the half dollar, weakness of strike is found in some of the same locations where friction is first noted. On the obverse, strike weakness is seen in the head and on the reverse in the eagle's breast, though the neck, legs, and wing feathers also may show slight incompleteness. Wear appears first on the head, breast, arms, gown, and baby on the obverse, with friction or hairlines also noted occasionally in the field. On the reverse, friction is first observed on the neck, breast, and legs of the eagle, with other wear sometimes noted on the wings, shield, and leaves of the branches. When stored in the original velvet-lined boxes, these coins often acquire a purplish toning, which may be fairly thick. This is usually a positive attribute, unless the toning becomes so thick that it obscures the luster. Other coins are seen with bright original surfaces and many other color and toning variations.

Pan-Pacific Gold Dollar (1915)

This is one of the most misunderstood coins of any metal in all of American numismatics. Incompleteness of strike is seen on the obverse in the same areas where friction is first noted: the cap, ear, and face. Often the cap will have slide marks or hairlines, but some of these result from die polishing. Strike weakness on the reverse is usually noted on the dolphins and the denomination—the same areas where friction is first noted. Several prototypes with an experimental Proof or matte-satin surface—similar to some of the regular 1915 coinage, such as the cent and nickel—were struck without the "S" mint mark. As with other commemorative gold coinage, these are usually found with a satin-to-frosty luster, and most are seen with satin-to-slightly frosty surfaces. These are usually not as colorful as other commemorative gold dollars, with many brilliant or lightly toned specimens noted. Occasionally, a deep green-gold or pastel-colored coin is encountered, probably the result of storage in the velvet-lined original box.

Pan-Pacific Quarter Eagle (1915)

Being one of only two commemorative quarter eagles issued in the series' classic era, this coin has been quite popular with collectors and investors. Although well-struck specimens are found, fully struck coins are nearly nonexistent, with weakness on the obverse seen on the head, body, "horse's" head, and other device elements. Reverse weakness is noted on the upper wing line, neck, breast, lower body, and legs of the eagle, with the perch sometimes also weak. Luster varies from satin to very frosty, with most coins having satin-to-slightly frosty surfaces. As with the Pan-Pacific gold dollar, this coin is usually found brilliant or lightly toned, though deeply toned coins are seen. Toned

specimens are usually deep green-gold in color, but pastel-colored and reddish-hued coins also are seen. Proofs should exist, and at least one has been reported, though not verified.

Pan-Pacific $50 Gold-Octagonal and Round (1915)

During the nineteenth century, the United States struck pattern $50 gold coins, the provisional mint in San Francisco produced octagonal "slugs" or fifties, and the private mints of Western territories and states issued both octagonal and round gold pieces of this kind. But the round and octagonal $50 gold pieces struck by the U.S. Mint for the Panama-Pacific Exposition were the only coins ever issued in that denomination by Uncle Sam. Always popular with collectors, investors, and hoarders alike, these huge coins are seldom found in pristine condition. Even those stored in original wire frames and velvet-lined boxes are usually found with marks, hairlines, or other surface disruptions. Luster is almost always satin-to-slightly frosty, with the surfaces uniform or with slight frost on the devices and lettering. The obverses of both types have strike weakness in Athena's helmet and hair, with wear first noted on the face. On the reverse, weakness can be seen in the entire owl and in the pinecones, though most notably in the central and lower area of the owl—the breast, legs, and claws. Wear is first seen on the beak, shoulder, breast, legs, and pinecones. No Proofs are known or reported.

McKinley Memorial Gold Dollar (1916–1917)

All luster variations are seen on this gold issue except for flat, with most coins frosty to semi-prooflike and satin and prooflike coins also common. Proofs, though extremely rare, are known for both years. These have deeply mirrored surfaces contrasting with frosted devices and lettering, and the strike is extraordinary. They should not be confused with the deeply prooflike regular issues, which do not have deep frost on the devices and lettering. Strike weakness on the obverse is noted on the top of the head, including the hair, as well as the ear and sometimes the facial features—the eye, nose, mouth, and chin. Wear is noted in these areas, plus in the face and neck, with the field sometimes showing hairlines or tiny nicks. Reverse striking weakness is found mainly on the building at the top, near the base of the flag, and in the central columns and steps, though sometimes the date is also weakly impressed. Marks or wear are first noted on the building. Many beautifully toned coins are seen for these issues, with light pastel, reddish, and green-gold colors found.

Illinois Half Dollar (1818)

Proofs of this 1918 coin are reported in satin and matte finish, but they are extremely rare and somewhat controversial. Regular strikes are usually seen with flat luster, a delicate satin luster, or slightly frosty luster—though frosty, semi-prooflike, and prooflike coins are sometimes seen. Strike weakness is noted on the obverse in the hair, ear, and cheek, with other areas such as Lincoln's jaw and coat sometimes slightly incomplete. Wear is first noted in the hair, forehead, cheek, jaw, and coat, with hairlines sometimes seen in the open field. Reverse strike weakness is seen in the eagle's wing, breast, and legs, as well as in other devices. Wear is first noted on the reverse on the eagle's wings, neck, breast, and legs, with the shield, sun, and other devices also showing friction. There is minimal field friction or hairlining on the reverse because of the lack of open area. These coins are often seen with a slightly dull gray color that is usually even. Others are seen occasionally with vibrant colors, with frosty luster beaming through the colors.

Maine Half Dollar (1920)

This 1920 coin is a difficult issue to find well struck, minimally marked, and with good luster. Luster variations range from flat to prooflike, but the typical specimen has flat, satin, or slightly frosty luster. Strike weakness is noted on nearly every specimen, including the ultra-rare matte-surface Proofs. The central detail of the shield on the obverse is almost always incomplete, with the figures on each side usually mushy in appearance.

Because of this prevalent weakness, plus marks and slide marks on the shield, the obverse of this coin usually is not attractive. Reverse strike weakness is noted mainly in the central lettering, though the wreath sometimes has incompleteness. Marks and other surface distractions usually are found on and among the central lettering, with the wreath also found with occasional markings. These coins are not often found with pretty toning; many are toned a steely gray, but an occasional coin is found with superior luster, with reds and blues around the periphery. These are the most attractive Maine half dollars usually encountered.

Pilgrim Half Dollar (1920–1921)

The only difference in these two issues is the 1921 date in the left obverse field; both are double-dated 1620–1920 on the reverse. These coins usually are found with a slightly frosty-to-very frosty luster, with occasional satin or semi-prooflike luster being seen. Flat-luster coins are rarely found, and no full prooflike specimens have been reported. A couple of Matte Proofs have been reported, but these are extremely rare. Weakness of strike is common for the issue, with the hat, hair, face, coat, Bible, and arm often incomplete. Wear is first noted on the hat, face, hair, and arm, with marks and hairlines fairly common for the large open field areas. Reverse incompleteness is noted on the ship—especially the center mast, including the crow's nest and the central part of the vessel. Other localized weakness is noted in the peripheral lettering of both the obverse and reverse. Wear and marks are noted on and about the ship and sails, with occasional markings in the surrounding field. Many coins are seen with brilliant surfaces or light, even golden or light yellow toning. Some spectacularly toned specimens have been found, some of them with peripheral reds and blues, probably the result of residing for years in cardboard holders.

Missouri Half Dollar— Plain and 2X4 (1921)

This is a very difficult issue to find with full-strike, superior luster, and minimal marks.

Issued to commemorate Missouri's admission to the Union in 1820, this coin bears the dual dates 1821–1921 because the centennial was celebrated in 1921. Luster is generally satin to slightly frosty, the only other variations being coins with flat and very frosty luster. There are no reports of semi-prooflike and prooflike coins, and only a single Matte Proof has been discovered—from the estate of John Sinnock, the U.S. Mint's former chief engraver, who was the source for much of the early Proof commemorative coinage. Strike weakness is almost always found on the obverse on the cap, ear, face, neck, and coat of the frontiersman; these are also the first areas of wear. Marks, nicks, and other surface disruptions are seen on the head, face, and bust of the frontiersman, along with the open field areas in front of and back of the head. Reverse weakness is seen on nearly every specimen, with the central areas of the Indian and frontiersman—especially the upper arm—being the areas most affected. There may be other localized areas of weakness, such as the heads of the figures, the lower parts of their bodies, or the peripheral lettering. Wear is seen first on the arms, shoulders, and central body of the frontiersman and on the central body of the Indian. Many of these coins have an even gray toning that may be neutral to slightly negative or positive. Relatively few coins are seen with spectacular toning or blazing luster, but there are quite a few with uneven, splotchy, or unattractive toning.

Alabama Half Dollar— Plain and 2X2 (1921)

These coins have the dual dates 1819–1919 on the reverse to denote the centennial of Alabama's statehood and 1921 on the obverse to denote the year of issue. The two heads portrayed on the obverse are those of Alabama's first and then-current governors, the latter being one of the few portrayals of a living person on a U.S. coin. Luster is usually slightly frosty to very frosty, with satin luster the only other variation seen. Proofs with matte finish are reported, with the Sinnock estate accounting for at least one of these. As with the Missouri half dollar, these coins are

almost always seen with central striking weakness on the cheek, ear, hair, and jaw of Governor Thomas Kilby. Wear is seen first on Kilby's head, face, and coat, with marks noted in these areas as well as in the field. Reverse weakness is almost always found in the central feathers right above the eagle's left leg, usually including this leg and the talons. The upper wing feathers and other parts of the eagle are also sometimes seen with weakness. Peripheral lettering of the obverse and reverse is sometimes seen with localized weakness. Wear is first noted on the central part of the eagle, with marks and other disruptions seen across the entire eagle and its perch. Although light and deeply toned coins are seen, many of the Alabama half dollars were stored in rolls and have survived with little toning. These frosty white lustrous coins are among the most attractive of all Alabama halves, along with the peripherally toned examples.

Grant Half Dollar—No Star and Star (1922)

These 1922 coins are common without the star and scarce with the star. Most of the Grant No-Star half dollars have a satin-to-very frosty luster, with semi-prooflike coins occasionally seen. Nearly all of the Grant Star half dollars have a semi-prooflike luster, with myriad die striations seen in the obverse field—the result of polishing the dies to remove clash marks. Although nearly all of these coins have a semi-prooflike luster, there is little reflectivity to the surface. Strike weakness is common for both types, with the hair above the ear up to nearly the top of the head usually incomplete. Wear is noted first in this area, as well as on the face and beard, with marks and other disturbances very common in the field. Reverse strike weakness is almost always seen in the trees directly above the house and sometimes in nearly all of the trees, as well as in the house itself. Wear and marks usually are seen in the trees, and marks are often noted on the house. Toned coins are very common, with flat gray toning seen on many specimens. Multicolored or peripherally toned coins are sometimes seen, but many of the most attractive

MS-65 *Grant half dollar obverse. This coin is lustrous, lightly toned, and well struck, with only a few ticks here and there. The hair behind the forehead is almost always incomplete.*

MS-65 *Grant half dollar reverse. Most Grant reverses have almost no marks, with slight incompleteness, even on the cabin and tree trunks on the left side.*

MS-63 *Grant half dollar obverse. A few field marks and one cut at the back of the head are seen.*

MS-63 *Grant half dollar reverse. As with most Grant reverses, there are very few marks visible in the intricate design. More-than-usual incompleteness is seen, with the cabin and tree trunks on the left side very weak.*

coins, especially the No-Star specimens, have a blazing white frosty luster.

Grant Gold Dollar—No Star and Star (1922)

These gold dollars were issued at the same time as the half dollars and mimicked their design, including the addition of the star. Proofs are unknown for both types, though they may exist with a matte finish. Luster is generally satin to slightly frosty, with very frosty coins the only other luster variation noted. Strike weakness and wear points are the same as for the half dollars, but the soft nature of gold results in more scrapes than on the silver halves. Obviously, these coins are much smaller than the half dollars, and the marks on them are usually in relation to the reduced size. These coins are seen brilliant, lightly toned, with pastel colors, and often

with deep green-gold colors, which are probably the most attractive of all.

Monroe Half Dollar (1923)

Luster on this 1923 issue is usually slightly frosty to very frosty, though some coins are seen with a satin luster. Some coins have a slight claim to semi-prooflike luster, usually with die polish in the fields. A couple of matte-finish Proofs have been reported, with the Sinnock estate accounting for at least one of these. Strike weakness is noted on most specimens, with John Quincy Adams' hair and face often incomplete. Wear is first noted on the top of the head, hair, face, and coat. Marks are noted across most of the obverse, especially on the face, as there is very little relief in the design. The reverse is almost always weak in the figures representing North and South America, with marks and other surface impairments very common in the flat, open field around the figures, as well as on the figures themselves. The best examples seen of this half dollar are untoned or lightly toned coins with a frosty luster, decent strikes, and minimal marks. Toned coins are often dull gray in color or splotchy and mottled, or are unevenly toned with mostly dull or flat colors.

Huguenot Half Dollar (1924)

This coin was issued to honor the tercentenary of an obscure event, the arrival of the Huguenots in New York State in 1624—hence the dual dates 1624–1924. Most examples have a satin-to-very frosty luster, with a few semi-prooflike coins noted—usually with the accompanying die polish. Strike is usually above average, though some coins have slight weakness on the obverse in the cap, face, and beard of the topmost head, that of Admiral Coligny. Wear is noted first on basically the same high points, with marks and other disruptions noted on the other head, that of Willem I ("William the Silent"), and in the surrounding field. Reverse weakness is usually seen in the masts and sails of the ship, with the central part of the ship and the waves below also sometimes weak. The field on the reverse is much more open, and marks, hairlines, and other impairments often are noted in these areas. An unusual feature seen fairly often on these coins is an unfinished area at the top left of the reverse, which appears as a shiny spot, like a wheel mark from a counting machine. Some of the most attractive Huguenot half dollars are untoned or lightly toned coins with a very frosty luster. There are many lightly toned coins, mainly an even gray color, and they are attractive when lustrous with minimal marks.

Stone Mountain Half Dollar (1925)

This 1925 coin usually is found with a slightly frosty-to-very frosty luster, though specimens are found occasionally with satin and semi-prooflike luster. Most examples are well struck, but some have slight weakness on Robert E. Lee's arm, hand, and leg, and

slight incompleteness also is noted in the portraits of "Stonewall" Jackson and Lee's horse. Friction is first noticed on the arm, hand, and leg of General Lee, with marks seen all over the obverse and very minute ones hidden in the devices. Reverse weakness, when found, is mainly seen on the eagle's breast, though the legs and wing feathers occasionally have slight weakness as well. The breast is also the point where friction is first noted, with all but the tiniest of marks visible across the entire reverse. Many examples have spectacular toning, as they were issued in holders that contained active chemicals such as sulfur. These coins may have reds, blues, yellows, and other bright colors, often in concentric circles with tab-toned centers. There also are many brilliant or lightly toned coins that have very positive eye appeal, as well as other toning variations—some positive and some negative.

Lexington Half Dollar (1925)

Examples of this 1925 coin were commonly distributed in wooden boxes, which often accompany the coins when they are sold. These boxes contain chemicals that give the enclosed coins a greenish cast, much like PVC coloring, when they are stored for a significant period of time. Most of these coins have a satin-to-frosty luster. A few have a very frosty luster, and there is an occasional semi-prooflike specimen—and even rarely, a proof-like example. A matte-finish Proof is reported from the Sinnock estate. Strike is not a real problem, as most coins are decently struck, though slight weakness is noted on some specimens on the minuteman. Friction appears first on the head, central area, and legs, with marks and other surface impairments often seen in the large open field. Reverse weakness, when present, usually is limited to the upper part of the belfry, the roof, and the corner facing the viewer. Slight friction is first noted on the top edge of the belfry and the line representing the corner facing the viewer. As noted previously, many of these coins have a greenish hue from storage in wooden boxes. Examples are sometimes found with brilliant surfaces or with an even, light, cream-colored toning, and these are among the most attractive specimens seen. Some of the frosty and semi-prooflike coins are seen with spectacular bullet toning, displaying bright, vibrant colors, and these are probably the best examples of this coin.

Fort Vancouver Half Dollar (1925)

This coin was issued to commemorate the centennial of the building of Fort Vancouver, Washington, hence the dual dates 1825–1925. It was struck at the San Francisco Mint without a mint mark. Although examples are seen with a satin to semi-prooflike luster, most specimens have frosty to very frosty surfaces—often with a blazing luster. Matte-finish Proofs have been reported, most likely from the Sinnock estate. Strike is usually decent, but many specimens have slight obverse weakness on the hair above the ear, the ear, and the top part of the coat. Friction is first noted on the hair, cheek, and coat, with marks and other surface disruptions in the field and other parts of the head. Reverse weakness usually is found in the central area, with the belly, gun, and upper legs sometimes slightly weak. Slight friction is first noted on the upper part of the frontiersman, his belly, the gun, and his legs, with the right leg showing the most noticeable wear. There may be marks on the other devices, though there is little open field area where impairments can occur. There are many toned examples of this coin, some with vibrant colors and quite attractive, others with uneven, mottled, or splotchy coloring that may be considered negative. Brilliant or lightly toned coins are seen and these, along with some of the brightly colored, vibrant coins, are the most attractive Vancouver half dollars.

California Half Dollar (1925)

This coin was struck to commemorate the diamond jubilee, or 75th anniversary, of California's statehood. Examples are seen with satin, frosty, semi-prooflike, and nearly full prooflike luster, with the frosty and semi-prooflike coins being the most common. Proofs are reported with a satin finish but are unverified, with only the Matte Proof from the Sinnock estate being confirmed. This

coin probably was struck for Sinnock in Philadelphia, as it lacks the "S" mint mark. Strike is usually very good for this coin, with occasional examples showing slight obverse weakness on the left arm and left leg. Obverse friction is noted on the miner's shoulder, left arm, and left leg, with marks and other disruptions typically found on the rest of the miner and in the open field. Reverse weakness is usually minor, with slight incompleteness sometimes seen on the bear's shoulder and hindquarters. Slight friction is first noticed on the bear, with high points at the top and middle and on the left front and rear legs. There may be other markings or impairments on the bear in some of the small open field areas, or on the lettering. Some of the frosty and semi-prooflike specimens are spectacular in appearance; typically, these are brilliant, have light, even toning that is often yellow or golden, or have glowing bright colors with a booming luster showing through.

Sesqui Half Dollar (1926)

This was one of two coins issued in 1926 to celebrate the sesquicentennial of American Independence. It carries conjoined busts of the nation's first president, George Washington, and the then-current president, Calvin Coolidge, on the obverse, and a view of the Liberty Bell on the reverse. Examples are found with a satin to semi-prooflike luster, and satin-to-slightly frosty coins are seen more often than are semi-prooflike ones. Proofs are reported in matte finish, with the Sinnock estate providing at least one example. Strike is a major problem with most pieces, due in part to the extremely low relief of the design. Weakness manifests itself as a grainy look on Washington's cheek, while incompleteness of the top, central portion, and bottom of the bell also will appear to the eye as graininess. Wear is first noted on Washington's hair and cheek and, for the reverse, on the bell and the support. Because of the design's low relief, marks and other impairments are commonplace across both sides, but the head and bell receive most of the marking. Most coins are brilliant, have an even, light toning (usually light yellow or golden), or are toned a dull shade of gray.

MS-65 *California half dollar obverse. This coin has blazing luster, with almost no marks or contact.*

MS-65 *California half dollar reverse. A few light marks are noted on the front legs of the bear.*

MS-63 *California half dollar obverse. Marks are seen on the miner and in the field, though not severe.*

MS-63 *California half dollar reverse. Light marks are seen, mainly on the bear, though a few are noted in the field.*

The most attractive coins have a frosty or semi-prooflike luster and are either brilliant or lightly toned. An occasional example is seen with vibrant colors, the result of being stored in a chemically active holder.

Sesqui Quarter Eagle (1926)

The companion $2.50 gold piece depicts a standing Miss Liberty on the obverse and Independence Hall on the reverse, with the sun's rays on both sides of the building. Most examples have a satin-to-slightly frosty luster, with a very frosty specimen being encountered occasionally, but no semi-prooflike or prooflike pieces. Matte Proofs are known, with the Sinnock estate contributing at least one specimen. Although the Sesqui quarter eagles are better struck overall than the half dollars, most specimens have slight incompleteness, with the obverse figure often

mushy in the central area. Friction, often just frost disturbance, is noted along the length of the body, especially on the legs. On the reverse, weakness takes the form of incompleteness in the building, usually in the tower and central part. The reverse reveals friction first in the building's central section, with marks being seen there, in the wings on both sides of the building, and in the field. The most attractive examples are brilliant and have light toning or deep green-gold color. A few coins have pastel colors or more vibrant toning, and these are very attractive as well.

Oregon Trail Half Dollar (1926, 1928, 1933–1934, 1936–1939)

This is the first of the marathon multi-year commemorative issues, being struck first in 1926 to celebrate the Oregon Trail and intermittently thereafter, until it finally was dis-

MS-67 *1939 Oregon half dollar obverse. This coin has blazing luster with a minor mark here and there—note the one on the upper right shoulder.*

MS-67 *1939 Oregon half dollar reverse. Careful study is required to find an imperfection. None is visible to the unaided eye.*

MS-66 *1939-D Oregon half dollar obverse. Minor marks appear on the upper and lower right leg.*

MS-66 *1939-D Oregon half dollar reverse. A few minor "hits" appear on the oxen and wagon.*

MS-65 *1936-S Oregon half dollar obverse. Minor marks are seen on the Indian and in the field.*

MS-65 *1936-S Oregon half dollar reverse. Light ticks appear on the oxen and wagon, with a few others noted, one on a sun ray.*

MS-64 *1934-D Oregon half dollar reverse. Marks, though none major, are noted on the upper body, the upper and lower leg showing slightly more.*

MS-64 *1934-D Oregon half dollar reverse. Marks are seen on the oxen, wagon, rays, and in the field, though nothing severe.*

MS-63 *1936 Oregon half dollar obverse. Light contact and scuffing is seen on the Indian, with a few field marks.*

MS-63 *1936 Oregon half dollar reverse. Light marks are seen across the surface, notable on the oxen and wagon, with scuffing above the date.*

MS-62 *1926 Oregon half dollar obverse. Marks and lines are seen across the Indian, with much contact in the field.*

MS-62 *1926 Oregon half dollar reverse. Surface marks and contact are seen over most of the coin with a line below the WE and T of TRUST.*

continued in 1939. Luster is usually slightly frosty to very frosty, though examples are also seen with flat, satin, and semi-prooflike luster. At least one matte-finish Proof is known for the 1926 issue, and it comes from the Sinnock estate. Strike weakness is not often noted; nearly every coin is fairly well struck. When incompleteness does occur, the obverse shows weakness in the central area or around the periphery, while weakness appears on the reverse in the wagon and oxen or around the periphery. Coins from several years are elliptical, or nearly egg-shaped, with thinner areas opposite each other on the two sides. On the obverse, slight friction is noticed first on the Indian's breast and right leg, with marks usually noted on the body and legs, or on the map. On the reverse, friction is noted first on the ribs of the wagon, the boards along the side of the wagon, and the oxen. Marks and other surface impairments are seen primarily on the wagon, on and among the rays, and on the ground below the wagon. There are many very attractive Oregon Trail half dollars for every date, ranging from frosty white examples to coins with spectacular rainbow toning. (Note: There are serious disagreements as to which side of this coin is the obverse. Many people consider the wagon side to be the obverse.)

Vermont Half Dollar (1927)

This coin, dual-dated 1777–1927, commemorates the Battle of Bennington during the American Revolution and honors Ira Allen, depicting this founder of Vermont on the obverse. Examples are found with a satin to semi-prooflike luster, with most being seen with frosty or semi-prooflike surfaces. A matte-finish Proof is reported, again from the Sinnock estate. Most Vermont half dollars are well struck, with obverse weakness sometimes noted on the hair curls directly behind the eye, upward to the top of the head, and also on the cheek. Friction is noted first on the cheek and hair. On the reverse, weakness is noted on the shoulder, upper midsection, and hindquarters of the catamount. Wear is first noted in approximately the same areas, but the legs may also show

some friction. Marks are often present on Allen's face and hair, as well as on the catamount. Vermont halves are found brilliant as well as spectacularly toned.

Hawaiian Half Dollar (1928)

Issued in 1928 to raise funds for the Captain Cook Memorial Collection and to celebrate the 150th anniversary of the discovery of the Hawaiian Islands by Cook, this scarce coin is highly treasured by collectors of commemoratives. Only 10,000 examples were struck and most have a satin-to-slightly frosty luster, though some are semi-prooflike. Fully prooflike specimens are not known, but this was the first silver commemorative since the Columbian half dollar to be struck in quantity in Proof. All known specimens are matte-finish Proofs, and some still survive in pristine condition. Hawaiian half dollars are usually well struck, with only slight weakness noted on the obverse on Captain Cook's cheek, hair, and coat. Marks are found on the face, hair, and coat and in the open field in front of the face. Weakness of strike is noted on the reverse on the body of the king, with the head, left hand, central area, and legs sometimes slightly incomplete. Marks are found on the reverse on the king and in the open area in front of the figure. Many of these coins are found with light yellow or yellow-green color, especially those from the small hoards that have surfaced over the years. These are among the most attractive Hawaiian halves when found with minimal marks and good luster.

Maryland Half Dollar (1934)

This 1934 coin marks the beginning of the onslaught of new commemoratives during the 1930s. It was issued to raise funds for the 300th anniversary of the arrival of settlers in what was to become Maryland. The coin is usually seen with a satin-to-slightly frosty luster, though some examples are found with frosty luster. Most pieces are well struck, but fully struck coins are seldom found; the obverse is often slightly incomplete—mainly in the center of the face, with the nose, eyebrows, and cheek being the affected areas. Marks are found on the face, hair, and coat and in the field. Weakness is more difficult to detect on the reverse, as the design is intricate, with a mushy or indistinct look on even the best-struck specimens. Maryland half dollars are found brilliant, lightly toned, and occasionally deeply colored, with colors including reds, blues, russets, and other attractive hues. When lustrous and well struck, these deeply toned coins are spectacular-looking and command significant premiums.

Boone Half Dollar (1934–1938)

This coin was issued to mark the 200th anniversary of Daniel Boone's birth and to raise funds for several restoration projects. It was the first U.S. commemorative to be issued in sets containing examples from multiple mints—one each from Philadelphia, Denver, and San Francisco. The coins were marketed to the public in sets, though Boone half dollars were struck only in Philadelphia in 1934, the first year of issue. Most examples are lustrous, ranging from satin to prooflike in nature. There is disagreement over whether Proofs exist; if they do, they probably are matte or satin finish. These half dollars are usually well struck, with only slight weakness sometimes being noted on the obverse in Boone's hair above the ear and the top of the head. Wear is first noted on the hair and cheek, with marks usually being confined to the head, though the open field is sometimes found with small marks. On the reverse, weakness may be noted in the details of the two figures, with the heads, arms, and central areas most affected. Wear first appears on the reverse in the upper parts of the two figures, and there may be small marks on the figures or in the open field. Examples are sometimes found with spectacular colors—and if they are minimally marked and lustrous, these are among the most attractive Boone commemoratives. They also are found brilliant, lightly toned, and with many other toning variations, since most of the yearly issues had limited mintages, were sold only in sets, and were saved by collectors and hoarders.

Texas Half Dollar (1934–1938)

This coin, another of the multi-year issues, first appeared in 1934 as a means of raising funds for Texas' centennial celebration. It was issued in three-coin sets from 1935 through 1938. Luster variations range from satin to nearly fully prooflike, though satin-to-frosty coins are the most prevalent. Some of the Denver and San Francisco issues are found with semi-prooflike or prooflike surfaces. No Proofs are known or reported. Most examples have some striking weakness, notably on the eagle's breast and left leg on the obverse, and on the breast, right arm, and right leg of the winged figure on the reverse. If marks are present on the obverse, they usually will be on the eagle's breast or legs, with the wings and open area around the eagle sometimes showing marks. Marks on the reverse are usually well hidden, as the intricate design camouflages all but the most severe marks. Texas half dollars sometimes are found with target toning, with blues, yellows, and reds around the periphery fading to brilliant or lightly toned centers. Brilliant, light cream-colored toning and other toning variations also are seen, as these coins were issued mainly in sets from 1935 through 1938 and the sets were bought primarily by collectors and speculators who carefully preserved them.

Connecticut Half Dollar (1935)

This one-year commemorative was issued in 1935 to celebrate the 300th anniversary of the formation of the first organized central government in Connecticut and also to raise money for various celebrations. Most of the surviving specimens have a satin-to-slightly frosty luster. Matte-finish Proofs are known, though they are extremely rare. Strike was a problem for most of these coins; the tree on the obverse almost always shows some weakness in the leaves, branches, and trunk. Marks are difficult to detect on the intricately designed tree, but severe ones are sometimes clearly visible. Wear is also hard to discern on the high points of the trunk and leaves. The Mint encountered even more serious striking problems with the reverse, with the wing, leg, and claws incomplete on most specimens. Sometimes there is almost no detail in the upper part of the wing, which also is among the first areas to reveal wear, along with the head and front part of the legs. Most examples have brilliant or lightly toned surfaces, with cream or light yellow color. Occasionally, a well-struck, lustrous coin with spectacular toning is noted.

Hudson Half Dollar (1935)

This is another single-year issue, struck in 1935 to commemorate the sesquicentennial of the incorporation of Hudson, New York. Surviving examples usually have a satin-to-frosty luster. Matte-finish Proofs are reported, but are extremely rare. This coin is almost never found fully struck; almost all specimens show weakness in the central designs. Obverse weakness is more difficult to detect, with Neptune usually slightly incomplete on the upper body and visible leg. Marks are often seen on the whale, with the first points of wear seen on Neptune, the whale, and the ribbon. The reverse almost always has weakness in the two center sails, with the lower sail seldom having the ribs visible. Marks are commonly seen on the sails, with the lower central sail and upper sails first showing friction. Hudson half dollars are often seen brilliant or with light gray, cream-colored, or silvery toning, although some examples are seen with bright peripheral colors. These target-toned coins are perhaps the most attractive of all when they are found with minimal marks and decent strikes.

San Diego Half Dollar (1935–1936)

This coin was struck in San Francisco in 1935 and in Denver in 1936 for sale at the World's Fair in San Diego. Most specimens have a slightly frosty-to-very frosty luster, although a few are satin in luster. Occasionally, semi-prooflike to prooflike coins are found, but the busy design makes reflectivity minimal. Matte-finish Proofs are reported, including one from the Sinnock estate, and at least one satin-finish Proof has been discovered. San Diego half dollars are seldom found fully struck, with slight incompleteness often noted on the obverse on the breast and knees of the figure (Minerva), and other slight weakness sometimes found on the head and central area. Marks, including nicks and

light lines, are common on the body of the figure, especially on the legs, and sometimes are found on the other devices and in the field as well. Weakness is more difficult to discern on the reverse, though most examples have slight incompleteness on the upper and lower parts of the tall building and the dome of the chapel. Marks are seen on the buildings and in the field and to the right of the tall building. San Diego halves are very common with brilliant surfaces. Many come from bags that have been distributed over the years (some of which probably are still intact). Most specimens have little toning, though occasional coins are seen with spectacular target toning, including blues, reds, yellows, and other vivid colors. These are among the most attractive San Diego commemoratives, especially when decently struck with minimal marks.

Spanish Trail Half Dollar (1935)

Another single-year 1935 issue, this coin was struck to raise funds for the celebration of the 400th anniversary of Cabeza de Vaca's trek from Florida to west Texas and possibly beyond. Most examples are satin to slightly frosty in luster. Some coins also have glittering surfaces—though semi-prooflike is a bit of a stretch, since there is usually no reflectivity. The Sinnock estate contained a matte-finish Proof. Most of these coins are well struck, with obverse weakness confined to the head of the cow and reverse weakness sometimes noted on the leaves and flower of the yucca tree. Marks are noted on the cow's head and often in the wide-open obverse field. There are often fine die-polish lines around the lower part of the cow's head. Reverse marks are noted mainly on the map and in the open field. Most of these coins are found brilliant or with light gray or silvery toning, with only an occasional coin being seen with bright-colored toning.

Arkansas Half Dollar (1935–1939)

This coin was issued to celebrate the centennial (1836–1936) of Arkansas statehood, though the first coins were issued in 1935 in three-piece sets. Sets were also issued from 1936 through 1939, with some issues being

MS-65 *1935-S Arkansas half dollar obverse. One mark is seen on the Indian's neck, though little else but light scuffing appears on this nicely toned specimen.*

MS-65 *1935-S Arkansas half dollar reverse. This coin is nearly mark-free, with a few rim marks from 8 o'clock to 9 o'clock.*

MS-63 *1935 Arkansas half dollar obverse. Scuffing and a few lines are noted on the faces.*

MS-63 *1935 Arkansas half dollar reverse. A few marks and contact are seen on the eagle and in the field, though nothing major. Some of the "lines" are die polish—above the RK of ARKANSAS.*

sold almost exclusively by the large coin dealers of the day. These coins are usually found with a satin-to-very frosty luster, though an occasional semi-prooflike specimen is encountered, mainly from the branch mints. There are reports of matte-finish Proofs, though they are unverified. Almost all examples are seen with slight weakness in the central areas. The obverse has incompleteness in the headbands of both figures, as well as in Miss Liberty's eyebrow and cheek. Marks and other disturbances usually are seen on the face and neck, with other impairments seen in the cap and open field. On the reverse, weakness is easily noted with the head, neck, and upper wing feathers almost always incomplete, and some specimens are very flat in these areas. Those very weak coins will often have incompleteness on the legs and inner wing feathers, where the wings join the

body. Many Arkansas half dollars have brilliant or lightly toned surfaces; usually, they are gray, light cream, or silvery in color. A few specimens are seen with more vibrant colors, but these are very attractive and command substantial premiums.

Rhode Island Half Dollar (1936)

This commemorative was issued in 1936, individually and in three-coin P-D-S sets, to celebrate the 300th anniversary of the founding of Rhode Island. Examples are seen satin to prooflike, with most of the Philadelphia and Denver coins found satin to slightly frosty and some of the San Francisco coins seen with prooflike surfaces. No Proofs are reported. Striking quality is usually very good, though slight incompleteness is seen on the obverse on the Indian, canoe, and Roger Williams, the figure in the canoe. Marks are fairly common, but usually are small, as are hairlines, slide marks, and other impairments—most being noted on the figures and the canoe. Weakness on the reverse usually is limited to the anchor and the design across the top of the anchor. Marks are often seen across the anchor and in the open field. Most of these coins are found brilliant or with light toning, usually creamy white or silvery. Some are seen with bright peripheral toning, others with even, bright toning, and these are the most attractive Rhode Islands.

Wisconsin Half Dollar (1936)

This 1936 coin was issued to celebrate the centennial of Wisconsin's attainment of territorial status. Luster is usually slightly frosty to very frosty. No Proofs of any finish are known. Wisconsin half dollars are generally well struck, though slight weakness is noted in the hand and the central part of the badger. There is confusion as to which side of this coin is the obverse. Mint reports refer to the badger side as the obverse, while convention dictates the side with the date as the obverse. Marks are usually seen on the arm holding the pick and in the open field. On the reverse, marks and other disturbances are noted mainly on the badger, but others may be scattered around the surrounding field and other devices. Examples of this half dollar are found brilliant, lightly toned, and deeply toned, with many toning variations noted. Some of the most spectacular coins have deep-green and gold colors mixed with reds, blues, and yellows. Some of these are incredibly attractive specimens and command substantial premiums when offered.

Cleveland Half Dollar (1936)

Another one-year, one-mint issue, this 1936 coin was struck to celebrate the 100th anniversary of the founding of the city of Cleveland and to promote the Great Lakes Exposition held in connection with that occasion. Most examples have a slightly frosty-to-very frosty luster, though some have satin surfaces. As with many of the later commemoratives, no Proofs are reported. On most examples, there is slight incompleteness in the hair, mainly above the ear, and in the

cheek. Marks are also noted on the face, hair, and shoulder, with occasional marks in the surrounding field. Incompleteness is more difficult to discern on the reverse, with the long arm of the compass slightly weak, especially near the top. Marks are noted on the long arm of the compass, as well as in the flat, surrounding field including the lakes. Cleveland half dollars usually are found mostly brilliant, with light creamy toning, or brightly colored. Specimens with reds, blues, yellows, and other vivid colors are always in demand and command premiums.

Cincinnati Half Dollar (1936)

This scarce but somewhat puzzling half dollar was issued mainly in three-coin sets in 1936. Although it bears the dates 1886 and 1936, it is unclear what 1886 event is being commemorated. Evidently, the coin was intended only to honor Cincinnati for its musical heritage. Luster ranges from satin to semi-prooflike, with most examples satiny to slightly frosty. Some of the San Francisco coins are seen with a semi-prooflike luster. No Proofs are reported for this issue. Although relatively few examples are fully struck, most are well-struck, with only slight obverse weakness noted on the hair, mainly right above the ear. Weakness on the reverse is easier to detect, generally taking the form of slight incompleteness on the breast, arm, and upper legs of the kneeling figure. Cincinnati half dollars are seen with brilliant surfaces and with many toning variations. Some spectacularly toned coins are encountered, with target toning of reds, blues, yellows, and other vibrant colors. These toned coins are among the most desirable.

Long Island Half Dollar (1936)

Struck only at the Philadelphia Mint in 1936, this coin was issued to celebrate the 300th anniversary of the first settlement on Long Island. Examples are seen in nearly every luster variation, except prooflike. No Proof has ever been reported. Most Long Island half dollars do not appear to be well struck; in actuality, they generally are, though the design is not crisp. Slight weakness is sometimes noted on the cheek and hair, mainly right behind the eye, but there is not much definition to the hair, so this is difficult to detect. Marks and other distractions are found across the entire head. The reverse has incompleteness that is easier to see, with the lower center sail almost always being found with roughness. This is the main area for marks and other impairments, though a granular roughness with the luster still intact indicates incomplete striking in this area. Many examples have brilliant or lightly toned surfaces, although some spectacularly toned pieces also are seen. These "holder-toned" coins sometimes have vivid reds, greens, yellows, and other bright colors. The coins with vibrant colors are among the most attractive Long Island half dollars.

York Half Dollar (1936)
This 1936 coin was issued for the tercentenary celebration of York County, Maine, and was struck only in Philadelphia. There is debate as to which side is the obverse. Some believe it is the side with the stockade, while others—including PCGS—regard the side with the date and shield as the obverse. York half dollars are found with a satin to frosty luster. No Proofs have ever been reported. Typically, most examples are very well-struck, if not fully struck, with only slight weakness sometimes noted in the tree and lines of the shield. On the reverse, the fort and buildings in the fort, along with the horseman below, are sometimes incomplete, and these same areas also are the first points of wear. There are many superb York half dollars with blazing luster, though often satin in nature, and wild, glowing toning with vivid colors. These, of course, are the most attractive of all specimens.

Columbia Half Dollar (1936)
This 1936 coin celebrated the sesquicentennial of the establishment of the city of Columbia, South Carolina, as the state capital. It was sold primarily in three-coin sets, often in a cardboard holder. Examples are encountered with luster ranging from flat to semi-prooflike. Again, no Proofs are known. Strike is well above average, with only slight obverse weakness noted in the figure, on the

breast, and sometimes on the head and upper skirt lines. Friction, whether marks or slide marks, can be noted first on the breast, with the head and skirt lines also being prone to wear. Weakness on the reverse is evident first in the palmetto trunk and leaves, with friction and slide marks also appearing on the tree. There are many tab-toned "holder" coins that are very attractive. When the three coins in a set have matching color, luster, and eye appeal, the set brings a premium.

Bridgeport Half Dollar (1936)
Famed showman P. T. Barnum is portrayed on the Bridgeport half dollar, which celebrated the 100th anniversary of the incorporation of that Connecticut city, where he resided. Most examples have a satin-to-very frosty luster, though all luster variations are seen. There are no Proofs reported. Bridgeport half dollars are well struck, but slight incompleteness is noted on the obverse in the cheek, ear, and hair above the ear, and this is sometimes granular in appearance, as on the Sesqui and Long Island half dollars. Friction is first noted in these areas and across the jaw and back part of the head. Marks and other disturbances also are noted on the forehead and in the field. The unusual eagle on the reverse does not have individual feathers, but rather only ridges separating the feather layers. Slight incompleteness is often noted, especially on the upper section of the right wing, which is granular in appearance like the obverse. This is the area where friction also appears first. There are great-looking Bridgeport half dollars with brilliant or light toning, as well as vivid multicolored specimens. The main problems are the granular-looking areas on both sides.

Lynchburg Half Dollar (1936)
Another Philadelphia-only product, this 1936 coin was struck to celebrate the 150th anniversary of the founding of Lynchburg, Virginia. This is another coin that violated the 1866 law prohibiting the depiction of living persons on coinage: Virginia Senator Carter Glass, depicted on the obverse, was alive at the time. Lynchburg half dollars usually are found with a satin-to-frosty luster.

There are no Proofs reported or rumored. Examples are usually found with slight-to-moderate incompleteness on the obverse, mainly on the cheek, ear, and hair above the ear. Marks are found on and around the head, along with the cheek, hair, and shoulder. On the reverse, incompleteness is noted on the breast and central area of the figure, with the head and leg also affected. Original detail is not crisp, even on the very best strikes. Marks and other disturbances are first noted on the breast and leg, with the head and central area of the body also affected. Light-to-moderate toning usually is seen on this issue. Some coins are encountered with multicolored toning, either all the way across or as target toning, and these are the most desired specimens.

Elgin Half Dollar (1936)

This is another 1936 commemorative struck only in Philadelphia, this time to raise funds for the Pioneer Memorial in Elgin, Illinois. Elgin half dollars are very common with a satin-to-frosty luster. Chief Engraver John Sinnock made one Matte Proof for the coin's designer, Trygve Rovelstad. This specimen is now in the reference collection of Bowers and Merena Galleries Inc. Almost all examples are slightly weak, especially on the reverse. On the obverse, the hair around the ear, the ear, and the top section of the beard often are slightly to moderately weak. Marks and other disturbances are noted mainly on the head of the pioneer, with the open field usually unmarked. The heads and upper bodies of the figures on the reverse are always mushy, sometimes with most of the statue, especially the baby in the woman's arms, indistinct. Marks or other disturbances sometimes are mixed with the granular look of the incomplete strike. There are brilliant and lightly toned Elgin halves, but the most attractive specimens are those with bright colors. Bullet, multicolored, even, and other toning variations are encountered, and many of these are very attractive.

Albany Half Dollar (1936)

This coin was issued in 1936 for the 250th anniversary of the 1686 issuance of the city charter of Albany, New York. The settlement date of 1614 also appears on the dated side of this coin, which most numismatists regard as the reverse. Most of the various luster variations are encountered, with most examples falling into the satin-to-slightly frosty categories. If there are Proofs, they have not been reported. Albany half dollars are generally well struck, with slight weakness noted occasionally on the hind part of the beaver—the same area where marks also first appear. The other parts of the beaver and open field are also sometimes seen with minor-to-moderate marks. The arms of the figures on the reverse (the dated side) are sometimes seen with slight weakness, as are the upper parts of the figures. Friction is first noted on the arms, head, and coats of the figures, and hairlines and slide marks also are commonplace. Marks are seen on the figures and occasionally in the field between and around them. Many examples are tab-toned from the holders that sometimes accompanied these coins. Some of these are essentially brilliant, except for the peripheral and tab-toning, with full brilliance, light even toning, and other toning variations also noted.

Bay Bridge Half Dollar (1936)

Issued to commemorate a contemporary event, the opening of the San Francisco–Oakland Bay Bridge in November 1936, this 1936 coin was even sold to motorists at drive-through kiosks near the bridge. Struck at the San Francisco Mint, it is normally found slightly frosty to very frosty, often with very deep frost on the bear. The date side is usually considered the reverse, which is probably incorrect, as it depicts the bridge. There are no known Proofs. Bay Bridge half dollars are almost always well struck, with slight weakness sometimes noted on the bear's face and chest. Slight marks or other detractions are first seen on the upper third of the bear, with other disturbances seen on the remainder of the bear and in the surrounding field. It is difficult to detect strike weakness or wear on the side with the bridge. The bridge's supports and the central area often have slight striking weakness, and the hills above the bridge are usually the first areas to show wear. Marks, unless severe, are difficult to detect on this intricately designed side. Bay Bridge halves were issued in cardboard holders, and some coins acquired light-to-fairly dark toning as a result, though the colors are often vibrant. Coins with bright colors are among the most attractive.

Delaware Half Dollar (1936)

This coin was authorized in 1936, struck in 1937, dated 1936, and carries the double dates 1638–1938 on the obverse. It was issued for the 300th anniversary of settlers' arrival in Delaware Bay in 1638. Examples are usually found with satin-to-frosty surfaces, with other luster variations also seen. No Proofs are known or reported. The ship side, usually considered the obverse, often has slight incompleteness in the lower center sail, which usually appears granular. This is also the area where friction and marks show up first; the other sails are prone to wear as well. On the reverse, weakness is sometimes noted as a granular area—mainly at the top of the church's door. Friction is noted first on the roof of the church, with marks and other impairments usually found around the building and in the surrounding field. Delaware half dollars sometimes still turn up in their original cardboard holders, often with attractive toning.

Robinson-Arkansas Half Dollar (1936)

This is another commemorative that violated the 1866 law barring the portrayal of a living person on U.S. coinage. In this case, the person was Arkansas Senator Joseph Robinson. This coin has the same reverse as the Arkansas half dollar, though Mint records indicate that this side is the obverse on the Robinson-Arkansas version. It does have the date and thus might be considered the obverse in a technical sense, but most numismatists refer to the portrait side as the obverse. Luster is usually seen on this issue as slightly frosty to very frosty, with some satin and semi-prooflike specimens also being encountered. Several satin-finish Proofs are known. Slight striking weakness is often noted on the cheek, ear, and hair, with friction first appearing on the cheek and forehead. Hairlines and slide marks are noted across these areas, as well as in the small open field. Weakness is easier to detect on the reverse, with the eagle's head, neck, breast, inner wing, and leg feathers often incomplete. Marks are usually more common than other impairments, and these are found mainly on the eagle or among the other devices. Robinson-Arkansas halves usually are brilliant or lightly toned, though specimens sometimes are found with vibrant colors in several toning variations.

Roanoke Half Dollar (1937)

This 1937 Philadelphia issue was struck to celebrate the 350th anniversary of both the settlement of the colony at Roanoke and the birth of Virginia Dare in 1587. Most examples have a satin-to-slightly frosty luster, though every luster variation is encountered. Satin-finish Proofs are reported to exist in quantity, although PCGS has never encountered one that is unquestionably of Proof status. Roanoke half dollars are usually well-struck, but slight weakness is sometimes noted on the hat, ear, hair above the ear, and upper beard of Sir Walter Raleigh. Marks and other detractions show up first in these areas, and also on the face, shoulder, and surrounding field and lettering. Weakness is somewhat easier to spot on the reverse, with the figure's head, arm, and upper skirt often slightly mushy and the baby also frequently indistinct. Friction first shows up on the head, arm, and baby, often in the form of hairlines and slide marks. Many specimens have attractive brilliance and light toning, but the highest-grade coins often have vivid, multicolored toning, whether bullet or tab or some other toning variation.

Gettysburg Half Dollar (1936)

The Gettysburg half dollar was struck to mark the 75th anniversary of one of the bloodiest battles of the Civil War—a battle that gave rise to a reunion in July of 1938 attended by surviving veterans from both armies. Although the dates 1863 and 1938 appear around the periphery, the coin is dated 1936 and was struck in 1937. Most luster variations are seen, except for fully prooflike, with most examples having a satin-to-slightly frosty luster. There are no Proofs known or reported. Nearly every specimen is well struck, with slight obverse weakness noted occasionally on the face and cap of the Union soldier. Friction and other disturbances, including hairlines and slide marks, are found across both faces and hats and sometimes are scattered over the figures and field. On the reverse, weakness is noted occasionally on the cords binding the fasces, as well as on the fasces themselves. Friction first shows up on the fasces and on the two shields on either side, which also are prone to marks. Hairlines and slide marks often appear across the shields, especially their tops, as well as on the fasces. Brilliant and lightly toned coins are seen more often than are multicolored coins, though the latter are also encountered and are usually very attractive.

Antietam Half Dollar (1937)

This is another coin honoring the 75th anniversary of a Civil War battle. It is dated 1937 and was issued for an observance in September of that year. Antietam half dollars usually are found with a satin-to-slightly frosty luster, though other luster variations are sometimes seen. No Proofs are known or reported. Almost all examples are well-struck, but slight weakness is sometimes noted on Robert E. Lee's eyebrow and cheek and the surrounding area on the obverse. Marks are found on and around the heads, with hairlines and slide marks also seen. Friction first shows up on Lee's face, hair, beard, and shoulder, but these coins are usually well preserved. On the reverse, slight weakness is sometimes noted on the bridge and the trees just above the center of the bridge. Marks are almost never seen on the reverse of this coin; friction is first noted on the tree leaves and bridge. Antietam halves are often very attractive and are seen with brilliance, light toning, medium toning, and multicolored toning.

Norfolk Half Dollar (1936)

This coin was issued in 1936 to celebrate the 300th anniversary of the original land grant for Norfolk, Virginia. Almost every example is found with a satin luster or very slightly frosty surfaces. There are no verified Proofs. Norfolk half dollars are almost always well struck or nearly fully struck, with only the slightest obverse weakness sometimes noted on the ship's sails. Marks and other disturbances are almost always minor, and the sails usually are the only affected area. The intricate design "hides" all but the most severe obverse disturbances, as well as most problems on the reverse. Slight striking weakness is sometimes noted on the Royal Mace on the reverse, especially at the top and center. Marks and other distractions usually do not have the granularity associated with weakness of strike. Although this issue is not often encountered with blazing luster, the lack of marks makes most specimens attractive. Norfolk halves enjoy the highest average grade of any pre-1955 commemorative and are found brilliant, lightly toned (often cream or light yellow), medium-toned, and vibrantly toned.

New Rochelle Half Dollar (1938)

Issued to celebrate the 300th anniversary of the settlement of the area where the city of New Rochelle, New York, later was founded, this 1938 coin bears both its date of issue and the city's incorporation date, 1899, on the obverse. Examples are found with every luster variation; most have a frosty to semi-prooflike luster, though prooflike coins are commonly encountered with great reflectivity. In fact, these coins are so mirrorlike that they often are confused with the brilliant Proofs, of which fifty supposedly were struck. Matte-finish Proofs also are reported, though none has surfaced recently. New Rochelle half dollars usually have slight incompleteness, mainly in the body of the calf on the obverse and on the flower of the *fleur de lis* on the reverse. These coins almost always have strong luster, so finding minimally marked, well-struck coins is the main concern. Brilliance, light toning, and other toning variations are commonplace, with many attractive specimens seen.

Iowa Half Dollar (1946)

When Congress passed legislation in 1939 prohibiting the issuance of any more examples of the pre-1939 commemoratives, it may have thought no other coins would be issued in this series. After a hiatus of seven years, however, a half dollar was authorized in 1946 to celebrate the centennial of Iowa's admission to the Union. Iowa half dollars are usually found with slightly frosty-to-very frosty luster, and there are a few examples that have semi-prooflike surfaces, though little reflectivity. No Proofs have ever been reported, and it is doubtful that any were struck. Most Iowa halves are well struck or fully struck. Occasional obverse weakness is noted on the central part of the eagle, head, and neck, and incompleteness occasionally appears on the wing feathers and on the lettering on the ribbon. Wear is first apparent on the head and neck of the eagle, but there is usually little disturbance on the obverse. There is almost no open field area—so marks, when noted, are usually small and appear on the eagle or other devices. Weakness is difficult to discern on the reverse, with the central part of the building sometimes slightly fuzzy. Marks and other minor impairments more often are found on the reverse, often on the clouds above the building. Many Iowa halves are brilliant or very lightly toned, although there are some spectacularly toned coins—some with target toning, and some sea-green mixed with reds and other colors.

Booker T. Washington Half Dollar (1946–1951)

Also authorized in 1946, the BTW half dollar ostensibly was issued to raise funds for a Birthplace Memorial honoring the famous black educator. This coin was sold singly and in P-D-S (Philadelphia, Denver, San Francisco) sets; production continued at all three mints every year through 1951. Most examples are found with a slightly frosty-to-frosty luster, though some semi-prooflike and prooflike specimens are seen, mainly among the San Francisco issues. There are no Proofs known or reported. Fully struck coins are scarce; most have slight incompleteness on the obverse, mainly on the eyes, nose, and lips—though the cheek and hair above the cheek also are sometimes slightly weak.

Marks and other disturbances often are seen on the face and occasionally on the forehead and in the field. The reverse has little open field area, but slight weakness is often seen on the central lettering, the building above, and the log cabin below. As a rule, only minor impairments are found on the reverse, with many coins seen essentially as struck. Although many specimens are brilliant or lightly toned, there are many toned coins as well, some with even toning, others mottled, and others with nearly every other toning variation.

Washington Carver Half Dollar (1951–1954)

This was the last coin from the golden age of U.S. commemorative coinage. It was authorized in 1951 and struck at all three mints each year from then through 1954. Examples are usually seen with a slightly frosty-to-frosty luster, but flat, satin, and semi-prooflike specimens also are encountered. Some of the San Francisco issues are nearly fully prooflike, though most have die polish that inhibits reflectivity. As with BTW half dollars, there are no Proofs known or reported. Striking quality is usually adequate, but most specimens show slight incompleteness, mainly in the form of granularity on the hair and face of George Washington Carver on the obverse. Marks and other impairments are common on the obverse, with Carver's head and face being the most affected areas. On the reverse, slight weakness is common-place on the map, with marks and other impairments noted on the map and in the open field. As with BTW half dollars, these coins are found brilliant and lightly toned, with nearly every other toning variation also seen. Some of the most attractive pieces have vibrant colors, usually across the entire coin, but finding mark-free specimens is more difficult than finding attractively toned examples.

Modern Commemoratives

Commemorate coinage was resumed in 1982 with the issuance of the Washington half dollar. Since 1982, many new coins have been issued to commemorate people, places, and

MS-70 *Commemorative Buffalo dollar obverse. The modern mint can make nearly perfect coins. There are no marks visible under 5-power magnification.*

MS-70 *Commemorative Buffalo dollar reverse. No marks or hairlines visible to the aided eye.*

MS-69 *Commemorative Buffalo dollar obverse. Only the slightest imperfections will be found using a 5-power loupe.*

MS-69 *Commemorative Buffalo dollar reverse. There is only the slightest disturbance noted under magnification.*

events from U.S. history. Nearly all of these coins possess superb quality of manufacture and grading them is not that difficult. Strike is nearly always full and luster is either very frosty or prooflike. So marks, hairlines, and other impairments are the main criteria that are use to judge grade. The same situation applies to the Proof issues. They are found with frosted devices and superb, deeply mirrored fields with only a few mint-caused problems, such as lint marks and planchet flaws. Thus, grading modern commemorative Proofs is almost identical to grading modern regular issue Proofs.

11 DOCTORED COINS

"Coin doctors" have become increasingly active in recent years in the rare-coin marketplace. Unfortunately, their role has not been to cure the market's ailments, but rather to spread an epidemic: the alarming proliferation of coins that have been chemically treated, or otherwise tampered with, to make them appear better—and more valuable—than they really are.

The "doctoring" of coins is a special concern as well as a constant challenge for PCGS. Over the years, practitioners of this black art have become ever more sophisticated in their methods, making it harder and harder to distinguish their wares from original, untreated coins. The PCGS grading staff identifies and intercepts the great majority of these coins when they are submitted for certification, returning them to their consignors as ungradable. Even with all of their expertise and vigilance, however, graders are occasionally fooled and certify one of these coins. When that happens, the company's guarantee covers any loss incurred by the ultimate purchaser. However, the fact that it happens at all is testament to the seriousness of the problem. It also serves to underscore the value of certification in a marketplace where such dangers are all too common.

Lumped with doctoring is the cleaning of coins that really do need it. This is an area of much confusion, as evidenced by letters written to coin publications about coins that have been graded and placed in holders after being "cleaned" by dipping them in a commercial solvent or dip. Not all coins that have been altered by chemicals are considered doctored. No matter how the results are achieved, many coins have been improved by judicious cleaning with commercial dips, solvents, or plain soap and water. PCGS grades many coins that have had their surfaces altered by the removal of "problems," perceived or otherwise. The coins it does not grade are the ones altered by adding substances to the surface or altering the surfaces by physical methods.

Fooling with Mother Nature

"All coins are doctored," an astute numismatist once observed. "It's just a matter of degree and by whom—Mother Nature or Joe Dipper." His point, one worth pondering, is that coins by their very nature are subject to chemical change because they are made from metals that, to a greater or lesser degree, are reactive. The surfaces of a coin begin to react with the environment from the very moment the coin is struck. Depending on how and where it is stored, the coin may change very little over time or, conversely, undergo a radical transformation. Sometimes the change is positive—spectacular color from a reactive holder. Other times it is very negative—PVC damage, salt-water damage, or other intrusive damage.

There is, however, a fundamental difference between the natural changes that occur in a coin's appearance because of environmental factors, on the one hand, and the artificial changes wrought by the intervention of larcenous profiteers who are, quite literally, fooling with Mother Nature to perpetrate a fraud. Natural toning, for instance, can greatly enhance the appearance of a coin in the eyes of many observers by embellishing its original color with dazzling rainbow hues. Artificial toning, by contrast, tends to be less attractive and is used all too often to conceal important flaws that could lower a coin's value if these flaws were visible. This, in fact, is one of the major ways in which coins are doctored: chemicals are used not to remove something from these coins, but to hide or obscure a problem.

Nearly every chemical known to man has been applied to the surfaces of coins to "improve" their look, and they have been subjected to bizarre and often ingenious forms of treatment, such as being washed in sulfur shampoo, blasted with cigarette smoke, even baked inside Idaho potatoes covered with corn oil! Some of the techniques are primitive, to be sure, but they can be effective in deceiving the unwary. And some of them are subtle and hard to detect.

Preservation or Exploitation?

Is doctoring inherently wrong and reprehensible? After all, no one cries "Foul!" when a painting is restored, and that involves the use of artificial means to enhance a collectible. Nor is there an outcry when museums "expertly clean" their ancient coins. At one time, in fact, it was common practice even among professionals to clean U.S. coins. It has been reported that coins in the National Numismatic Collection at the Smithsonian Institution were "polished to a high gloss" three times by the start of the twentieth century. In the early days of U.S. coin collecting, and even into the early 1900s, many hobbyists cleaned their coins with little regard for the consequences. The coins in some early U.S. collections were stored in wooden coin cabinets and regularly wiped to "improve" their look, giving rise to the term "cabinet friction." Today, these practices would be abhorrent to many—but at the time, they were accepted and looked upon as forms of enhancement as well as preservation.

The key difference between all of these practices and most of today's coin doctoring is that many of those engaged in such activities today are doing so for fraudulent gain. They are seeking to mislead others—the grading services and prospective purchasers, in particular—into accepting their coins at excessively high grade and price levels by disguising the deficiencies of those coins.

Beyond the issue of intent, the practice of doctoring can often be harmful to the health of the coins. Some of the processes and chemicals applied to coins actually do help preserve them in certain cases. The problem is, many of them do not. When an organic solvent such as alcohol or acetone is used to remove damage from the surfaces of coins that were stored in PVC flips, those coins are not only improved, but also probably saved from ruin. On the other hand, the use of abrasive or corrosive chemicals can directly cause irreparable damage, rather than save the coin. This damage may not be apparent at first, but over time the coin may change as the chemicals further react with the coin's metals. The instability of many altered coins is noted only with the passage of time, sometimes too late to "save" the patient.

Doctoring is practiced in several ways. Three of the major methods are *artificial toning, surface alteration*, and *etching*. No analysis of the subject could be totally comprehensive, since new techniques probably are being tried every day. However, this chapter will examine in detail the basic techniques coin doctors practice. It also will tell you how to recognize these practitioners and how to develop skills to avoid their deceit. When a coin's surfaces are doubtful and it is being offered at a bargain price, a red flag is raised. When something seems too good to be true, it probably is.

Questionable Toning

All U.S. coins tone to some degree. How and to what degree are determined by various factors. Their metal content, where and how they are stored, and atmospheric conditions play the biggest roles in determining the depth and color of the toning. When acquired naturally over time, toning is often viewed as a positive attribute of grading, unless it becomes too dark, thick, mottled, or splotchy. When the toning results from the application of chemicals to the surface of a coin over a short period of time, perhaps with the use of heat to speed the process, the coin is said to have artificial or questionable toning.

The most obvious difference between natural and questionable toning is the way in which the toning "lies" upon the surface of a coin. When an original coin tones over time, the toning appears to be attached to the surface from the "bottom up." There is an appearance of depth to the toning and the colors are rich and natural-looking. When a coin is toned quickly by the introduction of chemicals and/or heat to the coin's surfaces, the toning floats on the surface and the color lacks depth. The toning appears shallow and not "attached" to the surface, as with original color. The colors associated with this type of toning tend to be unnatural-looking, often called "crayon" colors because they look as though they were "colored" on the coin's surface—weak pastel colors "painted" by a first-grader.

Naturally Retoned Coins

Many coins that were cleaned in the past have since retoned naturally. In error, these are sometimes said to be questionably toned. This is a difficult area, since there is a very subtle difference between cleaned coins that have toned naturally and coins that have had the toning process enhanced by chemicals and/or heat. This is further discussed in chapter 5, Elements of a Coin's Grade, under the section about second toning. Because there are so many factors involved in original and artificial toning, discussion of every color and type of toning is impossible. However, understanding the processes of original and artificial toning is essential in recognizing the differences.

Once the original surface is removed from a coin by some type of commercial dip or cleaning, toning will no longer "adhere" in the same way it does with original coins. There are several chemical and physical reasons for this. One of the main reasons is that

in coinage alloys, the subordinate metal tends to "leach" out or migrate to the surface. When the coin is cleaned, the first several layers of molecules are removed—and if leeching has been occurring for a substantial period of time, more of the minority metal is removed by any cleaning. Because the mix of the metals is now different, any new toning, whether natural or artificial, will be different and will adhere differently from the original toning.

A cleaned coin also will have "slicker" surfaces at times, probably due to residue from the cleaning compound and/or the "flattening" of the flow lines. These flow lines—or stress lines, as they sometimes are called—occur when the metal flows into the recesses of the dies upon striking. This provides a rougher and minutely larger surface for the toning to adhere to—and when cleaning removes or "flattens" these flow lines, the toning will not adhere as easily and evenly as before. This contributes to the "floating" colors noted on second and artificial toning.

Showing True Colors

The chemicals in many of the old coin holders (the Wayte Raymond and Meghrig holders, for example) are responsible for the bright, usually peripheral, rainbow colors seen on many coins from old-time collections. These are among the colors that coin "chemists" try to duplicate with their concoctions. Another source of sometimes beautiful colors is the tissue in which the Mint wrapped Proof coins, and occasionally Mint State examples, from the 1850s onward. These colors, too, are widely imitated. However, these imitation colors are never quite right and do not "lie" correctly.

Toned original coins usually can be identified as such without much difficulty. However, there is little obvious difference between lightly cleaned coins that have retoned naturally over many years and coins that have been enhanced with chemicals and/or heat. By examining coins that you know have toned or retoned naturally over many years and comparing these with chemically enhanced coins, you will gain familiarity with the often subtle differences between these types of toning. You might also consider conducting your own experiments with inexpensive coins, applying nontoxic chemicals to their surfaces, then studying the reactions that occur. The results of such experiments will provide greater insight into the characteristics of artificial toning. How the colors and toning "lie" on the surfaces is one of the easiest-learned tools of the trade.

Chemicals, such as sulfur compounds, often result in "crayon" colors as opposed to more natural-looking greens, blues, reds, and yellows. Also, these "artificial" colors often do not blend as evenly as do original colors. When the colors are splotchy or uneven, there is a good chance Mother Nature did not cause them. Regardless of the process used, when the colors "float," have unusual lines, and are uneven, the coin is probably artificially enhanced. Sometimes these colors are applied just to the periphery, while other coins have the entire surface treated. Tab toning has also been simulated by chemically treating an original holder and applying heat to speed up the toning process. These are sometimes very deceptive, as the "tab" in the center of a coin is often taken as "proof" that a particular coin is original. Again, this applied toning will "float" and usually will have colors not seen on originally toned specimens. Other coins are noted with mottled toning, which often is applied over light original toning to make the colors appear "deeper" than they actually are. These mottled-toned coins usually have colors that are just a little off—"crayon" colors or unusual blues or greens. Another form of added toning is often seen on Proof coins that have had the toning "rubbed" off of the high points. Toning is added to the "rubbed" areas, often blending quite well with the original toning. This is occasionally seen on Mint State coins as well.

Another type of artificial toning used to hide defects is the kind produced by "smoking" or "hazing" a coin by bombarding it with cigarette or cigar smoke. This method leaves a filmy, usually slightly opaque haze on the surface of a coin—a look that is sometimes described as "smoky." Hazy toning also can be acquired naturally through storage in flips or envelopes. If the area affected by the haze is localized over marks or hairlines, it probably was applied artificially. This type of alteration could just as easily be listed in the next section on surface alteration techniques, since toning usually is associated with more vivid colors, and this technique results in a milky-white to a slightly creamy-white appearance.

Sophisticated Surface Alteration Techniques

There are other ways to hide or obscure surface problems besides adding color or toning. The most common of these surface techniques is the application of "nose" grease. This combination of skin oils and other skin chemicals often is used to dull shiny spots on the high points of coins that may represent slight wear or incomplete striking. Sometimes this method also is used on tiny marks or light hairlines in the fields, thought it is usually easier to detect in the open fields than on high points.

When the amount of nose grease used is minimal, this type of alteration may be difficult to detect, since the area doctored may be essentially clear and quite small. When larger amounts are used, the surfaces sometimes have a golden or light yellow-brown color and may be slightly opaque. Over time, most of the coins "done" by this method will start to discolor, the treated area becoming brown and splotchy. This technique is used on gold, silver, nickel, and copper coins, but it usually is more obvious on silver coins.

"Thumbing" and Other Techniques

One common variation of nose grease is a process called *thumbing*, which is used mainly on silver dollars. In this process, the skin oils are rubbed across the desired area, with the thumb acting like a brush, rubbing the oils into the "skin" of the coin. This method is often used to obscure shiny lines or marks on the face of Miss Liberty on Morgan and Peace dollars, and is sometimes so minor that it is nearly undetectable. The breast feathers on Morgan dollars are sometimes "dulled" by this method also, especially when there is a shiny area resulting from contact. When the oils are applied vigorously, the affected areas appear duller, with the luster inhibited. When the coin is tilted under a good light source, the marks or hairlines that have been obscured by the thumbing are visible—though some "thumb" experts are so skillful at this technique that their handiwork is difficult to detect. Once you become familiar with this method, you will usually have no trouble recognizing the telltale signs—principally the dullness associated with the thumbed area.

Dental wax and auto-body putty also are used for surface alteration. Dental wax is particularly subtle because it leaves a thin, clear layer on the area where it is applied. This substance is used much like nose grease. Nothing is contained in the wax to discolor a coin's surfaces, but sometimes, after the water and alcohol have evaporated, a white powdery residue can be seen.

Auto-body putty and other car products were first used on Morgan dollars to duplicate frosty devices or cover blemishes on Miss Liberty's face or the eagle's breast feathers. PCGS has seen this method used on three-cent nickels, where the head of Miss Liberty was "frosted" with these compounds. This is not considered a very deceptive method because it is easy to spot after having examined a few of the coins on which it was previously used. This is also considered a form of artificial frosting, therefore could have been listed in the next section on chemical etching and artificial frosting. It is listed here, however, because it is more a method of surface alteration than a chemical process.

Whizzing

Although it is used only occasionally, *whizzing* should be mentioned here, since light whizzing plus added toning can be deceptive. Whizzing is a technique in which surface metal is moved mechanically to cre-

ate the illusion of luster. Heavy whizzing produces unnatural surfaces whose brightness does not resemble original luster. The "cartwheel" effect is replaced by a "sheen" that causes light to bounce off the surface differently, often with a diffused effect. When whizzing is light and is covered by natural or artificial toning, it is much more difficult to detect. If a coin lacks sharp detail but the luster appears full, light whizzing may be the culprit.

Magnification is the best way to differentiate weakly struck coins from worn-die and lightly whizzed coins. On weakly struck coins, flow lines will still be present and luster will still "cartwheel." Worn-die coins may not have much "cartwheel" but still may have radial flow lines—often the result of die erosion. Whizzed coins will appear smooth, and because the flow lines have been disturbed, they will not have normal "cartwheel" luster, but rather a diffused look.

A sophisticated whizzing process is sometimes used on Proof coins, though PCGS has seen it on a few prooflike business strikes as well. This is a refinement of the process used to create the so-called "California Proof" Morgan and Peace dollars. The most common method involves the use of a high-speed drill, such as a dentist's drill, with some type of fine burr or attachment to "enhance" the surface and smooth away scratches, marks, and hairlines. Recently, PCGS has seen some very deceptive coins, mostly Proofs, with plated-looking surfaces, possibly produced by this method in combination with chemicals and/or heat. The plated appearance hides hairlines, planchet flaws, marks, and other defects. These surfaces have a "chromed" look that, once noticed, will appear very unnatural.

In yet another form of surface alteration, the surfaces of Proof coins are heated to actually melt the hairlines or other defects. This method may involve anything from a match held under the surface for a few seconds to a high-temperature torch selectively applied to a specific area. Coins altered in this manner sometimes have a wavy look or different "depth" to the mirrored surface. These clues are especially noticeable on Proof gold coins, since the surfaces are so delicate. Also, many Proof gold coins have "orange-peel" surfaces that are flattened by this method. If the mirrored fields vary across the surface of a coin, heat treatment of the fields is often the cause.

Chemical Etching and Artificial Frosting

To create the cameo devices seen on many U.S. coins, the Mint sometimes sandblasted the dies or pickled them in acid, then polished the fields, leaving the recesses of the dies with rough surfaces that produced the frosty devices. Before the introduction of completely hubbed dies, the die-making process also contributed to frosted letters and devices, because the ends of the punches were not always smooth. This roughness, and the pressure used to impart the letters and devices to the dies, often left the recessed areas with "frost." This resulted in frosty letters or devices from the letter- and device-punching process. Proof coins almost always were struck from these specially prepared dies, and some business-strike coins also were struck from the Proof dies and other dies treated in a similar way.

To recreate this frost, some coins are chemically treated on the devices, often with mild acids. PCGS also has seen some other coins, usually Proofs, which appear to have had their devices lightly sandblasted or acid-etched to imitate frosting. Other substances also are used to imitate frosting—among them auto-body putty, as mentioned in the previous section—but these will usually "dip off" in commercial dips or certain organic solvents. These treatments are applied most commonly to silver coins, but gold, nickel, and even copper coins also are sometimes seen with imitation frosted devices.

In their quest to find new methods to alter coins, the coin doctors have turned to a relatively modern technology, which is still quite expensive. Lasers have been used for quite a few years in many fields, but only recently has the intense light of these devices been turned onto the surfaces of coins. Usually, Proofs are the coins of choice for this sophisticated treatment, although a few Mint State examples have also been noted. Most collectors, and even dealers, will have a hard time recognizing this subtle alteration to a coin's surface. In most cases, a scratch or heavy hairline is heated with the laser to the point that the surfaces melt in this area. When the treatment is finished, the scratch or hairline is no longer obvious to the unaided eye. However, under magnification the surface will show disturbance, on silver coins this is very minor, but on gold coins, the "orange peel" surface is missing in the affected area. As noted, this technique is subtle and a trained eye is needed to detect the change. Buying a PCGS certified coin is the surest way to avoid a coin that may have been treated with a laser.

Learning To Detect Doctored Coins

Examining coins known to have been doctored in particular ways is the best way to learn how to recognize the various processes used and their results. Seeing such coins is worth even more than the "thousand words" of the old saying. No amount of discussion or analysis can fully instruct one about the subtle differences between original and altered coins. With experience, one will be able to spot certain doctored coins with just a casual glance. Once a particular process has been "seen," coins that result from that process may very well become extremely obvious.

Some of the alteration techniques are difficult to detect, and even experienced numismatists miss them at times. As more and more coins are examined and the "look" of totally original coins becomes increasingly familiar, any deviation from that look will serve as a tip-off to coins that have been altered in some way.

A coin is not necessarily ungradable just because it is not totally original. In some cases, in fact, altering a coin may actually improve its grade. One example of this would be dipping a coin that has splotchy, mottled, or dull toning and thereby revealing a blazing white gem. Another would be removing PVC flip damage with an organic solvent. Also, with gold, silver, and nickel coins, rinsing them in hot water sometimes is necessary to remove light surface contaminants. This should not be employed on copper coins, as the chemicals in the water plus the heat may affect the color and luster. Copper coins are much more difficult to work with, and in most cases should be left alone. If green corrosion appears on the surface of a copper coin, remove it mechanically, if possible, usually with a soft camel-hair brush. Copper aficionados sometimes have brushes they have used for decades, carefully protecting them. These "used" brushes have oils from years of use and their owners swear that these "protect" the surfaces of copper coins brushed by them. There is truth to this, as many coins brushed appear unchanged after many years. These, however, should only be used by knowledgeable copper experts, because even the fine camel hair can damage surfaces.

Only when this method has been tried and failed should one attempt to remove something chemically from the surface of a copper coin.

Obviously, one needs to learn what is *acceptable* alteration in order to know what is *not* acceptable. Once the original and non-original "looks" of coinage have been mastered, one must learn what is acceptable and not acceptable for coins that are not original. When unsure about a coin, ask the owner. Although the owner wants to sell you the coin, he or she does not want you to call six months later and ask why the coin has changed colors.

There are many subtle areas that only experience can clarify. The cloudiness on shipments of U.S. gold coins imported from Europe is very similar to the hazing or "smoking" seen on some altered coins. Second toning, in many cases, looks similar to artificial toning. The difference is subtle, but there are telltale signs that knowledgeable numismatists recognize. Learning the difference takes time and effort, but an "eye" can be developed for the "look."

12 THE FUNDAMENTALS OF COUNTERFEIT DETECTION

Since perhaps the very day coins were first produced, quick-buck artists and their counterparts throughout history have sought illicit gain by making copies—or counterfeits—of the genuine articles. From ancient times to the present, counterfeits have been an unwelcome reality, and they surely will continue to be a problem well into the future.

Initially, counterfeits were made merely with the objective of being spent. More recently, however, as some coins acquired substantial premium value as collectibles, there emerged a new crop of counterfeiters, bent on producing coins that would fool collectors rather than merchants. These more advanced malefactors utilized techniques extending far beyond the crude methods of earlier forgers. In time, the coin-buying public was confronted with a confusing array of cast copies, transfer-die counterfeits, spark-erosion counterfeits, electrotypes, and alterations—all deceptive and all decidedly dangerous to hobbyists' financial health.

Responding to its members' alarm about these counterfeits, the American Numismatic Association in 1972 created an agency called the American Numismatic Association Certification Service (ANACS) whose mission was to ferret out, identify, and expose spurious coins. Coins submitted to ANACS for inspection were determined to be genuine or not and were returned to their owners. It was ANACS's job to educate the public by publishing its findings and disclosing diagnostic features that would aid in determining the authenticity of a given coin.

In 1979, ANACS's role was broadened to encompass not only authentication but also grading. Within a few years, it was joined by other grading services, including PCGS. In each instance, these services had to establish with unwavering accuracy the authenticity of coins submitted for their review before they could assign grades to those coins. After all, a coin's grade is irrelevant if it is a counterfeit.

Fortunately, the art of counterfeit detection was far advanced by the time the grading services came into being, having had a head start of more than two decades, and a great deal of working knowledge was available. Still, it is relatively easy to produce counterfeits and alterations, and authenticators are constantly seeing new variations on old themes as they battle resourceful foes in the war against fakes and fakers.

What skills does one need to identify fakes? There is enough information in print about counterfeits to fill volumes. And that is where this guidebook will take a different tack. Rather than trying to determine why a particular coin is counterfeit, this book will offer secrets on how to determine a genuine coin's authenticity. It is easier and quicker to look for genuine diagnostics than it is to identify every counterfeit diagnostic. Many genuine rare coins were struck from a limited number of dies, making it easier to identify the real coin than to try to sort through what could be an infinite number of counterfeits.

Keep in mind that a counterfeiter can create many different variations of the same coin, but if only one or two dies were used by the U.S. Mint to produce a coin, the identifying characteristics of one of those dies will be present in every coin that was struck from them.

Cast Counterfeits

Cast **counterfeit** Continental dollar obverse. This is one of the most common modern cast counterfeits. Note the very granular surface and rough texture.

Cast **counterfeit** Continental dollar reverse. The surface looks pitted and has rough detail, characteristics of the casting process.

Cast **counterfeit** Continental dollar. Note the seam on the edge, the result of connecting the two cast halves to make the coin.

Having said all of this, it is still important to know what counterfeit coins look like—and at the outset, we will look at the different types of counterfeits that exist. However, the bulk of the text will deal with identifying genuine coins and their characteristics.

Overview
Cast Counterfeits

The most basic and most crude of all counterfeit coins are *cast copies*. These generally are manufactured not for the purpose of fraud, but to create a copy as a souvenir or promotional giveaway.

Usually the cast copy can be easily identified by a seam that runs around the outside edge or circumference of the coin. This seam appears at the point where two molds, obverse

and reverse, are joined. As the metal is poured or forced through the opening in the edge and fills the voids of the mold, a "coin" is produced.

Casting has come a long way from its early beginnings, and some cast copies today are made from plastic molds, using centrifugal force. These are of a slightly higher quality, but still can be detected by noting their faulty edges (unless they have been filed) and lack of surface detail.

The most commonly seen cast copies of American coins are colonial and territorial pieces. A number of crudely made cast pieces were manufactured for the sole purpose of being sold as souvenirs on historic occasions, and these are easily detected.

Electrotypes

Electrotype 1852 pattern ring cent obverse. The rough surfaces are the results of the electrolytic process to create the obverse.

Electrotype 1852 pattern ring cent reverse. As with the obverse, rough areas are seen on the surfaces, the results of the manufacturing process.

Electrotype 1852 pattern ring cent. Note the seam on the edge where the two halves were joined.

Virtually all cast counterfeits are underweight, compared with the genuine coins from which they are copied, due to the fact that base metals usually are used in place of any precious metals that would have been present in the original coins. The base metals most commonly used include pewter or some other combinations of tin, zinc, or lead.

Electrotypes

Over the years, electrotypes have been made legitimately and appropriately by museums. Many times museums display an imitation of a rare coin, rather than the real thing, for purposes of security or to show both the obverse and reverse of the coin, and they often create electrotypes for these purposes.

Electrotypes are made by impressing a genuine coin into a soft substance and electroplat-

ing the negative impression, thereby creating a positive shell. The process allows only one side to be produced at a time, which is ideal for a museum. With each side independent, the obverse and reverse can be displayed simultaneously. Problems developed for the coin-collecting public when these shells were matched, filled with a metallic composition, then fused to create an entire coin.

While the detail of an electrotype can be excellent, the edge will usually give it away. As with cast copies, many electrotypes have a seam along the outer edge. Also as with casts, electrotypes generally will not "ring." A ring test often is used on coins to determine whether a coin is solid and struck. When it is balanced on the tip of a finger and struck softly with a pen or pencil, a genuine coin usually will produce a high-pitched

Transfer Dies
*1906 Liberty Head quarter eagle obverse struck from trans-fer dies. These are the highest-quality **counterfeits** known, with fairly crisp detail, except under magnification.*

*1906 Liberty Head quarter eagle reverse struck from trans-fer dies. To the unaided eye, this coin is difficult to spot as a **counterfeit**.*

ring. Most electrotypes and cast copies will merely "thud" or "clunk." Since these pieces are not actually struck, they have relatively little solidity. Many times an electrotype will not be the proper weight; it may be either too light or too heavy, compared with a genuine coin.

A word of caution: Some counterfeiters who use electrotypes for the purpose of deception place a sliver of glass between the shells; because of this, plus the metallic substance joining the two halves, a ringing sound can be achieved when this kind of electrotype is tapped.

Transfer Dies

Transfer dies are the most common devices used by the modern counterfeiter whose sole intent is to defraud. In the transfer method, the counterfeiter actually creates a working die. In the crudest form, called an impact die, a genuine coin will be sacrificed in making this fake working die by impressing it into die steel, as if the coin were a working hub. Once a pair of dies has been created, the counterfeiter then produces fake coins.

While these counterfeits can be difficult to detect, a coin produced by this method will always be identifiable—for when the counterfeiter impresses the dies, any defects the original coin might have had are unavoid-

ably copied. Therefore, all subsequent copies the counterfeiter makes also will carry these defects, usually in the form of bag marks. Odds tell us that no two or more coins will contain identical contact marks in the exact same spots.

Sometimes the detector's job is made easier because the counterfeiter tried to remove the defects from the die and, in so doing, bungled the die and created what are known as *tooling marks*. Tooling marks appear on a coin as short, stubby raised lines. These result when the counterfeiter cuts grooves into the die in an effort to remove a raised lump—the lump that was creating the defective "bag mark." This lump was appearing on all the fakes, and the counterfeiter desperately wanted to remove it. By removing the repeating—yet unobtrusive—bag mark, the counterfeiter made detection easier by creating a coin that has obvious raised lines over the spot where a bag mark once was.

One of the shortcuts counterfeiters take is using the same undated side (usually the reverse) in combination with many dated sides (usually obverses). The U.S. Mint has rarely used the same undated dies from one year to the next, and the Mint's dies usually were in exemplary condition and did not show the common repeating defects evident on counterfeiters' dies.

Spark-Erosion Counterfeits

*1869 Indian Head cent obverse struck from spark erosion dies. The pebbly surface and fuzzy detail are characteristic of this **counterfeit** method.*

1869 Indian Head cent reverse struck from spark erosion dies. Lack of detail in the wreath and dentils is the result of incompleteness from the spark erosion process.

The transfer method is most commonly used to counterfeit gold coins. A few silver counterfeits also have been made this way, as have some fake copper coins. Interestingly, while entire date sets of counterfeit Indian quarter eagles, half eagles, and eagles have been seen, relatively few pre-1840 gold counterfeits exist. When they do appear, they generally are limited to certain dates.

Spark-Erosion Counterfeits

Spark-erosion counterfeits are quite easy to detect because of the way in which they are manufactured.

In the spark-erosion process, a model coin (usually genuine) is submersed in an electrolytic bath where the coin faces the counterfeiter's die steel. An electrical current is charged through the coin so that a spark jumps across the shortest gap between the coin and the die, thus etching the coin's design onto the steel die.

After both the obverse and reverse have undergone the electrical current process, the dies are highly polished. This is necessary because once the dies have been etched, they remain somewhat pitted. The polishing generally will clean up the fields, but often the design will retain the pitting, since counterfeiters tend not to polish the main devices. Either they are unable to get down into the design, or for time's sake they choose to leave the design elements alone.

In either case, these counterfeits are easy to detect, since their surfaces are glassy smooth—resembling a Proof finish—yet their devices are lumpy (remember, the pitting on the dies becomes raised lumps on the finished product). Because the excessive polishing makes the dies sharp, these counterfeits appear to be extremely well struck, with knifelike edges and rims.

These counterfeits usually are found on small-type coins such as cents and dimes, and on small-sized patterns such as those for Flying Eagle cents and dimes. PCGS has not encountered them on gold coins.

Contemporary Forgeries

Contemporary forgeries are counterfeits created at the time the Mint was issuing the coins from which they were copied, and made for the purpose of being spent. The counterfeiter would forge these pieces through the use of hand-cut dies, with which base-metal planchets would be struck. Then, he or she would simply spend the newly made fakes.

Due to the nature of the hand-cut dies, these forgeries are easily detected. The design elements, letters, and digits never quite match those of the genuine U.S. Mint products.

Contemporary Forgeries

Contemporary **counterfeit** 1837 Lettered Edge half dollar obverse. Struck counterfeit, with crude lettering and devices, in base metal made to pass at face value in commerce. Today this seems quaint, though fifty cents would buy quite a lot in 1837.

Contemporary **counterfeit** 1837 Lettered Edge half dollar reverse. Note the irregular look of the eagle and lettering.

Contemporary **counterfeit** 1837 Lettered Edge half dollar. Note the lettered edge, which was discontinued in 1836, when close-collar, reeded-edge half dollar strikings began. The contemporary counterfeiters probably were not aware of this when they made this specimen.

Contemporary copies frequently are seen for issues tied to financially burdensome times. These include fake 1861 three-cent silvers, presumably made and spent during the Civil War, and spurious 1933 half dollars that very likely were used during the Great Depression. An interesting series of copper-nickel counterfeits of Capped Bust half dollars carried dates from the 1820s into the 1840s, or after the series was discontinued, and may have been made as late as the Civil War.

Alterations

Alterations involve taking otherwise genuine coins and changing them into something they never were. Alterations run the gamut of coins as well as techniques.

One of the most frequently seen alterations is the addition of a mint mark to a coin that did not have one to begin with. By adding an "S"

mint mark to a genuine but common 1909 VDB Lincoln cent, for example, a forger makes it appear to be the highly coveted 1909-S VDB. Typically, the mint mark is added with epoxy glue, though alterations exist where a mint mark was soldered to the surface of the coin.

On other alterations the date has been changed. Many cases are known, for example, where the first "4" in the date of a 1944-D Lincoln cent has been altered to look like a "1"—making the coin appear, at least to the uninitiated, as a key-date 1914-D. Other such alterations might involve changing a 1941 Walking Liberty half dollar to a 1921 or a common-date Indian Head cent to an 1877.

Another form of alteration is the embossed mint mark. The results of this intricate process were first observed on Buffalo nick-

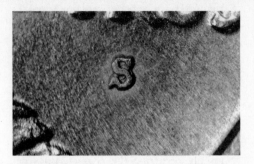

Alterations

*Close-up of **altered** 1917-S Obverse Walking Liberty half dollar obverse. Added "S" with the mint mark not square, bottom serif diagonal, and discolored area seen around the added mint mark.*

*Close-up of **altered** 1877 Indian Head cent obverse (from genuine Indian Head cent). This is a common, genuine coin with the date altered to that of a rarer issue.*

els. The counterfeiter would drill a hole through the edge of the coin in the area of the mint mark. From there, a raised mint mark would be embossed or created by inserting a pliers-like tool and squeezing the instrument. Presto—a mintmark!

The final form of alteration we will consider here is a process known as chasing, accomplished by building up metal from the field of the coin. With this built-up metal, a mint mark can be configured. This alteration generally is the easiest to detect, as it is by nature the sloppiest in execution.

Most altered coins will be found in the series from cents through silver dollars. Altered gold coins are seen much less frequently.

The Detection Process

While counterfeit detection obviously is important, such excellent information has been published in the recent past that the number of counterfeits being submitted to PCGS is minuscule. In fact, PCGS encounters only about 25 counterfeits per 10,000 coins, or an average rate of one quarter of 1 percent (0.25 percent).

The ultimate secret to counterfeit detection is knowledge of what the genuine coin should look like. If one knows the characteristics of

the genuine coin, everything else must be called into question.

Experts in various specialties generally find counterfeit detection easier in their particular fields. Experts in early large cents, Mercury dimes, or Morgan dollars will rarely get stung by a counterfeit in their specialty, because they have detailed knowledge of the genuine coins in their series. Therefore, they immediately question anything that appears strange. Their initial suspicion impels them to verify the coin's authenticity. Typically, the specialist will refer to reference books, notes, and inventory before reaching a conclusion. Comparison to the real coin will almost always solve the riddle.

In the next section, PCGS will share with you some of the secrets to counterfeit detection. We will start by examining the manufacture of genuine U.S. coins.

The Real Thing

Since the mid-1800s, U.S. coins have been made through a meticulous process that begins with the sculpting of a wax or clay positive of the intended design. A plaster or other composition negative then would be made of the model, and this negative then would be used to cast an iron positive of the design. Later, an electroplated galvano or shell would replace the iron casting.

The casting or galvano would be used on a reducing lathe to prepare a steel punch that would be used, in turn, to begin a master die. Letters, stars, and a rim would be added to finish the master die, which then would be used to raise up a master hub. This hub would be used to sink working dies, which were used to strike coins.

As the quality of the reducing lathes improved over the years, more and more detail such as the lettering and stars could be included on the original models. Beginning with the Saint-Gaudens $10s and $20s of 1907, the entire design, including the date, was reduced from the artist's model. This uniformity, though annoying to the variety collector, makes counterfeit detection easier.

Typically, all details will be sharp and crisp on a newly struck genuine coin. For most coin designs, the letters and digits will rise sharply from the fields of the coins. These same letters and digits will have sharply cornered tops. This is extremely important, as most counterfeiters lack the ability to reproduce this effect. It is because of the attention to detail that the U.S. Mint's products are unquestionably superior. Obviously for the few series where the letters and digits are rounded (such as the Peace dollar, Indian Head eagle, and Saint-Gaudens double eagle), counterfeits can sometimes be more deceptive.

Luster

We know how important luster can be in determining the grade of a coin, but it plays a major role in counterfeit detection as well. How often have you heard someone say that a coin "looks bad"? Have you ever wondered how someone could be so certain a coin was counterfeit just by its look? This again reflects the manufacturing process. Due to the one-to-one transfer that occurs with most counterfeits, their surfaces are totally uniform, which means the lustrous effects of the fields and devices are the same. On genuine coins, the fields usually contrast with the devices.

Perhaps this can be better explained another way: The smooth surface of the fields usually contrasts with the textured surface of the devices. The contrast is what gives genuine coins their particular look. *Genuine coins do not have a uniform appearance.* Two coin types that illustrate this particularly well are Morgan dollars and Liberty Head gold pieces.

Die Characteristics

Naturally occurring die characteristics detectable on a coin are most helpful in determining authenticity. These are the subtle clues that confirm a coin's genuineness. They include die-polish lines, die cracks, and die chips, striking anomalies, such as grease-filled dies and certain planchet characteristics.

Of the characteristics just mentioned, die polish lines are by far the most useful in determining a coin's authenticity. Just about every die is polished at one time or another—and when this is done, mint technicians leave small grooves on the surface of the die, which in turn become raised lines on the finished coin. These lines are almost always extremely crisp, well-defined, and purposeful.

The typical counterfeiter, on the other hand, rarely polishes the dies, being more interested in making coins as quickly and cheaply as possible. In addition, detail is lost when a counterfeiter transfers a model coin to an illicit die, which may totally eliminate or barely transfer existing die polish lines. The result is a counterfeit that shows very little, if any, evidence of die polishing. To effectively view these small lines, you need at least a 5X loupe and an incandescent, fluorescent, or halogen light source.

Knowledge is king. Knowing the characteristics of genuine coins will help you quickly weed out obvious fakes. With rare coins, remember that in most cases very few dies would have created them; therefore, their diagnostics are few. Counterfeiters can keep making their concoctions forever—but if they cannot duplicate the real thing, their duplicity will be easily detected.

13 IDENTIFYING GENUINE COINS— COMPARISONS WITH COUNTERFEIT SPECIMENS

The Real Deal

The key to spotting a counterfeit or an altered coin is knowing how to recognize the real thing. This has been said many times, but it bears repeating. Knowledge of die characteristics, the shapes of mint marks, the styles of digits, and how coins are made all come into play when confirming authenticity. The U.S. Mint is meticulous in its workmanship, and quality is inherent in its final products. Beyond that, the Mint treats its dies in ways that counterfeiters do not, imparting characteristics that counterfeiters find difficult to reproduce.

What are the characteristics authenticators look for?

The quality of the lettering, digits, and devices. On most U.S. coins, authenticators look for the letters, digits, and devices to erupt from the surface squarely in a sharp, defined manner. The tops of digits and letters must also be sharp and precise. Obviously there have been a few U.S. coin designs that were not sharp in nature, so authentication for these coins can be more difficult. However, for most U.S. coins, this standard can be applied.

Luster. While it might seem more important in grading a coin, luster is a factor in authentication as well. Typically, genuine U.S. coins have contrast between the fields and devices, attributable to the way coins are struck: the fields are essentially squeezed outward toward the edge, metal for the devices fills the dies, and the metallurgical flow results in contrast. For whatever reason—die preparation, striking pressure, or the types of

planchets used—counterfeiters tend to produce coins with uniform luster, which gives them a distinctive "look" that experienced authenticators immediately recognize.

Die characteristics. Most dies used by the U.S. Mint have been polished at one time or another or have developed cracks, clash marks, bulges, or other defects through use. While many counterfeiters see these defects as being detrimental, authenticators view them as clues to a genuine coin. Being able to recognize fine die-polish lines, small die cracks, or sharp die clashes makes it easier to separate the wheat—the genuine coin—from the chaff. Authenticators like to look into the most protected areas of a coin in search of the sharp, crisp, well-defined die polish marks. In the counterfeiter's attempt to reproduce coins, this slight but crucial evidence is almost always lost in the transfer. For this reason, it is one of the most useful tools in authentication. Additionally, die lines and die cracks are key diagnostics in identifying genuine dies.

The edge. This "third side" of a coin often is overlooked, yet it can yield vital evidence. The edge can tell the authenticator many things about the coin. It can aid in determining whether or not the coin was struck; it can help identify certain alterations; and it can help identify genuine diagnostics on the collars of certain coins, most notably Indian Head eagles and Saint-Gaudens double eagles.

Knowledge of date punches and mint marks. Perhaps the greatest single weapon in the authenticator's arsenal is knowledge of the

Quality of Lettering
Close-up of 1890 quarter eagle reverse, with sharp lettering.
Genuine *coins have well-formed lettering and numerals.*
Note how the lettering and numerals are crisp, sharp, and
fully detailed.

Die Characteristics
Massive die cracks on a very high-grade, well-struck 1796
Draped Bust dime. Strike is not always adversely affected
by die cracks, as this coin plainly exhibits.

Close-up of the RTY *of* LIBERTY *with die polish. Criss-cross*
lines are the results of the basining of the dies-more com-
monly called polishing. Although striking obliterates much
die polish, deeply recessed areas often retain these lines
through the life of the die. These lines are used by special-
ists to identify specific dies.

The Edge
Close-up of Indian Head eagle with tooling marks between
the stars on the edge. "Stock edge" found on many ***coun-***
terfeit *$10 Indians.*

Date Punches
Genuine *1856 Flying Eagle cent. Note how the ball of the*
"5" is chipped, flat instead of round. Also note that the ball
of the "5" is bisected by the front edge of the digit.

punches that were used in the production of genuine U.S. coins. This is particularly true for coins that are commonly altered. When you know the style of the date or mint-mark punch used for the genuine coin, you will become immediately suspicious of any coin that deviates from that style.

Weight and specific gravity. These tests are the least useful authentication tools for the vast majority of U.S. coins. Unfortunately, counterfeiters often use planchets of proper weight and fineness for their copies. Weight and specific gravity do become useful in checking the authenticity of many colonial coins, as well as some early U.S. coinage. For most other U.S. coins, however, these will not provide telling evidence.

The Specialist
Any individual who specializes in a given subject tends to know more about it than anyone else. This is certainly true with numismatics. Specialists not only know their particular field of interest inside and out, but also are quite proficient, as a rule, at detecting counterfeit and altered coins within their series.

References greatly contribute to the specialist's ability to identify forgeries. Reference books about early U.S. coins, for example, are a wonderful source of information, especially where they pertain to methods of manufacture and die varieties. Because of the typically low mintages of early U.S. coins, fewer dies were needed for their production. When the number of dies is known, the characteristics of those dies can be described and permanently recorded in a reference book. Knowledge of these dies and the characteristics they possess then will go far toward helping verify a coin's authenticity.

Even for someone who is not a specialist, merely having access to the many fine reference books currently available is a great advantage in coin authentication and attribution.

Inevitably, the counterfeiter will eventually create a coin that has the fundamental die characteristics described in the many references. There is always something, however, that the counterfeiter cannot reproduce from the genuine coin, which is why knowledge of microscopic details is so vital.

As we examine each series, we will see how the features of genuine coins compare and contrast with those of common counterfeits and alterations. In the end, experience will be the greatest teacher. Only after viewing thousands of coins can one become truly proficient at authentication.

Counterfeits by Series
In the colonial series, counterfeits have been seen for virtually every series. The counterfeit issues most commonly seen at PCGS and the styles in which they are found include:

Bermuda coinage—Cast copies

New England coinage—Cast copies

Higley's coppers—Cast copies

Continental dollars—Cast copies

Bar cents—Cast copies

With regular-issue coinage, counterfeits are many and varied. Let's explore each series and define the types of counterfeits encountered.

Half Cents

Weight:	1793–1795	6.74 grams
	1795–1857	5.44 grams
Composition:	1793–1857	100% copper
Specific Gravity:	1793–1857	8.92

Issues Affected:

1793—Electrotype

1811—High-grade cast copies

1831—Alterations of the date

1835—Transfer die copies

1840–49—Electrotype Proofs

The first place to look when authenticating half cents, as with most U.S. coinage, is reference books. In this particular case, the fine works of Walter Breen and Roger Cohen will aid in identifying the dies that struck these coins and the characteristics of those dies.

Counterfeits by Series

Genuine 1785 Bar Cent. The off-center strike is fairly common.

*Close-up of **genuine** 1785 Bar Cent. Notice how the "U" is under the "S" and the "S" is under the "A."*

*Close-up of **genuine** 1785 Bar Cent. Notice the die crack through the bar that is present on all **genuine** specimens.*

Half Cents

*"Bay Area" **counterfeit** 1835 half cent obverse.*

*"Bay Area" **counterfeit** 1835 half cent reverse.*

As a general rule, counterfeit and altered coins are not too abundant in this series; however, there are just enough to warrant discussion. Of particular interest are the electrotype counterfeits of the Proof-only half cents of 1840–1849. These are found in both the "original" and "restrike" versions. Electrotypes are direct copies and will contain general die characteristics such as date placement, letter placement, and so on. For this reason, reference books will not necessarily assist in determining authenticity in this instance. Instead, the tip-off will be the edge of the coin. Genuine half cents dated after 1797 have a flat, smooth edge, and the edge is even more fully defined beginning in 1836, when steam-powered coin production began at the U.S. Mint. With electrotypes, the edge represents the meeting place where two halves were joined, and so will display a seam or line along the circumference of the coin. Additionally, genuine coins will "ring" when tapped lightly with a pen or pencil while balanced on the tip of a finger. Electrotypes emit a dull thud, because these coins are not solid metal throughout.

The only half cent seen with a significant number of alterations is the 1831. Typically, these are 1834 cents altered by removing the diagonal and horizontal shafts of the "4," and these are easily detected.

The trickiest fakes in this series are the "Bay Area" counterfeits, named for the San Francisco area where they were first discovered. One known date for these is 1835, though others may exist. These deceptive pieces can be extremely difficult to detect, as they match the listed die variations. They are struck copies, thus not as easy to detect as electrotypes. Upon examination, very few repeating depressions of the kind so common on other counterfeits will be found. The real key to detecting them lies in their texture and coloration. Almost all of the Bay Area counterfeits have a very light, satiny and grainy finish. The color is usually tan-brown, with very little variation. While the numerals or letters may be slightly rounded, that in itself is not enough to truly condemn a piece.

Bay Area counterfeits have sharply formed letters and digits. The point where the letters, digits, and devices meet the field is sharp-edged and crisp. Extremely fine die polish can be found on genuine half cents. Refer to Cohen's book for notations on certain die lines that may be mentioned and can be useful in identifying genuine coins. Keep in mind, however, that the very faintest die lines are the most useful, as these are the most difficult to replicate.

Likelihood of non-genuine appearance: Average

Large Cents

Weight:	1793–1795	13.48 grams
	1795–1857	10.89 grams
Composition:	1793–1857	100% copper
Specific Gravity:	1793–1857	8.92

Issues Affected:

1793 Chain

AMERI. variety—Electrotype, one recent alteration from AMERICA

AMERICA variety—Electrotype

1793 Wreath—Electrotype

1799—Alterations from 1798, electrotype

1804—Electrotype, cast copies, alterations from other dates

1805—Recent transfer die copies

1851/81—Transfer die copies

1852—Transfer die copies

1853—Transfer die copies

The finest reference for early large cents for many years was unquestionably Dr. William H. Sheldon's *Penny Whimsy*. Recently, two new references have replaced this masterpiece and both have great photographs and new information. Published eight years after his death, *Walter Breen's Encyclopedia of Early United States Cents 1793-1814* is an excellent treatise on the subject with much of the final work done by Del Bland with Mark Borckardt serving as editor. Also, William C. Noyes' *United States Large Cents 1793-1814* is a superb reference book. These books thoroughly cover the die characteristics (both the Breen and Noyes works have utilized im-

Large Cents
Altered *1793 Chain cent obverse. The front is not altered.*

Altered *1793 Chain cent reverse. Remnants of the CA of AMERICA are slightly visible.*

Altered *1793 Chain cent. The CA of AMERICA is removed and replaced with a period to simulate the AMERI variety, which is more scarce.*

provements in the field of photography and have incredible pictures of every variety) needed to determine the authenticity of several frequently altered coins, most notably the rare 1799 cent. As a rule, this alteration will be created by changing the date on a 1798 cent. Since only two obverse and three reverse dies were used to strike 1799 cents, any example not matching the characteristics of one of these dies should immediately be viewed as being suspicious. Absolute confirmation of the alteration can be achieved by matching it to a 1798 die variety.

Counterfeits of 1793 large cents usually will be electrotypes or casts. These can often be exposed by inspecting the edge for a seam, or by weighing the coins. In many cases, electrotypes and cast pieces will be either too heavy or too light.

Like half cents, large cents typically have sharply formed letters and digits, and the junctions where the fields meet the letters, digits, and devices are sharp and crisp. Also like half cents, most large cents have fine die polish useful in identifying genuine coins. Keep in mind, though, that altered coins will exhibit these qualities as well, since they were genuine coins to begin with.

One interesting alteration recently seen, but certainly not widespread, is a 1793 Chain cent with the AMERI. variety altered from the 1793 AMERICA variety. PCGS encountered one piece where the CA of AMERICA was removed and a period was added, thus creating the AMERI. variety.

Like half cents, the "big sister" large cents have their share of Bay Area counterfeits.

Large Cents
*"Bay Area" **counterfeit** 1853 large cent obverse.*

*"Bay Area" **counterfeit** 1853 large cent reverse.*

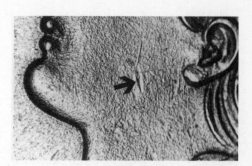

*Close-up of "Bay Area" **counterfeit** 1853 large cent. Notice the doubling effect on the date.*

*Close-up of "Bay Area" **counterfeit** 1853 large cent. Arrow points to repeating depression on cheek.*

These can be extremely difficult to detect because of the low number the counterfeiter seems to produce.

One such piece, the 1853 Bay Area counterfeit, displays some telltale features that absolutely are not found on genuine pieces. One is the unusual doubling in the date. The definitive diagnostic, however, is the repeating depression found on the jaw of Miss Liberty.

Likelihood of non-genuine appearance:
Below Average

Small Cents
Flying Eagle

Weight:	1856–1858	4.67 grams
Composition:	1856–1858	88% copper, 12% nickel
Specific Gravity:	1856–1858	8.92

Issues Affected:

1856—Alterations from 1858, spark-erosion die copies

1857—Spark-erosion copies

1858—Spark-erosion copies

With the start of the small cents, counterfeits and altered coins became more prevalent. In fact, the very first small cent—the 1856 Flying Eagle—is one of the most frequently forged. Knowledge of the genuine coin will enable you to easily discern the real thing from the typical fake.

Clues to identification of the genuine 1856 Flying Eagle cent include:

1. Note the digits. The ball of the "5" of the date is not completely round but in fact looks chipped or partial. Also, if a line was contin-

Small Cents—Flying Eagle
Genuine 1856 Flying Eagle cent obverse.

Genuine 1856 Flying Eagle cent reverse.

Close-up of genuine 1856 Flying Eagle cent obverse. Note the date with the defect on the ball of the "5" (flat area); the front edge of the "5" bisects the ball.

Close-up of genuine 1856 Flying Eagle cent obverse. Note the positioning of the A and the M of AMERICA.

Close-up of genuine 1856 Flying Eagle cent obverse. The inside of the O of OF is rectangular. On most 1857-8 coins, this is "D"-shaped.

Altered 1856 Flying Eagle cent (altered from genuine 1858).

Small Cents—Flying Eagle
*Close-up of **altered** 1856 Flying Eagle cent obverse (altered from genuine 1858). Note how the front line of "5" is in line with the front of the ball. Note how the ball is completely round.*

*Close-up of **altered** 1856 Flying Eagle cent obverse (altered from genuine 1858). Note how the A and M run together.*

ued down the back serif of the "5," it would split the defective ball in two.

2. The A and M of AMERICA do not quite touch, and the bases of these letters actually come together at an angle. When these are compared to 1857 cents or 1858 cents with either large or small letters, it becomes apparent that they were punched differently.

3. The O of OF is not actually round on the inside, but almost rectangular.

Most forgeries of this date are altered from 1858 Flying Eagle cents. The 1858 cents exhibit none of the characteristics cited here.

Likelihood of non-genuine appearance:
Above Average

Indian Head

Weight:	1859–1864	4.66 grams
	1864–1909	3.11 grams
Composition:	1859–1864	88% copper, 12% nickel
	1864–1909	95% copper, 5% tin and zinc
Specific Gravity:	1859–1864	8.92
	1864–1909	8.84

Issues Affected:

Various dates (rarer 1860s and 1870s)—Transfer die copies, spark-erosion die copies

1877—Alterations from other dates, transfer die copies

1909-S—Alterations via added mint mark, transfer die copies

Because of their generally low mintages, bronze Indian cents from 1864–1877 have been counterfeited with what are believed to be transfer dies. Very few examples of each date are ever seen.

Several of the rarer dates in the 1860s and 1870s are sometimes seen on counterfeits struck from spark-erosion dies. These are distinguished by the bubbles of metal on their surfaces—tiny lumps that result from the process by which the dies are created.

Genuine Indian cents exhibit the same sharp, crisp qualities as genuine half cents and large cents. The digits, letters, and devices all meet the fields at sharp, clear angles. Die polish can be found in the devices and fields of many of these coins, and the tops of the letters and digits show sharp angles and corners. These characteristics are important in distinguishing between genuine coins and the notorious Bay Area counterfeits. These fakes will display more rounded letters, digits, and devices. In addition, the Bay Area pieces fail

Small Cents—Indian Head
*Spark erosion **counterfeit** 1869 Indian Head cent obverse.*

*Spark erosion **counterfeit** 1869 Indian Head cent reverse.*

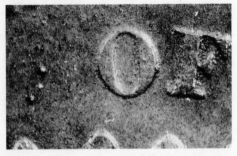

*Close-up of spark erosion **counterfeit** 1869 Indian Head cent obverse. Lumps in the field near OF are typical of a spark erosion counterfeit.*

to display sharp junctions where the letters and digits meet the fields.

The genuine characteristics of the two most commonly forged Indian cents, the 1877 and the 1909-S, are especially important to note.

An abnormality on the reverse of the 1877 cent helps determine its authenticity. Here are some guidelines:

1. Note the 7's in the date. On both the Proof and business strike, the 7's have a distinct style. The bottom of the second 7 is not actually rounded but exhibits an almost straight line on the left side.

2. On the reverse, the Ns of ONE and CENT and the E of CENT show weakness. This is a die flaw, not a weakness of strike, and it occurs on all of the business-strikes. The Proofs were struck from dies with normal, strong letters in ONE CENT.

Alterations from other business-strike issues almost always display strong letters in ONE CENT. Any business-strike 1877 cent seen with strong letters is an alteration. Struck counterfeits usually are crude and have roundedness in the letters, digits, and devices. In addition, many exhibit unusual lumps of metal on the surfaces, which are not associated with genuine coins.

The most important feature of the 1909-S Indian cent is the mint mark. Pay careful attention to the shape and style of the "S." Any deviation from the normal shape and style is indicative of an alteration.

Small Cents—Indian Head

*Close-up of **genuine** 1877 Indian Head cent obverse. The diagnostic die crack through the date is seen.*

*Close-up of **genuine** 1877 Indian Head cent obverse. Note the angular features at the base of 7's in the date.*

Genuine 1877 (business-strike) Indian Head cent obverse.

Genuine 1877 (business-strike) Indian Head cent reverse. Note the weakness on the N's and the E.

Struck counterfeits also exist for the 1909-S Indian cent. On the most common of these, unusual "spikes"—the products of a counterfeiter's gouges—extend from the rim into the field. The most noticeable one extends from the rim toward the mint mark; do not confuse this coin with a genuine piece based solely on the correct mint mark shape. As with most counterfeits, this fake will exhibit rounded features on the digits and letters.

Likelihood of non-genuine appearance: Below Average

Lincoln Head

Weight:	1909–1942	3.11 grams
	1943	2.69/2.75 grams
	1944–1982	3.11 grams
	1982–present	2.50 grams
Composition:	1909–1942	95% copper, 5% tin and zinc
	1943	Zinc-coated steel
	1944–1946	95% copper, 5% zinc
	1947–1962	95% copper, 5% tin and zinc
	1962–1982	95% copper, 5% zinc
	1982–present	97.5% zinc, 2.5% copper (pure copper plated to a core that is 99.2% zinc, 0.8% copper)

Small Cents—Indian Head
Altered 1877 Indian Head cent obverse.

Altered 1877 Indian Head cent reverse.

*Close-up of **altered** 1877 Indian Head cent reverse. Note the strong N's and E.*

*Close-up of **genuine** 1909-S Indian Head cent reverse. Note the open style of the S mint mark.*

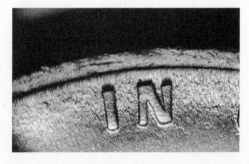

Small Cents—Lincoln
*Close-up of struck **counterfeit** 1909-S Lincoln cent obverse. Note the depression on the rim above the E of WE.*

*Close-up of struck **counterfeit** 1909-S Lincoln cent obverse. Note the depressed line along the rim above the I of IN.*

Small Cents—Lincoln

*Close-up of struck **counterfeit** 1909-S Lincoln cent reverse. Arrows point to repeating depressions through the top and bottom of O in ONE. This reverse also was used on some fake 1914-D cents.*

*Close-up of **altered** 1909-S VDB Lincoln cent obverse. Note the added "S."*

Specific Gravity:	1909–1942	8.84
	1943	7.80
	1944–1946	8.86
	1947–1962	8.84
	1962–1982	8.86
	1982–present	7.17

Issues Affected:

1909-S—Alterations via added mint mark, transfer die copies

1909-S VDB—Alterations via added mint mark, added VDB; transfer die copies

1914-D—Alterations via added mint mark, altered date

1922 "no-D"—Alterations via removed mint mark

1955 Doubled Die—Transfer die copies

1972 Doubled Die—Transfer die copies

Due to the number of valuable varieties and key dates in the Lincoln cent series, more counterfeit and altered coins will be seen. Because these rarities were produced with so few dies, the genuine characteristics are relatively easy to remember and recognize.

Five of these coins are the most frequently altered or counterfeited, with the predominant fake being the 1909-S VDB cent. With the following diagnostics, this coin plus the 1914-D, 1922 "no-D," 1955 Doubled-Die,

and 1972 Doubled-Die cents, easily can be identified as authentic.

1909-S VDB Cent

1. Identification of the mint mark. All 1909-S VDB cents were struck with the same shape and style mint mark. It is a very square, box-like "S" that contains a notch in the upper serif and a raised "dot" or lump in the upper loop.

2. The shape and style of the letters VDB (the initials of designer Victor D. Brenner) also are important. The "D" and "B" have a distinct shape: the lower portion of the "D" slopes at an angle, and the middle stroke of the "B" also slants at an angle.

3. Four dies were used to strike 1909-S VDB cents. The coins were struck with the mint mark in four slightly different positions below the date. Knowledge of these positions is important in weeding out several alterations.

4. Odd die characteristics seen on genuine coins include a short, raised die gouge protruding from the rim above the RU of TRUST in the obverse legend; a die chip in the B of LIBERTY; and raised die gouges extending from the left wheat sheaf into the field.

Small Cents—Lincoln
Genuine 1909-S VDB Lincoln cent obverse.

Genuine 1909-S VDB Lincoln cent reverse.

Close-up of **genuine** 1909-S VDB Lincoln cent date and mint mark. Note the square, boxy mint mark, the notch in the upper serif and the die chip in the upper loop of the "S."

Close-up of **altered** 1909-S VDB Lincoln cent. Note the added S.

A lack of these diagnostics does not condemn these coins; they occurred to the dies during production and thus appear on only some of the coins. They were not necessarily present on the dies from the start—but when they do appear, they go a long way toward confirming a coin's authenticity.

The most common alteration seen on this date displays a poorly shaped mint mark.

1914-D Cent

Compared with the 1909-S VDB cent, the 1914-D is seen less frequently either altered or counterfeit. On the genuine coin, the mint mark is decidedly angular. Its top and bottom are straight—and where it begins its outer right curve, the "D" appears to turn a corner, rather than being rounded. The inside of the "D" is also made up of angles. The

interior is almost a triangle, rather than being rounded throughout. Common alterations fail to reproduce the stylized mint mark correctly.

A few struck counterfeits exist, but these generally lack the sharp, crisp features that should be seen in the digits, letters, and devices. One semi-prooflike counterfeit does show up from time to time, with very sharp detail and lettering, as well as square, prooflike edges. The genuine 1914-D cent does not have the initials VDB on the edge of Lincoln's shoulder. These were not added until 1918, and are present on some alterations.

1922 "no-D" Cent

This coin, the product of overused dies, is notorious for its weakness of strike. Ironically,

Small Cents—Lincoln
*Close-up of **genuine** 1909-S VDB reverse. Note the shape of VDB-the curve of the "D" angles toward the base. The mid-section of the "B" is angled, not horizontal.*

***Altered** 1909-S VDB Lincoln cent obverse. Note the added "S."*

***Altered** 1909-S VDB Lincoln cent reverse.*

*Close-up of **genuine** 1909-S VDB Lincoln cent obverse. Note the die gouge from the rim above and between the RU of TRUST.*

*Close-up of **genuine** 1909-S VDB Lincoln cent obverse. Note the die chip in the B of LIBERTY.*

Small Cents—Lincoln
*Close-up of **genuine** 1914-D Lincoln cent obverse. The mint mark is boxy and the interior of the "D" is triangular.*

*Close-up of **genuine** 1914-D Lincoln cent obverse. There is a die crack connecting the bust to the rim.*

*Close-up of **altered** 1914-D Lincoln cent obverse. Note the added mint mark and the wrong style mint mark, with the "rough" area surrounding it.*

this overall lack of detail on the genuine coin is precisely what makes most altered coins so easy to detect.

PCGS currently recognizes four varying degrees of the 1922-D and no-D cent and its worn die states, including:

- The base 1922-D cent. This coin has a full, discernible mint mark.

- The 1922-D cent with a weak D. This coin will show a faint trace of the mint mark. Regardless of grade, PCGS will designate a coin as a "Weak-D" if the mint mark can be detected.

- The 1922-D no-D cent, weak reverse. This coin must show no trace of a mint mark. Also, the reverse will have been struck from a weak and overused reverse die. This worn

die state, unfortunately, resulted in a most confusing coin. In all of numismatics, few coins are subjective in nature when it comes to attribution—this coin is one of those issues, because this die combination is also seen with the "weak-D" obverse, sometimes in a later die state than the "no-D" strikings. Distinguishing the no-D coin from a weak-D example can sometimes be difficult. Therefore, PCGS demands that no trace of a mint mark be visible when describing a cent as a 1922 No-D, Weak Reverse.

- The 1922 no-D cent, strong reverse. This variety is the most sought-after and the easiest to identify. There will be no trace of a mint mark and the reverse will be strong, since the die was replaced at the time with a new, fresh die. Pay close attention to details on the obverse. The second "2" in the date will be

Small Cents—Lincoln
Close-up of **genuine** *1922-D Lincoln cent obverse. Note the normal mint mark.*

Genuine 1922-D *Lincoln cent obverse, weak "D" variety.*

Genuine 1922-D *Lincoln cent obverse, no "D," weak reverse variety.*

Genuine 1922-D *Lincoln cent obverse and reverse. No "D" strong reverse variety.*

Small Cents—Lincoln

Close-up of **genuine** 1922-D Lincoln cent obverse. No "D" strong reverse variety. Notice how the last "2" is stronger than the first three digits.

Close-up of **genuine** 1922-D Lincoln cent obverse. No "D" strong reverse variety. In the motto, notice that TRUST is stronger than IN GOD WE.

Genuine 1955 Doubled-Die Lincoln cent obverse.

Genuine 1955 Doubled-Die Lincoln cent reverse.

Close-up of **genuine** 1955 Doubled-Die Lincoln cent reverse. Note the die polish line to the left of the vertical shaft of the T in CENT.

Close-up of **genuine** 1972 Doubled Die Lincoln cent obverse. Note the gouge above the D of UNITED.

stronger than the rest of the digits. Likewise, the word TRUST will be stronger than the words IN GOD WE.

Should any purported weak-D or no-D coin be offered that has strong letters throughout all of the obverse legends, be wary of a possible alteration. While not exceptionally common, there also are alterations where the mint mark has been removed.

When a counterfeiter needs to remove a mint mark from a regular 1922-D cent, he or she has no choice but to use a coin that displays too much detail and too much strength. In other words, the coin being used for the alteration was struck from a set of dies too new to have produced a typical no-D example. The end result is a coin that looks too good—whose detail is impossible to find for this issue.

1955 Doubled-Die Cent

Fake versions of this coin are relatively easy to detect, as just one pair of dies was used to strike the genuine 1955 Doubled-Die cent.

Certain characteristics pertain to only the genuine coin. One diagnostic, in particular, is all one needs to check to establish whether a coin is genuine. This diagnostic is a faint pair of raised die-polish lines extending downward from the top of the T in CENT. The lines are to the left of the vertical shaft of the T. If it has this, it is good. If not, it is bad.

To see these lines adequately, it is recommended that the coin be turned perpendicular to a light source and viewed with a magnifier of at least 5X. The light will help create a shadowing of the lines so they become more apparent.

These die lines are well protected because they are so close to the letter; for that reason, they appear in grades as low as Good or Very Good.

1972 Doubled-Die Cent

This coin, the least forged of all the Lincoln cents in this discussion, is easily identified by a single diagnostic located on its reverse. Protruding from the rim toward the D of UNITED is a short, sharp die gouge. This is seen on all genuine 1972 Doubled-Die cents of the Type 1 (or prominent) variety.

The creator of one fake tried to reproduce this gouge but went too far, leaving too lengthy a spike.

Likelihood of non-genuine appearance: Above Average

Two-Cent Pieces

Weight:	1864–1873	6.22 grams
Composition:	1864–1873	95% copper, 5% tin and zinc
Specific Gravity:	1864–1873	8.84

Issues Affected:

1873 open-3 variety—Spark erosion dies

This series is rarely, if ever, seen counterfeited. Like most U.S. coins, the two-cent piece is found with sharp, squared-off letters and digits. The devices rise from the field in a distinct, crisp fashion.

One fake that does turn up is an 1873 two-cent piece struck from spark-erosion dies. Keep in mind that spark-erosion dies are easy to detect because of the many lumps on the surface of a coin produced with this process. The edge is extremely sharp, although this may not be conclusive, as the coin being replicated is a Proof.

Likelihood of non-genuine appearance: Low

Three Cents (Nickel)

Weight:	1865–1889	1.94 grams
Composition:	1865–1889	75% copper, 25% nickel
Specific Gravity:	1865–1889	8.92

Issues Affected:

Various dates—Contemporary counterfeits

This series, like the two-cent series, is rarely counterfeited. Any counterfeits seen are contemporary, being struck from easily de-

Three Cents (Silver)
*Contemporary **counterfeit** 1861 three-cent silver obverse. Note the crude shield, star, and lettering.*

*Contemporary **counterfeit** 1861 three-cent silver reverse. This counterfeiter would have to produce quite a few of these coins to make his or her operation profitable, though they were easily passed. These are very small coins, probably given only a cursory glance since this was not a lot of money, even in 1861.*

tectable hand-cut dies. The letters, digits, and devices do not match the style or quality of those on the genuine coin.

Genuine coins of this series display sharp, crisp lettering and digits. As on most U.S. coins, all of the raised devices erupt squarely from the fields, and the tops of the letters and digits are squared off.

Likelihood of non-genuine appearance: Low

Three Cents (Silver)

Weight:	1851–1853	.80 gram
	1854–1873	.75 gram
Composition:	1851–1853	75% silver, 25% copper
	1854–1873	90% silver, 10% copper
Specific Gravity:	1851–1853	10.11
	1854–1873	10.34

Issues Affected:

1861—Contemporary counterfeits

1864—Transfer die copies in "Proof" and Mint State formats

A few contemporary forgeries can be found for the 1861 three-cent silver and several other dates. These pieces are easily identified as they were struck from hand-cut dies. Due to the method of manufacture, the design el-

ements, letters, and digits are noticeably different from those on the genuine article.

This series, like the two-cent and three-cent nickel series, is rarely counterfeited. Only one deceptive fake has been seen to date—the 1864 Proof. Keep in mind that this piece is rarely encountered. The three-cent silver series has many of the attributes of other U.S. coins, and the lack of typical sharpness on the fake 1864 makes it easy to spot as a forgery.

Likelihood of non-genuine appearance: Low

Five Cents

Weight:	1866–present:	5.00 grams
Composition:	1866–1942	75% copper, 25% nickel
	1942–1945	56% copper, 35% silver, 9% manganese
	1946–present	75% copper, 25% nickel
Specific Gravity:	1866–1942	8.92
	1942–1945	9.25
	1946–present	8.92

Shield

Issues Affected:

Various dates—Contemporary counterfeits

Five Cents
Genuine 1912-S Liberty Head nickel obverse and reverse.

In this series, as with the three-cent series, very few counterfeits exist. The few that do are contemporary in origin and can be distinguished quite easily from the real thing.

Contemporary forgeries seen to date include the 1875 Shield nickel. This piece was made at a time when fake coins were meant to be something to spend and nothing more—the intent was to defraud a merchant, not a numismatist.

In making this fake nickel, the counterfeiter started by hand-cutting a set of dies. A planchet (or, most likely, a group of planchets) came next, usually composed of whatever base metals were handy. After striking the "coins," the counterfeiter had little trouble passing them off as genuine, as they were intended strictly for spending and most people would not have given them more than a cursory glance. Close inspection shows crude work that is not deceptive.

Likelihood of non-genuine appearance: Low

Liberty Head or "V"
Issues Affected:
1912-S—Alterations via added mint mark
1913–Alterations of the date

This series is rarely counterfeited. Perhaps the most popularly forged piece is the easily detected 1913 "V" nickel. Nearly all of the fakes seen for this date have been altered, usually by changing a 1910 to a 1913. There are a few contemporary counterfeits of common dates.

More deceptive alterations include the 1885 and the 1912-S. The 1885 is rarely encountered, while the 1912-S is slightly more plentiful. The genuine 1912-S nickel was made with the same mint-mark punch as the 1909-S VDB cent, which means the mint mark should be square and boxy, with a notch in the upper serif and a lump in the upper loop.

Almost all of the alterations commonly encountered show the mint mark with a rounded style and serifs that are angled, rather than squared off.

Likelihood of non-genuine appearance: Low

Indian Head or "Buffalo"
Issues Affected:
1913-S Type 1—Alterations via added mint mark

1913-D Type 2—Alterations via added mint mark

1913-S Type 2—Alterations via added mint mark

Most Denver and San Francisco issues in the teens and twenties—Added mint mark

1937-D "Three-Legged"—Alteration from regular 1937-D

Most Buffalo nickels from 1918 through 1927 have been seen at one time or another with added or embossed mint marks. While these are not necessarily prevalent, one must be aware of them, as the value of P-mint nickels from these years could be enhanced substantially, in most cases, simply by adding or embossing a mint mark.

Strangely, the author has seen no counterfeit 1916 Doubled-Die Buffalo nickels and relatively few altered 1937-D Three-Legged pieces.

The Buffalo nickel represents the greatest challenge in counterfeit detection within the entire realm of U.S. nickel coinage. Because there are so many rare dates, alterations abound. Fakes run the gamut from simple added mint marks on coins dated 1913 to 1927 to removal of a leg on 1937-D pieces. Knowledge of the genuine coins will go a long way toward helping one separate these from the fakes.

Coins with embossed mint marks victimize many collectors. This process involves drilling out the edge of a coin, sliding in an embossing tool in the shape of the desired mint mark, embossing the mint mark, filling the void or hole in the coin with metal, then smoothing off the edge. Many times, coins with embossed mint marks are sold in holders that do not allow the buyer to view the edge. If a coin is not certified, always ask to see the edge of any rare-date Buffalo nickel.

Of course, there are some alterations where the mint mark is affixed with epoxy or fused to the surface by heat. These can be exposed by looking for a seam between the mint mark and the field of the coin. A seam confirms that the two do not belong together.

Knowing the shapes and styles of the genuine mint marks will make it much easier to spot fakes. When studying a mint-marked Buffalo nickel, make sure the shape and size of the "D" or "S" correspond to the following:

1913–1917—Note that the mint-mark punches are the same ones are used for the 1909-S VDB cent and 1916-D dime.

1917-mid to late '20s—Mint mark is not as boxy in appearance and is taller and thinner, more stylized. "D" now has oval interior.

Other Key Dates
1918/7-D Nickel
A genuine 1918/7-D Buffalo nickel is easily identified because its characteristics are so distinctive. Notice how the 7 is formed through the 8 in the date. The overdate is actually the result of a doubled die. An unused 1917 die was reimpressed with a 1918 hub, resulting in the overdate. Look at the junction of the hair and braid at the back of the jaw. About 75 percent of the time, a die crack can be seen extending from this point toward the Indian's mouth. This diagnostic will appear even in the lowest grades. Next, look at the mint-mark area. Be sure the right edge of the E in FIVE lines up with the left edge of the mint mark. This positioning is diagnostic of the overdate. Finally, inspect the designer's initial F on the obverse. The field around the F is defective: the forward portion of the upper serif is depressed, sometimes giving it the appearance of a P. This little "blip" can be useful in determining authenticity.

1937-D Three-legged Nickel
This coin, not widely altered, has diagnostics that make a genuine coin easy to identify. Obviously, the first characteristic is the missing foreleg. What is important, however, is that on the genuine coin the hoof is still present. This error occurred due to polishing of an overworked, clashed die.

Other diagnostics of this coin include an eroded, moth-eaten appearance in the bison's hind leg and a similar appearance on the back of the Indian's neck. There also should be a series of lumps throughout the field of the reverse, which extend from the upper portion of the forward hind leg, then curve downward to the ground. Commonly referred to by an unflattering name, this char-

Five Cents—Liberty Head
*Close-up of **genuine** 1912-S Liberty Head nickel reverse, square, block style "S" mint mark. Note that it is the same mint-mark punch used on the 1909-S VDB Lincoln cent. Also note the die crack emerging from the rim into the field below the mint mark.*

Five Cents—Buffalo Nickel
***Altered** 1926-D Buffalo nickel obverse and reverse.*

*Close-up of **altered** 1926-D Buffalo nickel reverse with embossed mint mark.*

*Close-up of **altered** 1926-D Buffalo nickel edge. Note the edge area through which the embossed mint mark was added.*

Five Cents—Buffalo Nickel
Genuine 1918/7-D Buffalo nickel obverse and reverse.

*Close-up of **genuine** 1918/7-D Buffalo nickel obverse. Note the 7 through the 8. The right side of the upper loop and the left side of the lower loop of the 8 are filled by the 7. Also note the designer's initial, F, has a filled appearance, making it look like a P.*

*Close-up of **genuine** 1918/7-D Buffalo nickel obverse. The die crack extends into the jaw from the juncture of the hair and braid.*

*Close-up of **genuine** 1918/7-D Buffalo nickel reverse. The left side of the "D" is in line with the right side of the E of FIVE.*

Five Cents—Buffalo Nickel
*Close-up of **genuine** 1937-D Three-Legged Buffalo nickel reverse and obverse. Note the moth-eaten appearance of the back leg and neck.*

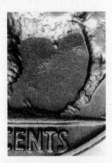

*Close-up of **genuine** 1937-D Three-Legged Buffalo nickel reverse. Note the raised die marks extending down from the bison's belly through the field between the legs.*

*Close-up of **genuine** 1937-D Three-Legged Buffalo nickel reverse. Note the missing front leg, removed by excessive die polishing. Also note that the hoof of the missing leg is still present.*

acteristic is a key to identifying the genuine coin.

Likelihood of non-genuine appearance: Average

Jefferson

Issues Affected:

Various dates—Contemporary counterfeits

1944—Contemporary counterfeit

Jefferson nickel forgeries seldom are seen, due in large part, no doubt, to the generally low premium value of coins from this series. Classic counterfeits do exist, however, for one Jefferson nickel that was never produced by the U.S. Mint—the 1944 Jefferson. Notice that it is not described as the 1944-P.

As the story goes, around 1950 a counterfeiter from New Jersey began producing Jef-

ferson nickels of several dates from 1939 through the late 1940s. He was doing well until he produced a 1944 nickel with no mint mark. At that time, the Mint was making nickels from a special wartime alloy and calling attention to this with a large mint mark above Monticello on each coin, including a large "P" on nickels produced in Philadelphia (which normally would not have carried a mint mark at all). Since the U.S. Mint never produced a "plain" 1944 nickel, the detection process is quite easy. Beyond this, however, there is one key diagnostic that identifies this fake, which happens to be found on other counterfeit Jefferson nickels as well. On 1944 fakes, a sizable hole appears in the center of the vertical upright of the R in PLURIBUS. Being cost-conscious, the counterfeiter used this same defective reverse die in making fake nickels of other dates. Any coin seen with this flaw is a counterfeit. Incidentally, this counterfeit was made to look well-worn.

Likelihood of non-genuine appearance: Low

Half Dimes

Weight:	1792–1837	1.34 grams
	1837–1853	1.35 grams
	1853–1873	1.24 grams
Composition:	1792–1837	89.2% silver, 10.8% copper
	1837–1873	90% silver, 10% copper
Specific Gravity:	1792–1837	10.32
	1837–1873	10.34

Issues Affected:

1795—Copy dies

1796—Crude transfer die copies

1802—Electrotype

1796–1873—Very scarce electrotypes exist; quite rare.

1853—Alterations via removed arrows

Half dimes have rarely been forged, the predominant counterfeit of the entire run being the 1795, a second-year issue.

Fortunately, this counterfeit is fairly crude and easy to identify. When it is viewed next to the real thing, there is no comparison. The devices, lettering, and digits of the fake are noticeably rounded. The denticles are virtually nonexistent, and several unusual raised lines and lumps are evident on the surfaces.

The 1802 half dime is rare as a genuine coin and equally rare as a counterfeit. One fake version seen of this coin is an electrotype. This slightly deceptive piece contains the telltale sign of the electrotype—a seam around the edge of the coin. Not being solid, the coin will not "ring" if it is tapped lightly with a pen or pencil.

Likelihood of non-genuine appearance: Low

Dimes

Weight:	1796–1853	2.70 grams
	1853–1873	2.49 grams
	1873–1964	2.50 grams
	1965–present	2.27 grams
Composition:	1796–1837	89.2% silver, 10.8% copper
	1837–1964	90% silver, 10% copper
	1965–present	75% copper, 25% nickel outer layers, bonded to a core of pure copper
Specific Gravity:	1796–1837	10.32
	1837–1964	10.34
	1965–present	8.92

Bust

Issues Affected:

Various dates—Electrotypes

Early U.S. dimes are fairly counterfeit-free. Occasionally an electrotype will be seen. As with fakes of other early U.S. coins, electrotype Bust dimes are detected by the edge and the lack of "ringing." After the two shells are joined, an electrotype displays a seam where the two halves were connected. And because it is not solid, the electrotype will not "ring" like a genuine coin.

Likelihood of non-genuine appearance: Low

Liberty Seated

Issues Affected:

Various dates—Contemporary counterfeits

1853—Alterations via removed arrows

1871–1874-CC—Alterations via added mint marks

1885-S—Alterations via added mint mark

Early Liberty Seated dimes are rarely found in a counterfeit state and only in the later years do alterations occur. One should be particularly wary of the rare Carson City issues of 1871–1874. Knowing the characteristics of genuine mint marks—the shape and style, in particular—helps one determine whether a coin is authentic. On one reverse die used from 1872 to 1874, there is a crack from the rim through the mint mark(s), extending to the end of the right ribbon. Knowing how to recognize coins struck with this die helps identify a genuine issue.

The 1871-CC dime can be distinguished from dimes struck at other mints by inspecting the edge. On the Carson City issue, only eighty-nine reeds were used on the collar. The Philadelphia and San Francisco pieces have more reeds on the edge, creating thinner reeds.

The rare-date 1885-S Liberty Seated dime can be authenticated readily by determining whether the "S" mint mark is the proper shape and style. In addition, one should check for a seam where the mint mark meets the field. A seam at this location would indicate that the mint mark is not part of the coin itself.

Likelihood of non-genuine appearance: Below Average

Barber
Issues Affected:
Various branch-mint issues—Alterations via added mint marks

There are several rare dates in this series, but few forgeries are encountered. Knowing the shapes and styles of genuine coins' mint marks is essential. On any suspicious piece, search for a seam where the mint mark joins the coin.

Likelihood of non-genuine appearance: Low

Winged Liberty or "Mercury"
Issues Affected:
1916-D—Alterations via added mint mark

1921—Alterations by changing date from 1941

1921-D—Alterations by changing date from 1941

Various Denver and San Francisco issues— Alterations via added mint marks

1942/1—Alterations by adding a "2" to a 1941 or adding a "1" to a 1942

1942/1-D—Alterations by adding a "2" to a 1941-D or adding a "1" to a 1942-D

1916-D Dime
Thousands of purported 1916-D Mercury dimes exist with an added "D" mint mark. You can spot them easily, however, by knowing the "look" of a genuine piece. The shape of the mint mark is crucial. On genuine pieces, the mint mark is boxy and squared off. As the curve of the "D" begins to take shape on the right side, the top and bottom are angled, not rounded. The inside of the "D" looks like a triangle. Also, the serifs of the genuine mint mark are square, not pointed. Does all of this sound familiar? It should, for the punch used here was the same one the Mint used for the 1914-D cent. Note also how the mint mark stands very tall on a genuine 1916-D dime. On many alterations, the mint mark is thin, with no height, and may have a rounded look, with pointy serifs and oval interiors.

Four reverse dies were used to strike the 1916-D dime. Two of these dies contained repunched mint marks. These can be identified by the notched effect in the upper left serif. Locating this notch is quite helpful in confirming authenticity, but since only two of the four dies had this feature, it is not essential. The Mercury dime is altered more often than any other U.S. dime.

1921 and 1921-D Dimes
The authenticity of a 1921 or 1921-D dime can be determined easily by noting the shape of the date. Since most alterations were 1941 dimes to begin with, several tip-offs can be used.

1. All genuine 1921 and 1921-D dimes have an open "9." The "9" does not touch itself. On altered coins, the "9" is closed, touching itself.

2. The base of the "2" has a slight curve, whereas altered pieces are usually flat.

1942/41 Dime
This coin, like the overdate Buffalo nickel, is the product of a doubled die. A 1941-dated die was reimpressed with a 1942-dated hub. Knowing this, it is important to look not just at the last digit in the date, but also at the third

Dimes
Altered 1916-D Mercury dime obverse and reverse. Note the added "D."

*Close-up of **genuine** 1916-D Mercury dime reverse. Note the mint-mark area and the style and shape of the mint mark.*

*Close-up of **altered** 1916-D Mercury dime reverse. Note the mint-mark area with an added "D," which is thinner and not shaped like a genuine mint mark.*

digit, the "4." On a genuine 1942/41 dime, the "4" was also reimpressed, creating a notched effect at the base of the "4." If any purported overdate lacks the notch, it is a fake.

One diagnostic that is found on all genuine 1942/41 dimes is located on the reverse; at the place where the olive branch meets the fasces, a die line will confirm this coin's authenticity.

1942/41-D Dime
The fundamental circumstances that created the overdate Philadelphia issue apply to the Denver overdate as well, but there are slight differences in the area of the date. Most important, the underlying "1" is not as apparent as on the Philadelphia issue. The key to this coin is the portion of the "1" under the left side of the "2." This "chip" of the "1" must be present. On the top left portion of the "2" is

the remnant of the serif of the "1." As with the Philadelphia issue, the "4" in the date is notched. The "D" mint mark is repunched.

Alterations are not as prevalent for this coin as they are for the Philadelphia piece.

Other Dates
Of the other scarce issues in the Mercury dime series, the 1926-S is the one most commonly altered. Knowing exactly what the mint mark should look like is the key to authenticating this piece. The mint-mark punches of that era made an "S" that is more elongated and stylized than earlier pieces mentioned in this chapter. Note that the serifs form two knobs.

On many alterations, the "S" is malformed and shows a seam where the mint mark was adhered to the surface of the coin.

Dimes
Genuine 1921-D Mercury dime obverse and reverse.

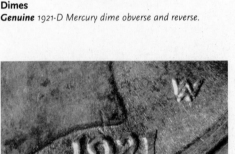

Close-up of **genuine** 1921-D Mercury dime obverse. Note the slightly curved base of the "2."

Likelihood of non-genuine appearance: Above Average

Roosevelt
Issues Affected:
1982—Alterations via removed mint mark

The only alteration seen in this series to date is a 1982 dime with the "P" removed. This crude alteration is easily detected. On the genuine coin, there are heavy die-polish lines running vertically on the reverse.

Likelihood of non-genuine appearance: Low

Twenty Cents

Weight:	1875–1878	5.00 grams
Composition:	1875–1878	90% silver, 10% copper
Specific Gravity:	1875–1878	10.34

Issues Affected:
1875—Transfer copy dies

1876—Transfer copy dies

Counterfeit twenty-cent pieces are seldom encountered, even in the case of the series' greatest rarity, the 1876-CC.

Genuine coins exhibit sharp lettering and digits and crisp angles from the fields to the letters and digits. Fine die polish can be found on the business strikes, which aids greatly in authentication.

Among the few counterfeits seen, the 1876 lacks these qualities. In addition, the forgeries have unusual lumps of extra metal in the field that do not occur on the genuine pieces. These "counterfeiter's lumps" are condemning evidence.

Dimes
Genuine 1942/1 Mercury dime obverse and reverse.

Close-up of **genuine** 1942/1 Mercury dime obverse. Note that the "4" is notched at the base. The "1" is clearly defined along the left edge of the "2."

Close-up of **genuine** 1942/1 Mercury dime reverse. The arrow points to the diagnostic die line connecting fasces to olive branch.

To date, the author has not encountered a fake 1876-CC twenty-cent coin. Since so few genuine pieces are extant, identifying a counterfeit would be relatively easy. All genuine 1876-CC coins were struck from a doubled obverse die most noticeable on LIBERTY.

Likelihood of non-genuine appearance: Low

Quarter Dollars

Weight:		
	1796–1837	6.74 grams
	1837–1853	6.68 grams
	1853–1873	6.22 grams
	1873–1964	6.25 grams
	1965–present	5.67 grams
	1976	5.75 grams (silver clad version)

Composition:		
	1796–1837	89.2% silver, 10.8% copper
	1837–1964	90% silver, 10% copper
	1965–present	75% copper, 25% nickel outer layers, bonded to a core of pure copper
	1976	40% silver, 60% copper (silver clad version)

Specific Gravity:		
	1796–1837	10.32
	1837–1964	10.34
	1965–present	8.93
	1976	9.53

Twenty Cents
Counterfeit 1876 Liberty Seated twenty-cent obverse and reverse.

*Close-up of **counterfeit** 1876 Liberty Seated twenty-cent obverse. Note the lumps in the field around the stars.*

*Close-up of **counterfeit** 1876 Liberty Seated twenty-cent obverse. Note the lumps in the field.*

Bust

Issues Affected:

1796—Transfer die copies in grade of About Good to Good

Early Bust quarters exhibit sharp details like so many of their early brothers and sisters. The devices, letters, and digits are sharp and crisp. They emerge squarely from the fields and have squared-off, flat tops. Some coins exhibit die polish as well as significant die cracks.

The forgeries, few and far between, lack many of the details just mentioned. The trickiest of the counterfeits for this series is the 1796 quarter. Its deceptiveness results from the condition of the coin chosen to be reproduced. Whereas most counterfeiters choose high-grade specimens to copy, this piece reflects a different strategy. One counterfeit 1796 quarter is in **G-VG** condition on the obverse, with an **AG** reverse. The repeating, identifying counterfeit diagnostics could easily be mistaken for damage, which they were on the genuine coin that was used as the model for this fake. Keep these marks in mind to avoid major financial damage.

This counterfeit has these diagnostics:

- A deep scratch in front of the face—a repeating, reproduced gouge

- A deep dent on the rim above the B of LIBERTY

- A heavy scratch above the eagle's head, extending into the wreath

- A major dent above the R of AMERICA

- A heavy dent on the last A in AMERICA

This and future forgeries of this nature can easily infiltrate the numismatic community for a time.

The rest of the Bust series is relatively fake-free. The few other counterfeits seen are usually of the cruder cast method, with an occasional electrotype. Knowing the characteristics of the genuine coins enables one to exclude these pieces easily and immediately.

Likelihood of non-genuine appearance: Low

Liberty Seated

Issues Affected:

Various dates—Contemporary counterfeits

1853—Alterations via removed arrows and rays

1870–73-CC—Alterations via added mint mark

Genuine Liberty Seated quarters, like genuine Bust quarters, display sharp, crisp lettering and digits. All devices are sharp as they emerge from the fields, and the lettering and digits have clear, angled features. Die polish abounds throughout this series and is useful for authentication. With many early U.S. coins, the dies became cracked, furnishing clues that can be extremely helpful in authentication.

Fakes are seldom seen for Liberty Seated quarters. The only strong candidates for alteration are the rare Carson City issues of 1870–1873. Knowledge of the genuine pieces leads to easy detection of altered coins.

The shape and style of the small, round mint marks can be used—in combination with their placement on the reverse—as points of reference in authenticating genuine coins. Counterfeiters have the difficult task of trying to position the mint marks in the right place every single time. Obviously, this does not happen, raising red flags regarding these coins' authenticity.

Contemporary counterfeits are encountered now and then, but these can be recognized easily by the crude nature of the dies and the base-metal planchets.

Likelihood of non-genuine appearance: Low

Barber

Issues Affected:

Various dates—Contemporary counterfeits

1896-S—Alterations via added mint mark

1901-S—Alterations via added mint mark

1913-S—Alterations via added mint mark

In general, this series is fake-free. The genuine coins were struck from sharp dies, with the lettering, digits, and devices erupting squarely from the fields. Like most U.S. coins of this era, the letters and devices are square and flat, typically exhibiting angular features. Die polish and die cracks are common and can be used as aids for authentication.

Alterations of the three key dates—1896-S, 1901-S, and 1913-S—were made by adding a mint mark to the corresponding Philadelphia issue. Knowing the shape and style of the genuine "S" mint mark can settle the question of authenticity in many instances.

Another factor to consider is the level of preservation of the coin. If you have an 1896-S quarter in Very Good condition, the mint mark must be commensurate with the rest of the coin. It is amusing to encounter an alteration where the coin is in Very Good condition and the "S" has the detail of a mint mark from an About Uncirculated coin. Remember that all portions of a coin are affected by wear—and in instances where the coin is in the lower grades of Good to Very Fine, the mint mark must show equal signs of wear.

Likelihood of non-genuine appearance: Below Average

Standing Liberty

Issues Affected:

1916—Alterations by changing low-grade and dateless 1917 quarters

Quarter Dollars—Standing Liberty
Genuine 1916 Standing Liberty quarter obverse.

*Close-up of **genuine** 1916 Standing Liberty quarter obverse. Note the single prominent hair strand, with the upper strand barely visible. On the 1917 Type I, there are two equally distinct hair strands. Also note the short, squat shield where the 1917 Type I is longer and thinner.*

*Close-up of **genuine** 1916 Standing Liberty quarter obverse. Gown extends to the toes at left, while on the 1917 Type I it traverses to mid-calf.*

*Close-up of **genuine** 1927-S Standing Liberty quarter obverse. Note the proper shape of the mint mark, which flows into the field.*

1918/7-S—Alterations by adding "7" to a 1918-S

1923-S—Alterations by adding mint mark

1927-S—Alterations by adding mint mark

Various Denver and San Francisco issues— Alterations by adding mint mark (1918–1923)

Genuine diagnostics are invaluable in authenticating Standing Liberty quarters. The design is not sharp and crisp, compared to its predecessors', but the lack of sharpness is not a predominant concern—knowing the genuine features *is*.

1916 Quarter

The first rarity found altered is the 1916 quarter. The only date suitable for this purpose is the 1917, since these are the only Type I issues in this series. But while quarters of these two dates share the same basic design, the hubs used to impress the dies were very different.

The best way to explore these differences is to use direct comparisons. The differences are so obvious that one can tell which year a coin was issued even if the date is worn off. Here are the features to check:

- The hair strands projecting from the back of the head. The 1916 has one prominent hair strand and a faint strand above it. The 1917 has two distinct hair strands.

- The shield being held by Miss Liberty. This is shorter and squatter on the 1916 quarter than on the 1917. *Note:* Once this area wears down, it is no longer useful.

Quarter Dollars—Standing Liberty
Altered 1923-S Standing Liberty quarter obverse and re-verse. Note the added "S."

*Close-up of **altered** 1923-S Standing Liberty quarter ob-verse. Note the added "S," which is misshapen and note how the bottom serif slants.*

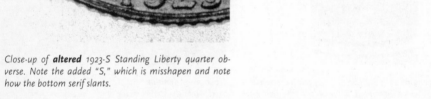

• Miss Liberty's gown. On the 1916, this extends to her foot. On the 1917, it travels up, connecting to her leg in the calf region.

With this information, identifying an alteration or confirming a legitimate 1916 Standing Liberty quarter is a snap.

1918/7-S Quarter
The 1918/7-S Standing Liberty quarter is not as easy to authenticate as the 1916, but it does have characteristics that aid in determining its authenticity.

The first thing to do is confirm the date. This overdate was created by impressing a Type 2 1917 die with a 1918-dated hub. The underlying "7" in the date forms a squared-off top to the "8," creates an angle through the right

side of the upper loop of the "8," and finishes off through the center and left part of the lower loop of the "8."

On many genuine overdates, a lump is found above and to the right of the date, just left of the wall that is parallel to Miss Liberty.

Many overdates are struck from clashed dies, but this is not diagnostic, so do not use it to either condemn or confirm this issue.

Other Dates
The rest of the Standing Liberty series is peppered with added mint marks from both branch mints. The most frequently seen of these is the 1927-S.

As with all other coins, knowing the style and shape of the mint mark is vital; so is ver-

Quarter Dollars—Washington
Close-up of genuine 1932-D Washington quarter reverse. Note the die polish around the mint mark, as well as the square, block-like "D."

Close-up of genuine 1932-S Washington quarter reverse. Note the square, tall, well-defined "S", as well as the often-seen die line above the D of DOLLAR.

ifying that the mint mark is actually part of the coin. Alterations do not always show the proper style of mint mark. In addition, most alterations will show a seam where the mint mark joins the surface of the coin.

The mint mark on a genuine 1927-S is a tall, thin, stylized "S" with upright serifs. Many of the alterations display a squat, thick "S" with a slanted bottom serif.

Other alterations seen in this series include the 1919-D, 1919-S, 1923-S, and other early Denver and San Francisco issues, though these are very rarely seen.

Likelihood of non-genuine appearance: Below Average

Washington

Issues Affected:
1932—Transfer die copies
1932-D—Alterations via added mint mark
1932-S—Alterations via added mint mark
1934—Transfer die copies
1936-D—Alterations via added mint mark
1965–1975—Various dates made in Vietnam during the war; always crude

The Washington quarter series has a surprisingly high number of counterfeits and alter-

ations. Alterations will be discussed first, as they are more likely to be encountered than are counterfeits.

1932-D Quarter
The 1932-D is the most frequently altered coin in the series. Genuine specimens are identified easily by their mint mark—a square, tall, and angular "D." In addition, the genuine 1932-D quarter is laden with die polish on the reverse. Tiny die lines are evident around the mint mark.

On altered pieces, the mint mark is usually ill-shaped—almost rounded, when compared to the real thing—and it sometimes lacks serifs. Often, it will be thin with no height. Since the coin used for the alteration is a 1932 Philadelphia issue, it is generally free from die polish. This "Philly" appearance alerts authenticators that something may not be right.

1932-S Quarter
On the genuine 1932-S, the mint mark is square and boxy in appearance. The serifs are parallel to each other, and the mint mark itself stands full against the field. On some examples, a large, raised die-polish line can be found above the D of DOLLAR on the reverse. Remember that this appears on only one die, thus cannot be used to disqualify a

coin. If it does appear, however, it endorses the piece as genuine.

On the few alterations that do exist, the mint mark is malformed and many times is thin and does not display any depth. Compared to the genuine pieces, these alterations look almost paper-thin.

On both the 1932-D and 1932-S, the mint mark will sometimes appear to be sitting on a lake or, in another instance, in a hole. When this effect is encountered in combination with the other confirming characteristics, the coin is conclusively genuine. The absence of this puddle or "hole" effect does not condemn a coin, but the presence of one or the other helps confirm its authenticity.

1936-D Quarter
The 1936-D Washington quarter, like the 1932-S, is not widely altered. The two coins also have something else in common: their mint-mark characteristics. On a genuine 1936-D, the "D" is squared-off and boxy, and stands tall.

Alterations often exhibit a mint mark that is rounded, thin, and sometimes without serifs.

Counterfeits
It is hard to believe, but struck copies of Washington quarters actually were made with the express intent to deceive. Even harder to believe are the dates chosen for this purpose: instead of focusing on the scarce dates in the series, the counterfeiter made a fistful of fakes dated 1932 and 1934. That's right—1932 and 1934 *Philadelphia* issues!

While relatively credible, these counterfeits are identifiable by several diagnostics. First, in a ceaseless pursuit of the dollar, the counterfeiter used one reverse to accommodate both the 1932 and 1934 obverse dies. On the right leg of the eagle (as you look at the coin), a repeating depression is evident. This most likely was damage on the genuine coin used as a model for the fake; it was picked up on the counterfeit dies and subsequently appeared on all of the forgeries. Also character-

istic of these fakes are the thin, depressed lines sprouting from the rim in a diagonal fashion, at 3 o'clock on the reverse. Additionally, these fakes are overly lustrous; they have too much "fire" for these particular issues. While genuine 1932 and 1934 quarters can be lustrous, these phonies go over the top. At times, in fact, they are so lustrous that subsequent owners have been known to tone down the coins through artificial means, hoping to disguise their obvious phoniness.

Finally, look at the edge of one of these fakes. It is almost "Proof"-like, and the reeds are so sharp they almost cut. Genuine pieces are not as square and have more beveled edges.

Likelihood of non-genuine appearance: Below Average

Half Dollars

Weight:	1794–1836	13.48 grams
	1836–1853	13.37 grams
	1853–1873	12.44 grams
	1873–1964	12.50 grams
	1965–1970	11.50 grams (silver clad version)
	1971–present	11.34 grams
	1976	11.50 grams (silver clad version)
Composition:	1794–1795	90% silver, 10% copper
	1796–1836	89.2% silver, 10.8% copper
	1836–1964	90% silver, 10% copper
	1965–1970	40% silver, 60% copper (silver clad version)
	1971–present	75% copper, 25% nickel outer layers, bonded to a core of pure copper
	1976	40% silver,

	60% copper (silver clad version)
Specific Gravity: 1794–1795	10.34
1796–1836	10.32
1836–1964	10.34
1965–1970	9.53
1971–present	8.92
1976	9.53 (silver clad version)

It seems that as coins get larger, more fakes appear. While this is not actually true, the half dollar series does contain more counterfeits and alterations than some of its smaller sisters. Rarity is the reason for the large number of fakes—but with rarity comes the fact that fewer dies were used to strike these coins, making their identification easier.

Bust

Issues Affected:

1796—Transfer die copies (or possibly spark-erosion dies)

1797—Transfer die copies (or possibly spark-erosion dies)

Various dates—Contemporary counterfeits

1838-O—Alterations via added mint mark

For the most part, Bust half dollars were struck with well-defined features. Like almost all early U.S. coins, their details are sharp, crisp, and prominent. The letters and digits emerge from the fields in abrupt, sharp angles. There is nothing rounded about the details on these coins.

The popular reference book *Early Half Dollar Die Varieties 1794–1836* by Al C. Overton is an excellent source about the many die varieties in the series; these die varieties can be used to verify and identify rarities.

The two dates of greatest concern in the Bust half dollar series are the 1796 and 1797. Two counterfeits, in particular, are quite deceptive and require multiple tests to confirm that they are forgeries.

These fakes appear fairly normal at first, except that they contain unusual "lint" marks on both the obverse and reverse. These marks are not generally seen on genuine coins of this series. They occur on genuine coins when threads or debris find their way between the die and planchet during striking. However, it is believed that these fakes result from high-quality casting techniques, so it is difficult to explain these lint marks. Perhaps they were copied from the original coin that served as the model.

Another deficient quality of the fakes is the edge. For some reason, counterfeiters tend to pay relatively little attention to the edges of their coins, and this case is no exception. Several letters, most notably the F in HALF, show extra lumps of metal.

Similar lumps can also be found, along with microscopic scratches or tooling, at the junctures where the devices and fields meet, giving the fakes a granular effect that permeates these coins. It is believed that this, too, results from the casting process.

A specific gravity test will go a long way toward establishing whether a given coin is authentic. Specific gravity measures the density of an object; the resulting number tells researchers the density of the object as measured against water, which has a specific gravity of 1. The specific gravity of the genuine 1796–1797 Bust half dollars is 10.32, while the specific gravity of the fake versions of these coins is a whopping 11.40. While that may seem almost acceptable to some, keep in mind that 100 percent pure silver has a specific gravity of 10.50. This would suggest that these counterfeits contain an alloy of gold or other heavy metal within the composition.

There are no other deceptive counterfeits or alterations to speak of in this series. What do exist are contemporary counterfeits struck from hand-cut dies. These pieces can be discerned easily for a couple of reasons:

- They will not be found in Overton's book.

- They were made of German silver, a copper-nickel alloy that contains no actual silver;

therefore, both their weight and specific gravity will be low, around 8.7.

Alterations are encountered for the exceptionally rare 1838-O half dollar. Since only twenty examples were produced, all in Proof, these are quite easy to detect. The coin used for these alterations is a business-strike 1838. Many times it will be polished to resemble a Proof. One should be wary and investigate all 1838-O half dollars.

Likelihood of non-genuine appearance: Average

Liberty Seated
Issues Affected:

Various dates—Contemporary counterfeits

1853—Alterations via removed arrows and rays

1870–1874-CC—Alterations via added mint mark

1878-CC—Alterations via added mint marks

1878-S—Alterations via added mint mark

Liberty Seated half dollars are seldom forged. As with other Liberty Seated coins, alterations will be the most commonly encountered fakes. Full-fledged counterfeits are quite rare.

Like their dime and quarter counterparts, the Carson City issues of 1870–1874 and 1878 are susceptible to alteration. As with the smaller denominations, knowledge of the shapes, styles, and positions of the mint marks enables one to confirm the genuine pieces and condemn the bad ones.

The other rare date in this series that is frequently altered is the 1878-S. On the reverse of the genuine piece, a raised die lump appears in the shield on the eagle. This lump is found at the top of the left white stripe. Any 1878-S half dollar without this diagnostic should arouse immediate suspicion.

Likelihood of non-genuine appearance: Low

Barber
Issues Affected:

Various dates—Contemporary counterfeits

Believe it or not, Barber half dollars are virtually free of counterfeits and alterations. There may be the occasional cheap cast copy or other low-quality fake, but otherwise, this is a clean series.

As with most U.S. coins up until this era, the details on genuine Barber halves are square, sharp-angled, and crisp. This in itself would not necessarily deter a counterfeiter, but for some reason the counterfeiters just have not discovered this series.

Likelihood of non-genuine appearance: Low

Walking Liberty
Issues Affected:

Various dates—Contemporary counterfeits

1917-S, S on obverse—Alterations via added mint mark

Various early Denver and San Francisco issues—Alterations via added mint marks

1921—Alterations via changed date from 1941

1921-D—Alterations via changed date from 1941-D

1921-S—Alterations via changed date from 1941-S

1938-D—Alterations via added mint mark

Unfortunately, alterations abound in this series, from added mint marks to altered dates to non-deceptive contemporary counterfeits. There are no decent counterfeits, so the alterations become the focus of attention. It is crucial to know the shapes and styles of mint marks, as well as the shapes of the digits on the 1921 half dollars.

A discussion of the most commonly altered coins follows.

1917-S, S-on-Obverse, Half Dollar
The genuine version of this coin was made with the same mint-mark punch as the 1909-S VDB cent. Notice how the mint mark is square, with parallel serifs. This boxy mint mark also has a notched serif, as well as a raised die lump within the upper loop of the "S." This punch was not used for the 1917-S half dollar with the mint mark on the re-

Half Dollars
Genuine 1917-S Obverse Walking Liberty half dollar obverse and reverse.

verse, indicating that the S-on-observe variety was produced first.

Alterations generally bear an ill-shaped mint mark that is not square and also appears "thinner," meaning it does not sit up off the field as high as the "S" on genuine pieces. The serifs are angled, particularly the bottom one.

1921-P, D, and S Half Dollars
All three of the low-mintage 1921 issues have been replicated by changing the date on a 1941-P, D, or S half dollar to 1921. On genuine coins, the shape of the "2" in the date is stylized. The base of the "2" is not perfectly straight, but rather has a slight curve to it.

On a suspected piece, check to see whether the digit appears to belong to the coin. Often, the alteration to the "2" appears foreign to the coin and does not look like it belongs with the other three digits.

1938-D Half Dollar
This alteration may be the most difficult to detect of all the fakes mentioned here. Close attention must be paid to the shape and style of this mint mark. The "D" should be boxy, with definite serifs. On many genuine pieces, the base of the "D" is machine-doubled. On some alterations, the "D" will be more rounded, sometimes having little in the way of serifs.

Other Dates
Other alterations seen occasionally include the 1917-D with the mint mark on the reverse, the 1919-D, and the 1919-S. Keys to authentication are being able to recognize the genuine mint marks and confirming that the "D" or "S" is indeed part of the coin.

Likelihood of non-genuine appearance: Average

Franklin and Kennedy
Issues Affected:
None

No counterfeits or alterations are reported for these series.

Dollars:

Weight:	1794–1803	26.96 grams
	1840–1935	26.73 grams
	1971–1978 (clad)	22.68 grams
	1971–1976 (40% silver)	24.59 grams
	1979–1981	8.10 grams
Composition:	1794–1795	90% silver, 10% copper
	1796–1803	89.2% silver, 10.8% copper
	1840–1935	90% silver, 10% copper

Half Dollars
Close-up of **genuine** *1917-S Obverse Walking Liberty half dollar obverse. Note the square, block-shaped mint mark with the notch in the upper serif, and the lump in the upper loop of the mint mark. This came from the same mint-mark punch used on the 1909-S VDB cent.*

Altered *1917-S Obverse Walking Liberty half dollar obverse and reverse. Note the added "S."*

Genuine *1921-S Walking Liberty half dollar obverse and reverse.*

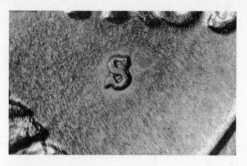

Half Dollars

*Close-up of **altered** 1917-S Obverse Walking Liberty half dollar obverse. Note the added "S," as well as the non-square mint mark. Note also that the mint mark has a diagonal bottom serif.*

*Close-up of **genuine** 1921-S Walking Liberty half dollar obverse. Note the shape of the "2"-the base of the "2" is flat.*

Altered *1917-D Reverse Walking Liberty half dollar obverse and reverse.*

*Close-up of **altered** 1917-D Reverse Walking Liberty half dollar reverse. Note the added "D"-serifs are pointy, not squared.*

	1971–1978	75% copper, 25% nickel outer layers, bonded to a core of pure copper
	1971–1976	40% silver, 60% copper (silver clad version)
	1979–1981	75% copper, 25% nickel outer layers, bonded to a core of pure copper
Specific Gravity:	1794–1795	10.34
	1796–1803	10.32
	1840–1935	10.34
	1971–1978	8.92
	1971–1976	9.53 (silver clad version)
	1979–1981	8.92

While U.S. dollars have their share of counterfeits and alterations, there also are plenty of references that provide tremendous assistance in ferreting out the fakes. The first of these excellent works is *The United States Early Silver Dollars from 1794 to 1803* by Milferd H. Bolender. His study of die varieties makes it clear when an alteration might be encountered. Alterations are rarely seen in the Bust dollar series, except for an occasional 1804 made by altering an 1801, 1802, or 1803.

The next outstanding reference, the *Comprehensive Catalogue and Encyclopedia of U.S. Morgan and Peace Dollars* by Leroy C. Van Allen and A. George Mallis, contains a mintmark study that is vitally important. Pay close attention to these mint marks and the eras when they were used. Often, a counterfeiter places the wrong style of mint mark on a phony rare-date coin, making it obvious that an alteration has occurred.

Q. David Bowers' two-volume *Silver Dollars & Trade Dollars of the United States* is a comprehensive study of all U.S. silver dollars and a must for counterfeit detection purposes.

Bust

Issues Affected:

1799—Transfer die copies

1804—Cast copies (very obvious), alterations from other dates (usually 1801–03)

The most commonly seen counterfeit Bust dollar is the 1799. When compared to the genuine piece, the counterfeit has many defective traits. First, the counterfeit looks as if it were struck in a collar. All specimens of this fake are perfectly round and not irregular like the genuine pieces. The edge is extremely sharp, and one might think by looking strictly at its edge that this fake is a Proof.

Counterfeit diagnostics include the following:

- A hole in the R of LIBERTY. This defect may have been carried over from the genuine coin used as the model. This repeating depression appears on all of the fakes made by this counterfeiter.

- A light, diagonal, repeating depression about two-thirds of the way up the vertical shaft of the D of UNITED.

Fakes are also seen for the "King of American Coins," the 1804 Bust dollar. These fakes are exceptionally easy to detect as most are cheap, obviously cast copies. They are light in weight and have many lumps on their surfaces, and the edges usually are badly flawed due to the casting process. Alterations of the last digit to a "4" from genuine 1801–1803 Bust dollars also are seen occasionally, though few of these are very deceptive. Comparing these with known die varieties of these dates in the Bolender reference is the easiest way to discover which date was used for the alteration.

Likelihood of non-genuine appearance:
Below Average

Liberty Seated

Issues Affected:

1870–1873-CC—Alterations via added mint mark

Dollars—Draped Bust
*Close-up of **counterfeit** 1799 Draped Bust dollar obverse.
Note the hole in the R of LIBERTY.*

***Counterfeit** 1799 Draped Bust dollar reverse. The arrow
points to the diagonal depression on the vertical shaft of
the D of UNITED.*

This is a series seldom seen counterfeited or altered. Once in a great while, one of the rare Carson City issues will be found altered. As with the Carson City issues of other Liberty Seated denominations, one needs to verify the shapes and styles of the mint marks. The "CC" mint marks are tall and have well-defined serifs. In checking the proper positions of these mint marks, a book such as *Walter Breen's Complete Encyclopedia of U.S. and Colonial Coins* can be a great source of information.

Likelihood of non-genuine appearance: Low

Morgan
Issues Affected:
1879-CC—Alterations via added mint marks

1883-S—Alterations via added mint mark

1884-S—Alterations via added mint mark

1886-O—Alterations via added mint mark

1888-S—Alterations via added mint mark

1889-CC—Alterations via added mint marks

1892-S—Alterations via added mint mark

1893-S—Alterations via added mint mark, altered date

1894—Alterations via removed mint mark

1895—Alterations via removed mint mark

1896-O—Alterations via added mint mark

1896-S—Alterations via added mint mark

1897-O—Alterations via added mint mark

1901—Alterations via removed mint mark

1903-S—Alterations via added mint mark

1904-S—Alterations via added mint mark

The great reference books on silver dollars, notably those by Van Allen-Mallis and by Q. David Bowers, help immensely in recognizing genuine Morgan silver dollars and in exposing fakes. In addition, several die characteristics make it easy to discern genuine coins from their altered counterparts.

Of the often-seen Morgan dollar fakes, a few will be detailed here, as they contain certain die characteristics that make it extremely easy to identify the real coins. As for the others, studying the genuine pieces in the books of Van Allen-Mallis and Bowers, learning the shapes and styles of the mint marks, and determining whether a mint mark truly belongs on a coin will help resolve any questions about authenticity.

1879-CC Dollar
While this coin is found with added mint marks, one of the genuine dies has created the most confusion regarding this issue. Indeed, the 1879-CC "Capped Die" variety has confused collectors—and even some dealers—for a very long time.

The Philadelphia Mint produced all working dies for the various mints, and techni-

Dollars—Morgan
Genuine 1879-CC *"Capped Die" Morgan dollar obverse and reverse.*

Dollars—Morgan
*Close-up of **genuine** 1879-CC "Capped Die" Morgan dollar reverse. Note the rusted die effect on the mint mark.*

cians in Philadelphia also placed the mint marks on the dies. In early 1879, a reverse die of the "Reverse of 1879" type was mint-marked with the "small-CC" punch used for the 1878-CC dies, which were all of the "Reverse of 1878" type. Apparently, it was then decided to use the "large-CC" punch from the discontinued Trade dollar series on the Morgan dollar dies. The two small C's were then repunched with two large C's, though the tops of the small C's remained as "caps" or hats atop the large C's. The result is the "Capped Die" variety—a coin with an irregular mint mark that looks fake but is indeed genuine.

1886-O Dollar

Most fake 1886-O dollars are 1886 Philadelphia issues with a soldered or glued "O" mint mark. Knowledge of the look and feel of Philadelphia and New Orleans Morgan dollars generally enables one to spot this alteration. Sometimes, however, a coin is cleaned to obscure the counterfeiter's work. Check the mint mark for a seam or the area around the mint mark for discoloration, which creates a halo effect.

1889-CC Dollar

For coins of this frequently altered date-and-mint issue, one of the first places to look is the mint mark. Be sure the letters "CC" are properly formed and part of the coin. By viewing a coin with a high-powered loupe, one can determine whether the mint mark flows into the field. This verifies that the mint mark is part of the coin—connected, if you will. Many alterations display mint

Dollars—Morgan
Altered 1886-O Morgan dollar obverse and reverse. Note the added "O."

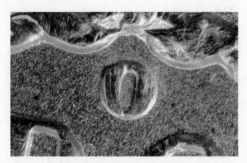

Close-up of **genuine** 1886-O Morgan dollar reverse. Note the strength, height, and shape of the "O."

Close-up of **altered** 1886-O Morgan dollar reverse. Note the added "O." The "O" is narrow, not wide like the genuine piece.

Close-up of **genuine** 1889-CC Morgan dollar obverse. The die crack through the date is seen on some specimens.

marks that are glued to the surface and show a seam where the mint mark joins the field.

Several die characteristics help confirm this coin's authenticity.

One characteristic of the genuine coin is a raised die line in Miss Liberty's cap, between the banner that bears the word LIBERTY and the leaf in the cap. Unfortunately, this die line does not appear on every specimen, but if it is present, it can confirm the coin's authenticity. The die line will be visible down to the lowest grades.

Die cracks permeate genuine 1889-CC dollars. Not all of them have these die cracks, but if they are present they confirm a coin's authenticity. Look first at the date. A faint die crack often begins at the point of the bust and extends through the four digits of the date. Later die states show continuing cracks through the stars around the obverse, with another die crack extending from 12 o'clock into the cap. If you have this late die state, it definitely denotes a genuine 1889-CC.

1893-S Dollar

This date is the easiest to authenticate in the entire Morgan series.

Since only 100,000 coins were struck, just one obverse die was used in combination with two reverse dies. This one obverse die has key diagnostics with which one can determine a coin's authenticity readily and conclusively. Simply put, if an 1893-S dollar does not contain these characteristics, it is not genuine. By inspecting the obverse, one never needs to check to see whether the mint mark is part of the coin or has been added.

The close-up photos of the word LIBERTY in the headband illustrate these characteristics:

- In the foot of the R of LIBERTY is a die chip, known as the "rabbit ear." This raised chip is found only on genuine 1893-S dollars.

- The T of LIBERTY has a raised diagonal die line through the top of the letter.

These characteristics will be identifiable down to the lowest grades because they are found in protected areas of the coin.

Besides the die lines, also notice the date position for the genuine 1893-S. The "1" is squarely over a denticle. As the date progresses, notice how it tends to slope up. This, in combination with the die lines, is conclusive evidence of a coin's authenticity.

By checking these characteristics, one can positively identify and authenticate a coin as a genuine 1893-S dollar—or, conversely, determine that an altered coin is a fake.

1894 Dollar

This is another coin with a low mintage and diagnostics that conclusively determine authenticity. The difference between this date and the 1893-S is that only one reverse die was used for the 1894-P.

- On a genuine 1894 dollar, a short, thick, raised horizontal die line is visible in the area between the leg and claw of the eagle's right leg (as we view it).

- Along the upper right leg of the eagle (again, as we view it) and next to the tail can be found a pair of crisscrossing die-polish lines.

As in the case of the 1893-S, these diagnostics will be found in even the lowest grades. Again, this is due to the fact that these characteristics are located in protected, recessed areas.

Note: These two die characteristics pertain to business strikes only, not to Proofs. The authenticity of an 1894 dollar can be determined conclusively by examining these characteristics. If they are not present and the coin is clearly not a Proof, the piece cannot be genuine.

When inspecting other rare-date or expensive coins in the Morgan dollar series, use references such as the Van Allen-Mallis or Bowers books on dollars, and refer especially

Dollars—Morgan
Genuine 1893-S Morgan dollar obverse and reverse.

*Close-up of **genuine** 1893-S Morgan dollar obverse. Note the die line through the top of the T and the "rabbit ears" die chip in the foot of the R of LIBERTY.*

*Close-up of **genuine** 1893-S Morgan dollar obverse. Note that the date slants up to the right. The "1" of the date is centered over the dentil.*

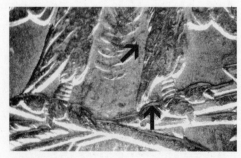

*Close-up of **genuine** 1894 Morgan dollar reverse. Note the heavy, straight die gouge in the crook of the eagle's left foot. Also, on the right side of the tail three-fourths of the way up, the eagle's left leg is a raised die line that resembles a "Y."*

to the mint-mark styles used during different time periods. These books go a long way toward identifying die characteristics that are useful in authentication. Digit punches also are outlined. Armed with these powerful tools, one will seldom be fooled by alterations.

Other Characteristics
Luster

Have you ever wondered how some people can look at a Morgan dollar and tell just from the obverse the mint at which it was struck?

This is an ability built upon experience. If asked to explain how they do it, many people will offer some intangible, mysterious explanation. While the full answer could take pages, it all boils down to knowing how the dies were prepared.

Once each mint received its allotted dies, it was allowed to prepare them for striking any way it chose. Some mints lapped or prepared their dies more aggressively than others. This lapping of the dies was a polishing method used to get them ready for production. For example, Carson City and San Francisco lapped their dies in a way that almost always resulted in bright, lustrous finishes on the coins—usually with a frosty, semi-prooflike, or proof-like luster. Conversely, New Orleans and Philadelphia prepared their dies in a way that usually resulted in a flat or satin luster.

While these are generalizations, they explain how some people can identify mint origin.

How does this help in authentication? Since so many Morgan dollars are found in Uncirculated condition, these qualities can help ferret out coins that might be altered. For instance, when inspecting a purported 1889-CC dollar, the coin may have a distinctive "Philadelphia" look. Suspicion is immediately raised, then perhaps confirmed by inspection of the die characteristics and mint marks.

Strike

Coins struck at different mints often had striking characteristics peculiar to each particular mint. New Orleans issues are almost always softly struck, while those from San Francisco are usually well struck. Philadelphia and Carson City issues are often well struck, but weaknesses are noted on some dates. Denver struck Morgan dollars only in 1921, and these have not been targeted for fraud to this point.

Likelihood of non-genuine appearance: Above Average

Peace
Issues Affected:
1928—Alterations via removed mint mark
1934-S—Alterations via added mint mark

Peace dollars are seldom found altered—but when they are, the rare dates are the targets. Added mint marks have been found on 1934-S dollars and mint marks have been removed from 1928-S dollars to make them look like the much-scarcer 1928 issue from Philadelphia.

As always, knowing the shapes and styles of mint marks is invaluable. As with the Morgan series, the Van Allen and Mallis and Bowers books can aid in determining what mint-mark styles and shapes should appear on these rare-date coins. Any die information that can be gleaned from these or other references, or from one's own experience, also can be enormously helpful in authentication.

Die characteristics are particularly useful in identifying a genuine 1928 Peace dollar. It is believed that only three obverse dies were used to strike this issue, and each of them exhibits specific die lines. They are:

- Die 1—A raised, short die line extends from the B of LIBERTY past the ray.

- Die 2—A swirling series of raised die-polish lines is found after the B of LIBERTY. On later

Dollars—Peace
Genuine 1928 Peace dollar obverse and reverse.

states of this die, a series of unusual raised lines can be seen extending through the mid-section of the E of LIBERTY and into the field.

- Die 3—A short, thick die line appears in the folds of Miss Liberty's hair. Be sure to position your light source from either 9 o'clock or 3 o'clock so the line will be visible during inspection.

Any 1928 dollar with one of these diagnostics will be genuine. If none of these characteristics can be found, look at the reverse for evidence that a mint mark has been removed. However, ANACS did examine a single specimen of a *fourth* 1928-P obverse die with no indication of a removed mint mark.

For Peace dollars as with Morgans, being able to identify mint traits through visual inspection also can aid in authenticating scarce issues.

Likelihood of non-genuine appearance: Low

Eisenhower and Susan B. Anthony
Issues Affected:
None

No counterfeits or alterations inspected

Trade

Weight:	1873–1885	27.21 grams
Composition:	1873–1885	90% silver, 10% copper
Specific Gravity:	1873–1885	10.34

Issues Affected:
Various dates—Cast copies

1884—Transfer copy dies

1885—Unknown, but may have been made from the fake 1884 pieces

The Trade dollar series is not especially rife with deceptive counterfeits, but lesser-quality, base metal cast copies will be found. These fakes are easy to detect and to confirm by measuring their weight and, if necessary, performing a specific gravity test. The low-quality cast pieces made with low-grade silver—or no silver at all—usually are 2 grams light and register a specific gravity under 9.5.

The quality of the typical counterfeit coin is crude, displaying many lumps, uneven fields, poorly formed edge reeding, and lack of sharp detail.

On the other hand, genuine coins are similar in quality to all of the other type coins from this era. They exhibit sharp, crisp lettering and digits and possess pronounced detail that

Dollars—Peace

Close-up of genuine 1928 Peace dollar obverse. Note the die line extending from the B of LIBERTY past the ray.

Close-up of genuine 1928 Peace dollar obverse. Note the die lines extending through the middle part of the E in LIB-ERTY.

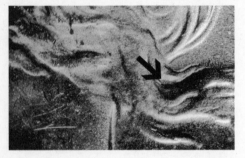

Close-up of genuine 1928 Peace dollar obverse. Note the die line in the fold of the hair.

emerges from the field in a sharp, angular fashion. Further, the tops of the letters and digits are uniform, square, and flat.

Likelihood of non-genuine appearance: Below Average

Gold

As we turn to gold coins, counterfeits become much more prevalent. No longer will alterations be the most commonly seen fakes.

Because gold counterfeits are usually struck copies, they can be identified by looking for repeating flaws—typically depressions. These are actually bag marks, scratches, and the like that were transferred from an original "model" coin to the counterfeiter's dies. These defects then repeat themselves on all of the coins the counterfeiter strikes. Sometimes the counterfeiter will notice such a flaw

and attempt to correct it on the die. When this is done, the counterfeiter invariably tools down the defect, making the flaw even more noticeable. The tool marks are usually short, thick, concentrated lines that are raised on the coins, corresponding to the grooves that have been cut in the surface of the die.

Counterfeit gold coins usually display a uniform and unnatural luster. This, too, results from the transfer process. Genuine coins have a luster that reflects their manufacture.

The devices of genuine coins, being raised, have a textured-type surface when compared to the fields, which are usually smooth. In studying the minting process, one will discover that the Mint polishes the fields of each die while leaving the devices relatively untouched, which results in differences between their surfaces. As a coin is struck, the metal from the planchet fills the voids in each die, producing the devices, and flows across the fields to the outer edge. These differing flows of metal cause the unique look and luster typically observed on a genuine coin.

Counterfeiters do not spend nearly as much time producing their coins, as does the Mint—and, consequently, defects and lack of craftsmanship permeate their work. Luster is one of these flaws. During the transfer process, the dies retain a uniform, typically granular surface. The average counterfeiter does not prepare dies by polishing them, as a rule, and this results in coins that look too uniform, too even. Many dealers can spot this "look" at a glance and quickly declare the coin a fake.

The other important factor distinguishing the genuine coin from the fake is the coin's detail of design. Genuine U.S. gold coins are famous for their sharp, crisp detail. The lettering and digits are almost always sharp, protruding at crisp angles from the fields. These letters and digits are square and flat and display sharp, angular features at the top.

Genuine gold coins also show plenty of sharp, crisp die polish throughout the fields and devices. Occasionally, the dies cracked, leaving telltale evidence that also is sharp and well defined.

Die-clash marks provide yet another way to authenticate a coin, but this is the least-used tool because these marks can be copied by the counterfeiter.

For the most part, the counterfeiter has a difficult time reproducing the many subtle features of the genuine coin. During the transfer process, he or she loses the sharpness of detail, the die polish, the definition of die cracks, and the overall quality of the genuine coin.

With this in mind, this section will explore U.S. gold coins according to the eras in which they were produced, rather than on a series-by-series basis. We will look at early U.S. gold coins (1795–1839), mid-era issues (1840–1908), and the Indian and Saint-Gaudens series (1907–1933).

Interestingly, very few forgeries are encountered for coins from the early years, while the mid-era and late series are rampant with counterfeits. In fact, entire series of Indian quarter eagles, half eagles, and eagles have been seen in counterfeit form. Hopefully, with the information provided here, it will be easy to weed out the bad from the good.

Counterfeiting is a problem with gold dollars and three-dollar gold pieces, from their earliest issues in the mid-nineteenth century. With the quarter eagle, half eagle, eagle, and double eagle Liberty Head coinage, however, the problem is limited largely to issues from 1880 onward. It is possible to assemble complete or almost complete date sets of fakes from every gold coin series from 1880 through 1933. With Indian Head quarter eagles, half eagles, and eagles and Saint-Gaudens double eagles, nearly every single date-and-mint issue has been forged; as well as some dates and mint-mark combinations that were not issued.

Early U.S. Gold
Issues Affected:
1811 half eagle—Transfer copy dies

1799 eagle—Transfer copy dies

As mentioned in the preceding text, very few counterfeits exist for the early U.S. gold coins. In fact, only two commonly seen counterfeits qualify for this section.

1811 Five Dollar
The genuine coin is sharp and crisp—the same way virtually all U.S. coins of this era are found. The angular features of the letters, digits, and devices are clear and well-defined.

The counterfeit, on the other hand, lacks crisp, sharp detail and its luster is unnaturally uniform. The fake even has a "new" look, as if it were made recently (which, by the way, it was!).

Diagnostics for this fake include a repeating depression directly next to the star just to the right of the date. Additionally, the digits in the date have a concave appearance. These features are not present on the genuine coin, and it is not known why they occur on these fakes.

Early U.S. Gold
Genuine 1799 eagle obverse and reverse.

*Close-up of **genuine** 1799 eagle obverse. Note the sharpness of the date and die polish.*

*Close-up of **genuine** 1799 eagle obverse. Note the sharp, crisp lettering.*

*Close-up of **genuine** 1799 eagle obverse. Note the sharp, crisp lettering and the planchet adjustment lines through the letters.*

Early U.S. Gold
Counterfeit 1799 eagle obverse and reverse.

*Close-up of **counterfeit** 1799 eagle obverse. Note the lump to the right of the date.*

*Close-up of **counterfeit** 1799 eagle obverse. Note the lump to the left of LIBERTY.*

1799 Ten Dollar

The fake version of this other early gold piece is an even worse copy than the counterfeit 1811 half eagle. It is rounded in detail and has an even, uniform luster or glow. It also has that "new" look.

Diagnostically, this coin is loaded with flaws imparted to it by the hapless counterfeiter. It shows many lumps of extra metal throughout the fields, the most prominent being in the field above the cap of Miss Liberty. This large lump, along with the other lumps throughout the coin, the uniform luster, and the rounded details, will make this coin relatively easy to identify as a fake.

Middle Era (1840–1908)

This is the era when counterfeits flourish.

Genuine coins from this period have sharp, distinct, crisp, and well-defined features and

are found with ample die polish, die cracks, and other die information that make it possible to distinguish them from their counterfeit counterparts.

All issues are heavily counterfeited, with the gold dollar and three-dollar piece being most prevalent. The quarter eagle, half eagle, eagle, and double eagle are heavily counterfeited for issues dated mostly after the mid-1870s. For whatever reason, it is unusual to find a pre-1875 counterfeit from any of the Liberty Head series. Among the double eagle series, it is extremely rare to find a Type I or Type II (1850–1876) counterfeit. Another unusual sighting would be a mint-marked counterfeit from this era.

Some counterfeiters used the same undated-side die to produce gold pieces of many different dates. In the case of gold dollars and

Gold Dollars
Genuine 1862 gold dollar obverse and reverse.

three-dollar gold pieces, the obverse is the undated side. Thus, fake versions of Type III (1856–1889) gold dollars show the same counterfeit obverse paired with many differently dated reverses. The same is true with the three-dollar series. Obviously, it is much cheaper and easier to reuse the undated side of a die pair to produce more coins. By doing this, however, the counterfeiter makes it somewhat easier to track down and expose his or her handiwork.

The U.S. Mint, by contrast, seldom used an undated die for more than two consecutive years during the period in question unless the mintages were exceptionally low. One glaring exception is the obverse of the genuine 1869–1871 business-strike gold dollars. This die, with a heavy gouge through Miss Liberty, can be found on gold dollars for all three of these dates.

Some of the more common counterfeits will now be explored, along with the genuine characteristics.

Gold Dollars

Issues Affected:

1850-C—Transfer die copies

1850-O—Transfer die copies

1862—Transfer die copies

1874—Transfer die copies

Various dates (many of the 1880s issues)— Transfer die copies

1862 Gold Dollar

This commonly seen counterfeit has several telltale signs. Counterfeiters have been known to use the same obverse on differently dated reverses. Therefore, the diagnostics that follow can be used to identify other dated counterfeits:

- Two raised dots above and slightly left of the O of OF.

- A depressed line running from the rim to Miss Liberty's headdress between the E and S of STATES.

On genuine issues of all dates, plenty of sharp, crisp die polish can be seen running in a vertical fashion. This, along with the sharp, angular features of the lettering and devices, will help distinguish the good from the bad. The luster of the genuine coin also will aid in spotting a fake. The fake will have the usual uniform, even luster that is so common with counterfeit gold.

1874 Gold Dollar

Here is another classic counterfeit with all of the usual characteristics: spikes from the rims, repeating depressions, rounded letters and devices, and uniform luster.

When a fake is compared to the genuine article, its flaws become obvious. Especially no-

Gold Dollars
Close-up of **genuine** *1862 gold dollar obverse. Note the die polish through OF.*

Counterfeit *1862 gold dollar obverse and reverse.*

Close-up of **counterfeit** *1862 gold dollar obverse. Note the repeating depressed line running from the rim to the head-dress between the E and the S of STATES and the two lumps above and to the left of the O of OF. This fake obverse is seen on many Type III gold dollars.*

Close-up of **genuine** *1869 gold dollar obverse. Note the die gouge through the ear and the die polish under the ear. This obverse die is used on business strikes through 1871.*

Quarter Eagles
Counterfeit 1904 Liberty Head quarter eagle obverse and reverse.

Close-up of **counterfeit** 1904 Liberty Head quarter eagle obverse. The digits of the date have a rough texture, the digits are not square and well-defined and the digits do not emerge from the field in a crisp manner.

tice the heavy spikes that protrude from the reverse rim at 3 o'clock.

The genuine coin, by contrast, has well-defined letters and devices, plus sharp, crisp die polish. Coins from this era of U.S. coinage are famous for their sharpness, die polish, and die cracks.

Note on gold dollar counterfeits: Be wary of all Philadelphia issues. Few branch-mint issues are forged, the exceptions being the 1850-C and 1850-O. Most branch-mint coins are found in such wretched condition, reflecting poor die maintenance, which counterfeiters may feel they would be too ugly to reproduce and sell to the average person. Just the same, these poorly preserved dies produced coins with very identifiable and useful die abnormalities, such as lumps from rusted dies, cuds, and heavy gouges.

Quarter Eagles, Half Eagles, Eagles, and Double Eagles

Issues Affected:
Various dates in all series—Transfer die copies

Various dates—Contemporary counterfeits in gold and gold-plated base metal

Oddly, very little counterfeiting has taken place in these four series for coins of the early years (1839 through the mid-1870s). The creation of fakes swung into high gear, however, for issues dated from the mid-1870s to 1908. Contemporary counterfeits are all quite rare and sometimes were made with very crude imitation dies.

Like all counterfeits, fakes from these series lack the characteristics of genuine coins. Look for rounded lettering and devices, repeating depressions, unusual gouges and

Counterfeit 1906 Liberty Head quarter eagle obverse and reverse.

tooling lines, and uniform and evenly textured surfaces. The genuine pieces will be sharp and crisp, many times displaying die polish or die cracks, well-defined letters, digits, and devices, and sharp, angular features in the letters and digits.

As with gold dollars, relatively few fakes exist for branch-mint pieces. The forgers tend to focus on the Philadelphia issues. Of the four denominations, the eagle is probably the least counterfeited in the Liberty Head series. The Liberty Head quarter eagle is king of the fakes in this series, with the Liberty Head half eagle and double eagle holding the middle ground.

Three Dollars

Issues Affected:
Various dates (mainly Philadelphia)—Transfer die copies

1854—Transfer die copies

1857—Transfer die copies (very common)

1874—Transfer die copies (common)

1878—Transfer die copies (very common)

1882—Transfer die copies (very common)

This series is heavily counterfeited throughout. As with all gold coins from this era, fakes reveal themselves through rounded details, repeating depressions and tooling lines, and uniform, even luster.

The genuine coins are sharp and crisp, with considerable die polish, an occasional die crack, and other diagnostics that can be used to distinguish them from fakes. One stock obverse has the upper left serif of the letter I in UNITED and AMERICA missing, as copied from a genuine 1857 three-dollar gold piece with this characteristic. It was used to make counterfeits of several dates, including 1857.

The 1878 three-dollar gold piece is one of the most commonly counterfeited U.S. gold coins. Numerous counterfeits of this date exist from varying dies. Nonetheless, knowing the characteristics of the genuine piece will remove any questions regarding authenticity.

Two pairs of dies were used in 1878 for the genuine business-strike three-dollar pieces. The first one is identifiable by two lumps on the face—one behind the eye and another at the bottom of the neck, near the hair lock. These lumps can be transferred in the counterfeiting process and have been seen in a degraded state on forgeries.

The reverse of one genuine variety exhibits short, crisp, raised vertical lines inside the bow of the wreath. No counterfeits have been seen where these lines are duplicated successfully.

Quarter Eagles

*Close-up of **counterfeit** 1906 Liberty Head quarter eagle obverse. Note the line from the coronet to the star.*

*Close-up of **counterfeit** 1906 Liberty Head quarter eagle obverse. Note the spikes from the rim.*

*Close-up of **counterfeit** 1906 Liberty Head quarter eagle obverse. Note the depressed line through the fraction bar and denomination.*

*Close-up of **genuine** 1890 Liberty Head quarter eagle obverse. Note the crisp, sharp digits of the date.*

*Close-up of **genuine** 1890 Liberty Head quarter eagle obverse. Note the crisp, sharp detail and the contrast between the device and the field.*

*Close-up of **genuine** 1890 Liberty Head quarter eagle reverse. Note the minute die polish in the wings around the shield.*

Quarter Eagles
*Close-up of **genuine** 1890 Liberty Head quarter eagle reverse. Note the crisp, sharp lettering and numerals.*

Eagles
***Genuine** 1902 eagle obverse and reverse.*

*Close-up of **genuine** 1902 eagle obverse. Note the die polish through LIBERTY.*

*Close-up of **genuine** 1902 eagle reverse. Note the die line from the back of the arrow feathers to the wing.*

Eagles
Counterfeit 1892 eagle obverse and reverse.

Double Eagles
Genuine 1904 double eagle obverse and reverse.

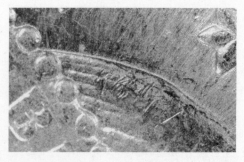

Close-up of **genuine** 1904 double eagle obverse. Note the hub line from the Y of LIBERTY, found on all Type III Liberty Head double eagles.

Close-up of **counterfeit** 1904 double eagle obverse. Note the tooling marks in the hair above the coronet.

Three Dollars
Counterfeit 1857 three-dollar gold obverse and reverse.

*Close-up of **counterfeit** 1857 three-dollar gold obverse. Note the tooling marks in the field between the chin and the N of UNITED. The broken top left serif of the I of UNITED is found on some genuine 1857 three-dollar coins, though this counterfeit obverse is paired with an 1882 and other date reverses. When this characteristic is found on dates other than 1857, the coin is definitely not genuine.*

*Close-up of **counterfeit** three-dollar gold obverse. The stock obverse with the depression between the I and B of LIBERTY is used with various dates.*

The second genuine obverse can be identified by a raised "horseshoe" between the E and R of LIBERTY. To date, this feature has not been seen on any counterfeits, perhaps because of how thinly raised it is.

Four Dollars (Stella)
Issues Affected:

None—though some gold-plated copper and aluminum issues are offered as gold

Four-dollar gold pieces are even rarer in the counterfeit state than they are as genuine coins. In fact, they are so rare that there are no known counterfeits to discuss in this chapter.

The only concern would be to watch for gold-plated copper or aluminum pieces. Their weight would make it easy to distinguish these from the regular gold issues.

Late Era Gold (1907–1933)

This era introduces the incuse designs of the Indian Head quarter eagles and half eagles, as well as the highly artistic Indian Head eagles and Saint-Gaudens double eagles.

Because of their "sunken" designs, the Indian Head quarter eagles and half eagles are among the most difficult of all U.S. coins to authenticate. No longer is the usual sharpness available as a diagnostic. The luster is not always helpful, either. These coins do exhibit a great deal of die polish, however. Looking to the deepest recesses, one can find sharp die polish on genuine coins. Usually, these deepest recesses will bear the outlines to the design.

Indian Head Quarter Eagle
Issues Affected:
All dates—Transfer die copies

Three Dollars
Genuine 1874 three-dollar gold obverse and reverse.

Close-up of **genuine** 1874 three-dollar gold reverse. Note the die polish through the bow of the wreath.

Close-up of **genuine** 1878 three-dollar gold reverse. Note the vertical die polish in the bow of the wreath.

Close-up of **genuine** 1878 three-dollar gold obverse. Note the raised "horseshoe" die characteristic between the E and R of LIBERTY.

Indian Head Quarter Eagle
Altered 1911-D Indian Head quarter eagle obverse and reverse.

*Close-up of **altered** 1911-D Indian Head quarter eagle reverse. The mint mark is formed from the field (chased).*

*Close-up of **genuine** 1911-D Indian Head quarter eagle reverse. The arrow points to the raised die line in the recess between the arrow tips and field, found even on very low-grade specimens.*

Genuine 1911-D Indian Head quarter eagle obverse and reverse.

Indian Head Quarter Eagle
Counterfeit 1914-D Indian Head quarter eagle obverse and reverse.

*Close-up of **counterfeit** 1914-D Indian Head quarter eagle obverse. Note the repeating depression above and between the "1" and "4" in the date.*

1911-D—Transfer die copies, added mint mark, "chased" mint mark

1911-D Quarter Eagle

The 1911-D quarter eagle perennially ranks among the most popular of all U.S. gold coins. With that popularity—and the corresponding value—comes the threat of counterfeits. Two or three times a month, PCGS sees a counterfeit example of this date; usually the fake is a struck copy, though now and then an added mint mark is seen. Oddly, the added mint mark is invariably created through "chasing"—a method of moving the metal in the fields to create the fake "D." PCGS has never encountered a fake 1911-D with a glued-on or soldered mint mark.

Fortunately, authentication of genuine 1911-D quarter eagles is made easier by the low mintage of this issue. Only two dies were used, and most of the survivors are from one die combination that offers an infallible diagnostic. The diagnostic is *not* the wire rim on the obverse, as not all genuine pieces show this characteristic. Rather, it is a short, raised vertical die polish line in the recess just to the left of the arrowheads, clutched by the eagle on the reverse.

To view this characteristic under the most ideal conditions, you will want to observe the coin with at least a 5X magnifier, with the light source beaming at a 90-degree angle to the die line. This diagnostic is so reliable it can be used to authenticate coins with either strong or weak mint marks—and because it is located in a protected area, it can be found even on the lowest-grade coins.

For the bulk of the counterfeit incuse gold pieces, one characteristic almost invariably shows up. It takes the form of raised horizontal "tool marks" at the back of the Indian's neck. It is uncertain why these marks occur with such regularity, but they will be found on many counterfeit Indian Head quarter eagles and half eagles.

Other times, localized tool marks will be found. One example is the shared counterfeit obverse die used for 1914 and 1914-D quarter eagles.

The 1914 quarter eagle is an ultra-popular coin because of its relatively low mintage and elusiveness in higher grades. The counterfeits of this date that appear on the market today are usually of **MS-62/63** quality, with good color and strike. The 1914 obverse is also seen paired with a fake "D" reverse at times, but the "Philadelphia" reverse is much more prevalent.

There are two varieties of this counterfeit. In its early die state, there is a depression above the "4" of the date, caused by a lump on the die. The later die state is characterized by tooling in this area, as the counterfeiter tried to remove the lump on the die, which created the depression on the coin.

Another diagnostic of this counterfeit can be seen on the Indian's bust, just below the necklace. Once again, tooling and/or filing have taken place on the die to remove lumps, and the results have actually made it easier to detect that the coin is counterfeit.

Indian Head Half Eagle
Issues Affected:
All dates—Transfer die copies

As with the Indian Head quarter eagles, counterfeits are known for nearly every date in the half eagle series, and some are quite deceptive. The same diagnostics used for the quarter eagles are applicable here—including the presence of "tool marks" on the back of the Indian's neck. The luster on these coins is often "off," with the open field areas on the reverse sometimes "fading" when tilted under a good light source.

Crumbled letters or stars also are found on many Indian Head quarter and half eagle counterfeits—but these alone should not condemn a coin, as some genuine coins struck from worn dies also exhibit these characteristics. Additionally, the mint mark may be poorly formed on some genuine issues, especially those from San Francisco. The mint mark on some of these coins is also found flattened and quite weak.

Fantasy fakes exist for dates such as 1915-D, which never were produced by the Mint, and these are obviously not genuine. Most of these fantasy issues are not of the same high quality as most other Indian Head half eagle counterfeits.

Indian Head Eagle
Issues Affected:
Most dates—Transfer die copies

As we move on to Indian Head eagles, we leave incuse-relief designs behind and resume the traditional approach to authentication.

Unfortunately, the design of the Indian Head eagle—while strikingly handsome—is not sharp in nature. The letters and devices are rounded, making authentication slightly more dependent upon identifying die polish, die cracks, and the luster associated with genuine coins. To complicate matters, counterfeits may sometimes exhibit tooling marks that are often confused with die polish.

One area where the counterfeiters became lackadaisical is the edge. This "third side" of the coin plays an important role in authentication, as counterfeiters tend to use a "common" or "stock" edge to produce all of their fakes. Just as they use the undated side of a single coin to pair with many dated sides, the forgers tend to use the same edge or collar to strike many different dates of Indian Head eagles.

The common or stock edge encountered on fake Indian Head eagles has raised, short, thick lines clustered between some, but not all, of the stars. These clusters of tooling lines will not be found on genuine examples.

One of the dates most frequently seen on counterfeit Indian Head eagles is the 1926.

Indian Head Half Eagle
Genuine 1909-D Indian Head half eagle obverse and reverse.

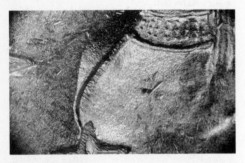

Close-up of **genuine** 1909-D Indian Head half eagle obverse. Note the crisp, sharp die polish in the recessed area in front of the neck.

Close-up of **genuine** 1909-D Indian Head half eagle obverse. No tooling lines are seen in the neck.

Counterfeit 1911-D Indian Head half eagle obverse and reverse.

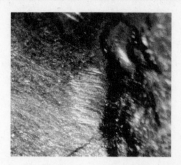

Indian Head Half Eagle

Close-up of *counterfeit* 1911-D Indian Head half eagle obverse. Note the fuzzy detail on the necklace.

Close-up of *counterfeit* 1911-D Indian Head half eagle obverse. Note the tooling marks at the back of the neck.

Close-up of *genuine* 1914-S Indian Head half eagle reverse. Note the shape and style of the mint mark, which is square and boxy. This came from the same punch that was used on the 1909-S VDB Lincoln cent.

Close-up of *counterfeit* 1911-S Indian Head half eagle reverse. Note the poorly formed and wrong-style mint mark. This mint mark is commonly referred to as the "snake S."

Counterfeit 1915-D Indian Head half eagle obverse and reverse. An impossible coin—none was struck in Denver. The counterfeiters were unaware of this combination of date and mint mark impossibility.

Indian Head Eagle
Counterfeit 1913-S Indian Head eagle obverse and reverse.

Close-up of *counterfeit* 1913-S Indian Head eagle reverse. Note the tooling marks below the leaves. This reverse is used on other-date counterfeits.

Close-up of *counterfeit* 1926 Indian Head eagle obverse. Note the incuse lines extending from the right side of the "9" in the date.

Genuine 1932 Indian Head eagle obverse and reverse.

Indian Head Eagle
*Close-up of **genuine** 1932 Indian Head eagle obverse. Note the sharp, crisp die polish through the date.*

*Close-up of **counterfeit** 1932 Indian Head eagle obverse. Note the diagnostic raised line extending from the rim to the "2" in the date.*

***Counterfeit** 1913-D Indian Head eagle obverse and reverse—another date that the Denver Mint did not strike.*

The principal characteristic for detecting this fake is a patch of recessed lines near the right side of the lower loop of the "9." If this diagnostic is found, it is proof that the coin is not genuine. Compare this with most genuine 1926 Indian Head eagles, which have plenty of die polish throughout the obverse, particularly in the area of the date. The edge of the genuine coin also will not show the typical counterfeit's trademark: the short, stubby tool lines between the stars.

Another late-date Indian Head eagle that displays a great deal of die polish is the genuine 1932 issue. This coin exhibits plenty of raised die polish throughout the fields and through the date area.

Unfortunately, earlier-dated Indian Head eagle counterfeits are not as easy to detect as fakes of these two pieces, for the minting process tended to produce more uniform-looking coins, with little die polish evident. Certainly the edge is one area to inspect, as counterfeiters are notorious for using the "stock edge."

As with the half eagles, counterfeit eagles are found with fantasy dates, such as 1913-D—and these are obviously fake, since no genuine coins were struck in Denver in 1913. These fantasy issues usually are not of the same high quality as many of the other counterfeit Indian Head eagles that were struck.

Saint-Gaudens Double Eagle

Issues Affected:

Various dates (mainly common Philadelphia issues)—Transfer die copies

As with Indian Head eagles, more traditional counterfeit-detection methods are employed with Saint-Gaudens double eagles. Many of these coins do not have the sharpness associated with earlier gold issues, such as the Liberty Head series. Luster, die polish, die cracks, and other identifying characteristics are very helpful in distinguishing genuine issues from fakes. Again, the counterfeiters used a shortcut with many of the common dates, especially those in the 1920s. The same edge collar was used with multiple dates, and this makes many of these deceptive counterfeits fairly easy to identify.

On Saint-Gaudens double eagles, the common or stock edge can be identified by a raised, curved line that extends from the middle bar of the E in E PLURIBUS UNUM back toward the body of the E.

The 1907 Roman-numeral high-relief double eagle is a numismatic treasure, eagerly sought by collectors around the world. Unfortunately, its popularity also makes it the focus of many counterfeiters. Fortunately, it has plenty of diagnostics to offer, which make it fairly easy to distinguish the real thing from the numerous fakes.

High-relief "Saints" generally were struck from highly polished dies, resulting in many finely raised, swirling lines on the fields of both the obverse and reverse. One area to observe this die polish is beneath the outstretched arm of Miss Liberty.

On one genuine reverse die, the U of UNITED has an area missing from the left vertical portion of the letter. Evidently this occurred on only one reverse die. Although this characteristic could be transferred to a counterfeiter's die, most fakes do not exhibit this feature.

The obverse of the most famous counterfeit high-relief Saint has tooling marks above the first M in the date. This famous—or rather, notorious—high-relief fake was "signed" with an omega in the claw of the eagle. It is speculated that this is the "mark" of a brazen counterfeiter, put there proudly by the forger to identify the work. This omega also is

found on other gold counterfeits, including some three-dollar gold issues.

Not every high-relief Saint will display all of these characteristics, since the Mint used more than one pair of dies; however, the diagnostic die polish is found on most of the high-relief pieces inspected at PCGS.

Like later-date Indian Head eagles, later-date Saint-Gaudens double eagles will be found with plenty of die polish. The crisp, sharp die polish will most likely be found on the reverse, between the rays below the eagle. Some swirling die polish may be found throughout the obverse, but the most reliable traces of die polish will be in the area mentioned on the reverse.

An interesting note as it pertains to luster for all late-era gold coinage is that the coins in the 1907–1915 period often display a flat or dull luster, whereas the later dates (1916–1933) display a more frosty, satiny, fresh luster. There are always exceptions, such as the 1909-D half eagle, 1907 Arabic Numerals double eagle, and 1908 No-Motto double eagle, but for the most part the early dates do not display the fire of the later issues. This can be useful in counterfeit detection when checking a suspicious coin. Should one encounter an overly lustrous 1911 double eagle with other questionable characteristics, it may indeed be counterfeit. Not many 1911 double eagles will have the same lustrous effect as a 1927 or 1928 double eagle.

As with other later-date gold issues, fantasy dates such as 1918 and 1919 turn up occasionally, but these are not particularly deceptive.

Commemoratives
Issues Affected:
All gold issues—Transfer die copies

Albany—Transfer die copies

Antietam—Transfer die copies

Boone—Transfer die copies

Cincinnati—Transfer die copies

Connecticut—Transfer die copies

Saint-Gaudens Double Eagle
Genuine Saint-Gaudens High Relief double eagle obverse and reverse.

*Close-up of **genuine** Saint-Gaudens High Relief double eagle obverse. Note the die polish under the branch.*

*Close-up of **genuine** Saint-Gaudens High Relief double eagle reverse. Note the notch out of the left side of the U of* UNITED. *Also note the fine die polish through the letters.*

Counterfeit *Saint-Gaudens High Relief double eagle obverse and reverse.*

Saint-Gaudens Double Eagle

*Close-up of **counterfeit** Saint-Gaudens High Relief double eagle obverse. Note the tooling marks on the ray above the first "M" in the date.*

*Close-up of **counterfeit** Saint-Gaudens High Relief double eagle reverse. Note the "omega" sign within the claw of the eagle.*

*Close-up of **genuine** 1926 Saint-Gaudens double eagle edge. Note the sharp, crisp "E" on the edge.*

*Close-up of **counterfeit** 1920 Saint-Gaudens double eagle edge. The "stock edge" shows the curved line shooting off the middle stroke of the "E." This edge was used for multiple dates.*

***Genuine** 1926 Saint-Gaudens double eagle obverse and reverse.*

Saint-Gaudens Double Eagle
*Close-up of **genuine** 1926 Saint-Gaudens double eagle obverse. Note the die polish through the head and letters.*

*Close-up of **genuine** 1926 Saint-Gaudens double eagle reverse. Note the die polish through the sun's rays under the eagle.*

*Close-up of **counterfeit** 1926 Saint-Gaudens double eagle obverse. Note the repeating depression above the date in the rays.*

Grant w/star—Alterations via added star

Hawaiian—Transfer die copies

Hudson—Transfer die copies

Missouri—Transfer die copies

Panama/Pacific—Transfer die copies

Pilgrim—Transfer die copies

Spanish Trail—Transfer die copies

Stone Mountain—Transfer die copies

Vancouver—Transfer die copies

Lafayette dollar—Transfer die copies

While the silver commemorative series has some counterfeits, few are seen at PCGS. The same cannot be said for the gold commemorative pieces: with these, many counterfeits will be found, with the Pan-Pacific dollar and quarter eagle and the Sesqui quarter eagle among the most often seen.

Fortunately, for authentication purposes, all of the silver commemoratives most frequently counterfeited have genuine characteristics that separate them from the fakes. Additionally, five of the coins on the list—the Antietam, 1937 Boone, Connecticut, Panama-Pacific, and Stone Mountain half dollars—are less numerous than the others in counterfeit form. The others, being more valuable, are more commonly found as fakes.

It is not unusual to find plenty of die polish on many of the genuine silver commemorative half dollars. This important feature easily distinguishes the genuine coins from many of the fakes. The counterfeits seen at PCGS generally have not exhibited this fine, crisp die polish. Die cracks also are seen on some genuine coins, and these are not usually reproduced with clarity on counterfeits.

Commemoratives
Counterfeit Sesqui commemorative quarter eagle obverse
and reverse.

Close-up of **counterfeit** Sesqui commemorative quarter
eagle reverse. Note the depressed line from the building to
the word TRUST.

Throughout the years, two varieties of counterfeits have appeared for the Cincinnati, Hawaiian, Hudson, Missouri, Spanish Trail, and Vancouver half dollars.

The first style exhibits a dull gray finish, devoid of the die polish seen on most authentic coins. Beyond this, these counterfeits display repeating flaws that make them readily identifiable.

The second style common to fakes of these six coins is also seen on counterfeits of the Panama-Pacific half dollar. Here, too, the coins are devoid of any genuine die polish, yet they display tremendous luster. In fact, they are too lustrous for these issues: They look as though they were made only yesterday. Their surfaces are granular and lack the details of the genuine article. Beware of coins of this kind that are toned down—the luster may be disguised, but the granular features remain.

Counterfeits of more common commemorative coins are deceptive only because most people assume they would not be candidates for such treatment. The element of surprise boosts the sale of these coins. However, like all other fakes, they contain numerous, repeating flaws.

In 1980, E. G. V. Newman of the British-based International Bureau for the Suppression of Counterfeit Coins (IBSCC) released information about fake U.S. commemorative coins. One of those coins, a 1937 Antietam half dollar, did not seem a likely coin to counterfeit. After the initial release of this information, very few were ever seen.

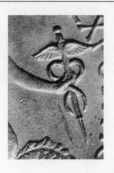

Commemoratives

*Close-up of **genuine** 1903 McKinley commemorative gold dollar obverse. Note the heavy die polish in the field in front of the face.*

*Close-up of **genuine** Pan-Pacific commemorative quarter eagle obverse. Note the swirling die polish under the staff.*

*Close-up of **genuine** Pan-Pacific commemorative quarter eagle reverse. Note the fine, swirling die polish under the eagle.*

Typically, these fakes have a dull gray finish and lack luster. In addition, there are numerous other characteristics that brand them conclusively as fakes.

First examine the cheek area for what look like bag marks. These are actually depressions that repeat from fake to fake. In addition, odd raised lines can be found through the letters of ANNIVERSARY. Another depression can be found on the D of UNITED.

Sometimes the best fakes are coins one would least suspect of being counterfeit. The Antietam, Stone Mountain, and 1937-D Boone half dollars are three coins that can easily fool many buyers, simply because these are not thought of as being worthy to counterfeit. While they are encountered only infre-

quently, keep in mind that just about anything can be copied.

On the altered side of the ledger, one may run across a genuine Grant half dollar with a star punched by hand. Always keep the genuine piece in mind, for its characteristics will invariably determine whether or not the coin being examined is genuine.

Because the star was a raised element on the die, it attracted plenty of die polish. Therefore, one should look for genuine die polish on the star, which will run in a vertical fashion.

The stars on altered pieces are punched in and many times show nothing but uninterrupted metal, with no lines whatsoever.

Commemoratives
Genuine *Lafayette commemorative silver dollar obverse and reverse.*

Close-up of ***genuine*** *Lafayette commemorative silver dollar reverse. Note the swirling die polish under the horse.*

Close-up of ***genuine*** *Lafayette commemorative silver dollar reverse. Note the die cracks through the date.*

Close-up of ***genuine*** *Lafayette commemorative silver dollar obverse. Note the die cracks through the lettering.*

Commemoratives
Counterfeit Antietam commemorative half dollar obverse
and reverse.

*Close-up of **counterfeit** Antietam commemorative half dollar obverse. Note the repeating depression on the cheek of General Lee.*

*Close-up of **counterfeit** Antietam commemorative half dollar obverse. Note the repeating depression on the vertical shaft of the D of UNITED.*

*Close-ups of **genuine** Vancouver commemorative half dollar reverse. Note the die polish through the lettering.*

Territorials
Counterfeit 1853 United States Assay Office twenty-dollar gold obverse and reverse.

*Close-up of **counterfeit** 1853 United States Assay Office twenty-dollar gold obverse. The arrow points to the depression near the end of the branch.*

*Close-up of **counterfeit** 1853 United States Assay Office twenty-dollar gold obverse. The arrow points to the depression in the field between the legend and banner.*

Other times, circular lines may be present on the altered star.

Overall, look for well-defined die polish and appropriate luster. Sharpness in the letters and digits is not as useful for authentication in the commemorative series as it is for regular-issue coinage, due to the roundness typically found in these features on genuine commemorative coins.

Territorials

Surprisingly little U.S. territorial gold coinage has been forged. Besides the common replicas of the California fractional gold series, counterfeits are limited primarily to the United States Assay Office of Gold issues of 1852 and 1853. The most common of these is the 1853 Assay twenty-dollar coin.

This counterfeit piece is prooflike in appearance and rounded in its details, and exhibits several depressions that repeat from fake to fake. The genuine Assay issues have sharp details and a great deal of die flow in the fields, and are well-defined pieces.

On the counterfeit, look for a repeating depression on the base of the branch being held by the eagle. This depression, which looks like a bag mark, is a key counterfeit diagnostic. Also, a repeating depression is seen in the field between the legend and the banner on this issue.

The counterfeit version of the 1852 ten-dollar Assay piece is likewise prooflike, and exhibits repeating depressions. The most prominent is a circular depression between the N and I of CALIFORNIA on the reverse.

Genuine pieces do not possess the prooflike appearance of the counterfeit. Rather, their fields are rough and textured, with considerable die flow. The devices, letters, and digits on the genuine pieces are sharp and well-defined, erupting from the fields and having sharp, angular features.

Other than these two deliberate counterfeits, the rest of the territorial coins found in fake form are common, cheap replicas. These are made of base metal and are detected easily by the presence of a seam along the edge. Also, the weights of these replicas are considerably lower than what they should be.

14 FREQUENTLY SEEN COUNTERFEIT COINS

Counterfeit and altered coins are considerably less common today than they were twenty years ago, attesting to the success of efforts by ANACS and others to curb these problems. However, it would be foolish—and false—to say that these abuses have been rendered insignificant.

During a typical month, PCGS sees about 100 counterfeit and altered coins among the submissions it receives. That is only about one-quarter of 1 percent (.25 percent) of all the coins submitted to the service, undoubtedly, the percentage in the numismatic marketplace is somewhat higher than that; as many counterfeit and altered coins are weeded out by the dealer network before they ever make it to PCGS. Still, the number of fakes in the marketplace today is considerably lower than in the past, due to the greater knowledge and information now available.

The counterfeit and altered coins most often seen today are basically the same ones that have been seen for years. A summary of the most frequent fakes follows.

1909-S VDB Cent
Without a doubt, the most commonly seen counterfeit or altered coin is the 1909-S VDB Lincoln cent. This often-encountered alteration is made by taking an otherwise common 1909 VDB cent and adhering an "S" mint mark to it. This particular fake exploded in popularity in the 1960s and 1970s, and the many altered pieces made at that time remain today. The mint marks reportedly were mass-produced on cookie sheets and sold in vials, with instructions that epoxy glue worked just fine as an adhesive.

Knowledge of the genuine-style mint mark will make it quite easy to detect this alteration. It can always be identified through the misshaped "S" mint mark.

1916-D Dime
Close on the heels of the 1909-S VDB cent is the 1916-D Winged Liberty ("Mercury") dime. This fake, like the cent, is the product of alteration. The forger will take a common, inexpensive 1916 dime and typically attach a "D" mint mark to the reverse with epoxy. Detecting such pieces is easy in most cases, as the forger rarely uses the proper-style mint mark. Typically, an altered piece does not have the squared-off serifs, the boxy shape of the mink mark itself, or the triangular effect in the interior of the "D." Many times, the phony mint mark looks wafer-thin, with no body or height. Genuine mint marks always stand tall, even when a coin is circulated.

After these two "kings of the hill" are accounted for, the rankings on the list of commonly encountered counterfeits start to run together.

1893-S Morgan Dollar
The next prominent piece is the 1893-S Morgan silver dollar. Like the 1909-S VDB cent and the 1916-D dime, this coin—when faked—is almost always the product of alteration. This time, however, one will find not only added mint marks, but also altered dates. Fake 1893-S dollars have been created from both 1898 and 1898-S dollars. There is a special satisfaction in exposing a bogus 1893-S dollar that not only has an added "S" but also has had its date changed from 1898.

1909-S VDB Cent
Altered 1909-S VDB Lincoln cent obverse and reverse. Note the added "S."

Close-up of ***altered*** 1909-S VDB Lincoln cent obverse. Note the added and misshapen "S."

1916-D Dime
Close-up of ***altered*** 1916-D Mercury dime reverse. Note the added "D," which is misshapen.

1916-D Dime
Altered 1916-D Mercury dime obverse and reverse. Note the added "D."

1893-S Morgan Dollar

*Close-up of **genuine** 1893-S Morgan dollar obverse. The date slants up to the right. The "1" of the date is centered over the dentil.*

*Close-up of **genuine** 1893-S Morgan dollar obverse. Note the die line through the top of the T and the "rabbit ears" die chip in the foot of the R of LIBERTY.*

1955 Doubled Die Cent

*Close-up of **genuine** 1955 Doubled-Die Lincoln cent obverse. Note the separation of the numerals in the doubling of the date.*

*Close-up of **genuine** 1955 Doubled-Die Lincoln cent reverse. Note the "V"-shaped die line along the shaft of the T of CENT.*

Fortunately, fakes of this coin are detected easily because the diagnostics on the genuine coin's obverse are readily recognizable. The die characteristics in the word LIBERTY and the unique placement of the date, both exclusive to this issue, make it extremely easy to identify a genuine 1893-S dollar, down to the lowest grades. In recent years, 1893-S dollars have been seen with an embossed mint mark added.

1955 Doubled-Die Cent

Unlike all of the preceding coins in this list, fraudulent versions of the 1955 Doubled-Die Lincoln cent inevitably are counterfeits, rather than alterations. This particular fake, once truly rampant, has been scaled back a bit, but still is encountered now and then. Once again, it can be ferreted out quite readily because of the relative ease in identifying

the genuine coin. Just one set of dies was used to strike the genuine pieces, so certain diagnostics will be common to all of them. Always look for the telltale die lines to the left of—and parallel to—the T in CENT on the reverse. These crisscrossing die lines are fairly well-protected, being next to the vertical shaft of the T, and can be observed right down to the grade of Very Good to Fine. Since most fakes of this coin are encountered in the Extremely Fine to Mint State range, the absence of these characteristics would be a dead giveaway that they were bogus. To date, no counterfeits seen at PCGS have been found with genuine die characteristics.

High-Relief Saint-Gaudens Double Eagle

The first gold coin on the list of frequently encountered fakes is the 1907 high-relief

High-Relief Saint-Gaudens Double Eagle
Counterfeit Saint-Gaudens High Relief double eagle obverse and reverse.

Close-up of *counterfeit* Saint-Gaudens High Relief double
eagle reverse. Note the "omega" sign within the claw of the
eagle.

Close-up of *counterfeit* Saint-Gaudens High Relief double
eagle obverse. Note the tooling marks on the ray above the
first "M" of the date.

Saint-Gaudens $20 gold piece. The most
commonly seen forgery of this piece is the
so-called "Omega" counterfeit. There are
many theories and anecdotes associated
with this fake, the most famous being that
the counterfeiter, wanting to "sign" his
work, treated the reverse die so the resulting coins would bear evidence of the Greek
letter omega, or at least a facsimile of it. No
one knows for sure how this came about,
or whether it was deliberate, but similar
omegas also appear on other counterfeit
gold coins. One thing is certain, however: it
is an easy way to detect this particular fake.
Even without this tool, other diagnostics
give this piece away. Most notable are the
tool marks in the rays above the date. It is
wise to focus here, as many times the omega
is buffed out in an effort to disguise or bury
the evidence.

1804 Bust Dollar

The 1804 silver dollar, widely known as the
"King of American Coins," also is one of the
most frequently forged. In most cases, however, these forgeries apparently were intended not to defraud anyone, but just to give
the owner a replica of this rare and famous
coin. In fact, most fakes of this coin are crude
casts. These are almost always lightweight
and poorly defined, and sometimes even
have reeded edges. Remember, the genuine
coins were made in proof quality with lettered edges. Low-grade specimens of genuine 1801, 1802, and 1803 dollars occasionally
have had their last digit altered to a "4," but
the perpetrators of this deception seldom
match the correct characteristics of the "4."
Using reference books such as Milferd H.
Bolender's classic work *The United States
Early Silver Dollars from 1794 to 1803*, the

1856 Flying Eagle Cent
*Close-up of **genuine** 1856 Flying Eagle cent obverse. Note the chip on the ball of the "5" in the date. Also note how the front edge of the "5" bisects the ball.*

*Close-up of **altered** 1856 Flying Eagle cent obverse (from genuine 1858 cent). Note how the front line of the "5" is in line with the front of the ball. Note how the ball is completely round.*

*Close-up of **genuine** 1856 Flying Eagle cent obverse. Note the positioning of the A and M of AMERICA.*

*Close-up of **altered** 1856 Flying Eagle cent obverse (from genuine 1858 cent). Note how the A and M of AMERICA run together.*

date and variety used for such alterations can be located.

1856 Flying Eagle Cent

The 1856 Flying Eagle cent brings us back to the realm of alterations. Fake versions of this coin almost always are altered from 1858 Flying Eagle cents. Because of the unique characteristics of the 1856, the altered specimens are easy to weed out.

Make sure the ball of the "5" in the date is chipped or abbreviated. All genuine 1856 Flying Eagle cents have this characteristic. Note also how the backside of the "5" actually bisects the ball of the digit. On the altered pieces, the ball of the "5" is complete and round and is tucked within the "5," not allowing the backside of the "5" to bisect it.

The positioning of the letters A and M of AMERICA on genuine 1856 cents is found on some 1857 cents but never on those dated 1858, so this is an easy way to separate the wheat from the chaff. Notice how the letters meet at an angle on the genuine coin, but do not actually touch. With altered pieces, the letters will either be joined together in a defined line (on 1858 cents of the large-letters variety) or well-separated (on the small-letters variety). The last place to look would be the inside of the word OF. On genuine pieces, the interior of the O is rectangular. On altered pieces, the interior is oval and lacks the distinct angles of the genuine piece.

Cincinnati Half Dollar

In the world of commemorative coins, certain pieces have become particular favorites with forgers. Of these, the 1936 Cincinnati half

Cincinnati Half Dollar
Counterfeit Cincinnati commemorative half dollar obverse and reverse.

Close-up of **counterfeit** Cincinnati commemorative half dollar obverse. Note the repeating depression in the hair.

dollar is at or near the top of the list—due in large measure, no doubt, to its relatively high premium value. Counterfeits of this coin were widely seen during the 1970s and still turn up with some regularity to this day.

The most commonly seen Cincinnati half dollar fakes are identified easily by the two indentations in the hair of Stephen Foster. These repeating depressions occur because the model coin had these defects. When transferred to the counterfeiter's die, the depressions actually are lumps. These lumps on the die then produce the repeating depressions on all of the coins subsequently struck.

Embossed-Mint-Mark Buffalo Nickels

The next frequently seen forgery is not so much an individual coin, but rather a method of alteration: the creation of embossed mint marks on rare-date Indian Head (or Buffalo) nickels. What an ingenious way to alter rare Buffalo nickels! Where most alterations typically are performed by using epoxy to adhere a mint mark to the surface of a coin, this method broke new ground in technology and technique.

In this instance, some ingenious malefactor decided to drill into the edge of a common P-mint nickel just below the spot where a mint mark would be located on a branch-mint issue. The counterfeiter then inserted an embossing tool similar to a needle-nosed pliers, with one end shaped like an "S" or a "D." By squeezing the tool, a mint mark would rise magically from the field of the coin, as if it had been struck in the regular minting process. The forger then filled the hole with a

Embossed-Mint-Mark Buffalo Nickels
*Close-up of **altered** 1926-D Buffalo nickel edge. Note the area of the edge through which an embossed mint mark was applied.*

*Close-up of **altered** 1926-D Buffalo nickel reverse. Note the embossed mint mark and its lack of height.*

nickel composition and buffed the edge smooth to hide the handiwork.

Initially, Buffalo nickels altered in this manner were sold in hard plastic holders to divert attention from the edge and to help the coins infiltrate the numismatic world.

One of the first clues to look for on these pieces is the absence of a seam where the mint mark meets the field. On just about every other alteration involving a mint mark, a seam of this kind will be present, as the mint mark never was part of the coin to begin with. But with an embossed piece, the mint mark is very much a part of the coin, since it was squeezed up from the field and therefore was created from the actual coinage metal.

Detecting a coin with an embossed mint mark will be easier if one has access to the edge of the coin. In fact, it is imperative to be able to view the edge, and these alterations underscore the importance of examining the "third side" of a coin. On an embossed alteration, the edge will appear inconsistent and look as though it had been treated at the point of drilling. Sometimes the color will be different there from the rest of the edge because of the forger's inability to match the metal used to fill the void with the metal surrounding it.

Saint-Gaudens Double Eagles

The last commonly seen fake also is not an individual coin, but rather a type of fake that turns up on coins of many different dates. It is what is known in numismatic circles as the *stock-edge* counterfeit Saint-Gaudens $20 gold piece, the term referring to a commonly used collar containing certain defects that almost always appear on the edges of the coins it was used to produce. The telltale sign of the counterfeit edge is an unusual raised line that curves upward from the middle bar of the E. While not every counterfeit $20 has this edge, the vast majority do—and when a piece has this characteristic, it can be ruled conclusively a forgery.

Interestingly, the counterfeiter used this style of edge in striking fake $20s dated 1928. This is noteworthy because the Mint changed its collar style at that time, and genuine 1928 "Saints" carry letters on the edge that are thicker and more block-like than those on previous issues. Nevertheless, the counterfeiter continued to use the fake collar with the outdated style of lettering.

Summing Up

These top ten counterfeits represent the forgeries most commonly seen, not only at PCGS but also throughout the numismatic marketplace. This list could have included

Saint-Gaudens Double Eagles
Counterfeit 1920 Saint-Gaudens double eagle obverse and reverse.

Close-up of **counterfeit** *1920 Saint-Gaudens double eagle edge. The "stock edge" shows the curved line shooting off the middle stroke of the E of E PLURIBUS UMUM.*

other fakes, among them rip-offs of the entire Indian Head quarter eagle and half eagle series. But many of these are not as deceptive as the ones actually listed. Because of heightened public awareness and the hobby's aggressive campaign against fakes and fakers, fewer new counterfeits have appeared in recent years.

Counterfeit detection is a learned skill, acquired through the experience of looking at thousands of coins. At the same time, the first line of defense is to know what genuine coins look like and what their diagnostics are. Once you master these skills and examine more and more coins, you will find it increasingly easier to recognize counterfeit and altered coins.

Generally, the coins you see will be genuine pieces; in fact, the vast majority will be genuine. You should always reserve judgment, though, when contemplating the purchase of a rare coin or a coin whose price seems too good to be true. Check it out thoroughly— for as the saying goes, it is better to be safe than sorry.

GLOSSARY

AG (About Good)
Abbreviation. See definition below.

ANA (American Numismatic Association)
A nonprofit organization founded in 1888 for the advancement of numismatics.

ANACS (American Numismatic Association Certification Service)
A service established by the ANA in 1972 to authenticate coins; its mission was broadened in 1979 to include coin grading as well. The ANA subsequently sold the grading portion of the service to Amos Press Inc. of Sidney, Ohio, which operates it today under the acronym ANACS, although those letters no longer are shorthand for the full original name.

AU (Almost Uncirculated or About Uncirculated)
Abbreviation. See definition below.

About Good
The grade AG-3. The grade of a coin that falls short of Good. Only the main features of the coin are present in this grade. Peripheral lettering, date, stars, etc., sometimes are worn away partially.

adjustment marks
Pre-striking file marks seen mainly on gold and silver coins made prior to 1840. These removed excess metal from overweight planchets.

album friction
Similar to album slide marks, though the friction may be only slight rubbing on the high points.

album slide marks
Lines, usually parallel, imparted to the surface of a coin by the plastic "slide" of an album.

alloy
A combination of two or more metals.

Almost Uncirculated (*alt.* About Uncirculated)
The term(s) corresponding to the grades AU-50, 53, 55, and 58. A coin that at first glance appears Uncirculated but upon closer inspection has slight friction or rub.

alteration
A coin that has a date, mint mark, or other feature that has been changed, added, or removed, usually to simulate a rarer issue.

annealing
The heating of a die or planchet to soften the metal before preparation of the die or striking of the coin.

anvil die
The lower die, usually the reverse—although on some issues with striking problems, the obverse was employed as the lower die. Because of the physics of minting, the fixed lower-die impression is slightly better struck than the upper-die impression.

artificial toning
Coloring added to the surface of a coin by chemicals and/or heat. Many different methods have been employed over the years.

attributes
The elements that make up a coin's grade. The main ones are marks (hairlines for Proofs), luster, strike, and eye appeal.

BN (Brown)
A PCGS grading suffix used for copper coins that meet Brown standards. See definition below.

BU (Brilliant Uncirculated)
Abbreviation. See definition below.

bag friction
Coin-on-coin friction that is the result of coins rubbing against each other in a bag. See *"coin" friction, roll friction*.

bag mark
A generic term applied to a mark on a coin from another coin; it may, or may not, have been incurred in a bag.

bag toning
Coloring acquired from the bag in which a coin was stored. The cloth bags in which coins were transported contained sulfur and other reactive chemicals. When stored in such bags for extended periods, the coins near and in contact with the cloth often acquired beautiful red, blue, yellow, and other vibrant colors. Sometimes the pattern of the cloth is visible in the toning; other times, coins have crescent-shaped toning because another coin was covering part of the surface, preventing toning. Bag toning is seen mainly on Morgan silver dollars, though occasionally on other series.

basal state
The condition of a coin that is identifiable only as to date and type; one-year-type coins may not have a date visible.

basal value
The value base from which Dr. William H. Sheldon's 70-point grade/price system started; this lowest-grade price was one dollar for the 1794 large cent upon which he based his system.

basining
The process of polishing a die to impart a mirrored surface or to remove clash marks or other injuries from the die.

beaded border
Small, round devices around the edge of a coin, often seen on early U.S. coins. These were replaced by dentils.

blank
The flat disk of metal before it is struck by the dies and made into a coin. See *planchet*.

blended
A term applied to an element of a coin (design, date, lettering, etc.) that is worn into another element or the surrounding field.

branch mint
One of the various subsidiary government facilities that struck, or still strikes, coins.

brilliant
A coin with full luster, unimpeded by toning, or impeded only by extremely light toning.

Brilliant Uncirculated
A generic term applied to any coin that has not been in circulation. It often is applied to

coins with little "brilliance" left, which properly should be described as simply Uncirculated.

bronze
An alloy of copper, tin, and zinc, with copper the principal metal.

Brown
The term applied to a copper coin that no longer has the red color of copper. There are many "shades" of brown color—mahogany, chocolate, etc. (abbreviated as BN when used as part of a grade).

buckled die
A die that has "warped" in some way, possibly from excess clashing, and that produces coins which are slightly "bent." This may be more apparent on one side and occasionally apparent only on one side.

bulged die
A die that has clashed so many times that a small indentation is formed in it. Coins struck from this die have a "bulged" area.

bullet toning
See *target toning*.

burnishing
A process by which the surfaces of a planchet or a coin are made to shine through rubbing or polishing. This term is used in two contexts—one positive, one negative. In a positive sense, Proof planchets are burnished before they are struck—a procedure done originally by rubbing wet sand across the surfaces to impart a mirrorlike finish. In a negative sense, the surfaces on repaired and altered coins sometimes are burnished by various methods. In some instances, a high-speed drill with some type of wire brush attachment is used to achieve this effect.

burnishing lines
Lines resulting from burnishing, seen mainly on open-collar Proofs and almost never found on close-collar Proofs. These lines are incuse in the fields and go under lettering and devices.

burn mark
See *counting-machine mark*.

business strike (*alt.* regular strike)
A regular-issue coin, struck on regular planchets by dies given normal preparation. These are coins struck for commerce that the government places into circulation.

bust
The head and shoulders of the emblematic Liberty seen on many U.S. coins. See *Capped Bust* and *Draped Bust*.

***CAM (cameo) (*alt. *CA*)**
A PCGS grading suffix used for Proofs that meet cameo standards. See definition below.

cabinet friction
Slight disturbance seen on coins (usually on the obverse) that were stored in wooden cabinets used by early collectors to house their specimens. Often a soft cloth was used to wipe away dust, causing light hairlines or friction.

cameo
A term applied to coins, usually Proofs and prooflike coins, that have frosted devices and lettering that contrast with the fields. When this is deep, the coins are said to be "black-and-white" cameos. Occasionally, frosty coins have "cameo" devices that do not contrast as dramatically with the fields. Specifically applied by PCGS to Proofs that meet cameo (CAM) standards.

Capped Bust
A term describing any of the various incarnations of the head of Miss Liberty represented on early U.S. coins by a bust with a floppy cap. This design is credited to John Reich.

carbon spot
A spot seen mainly on copper and gold coins, though also found occasionally on nickel U.S. coins (which are 75 percent copper) and

silver coins (which are 10 percent copper). Carbon spots are brown to black spots of oxidation that range from minor to severe—some so large and far advanced that the coin is not graded because of environmental damage. See *copper spot.*

cartwheel
The pleasing effect seen on some coins when they are rotated in a good light source. The luster rotates around like the spokes of a wagon wheel. A term applied mainly to frosty Mint State coins, especially silver dollars, to describe their luster. Also, a slang term for a silver dollar.

Castaing machine
A device invented by French engineer Jean Castaing, which added the edge lettering and devices to early U.S. coins before they were struck. Some have speculated that reeding on early U.S. coins was also added using this device, but the data is inconclusive.

cast blanks
Planchets made by a mold method, rather than being cut from strips of metal.

cast counterfeit
A replication of a genuine coin usually created by making molds of the obverse and reverse, then casting base metal in the molds. A seam is usually visible on the edge unless it has been ground away.

cent
A denomination valued at one-hundredth of a dollar, struck continuously by the U.S. Mint since 1793 except for 1815.

chasing
A method used by forgers to create a mint mark on a coin. It involves heating the surfaces and moving the metal to form the mint mark.

choice
An adjectival description applied to a coin's grade, e.g., choice Uncirculated, choice Very Fine, etc. Used to describe an especially attractive example of a particular grade.

circulated
A term applied to a coin that has wear, ranging from slight rubbing to heavy wear.

clad
A term for any of the modern "sandwich" coins that have layers of different alloys.

clashed dies
Dies that have been damaged by striking each other without a planchet between them. Typically, this imparts part of the obverse image to the reverse die and vice versa.

clash marks
The images of the dies seen on coins struck from clashed dies. The obverse will have images from the reverse and vice versa.

cleaned
A term applied to a coin whose original surface has been removed. The effects may be slight or severe, depending on the method used.

clipped
A term for an irregularly cut planchet. A clip can be straight or curved, depending upon where it was cut from the strip of metal.

clogged die
A die that has grease or some other contaminant lodged in the recessed areas. Coins struck from such a die have diminished detail, sometimes completely missing.

close(d) collar
The edge device, sometimes called a collar die, that surrounds the lower die. Actually, open and close collars are both closed collars, as opposed to segmented collars. The close collar imparts either reeding or a smooth, plain edge.

coin
Metal formed into a disk of standardized weight and stamped with a standard design to enable it to circulate as money authorized by a government body.

"coin" friction

Coin-on-coin friction imparted to coins when they rub together in rolls or bags and a light amount of metal is displaced. See also *roll friction* and *bag friction*.

collar

A device placed around the lower die to prevent excessive spreading or later to impart reeding or devices to the edge.

commemoratives

Coins issued to honor some person, place, or event and, in many instances, to raise funds for activities related to the theme. Sometimes called NCLT (noncirculating legal tender) commemoratives.

commercial grade

A grade that is usually one level higher than the market grade; refers to a coin that is "pushed" a grade, such as an EF/AU coin (corresponding to 45+) sold as AU-50.

consensus grading

The process of determining the condition of a coin by using multiple graders.

contact marks

Marks on a coin that are incurred through contact with another coin or a foreign object. These are generally small, compared to other types of marks such as gouges. See *bag marks*.

contemporary counterfeit

A coin, usually in base metal, struck from crudely engraved dies and made to pass for face value at the time of its creation. Sometimes such counterfeits are collected along with the genuine coins, especially in the case of American Colonial issues.

copper spot (stain)

A spot or stain commonly seen on gold coinage, indicating an area of copper concentration that has oxidized. Copper spots or stains range from tiny dots to large blotches.

copy

Any reproduction, fraudulent or otherwise, of a coin.

copy dies

Dies made at a later date, usually showing slight differences from the originals. An example would be the reverse of 1804 Class 2 silver dollars, although the "original" Class 1 dies also could be called copy dies, as they are different than the 1798–1803 dies. Also used to denote counterfeit dies copied directly from a genuine coin.

corrosion

Damage that results when reactive chemicals act upon metal. When toning ceases to be a "protective" coating and instead begins to damage a coin, corrosion is the cause. Usually confined to copper, nickel, and silver regular issues, although patterns in aluminum, white metal, tin, etc., also are subject to this harmful process.

counterfeit

Literally, a coin that is not genuine. There are cast and struck counterfeits and the term is also applied to issues with added mint marks, altered dates, etc.

counting-machine mark

A dense patch of lines caused by the rubber wheel of a counting machine where the wheel was set with insufficient spacing for the selected coin. Many coins have been subjected to counting machines—among these are Mercury dimes, Buffalo nickels, Walking Liberty half dollars, Morgan and Peace dollars, and Saint-Gaudens double eagles.

cud

An area of a coin struck by a die that has a complete break across part of its surface. A cud may be either a *retained cud*, where the faulty piece of the die is still retained, or a *full cud*, where the piece of the die has fallen away. Retained cuds usually have dentil detail, while full cuds do not.

cupro-nickel

Any alloy of copper and nickel. Now used primarily in referring to the modern "sandwich" coinage. The Flying Eagle and early

Indian Head cents, nickel three-cent pieces, and nickel five-cent pieces also are cupro-nickel coins.

DCAM (Deep Cameo)
A PCGS grading suffix used for Proofs that meet deep cameo standards. See definition below.

DMPL (Deep Mirror Prooflike)
A PCGS grading suffix used for Morgan dollars that meet deep mirror prooflike standards. See definition below.

date
The numerals on a coin representing the year in which it was struck. Restrikes are made in years subsequent to the one that appears on them.

deep cameo
A term applied to coins, usually Proofs and prooflike coins, that have deeply frosted devices and lettering that contrast with the fields—often called "black-and-white" cameos. Specifically applied to those Proofs that meet deep cameo (DCAM) standards.

deep mirror prooflike
A term applied to any coin that has deeply reflective mirrorlike fields, especially Morgan dollars. Those Morgan dollars that meet PCGS standards are designated deep mirror prooflike (DMPL).

denomination
The value assigned by a government to a specific coin.

dentils (*alt.* denticles)
The tooth-like devices seen around the rim on many coins. Originally, these were somewhat irregular; later, they became much more uniform—the result of better preparatory and striking machinery.

design type
A specific motif placed upon coinage which may be used for several denominations and sub-types, e.g., the Liberty Seated design type used for silver coins from half dimes through dollars and various sub-types therein.

device
Any specific design element. Often refers to the principal design element, such as the head of Miss Liberty.

device punch
A steel rod with a raised device on the end used to punch the element into a working die. This technique was used before hubbed dies became the norm.

die
A steel rod that is engraved, punched, or hubbed with devices, lettering, the date, and other emblems.

die alignment
The condition in which the obverse and reverse dies are aligned properly and therefore strike a coin evenly. When the dies are out of alignment, two things can happen: If the dies are out of parallel, weakness may be noted in a quadrant of the coin's obverse and the corresponding part of the reverse; and if the dies are spaced improperly, the resultant coins may have overall weakness.

die break
A defect in a die that has cracked during use; if not removed from service, such a die may break eventually. See also *die crack*.

die crack (*alt.* die break)
A defect in a die. When dies crack, the coins struck from those dies have raised, irregular lines ranging from very slight to very large—some of them quite irregular. When a die breaks apart totally, the break will result in a full—or retained—cud, depending upon whether the broken piece falls from the die.

die line (*alt.* die scratch)
A polish line on a die; being incuse, it results in a raised line on the coins struck with that die.

die rust
Rust that has accumulated on a die that was not stored properly. Often such rust was pol-

ished away, so that only the deeply recessed parts of the die still exhibited it. A few examples are known of coins that were struck with extremely rusted dies—the 1876-CC dime, for one.

die state
A readily identified point in the life of a coinage die. Often dies clash and are polished, crack, break, etc., resulting in different stages of the die. These are called die states. Some coins have barely distinguishable die states, while others go through multiple distinctive ones.

die striations
Raised lines on coins that were struck with polished dies. As more coins are struck with such dies, the striations become fainter until most or all disappear.

die variety
A coin that can be linked to a given set of dies because of characteristics possessed by those dies and imparted to the coin at the time it was struck. In the early years of U.S. coinage history, when dies were made by hand engraving or punching, each die was slightly different. The coins from these unique dies are die varieties and are collected in every denomination. By the 1840s, when dies were made by hubbing and therefore were more uniform, die varieties resulted mainly from variances in the size, shape, and positioning of the date and mint mark.

die wear
Deterioration in a die caused by excessive use. This may evidence itself on coins produced with that die in a few indistinct letters or numerals or, in extreme cases, a loss of detail throughout the entire coin. Some coins, especially certain nickel issues, have a fuzzy, indistinct appearance even on Uncirculated examples.

dime (*alt.* disme)
A denomination, one-tenth of a dollar, that has been struck from 1796 to date, with the exception of only a few years.

ding
Slang term for a small to medium-size mark on a coin. See *rim ding*.

dipped
A term applied to a coin that has been placed in a commercial "dip" solution, a mild acid wash that removes the toning from most coins. Some dip solutions employ other chemicals, such as bases, to accomplish a similar result. The first few layers of metal are removed with every dip, so coins dipped repeatedly will lose luster, hence the term *over dipped*.

dipping solution
Any of the commercial "dips" available on the market, usually acid-based.

dollar
The basic unit, along with the eagle, for the currency of the United States. At the time of the Mint Act of 1792 establishing the U.S. coinage system, a dollar was comparable to the Central European thaler and the Spanish silver peso of 8 reales, containing nearly an ounce of silver. Its legal value in silver and gold was modified over the years on a number of occasions. Today, it is a fiat-money unit with no fixed legal equivalent in silver or gold; rather, its purchasing power rises or falls, in a general way, in accordance with fluctuations in the market value of gold.

doubled die
A die that has been struck more than once by a hub in misaligned positions, resulting in doubling of design elements. Before the introduction of hubbing, the individual elements of a coin's design were either engraved or punched into the die, so any doubling was limited to a specific element. With hubbed dies, multiple impressions are needed from the hub to make a single die with adequate detail. When shifting occurs in the alignment between the hub and the die, the die ends up with some of its features doubled—then imparts this doubling to every coin it strikes. The coins struck from such dies are called doubled-die errors—the most famous being the 1955 Doubled-Die Lincoln cent.

double eagle

Literally two eagles, or twenty dollars. A twenty-dollar U.S. gold coin issued from 1850 through 1932. (One double eagle dated 1849 is known and is part of the National Numismatic Collection at the Smithsonian Institution. Nearly half a million examples dated 1933 were struck by the U.S. Mint, but virtually all were melted when private gold ownership was outlawed that year, and currently federal officials claim it is illegal to own any specimens that survive, except the single coin that was sold in 2002 and was monetized by the Treasury.)

double-struck

A condition that results when a coin is not ejected from the dies and is struck a second time. Such a coin is said to be double-struck. Triple-struck coins and other multiple strikings also are known. Proofs are usually double-struck on purpose in order to sharpen their details; this is sometimes visible under magnification.

Draped Bust (*alt.* Turban Head)

A design by Robert Scot used on certain U.S. coins—half dimes through eagles—from 1795 until 1807. Miss Liberty has a prominent drape across her bust and wears a turban-type hat.

drawbar lines

See *roller marks*.

drift mark

An area on a coin, often rather long, that has a discolored, streaky look. This is the result of impurities or foreign matter in the dies. One theory is that burnt wood was rolled into the planchets, resulting in these black streaks.

EAC (Early American Coppers)

Abbreviation for an association made up of collectors who specialize in early U.S. copper coins, especially large cents, which they generally collect by Sheldon numbers.

EF (Extremely Fine or Extra Fine)

Abbreviation. See definition below.

eagle

A gold coin with a face value of ten dollars. Along with the dollar, this was the basis of the U.S. currency system from 1792 until 1971. No U.S. gold coins were struck for circulation after 1933, and all gold coins issued prior to that time were recalled from circulation. The only exceptions were coins of value to collectors. Also, in grading, the bird found on many U.S. coins.

edge

The third side of a coin. It may be plain, reeded, or ornamented—with lettering or other elements raised or incuse.

edge device

A group of letters or emblems on the edge of a coin. Examples would be the stars and lettering on the edge of Indian Head eagles and Saint-Gaudens double eagles.

electrotype

A duplicate coin created by the electrolytic method, in which metal is deposited into a mold made from the original. The obverse and reverse metal shells are then filled with metal and fused together—after which the edges sometimes are filed to obscure the seam.

elements

For the purposes of this book, the various components of grading. In other numismatic contexts, this term refers to the various devices and emblems seen on coins.

emission sequence

The order in which die states are struck. Also, the order in which coins of a particular date or series are struck.

engraver

The person responsible for the design and/or punches used for a particular coin.

envelope toning

A term applied to toning that results from storage in 2 X 2 manila envelopes; most paper envelopes contain reactive chemicals.

environmental damage
Damage to a coin that results from exposure to the elements. This may be minor, such as toning that is nearly black, or major—as when a coin found in the ground or water has severely pitted surfaces. PCGS does not grade coins with more than very minor environmental damage.

eroded die
See *worn die*.

error coin
A coin with a mint-caused abnormality, such as a clipped planchet, off-center striking, large planchet flaw, and so on that is graded and described; PCGS encapsulates those issues as error coins with an E preceding the coin number.

Extremely Fine (*alt.* Extra Fine)
The term corresponding to the grades EF-40 and EF-45 (or XF-40 and XF-45). Coins in these grades have nearly full detail with only the high points worn and the fields lightly rubbed; often, luster still clings in protected areas.

eye appeal
The element of a coin's grade that "grabs" the viewer. The overall look of a coin.

F (Fine)
Abbreviation. See later definition below.

FB (full bands)
A PCGS grading suffix used for Mercury dimes that meet the standards for full bands. Also, the grading suffix used for Roosevelt dimes that meet the standards for full bands. See later definition below.

FBL (full bell lines) (*alt.* FL)
A PCGS grading suffix used for Franklin half dollars that meet the standards for full bell lines. See later definition below.

FH (full head)
A PCGS grading suffix used for Standing Liberty quarters that meet the standards for a full head. See later definition.

FR (Fair)
Abbreviation. See later definition.

FS (full steps)
A PCGS grading suffix used for Jefferson nickels that meet the standards for full steps. See later definition.

Fair
The adjective corresponding to the grade FR-2. In this grade, there is heavy wear with the lettering, devices, and date partially visible.

fantasy piece
A term applied to coins struck at the whim of Mint officials. Examples include the 1868 large cent Type of 1857 and the various 1865 Motto and 1866 No Motto coins.

fasces
A Roman symbol of authority used as a motif on the reverse of Mercury dimes. It consists of a bundle of rods wrapped around an ax with a protruding blade. The designation *full bands* refers to fasces on which there is complete separation in the central bands across the rods.

field
The portion of a coin where there is no design—generally the flat part (although on some issues, the field is slightly curved).

finalizer
A PCGS grader who, before computers were used for this task, compared his own grade with those of other graders and determined the final grade. The *verifier* replaced the finalizer after PCGS began inputting the grades by computer.

Fine
The adjective corresponding to the grades F-12 and 15. In these grades, most of a coin's detail is worn away. Some detail is present in the recessed areas, but it is not sharp.

first strike
A coin struck early in the life of a die. First strikes sometimes are characterized by stri-

ated or mirror-like fields if the die was polished. Almost always full or well struck, with crisp detail.

flat luster

A subdued type of luster seen on coins struck from worn dies. Often these coins have a gray or otherwise dull color that makes the fields seem even more lackluster.

flip

A clear plastic holder, usually pliable, that is used to store an ungraded ("raw") coin. Flips are used to house coins when they are submitted to PCGS, but are not recommended for long-term storage if they contain polyvinyl chloride, or PVC. Care should be taken with PVC-free flips, as they usually are very brittle and can damage the delicate surfaces of a coin. (See *PVC*.)

flip rub

Discoloration, often only slight, on the highest points of a coin resulting from contact with a flip. On occasion, highly desirable coins sold in auctions have acquired minor rub from being examined repeatedly in flips by eager bidders.

flow lines (*alt.* stress lines)

Lines, sometimes visible, resulting when the metal flows outward from the center of a planchet as it is struck. "Cartwheel" luster is seen when light is reflected from these radial lines.

focal area

The area of a coin to which a viewer's eye is drawn. An example is the cheek of a Morgan dollar.

four-dollar gold piece

An experimental issue, also known as a *stella*, struck in 1879-1880 as a pattern. Often collected along with regular-issue gold coins, this was meant to be an international coin approximating the Swiss and French twenty-franc coins, the Italian twenty lira, etc.

friction

Slight wear on a coin's high points or in the fields.

frost

A crystallized-metal effect seen in the recessed areas of a die, thus the raised parts of a coin struck with that die. This is imparted to dies by various techniques, such as sandblasting them or pickling them in acid, then polishing the fields, leaving the recessed areas with frost.

frosted devices

Raised elements on coins struck with treated dies that have frost in their recessed areas. Such coins have crystalline surfaces that resemble frost on a lawn.

frosty luster

The crystalline appearance of coins struck with dies that have frost in their recessed areas. Such coins show vibrant luster on their devices and/or surfaces; the amount of crystallization may vary.

full bands (*alt.* full split bands)

A term used to describe the central bands of the fasces on a Mercury dime's reverse when they are fully separated. Also, the term used for the upper and lower horizontal bands on the torch of Roosevelt dimes when they are fully separated. The FB designation indicates an unusually sharp strike and is highly desired by collectors. To qualify for this designation, a coin can have no disturbance of the separation for Mercury dimes and only the slightest disturbance for Roosevelt dimes.

full bell lines

A condition in which the lower sets of lines on the Liberty Bell are fully visible on Franklin half dollars. Very slight disturbance of several lines is acceptable. Full bell lines (FBL or FL) indicate sharpness of strike and seldom are seen on coins of certain dates.

full head

A term used to describe Miss Liberty's head on Standing Liberty quarters when the helmet on her head has full detail. The FH designation can apply to both Type I and Type II coins, but the criteria are different. See chapter 5 for full-head standards.

full steps
A term applied to Jefferson nickels when 5 1/2 or 6 steps are fully defined in the portrait of Monticello, Thomas Jefferson's home, on the reverse.

G (Good)
Abbreviation. See definition below.

galvano
The large metal relief used in the portrait lathe from which a positive reduction, called a hub, is made.

gem
Adjectival description applied to Mint State and Proof-65 coins. It also is used for higher grades and as a generic term for a superb coin.

Good
The adjective corresponding to the grades G-4 and G-6. Coins in these grades usually have little detail but outlined major devices. On some coins, the rims may be worn to the tops of some letters.

grade
The level of preservation of a particular coin. For circulated coins, this is mainly a function of wear, whereas marks, luster, strike, and eye appeal are the principal elements used to determine the grades of Mint State and Proof coins.

grader
An individual who evaluates the condition of coins.

grading
The process of numerically quantifying the condition of a coin. Before the adoption of the Sheldon numerical system, coins were given descriptive grades such as Good, Very Good, Fine, and so forth.

grading standards
The rules, descriptions, and conventions applied to the grading of coins. PCGS has written standards as well as a grading set representing these standards.

hairlines
Fine cleaning lines found mainly in the fields of Proof coins, although they sometimes are found across an entire Proof coin as well as on business strikes.

half cent
The lowest-value coin denomination ever issued by the United States, representing one-two hundredth of a dollar. Half cents were struck from 1793 until the series was discontinued in 1857.

half dime (*alt.* half disme)
A coin denomination, one-twentieth of a dollar, struck from 1792 until it was discontinued in 1873.

half dollar
A coin denomination, one half of a dollar, struck nearly continuously since 1794.

half eagle
A coin denomination, valued at five silver dollars, struck from 1795 until 1916 and again in 1929. Half eagles were recalled, as were all U.S. gold coins, in 1933.

halogen light
A powerful light source that enables a viewer to examine coins closely. This type of light reveals even the tiniest imperfections.

hammer die (*alt.* hammered die)
The upper die—usually the obverse, although on some issues with striking problems the reverse die was placed on top to improve striking quality. In early minting terminology, a hammer die was literally that: the lower die was fixed in a tree stump, the planchet was placed on top of it, and the upper die then was placed upon the planchet and struck with a hammer.

haze

A cloudy film, original or added, seen on both business-strike coins and Proofs. This film can range from a light, nearly clear covering with little effect on the grade to a heavy, opaque layer that might prevent the coin from being graded.

high-end

A term applied to any coin at the upper end of a particular grade. See *premium quality*.

high relief

A condition in which the design elements of a coin stand out dramatically above the flat fields. This three-dimensional effect is achieved through the use of dies with deeply recessed devices and multiple strikings. The term *high relief* is applied specifically to Saint-Gaudens double eagles with the Roman numerals date MCMVII (1907). Coins with high relief often do not strike up properly in a single blow from the dies, leading to weak central detail.

holder

Any device for housing a coin. PCGS holders are made of hard, inert plastic and are sonically sealed and tamper-resistant.

holder toning

Any toning acquired by a coin as a result of storage in a holder. Mainly refers to toning seen on coins stored in Wayte Raymond-type cardboard holders, which contained sulfur and other reactive chemicals. Sometimes vibrant, spectacular reds, greens, blues, yellows, and other colors are seen on coins stored in these holders.

hub

Minting term for the steel device from which a die is produced. The hub is produced with the aid of a portrait lathe or reducing machine and bears a "positive" image of the coin's design—that is, it shows the design as it will appear on the coin itself. The image on the die is "negative"—a mirror image of the design.

impaired Proof

A Proof coin that grades less than PR-60; a circulated Proof. See *mishandled Proof*.

incandescent light

Direct light from a lamp, as opposed to indirect light such as that from a fluorescent bulb.

incomplete strike

A coin that is missing design detail because of a problem during the striking process. The incompleteness may be due to insufficient striking pressure or improperly spaced dies.

incuse design

The intaglio design used on Indian Head quarter eagles and half eagles. These coins were struck from dies which had fields recessed, so that the devices—the areas usually raised—were recessed on the coins themselves. This was an experiment to try to deter counterfeiting and improve wearing quality.

iridescence

A "glow" displayed by a coin, often gleaming through light pastel colors.

Janvier reducing machine (*alt.* Janvier lathe)

The portrait lathe introduced at the U.S. Mint in 1905, which replaced the old Contamin portrait lathe in use since the 1830s. Completely hubbed dies, including the date, were produced from the hubs created by this device.

lamination

A thin piece of metal that has nearly become detached from the surface of a coin. If this breaks off, an irregular hole or planchet flaw is left.

large cent

A large copper U.S. coin, one-hundredth of a dollar, issued from 1793 until 1857, when it was replaced by a much smaller cent made from a copper-nickel alloy. The value of copper in a large cent had risen to more than one cent, requiring the reduction in weight.

lasering

A technique using a laser to alter the surface of a coin.

legend
A phrase that appears on a coin—for instance, UNITED STATES OF AMERICA.

lettered edge
A coin edge that displays an inscription or other design elements, rather than being reeded or plain. The lettering can be either incuse (recessed below the surface) or raised. Incuse lettering is applied before a coin is struck; the Mint did this with a device called the Castaing machine. Raised lettering is found on coins struck with segmented collars; the lettering is raised during the minting process, and when the coin is ejected from the dies, the collar "falls" apart, preventing the lettering from being sheared away.

lettering
The alphabet characters used in creating legends, mottos, and other inscriptions on a coin, whether on the obverse, reverse, or edge.

Liberty
The symbolic figure used in many U.S. coin designs. Also, when in all caps in the text, it refers to the word found on the headband or shield of many coins.

Liberty Cap
The head of Miss Liberty, with a cap on a pole by her head, used on certain U.S. half cents and large cents.

Liberty Head
The design used on most U.S. gold coins from 1838 until 1908. This design was first employed by Christian Gobrecht, with later modifications by Robert Ball Hughes and James Longacre. Morgan dollars and Barber coinage sometimes are referred to as Liberty Head coins.

light line
The band of light seen on photographs of coins, especially Proofs. This band also is seen when a coin is examined under a light.

liner
A coin that is on the cusp between two different grades. A 4/5 liner is a coin that is either a high-end MS/PR-64 or a minimum-standard MS/PR-65. See *high-end* and *premium quality*.

lint mark
A repeating depression on a coin, usually thin and curly, caused by a thread that adhered to a die during the coin's production. Lint marks are found primarily on Proofs. After dies are polished, they are wiped with a cloth, and these sometimes leave tiny threads.

loupe
A magnifying glass used to examine coins. Loupes are found in varying strengths or "powers."

luster (*alt.* lustre)
In numismatics, the amount and strength of light reflected from a coin's surface; original mint bloom. Luster is the result of light reflecting on a coin's flow lines, whether those are visible or not.

lustrous
A term used to describe coins that still have original mint bloom.

MS (Mint State)
Abbreviation. See definition below.

major variety
A coin that is easily recognized as having a major difference from other coins of the same design, type, date, and mint. See *minor variety*.

market grading
A numerical grade that matches the grade at which a particular coin generally is traded in the marketplace. The grading standard used by PCGS.

marks
Imperfections acquired after striking. These range from tiny to large hits and may be caused by other coins or foreign objects.

master die
The main die produced from the master hub. Many working hubs are prepared from this

single die. See *master hub, working die,* and *working hub*.

master hub
The original hub created by the portrait lathe. Master dies are created from this hub.

Matte Proof
An experimental Proof striking, produced by the U.S. Mint mainly from 1907 to 1916, which has sandblasted or acid-pickled surfaces. These textured surfaces represented a radical departure from brilliant Proofs, having even less reflectivity than business strikes.

medal press
A high-pressure coining press acquired by the U.S. Mint, probably in 1858, to strike medals, patterns, restrikes, and regular-issue Proofs.

metal stress lines
Radial lines, sometimes visible, that result when the metal flows outward from the center of the planchet during the minting process. See *flow lines*.

milling machine (*alt.* upsetting machine)
The mechanical device to which planchets are fed to upset their rims. These are sometimes referred to as Type II planchets, and this process makes it easier to strike the higher rims associated with close-collar dies. This results in longer die life.

milling mark
A mark that results when the reeded edge of one coin hits the surface of another coin. Such contact may produce just one mark or a group of staccato-like marks. See *reeding mark*.

minor variety
A coin that has a minor difference from other coins of the same design, type, date, and mint. This minor difference is barely discernible to the unaided eye. The difference between a major variety and a minor variety is a matter of degree. See *major variety*.

mint
A coining facility.

mintage
The number of coins struck at a given mint during a particular year.

mint bloom
Original luster that is still visible on a coin. See *luster* and *lustrous*.

mint mark (*alt.* mintmark)
The tiny letter(s) stamped into the dies to denote the mint at which a particular coin was struck.

Mint State
The term corresponding to the numerical grades MS-60 through MS-70, used to denote a business-strike coin that never has been in circulation. A Mint State coin can range from one that is covered with marks (MS-60) to a flawless example (MS-70).

mishandled Proof
A Proof coin that has been circulated, cleaned, or otherwise reduced to a level of preservation below PR-60. See *impaired Proof*.

mottled toning
Uneven toning, usually characterized by splotchy areas of drab colors.

motto
An inscription on a coin—especially IN GOD WE TRUST, which first appeared on the 1864 two-cent piece and now is required on all U.S. coinage.

multiple-struck
See *double-struck*.

mutilated
A term used to describe a coin that has been damaged to the point where it no longer can be graded.

new
A term for a coin that never has been in circulation.

nickel
Popular term for a five-cent piece struck in cupro-nickel alloy (actually 75 percent copper, 25 percent nickel).

numerical grading
A system for grading coins that uses the Sheldon 1-70 scale; it is employed by PCGS and others.

obverse
The front, or heads side, of a coin. Usually the date side.

off center
A term for a coin struck on a blank that was not properly centered over the anvil (or lower) die. To be graded by PCGS, in most cases, a coin can be no more than 5 percent off center. For some coins that are less than 5 perfect off center, and for all coins that are more than 5 percent off center.

open collar
Its name notwithstanding, a closed collar that surrounded the anvil (or lower) die used in striking early U.S. coins on planchets whose edges already had been lettered or reeded. An open collar was a restraining collar that made it easier to position a planchet atop the lower die, and also sometimes kept the planchet from expanding.

"orange-peel" surfaces
The dimple-textured fields seen on many Proof gold coins; their surfaces resemble those of an orange, hence the descriptive term. Some Mint State gold dollars and three-dollar gold coins exhibit this effect to some degree.

original
A term used to describe a coin that never has been dipped or cleaned, or a coin struck from original dies in the year whose date it bears. (The early U.S. Mint often used dies with dates of previous years, as die steel and die making were expensive. Thus, coins struck with these prior-year dies are still regarded as originals.) See *restrike*.

original roll
Coins in fixed quantities wrapped in paper and stored at the time of their issuance. The quantities vary by denomination, but typically include 50 one-cent pieces, 40 nickels, 50 dimes, 40 quarters, 20 half dollars and 20 silver dollars. U.S. coins were first shipped to banks in kegs, later in cloth bags, and still later in rolls. Silver and gold coins stored in such rolls often have peripheral toning and untoned centers. Obviously, coins stored in rolls suffered fewer marks than those in kegs or bags.

original toning
Color acquired naturally by a coin that never was cleaned or dipped. Original toning ranges from the palest yellow to extremely dark blues, grays, browns, and finally black.

overdate
A coin struck with a die on which one date is engraved over a different date. With few exceptions, the die overdated is an unused die from a previous year. Sometimes an effort was made to polish away evidence of the previous date. PCGS will not recognize a coin as an overdate variety unless the overdate is visible.

over-mint mark
A coin struck with a die on which one mint mark is engraved over a different mint mark. In rare instances, branch mints returned dies that already had mint marks punched into them; on occasion, these were then sent to different branch mints and the new mint punched its mint mark over the old one. Examples include the 1938-D/S Buffalo nickel and the 1900-O/CC Morgan dollar.

PCGS (P.C.G.S.)
The Professional Coin Grading Service. Founded in 1985 (with the first coins being graded in February 1986) by David Hall, Bruce Amspacher, John Dannreuther, and Gordon Wrubel. The first commercial coin-grading service; the first grading service to guarantee the grade and authenticity of encapsulated coins.

PCGS Grading Standards
The written standards in chapter 4 of this book, along with the PCGS grading set.

PCGS holders
Hard plastic holders in which coins are encapsulated after the grading process at PCGS. Each coin is placed in an inert, pliable ring, which then is put into the bottom half of the holder. The top half is then carefully snapped on and the holder is sonically sealed.

PL (prooflike)
A PCGS grading suffix used for Morgan dollars that meet prooflike standards. See later definition.

PO (Poor)
Abbreviation. See definition below.

PQ (premium quality)
Abbreviation. See later definition.

PR (Proof)
Abbreviation. See later definition.

PVC (polyvinyl chloride)
Abbreviation. A chemical used in coin flips to make them pliable.

PVC damage
A film, usually green, left on a coin after storage in flips that contain PVC. During the early stage, this film may be clear and sticky.

PVC flip
Any of the various soft coin flips that contain PVC.

pattern
A test striking of a coin produced to demonstrate a proposed design, size, or composition (whether adopted or not). Patterns often are made in metals other than the one proposed; examples of this include aluminum and copper patterns of the silver Trade dollar.

pedigree
A listing of a coin's current owner plus all known previous owners.

penny
In American numismatics, slang for a one-cent coin.

peripheral toning
Light, medium, or dark coloring around the edge of a coin.

plain edge
A flat, smooth edge seen mainly on small-denomination coinage. See *lettered edge* and *reeded edge*.

planchet (*alt.* flan)
A blank disk of metal before it is struck by a coining press, transforming it into a coin. Type I planchets are flat. Type II planchets have upset rims imparted by a milling machine to facilitate striking in close collars. See *blank*.

planchet defects
Any of the various abnormalities found on coin blanks. These include drift marks, laminations, clips, and so forth.

planchet flaw
An irregular hole in a coin blank, often the result of a lamination that has broken away.

planchet striations
Fine, incuse lines found on some Proof coins, though rarely on business strikes, usually the result of polishing blanks to impart mirror-like surfaces prior to striking. See *adjustment marks, burnishing lines, die striations*, and *roller marks*.

plated
A term used to describe a coin to which a thin layer of metal has been applied—for example, gold-plated copper strikings of certain U.S. pattern coins.

plugged
A term used to describe a coin that has had a hole filled, often so expertly that it can be discerned only under magnification.

polished coin

A coin that has had some type of commercial polish, jeweler's rouge, or similar substance applied to its surface. Polished coins are not graded by PCGS.

polished die

A die that has been basined to remove clash marks or other die injury. In a positive sense, Proof dies were basined to impart mirrorlike surfaces, resulting in coins with reflective fields. See *basining*.

Poor

The grade PO-1. A coin with a readable date but little more, barely identifiable as to type. (One-year type coins do not require a readable date to qualify for this grade.)

portrait lathe (*alt.* transfer lathe)

A mechanical device that reduces a cast (or galvano) of a design to coin size. From this miniature model, a hub and dies are fabricated. See *Janvier reducing machine*.

premium quality

A term applied to coins that are the best examples within a particular grade. See *high-end*.

presentation striking

A coin, often a Proof or an exceptionally sharp business strike, specially struck and given to a dignitary or other person.

press

Any of the various coining machines. Examples include the screw press and the steam-powered knuckle press.

pristine

A term applied to coins in original, unimpaired condition. These coins typically are graded MS/PR-67 and higher.

Proof (*alt.* proof)

A coin typically struck with specially prepared dies on a specially prepared planchet. Ordinarily, Proofs are given more than one blow with the coining dies and struck with presses operating at slower speeds and higher striking pressure. Because of this extra care, Proofs usually exhibit much sharper detail than circulation-quality coins, or business strikes. PCGS applies the term Proof (PR) to special U.S. coins struck in 1817 and later. Similar coins struck prior to 1817 are recognized by PCGS as specimen strikes (SP).

Proof dies

Specially prepared dies, often sandblasted or acid-pickled, that are used to strike Proof coins. Often, the fields are highly polished to a mirrorlike finish, while the recessed areas are left "rough"; on coins struck with such dies, the devices are frosted and contrast with highly reflective fields. Matte, Roman, and Satin Proof dies are not polished to a mirrorlike finish.

prooflike

A term used to describe the mirror-like surfaces on business-strike coins that resemble Proofs, particularly Morgan silver dollars. Morgan dollars that meet PCGS standards for prooflike quality are designated PL. See *deep mirror prooflike*.

Proof-only issue

A coin struck only in Proof, with no business-strike counterpart.

Proof set

A coin set containing Proof issues from a particular year. A few sets contain anomalies such as the 1804 dollar and eagle in 1834 Proof presentation sets.

punch

A steel rod with a device, lettering, date, star, or some other symbol on the end that was sunk into a working die by hammering on the opposite end of the rod.

quarter dollar

A U.S. coin denomination, one-fourth of a dollar, first struck in 1796, minted sporadically until 1840, then issued virtually without interruption to the present.

quarter eagle

A U.S. gold coin denomination, two-and-a-half dollars or one-fourth of an eagle, first struck in 1796, issued sporadically thereafter, and discontinued as a regular issue in 1929.

questionable toning

Coloring on a coin that may not be original. After a coin is dipped or cleaned, any subsequent toning, whether acquired naturally or induced artificially, will look different from the original toning. PCGS will not grade coins with questionable color.

RB (Red and Brown)

A PCGS grading suffix used for copper coins that meet the standards for designation as Red and Brown. See *Red-Brown*.

RD (Red)

A PCGS grading suffix used for copper coins that meet the standards for designation as Red. See *Red*.

rare

A general term, often overused, to describe the availability of a particular coin. Truly rare coins usually have fewer than 50 to 75 specimens known; however, the term often is used to describe a coin such as the 1856 Flying Eagle cent, of which several thousand examples exist.

rarity scale

A system for denoting the relative rarity of different coins. As with the 1–70 numerical grading system, the most commonly used rarity scale is credited to Dr. William H. Sheldon, who adapted it from a nineteenth-century rarity scale. The system uses the terms R-1 through R-8, with an R-8 coin having one to three examples known and an R-1 coin having 1,251 or more examples known.

raw

Numismatic slang for a coin that has not been encapsulated by a grading service.

real

Numismatic slang for genuine coin. See *counterfeit* and *alteration*.

Red

A copper coin that still retains 95 percent or more of its original mint bloom or color. PCGS will award this designation (RD) if a coin has only slight mellowing of color, but not beyond that.

Red-Brown

A copper coin that has from 5 to 95 percent of its original mint color remaining (RB).

reeded edge (*alt.* milled edge, reeding)

The grooved notches on the edges of some coins. These were first imparted by the Mint's edge-lettering machine, later in the minting process by the use of a close collar, which sometimes is described as the third die or a collar die.

reeding mark(s)

A mark or marks caused when the reeded edge of one coin hits the surface of another coin. The contact may leave just one mark or a series of staccato-like marks. See *milling mark*.

Registry coin

A coin that is included in a collection listed in the PCGS Set Registry™. Also, some use the term to indicate a coin that would be in the condition census (top 6–10 coins) and thus would add points to a collection listed in the Set Registry. See *Set Registry*.

Registry set

A collection that is listed in the PCGS Set Registry. See *Set Registry*.

relief

The height of the devices of a particular coin design, expressed in relation to the fields.

replica

A copy, or reproduction, of a particular coin.

restrike

A coin struck later than indicated by its date, often with different dies. Occasionally, a different reverse design is used, as in the case of restrike 1831 half cents made with the reverse type used from 1840–1857.

retoned

A term used to describe a coin that has been dipped or cleaned and then has reacquired color, whether naturally or artificially.

reverse

The back, or tails side, of a coin. Usually opposite the date side.

rim

The raised area around the edges of the obverse and reverse of a coin. Pronounced rims resulted from the introduction of the close collar, first used in 1828 for Capped Bust dimes.

rim ding

Numismatic slang for a mark or indentation on the rim of a coin.

ring test

A test used to determine whether a coin was struck or is an electrotype or cast copy. The coin in question is balanced on a finger and gently tapped with a metal object—a pen, another coin, and so on. Struck coins have a high-pitched ring or tone, while electrotypes and cast copies have none. This test is not infallible; some struck coins do not ring because of planchet defects such as cracks or gas occlusions.

rolled edge (*alt.* rounded edge)

Numismatic slang for a raised rim. This has become part of the vernacular because of the Rolled Edge Indian Head eagle.

roller marks (*alt.* roller lines, drawbar lines)

Marks imparted to a planchet by the giant steel rollers used in reducing sheets of coinage metal to the proper thickness. (Today, strong evidence is that these lines are from the drawbar, the machine through which the strips are pulled through to produce the final thickness.) During this procedure, the strips of metal are passed through the rollers several times, if necessary, in order to achieve the desired thickness. With each succeeding pass, the rollers are placed closer together until the proper thickness is attained. Sometimes pieces of metal became imbedded in the rollers and these impart parallel grooves or lines to the metal strips. When planchets are cut from these strips, some display lines called roller marks or roller lines. Most of these disappear during the minting process, but some make it through to the finished coins. Lines of this kind are fairly common on some coins, such as 1902-S Morgan dollars.

roll friction

Minor displacement of metal, mainly on the high points, seen on coins stored in rolls. See *"coin" friction* and *bag friction*.

Roman finish

An experimental Proof surface used mainly on U.S. gold coins of 1909 and 1910. This is a hybrid surface with more reflectivity than Matte surfaces but less than brilliant Proofs. The surface is slightly scaly, similar to that of Satin Proofs.

rub (*alt.* rubbing)

A numismatic term for slight wear, often referring to just the high points or the fields. See *friction*.

SMS (Special Mint Set)

Abbreviation. See definition below.

SP (Specimen)

Abbreviation. See later definition.

Saints (*alt.* Saint-Gaudens)

Slang term for U.S. double eagles struck from 1907–1933, which were designed by the illustrious sculptor Augustus Saint-Gaudens at the behest of President Theodore Roosevelt.

Satin finish

Another of the experimental Proof surfaces used on U.S. gold coins after 1907. The dies were treated in some manner to create the silky surfaces imparted to the coins.

satin luster

Fine, silky luster seen on many coins, especially copper and nickel issues. Almost no "cartwheel" effect is seen on coins with this type of luster.

scratch

A detracting line that is more severe than a hairline. The size of the coin determines the point at which a line ceases to be viewed as a hairline and instead is regarded as a scratch; the larger the coin, the greater the tolerance. A heavy scratch may result in a coin's not being graded by PCGS.

screw press

The first type of coining press used at the U.S. Mint. Invented by Italian craftsman Donato Bramante, this press had a fixed anvil (or lower) die, with the hammer (or upper) die being attached to a rod with screw-like threads. When weighted arms attached to the rod were rotated, the screw mechanism quickly moved the rod with the die downward, striking the planchet placed into the lower die. The struck coin then was ejected and the process was repeated.

seawater damage

Damage incurred by a coin through exposure to seawater, as with coins found in sunken treasure ships. The copper in gold and silver alloys reacts with seawater and, over time, is "eaten" away. The surfaces of these coins appear dull and lightly pitted. PCGS will not grade such coins unless the damage is extremely minor. Research has shown that the movement of sand over the surfaces of a coin is perhaps the real culprit for seawater damage.

second toning

Any toning, natural or artificial, that results after a coin is dipped or cleaned. This second toning is seldom as attractive as original toning, though some coins "take" second toning better than others.

segmented collar

A multiple-piece collar that imparts raised lettering and devices to a coin's edge. Jean-Pierre Droz, a Swiss craftsman, invented this device, which comes apart when the coin is ejected from the lower die, allowing raised edge lettering and devices. See *close(d) collar*.

semi-prooflike

A term used to describe a coin that has some mirror-like surface mixed with satin or frosty luster. Reflectivity is obscured on such a specimen, unlike the reflectivity on prooflike and deep mirror prooflike coins.

Set Registry™

An Internet listing of partial and complete sets of coins that are ranked according to grade and completeness. PCGS developed this popular concept in the 1990s, as a method for collectors to determine how their collections matched up to other current sets and some of the great collections of the past.

Sheldon scale

The 1-to-70 grading system devised for U.S. large cents by Dr. William H. Sheldon and adopted for all coins by the coin industry. PCGS based its grading system on this scale with certain refinements, such as the inclusion of intermediate grades (61, 62, 64, and so on).

"shiny" spots

Areas on Matte, Roman, and Satin Proofs where the surface has been disturbed. On brilliant Proofs, dull spots appear where there are disturbances; on textured-surface coins such as Matte, Roman, and Satin Proofs, these disturbances create "shiny" spots.

silver-clad

The composition of Kennedy half dollars struck from 1965 to 1970, whose overall content is 40 percent silver and 60 percent copper. These are commonly referred to as silver-clad halves because two outer layers containing primarily silver are bonded to a core made primarily of copper.

silver dollar

The silver coin that served as a cornerstone of U.S. currency from 1792 until 1964. (The gold eagle played a similar role from 1792 until 1971.) First struck in 1794 and issued sporadically thereafter until 1935. Defined as so many grains of silver, changing with market conditions. See *dollar* and *Trade dollar*.

slab
Numismatic slang for the holder in which a coin is encapsulated by a grading service. The coin contained therein is said to be *slabbed*.

slide marks (*alt.* album slide marks)
Detracting lines imparted to a coin when the plastic slides in a coin album rub across the high points of the coin as the slides are inserted or removed.

slider
A term used to describe an AU coin that looks, or can be sold as, Uncirculated. Occasionally used in reference to another grade; a slider EF coin, for example, would be a VF/EF coin that is nearly EF.

spark-erosion die
A die made by an electrolytic deposition method. The surfaces of such a die are very rough, so they usually are polished extensively to remove the "pimples." The recessed areas of the die, and the relief areas of any coin struck with the die, still have rust-like surfaces with tiny micro pimples.

spark-erosion strike
A coin made from spark-erosion dies. These are characterized by the telltale "pimples" noted mainly on the areas in relief.

Special Mint Set
A set of special coins—neither business strikes nor Proofs—first struck in limited quantities in 1965 and officially released in 1966–1967 to replace Proof sets, which were discontinued as part of the U.S. Mint's efforts to stop coin hoarding. The quality of many of the 1965 coins was not much better than that of business strikes—but by 1967, some Special Mint Set (SMS) coins resembled Proofs. In fact, the government admitted as much when it revealed how the 1967 issues were

struck. In 1968, Proof coinage resumed. There have been similar issues since; the 1994 and 1997 Matte-finish Jefferson nickels, for example, are frosted SMS-type coins. Also, a limited number of 1964 coins received this special treatment.

Special striking
A coin made for a particular purpose or person that does not meet the definition of a Proof striking, but is of higher (or different) quality than a business strike. See *presentation striking*.

specimen (*alt.* specimen strike)
A special coin struck at the Mint from 1792 to 1816 that displays many characteristics of the later Proof coinage. Prior to 1817, the minting equipment and technology were limited, so specimen coins do not have the "watery" surfaces of later Proofs or the evenness of strike of the close-collar Proofs. PCGS designates these coins SP.

split grade
A situation where separate and different grades are assigned to the obverse and reverse of the same coin. A coin graded MS-63/65, for example, has an MS-63 obverse and an MS-65 reverse. Since reverses often receive higher grades than obverses, split grading has been employed to infer a superior coin. The obverse grade is more important than the reverse; thus, an MS-63/65 coin would be graded MS-63 by PCGS.

splotchy toning
Color that is uneven, both in shade and in composition.

"square" edge (*alt.* squared-off edge)
An edge that is unusually flat. Most Proof coins are seen with such edges, which are said to be "square." Some business strikes exhibit this also, though most have rounding or beveling where the edges meet the rims.

standard silver
The official composition of U.S. silver coinage, set by the Mint Act of 1792 at ap-

proximately 89 percent silver and 11 percent copper, later changed to 90 percent silver and 10 percent copper—the composition seen in most U.S. silver coins.

star

A device used as a motif on many U.S. coins. On the earliest U.S. coins, thirteen stars were depicted, representing the thirteen original colonies/states. As new states were admitted into the Union, more stars were added; up to sixteen appeared on some coins. Adding stars for each state was impractical, however, so the number was reduced to the original thirteen. Exceptions include the forty-six stars, later forty-eight stars, around the periphery of Saint-Gaudens double eagles, reflecting the number of states in the Union at the time those coins were issued.

steam-powered press

A coining press driven by a steam-powered engine. This type of press, more powerful than its predecessors, was installed in the United States Mint in 1836, replacing the hand and horse-powered screw presses.

stella

A term applied to the experimental four-dollar gold coins struck by the U.S. Mint in 1879–1880. So named for the large star on the coins' reverse.

stock edge

A counterfeit edge collar used for various-dated fakes. These have the same repeating characteristics.

striations (*alt.* striae)

Incuse polish lines on a die that result in raised lines on coins struck with that die. These are usually fine, parallel lines, though on some coins they are swirling and still others have crisscross lines. Planchet striations are burnishing lines not struck away by the minting process.

strike

n. The completeness, or incompleteness, of a coin's detail. *v.* The act of minting a coin.

striking

n. A coin. *adj.* The process of minting.

strip

The flat metal, rolled to proper thickness, from which planchets are cut.

struck

A term used to describe a coin produced from dies and a coining press.

struck copy

A replica of a particular coin made from dies not necessarily meant to deceive.

struck counterfeit

A fake coin produced from false dies.

surface preservation

The condition of the surface of a coin. On weakly struck coins, this is a better indicator of grade than is the coins' detail.

surfaces

The entire obverse and reverse of a coin, though often used to mean just the field areas.

sweating

A procedure in which coins are placed in a bag and shaken vigorously to knock off small pieces of metal. Later these bits of metal are gathered and sold, producing a profit as the coins are returned to circulation at face value. Mainly employed with gold coins, leaving their surfaces peppered with tiny nicks.

tab toning

Toning often seen on commemorative coins which were sold in cardboard holders with a round tab. Coins toned in these holders have a circle in the center and are said to have tab toning.

target toning (*alt.* bullet toning)

Toning that resembles an archery target, with deeper colors on the periphery often fading to white or cream color at the center.

technical grading

A method of grading that takes into account only the surfaces of a coin, ignoring luster, strike, and eye appeal. The surfaces of a particular coin may be nearly mark-free, so its technical grade may be MS-65 or higher. But if it is poorly struck and has flat luster, its market grade—the grade assigned by PCGS—may be only MS-63.

tensor light

A small, direct light source used by some numismatists to examine and grade coins.

three-cent piece (*alt.* trime)

A U.S. coin denomination used for two separate nineteenth-century series—one struck in copper-nickel, the other in silver. The silver three-cent piece was first struck in 1851, in debased silver, to facilitate the purchase of postage stamps; the composition was changed to standard silver in 1854, and production continued until 1873. The nickel three-cent piece was introduced in 1865 and was issued until 1889.

three-dollar piece

A U.S. gold coin struck from 1854 until 1889.

thumbed

A term used to describe a coin that has been doctored in a specific way to cover marks, hairlines, or other disturbances. Often associated with silver dollars, it actually is used on many issues, mainly business strikes. The thumb is rubbed lightly over the disturbances, and the oils in the skin help to disguise any problems.

tissue toning

Color, often vibrant, acquired by coins stored in original Mint paper. Originally, this was fairly heavy paper; later, very delicate tissue. Sometime during the nineteenth century, the Mint began wrapping Proof coins, and occasionally business strikes, in this paper. The paper contained sulfur; as a result, the coins stored in it for long periods of time acquired blues, reds, yellows, and other attractive colors.

toning (*alt.* patina)

The color seen on many coins. Infinite numbers of shades, hues, and pattern variations are seen, depending upon how, where, and how long a coin has been stored. Every coin begins to tone the second it leaves the dies, as all U.S. coins contain reactive metals in varying degrees.

tooling mark

A line, usually small and fine, found on both genuine and counterfeit coins. On genuine coins, such lines result when Mint workmen touch up dies to remove remnants of an overdate or other unwanted area. On counterfeits, they often appear in areas where the die was flawed and the counterfeiter has attempted to "fix" the problem.

Trade dollar

A U.S. silver coin, slightly heavier than the regular silver dollar, issued from 1873 until 1885 and intended specifically to facilitate trade in the Far East—hence its name. Trade dollars were made with marginally higher silver content than standard silver dollars in an effort to gain acceptance for them in commerce.

transfer die

A die created by sacrificing a coin for a model.

transitional issue

A coin struck after a series ends, such as the 1866 No Motto issues. A coin struck before a series starts, such as the 1865 Motto issues. A coin struck with either the obverse or the reverse of a discontinued series, an example being the 1860 half dime With Stars. A coin struck with the obverse or reverse of a yet-to-be-issued series, an example being the 1859 Stars half dime with the No Legend-type reverse.

trime

See *three-cent piece.*

Turban Head

See *Draped Bust.*

two-cent piece
A U.S. coin struck from 1864 until 1873, in part to facilitate the purchase of postage stamps, whose price had been reduced to two cents each.

type
A variation in design, size, or metallic content of a specific coin design. Examples include the Small and Heraldic Eagle types of Draped Bust coinage, Large-Size and Small-Size Capped Bust quarters, and the 1943 Lincoln cent struck in zinc-coated steel.

Uncirculated
A term used to describe a coin that has never been in circulation, a coin without wear. See *Brilliant Uncirculated, Mint State,* and *new.*

upset rim
The edge of a coin blank, or planchet, that has passed through a milling machine. This machine raises the edge, making it easier to strike the rim and also prolonging die life. Also called Type II planchets. See *milling machine.*

used
A term used to describe a coin that has light to heavy wear or circulation. See *circulated, friction,* and *rub.*

VF (Very Fine)
Abbreviation. See definition below.

VG (Very Good)
Abbreviation. See definition below.

variety
A coin of the same date and basic design as another but with a discernible difference. PCGS recognizes all major varieties; there are thousands of minor varieties, most of which have significance only to specialists in the particular series.

verifier
The grader at PCGS who looks at graded coins and decides whether the indicated grade is correct. He may tag a coin to be looked at again by the graders.

Very Fine
The term corresponding to the grades VF-20, 25, 30, and 35. This has the broadest range of any circulated grade, with nearly full detail on some VF-35 coins and less than half on some VF-20 specimens.

Very Good
The term corresponding to the grades VG-8 and VG-10. In these grades, between Good and Fine, a coin shows slightly more detail than in Good, usually with full rims except on certain series such as Buffalo nickels.

"watery" look
A look seen on the surfaces of most close-collar Proof coins. Highly polished planchets and dies give the surfaces an almost "wavy" look—hence the term.

weak strike
A term used to describe a coin that does not show intended detail because of improper striking pressure or improperly aligned dies.

wear
See *circulated, friction, rub,* and *used.*

wheel mark
See *counting-machine mark.*

whizzing
The process of mechanically moving the metal of a lightly circulated coin to simulate luster. Usually accomplished by using a wire brush attachment on a high-speed drill.

wire edge (alt. knife edge, wire rim)
The thin, knife-like projection seen on some rims created when metal flows between the collar and the die.

wonder coin
Numismatic slang for a coin whose condition is particularly superb.

working die
A die prepared from a working hub and used to strike coins.

working hub
A hub created from a master die and used to create the many working dies required for coinage.

worn die (*alt.* eroded die)
A die that has lost detail because of extended use. In earlier periods of U.S. coinage history, dies were often used until they wore out, became excessively cracked, or broke apart. Coins struck from worn dies often appear to be weakly struck, but no amount of striking pressure will produce detail on a coin that does not exist on the die.

XF (Extremely or Extra Fine)
An abbreviation sometimes used interchangeably with EF. See definitions for *Extra Fine* and *Extremely Fine*.

INDEX